LAUREN E. ANDERSON

Lowrey's International Trumpet Discography

Alvin Lowrey

Lowrey's International Trumpet

Discography

VOLUME II

CAMDEN HOUSE

Published by Camden House, Inc.
Drawer 2025
Columbia, SC 29202 U.S.A.

Copyright © 1990 by
Alvin L. Lowrey

First Edition
ISBN: 0-938100-79-3

Printed by Thomson-Shore Inc.
Dexter, Michigan

Library of Congress Cataloging-in-Publication Data

Lowrey, Alvin.
     Lowrey's international trumpet discography.

     Includes bibliographical references.
     1. Trumpet players--Discography. I. Title.
ML156.4.T8L68   1990   016.7889'2'0266   89-23960
ISBN 0-938100-79-3 : (alk. paper) :

Abramyan, Eduard
See: Aramyan, Eduard Aramovich

Absil, Jean, 1893-1974

₍Contes (3), trumpet & piano₎
Trois Contes pour trompette et piano
(Three Tales for Trumpet and Piano)
Gardner, Ned
Orvid, Georgy

₍Suite, trumpet & piano, op. 149₎
Suite for Trumpet and Piano, op. 149
Phillippe, André

Adam, Adolphe-Charles, 1803-1856

₍Cantique de Noël; arr. children's voices, trumpet & orchestra₎
Cantique de Noël
(Minuit, Chrétiens)
(O Holy Night)
André, Maurice, 166)

₍Cantique de Noël; arr. trumpet & organ₎
Cantique de Noël
(Minuit, Chrétiens)
(O Holy Night)
Schultz, Erik, 3)

₍Cantique de Noël; arr. trumpet & piano₎
Cantique de Noël
(Minuit, Chrétiens)
(O Holy Night)
Stith, Marice, 9)

Adams, A. Emmett, *d.* 1938

₍Bells of St. Mary's; arr. 3 trumpets, clarinet/bass clarinet & rhythm₎
The Bells of St. Mary's
Victorian Trumpet Trio

Adams, Stephen, 1844-1913
Maybrick, Michael

₍Holy City, voice & piano; arr. cornet & organ₎
The Holy City
McCann, Phillip

₍Holy City, voice & piano; arr. trumpet & dance band₎
The Holy City
Jacoby, Don

⌜Holy City, voice & piano; arr. trumpet & organ⌝
The Holy City
Stephen Adams was a pseudonym for Michael Maybrick.
Stith, Marice, 9)
Tolley, Richard

Addinsell, Richard, 1904-1977

⌜Warsaw Concerto; arr. trumpet & orchestra⌝
Warsaw Concerto
(Concerto de Varsovie)
Excerpt from music for the film, *Dangerous Moonlight*, (1942).
André, Maurice, 4)

Addison, John, 1920-
Addison, John Mervyn

⌜Concerto, trumpet, strings, (optional percussion), (1947)⌝
Concerto for Trumpet and Strings
¹Allegretto / ²Adagio misterioso / ³Allegro con brio
Rapier, Leon, 5)

Adson, John, *d.* 1640

⌜Courtly Masquing Ayres, (1621). Suite a 5⌝
Courtly Masquing Ayres a 5
Smithers, Don, 2)

⌜Courtly Masquing Ayres, (1621). Suite a 6⌝
Courtly Masquing Ayres a 6
Smithers, Don, 2)

Ahlstrom, David, 1927-

⌜Scherzo, trumpet & orchestra (1959); arr. trumpet & chamber ensemble⌝
Scherzo for Solo Cup-Muted Trumpet, Winds and Percussion
Chamber ensemble includes: 2 flutes, piano (4 hands), 2 percussion & bass.
Logan, Jack

Aichinger, Gregor, 1564-1628

⌜Laudate Dominum, mixed voices, 2 trumpets, 2 trombones & strings⌝
Laudate Dominum
Thibaud, Pierre, 10)

Akira, Nakata, 1886-1951

⌜Soshunfu; arr. trumpet & piano⌝
Soshunfu
(Early Spring Song)
Dokshitser, Timofei, 19)

Albéniz, Isaac, 1860-1909

⌐Suite Espagnole, piano, no. 1, op. 47. No. 3: Sevilla; arr. trumpet & guitar┐
Sevilla
(Sevillanas)
Méndez, Rafael, 14)

⌐Suite Espagnole, piano, no. 1, op. 47. No. 3: Sevilla; arr. trumpet & orchestra┐
Sevilla
(Sevillanas)
Méndez, Rafael, 9), 24)

Alberti, Giuseppe Matteo, 1685-1751

⌐Sinfonia Teatrale, 4 trumpets, strings & continuo, D major┐
Sinfonia Teatrale con 4 Trombe in Re maggiore
Touvron, Guy, 2)
Wallace, John, 4)

⌐Sonata, 2 trumpets, timpani, strings & continuo, D major┐
Sonata a 4 con due Trombe in Re maggiore
[1]Allegro / [2]Grave / [3]Allegro
Wobisch, Helmut, 4), 11)

⌐Sonata, 2 trumpets, violins & continuo, D major┐
Sonata con due Trombe e Violini in Re maggiore
[1]Allegro / [2]Adagio / [3][Allegro]
André, Maurice, 143)
Scherbaum, Adolf, 20)
Vaillant, Ludovic, 6)

Albertin, Alfons, 18th cent.

⌐Sonata, "Per la Festa di Pasqua", 4 organs, 4 trumpets, 4 horns & timpani,
D major┐
Sonata in D major, "Per la Festa di Pasqua"
Unidentified, Trumpet(s), 21)

Albinoni, Tomaso Giovanni, 1671-1751
Albinoni, Tommaso

⌐Concerti a cinque, op. 7. No. 3: oboe, strings & continuo, (T. VII, 3), B$^\flat$ major;
arr. trumpet & organ┐
Concerto in B$^\flat$ major for Trumpet and Organ, op. 7, no. 3
[1]Allegro / [2]Adagio / [3]Allegro
Güttler, Ludwig, 6)
Jorand, Jean-Claude

3

ɾConcerti a cinque, op. 7. No. 3: oboe, strings & continuo, (T. VII, 3), B♭ major; arr. trumpet, strings & continuoɹ

Concerto in B♭ major for Trumpet, Strings and Continuo, op. 7, no. 3

¹Allegro / ²Adagio / ³Allegro

> **André, Maurice**, 3), 35), 51), 67), 74), 86), 117), 169)
> **Bernard, André**, 1)
> **Dassé, Jean-Luc**
> **Güttler, Ludwig**, 7)
> **Schultz, Erik**, 5)
> **Touvron, Guy**, 1)

ɾConcerti a cinque, op. 7. No. 5: 2 oboes, strings & continuo, (T. VII, 5), C major; arr. 2 trumpets, strings & continuoɹ

Concerto in C major for 2 Trumpets, Strings and Continuo, op. 7, no. 5

³Allegro

> **Basch, Wolfgang**, 10)

ɾConcerti a cinque, op. 7. No. 6: oboe, strings & continuo, (T. VII, 6), D major; arr. trumpet & organɹ

Concerto in D major for Trumpet and Organ, op. 7, no. 6

¹Allegro / ²Adagio / ³Allegro

> **Basch, Wolfgang**, 11)
> **Schultz, Erik**, 2)
> **Zapf, Gerd**

ɾConcerti a cinque, op. 7. No. 6: oboe, strings & continuo, (T. VII, 6), D major; arr. trumpet, strings & continuoɹ

Concerto in D major for Trumpet, Strings and Continuo, op. 7, no. 6

¹Allegro / ²Adagio / ³Allegro

> **André, Maurice**, 51), 67), 109)
> **Wilbraham, John**, 24)

ɾConcerti a cinque, op. 9. No. 2: oboe, strings & continuo, (T. IX, 2), d minor; arr. trumpet & organɹ

Concerto in d minor for Trumpet and Organ, op. 9, no. 2

¹Allegro e non presto / ²Adagio / ³Allegro

> **André, Maurice**, 50), 76), 139), 218), 227)
> **Güttler, Ludwig**, 2), 6)
> **Mertens, Theo**, 4)
> **Murphy, Maurice**
> **Schultz, Erik**, 10)

[Concerti a cinque, op. 9. No. 2: oboe, strings & continuo, (T. IX, 2), d minor;
arr. trumpet, strings & continuo]
Concerto in d minor for Trumpet, Strings and Continuo, op. 9, no. 2
[1]Allegro e non presto / [2]Adagio / [3]Allegro
André, Maurice, 38), 41), 62), 67), 68), 226),
227)
Blair, Stacy
Zapf, Gerd

[Concerti a cinque, op. 9. No. 3: 2 oboes, strings & continuo, (T. IX, 3), F major;
arr. 2 trumpets, strings & continuo]
Concerto in F major for 2 Trumpets, Strings and Continuo, op. 9, no. 3
[1]Allegro / [2]Adagio (non troppo) / [3]Allegro
André, Maurice, 48), 58)

[Concerti a cinque, op. 9. No. 6: 2 oboes, strings & continuo, (T. IX, 6), G major;
arr. 2 trumpets, strings & continuo]
Concerto in G major for 2 Trumpets, Strings and Continuo, op. 9, no. 6
[1]Allegro / [2]Adagio (non troppo) / [3]Allegro
André, Maurice, 58)

[Concerti a cinque, op. 9. No. 9: 2 oboes, strings & continuo, (T. IX, 9), C major;
arr. 2 trumpets, strings & continuo]
Concerto in C major for 2 Trumpets, Strings and Continuo, op. 9, no. 9
[1]Allegro / [2]Adagio (non troppo) / [3]Allegro
André, Maurice, 3), 58), 74), 86), 153)
Potpourri, 10)
Sauter, Hermann, 25)

[Concerti a cinque, op. 9. No. 11: oboe, strings & continuo, (T. IX, 11),
B♭ major; arr. trumpet & organ]
Concerto in B♭ major for Trumpet and Organ, op. 9, no. 11
Braz, Dirceu, 4)

[Concerti a cinque, op. 9. No. 12: 2 oboes, strings & continuo, (T. IX, 12),
F major; arr. 2 trumpets, strings & continuo]
Concerto in D major for 2 Trumpets, Strings and Continuo, op. 9, no. 12
[1]Allegro / [2]Adagio / [3]Allegro
André, Maurice, 58)

[Concerto, trumpet, 3 oboes, bassoon & continuo, (T. *Mi* 3), C major]
Concerto in C major for Trumpet, 3 Oboes, Bassoon and Continuo, (T. *Mi* 3)
(Concerto C-dur für Trompete, 3 Oboen, Fagott und Basso continuo)
[1]Allegro moderato / [2]Affettuoso / [3]Presto
> **Erb, Helmut, 6)**
> **Fink, Werner**
> **Güttler, Ludwig, 4)**
> **Läubin, Hannes, 1)**
> **Schwarz, Gerard, 8)**
> **Wallace, John, 4)**
> **Wilbraham, John, 4), 5)**

[Sinfonie e concerti a cinque, op. 2. No. 8: Concerto No. 4, violin, strings & continuo, (T. II, 8), G major; arr. trumpet & organ, F major]
Concerto in F major for Trumpet and Organ, op. 2, no. 8
[1]Allegro / [2]Adagio / [3]Allegro
The odd numbers of Opus 2 are sonatas, and the even numbers are concertos; hence *Concerto No. 4* is op. 2, no. 8.
> **André, Maurice, 76), 134)**
> **Gabel, Bernard, 1)**
> **Groth, Konradin**
> **Riggione, Angelo**

[Sinfonie e concerti a cinque, op. 2. No. 8: Concerto No. 4, violin, strings & continuo, (T. II, 8), G major; arr. trumpet, organ, bass & drums, F major]
Concerto in F major for Trumpet and Organ, op. 2, no. 8
[1]Allegro / [2]Adagio / [3]Allegro
> **Molénat, Claude**

[Sinfonie e concerti a cinque, op. 2. No. 10: Concerto No. 5, violin, strings & continuo, (T. II, 10), C major; arr. trumpet, strings & continuo]
Concerto in C major for Trumpet, Strings and Continuo, op. 2, no. 10
The odd numbers of Opus 2 are sonatas, and the even numbers are concertos; hence *Concerto No. 5* is op. 2, no. 10.
> **Güttler, Ludwig, 3), 25)**

[Sonata, trumpet, strings & continuo, (T. *Si* 1), D major]
Sonata No. 2 for Solo Trumpet and Strings, T 180
[1]Allegro / [2]Grave - Presto - Adagio / [3]Allegro
Michael Talbot originally catalogued this work as "T 180", but later changed his cataloguing system. It is now catalogued as "T. *Si* 1."
> **Wallace, John, 4)**

[Sonata, trumpet, strings & continuo, (T. *So* 1), C major]
Sonata in C major for Solo Trumpet, Strings and Continuo, T 159
(Sonata a 6 con Tromba)
(Concerto in C major for Trumpet, Strings and Continuo)
¹Grave / ²Allegro / ³Grave / ⁴Allegro
Michael Talbot originally catalogued this work as "T 159", but later changed his cataloguing system. It is now catalogued as "T. *So* 1."

> **Dokshitser, Timofei**, 4), 14), 36)
> **Potpourri**, 21), 34), 35), 65)
> **Reinhart, Carole Dawn**, 1)
> **Steele-Perkins, Crispian**, 2)
> **Wallace, John**, 4)

[Suonate a tre, op. 1. No. 3: 2 violins & continuo, (T. I, 3), A major; arr. Suite, 2 trumpets & 4 trombones]
Suite in A major
¹Grave / ²Allegro / ³Grave / ⁴Allegro

> **André, Maurice**, 173)

[Trattenimenti armonici, op. 6. No. 4: Sonata, violin & continuo, (T. VI, 4), d minor; arr. Concerto, trumpet & orchestra]
Concerto in d minor for Trumpet and Orchestra, op. 6, no. 4
¹Grave / ²Allegro / ³Adagio / ⁴Allegro

> **André, Maurice**, 54), 195), 197), 200)
> **Potpourri**, 42), 45)

[Trattenimenti armonici, op. 6. No. 4: Sonata, violin & continuo, (T. VI, 4), d minor; arr. Concerto, trumpet, organ, bass & drums]
Concerto in d minor, op. 6, no. 4
¹Grave / ²Allegro / ³Adagio / ⁴Allegro

> **Molénat, Claude**

[Trattenimenti armonici, op. 6. No. 5: Sonata, violin & continuo, (T. VI, 5), F major; arr. trumpet & organ]
Sonata in F major for Trumpet and Organ, op. 6, no. 5
(Concert en Fa majeur pour trompette & piano ou orgue)
¹Grave / ²Allegro / ³Adagio / ⁴Allegro

> **André, Maurice**, 76), 118)

[Trattenimenti armonici, op. 6. No. 5: Sonata, violin & continuo, (T. VI, 5), F major; arr. trumpet & organ, C major]
Sonata in C major for Trumpet and Organ, op. 6, no. 5
¹Grave / ²Allegro / ³Adagio / ⁴Allegro

> **Hickman, David**, 6)

[Trattenimenti armonici, op. 6. No. 6: Sonata, violin & continuo, (T. VI, 6), a minor; arr. trumpet & organ]
Sonata in a minor, op. 6, no. 6
(Adagio aus "Sonate a-moll")
¹Grave adagio

> **André, Maurice**, 40), 59)

ₜTrattenimenti armonici, op. 6. No. 7: Sonata, violin & continuo, (T. VI, 7),
D major; arr. trumpet & organₗ
Sonata in D major for Trumpet and Organ, op. 6, no. 7
[1]Lento / [2]Allegro non troppo / [3]Lento / [4]Allegro
André, Maurice, 76), 118)

ₜTrattenimenti armonici, op. 6. No. 11: Sonata, violin & continuo, (T. VI, 11),
A major; arr. Concerto, trumpet & clarinet sextet, A majorₗ
Concerto in A major, "Saint Marc", op. 6, no. 11
(Trompetenkonzerte A-dur, "St. Markus", op. 6, no. 11)
[2]Allegro / [3]Adagio / [4]Allegro
The first movement is not included in this transcription.
André, Maurice, 173), 190), 193), 194), 197)
Potpourri, 44)

ₜTrattenimenti armonici, op. 6. No. 11: Sonata, violin & continuo, (T. VI, 11),
A major; arr. Concerto, trumpet & organ, A majorₗ
Concerto in A major, "Saint Marc", op. 6, no. 11
(Sonata in A major for Trumpet and Organ, op. 6, no. 11)
[1]Grave adagio / [2]Allegro / [3]Adagio / [4]Allegro
Hardy, Francis

ₜTrattenimenti armonici, op. 6. No. 11: Sonata, violin & continuo, (T. VI, 11),
A major; arr. Concerto, trumpet & strings, B♭ majorₗ
Concerto in B♭ major, "Saint Marc", op. 6, no. 11
(Concerto en si bémol majeur pour trompette et orchestre à cordes, op. 6,
no. 11)
(Konzert für Trompete und Streichorchester B-dur, op. 6, no. 11)
[1]Grave adagio (adagietto) / [2]Allegro / [3]Adagio / [4]Allegro
André, Maurice, 3), 42), 56), 67), 83), 86),
117), 154), 135), 210), 217), 169)
Berinbaum, Martin
Blair, Stacy
Erb, Helmut, 6)
Touvron, Guy, 1)

Albrecht, Gerd, 1935-
ₜMusikinstrumente und wie man sie spieltₗ
Musikinstrumente und wie man sie spielt
(Musical instruments and how they are played)
Adelbrecht, Henri, 1)

Albrechtsberger, Johann Gregor, 1736-1809

[Concertino, trumpet, violin, viola, cello & piano, E♭ major, (1771)]
Concertino in E♭ a cinque strumenti
[1]Moderato / [2]Menuett / [3]Larghetto / [4]Vivace
The original instrumentation designation was: Violino, Viola,
Basso, Tromb. e Cembalo. (The term *Tromb.* has been translated
as *Tromba*, i.e., trumpet, but may have meant *Trombula*, i.e.,
Jew's harp.)
Ghitalla, Armando, 2)
Wilbraham, John, 4), 7), 15)

Albrici, Vincenzo, 1631-1696
Alberici, Vincenzo

[Sonata, 2 trumpets, 2 violins & bassoon]
Sonata a 5, 2 Trombetta, 2 Violini con Fagotto
[1][Allegro] / [2][Allegro]
Keavy, Stephen

Alcock, John, 1715-1806
Alcock "the elder", John
Alcock "der Ältere", John
Alcock "l'aîné", John

[Voluntary, keyboard, D major; arr. trumpet & organ]
Voluntary in D major
Which of Alcock's ten voluntaries is (are) recorded has not been
ascertained.
Basch, Wolfgang, 5)
Carroll, Edward, 6)
Fink, Werner
Güttler, Ludwig, 24)
Sautter, Fred

Aldrovandini, Giuseppe Antonio Vincenzo, *ca.* 1672-1707

[Sinfonia, 2 trumpets, strings & continuo, D major]
Sinfonia in D major for 2 Trumpets, Strings and Continuo
[1]Allegro / [2]Grave / [3]Allegro
This work, specified as *Sinfonia* on the albums, is published as
Sonata in C for 2 Trumpets and Piano by the International Music
Company of New York.
André, Maurice, 79), 105)

[Sonata, trumpet & strings, D major]
Sonata con Tromba in D major
(Sonata in D major for Trumpet and Strings)
Güttler, Ludwig, 19)

⌈Sonata, trumpet & strings, D major; arr. trumpet & organ⌉
Sonata in D major for Trumpet and Organ
(Sonata con Tromba in D major)
Haas, Wolfgang

⌈Sonata, 2 trumpets & continuo, op. 5, D major⌉
Sonata a 3 in D major, op. 5
Güttler, Ludwig, 14)

⌈Sonatas (2), 2 trumpets, strings & continuo, D major⌉
Sonata in D major for 2 Trumpets, Strings and Continuo
There are at least 2 sonatas and 1 sinfonia for 2 trumpets by
Aldrovandini. The sonatas are not separately identified here (and
any of the following recordings may actually include the sinfonia
rather than the designated sonata).
Molénat, Claude
Soustrot, Bernard, 7)
Touvron, Guy, 2)
Wobisch, Helmut, 6)

Alexander, Josef, 1907-

⌈Burlesque and Fugue, trumpet & piano, (1970)⌉
Burlesque and Fugue for Trumpet and Piano
Ware, John

Alexandrov, Yuri Mikhailovich, 1914-

⌈Sonata, trumpet & orchestra, B♭ major⌉
Sonata in B♭ major for Trumpet and Orchestra
Orvid, Georgy

Alexius, Carl John, 1928-

⌈Sonatina, trumpet & piano (1959)⌉
Sonatina for Trumpet and Piano
Tarr, Edward, 6)

Allen, Harold, 1917-

⌈Cumana; arr. trumpet trio, clarinet & rhythm⌉
Cumana
Victorian Trumpet Trio

Altenburg, Johann Ernst, 1734-1801

⌈Trompeter- und Pauker-Kunst, (1795). Chorale, "Aus meines Herzensgrunde",
4 trumpets⌉
Chorale, "Aus meines Herzensgrunde"
Tarr, Edward, 21)

[Trompeter- und Pauker-Kunst, (1795). Concerto, 7 trumpets & timpani; version in A♭ major]
Concerto a VII Clarini con Tympani
[1]Allegro / [2]Andante / [3]Vivace
> Voisin, Roger, 5), 8)

[Trompeter- und Pauker-Kunst, (1795). Concerto, 7 trumpets & timpani; version in C major]
Concerto a VII Clarini con Tympani
[1]Allegro / [2]Andante / [3]Vivace
> Immer, Friedemann, 18)
> Potpourri, 16)
> Tarr, Edward, 21)

[Trompeter- und Pauker-Kunst, (1795). Concerto, 7 trumpets & timpani; version in D major]
Concerto a VII Clarini con Tympani
[1]Allegro / [2]Andante / [3]Vivace
> Potpourri, 29)
> Schwarz, Gerard, 7)
> Smithers, Don, 10)
> Wallace, John, 5)
> Wilbraham, John, 14), 17)

[Trompeter- und Pauker-Kunst, (1795). Polonaise, 3 trumpets, C major]
Polonaise (Tricinium)
> Rehm, Klaus

Ameller, André-Charles, 1912-

[In the Glow of Sunset, trumpet & piano, (1953)]
In the Glow of Sunset
> Ode, James

Anders, Bob

[Samba Si — Samba No, trumpet, rhythm & orchestra]
Samba Si — Samba No
> Andersen, Ole

Anderson, Leroy, 1908-1975

[Bugler's Holiday, 3 trumpets & orchestra; also arr. 3 trumpets & piano]
Bugler's Holiday
> Burke, James, 3)
> Hirt, Al
> Méndez, Rafael, 11)
> Sullivan, William
> Tobe, Yutaka

[Serenata, strings; arr. trumpet & orchestra]
Serenata
> André, Maurice, 7)

11

ſTrumpeter's Lullaby, trumpet & orchestra; also arr. trumpet & piano꜒
A Trumpeter's Lullaby
Burke, James, 1)
Christensen, Ketil
Haynie, John, 1)
Head, Emerson
Hirt, Al
Lieberman, Harold J.
Méndez, Rafael, 19)
Nagel, Robert, 15)
Stith, Marice, 5)
Sullivan, William
Tobe, Yutaka
Wilder, Joseph B.

Anderson, Thomas Jefferson, 1928-

ſVariations (theme by M.B. Tolson), soprano & chamber ensemble, (1969)꜒
Variations on a Theme by M.B. Tolson
Chamber ensemble includes: alto saxophone, trumpet, trombone, violin, cello & piano.
Dean, Allan, 7)

André, Maurice, 1933-

ſChristmas Bugle, trumpet & orchestra꜒
Christmas Bugle
André, Maurice, 66)

ſPrintemps, trumpet & orchestra꜒
Printemps
(Springtime)
André, Maurice, 66)

ſRomance, trumpet & orchestra꜒
Romance
André, Maurice, 66)

Andriasyan, Iosif Arshakovich, 1933-

ſConcerto, trumpet & orchestra, D♭ major꜒
Concerto in D♭ major for Trumpet and Orchestra
Dokshitser, Timofei, 13)

Andriessen, Jurriaan, 1925-

ſMovimenti, 9 instruments, (1965)꜒
Movimenti (1965)
Included in the nine instruments are: trumpet, horn, trombone and timpani.
Unidentified, Trumpet(s), 10)

Andrieu, Jean-François d'
See: Dandrieu, Jean-François

Anisimov, Boris Ivanovich, 1907-

rConcertino, trumpet & piano, f minorꞁ
     Concertino in f minor for Trumpet and Piano
         Sveshnikov, Mikhail

Antegnati, Costanzo, 1549-1624
Antegnati, Constanzo

rCanzoni per Sonare..., (1608). No. 9: "La Battera"; arr. 2 trumpets & 2
    trombonesꞁ
     Canzona nona a quattro, "La Battera"
         [from *Canzoni per Sonare con ogni sorti di Stromini, a Quattro,*
         Cinque, & Otto, con il suo Basso generale per l'Organo,
         Nouamente raccolte da diversi Eccellentissimi Musici, & date in
         luce. Venice, Alessandro Rauerij.]
         Carroll, Edward, 7)

Antheil, George, 1900-1959
Antheil, Georg Johann Carl

rSonata, trumpet & piano, (1952)ꞁ
     Sonata for Trumpet and Piano
         Gardner, Ned
         Stevens, Thomas, 9)
         Stith, Marice, 8)

Appledorn, Mary Jeanne van
See: van Appledorn, Mary Jeanne

Aquin, Claude d'
See: Daquin, Claude

Aramyan, Eduard Aramovich, 1930-
Abramyan, Eduard

rConcert-Scherzo, trumpet & pianoꞁ
     Concert-Scherzo
         Usov, Yuri

Arban, Joseph Jean Baptiste Laurent, 1825-1889

rCavatine (theme from Bellini's Zaïra), cornet & pianoꞁ
     Cavatine de La Zaïra
         Urfer, Eric

₍Cavatine (theme from Rossini's Barber of Seville), cornet & piano; arr. cornet & brass ensemble₎
Cavatine de Le Barbier de Seville de Rossini
Caens, Thierry

₍Fantaisie (based on Verdi's Aïda), cornet & piano₎
Aïda
(Fantaisie sur l'Opera de Verdi)
(Fantasy on themes from Verdi's Aïda)
Includes excerpted themes: soprano aria from Act I, soprano aria from Act III, tenor aria from Act IV, and the Triumphal March (with variations) from Act II.
Burke, James, 2)

₍Fantaisie (themes from Bizet's Carmen), cornet & piano; arr. cornet & brass ensemble₎
Fantaisie sur Carmen de Bizet
(Fantasy on themes from Bizet's Carmen)
Caens, Thierry

₍Fantaisie (themes from Verdi's Rigoletto), cornet & piano, (1868)₎
Fantaisie sur l'opéra Rigoletto de Verdi
(Fantasy on themes from Verdi's Rigoletto)
Impett, Jonathan

₍Fantaisie brillante, cornet & piano (no. 1)₎
Fantaisie Brillante
Arban's Complete Conservatory Method for Trumpet (Cornet), "Twelve Celebrated Fantaisies and Airs Variés", **No. 3**, (New York: Carl Fischer, 1936).
Célèbre Methode Complète de Trompette, Cornet à pistons et Saxhorn, "Airs Variés", No. 3, (Paris: Alphonse Leduc, 1956).
Urfer, Eric

₍Fantaisie brillante, cornet & piano (no. 1); arr. cornet & band₎
Fantaisie Brillante
André, Maurice, 120), 212)

₍Fantaisie brillante, cornet & piano (no. 1); arr. cornet & wind ensemble₎
Fantaisie Brillante
Marsalis, Wynton, 4)

₍Fantaisie brillante, cornet & piano (no. 1); arr. trumpet & piano₎
Fantaisie Brillante
Endsley, Gerald

₍Fantaisie brillante, cornet & piano, No. 2₎
Deuxième Fantaisie Brillante
Burke, James, 2)

₍Grand Solo, cornet & piano, No. 2₎
Deuxième Grand Solo
Burke, James, 2)

ₜMethod. Characteristic Etudes (14), trumpet or cornet: No. 13; arr. cornet &
brass quartetₜ
Étude Caractéristique
Howarth, Elgar

ₜMethod. Characteristic Etudes (14), trumpet or cornet: Nos. 1-7; arr. trumpet &
pianoₜ
Characteristic Etudes
(Études Caractéristiques)
Thibaud, Pierre, 12)

ₜMethod. Etudes, trumpet (cornet), Nos. 18-36ₜ
Etudes Nos. 18 - 36
Arban's Complete Conservatory Method for Trumpet (Cornet).
Etudes Nos. 18-36, pp. 28-36. edited by Edwin Franko Goldman
& Walter M. Smith, (New York: Carl Fischer, 1936).
Méndez, Rafael, 23)

ₜVariations (Carnival of Venice), cornet & pianoₜ
Fantaisie and Variations on The Carnival of Venice
(Variations sur le Carnaval de Venise)
(Variationen über dem Karneval von Venedig)
Arban's Complete Conservatory Method for Trumpet (Cornet),
"Twelve Celebrated Fantaisies and Airs Variés", No. 11, (New
York: Carl Fischer, 1936).
Célèbre Methode Complète de Trompette, Cornet à pistons et
Saxhorn, "Airs Variés", No. 12, (Paris: Alphonse Leduc, 1956).
Schwarz, Gerard, 19)
Urfer, Eric

ₜVariations (Carnival of Venice), cornet & piano; arr. cornet & bandₜ
Fantaisie and Variations on The Carnival of Venice
Burke, James, 2), 8)

ₜVariations (Carnival of Venice), cornet & piano; arr. cornet & brass ensembleₜ
Fantaisie and Variations on The Carnival of Venice
Caens, Thierry

ₜVariations (Carnival of Venice), cornet & piano; arr. cornet & wind ensembleₜ
Fantaisie and Variations on The Carnival of Venice
Marsalis, Wynton, 4)

ₜVariations (Carnival of Venice), cornet & piano; arr. flügelhorn & bandₜ
Fantaisie and Variations on The Carnival of Venice
André, Maurice, 120), 212)

ₜVariations (Carnival of Venice), cornet & piano; arr. trumpet & bandₜ
Fantaisie and Variations on The Carnival of Venice
Dokshitser, Timofei, 23)

ₜVariations (Carnival of Venice), cornet & piano; arr. trumpet & brass ensembleₜ
Fantaisie and Variations on The Carnival of Venice
Grin, Freddy, 2)

[Variations (Carnival of Venice), cornet & piano; arr. trumpet & orchestra]
Fantaisie and Variations on The Carnival of Venice
André, Maurice, 5), 7)

[Variations (Carnival of Venice), cornet & piano; arr. trumpet & piano]
Fantaisie and Variations on The Carnival of Venice
Endsley, Gerald

[Variations (theme from Auber's Actéon), cornet & piano]
Fantaisie and Variations on Actéon
(Fantaisie et Variations sur Actéon)
Arban's Complete Conservatory Method for Trumpet (Cornet), "Twelve Celebrated Fantaisies and Airs Variés", No. 2, (New York: Carl Fischer, 1936).
Célèbre Methode Complète de Trompette, Cornet à pistons et Saxhorn, "Airs Variés", No. 2, (Paris: Alphonse Leduc, 1956).
Urfer, Eric

[Variations (theme from Bellini's Norma), cornet & piano]
Variations on a Theme from Norma by V. Bellini
(Variations sur La Norma)
(Variationen über Norma)
Arban's Complete Conservatory Method for Trumpet (Cornet), "Twelve Celebrated Fantaisies and Airs Variés", No. 12, (New York: Carl Fischer, 1936).
Célèbre Methode Complète de Trompette, Cornet à pistons et Saxhorn, "Airs Variés", No. 4, (Paris: Alphonse Leduc, 1956).
Hardenberger, Håkan
Urfer, Eric

[Variations (theme from Bellini's Norma), cornet & piano; arr. cornet & chamber ensemble]
Variations on a Theme from Norma by V. Bellini
Schwarz, Gerard, 5)

[Variations (theme from Verdi's La Traviata), cornet & piano; arr. cornet & band]
Variations sur un thème de La Traviata de Verdi
(Variations on a Theme from La Traviata by Verdi)
André, Maurice, 120), 212)

[Variations (Tyrolean Song), cornet & piano]
Variations on a Tyrolean Song
(Variations sur La Tyrolienne)
(Variationen über ein Tirolerlied)
Arban's Complete Conservatory Method for Trumpet (Cornet), "Twelve Celebrated Fantaisies and Airs Variés", No. 4, (New York: Carl Fischer, 1936).
Célèbre Methode Complète de Trompette, Cornet à pistons et Saxhorn, "Airs Variés", No. 5, (Paris: Alphonse Leduc, 1956).
Urfer, Eric

₍Variations (Tyrolean Song), cornet & piano; arr. trumpet & orchestra₎
Variations on a Tyrolean Song
(Variations sur La Tyrolienne)
André, Maurice, 5)

Arbeau, Thoinot, 1520-1595
Tabourot, Jehan

₍Dances (4); arr. trumpet, harp & percussion₎
Vier franko flämische Tänze
(Four Franko-Flemish Dances)
¹Tourdion / ²Gaillard, "La traditore my fa morire" / ³Pavane, "Belle qui tient ma vie" / ⁴Basse danse, "Jouissance vous donnerai"
Thoinot Arbeau is an anagram of the composer's real name, Jehan Tabourot.
André, Maurice, 64)

Arensky, Anton Stepanovich, 1861-1906

₍Concert Waltz, trumpet & piano₎
Concert Waltz
Dokshitser, Timofei, 5), 7), 9), 23), 27), 35), 39)

Arlen, Harold, 1905-1986
Arluck, Hyman

₍Wizard of Oz, (1939). Over the Rainbow; arr. trumpet & orchestra₎
Over the Rainbow
Harold Arlen is a pseudonym for Hyman Arluck.
Méndez, Rafael, 20)

Arne, Thomas Augustine, 1710-1778

₍Alfred. Rule Britannia; arr. trumpet & piano₎
Rule Britannia from *Alfred*
This song is included as the first movement of *English Suite* arranged by Bernard Fitzgerald.
Masters, Edward L.
Ritter, David
Schwarz, Gerard, 14)

Arnold, Malcolm, 1921-
Arnold, Malcolm Henry

₍Concerto, trumpet & orchestra, op. 125₎
Concerto for Trumpet and Orchestra, op. 125
Wallace, John, 1)

Arutiunian, Aleksandr Grigor'evich, 1920-
Arutunian, Alexander
Aroutounian, Alexandre
Arutjunjan, Alexander
Harut'unyan, Alexander Grigori

₍Concert Vocalise, trumpet & piano, No. 1₎
Concert Vocalise No. 1
Balyan, Yuri

₍Concerto, trumpet & orchestra, A♭ major, (1949)₎
Concerto in A♭ major for Trumpet and Orchestra
André, Maurice, 155), 147), 168)
Dokshitser, Timofei, 11), 33)
Erb, Helmut, 4)
Hickman, David, 1)
Junek, Václav, 2)
Maximenko, Anatoly, 5)
Potpourri, 7), 39)
Tobe, Yutaka

₍Concerto, trumpet & orchestra, A♭ major, (1949); arr. trumpet & band₎
Concerto in A♭ major for Trumpet and Band
Hickman, David, 7)

₍Scherzo, trumpet & piano₎
Scherzo
Balyan, Yuri

₍Theme and Variations, trumpet & orchestra, B♭ major, (1984)₎
Theme and Variations in B♭ for Trumpet and Orchestra
Balyan, Yuri
Dokshitser, Timofei, 26)

Arutiunian, Erik, 1933-
Arutunian, Erik
Aroutounian, Erik
Arutjunjan, Erik

₍Sonata, trumpet & piano₎
Sonata for Trumpet and Piano
Balyan, Yuri

Asafiev, Boris, 1884-1949
Asaf'yev, Boris Vladimirovich

₍Sonata, trumpet & piano, B♭ major₎
Sonata in B♭ for Trumpet and Piano
Usov, Yuri

Astier, André

ₜFanfare valse, flügelhorn & accordion bandₜ
Fanfare valse
André, Maurice, 61)

ₜFlons flons champêtres, flügelhorn & accordion bandₜ
Flons flons champêtres
André, Maurice, 61)

ₜGais virtuoses, flügelhorn & accordion bandₜ
Les gais virtuoses
André, Maurice, 61)

ₜGouttes d'eau, flügelhorn & accordion bandₜ
Gouttes d'eau
André, Maurice, 61)

ₜJoli coeur, flügelhorn & accordion bandₜ
Joli coeur
André, Maurice, 61)

ₜTrompetissimo, flügelhorn & accordion bandₜ
Trompetissimo
André, Maurice, 61)

ₜVive l'Auvergne, flügelhorn & accordion bandₜ
Vive l'Auvergne
André, Maurice, 61)

Attaingnant, Pierre, *ca.* 1494-1552

ₜDances, lute, (1529); arr. trumpet & organₜ
Sept Danceries de la Renaissance Française
(Seven Dances from the French Renaissance)
[1]Pavane [Gervaise] / [2]Gaillarde [Gervaise] / [3]Branle de Bourgogne [Anonymous] / [4]Branle de Champagne [Gervaise] / [5]Branle gai, "Que ie chatoulle ta fossette" [Anonymous] / [6]Branle simple [Anonymous] [7]Allemande [Gervaise]

André, Maurice, 50), 118[1-2+7+3-6])
Basch, Wolfgang, 5)
Bernard, André, 4)
Bouche
Gaudon, Jean-Jacques
Giangiulio, Richard
Pearson, Byron
Schultz, Erik, 10)
Touvron, Guy, 20)

Aubert, Jacques, 1689-1753

ᵣConcert de symphonies. Suite No. 2: Fanfareᵤ
Concert de symphonies (Suite No. 2)
The orchestration includes trumpets, oboes & flutes.
Delmotte, Roger, 23)

Austin, James, 20th cent.

ᵣLesson Course for the Serious Student, trumpet, Vol. 1ᵤ
Lesson Course for the Serious Student, Vol. I
Austin, James

Babbitt, Milton, 1916-
Babbitt, Milton Byron

ᵣAll Set, 2 saxophones, trumpet, trombone & rhythm (1957)ᵤ
All Set, for Jazz Ensemble
Dean, Allan, 7)

Bacewicz, Grażyna, 1909-1969
Bacewicz, Grażyna Wanda

ᵣMusic, 5 trumpets, percussion & strings (1958)ᵤ
Music for Strings, Trumpets and Percussion
(Muzyka na smyczki, trąbki i perkusję)
Piórkowski, Zygmunt
Unidentified, Trumpet(s), 17)

Bach, Carl Philipp Emanuel, 1714-1788
Bach, Karl Philipp Emanuel

ᵣMarch and Fanfare, 3 trumpets & timpani, No. 1, D major, Wq 185,1ᵤ
Marsche und Fanfare, Wq 185,1
(March and Fanfare No. 1 in D major, Wq 185,1)
Fink, Werner

ᵣMarsch für die Arche, 3 trumpets & timpani, C major, Wq 188ᵤ
Marsch für die Arche, Wq 188
Potpourri, 1)
Tarr, Edward, 28)
Voisin, Roger, 5), 8)
Wilbraham, John, 17)

ᵣSonata, flute & continuo, Wq 131, D major; arr. trumpet & organᵤ
Sonata in D major, Wq 131
(Sonata in D major for Flute and Continuo, Wq 131)
[1]Andante / [2]Allegretto / [3]Allegro
André, Maurice, 45), 59)

[Sonata, organ, No. 4, g minor, Wq 70,4; arr. trumpet & organ]
Sonata in g minor, Wq 70,4
(Sonata No. 4 in g minor for Organ, Wq 70,4)
[1]Adagio / [2]Allegro / [3]Vivace
André, Maurice, 141)

Bach, Johann Christian, 1735-1782

[Magnificat, double chorus & orchestra]
Magnificat
Sauter, Hermann, 29)

[Sonata, flute & continuo, E^b major; arr. trumpet & organ]
Sonate en mi bemol majeur pour trompette et orgue
(Sonata in E^b major for Flute and Continuo)
[1]Adagio / [2]Allegretto / [3]Allegro assai
The title indicated on the album is "Concerto", but the title on
the published transcription is "Sonate".
André, Maurice, 134)

Bach, Johann Sebastian, 1685-1750

[Brandenburgischen Konzerte, S. 1046-1051, (1721). No. 1, 3 oboes, bassoon, 2
horns (2 trumpets), violino piccolo, strings & continuo, F major, S. 1046]
Brandenburg Concerto No. 1 in F major, S. 1046
[1][Allegro] / [2]Adagio / [3]Allegro / [4]Menuetto - Trio I - Menuetto -
Polacca - Menuetto - Trio II - Menuetto
Clift, Dennis

[Brandenburgischen Konzerte, S. 1046-1051, (1721). No. 2, flute (recorder), oboe,
trumpet (horn), violin, strings & continuo, F major, S. 1047]
Brandenburg Concerto No. 2 in F major, S. 1047
[1][Allegro] / [2]Andante / [3]Allegro assai
Tuckwell, Barry

[Brandenburgischen Konzerte, S. 1046-1051, (1721). No. 2, flute (recorder), oboe,
trumpet, violin, strings & continuo, F major, S. 1047]
Brandenburg Concerto No. 2 in F major, S. 1047
[1][Allegro] / [2]Andante / [3]Allegro assai
André, Maurice, 38[3]), 41), 46), 57), 93), 171),
180), 194[3]), 201), 211), 152), 220), 226),
227)
Baker, Bernard
Basch, Wolfgang, 8), 10[1])
Berinbaum, Martin
Bernard, André, 12)
Broiles, Melvin
Clift, Dennis
Cohen, Sol
Csiba, József
Delmotte, Roger, 3)
DiVall, Robert

ₜBrandenburgischen Konzerte, S. 1046-1051, (1721). No. 2, flute, oboe, trumpet (soprano saxophone), violin, strings & continuo, F major, S. 1047ₙ
Brandenburg Concerto No. 2 in F major, S. 1047
¹[Allegro] / ²Andante / ³Allegro assai
Mule, Marcel

ₜBrandenburgischen Konzerte, S. 1046-1051, (1721). No. 3, 3 violins, 3 violas, 3 cellos & continuo, G major, S. 1048. 1. [Allegro]; arr. trumpet, organ, bass & drumsₙ
Brandenburg Concerto No. 3 in G major, S. 1048
André, Maurice, 70)

ₜCantatas. No. 2, Ach Gott, vom Himmel sieh' dareinₙ
Cantata No. 2, "Ach Gott, vom Himmel sieh' darein"
Instrumentation: 2 oboes, 4 trombones (cornetto & 3 trombones), strings & continuo.
Bryant, Ralph, 1)
Potpourri, 26^{1+6})
Wolf, Hans, 4), 6)

ₜCantatas. No. 4, Christ lag in Todesbandenₙ
Cantata No. 4, "Christ lag in Todesbanden"
Instrumentation: cornetto (trumpet), 3 trombones, strings & continuo.
Bryant, Ralph, 1)
Lachenmeir, Paul
Sauter, Hermann, 17)
Unidentified, Trumpet(s), 13)

ₜCantatas. No. 4, Christ lag in Todesbanden. 4. Chorale; arr. trumpet & organₙ
Chorale, "Jesus Christus, Gottes Sohn" from Cantata No. 4
This arrangement may be for a modern valved "corno da caccia" with organ.
Güttler, Ludwig, 15)

ₜCantatas. No. 5, Wo soll ich fliehen hinₙ
Cantata No. 5, "Wo soll ich fliehen hin"
Instrumentation: 2 oboes, tromba da tirarsi (trumpet), strings & continuo.
Spindler, Josef, 11)
Wolf, Hans, 4), 9)

ₜCantatas. No. 6, Bleib' bei uns, denn es will Abend werden. 3. Chorale; arr. trumpet & organₙ
Chorale, Ach bleib' bei uns, Herr Jesu Christ", from Cantata No. 6
This arrangement may be for a modern valved "corno da caccia" with organ.
Güttler, Ludwig, 15)

ₜCantatas. No. 6, Bleib' bei uns, denn es will Abend werden. 3. Chorale; arr.
trumpet & stringsₜ
Chorale, Ach bleib' bei uns, Herr Jesu Christ", from Cantata No. 6

Touvron, Guy, 9)

ₜCantatas. No. 10, Meine Seel' erhebt den Herren!ₜ
Cantata No. 10, "Meine Seel' erhebt den Herren!"
Instrumentation: 2 oboes, trumpet (tromba da tirarsi), strings &
continuo.

Jones, Philip, 5)
Potpourri, 51)
Wolf, Hans, 8)

ₜCantatas. No. 11, Lobet Gott in seinen Reichenₜ
Cantata No. 11, "Lobet Gott in seinen Reichen"
Instrumentation: 2 flutes, 2 oboes, 3 trumpets, timpani, strings &
continuo.

André, Maurice, 123)
Güttler, Ludwig, 16[11])
Laird, Michael, 23[11])
Potpourri, 51)
Schmid, Bernhard, 10)

ₜCantatas. No. 12, Weinen, Klagen, Sorgen, Zagenₜ
Cantata No. 12, "Weinen, Klagen, Sorgen, Zagen"
Instrumentation: oboe, bassoon, trumpet (tromba da tirarsi),
strings & continuo.

Bryant, Ralph, 2)
Güttler, Ludwig, 16[7])
Sauter, Hermann, 10), 32[7])

ₜCantatas. No. 13, Meine Seufzer, meine Tränen. 3. Chorale; arr. trumpet &
organₜ
Chorale, "Der Gott, der mir hat versprochen", from Cantata No. 13

Michel, Jean-François

ₜCantatas. No. 14, Wär' Gott nicht mit uns diese Zeitₜ
Cantata No. 14, "Wär' Gott nicht mit uns diese Zeit"
Instrumentation: 2 oboes, corno da caccia, strings & continuo.
(The horn used for these recordings may vary and may be a
natural horn, modern valved horn or a modern valved "corno da
caccia".)

Bryant, Ralph, 2)
Güttler, Ludwig, 17)
Schmid, Bernhard, 10)

Cantata No. 19, "Es erhub sich ein Streit"
Instrumentation: 2 oboes, 2 oboes d'amore, oboe da caccia, 3 trumpets, timpani, strings & continuo.
André, Maurice, 107)
Güttler, Ludwig, 16⁵)
Sauter, Hermann, 8), 32⁷), 33¹)
Spindler, Josef, 12)

Cantata No. 20, "O Ewigkeit, du Donnerwort"
Instrumentation: 3 oboes, tromba da tirarsi (trumpet), strings & continuo.
Sauter, Hermann, 5), 32⁷)
Spindler, Josef, 12)

Cantata No. 21, "Ich hatte viel Bekümmernis"
Instrumentation: oboe, bassoon, 3 trumpets, 4 trombones, timpani, strings, organ & continuo.
Potpourri, 52)
Sauter, Hermann, 19)
Unidentified, Trumpet(s), 14)

Cantata No. 23, "Du wahrer Gott und Davids Sohn"
Potpourri, 52)

Cantata No. 24, "Ein ungefärbt Gemüte"
Instrumentation: 2 oboes, 2 oboes d'amore, "clarino" (trumpet or horn), strings & continuo.
Bryant, Ralph, 3)
McGregor, Rob Roy, 2), 7)

Cantata No. 25, "Es ist nichts Gesundes an meinem Leibe"
Instrumentation: 3 flutes (recorders), 2 oboes, cornetto, 3 trombones, strings & continuo.
Bryant, Ralph, 3)
Potpourri, 17)
Wolf, Hans, 2)

Cantata No. 26, "Ach wie flüchtig, ach wie nichtig"
Instrumentation: flute, 3 oboes, horn, strings & continuo. (The horn doubles the soprano voice part and may be replaced by cornetto while the other voice parts may be doubled using 3 trombones.)
Bryant, Ralph, 3)
Gleissle, Walter, 5)
Schmid, Bernhard, 6)

[Cantatas. No. 28, Gottlob! nun geht das Jahr zu Ende]
Cantata No. 28, "Gottlob! nun geht das Jahr zu Ende"
Instrumentation: 2 oboes, oboe da caccia, cornetto, 3 trombones, strings & continuo.
Lagorce, Marcel
Potpourri, 53)

[Cantatas. No. 29, Wir danken dir, Gott, wir danken dir]
Cantata No. 29, "Wir danken dir, Gott, wir danken dir"
Instrumentation: 2 oboes, 3 trumpets, timpani, strings, organ & continuo.
Carroll, Edward, 3[1])
Held, Friedrich
Holy, Walter, 3)
Läubin, Hannes, 7)
Potpourri, 53)

[Cantatas. No. 29, Wir danken dir, Gott, wir danken dir. 1. Sinfonia; arr. (trumpet), brass ensemble & organ]
Sinfonia in D major from Cantata No. 29
("Wir danken dir, Gott, wir danken dir")
("Nous te remercions, Dieu")
André, Maurice, 185)
Potpourri, 41), 43)

[Cantatas. No. 29, Wir danken dir, Gott, wir danken dir. 1. Sinfonia; arr. 2 trumpets, organ & chamber orchestra]
Sinfonia in D major from Cantata No. 29
Voisin, Roger, 1)

[Cantatas. No. 31, Der Himmel lacht, die Erde jubilieret]
Cantata No. 31, "Der Himmel lacht, die Erde jubilieret"
Instrumentation: 3 oboes, oboe da caccia, bassoon, 3 trumpets, timpani, strings & continuo.
André, Maurice, 100)
Güttler, Ludwig, 16⁹)
Sauter, Hermann, 21), 34[1])
Spindler, Josef, 13)

[Cantatas. No. 31, Der Himmel lacht, die Erde jubilieret. 1. Sonata, C major; arr. 3 trumpets, timpani & organ]
Sonata in C major from Cantata No. 31
This sonata was originally for 3 oboes, oboe da caccia, bassoon, 3 trumpets, timpani, strings & continuo.
Läubin, Hannes, 2)

[Cantatas. No. 33, Allein zu dir, Herr Jesu Christ. 3. Aria; arr. trumpet, organ, bass & drums]
Aria, "Wie furchtsam wankten meine Schritte" from Cantata No. 33
André, Maurice, 70)

ₜCantatas. No. 33, Allein zu dir, Herr Jesu Christ. 5. Duetto, tenor, bass, 2 oboes, organ & continuo, e minor; arr. 2 trumpets & organ₎

Aria Duetto, "Gott, der du die Liebe heisst", from Cantata No. 33

Butler, Barbara

ₜCantatas. No. 34, O ewiges Feuer, o Ursprung der Liebe₎

Cantata No. 34, "O ewiges Feuer, o Ursprung der Liebe"

Instrumentation: 2 flutes, 2 oboes, 3 trumpets, timpani, strings & continuo.

> **Potpourri, 11)**
> **Sauter, Hermann, 9), 32^5), 33^1)**
> **Spindler, Josef, 13)**
> **Unidentified, Trumpet(s), 13)**

ₜCantatas. No. 37, Wer da glaubet und getauft wird. 3. Chorale; arr. trumpet & organ₎

Chorale, "Herr Gott Vater, mein starker Held" from Cantata No. 37

This arrangement may be for a modern valved "corno da caccia" with organ.

> **Güttler, Ludwig, 15)**

ₜCantatas. No. 38, Aus tiefer Not schrei' ich zu dir₎

Cantata No. 38, "Aus tiefer Not schrei' ich zu dir"

Instrumentation: 2 oboes, 4 trombones (soprano, alto, tenor, bass), strings & continuo. (The soprano trombone part is played on trumpet.)

> **Schmid, Bernhard, 5)**

ₜCantatas. No. 41, Jesu, nun sei gepreiset₎

Cantata No. 41, "Jesu, nun sei gepreiset"

Instrumentation: 3 oboes, 3 trumpets, timpani, strings, organ & continuo.

> **Sauter, Hermann, 13), 32^6), 33^1), 35)**
> **Spindler, Josef, 14)**

ₜCantatas. No. 41, Jesu, nun sei gepreiset. 6. Chorale; arr. 3 trumpets, timpani & organ₎

Chorale, "Dein ist allein die Ehre" from Cantata No. 41

> **Laubin, Hannes, 2)**
> **Voisin, Roger, 2)**

ₜCantatas. No. 43, Gott fähret auf mit Jauchzen₎

Cantata No. 43, "Gott fähret auf mit Jauchzen"

Instrumentation: 2 oboes, 3 trumpets, timpani, strings & continuo.

> **Gleissle, Walter, 7)**
> **Immer, Friedemann, 6)**
> **Spindler, Josef, 15)**

[Cantatas. No. 43, Gott fähret auf mit Jauchzen. 3. Aria, bass, trumpet &
continuo, C major; arr. trumpet & piano]

Aria, "Er ist's, der ganz allein" from Cantata No. 43

This arrangement remains in the orignal key, but transposes the
trumpet part down an octave.

Nagel, Robert, 10)

[Cantatas. No. 46, Schauet doch und sehet, ob irgend ein Schmerz sei]

Cantata No. 46, "Schauet doch und sehet"

Instrumentation: 2 flutes (recorders), 2 oboes da caccia, trumpet
(tromba da tirarsi / corno da tirarsi), strings & continuo.

Holy, Walter, 1)
McGregor, Rob Roy, 3), 7)
Spindler, Josef, 15)
Stracker, Wilhelm

[Cantatas. No. 48, Ich elender Mensch, wer wird mich erlösen]

Cantata No. 48, "Ich elender Mensch, wer wird mich erlösen"

Instrumentation: oboe solo, 2 oboes, trumpet (tromba da tirarsi),
strings & continuo.

Potpourri, 54)
Sauter, Hermann, 32^{3+7})
Unidentified, Trumpet(s), 5)

[Cantatas. No. 49 & 169. Sinfonias, E major & D major; arr. concerto, trumpet &
chamber orchestra, F major]

Concerto in F major for Trumpet

(arr. of Sinfonias from Cantatas Nos. 49 and 169)

The sinfonia from Cantata No. 49 was originally for oboe
d'amore, strings, organ & continuo; and the sinfonia from
Cantata No. 169 was originally for 2 oboes, oboe da caccia,
strings, organ & continuo.

André, Maurice, 73), 214), 165)

[Cantatas. No. 50, Nun ist das Heil und die Kraft]

Cantata No. 50, "Nun ist das Heil und die Kraft"

Instrumentation: 3 oboes, 3 trumpets, timpani, strings, organ &
continuo.

André, Maurice, 107)
Läubin, Hannes, 8)
Potpourri, 54)

[Cantatas. No. 51, Jauchzet Gott in allen Landen]

Cantata No. 51, "Jauchzet Gott in allen Landen"

Instrumentation: trumpet, strings & continuo.

André, Maurice, 1), 11), 48), 192), 223)
Bauer, Willibald, 1)
Ghitalla, Armando, 3)
Güttler, Ludwig, 17)
Heinrich, Robert
Holmgren, Fred
Hunger, Helmut, 2)
Jackson, Harold

Läubin, Hannes, 6)
Reinhart, Carole Dawn, 2)
Ridder, Jean de
Smithers, Don, 13)
Steele-Perkins, Crispian, 16)
Thibaud, Pierre, 6)
Wobisch, Helmut, 1)

₍Cantatas. No. 51, Jauchzet Gott in allen Landen. 4. Chorale; arr. trumpet, 2
violins & continuo₎
Chorale, "Sei Lob und Preis mit Ehren" from Cantata No. 51
André, Maurice, 211), 215)

₍Cantatas. No. 51, Jauchzet Gott in allen Landen. 4. Chorale; arr. 2 trumpets,
strings & continuo₎
Chorale, "Sei Lob und Preis mit Ehren" from Cantata No. 51
This arrangement most likely also includes the concluding
"Alleluia".
André, Maurice, 85), 153)

₍Cantatas. No. 51, Jauchzet Gott in allen Landen. 5. Aria, soprano, trumpet,
strings & continuo, C major; arr. 2 trumpets & strings₎
Aria, "Alleluja", from Cantata No. 51
Carroll, Edward, 5)

₍Cantatas. No. 59, Wer mich liebet, der wird mein Wort halten₎
Cantata No. 59, "Wer mich liebet, der wird mein Wort halten"
Instrumentation: 2 trumpets, timpani, strings & continuo.
Groot, Willem (Wim)
Potpourri, 23), 55)
Sauter, Hermann, 24)

₍Cantatas. No. 60, O Ewigkeit, du Donnerwort₎
Cantata No. 60, "O Ewigkeit, du Donnerwort"
Instrumentation: 2 oboes d'amore, horn (tromba da tirarsi),
strings & continuo.
McGregor, Rob Roy, 5), 7)
Potpourri, 55)

₍Cantatas. No. 62, Nun komm, der Heiden Heiland₎
Cantata No. 62, "Nun komm, der Heiden Heiland"
Instrumentation: 2 oboes, horn (cornetto), strings & continuo.
Potpourri, 26^{1+5-6}), 56)
Schmid, Bernhard, 7)

₍Cantatas. No. 62, Nun komm, der Heiden Heiland. 4. Aria; arr. trumpet & brass
ensemble₎
Aria, "Streite, siege, starker Held" from Cantata No. 62
Michel, Jean-François

[Cantatas. No. 63, Christen, ätzet diesen Tag]

Cantata No. 63, "Christen, ätzet diesen Tag"
Instrumentation: 3 oboes, bassoon, 4 trumpets, timpani, strings, organ & continuo.
> **Potpourri, 23), 27[1+7]), 56)**
> **Sauter, Hermann, 7)**
> **Schmid, Bernhard, 4)**

[Cantatas. No. 63, Christen, ätzet diesen Tag. Excerpts; arr. 4 trumpets, timpani & organ]

Cantata No. 63, "Christen, ätzet diesen Tag"
[1]Chorus, "Christen, ätzet diesen Tag" / [7]Chorus, "Höchster, schau' in Gnaden an"
> **Hickman, David, 6)**

[Cantatas. No. 64, Sehet, welch eine Liebe hat uns der Vater erzeiget]

Cantata No. 64, "Sehet, welch eine Liebe hat uns der Vater erzeiget"
Instrumentation: oboe d'amore, cornetto, 3 trombones, strings, organ & continuo.
> **Potpourri, 17), 56)**
> **Wolf, Hans, 3)**

[Cantatas. No. 64, Sehet, welch eine Liebe hat uns der Vater erzeiget. 4. Chorale; arr. trumpet & organ]

Chorale, "Was frag ich nach der Welt", from Cantata No. 64
Michel, Jean-François

[Cantatas. No. 68, Also hat Gott die Welt geliebt]

Cantata No. 68, "Also hat Gott die Welt geliebt"
Instrumentation: 2 oboes, oboe da caccia, cornetto, horn, 3 trombones, strings & continuo. (The cornetto and horn parts double the soprano voice part and may be performed by cornetto, horn or trumpet.)
> **Potpourri, 2), 11), 24), 25), 57)**

[Cantatas. No. 68, Also hat Gott die Welt geliebt. 2. Aria; arr. trumpet & organ]

Aria, "Mein gläubiges Herze" from Cantata No. 68
André, Maurice, 40), 52), 67)

[Cantatas. No. 68, Also hat Gott die Welt geliebt. 2. Aria; arr. trumpet & strings]

Aria, "My Heart Ever Faithful"
(Aria, "Mein gläubiges Herze" from Cantata No. 68)
Carroll, Edward, 5)

ₜCantatas. No. 69, Lobe den Herrn, meine Seele₎

Cantata No. 69, "Lobe den Herrn, meine Seele" [version a, 1724]

Cantata No. 69 (version a) = Cantata No. 69 (without further designation).

Instrumentation: 3 oboes, oboe d'amore, bassoon, 3 trumpets, timpani, strings & continuo.

Potpourri, 24)
Sauter, Hermann, 12), 36⁶)

ₜCantatas. No. 69a, Lobe den Herrn, meine Seele₎

Cantata No. 69, "Lobe den Herrn, meine Seele" [version b, 1730]

Cantata No. 69 (version b) = Cantata No. 69a.

Instrumentation: 3 oboes, oboe d'amore, bassoon, 3 trumpets, timpani, strings & continuo.

Spindler, Josef, 16)

ₜCantatas. No. 70, Wachet! Betet! Betet! Wachet!₎

Cantata No. 70, "Wachet! Betet! Betet! Wachet!"

Instrumentation: oboe, bassoon, trumpet, strings & continuo.

André, Maurice, 138)
Potpourri, 24), 27⁷)
Sauter, Hermann, 6), 33¹), 35)
Spindler, Josef, 16)

ₜCantatas. No. 71, Gott ist mein König₎

Cantata No. 71, "Gott ist mein König"

Instrumentation: 2 flutes (recorders), 2 oboes, bassoon, 3 trumpets, timpani, strings & organ.

Potpourri, 24)
Sauter, Hermann, 17)
Spindler, Josef, 16)

ₜCantatas. No. 74, Wer mich liebet, der wird mein Wort halten₎

Cantata No. 74, "Wer mich liebet, der wird mein Wort halten"

Instrumentation: 2 oboes, oboe da caccia, 3 trumpets, timpani, strings & continuo.

Potpourri, 24)
Sauter, Hermann, 9), 33¹)
Smithers, Don, 14)

ₜCantatas. No. 75, Die Elenden sollen essen₎

Cantata No. 75, "Die Elenden sollen essen"

Instrumentation: 2 oboes, oboe d'amore, bassoon, trumpet, strings & continuo.

Sauter, Hermann, 4), 34⁸)
Smithers, Don, 14)

[Cantatas. No. 75, Die Elenden sollen essen. 7. Chorale; arr. trumpet & strings]
Chorale, "Was Gott tut, das ist wohlgetan" from Cantata No. 75
Touvron, Guy, 9)

[Cantatas. No. 75, Die Elenden sollen essen. 8. Sinfonia, trumpet, strings & continuo, G major]
Sinfonia in G major from Cantata No. 75
Schneidewind, Helmut, 7)
Touvron, Guy, 9)

[Cantatas. No. 76, Die Himmel erzählen die Ehre Gottes]
Cantata No. 76, "Die Himmel erzählen die Ehre Gottes"
Instrumentation: 2 oboes, oboe d'amore, trumpet, strings and continuo.
Gleissle, Walter, 2)
McGregor, Rob Roy, 1), 7)
Potpourri, 26^{14}), 58)

[Cantatas. No. 77, Du sollst Gott, deinen Herren, lieben]
Cantata No. 77, "Du sollst Gott, deinen Herren, lieben"
Instrumentation: 2 oboes, tromba da tirarsi, strings & continuo.
Güttler, Ludwig, 16^5)
Potpourri, 58)
Sauter, Hermann, 11)

[Cantatas. No. 77, Du sollst Gott, deinen Herren, lieben. 3. Aria; arr. trumpet & organ]
Aria, "Mein Gott, ich liebe dich von Herzen" from Cantata No. 77
Basch, Wolfgang, 11)

[Cantatas. No. 77, Du sollst Gott, deinen Herren, lieben. 5. Aria, alto, trumpet & continuo, d minor; arr. trumpet & piano]
Aria, "Ach, es bleibt in meiner Liebe", from from Cantata No. 77
This arrangement remains in the original key, but the trumpet part is transposed down an octave.
Nagel, Robert, 10)

[Cantatas. No. 78, Jesu, der du meine Seele]
Cantata No. 78, "Jesu, der du meine Seele"
Instrumentation: flute, 2 oboes, horn, strings, organ & continuo.
(The horn may be replaced by tromba da tirarsi.)
Basch, Wolfgang, 1)
Gleissle, Walter, 4)
Potpourri, 58)
Unidentified, Trumpet(s), 8)

[Cantatas. No. 78, Jesu, der du meine Seele. 2. Aria, soprano, alto & continuo,
B♭ major; arr. trumpet, organ, bass & drums]

Aria Duetto, "Wir eilen mit schwachen, doch emsigen Schritten", from Cantata No. 78
André, Maurice, 69)

[Cantatas. No. 78, Jesu, der du meine Seele. 2. Aria, soprano, alto & continuo,
B♭ major; arr. 2 trumpets, strings & continuo]

Aria Duetto, "Wir eilen mit schwachen, doch emsigen Schritten", from Cantata No. 78
André, Maurice, 43), 57), 85), 211), 215), 153)

[Cantatas. No. 79, Gott, der Herr, ist Sonn' und Schild. 3. Chorale; arr. trumpet
& organ]

Chorale, "Nun danket alle Gott" from Cantata No. 79
Hardy, Francis

[Cantatas. No. 79, Gott, der Herr, ist Sonn' und Schild. 3. Chorale; arr. 2
trumpets, timpani, organ & bassoon]

Chorale, "Nun danket alle Gott" from Cantata No. 79
Voisin, Roger, 2)

[Cantatas. No. 80, Ein feste Burg ist unser Gott]

Cantata No. 80, "Ein feste Burg ist unser Gott"
Gleissle, Walter, 3)
Potpourri, 26^{1+5+8})
Sauter, Hermann, 20)
Tarr, Edward, 24)
Unidentified, Trumpet(s), 23)

[Cantatas. No. 89, Was soll ich aus dir machen, Ephraim?]

Cantata No. 89, "Was soll ich aus dir machen, Ephraim?"
Instrumentation: 2 oboes, horn, strings & continuo.
(One recording uses piccolo trumpet with a wool hat in place of
the horn.)
Groot, Willem (Wim)
McGregor, Rob Roy, 4)
Potpourri, 17)
Smithers, Don, 15)

[Cantatas. No. 90, Es reifet euch ein schrecklich Ende]

Cantata No. 90, "Es reifet euch ein schrecklich Ende"
Instrumentation: trumpet, strings & continuo.
André, Maurice, 99)
Groot, Willem (Wim)
McGregor, Rob Roy, 5), 7)
Smithers, Don, 15)

ₜCantatas. No. 95, Christus, der ist mein Lebenₒ

Cantata No. 95, "Christus, der ist mein Leben"

Instrumentation: 2 oboes, 2 oboes d'amore, cornetto (or trumpet), strings & continuo.

Bryant, Ralph, 4)
Köpp, Rudolf

ₜCantatas. No. 99, Was Gott tut, das ist wohlgetanₒ

Cantata No. 99, "Was Gott tut, das ist wohlgetan"

Instrumentation: flute, oboe d'amore, horn (or cornetto), strings & continuo.

Bryant, Ralph, 5)

ₜCantatas. No. 101, Nimm von uns, Herr, du treuer Gottₒ

Cantata No. 101, "Nimm von uns, Herr, du treuer Gott"

Instrumentation: flute, 2 oboes, oboe da caccia, cornetto, 3 trombones, strings & continuo.

Bryant, Ralph, 5)

ₜCantatas. No. 103, Ihr werdet weinen und heulenₒ

Cantata No. 103, "Ihr werdet weinen und heulen"

Instrumentation: piccolo, flute, 2 oboes d'amore, trumpet, strings & continuo.

Güttler, Ludwig, 16⁵)
Potpourri, 59)
Wolf, Hans, 11)

ₜCantatas. No. 105, Herr, gehe nicht ins Gericht mit deinem Knechtₒ

Cantata No. 105, "Herr, gehe nicht ins Gericht mit deinem Knecht"

Instrumentation: 2 oboes, horn (cornetto), strings & continuo. (While a real horn is used on one recording, a cornetto on another, yet another uses piccolo trumpet with a wool hat.)

André, Maurice, 100)
McGregor, Rob Roy, 3)
Potpourri, 17), 59)

ₜCantatas. No. 107, Was willst du dich betrübenₒ

Cantata No. 107, "Was willst du dich betrüben"

Instrumentation: 2 flutes, 2 oboes d'amore, horn (corno da caccia or tromba da tirarsi), strings, organ & continuo.

Potpourri, 60)

ₜCantatas. No. 109, Ich glaube, lieber Herr, hilf meinem Unglauben!ₒ

Cantata No. 109, "Ich glaube, lieber Herr, hilf meinem Unglauben!"

Instrumentation: 2 oboes, corno da caccia (tromba da tirarsi), strings & continuo.

Potpourri, 60)

₍Cantatas. No. 110, Unser Mund sei voll Lachens₎
Cantata No. 110, "Unser Mund sei voll Lachens"
Instrumentation: 2 flutes, 3 oboes, oboe d'amore, oboe da caccia, bassoon, 3 trumpets, timpani, strings, organ & continuo.
Gleissle, Walter, 6)
Potpourri, 22), 60)
Sauter, Hermann, 14), 30), 33[6]), 36[7])

₍Cantatas. No. 111, Was mein Gott will, das g'scheh' allzeit. 4. Aria, alto, tenor, strings & continuo, G major; arr. 2 trumpets & organ₎
Aria Duetto, "So geh' ich mit beherzten Schritten", from Cantata No. 111
Butler, Barbara

₍Cantatas. No. 112, Der Herr ist mein getreuer Hirt₎
Cantata No. 112, "Der Herr ist mein getreuer Hirt"
Instrumentation: 2 oboes d'amore, 2 horns (2 "clarinhorns"), strings & continuo.
Läubin, Hannes, 6)
Potpourri, 61)

₍Cantatas. No. 114, Ach, lieben Christen, seid getrost₎
Cantata No. 114, "Ach, lieben Christen, seid getrost"
Instrumentation: flute, 2 oboes, horn (trompetenhorn), strings & continuo.
Potpourri, 61)

₍Cantatas. No. 115, Mache dich, mein Geist, bereit₎
Cantata No. 115, "Mache dich, mein Geist, bereit"
Instrumentation: flute, oboe d'amore, horn (cornetto), strings & continuo.
Schmid, Bernhard, 5)

₍Cantatas. No. 116, Du Friedefürst, Herr Jesu Christ₎
Cantata No. 116, "Du Friedefürst, Herr Jesu Christ"
Instrumentation: 2 oboes d'amore, horn (cornetto), strings & continuo.
Schmid, Bernhard, 7)

₍Cantatas. No. 119, Preise, Jerusalem, den Herrn₎
Cantata No. 119, "Preise, Jerusalem, den Herrn"
Instrumentation: 2 flutes (recorders), 3 oboes, 2 oboes da caccia, 4 trumpets, timpani, strings & continuo.
Güttler, Ludwig, 16[7])
Lagorce, Marcel
Potpourri, 17)
Schmid, Bernhard, 3)

ₜCantatas. No. 120, Gott, man lobet dich in der Stilleₕ

Cantata No. 120, "Gott, man lobet dich in der Stille"
Instrumentation: 2 oboes d'amore, 3 trumpets, timpani, strings & continuo.
> **Potpourri,** 62)
> **Sauter, Hermann,** 12), 33²)

ₜCantatas. No. 121, Christum wir sollen loben schonₕ

Cantata No. 121, "Christum wir sollen loben schon"
Instrumentation: oboe d'amore, cornetto (trumpet), 3 trombones, strings & continuo.
> **Potpourri,** 62)
> **Schmid, Bernhard,** 8)

ₜCantatas. No. 124, Meinen Jesum lass' ich nichtₕ

Cantata No. 124, "Meinen Jesum lass' ich nicht"
Instrumentation: oboe d'amore, horn (cornetto), strings & continuo.
> **Potpourri,** 63)

ₜCantatas. No. 125, Mit Fried' und Freud' ich fahr' dahinₕ

Cantata No. 125, "Mit Fried' und Freud' ich fahr' dahin"
Instrumentation: flute, oboe, oboe d'amore, horn (cornetto), strings & continuo.
> **Potpourri,** 63)

ₜCantatas. No. 126, Erhalt' uns, Herr, bei deinem Wortₕ

Cantata No. 126, "Erhalt' uns, Herr, bei deinem Wort"
Instrumentation: 2 oboes, trumpet, strings & continuo.
> **Miller, Rodney**
> **Potpourri,** 26¹⁺³⁺⁶), 63)
> **Tarr, Edward,** 26)
> **Thibaud, Pierre,** 7)

ₜCantatas. No. 127, Herr Jesu Christ, wahr' Mensch und Gottₕ

Cantata No. 127, "Herr Jesu Christ, wahr' Mensch und Gott"
Instrumentation: 2 flutes (recorders), 2 oboes, trumpet (tromba da caccia), strings & continuo.
> **Potpourri,** 63)
> **Wolf, Hans,** 10)

ₜCantatas. No. 128, Auf Christi Himmelfahrt alleinₕ

Cantata No. 128, "Auf Christi Himmelfahrt allein"
Instrumentation: 2 oboes, oboe d'amore, oboe da caccia, 2 horns, trumpet, strings & continuo.
> **Immer, Friedemann,** 5), 14)

₍Cantatas. No. 129, Gelobet sei der Herr, mein Gott₎
Cantata No. 129, "Gelobet sei der Herr, mein Gott"
Instrumentation: flute, 2 oboes, oboe d'amore, 3 trumpets, timpani, strings & continuo.
Carroll, Edward, 3[1])
Immer, Friedemann, 14)
Läubin, Hannes, 3)

₍Cantatas. No. 129, Gelobet sei der Herr, mein Gott. 5. Chorale; arr. 2 trumpets, organ & chamber orchestra₎
Chorale, "Awake thou wintry earth" from Cantata No. 129
(Chorale, "Dem wir das Heilig itzt mit Freuden lassen klingen")
Voisin, Roger, 1)

₍Cantatas. No. 129, Gelobet sei der Herr, mein Gott. 5. Chorale; arr. 3 trumpets, timpani, organ & continuo₎
Chorale, "O Gott, du frommer Gott"
(Chorale, "Dem wir das Heilig itzt mit Freuden lassen klingen" from Cantata No. 129)
Smithers, Don, 6)

₍Cantatas. No. 130, Herr Gott, dich loben alle wir₎
Cantata No. 130, "Herr Gott, dich loben alle wir"
Instrumentation: flute, 3 oboes, 3 trumpets, timpani, strings & continuo.
Gleissle, Walter, 5)
Güttler, Ludwig, 16[3])
Immer, Friedemann, 14)
Sauter, Hermann, 15), 33[1])

₍Cantatas. No. 130, Herr Gott, dich loben alle wir. 6. Chorale; arr. 3 trumpets, timpani & organ₎
Chorale, "Darum wir billig loben dich" from Cantata No. 130
Läubin, Hannes, 2)
Voisin, Roger, 2)

₍Cantatas. No. 134, Ein Herz, das seinen Jesum lebend weiss. 4. Aria, alto, tenor, strings & continuo, E♭ major; arr. 2 trumpets & organ₎
Aria Duetto, "Wir danken", from Cantata No. 134
Butler, Barbara

₍Cantatas. No. 135, Ach Herr, mich armen Sünder₎
Cantata No. 135, "Ach Herr, mich armen Sünder"
Instrumentation: 2 oboes, cornetto, trombone, strings & continuo.
Holy, Walter, 3)
Laird, Michael, 23[1+6])
Wolf, Hans, 7)

₍Cantatas. No. 136, Erforsche mich, Gott, und erfahre mein Herz₎

Cantata No. 136, "Erforsche mich, Gott, und erfahre mein Herz"

Instrumentation: oboe d'amore, horn, strings & continuo. (One recording uses a "clarinhorn" in A.)
Immer, Friedemann, 15)
McGregor, Rob Roy, 2)
Potpourri, 17)

₍Cantatas. No. 137, Lobe den Herren, den mächtigen König der Ehren₎

Cantata No. 137, "Lobe den Herren, den mächtigen König der Ehren"

Instrumentation: 2 oboes, 3 trumpets, timpani, strings & continuo.
Immer, Friedemann, 15)
Tarr, Edward, 23)
Wolf, Hans, 12)

₍Cantatas. No. 137, Lobe den Herren, den mächtigen König dr Ehren. 1. Chorale; arr. 3 trumpets, timpani & organ₎

Chorale, "Lobe den Herren, was in mir ist" from Cantata No. 137

Läubin, Hannes, 2)
Voisin, Roger, 2)

₍Cantatas. No. 140, Wachet auf, ruft uns die Stimme. 1. Chorale; arr. trumpet & strings₎

Chorale, "Wachet auf, ruft uns die Stimme" from Cantata No. 140

André, Maurice, 35), 43), 57), 85), 133), 211), 227)

₍Cantatas. No. 140, Wachet auf, ruft uns die Stimme. 3. Aria, soprano, bass, violin & continuo, c minor; arr. 2 trumpets & organ₎

Aria Duetto, "Wann kommst du, mein Heil?" from Cantata No. 140

Butler, Barbara

₍Cantatas. No. 140, Wachet auf, ruft uns die Stimme. 4. Chorale; arr. trumpet & orchestra₎

Chorale, "Zion hört die Wächter singen", from Cantata No. 140
Touvron, Guy, 9), 13)

₍Cantatas. No. 140, Wachet auf, ruft uns die Stimme. 4. Chorale; arr. trumpet & organ₎

Chorale, "Zion hört die Wächter singen", from Cantata No. 140
Erb, Helmut, 5)

₍Cantatas. No. 140, Wachet auf, ruft uns die Stimme. 4. Chorale; arr. trumpet, guitar & orchestra₎
Sleepers Awake!
(Chorale No. 4, "Zion hört die Wächter singen", from Cantata No. 140)
Schultz, Erik, 8)

₍Cantatas. No. 142, Uns ist ein Kind geboren. Excerpts; arr.₎
Concerto and Chorale from Cantata No. 142
¹Concerto in a minor / ⁸Chorale, "Alleluia, gelobet sei Gott"
Voisin, Roger, 1)

₍Cantatas. No. 143, Lobe den Herrn, meine Seele₎
Cantata No. 143, "Lobe den Herrn, meine Seele"
Instrumentation: 3 corni da caccia, bassoon, timpani, strings & continuo. (The 3 "corni da caccia" used for this recording are modern valved instruments.)
Güttler, Ludwig, 17)

₍Cantatas. No. 143, Lobe den Herrn, meine Seele. 2. Chorale; arr. corno da caccia & organ₎
Chorale, "Du Friedefürst, Herr Jesu Christ", from Cantata No. 143
The "corno da caccia" used in this arrangement is a modern valved instrument.
Güttler, Ludwig, 24)

₍Cantatas. No. 145, Ich lebe, mein Herze, zu deinem Ergötzen₎
Cantata No. 145, "Ich lebe, mein Herze, zu deinem Ergötzen"
Schmieder lists this cantata as "Auf, mein Herz, des Herren Tag". The first two sections of the cantata as listed by Schmieder are omitted from this recording. (Presumably the first two sections are not considered authentic, hence, the difference in titles.) Instrumentation: flute, 2 oboes d'amore, trumpet, strings & continuo.
Friedrich, Reinhold

₍Cantatas. No. 146, Wir müssen durch viel Trübsal in das Reich Gottes eingehen. 7. Duetto, tenor, bass, 2 oboes, strings & continuo; arr. 2 trumpets & organ₎
Duet Aria, "My Spirit be Joyful" from Cantata No. 146
(Duetto, "Wie will ich mich freuen")
Voisin, Roger, 1)

[Cantatas. No. 147, Herz und Mund und Tat und Leben]

Cantata No. 147, "Herz und Mund und Tat und Leben"
Instrumentation: 2 oboes, oboe d'amore, 2 oboes da caccia,
bassoon, trumpet, strings & continuo.

André, Maurice, 99)
Basch, Wolfgang, 1)
Carroll, Edward, 3[10])
Gleissle, Walter, 8)
Güttler, Ludwig, 13[10])
Laird, Michael, 23[10])
Sauter, Hermann, 23)
Schmid, Bernhard, 2)
Steele-Perkins, Crispian, 17[10])
Wilbraham, John, 22)

[Cantatas. No. 147, Herz und Mund und Tat und Leben. 10. Chorale; arr. brass & organ]

Chorale, "Jesus bleibet meine Freude" from Cantata No. 147
(Chorale, "Jésus, que ma joie demeure")
(Chorale, "Jesu, Joy of Man's Desiring")

André, Maurice, 185), 198)

[Cantatas. No. 147, Herz und Mund und Tat und Leben. 10. Chorale; arr. trumpet & organ]

Chorale, "Jesus bleibet meine Freude" from Cantata No. 147
(Chorale, "Jésus, que ma joie demeure")
(Chorale, "Jesu, Joy of Man's Desiring")

André, Maurice, 40), 42), 50), 76), 78), 118),
    215), 218), 227)
Basch, Wolfgang, 11)
Bernard, André, 4), 9), 11)
Braz, Dirceu, 4)
Carroll, Edward, 3)
Delmotte, Roger, 38)
Erb, Helmut, 5)
Güttler, Ludwig, 2)
Läubin, Hannes, 2)
Lewark, Egbert
Pliquett, Joachim
Potpourri, 41), 43), 44)
Schetsche, Walter
Schultz, Erik, 3)
Smithers, Don, 6), 9)
Stringer, Alan, 3)
Tschotschev, Nicolai-Dimitrov

[Cantatas. No. 147, Herz und Mund und Tat und Leben. 10. Chorale; arr. trumpet & strings]

Chorale, "Jesus bleibet meine Freude" from Cantata No. 147
(Chorale, "Jésus, que ma joie demeure")
(Chorale, "Jesu, Joy of Man's Desiring")
Carroll, Edward, 5)
Touvron, Guy, 9), 13)

[Cantatas. No. 148, Bringet dem Herrn Ehre seines Namens]

Cantata No. 148, "Bringet dem Herrn Ehre seines Namens"
Instrumentation: 3 oboes, trumpet, strings & continuo.
Güttler, Ludwig, 16¹)
McGregor, Rob Roy, 4), 7)
Tarr, Edward, 25)

[Cantatas. No. 149, Man singet mit Freuden vom Sieg]

Cantata No. 149, "Man singet mit Freuden vom Sieg"
Instrumentation: 3 oboes, bassoon, 3 trumpets, timpani, strings & continuo.
Läubin, Hannes, 5)
Tarr, Edward, 26)
Unidentified, Trumpet(s), 15)

[Cantatas. No. 156, Ich steh' mit einem Fuss im Grabe. 1. Sinfonia, oboe, strings & continuo, F major; arr. trumpet & organ]

Sinfonia in F major from Cantata No. 156
Berinbaum, Martin
Michel, Jean-François

[Cantatas. No. 156, Ich steh' mit einem Fuss im Grabe. 1. Sinfonia, oboe, strings & continuo, F major; arr. trumpet & piano]

Sinfonia in F major from Cantata No. 156
Ghitalla, Armando, 11)
Stith, Marice, 5)

[Cantatas. No. 156, Ich steh' mit einem Fuss im Grabe. 1. Sinfonia, oboe, strings & continuo, F major; arr. trumpet & strings]

Sinfonia in F major from Cantata No. 156
Cowell, Johnny

[Cantatas. No. 162, Ach, ich sehe, itzt, da ich zur Hochzeit gehe]

Cantata No. 162, "Ach, ich sehe, itzt, da ich zur Hochzeit gehe"
Instrumentation: corno da tirarsi (trumpet), bassoon, strings & continuo.
Sauter, Hermann, 22)

[Cantatas. No. 167, Ihr Menschen, rühmet Gottes Liebe]

Cantata No. 167, "Ihr Menschen, rühmet Gottes Liebe"
Instrumentation: oboe, oboe da caccia, trumpet, strings & continuo.
Laird, Michael, 23⁵)
Sauter, Hermann, 15)

ₜCantatas. No. 167, Ihr Menschen, rümet Gottes Liebe. 5. Chorale; arr. trumpet & stringsₗ

Chorale, "Sei Lob und Preis mit Ehren" from Cantata No. 167
Touvron, Guy, 9)

ₜCantatas. No. 171, Gott, wie dein Name, so ist auch dein Ruhmₗ

Cantata No. 171, "Gott, wie dein Name, so ist auch dein Ruhm"
Instrumentation: 2 oboes, 3 trumpets, timpani, strings & continuo.
Send, Peter
Tarr, Edward, 15)

ₜCantatas. No. 172, Erschallet, ihr Lieder, erklinget, ihr Saiten!ₗ

Cantata No. 172, "Erschallet, ihr Lieder, erklinget, ihr Saiten!"
Instrumentation: 3 trumpets, timpani, strings, organ, bassoon & continuo.
Potpourri, 2)
Sauter, Hermann, 18), 33[1])

ₜCantatas. No. 174, Ich liebe den Höchsten von ganzem Gemüteₗ

Cantata No. 174, "Ich liebe den Höchsten von ganzem Gemüte"
Instrumentation: 2 oboes, oboe da caccia, bassoon, corno da caccia, strings & continuo. (The "corno da caccia" used for this recording is a modern valved instrument.)
Güttler, Ludwig, 13[1])

ₜCantatas. No. 175, Er rufet seinen Schafen mit Namenₗ

Cantata No. 175, "Er rufet seinen Schafen mit Namen"
Instrumentation: 3 flutes (recorders), 2 trumpets, strings & continuo.
Potpourri, 11), 25)
Zeh, Karl Heinz

ₜCantatas. No. 175, Er rufet seinen Schafen mit Namen. 6. Aria, bass, 2 trumpets & continuo, D major; arr. 2 trumpets & piano, B♭ majorₗ

Aria, "Öffnet euch, ihr beiden Ohren", from Cantata No. 175
Nagel, Robert, 11)

ₜCantatas. No. 181, Leichtgesinnte Flattergeisterₗ

Cantata No. 181, "Leichtgesinnte Flattergeister"
Instrumentation: flute, oboe, trumpet, strings & continuo.
Sauter, Hermann, 16), 31), 33[5])

ₜCantatas. No. 190, Singet dem Herrn ein neues Liedₗ

Cantata No. 190, "Singet dem Herrn ein neues Lied"
Instrumentation: 3 oboes, oboe d'amore, 3 trumpets, strings & continuo.
Potpourri, 17)
Tarr, Edward, 23)
Wolf, Hans, 3)

[Cantatas. No. 191, Gloria in excelsis Deo]

Cantata No. 191, "Gloria in excelsis Deo"
Instrumentation: 2 flutes, 2 oboes, 3 trumpets, timpani, strings & continuo.

Potpourri, 27[1+3])

Sauter, Hermann, 8)

[Cantatas. No. 193, Ihr Tore zu Zion]

Cantata No. 193, "Ihr Tore zu Zion"
Instrumentation: 2 oboes, strings & continuo. (3 trumpets are listed on this recording, but are not indicated by Schmieder.)

Läubin, Hannes, 4)

[Cantatas. No. 195, Dem Gerechten muss das Licht immer wieder aufgehen]

Cantata No. 195, "Dem Gerechten muss das Licht immer wieder aufgehen"
Instrumentation: 2 flutes, 2 oboes, 2 oboes d'amore, 2 horns, 3 trumpets, timpani, strings & continuo.

Schmid, Bernhard, 11)

[Cantatas. No. 197, Gott ist unsre Zuversicht]

Cantata No. 197, "Gott ist unsre Zuversicht"
Instrumentation: 2 oboes, 2 oboes d'amore, bassoon (obligato), 3 trumpets, timpani, strings & continuo.

Läubin, Hannes, 8)

[Cantatas. No. 201, Geschwinde, geschwinde, ihr wirbelnden Winde]

Cantata No. 201, "Geschwinde, geschwinde, ihr wirbelnden Winde"
(Dramma per musica. "Der Streit zwischen Phoebus und Pan")
Instrumentation: 2 flutes, 2 oboes, oboe d'amore, 3 trumpets, timpani, strings & continuo.

Zickler, Heinz, 1)

[Cantatas. No. 206, Schleicht, spielende Wellen]

Cantata No. 206, "Schleicht, spielende Wellen"
Instrumentation: 3 flutes, 2 oboes, 2 oboes d'amore, 3 trumpets, timpani, strings & continuo.

Zickler, Heinz, 2)

[Cantatas. No. 207, Vereinigte Zwietracht der wechselnden Saiten. Excerpts]

Cantata No. 207, "Vereinigte Zwietracht der wechselnden Saiten"
[1]March / [2]Chorus
Instrumentation: 2 flutes, 2 oboes d'amore, oboe da caccia, 3 trumpets, timpani, strings & continuo.

Carroll, Edward, 3[1-2])

[Cantatas. No. 207, Vereinigte Zwietracht der wechselnden Saiten. 1. Marcia, 3 trumpets, timpani, strings & continuo, D major; arr. 3 trumpets, timpani, organ & bassoon]

Marcia from "Vereinigte Zwietracht der wechselnden Saiten"
Carroll, Edward, 11)

₍Cantatas. No. 207a, Auf, schmetternde Töne der muntern Trompeten₎
Cantata No. 207a, "Auf, schmetternde Töne der muntern Trompeten"
Instrumentation: 2 flutes, 2 oboes d'amore, oboe da caccia, 3 trumpets, timpani, strings & continuo.
Holy, Walter, 2)

₍Cantatas. No. 214, Tönet, ihr Pauken! Erschallet, Trompeten!₎
Cantata No. 214, "Tönet, ihr Pauken! Erschallet, Trompeten!"
Instrumentation: 2 flutes, 2 oboes, 3 trumpets, timpani, strings & continuo.
Güttler, Ludwig, 16^1)
Holy, Walter, 2)

₍Cantatas. No. 215, Preise dein Glücke, gesegnetes Sachsen₎
Cantata No. 215, "Preise dein Glücke, gesegnetes Sachsen"
Instrumentation: 2 flutes, 2 oboes, 2 oboes d'amore, 3 trumpets, timpani, strings & continuo.
Wolf, Haas, 1)

₍Cantatas. No. 249a, Enfliehet, verschwindet, entweichet, ihr Sorgen₎
Cantata No. 249a, "Enfliehet, verschwindet, entweichet, ihr Sorgen"
Instrumentation: 2 recorders, flute, 2 oboes, bassoon, 3 trumpets, timpani, strings & continuo.
Zickler, Heinz, 3)

₍Capriccio, harpsichord, B$^\flat$ major, S. 992, (1704). 5. Aria di Postiglione; arr. trumpet & organ₎
Aria di Postiglione from *Capriccio in B$^\flat$ major*, S. 992
Basch, Wolfgang, 11)

₍Capriccio, harpsichord, B$^\flat$ major, S. 992, (1704). 5. Aria di Postiglione; arr. trumpet & strings₎
Aria di Postiglione from *Capriccio in B$^\flat$ major*, S. 992
André, Maurice, 219)
Potpourri, 32)

₍Choräle zu Trauungen, S. 250-252; arr. 2 trumpets & organ₎
Three Wedding Chorales
(Drei Choräle zu Trauungen)
   a) "Was Gott tut, das ist wohlgetan", S. 250
   b) "Sei Lob und Ehr' dem höchsten Gut", S. 251
   c) "Nun danket alle Gott", S. 252
Voisin, Roger, 2)

₍Choralchor (motet). Sei Lob und Preis mit Ehren, mixed voices; arr. mixed voices, trumpet & organ₎
Choralchor, "Sei Lob und Preis mit Ehren", S. 231
Krystek, Ulrich

ₓChorale preludesₓ
Chorale preludes
SEE: Chorale preludes, organ.
SEE also: Kirnberger Chorales.
SEE also: Leipzig Chorales.
SEE also: Schübler Chorales.

ₓChorale preludes, organ. Aus tiefer Not schrei' ich zu dir, S. 686; arr. (trumpet), brass ensemble & organₓ
Chorale Prelude, "Aus tiefer Not schrei' ich zu dir", S. 686
André, Maurice, 185)

ₓChorale preludes, organ. Aus tiefer Not schrei' ich zu dir, S. 686; arr. trumpet & organₓ
Chorale Prelude, "Aus tiefer Not schrei' ich zu dir", S. 686
Hardy, Francis

ₓChorale preludes, organ. Der Tag, der ist so freudenreich, S. 605; arr. trumpet & organₓ
Chorale Prelude, "Der Tag, der ist so freudenreich", S. 605
Delmotte, Roger, 38)

ₓChorale preludes, organ. Erbarm' dich mein, o Herre Gott, S. 721; arr. trumpet & chamber orchestraₓ
Chorale Prelude, "Erbarm' dich mein, o Herre Gott", S. 721
Touvron, Guy, 9)

ₓChorale preludes, organ. Erbarm' dich mein, o Herre Gott, S. 721; arr. trumpet & organₓ
Chorale Prelude, "Erbarm' dich mein, o Herre Gott", S. 721
André, Maurice, 185)
Hardy, Francis
Touvron, Guy, 12)

ₓChorale preludes, organ. Gottes Sohn ist kommen, S. 600; arr. 2 trumpets & organₓ
Chorale Prelude, "Gottes Sohn ist kommen", S. 600
(or "Gott, durch deine Güte")
André, Maurice, 185)

ₓChorale preludes, organ. Herzlich tut mich verlangen, S. 727; arr. trumpet & organₓ
Chorale Prelude, "Herzlich tut mich verlangen", S. 727
André, Maurice, 185)
Bernard, André, 4)
Pliquett, Joachim

ₓChorale preludes, organ. Ich ruf' zu dir, Herr Jesu Christ", S. 639; arr. trumpet & organₓ
Chorale Prelude, "Ich ruf' zu dir, Herr Jesu Christ", S. 639
Delmotte, Roger, 38)

[Chorale preludes, organ. Kyrie, Gott Vater in Ewigkeit, S. 669; arr. trumpet & organ]

Chorale Prelude, "Kyrie, Gott Vater in Ewigkeit", S. 669
Hardy, Francis

[Chorale preludes, organ. Lob sei dem allmächtigen Gott; arr. trumpet & organ]

Chorale Prelude, "Lob sei dem allmächtigen Gott", S. 602
Delmotte, Roger, 38)

[Chorale preludes, organ. Nun freut euch, lieben Christen g'mein; arr. 2 trumpets & organ]

Chorale Prelude, "Nun freut euch, lieben Christen g'mein", S. 734
André, Maurice, 185)

[Chorale preludes, organ. Wir glauben all' an einen Gott, S. 740; arr. (trumpet), brass ensemble & organ]

Chorale Prelude, "Wir glauben all' an einen Gott", S. 680
André, Maurice, 185)

[Chorale preludes, organ. Wir glauben all' an einen Gott, S. 740; arr. trumpet & organ]

Chorale Prelude, "Wir glauben all' an einen Gott", S. 740
Smithers, Don, 6)

[Christmas Oratorio, S. 248]

Christmas Oratorio, S. 248
SEE: Weihnachts-Oratorium, S. 248.

[Concerto (Fragment), violin, 2 oboes, 3 trumpets, timpani, strings & continuo, D major, S. 1045]

Concerto Movement (Sinfonia) in D major, S. 1045
Konzert D-dur (Fragment)
Güttler, Ludwig, 18)

[Concerto, oboe, violin, strings & continuo, c minor, S. 1060, (1730); arr. trumpet, violin, strings & continuo, d minor]

Concerto in d minor for Trumpet and Violin, S. 1060
[1]Allegro / [2]Adagio / [3]Allegro
André, Maurice, 43), 57), 133), 211)

[Concertos, harpsichord, (16), S. 972-987. No. 1, D major, S. 972; arr. trumpet & organ]

Concerto in D major for Harpsichord, S. 972
[1][tempo not indicated] / [2]Larghetto / [3][tempo not indicated] / [4]Allegro
Michel, Jean-François

[Concertos, harpsichord, (16), S. 972-987. No. 5, a minor, S. 976; arr. trumpet & organ]

Concerto in a minor for Harpsichord, S. 976
[1][tempo not indicated] / [2]Largo / [3]Allegro
Berinbaum, Martin

₍Concertos, organ, S. 592-597. No. 1, G major, S. 592, (1708-17); arr. trumpet & organ₎

Concerto in G major for Organ, S. 592
[1][tempo not indicated] / [2]Grave / [3]Presto
Michel, Jean-François

₍Easter Oratorio, S. 249₎

Easter Oratorio, S. 249
SEE: Oster-Oratorium, S. 247

₍Fugues, organ, S. 574-581. No. 5, "Little", g minor, S. 578, (1709); arr. trumpet, organ, bass & drums₎

Fugatissimo
(based on Fugue in g minor, "Little", S. 578)
André, Maurice, 70)

₍Johannespassion, S. 245, (1722/23). No. 68, Chorale; arr. trumpet, brass ensemble & organ₎

Final Chorale from *Saint John Passion*, S. 245
(Johannespassion)
[68]Chorale, "Ach Herr, lass dein' lieb' Engelein
André, Maurice, 185), 198)
Potpourri, 41), 43)

₍Kirnberger Chorales, organ, S. 690-713a, (1708-17). No. 17, Liebster Jesu, wir sind hier, A major, S. 706; arr. trumpet & Irgan₎

Kirnberger Chorale, "Liebster Jesu, wir sind hier", S. 706
Pliquett, Joachim

₍Kunst der Fuge, S. 1080, (1749-50); arr. chamber ensemble & chamber orchestra₎

Die Kunst der Fuge, S. 1080
(The Art of the Fugue, S. 1080)
Chamber ensemble includes: 2 flutes, oboe, trumpet, trombone & cello.
Delmotte, Roger, 30)

₍Leipzig Chorales, organ, S. 651-668, (1747-49). No. 1, Fantasia on Komm, Heiliger Geist, Herre Gott, F major, S. 651; arr. trumpet & organ₎

Leipzig Chorale, "Komm, Heiliger Geist, Herre Gott", S. 651
Gaudon, Jean-Jacques

₍Leipzig Chorales, organ, S. 651-668, (1747-49). No. 9a, Fantasia on Nun komm' der Heiden Heiland, S. 659a; arr. cornetto & organ₎

Leipzig Chorale, Fantasia on "Nun komm' der Heiden Heiland", S. 659
Smithers, Don, 6)

₍Magnificat, D major, S. 243, (1723)₎

Magnificat in D major, S. 243

Solo voices, mixed voices & chamber orchestra.
Chamber orchestra includes: 2 flutes, 2 oboes, 2 oboes d'amore, 3
trumpets, timpani, strings, organ & continuo.

André, Maurice, 11), 110)
Holmgren, Fred
Immer, Friedemann, 17)
Potpourri, 22)
Steele-Perkins, Crispian, 16)
Unidentified, Trumpet(s), 8)

₍Magnificat, D major, S. 243, (1723). Excerpts; arr. trumpet & piano₎

Two Arias from *Magnificat in D major*, S. 243

³Soprano Aria, "Quia respexit" / ⁸Tenor Aria, "Deposuit"
Kafelnikov, Vladimir³⁺⁸

₍Magnificat, D major, S. 243, (1723). No. 1, Chorus; arr. trumpet, organ, bass &
drums₎

Chorus, "Magnificat anima mea Dominum" from *Magnificat in D major*, S. 243

André, Maurice, 206), 207)

₍Messe, b minor, S. 232, (1733)₎

Messe in h-moll, S. 232

(Mass in b minor, S. 232)

Solo voices, mixed voices & chamber orchestra.
Chamber orchestra includes: 2 flutes, 3 oboes, 2 oboes d'amore, 2
bassoons, 3 trumpets, horn (corno da caccia), timpani, strings &
continuo.

André, Maurice, 16)
Broiles, Melvin
Gleissle, Walter, 11)
Holmgren, Fred
Immer, Friedemann, 10)
McGregor, Rob Roy, 6)
Sauter, Hermann, 26)
Scherbaum, Adolf, 9)
Spindler, Josef, 10)
Steele-Perkins, Crispian, 3)

₍Messe, b minor, S. 232, (1733). No. 17, Chorus; arr. trumpet, organ, bass &
drums₎

Chorus, "Et resurrexit" from *Mass in b minor*, S. 232

André, Maurice, 206), 207)

₍Musikalisches Opfer, S. 1079, (1747). No. 5, Ricercar a 6, c minor; arr. trumpet,
trombone & organ₎

Ricercar a 6 from *Musical Offering*, S. 1079

Tamiya, Kenji

⌜Oster-Oratorium, S. 249, (1736)⌝
Oster-Oratorium, S. 249
(Easter Oratorio, S. 249)
Solo voices, mixed voices, & chamber orchestra.
Chamber orchestra includes: flute, recorder, 2 oboes, 2 oboes
d'amore, bassoon, 3 trumpets, timpani, strings & continuo.
André, Maurice, 106)
Güttler, Ludwig, 16[1])
Schmid, Bernhard, 9)

⌜Oster-Oratorium, S. 249, (1736). 1. Sinfonia; arr. 3 trumpets, timpani & organ⌝
Sinfonia from *Easter Oratorio*, S. 249
Hickman, David, 6)

⌜Partita, harpsichord, A major, S. 832. 2. Air pour les trompettes; arr. 2 solo
trumpets, horn, trombone & tuba⌝
Air pour les trompettes from *Partita in A major*, S. 832
Canadian Brass, 2)

⌜Preludes and fugues. Fugue, organ, g minor, S. 542, (1720); arr. trumpet, organ,
bass & drums⌝
Sur un air de Bach
(based on Fugue in g minor, S. 542)
André, Maurice, 70)

⌜Preludes, organ, various; arr. trumpet & organ⌝
Organ Preludes
Prelude in g minor, "Nun komm' der Heiden Heiland", S. 659 /
Prelude in f minor, "Ich ruf' zu dir, Herr Jesu Christ", S. 639 /
Prelude in d minor, S. 539 / Prelude in E♭ major, S. 552
These arrangements are not cross-referenced separately under the
respective sources of each prelude.
Dokshitser, Timofei, 18)

⌜Saint John Passion, S. 245⌝
Saint John Passion, S. 245
SEE: Johannespassion, S. 245.

⌞Schübler Chorales, organ, S. 645-650, (1746-50). No. 1, Wachet auf, ruft uns die
Stimme, E♭ major, S. 645; arr. trumpet & organ⌝
Schübler Chorale, "Wachet auf, ruft uns die Stimme", S. 645
André, Maurice, 40), 45), 65)
Bernard, André, 9)
Gaudon, Jean-Jacques
Güttler, Ludwig, 2)
Hardy, Francis
Schultz, Erik, 3)

⌜Schübler Chorales, organ, S. 645-650, (1746-50). No. 1, Wachet auf, ruft uns die
Stimme, E♭ major, S. 645; arr. trumpet, organ, bass & drums⌝
Schübler Chorale, "Wachet auf, ruft uns die Stimme", S. 645
André, Maurice, 69)

[Schübler Chorales, organ, S. 645-650, (1746-50). No. 2, Wo soll ich fliehen hin, e minor, S. 646; arr. trumpet & organ]
Schübler Chorale, "Wo soll ich fliehen hin", S. 646
(or "Auf meinen lieben Gott")
Hardy, Francis

[Schübler Chorales, organ, S. 645-650, (1746-50). No. 3, Wer nur den lieben Gott lässt walten, c minor, S. 647; arr. trumpet & organ]
Schübler Chorale, "Wer nur den lieben Gott lässt walten", S. 647
André, Maurice, 118)
Hardy, Francis

[Schübler Chorales, organ, S. 645-650, (1746-50). No. 4, Meine Seele erhebet den Herrn, d minor, S. 648; arr. trumpet & organ]
Schübler Chorale, "Meine Seele erhebet den Herrn", S. 648
Hardy, Francis

[Schübler Chorales, organ, S. 645-650, (1746-50). No. 6, Kommst du nun, Jesu, vom Himmel herunter, G major, S. 650; arr. trumpet & organ]
Schübler Chorale, "Kommst du nun, Jesu, vom Himmel herunter", S. 650
Güttler, Ludwig, 6), 21)
Hartog, Thomas

[Sonatas and partitas, violin solo, S. 1001-1006a, (1720). Partita No. 3, E major, S. 1006. 3. Gavotte en Rondeau; arr. trumpet & clarinet sextet]
Gavotte en Rondeau from *Partita No. 3 for Violin*, S. 1006
Ménardi, Louis

[Sonatas and partitas, violin solo, S. 1001-1006a, (1720). Partita No. 3, E major, S. 1006. 3. Gavotte en Rondeau; arr. trumpet & organ]
Gavotte en Rondeau from *Partita No. 3 for Violin*, S. 1006
André, Maurice, 40), 52), 67)

[Sonatas, flute, (3), S. 1030-1032, (1720). No. 2, E♭ major, S. 1031. 2. Siciliano; arr. trumpet & strings]
Siciliano from *Sonata in E♭ major for Flute and Continuo*, S. 1031
André, Maurice, 85), 215), 153)

[Sonatas, flute, (3), S. 1030-1032, (1720). No. 2, E♭ major, S. 1031; arr. trumpet & organ]
Sonata in E♭ major for Flute and Continuo, S. 1031
Sonata II (Es-dur)
[1]Allegro moderato / [2]Siciliano / [3]Allegro
André, Maurice, 39)
Michel, Jean-François

₍Sonatas, flute, (3), S. 1033-1035, (1720). No. 1, C major, S. 1033; arr. trumpet & organ₎

Sonata in C major for Flute and Continuo, S. 1033
Sonata I (C-dur)
[1]Andante / [2]Presto / [3]Allegro / [4]Adagio / [5]Menuetto I & II
Groth, Konradin

₍Sonatas, flute, (3), S. 1033-1035, (1720). No. 2, e minor, S. 1034. 3. Andante, G major; arr. trumpet & organ₎

Sonata in e minor for Flute and Continuo, S. 1034
Sonata II (e-moll)
Groth, Konradin

₍Sonatas, violin (6), S. 1014-1019a, (1720). No. 2, A major, S. 1015. Largo; arr. trumpet & harp₎

Sonata in A major for Violin and Continuo, S. 1015
Sonata II (A-dur)
The source for the listing of this album suggests that this "largo" is the fourth movement; however, the movements listed by Schmieder for S. 1015 are: 1. (dolce) / 2. Allegro assai / 3. Andante un poco / 4. Presto. (Perhaps this arrangement is actually the third movement.)
André, Maurice, 84)

₍Suites, cello, S. 1007-1012, (1720). No. 4, cello solo, E♭ major, S. 1010. 6. Bourrée II; arr. trumpet & organ₎

Bourrée II from *Suite No. 4 in E♭ major for Cello, S. 1010*
André, Maurice, 40), 52), 67)

₍Suites, orchestra. No. 2, flute, strings & continuo, b minor, S. 1067, (1721). 4. Bourrée I & II; arr. trumpet, organ, bass & drums₎

Bourrée I & II from *Suite No. 2 in b minor for Orchestra*, S. 1067
André, Maurice, 69)

₍Suites, orchestra. No. 2, flute, strings & continuo, b minor, S. 1067, (1721). 7. Badinerie; arr. trumpet, organ, bass & drums₎

Badinerie from *Suite No. 2 in b minor for Orchestra*, S. 1067
André, Maurice, 69)

₍Suites, orchestra. No. 2, flute, strings & continuo, b minor, S. 1067, (1721); arr. trumpet & organ₎

Suite No. 2 in b minor for Orchestra, S. 1067
(Ouvertüre h-moll, [Nr. 2])
[1]Lentement - [Allegro] - Lentement / [2]Rondeau / [3]Sarabande / [4]Bourrée I & II / [5]Polonaise - Double - Polonaise / [6]Menuet / [7]Badinerie
André, Maurice, 39)
Winslow, Richard

₍Suites, orchestra. No. 2, flute, strings & continuo, b minor, S. 1067, (1721); arr. trumpet, strings & continuo₎

Suite No. 2 in b minor for Orchestra, S. 1067
(Ouvertüre h-moll, [Nr. 2])

[1]Lentement - [Allegro] - Lentement / [2]Rondeau / [3]Sarabande / [4]Bourrée I & II / [5]Polonaise - Double - Polonaise / [6]Menuet / [7]Badinerie

> **André, Maurice,** 35), 42), 43), 44), 53), 83), 85), 133), 168), 211), 213), 217), 227)
>
> **Smedvig, Rolf**

₍Suites, orchestra. No. 3, 2 oboes, 3 trumpets, timpani, strings & continuo, D major, S. 1068, (1727-1736)₎

Suite No. 3 in D major for Orchestra, S. 1068
(Ouvertüre D-dur, [Nr. 3])

[1][Lent] - Vite / [2]Air / [3]Gavotte I / [4]Gavotte II / [5]Bourrée / [6]Gigue

> **André, Maurice,** 26), 95), 183), 194), 195[2]), 199), 209[2])
>
> **Carroll, Edward,** 3[3])
>
> **Clift, Dennis**
>
> **Delmotte, Roger,** 20)
>
> **Güttler, Ludwig,** 11), 13[2])
>
> **Junge, Harald**
>
> **Kejmar, Miroslav,** 8)
>
> **Laird, Michael,** 22)
>
> **Nowak, Henry**
>
> **Potpourri,** 4[2]), 44[1+5])
>
> **Ridder, Jean de**
>
> **Scherbaum, Adolf,** 26[2]), 31)
>
> **Schwarz, Gerard,** 2[2])
>
> **Spindler, Josef,** 8)
>
> **Stringer, Alan,** 2[2])
>
> **Tarr, Edward,** 42)
>
> **Touvron, Guy,** 4)
>
> **Wilbraham, John,** 28), 30[2])
>
> **Wobisch, Helmut,** 12[2])

₍Suites, orchestra. No. 3, 2 oboes, 3 trumpets, timpani, strings & continuo, D major, S. 1068, (1727-1736). Excerpts; arr. trumpet, organ, bass & drums₎

Air and Gavotte from *Suite No. 3 in D for Orchestra*, S. 1068
André, Maurice, 69)

₍Suites, orchestra. No. 3, 2 oboes, 3 trumpets, timpani, strings & continuo, D major, S. 1068, (1727-1736). 2. Air, strings & continuo; arr. flügelhorn & organ, E♭ major₎

Air from *Suite No. 3 in D for Orchestra*, S. 1068
Tolley, Richard

[Suites, orchestra. No. 3, 2 oboes, 3 trumpets, timpani, strings & continuo, D major, S. 1068, (1727-1736). 2. Air, strings & continuo; arr. trumpet & brass ensemble]

Air from *Suite No. 3 in D for Orchestra*, S. 1068
Grin, Freddy, 7)

[Suites, orchestra. No. 3, 2 oboes, 3 trumpets, timpani, strings & continuo, D major, S. 1068, (1727-1736). 2. Air, strings & continuo; arr. trumpet & orchestra]

Air from *Suite No. 3 in D for Orchestra*, S. 1068
(Air on a G String)
Cowell, Johnny

[Suites, orchestra. No. 3, 2 oboes, 3 trumpets, timpani, strings & continuo, D major, S. 1068, (1727-1736). 2. Air, strings & continuo; arr. trumpet & organ]

Air from *Suite No. 3 in D for Orchestra*, S. 1068
André, Maurice, 39), 40), 42), 44), 52), 67), 227)
Bernard, André, 9), 11)
Braz, Dirceu, 1)
Capouillez, Luc
Gaudon, Jean-Jacques
Mertens, Theo, 2)
Michel, Jean-François

[Suites, orchestra. No. 4, 3 oboes, bassoon, 3 trumpets, timpani, strings & continuo, D major, S. 1069, (1727-1736)]

Suite No. 4 in D major for Orchestra, S. 1069
(Ouvertüre D-dur, [Nr. 4])
[1][Grave] - [Allegro] / [2]Bourrée I / [3]Bourrée II / [4]Gavotte / [5]Menuet I / [6]Menuet II / [7]Réjouissance
André, Maurice, 95), 182), 194[5]), 199), 204)
Clift, Dennis
Delmotte, Roger, 20)
Güttler, Ludwig, 11), 13[5]), 21[5])
Junge, Harald
Kejmar, Miroslav, 8)
Laird, Michael, 22)
Nowak, Henry
Scherbaum, Adolf, 31)
Spindler, Josef, 8)
Touvron, Guy, 4)
Wilbraham, John, 28)

[Toccata, organ, C major, S. 564, (1709). Adagio; arr. trumpet & orchestra]

Adagio from *Toccata in C major for Organ*, S. 564
André, Maurice, 153), 215)

[Toccata, organ, C major, S. 564, (1709). Adagio; arr. trumpet & organ]

Adagio from *Toccata in C major for Organ*, S. 564
Hunger, Helmut, 5)

[Weihnachts-Oratorium, S. 248, (1734)]
Weihnachts-Oratorium, S. 248
(Christmas Oratorio, S. 248)
>Solo voices, mixed voices, chamber orchestra & continuo
>Chamber orchestra includes: 2 flutes, 2 oboes, 2 oboes d'amore, 2 oboes da caccia, bassoon, 2 horns (corni da caccia), 3 trumpets, timpani, strings, organ & continuo.
>>**André, Maurice**, 17), 94)
>>**Bauer, Willibald**, 4)
>>**Carroll, Edward**, 3[1+64])
>>**Güttler, Ludwig**, 16[8+64]), 28)
>>**Laird, Michael**, 15), 23[23+42+64])
>>**Steele-Perkins, Crispian**, 4)
>>**Tarr, Edward**, 17)
>>**Touvron, Guy**, 10)
>>**Zeyer, Adam**

[Weihnachts-Oratorium, S. 248, (1734). Excerpts; arr. trumpet & organ]
Arias and Chorale from *Christmas Oratorio*, S. 248
>[8]Bass Aria, "Grosser Herr und starker König" / [12]Chorale, "Brich an, o schönes Morgenlicht" / [15]Tenor Aria, "Frohe Hirten, eilt, ach eilet" / [41]Tenor Aria, "Ich will nur di Ehren leben"
>>**Schultz, Erik**, 3)

[Weihnachts-Oratorium, S. 248, (1734). No. 1, Chorus; arr. chamber orchestra]
Chorus, "Jauchzet, frohlocket!", from *Christmas Oratorio*, S. 248
>Chamber orchestra includes: 2 flutes, 2 oboes, 2 [3] trumpets, timpani, strings & continuo. (There is no choir in this arrangement.)
>Chorus No. 1 of the *Christmas Oratorio* is the same as Chorus No. 1 of Cantata No. 214, "Tönet, ihr Pauken! Erschallet, Trompeten!".
>>**Carroll, Edward**, 5)

[Weihnachts-Oratorium, S. 248, (1734). No. 5, Chorale; arr. 3 trumpets, timpani, organ & continuo]
Chorale, "Herzlich tut mich verlangen"
>(Chorale No. 5, "Wie soll ich dich empfangen", from *Christmas Oratorio*, S. 248)
>>**Smithers, Don**, 6)

[Weihnachts-Oratorium, S. 248, (1734). No. 9, Chorale; arr. 3 trumpets, timpani & organ]
Chorale, "Ach, mein herzliebes Jesulein!" from *Christmas Oratorio*, S. 248
>>**Carroll, Edward**, 11)
>>**Voisin, Roger**, 2)

ₜWeihnachts-Oratorium, S. 248, (1734). No. 9, Chorale; arr. 3 trumpets, timpani, organ & continuoₒ

Chorale, "Vom Himmel hoch, da komm' ich her"
(Chorale No. 9 "Ach, mein herzliebes Jesulein!" from *Christmas Oratorio*, S. 248)
> This arrangement is the fourth setting of the same chorale melody, "Vom Himmel hoch", although the text of the *Christmas Oratorio* setting is different.
> **Smithers, Don,** 6)

ₜWeihnachts-Oratorium, S. 248, (1734). No. 64, Chorale; arr. 2 trumpets & organₒ

Final Chorale from *Christmas Oratorio*, S. 248
⁶⁴"Nun seid ihr wohl gerochen"
> **Butler, Barbara**
> **Voisin, Roger,** 1)

ₜWeihnachts-Oratorium, S. 248, (1734). No. 64, Chorale; arr. 3 trumpets, timpani, organ & continuoₒ

Final Chorale from *Christmas Oratorio*, S. 248
> **Carroll, Edward,** 11)

ₜWeihnachts-Oratorium, S. 248, (1734). No. 8, Aria, bass, trumpet, strings & continuo, D majorₒ

Aria, "Grosser Herr und starker König" from *Christmas Oratorio*, S. 248
> **Reinhart, Carole Dawn,** 2)

ₜWeihnachts-Oratorium, S. 248, (1734). Sinfonia; arr. trumpet & organₒ

Sinfonia from *Christmas Oratorio*, S. 248
> **Falentin, Paul,** 5)

ₜWohltemperierte Klavier, v. 1, S. 846-869, (1722). No. 22, b♭ minor, S. 867. Praeludium; arr. trumpet & violin ensembleₒ

Prelude No. 22 in b♭ minor from *The Well-tempered Klavier*, v. 1
> **Dokshitser, Timofei,** 14), 36), 38), 39)

ₜWohltemperierte Klavier, v. 1, S. 846-869, (1722). Selections; arr. trumpet & organₒ

Preludes from *The Well-tempered Klavier*, v. 1
⁸Prelude in e♭ minor, S. 853 / ¹²Prelude in f minor, S. 857 / ¹⁷Prelude in A♭ major, S. 862 / ²⁰Prelude in a minor, S. 865 / ²²Prelude in b♭ minor, S. 867
> **Dokshitser, Timofei,** 18)

ₜWohltemperierte Klavier, v. 2, S. 870-893, (1744). No. 15, G major, S. 884. Praeludium; arr. trumpet & orchestraₒ

Prelude No. 15 in G major from *The Well-tempered Klavier*, v. 2
> **Wilbraham, John,** 24)

[Wohltemperierte Klavier, v. 2, S. 870-893, (1744). No. 5, D major, S. 874.
Praeludium; arr. cornet & piano]
Prelude No. 5 in D major from *The Well-tempered Klavier*, v. 2
Smith, Leonard B.

[Wohltemperierte Klavier, v. 2, S. 870-893, (1744). Selections; arr. trumpet &
organ]
Preludes from *The Well-tempered Klavier*, v. 2
[5]Prelude in D major, S. 874 / [9]Prelude in E major, S. 878 / [11]Prelude
in F major, S. 880
Dokshitser, Timofei, 18)

Bach, Karl Philipp Emanuel
See: Bach, Carl Philipp Emanuel

Bach, P.D.Q., 1807-1742 ?

[Iphigenia in Brooklyn, countertenor, harpsichord, trumpet mouthpiece,
double-reeds, wine-bottle & strings, S. 53162]
Cantata, "Iphigenia in Brooklyn" (S. 53162)
[1]Aria, "As Hyperion" / [2]Recitative, "And lo, she found herself" /
[3]Ground, "Dying" / [4]Recitative, "And in a vision" / [5]Aria, "Running
knows"
Reconstructed by Peter Schickele.
Platt, Seymour

Bach, Vincent, 1890-1976

[Hungarian Melodies, cornet & piano; arr. cornet & chamber ensemble]
Hungarian Melodies, Fantasy brillante for Cornet Solo
(Magyar Dallamok)
Schwarz, Gerard, 5)

Bacharach, Burt F., 1928-

[Best That You Can Do. Arthur's Theme; arr. trumpet & orchestra]
Arthur's Theme
Music for the film, *Best That You Can Do*.
Schultz, Erik, 8)

Bakaleinikov, Vladimir Romanovich, 1885-1953
Bakaleinikoff, Vladimir Romanovitch

[Polonaise, trumpet & piano]
Polonaise
Nagel, Robert, 15)

[Serenade, trumpet & piano]
Serenade
Ghitalla, Armando, 11)
Haynie, John, 2)

Baker, Richard D.

₍Anthem, "His Way — Mine"; arr. trumpet & piano₎
His Way — Mine
Blair, Stacy

Balay, Guillaume, 1871-1943

₍Andante and Allegro, cornet or saxhorn or trumpet & piano, f minor/A♭ major₎
Andante et Allegro
(Andante et Allegretto)
Published by Leduc as *Andante et Allegro* and by Southern Music
as *Andante et Allegretto*.
Benedetti, Donald
Crisara, Raymond, 8)

₍Petite Pièce Concertante, cornet & piano, G♭ major/E♭ major₎
Petite Pièce Concertante
Burkart, Richard
Burke, James, 7)
Masters, Edward L.
Schwarz, Gerard, 15)

₍Prelude and Ballad, cornet & piano, b♭ minor/D♭ major₎
Prélude et Ballade
The sections are marked Andante and Allegro moderato.
Masters, Edward L.
Schwarz, Gerard, 16)

Balbastre, Claude-Bénigne, 1727-1799

₍Votre bonté grand Dieu; arr. 3 trumpets, organ & timpani₎
Votre bonté grand Dieu
Held, Friedrich

Baldassare, Pietro, *fl.* 1700

₍Sonatas. No. 1: cornetto, strings & continuo, F major; also arr. trumpet & organ₎
Sonata No. 1 in F major for Cornetto, Strings & Continuo
[1]Allegro / [2]Grave / [3]Allegro
Burns, Stephen
Güttler, Ludwig, 2), 7)
Nystrom, Kaj
Schultz, Erik, 6)
Stringer, Alan, 3)

₍Sonatas. No. 2: cornetto, strings & continuo, F major; also arr. trumpet & organ₎
Sonata No. 2 in F major for Cornetto, Strings & Continuo
[1]Allegro / [2]Grave / [3]Allegro
Güttler, Ludwig, 14)
Rippas, Claude

Baldwin (arr.), David, 20th cent.

₍Consort Music; arr. 3 trumpets₎
Consort Music
¹Madrigal, "So Light is Love" [Wilbye] / ²Fantasia [White] /
³Madrigal, "What Shall I Doe" [Wilbye]
Carroll, Edward, 10$^{1-3}$)

Bales, Gerald Albert, 1919-

₍Fanfare for Easter Day, 2 trumpets, 2 trombones, organ & timpani, (1964)₎
Fanfare for Easter Day
(Fanfare on "Jesus Christ is risen today")
Chenette, Stephen

₍Festival Fanfare, 3 trumpets, 3 trombones & timpani, (1953)₎
Festival Fanfare
Chenette, Stephen

₍Jubilate Deo, mixed voices, 3 trumpets, 3 trombones, organ & percussion₎
Jubilate Deo
Chenette, Stephen

₍Te Deum Laudamus, mixed voices, 3 trumpets, organ & timpani₎
Te Deum Laudamus
Chenette, Stephen

Balin, Isodore
See: Berlin, Irving

Ball, Eric, 1903-
Ball, Eric John Walter

₍Challenge; arr. trumpet & band₎
The Challenge
Reinhart, Carole Dawn, 10)
Smith, Philip, 2), 4)

₍Song of Courage; arr. for trumpet & piano₎
Song of Courage
Smith, Philip, 3)

Ballif, Claude, 1924-
Ballif, Claude André François

₍Battements du cœur de Jésus, mixed voices, trumpet & trombone₎
Les Battements du cœur de Jésus
Kemblinsky, A.

₍Prière au seigneur, mixed voices, trumpet & trombone, op. 45₎
Prière au seigneur, op. 45
Kemblinsky, A.

Balsamo

⌜Sicilian Tarantella; arr. trumpet trio, clarinet/bass clarinet & rhythm⌝
Sicilian Tarantella
"Sicilian" is spelled "Sicillian" on the album.
Victorian Trumpet Trio

Balyan, Yuri

⌜Melody and Dance, trumpet & piano⌝
Melody and Dance
Balyan, Yuri

Barat, Joseph Edouard, 1882-1963

⌜Andante and Scherzo, trumpet & piano⌝
Andante et Scherzo
The "Andante" section is marked "Lent-Più vivo-Lent".
Benedetti, Donald
Crisara, Raymond, 8)
Masters, Edward L.
Orvid, Georgy
Sveshnikov, Mikhail
Tolley, Richard

⌜Fantasie, cornet or trumpet & piano, e♭ minor/E♭ major⌝
Fantasie en mi bémol
(Fantasie in e♭)
Reinhart, Carole Dawn, 9), 13)
Smith, Leonard B.

⌜Orientale, cornet or trumpet & piano⌝
Orientale
Amstutz, Keith

Barber, Samuel, 1910-1981

⌜Capricorn Concerto, flute, oboe, trumpet & strings, op. 21, (1944)⌝
Capricorn Concerto for Flute, Oboe, Trumpet and Strings, op. 21
[1]Allegro ma non troppo - Andante con moto - Allegro / [2]Allegretto / [3]Allegro con brio
Friestadt, Harry
Maximenko, Anatoly, 2)
Mear, Sidney, 2), 4)
Plog, Anthony, 1), 3)

Barolsky, Michael, 1947-

⌜Cries and Whispers, mezzo-soprano & chamber ensemble⌝
Cries and Whispers
Perry, Brian

Baronville

ꜛOrdonnance des Dragons du Roy, chamber orchestraꜜ
Ordonnance des Dragons du Roy
Delmotte, Roger, 8)

Barraud, Henry, 1900-

ꜛSymphonie concertante, trumpet & orchestra (1966)ꜜ
Symphonie concertante pour trompette et orchestre
¹Largamente e cantabile - Allegro giocoso / ²Aria cantabile / ³Con
brio
Delmotte, Roger, 34)

Barre, Michel de la, *ca.* 1675-1743

ꜛSuite, flute & continuo, D major; arr. trumpet & organꜜ
Suite in D major
¹Prélude (Gravement) / ²Allemande: l'Angélique / ³Air: le Badin /
⁴Gavotte: la Chevry / ⁵Air: la Coquette / ⁶Allemande: La Magdelon /
⁷Gigue: Langloise
André, Maurice, 65)

Barrett, John, *ca.* 1676-1719?

ꜛVoluntary, keyboard, C major; arr. 2 trumpets & organꜜ
Voluntary in C major
Formerly attributed dubiously to Henry Purcell, Z. D241.
Carroll, Edward, 6)
Delmotte, Roger, 14), 23)
Ghitalla, Armando, 5)
Tarr, Edward, 41)
Voisin, Roger, 3)

Barris, Harry, 1905-1962

ꜛI Surrender Dear; arr. trumpet & orchestraꜜ
I Surrender Dear
Méndez, Rafael, 21)

Barro, Joao de
See: Vianna, C.A.

Barrow, Edgar L., 20th cent.

ꜛScherzo, trumpet & piano, (c. 1959)ꜜ
Scherzo
Crisara, Raymond, 7)
Reynolds, George

Barsanti, Francesco, 1690-1772

⌈Concerto grossi, op. 3. No. 10: 2 oboes, trumpet, timpani & strings, D major⌉
Concerto grosso in D major, op. 3, no. 10
André, Maurice, 62), 68), 194), 196)
Cuvit, Michel
Potpourri, 37), 42)
Sauter, Hermann, 1)

Barsoti

⌈Tally Ho; arr. post horn & chamber ensemble⌉
Tally Ho
Smith, Bramwell "Bram"

Barsotti, Roger, 20th cent.

⌈Nautical Galop, post horn & band, (1962)⌉
A Nautical Galop
Head, Emerson

Barthali, Giovanni Antonio, 1605-1669
Bertali, Giovanni Antonio

⌈Sonata, "Sancti Leopoldi", 2 trumpets, 3 cornetti, 4 trombones, strings & continuo⌉
Sonata "Scti Leopoldi"
(Sonata "Sancti Leopoldi")
Güttler, Ludwig, 1)

Bartók, Béla, 1881-1945

⌈Roumanian Folk Dances, piano, Sz 56, 1-6; arr. trumpet & brass ensemble⌉
Roumanian Folk Dances, Sz 56
(Rumänische Volkstänze, Sz 56)
(Roemeense dansen)
Mertens, Theo, 3)

Bartolomeo, Padre Francesco, *fl.* 1638
Bartolomeo de Selma y Salaverde, Francesco

⌈Canzon, cornetto & continuo, (1638)⌉
Canzon a due
Continuo instruments used are organ and trombone.
Eichhorn, Holger

⌈Canzona, violin, cornetto & continuo⌉
Canzona a 2
Dickey, Bruce

⌈Festiva i colli passaggiato, violin, cornetto & continuo⌉
Festiva i colli passaggiato a 2
Dickey, Bruce

Bassani, Giovanni
See: Bassano, Giovanni

Bassano, Anthony, *fl.* 1620

₍Pavan, diverse instruments, No. 16; arr. 2 trumpets & 4 trombones₎
Pavan No. 16
André, Maurice, 176)

Bassano, Giovanni, *ca.* 1558-1617
Bassani, Giovanni

₍Aria, "Quel che dice", soprano & organ (with trumpet?)₎
Aria, "Quel che dice"
Schetsche, Walter

Bassano, Jerome, *fl. ca.* 1700

₍Fantasia, diverse instruments; arr. 2 trumpets & 4 trombones₎
Fantasia
André, Maurice, 176)

Batsevich, Grażyna
See: Bacewicz, Grażyna

Bazelon, Irwin, 1922-
Bazelon, Irwin Allen

₍Concerto, chamber ensemble & 4 electronic instruments, (1970)₎
Chamber Concerto
Chamber ensemble includes: flute, clarinet, saxophone, horn, 3
trumpets, 2 trombones & 3 percussion.
Crisara, Raymond, 2)

Bazil, Ludwig, 1931-

₍Lobgesang des Heiliger Franz von Assisi, soprano, trumpet, violin, cello & organ₎
Lobgesang des Heiliger Franz von Assisi
(Songs of Praise by St. Francis of Assisi)
Scherbaum, Adolf, 32)

Beckwith, John, 1927-

₍Trumpets of Summer, narrator, soli & chamber ensemble, (1964)₎
The Trumpets of Summer
Chamber ensemble includes: flute, bassoon, trumpet, percussion,
harp & cello.
Umbrico, Joseph

Beecroft, Norma, 1934-
Beecroft, Norma Marian

[Consequences, piano, trumpet, horn, trombone & electronic ensemble (1977)]
Consequences for 5
Malone, Michael

Beethoven, Ludwig van, 1770-1827

[Albumblatt für Elise, piano, WoO 59, a minor; arr. trumpet & orchestra]
Albumblatt für Elise, WoO 59
Scherbaum, Adolf, 34)

[Romance, violin & orchestra, No. 1, op. 40, G major; arr. trumpet & organ]
Romanze, G-dur, op. 40
(Romance No. 1 in G major, op. 40)
Falentin, Paul, 5)

[Romance, violin & orchestra, No. 2, op. 50, F major; arr. trumpet & orchestra]
Romanze, F-dur, op. 50
(Romance No. 2 in F major, op. 50)
Geiger, György

[Sonatas, piano, op. 27. No. 2, c# minor: Adagio sostenuto; arr. trumpet & harp]
Sonata No. 14 in c# minor for Piano, op. 27, no. 2
(Mondschein)
(Clair de Lune)
(Moonlight Sonata)
André, Maurice, 84)

[Sonatas, piano, op. 27. No. 2, c# minor: Adagio sostenuto; arr. trumpet & orchestra]
Sonata No. 14 in c# minor for Piano, op. 27, no. 2
(Mondschein)
(Clair de Lune)
(Moonlight Sonata)
Méndez, Rafael, 16)

[Song of Joy; arr. trumpet & orchestra]
Song of Joy
(Theme from Symphony No. 9, 4th movement)
Cowell, Johnny

[Suite, mechanical organ, WoO 33, F major. Adagio; arr. 2 trumpets & organ]
Adagio in F major
Loustalot, Alain

Bellini, Vincenzo, 1801-1835

[Concerto, oboe & strings, E♭ major; arr. trumpet & strings]
Concerto in E♭ major
(Concerto in E♭ major for Oboe)
[1]Maestoso e deciso / [2]Larghetto cantabile / [3]Allegro (alla polonese)
André, Maurice, 74), 158), 169), 214)

₍Norma, (1831). Act I: Cavatine, "Casta Diva, che inargenti"; arr. trumpet & orchestra₎
Cavatine de Norma, "Casta Diva, che inargenti"
André, Maurice, 161)

₍Norma, (1831). Act I: Cavatine, "Casta Diva, che inargenti"; arr. trumpet & organ₎
Cavatine de Norma, "Casta Diva, che inargenti"
André, Maurice, 39)

₍Norma, (1831). Act I: Cavatine, "Casta Diva, che inargenti"; arr. trumpet, mixed voices & orchestra₎
Cavatine de Norma, "Casta Diva, che inargenti"
André, Maurice, 37)

₍Puritani, (1835). Act I: Aria, "Son vergin vezzosa"; arr. trumpet & orchestra₎
Aria, "Son vergin vezzosa"
(Polonaise)
André, Maurice, 37)

Bellstedt, Herman, 1858-1926

₍Variations, Napoli, cornet & band; arr. cornet & wind ensemble₎
Napoli
(Canzone Napolitana con Variazioni)
The theme of these variations is the song, *Funiculì, Funiculà* by Luigi Denza (1846-1922).
Marsalis, Wynton, 4), 7)

₍Variations, Napoli, cornet & band; arr. trumpet & band₎
Napoli
(Canzone Napolitana con Variazioni)
Head, Emerson
Jacoby, Don

₍Variations, Napoli, cornet & band; arr. trumpet & orchestra₎
Napoli
(Canzone Napolitana con Variazioni)
Cowell, Johnny

Benatzky, Ralph, 1884-1957
Benatzky, Rudolf Josef František

₍Im weissen Rössl. Im Salzkammergut; arr. flügelhorn & accordion band₎
Im Salzkammergut aus *Im weissen Rössl*
(from *The White Horse Inn*)
André, Maurice, 61)

Bendinelli, Cesare, *fl.* 1600

₍Tutta l'arte della trombetta (1614). No. 336: Sonata, 5 trumpets & timpani, E♭ major₎
Sonata No. 336 in E♭ major
Tarr, Edward, 34)

Benedict, Sir Julius, 1804-1885

₍Variations, Carnival of Venice; arr. trumpet & orchestra₎
Variations sur "Le Carnaval de Venise"
André, Maurice, 5)

Bennard, George, 1873-1958

₍Speak, My Lord; arr. trumpet & organ₎
Speak, My Lord
Reinhart, Carole Dawn, 13)

Bennett, John, *ca.* 1725-1784

₍Voluntary, keyboard; arr. trumpet & organ₎
Trumpet Voluntary
Basch, Wolfgang, 11)
Hunger, Helmut, 5)

Bennett, Richard Rodney, 1936-

₍Calendar, chamber ensemble₎
Calendar for Chamber Ensemble
Chamber ensemble includes: flute, clarinet, bassoon, trumpet, trombone, 2 percussion, piano, violin, viola & cello.
Jones, Philip, 2)

Bennett, Robert Russell, 1894-1981

₍Rose Variations, trumpet & band₎
Rose Variations
Introduction: "The Garden Gate" / Theme: "Carolina (wild) rose" / Variation I: "Dorothy Perkins (rambler) rose" / Variation II: "Fran Karl Druschki (white) rose" / Variation III: "Cinnamon Rose (with humming birds)" / Variation IV: "American Beauty (red) rose"
Chunn, Michael
Haynie, John, 4)

₍Rose Variations, trumpet & band; arr. trumpet & piano₎
Rose Variations
Introduction: "The Garden Gate" / Theme: "Carolina (wild) rose" / Variation I: "Dorothy Perkins (rambler) rose" / Variation II: "Fran Karl Druschki (white) rose" / Variation III: "Cinnamon Rose (with humming birds)" / Variation IV: "American Beauty (red) rose"
Hickman, David, 3)

Benson, Warren, 1924-

[Prologue, trumpet & piano]
Prologue
Levy, Robert

Berg, Alban, 1885-1935
Berg, Alban Maria Johannes

[Chamber Concerto, piano, violin & 13 wind instruments, (1925)]
Kammerkonzert für Klavier, Violine und 13 Blasinstrumente
(Chamber Concerto for Piano, Violin and 13 Wind Instruments)
Wind ensemble includes: 2 flutes (piccolo), oboe, English horn, 2 clarinets, bass clarinet, bassoon, contrabasson, 2 horns, trumpet & trombone.
Rudolf, Richard
Zikov, Vladimir

Berg, Josef, 1927-1971

[Eufrides before the Gates of Tymen, tenor & trumpet, (1966)]
Eufrides před branami Tymén
(Eufrides before the Gates of Tymen)
Schwarz, Gerard, 22)

Berger, Arthur, 1912-
Berger, Arthur Victor

[Chamber Music, chamber ensemble, (1956)]
Chamber Music for 13 Players
[1]Variations / [2]Fantasy
Chamber ensemble includes: flute, oboe, clarinet, bassoon, horn, trumpet, harp, celeste, 2 violins, viola, cello & bass.
Nagel, Robert, 3)

Berio, Luciano, 1925-

[Laborintus 2, 3 vocalists, speaker, mixed voices, chamber ensemble & electronic tape, (1965)]
Laborintus 2
Chamber ensemble includes: flute, 3 clarinets, 2 trumpets, 3 trombones, 2 percussion, 2 harps, 2 celli & bass.
Thibaud, Pierre, 13)

Berlin, Irving, 1888-
Balin, Isodore "Izzy"
Balin, Israel
Baline, Israel

[White Christmas; arr. children's voices, trumpet & orchestra]
White Christmas
Irving Berlin is a pseudonym for Isodore Balin.
André, Maurice, 166)

Berlioz, Gabriel Pierre, 1916-

[Air gai; arr. trumpet & organ]
Air gai
Braz, Dirceu, 1)

Berlioz, Hector, 1803-1869
Berlioz, Louis-Hector

[Damnation de Faust, op. 24, (1845-46). Danse des Sylphes; arr. trumpet & harp]
Danse des Sylphes
(Danse des Sylphes from *La Damnation de Faust*)
André, Maurice, 84)

Bernard, Felix, 1897-1944

[Winter Wonderland (1934); arr. trumpet quartet]
Winter Wonderland
Blackburn, Roger

Bernstein, Leonard, 1918-
[Rondo for Lifey, trumpet & piano, (1950)]
Rondo for Lifey
Although published separately, this work is from a collection of Brass Music composed by Bernstein and commissioned by the Juilliard School of Music. Other works in the series are: *Elegy for Mippy I* (horn & piano); *Elegy for Mippy II* (solo trombone); *Waltz for Mippy III* (tuba & piano); *Fanfare for Bima* (trumpet, horn, trombone & tuba).
Amstutz, Keith
Schwarz, Gerard, 15)
Stevens, Thomas, 9)

Berrios, Pedro
See: Vianna, C.A.

Betti, Henri, 1917-

[C'est si bon; arr. trumpet & orchestra]
C'est si bon
André, Maurice, 170)

Biber, Carl Heinrich, 1681-1749

[Sonata, trumpet, strings & continuo, C major]
Sonate C-dur für Trompete und Streichorchester
[1]Allegro / [2]Adagio / [3]Presto
Sauter, Hermann, 1)

[Sonata, trumpet, strings & continuo, D major]
Sonate D-dur für Trompete und Streichorchester
[1]Vivace / [2]Adagio / [3]Allegro
Sauter, Hermann, 1)

[Sonata, 4 trumpets, timpani, 2 violins & continuo, C major]
Sonata in C major for 4 Trumpets, Timpani, 2 Violins and Continuo
[1]Un poco allegro / [2]Adagio / [3]Presto
Schwarz, Gerard, 20)

[Sonata, 5 trumpets, timpani, strings & continuo, C major]
Sonata per tromba sola con 4 trombe ripieni
[1]Presto / [2]Adagio / [3]Presto
Smithers, Don, 10)

[Sonata, 8 trumpets, timpani, 2 violins & continuo, C major, (1744)]
Sonata a due cori per 8 Trombe, Timpani, Archi e Continuo
Schwarz, Gerard, 20)
Smithers, Don, 10)

Biber, Heinrich Ignaz Franz, 1644-1704
Biber von Bibern, Heinrich Ignaz Franz

[Sonata "Scti Polycarpi", 8 trumpets, timpani & continuo, C major]
Sonata "Scti Polycarpi" a 9 in C major
(Sonata "Sancti Polycarpi")
Eklund's Baroque Ensemble
Immer, Friedemann, 18)
Marsalis, Wynton, 6)
Schwarz, Gerard, 7)
Smithers, Don, 10)
Spindler, Josef, 7)
Tarr, Edward, 3)

[Sonata, trumpet, strings & continuo, B♭ major]
Sonata a 6 in B♭ major for Trumpet, Strings and Continuo
[1]Allegro / [2]Adagio / [3]Allegro
Dokshitser, Timofei, 32)
Svejkovský, Josef
Voisin, Roger, 4), 8)

[Sonata, 6 trumpets, timpani & continuo, C major, (1668)]
Sonata a 7 für 6 Trompeten, Pauken und Basso continuo
(in one movement)
> Carroll, Edward, 10)
> Güttler, Ludwig, 1)
> Immer, Friedemann, 18)
> Potpourri, 32)
> Schwarz, Gerard, 20)
> Smithers, Don, 10)
> Spindler, Josef, 9)
> Tarr, Edward, 34)
> Wobisch, Helmut, 4), 11)

[Sonatae tam aris... (1676). Duets (12), 2 trumpets]
12 Trumpet Duets
(12 Duos per trombe)
[1](alla breve: quarter = 116) / [2](alla breve: quarter = 116) / [3](3/2:
half = 96) / [4]Presto-Adagio-Presto-Adagio-Presto / [5](6/8: dotted
quarter = 86) / [6](alla breve: quarter = 126) / [7](3/2: half = 112) / [8](a
breve: quarter = 132) / [9](6/4: quarter = 144) / [10](6/4: quarter = 152) /
[11]Adagio (quarter = 80) / [12](3/2: half = 152)
The tempo markings are from the Brass Press edition.
> Pohle, Wolfgang[1-2+5+11]
> Smithers, Don, 7[1+4+7+11+10+5])
> Tarr, Edward, 34[1-4+11+5])

[Sonatae tam aris... (1676). No. 1: 2 trumpets, 2 violins, 2 violas, cello &
continuo, C major]
Sonata I a otto in Do maggiore
(Sonata No. 1 in C major for 2 Trumpets, Strings and Basso continuo)
[1]Allegro / [2]Adagio - Presto - Adagio - Allegro / [3]Allegro
> Jones, Philip, 10)
> Scherbaum, Adolf, 16)
> Spindler, Josef, 9)
> Steele-Perkins, Crispian, 10)

[Sonatae tam aris... (1676). No. 4: trumpet, violin, 2 violas & continuo, C major]
Sonata IV a cinque in Do maggiore
(Sonata No. 4 in C major for Trumpet, Violin, 2 Violas and Basso
continuo)
[1][Allegro] / [2][Adagio] - Allegro / [3]Presto / [4]Adagio - Allegro
> André, Maurice, 50)
> Braz, Dirceu, 3)
> Jones, Philip, 10)
> Potpourri, 21), 34), 35)
> Sauter, Hermann, 3)
> Smithers, Don, 10)
> Steele-Perkins, Crispian, 10)
> Zickler, Heinz, 7)

₍Sonatae tam aris... (1676). No. 7: 2 trumpets, 2 violins, cello & continuo, C major₎

Sonata VII a cinque in Do maggiore
(Sonata No. 7 in C major for 2 Trumpets, Strings and Basso continuo)
Steele-Perkins, Crispian, 10)

₍Sonatae tam aris... (1676). No. 10: trumpet, violin, 2 violas, cello & continuo, g minor₎

Sonata X a cinque in sol minore
(Sonata No. 10 in g minor for Trumpet, Violin, 2 Violas, Cello and Basso Continuo)
[1]Adagio / [2]Allegro / [3]Adagio - Presto - Adagio
Friedrich, Reinhold
Jones, Philip, 10)
Steele-Perkins, Crispian, 5), 10)

₍Sonatae tam aris... (1676). No. 12: 2 trumpets, 2 violins, 2 violas, cello & continuo, C major₎

Sonata XII a otto in Do maggiore
(Sonata No. 12 in C major for 2 Trumpets, Strings and Basso continuo)
[1]Allegro / [2]Adagio - Allegro / [3]Adagio - Presto
Jones, Philip, 10)
Scherbaum, Adolf, 16)
Spindler, Josef, 9)
Steele-Perkins, Crispian, 10)

Bichkov, Anatoly

₍Kyui-Fantasia, trumpet & orchestra₎

Kyui-Fantasia
Klushkin, Yuri

Bilik, Jerry H., 1933-

₍Concerto, trumpet & band₎

Concerto for Trumpet and Band
Hickman, David, 8)

Biscogli, Francesco, 18th cent.

₍Concerto, oboe, bassoon, trumpet, violins & continuo, D major₎

Concerto in D major for Trumpet, Oboe, Bassoon, Violins & Continuo
[1]Largo maestoso - Grazioso / [2]Largo e staccato / [3]Allegro con spirito
André, Maurice, 63), 68), 124)
Güttler, Ludwig, 19), 21³)
Petz, Pál
Schultz, Erik, 7)
Vaillant, Ludovic, 4)

Bishop, Henry (Rowley), 1786-1855

ₜThine for Ever, soprano, slide trumpet & piano, (1837)₁
Thine for Ever
Arranged by Thomas Harper, Jr.
Impett, Jonathan

Bitsch, Marcel, 1921-

ₜVariations, theme by Domenico Scarlatti, trumpet or cornet & piano₁
Quatre Variations sur un Thème de Domenico Scarlatti
(Four Variations on a Theme by Domenico Scarlatti)
Chunn, Michael

Bizet, Georges, 1838-1875
Bizet, Georges Alexandre César Léopold

ₜAgnus Dei; arr. trumpet & organ₁
Agnus Dei
Melody extracted from *l'Arlésienne.*
André, Maurice, 66), 205)

ₜCarmen, (1873-74). Act I: Habañera; arr. cornet & orchestra₁
Aria, "l'Amour est un oiseau rebelle"
(Habañera)
McCann, Phillip

ₜCarmen, (1873-74). Act I: Habañera; arr. trumpet & orchestra₁
Habañera
Méndez, Rafael, 20)

ₜCarmen, (1873-74). Act I: Séguidille; arr. trumpet & orchestra₁
Aria, "Près des remparts de Séville"
(Séguidille)
André, Maurice, 37)

ₜCarmen, (1873-74). Act II: Toreador Song; arr. trumpet & orchestra₁
Toreador Song
Ghitalla, Armando, 14)

ₜCarmen, (1873-74). Danse Bohème; arr. trumpet & orchestra₁
Danse Bohème
(Bohemian Dance)
Méndez, Rafael, 2), 10), 24)

ₜPêcheurs de Perles, (1862-63). Act I: Je crois entendre encore; arr. trumpet & orchestra₁
Romance de Nadir, "Je crois entendre encore"
André, Maurice, 161), 212)

Bjerre, Bent Fabricius, 1924-
Fabricius-Bjerre, Bent

[Matador, trumpet & orchestra]
Matador
Andersen, Ole

Bjorklund, Ingegerd, 20th cent.

[Now Thank We All Our God, soprano & trumpet (or flügelhorn)]
Now Thank We All Our God
This work may actually be for organ alone.
Nystrom, Kaj

Blacher, Boris, 1903-1975

[Divertimento, trumpet, trombone & piano, op. 31, (1944)]
Divertimento für Trompete, Posaune und Klavier, op. 31
(Divertimento for Trumpet, Trombone and Piano, op. 31)
[1]Allegro / [2]Andantino / [3]Presto / [4]Moderato / [5]Allegretto /
[6]Moderato / [7]Presto
Nagel, Robert, 8)

Black, James M., 1856-1938

[When the Roll Is Called Up Yonder; arr. trumpet & orchestra]
When the Roll Is Called Up Yonder
Driscoll, Phil

Black, Johnny Stewart, 1896-

[Paper Doll; arr. trumpet & orchestra]
Paper Doll
Méndez, Rafael, 20)

Blake, Eubie, 1883-1983
Blake, James Hubert

[Memories of You; arr. trumpet & orchestra]
Memories of You
Méndez, Rafael, 21)

Blamont, François Colin de, 1690-1760
Collin de Blamont, François

[Suite, d minor; arr. trumpet & organ]
Suite en ré mineur
(Suite in d minor)
Morisset, Michel

Blanchard, Henri-Louis, 1791-1858

₍Te Deum. Prélude; arr. trumpet & organ₎
Prélude avec trompette du *Te Deum*
(Prelude [with trumpet] from *Te Deum*)
Morisset, Michel

Blankenship, 20th cent.

₍Come to Him; arr. trumpet & organ₎
Come to Him
Blair, Stacy

Bloch, Ernest, 1880-1959

₍Proclamation, trumpet & orchestra (1955)₎
Proclamation
Rapier, Leon, 2)

Boccherini, Luigi, 1743-1805

₍Minuet; arr. trumpet & orchestra₎
Menuet
André, Maurice, 4)

Böhm, Georg, 1661-1733

₍Chorale prelude, "Vater unser im Himmelreich"; arr. trumpet & organ₎
Chorale Prelude, "Vater unser im Himmelreich"
Delmotte, Roger, 39)

₍Suite, organ, D major; arr. trumpet & organ₎
Suite in D major
[1]Ouverture / [2]Air / [3]Rigaudon / [4]Menuet / [5]Rondeau / [6]Rigaudon
(da Capo)
André, Maurice, 141)

Böhme, Oskar, 1870-1938

₍Concerto, trumpet & piano, op. 18, f minor, (1899)₎
Concerto in f minor for Trumpet, op. 18
[1]Allegro moderato / [2]Adagio religioso / [3]Rondo: Allegro scherzando
Sommerhalder, Max

₍Concerto, trumpet & piano, op. 18, f minor, (1899); arr. trumpet & band₎
Concerto in f minor for Trumpet and Band, op. 18
[1]Allegro moderato / [2]Adagio religioso / [3]Rondo: Allegro scherzando
Dokshitser, Timofei, 23)

ₜConcerto, trumpet & piano, op. 18, f minor, (1899); arr. trumpet & orchestra,
e minorₗ
Concerto in e minor for Trumpet and Orchestra, op. 18
[1]Allegro moderato / [2]Adagio religioso / [3]Rondo: Allegro scherzando
Presumably, this orchestration restores the original tonality.
Naess, Lars

ₜDanse russe, trumpet & piano, op. 32, b♭ minorₗ
Danse russe en si bémol mineur, op. 32
(Russian Dance in b♭ minor, op. 32)
Naess, Lars
Sommerhalder, Max

ₜNapolitaine, cornet & piano, op. 25ₗ
La Napolitaine, op. 25
Sommerhalder, Max

ₜNapolitaine, cornet & piano, op. 25; arr. trumpet & orchestraₗ
La Napolitaine, op. 25
(Tarantelle)
Geiger, György

ₜScène de Ballet, cornet & piano, op. 31ₗ
Scène de Ballet, op. 31
Sommerhalder, Max

ₜSoirée de St. Pétersbourg, cornet & piano, op. 23ₗ
Soirée de St. Pétersbourg, op. 23
Sommerhalder, Max

Boismortier, Joseph Bodin de, *ca.* 1691-1755

ₜSonata, flute (oboe or violin) & continuo, g minor, op. 34, no. 1; arr. trumpet &
organₗ
Sonata in g minor for flute, oboe or violin, op. 34, no. 1
[1]Gayement / [2]Gracieusement / [3]Gayement
André, Maurice, 77), 156)

Bolling, Claude, 1930-

ₜToot Suite, trumpet(s)/cornet/flügelhorn, piano, bass & drumsₗ
Toot Suite
[1]Allègre (C-trumpet) / [2]Mystique (E♭-trumpet) / [3]Rag-Polka
(cornet) / [4]Marche (piccolo trumpet) / [5]Vespérale (flügelhorn) /
[6]Spirituelle (piccolo trumpet)
André, Maurice, 8)

Bond, Capel, 1730-1790

₍Concerto, trumpet, strings & continuo, D major, (1760)₎
Concerto in D major for Trumpet, Strings and Continuo
¹Con spirito / ²Allegro / ³Larghetto
André, Maurice, 175)
Bodenröder, Robert

Bond, Carrie Minetta Jacobs, 1862-1946

₍Perfect Day, voice & piano; arr. trumpet & instrumental ensemble₎
A Perfect Day
Andersen, Ole
Smith, Bramwell "Bram"

Bononcini, Giovanni, 1670-1747

₍Griselda, (1722). Aria, "Per la gloria d'adorarvi"; arr. trumpet & piano₎
Aria, "Per la gloria d'adorarvi" from *Griselda*
Crisara, Raymond, 6)

₍Griselda, (1722). Aria, "Per la gloria d'adorarvi", tenor, trumpet & strings₎
Aria, "Per la gloria d'adorarvi" from *Griselda*
Mantovani, Alberto

₍Rondeau; arr. trumpet & piano₎
Rondeau
Included in a "Baroque Suite" arranged by Robert Getchell.
Geyer, Charles

₍Sinfonie a 5, 6, 7, e 8 Istromenti..., op. 3, (1685). No. 8: trumpet, strings & continuo, D major₎
Sinfonia ottava a 6 con Tromba, op. 3
¹Adagio - Allegro / ²Adagio - Vivace / ³Adagio - Allegro spiccato
Smithers, Don, 5)
Vaillant, Ludovic, 6)

₍Sinfonie a 5, 6, 7, e 8 Istromenti..., op. 3, (1685). No. 10: trumpet, strings & continuo, D major₎
Sinfonia decima a 7 con due Trombe, op. 3
¹Adagio - Allegro / ²Grave - Vivace / ³Adagio - Largo - Allegro
André, Maurice, 143)
Güttler, Ludwig, 14)
Keavy, Stephen
Petit, Gilbert
Smithers, Don, 4)
Vaillant, Ludovic, 6)
Wallace, John, 4)

Borden, David, 1938-

₍Dialogues (6), trumpet & trombone₎
Six Dialogues for Trumpet and Trombone
Stevens, Thomas, 7)

Borel-Clerc, Charles, 1879-1959
Clerc, Charles

₍Mattchiche (1903); arr. flügelhorn & accordion band₎
La Mattchiche
André, Maurice, 61)

Borg, Oscar, 1851-1930

₍Summer Mood, trumpet & brass ensemble₎
Summer Mood for Trumpet and Brass Ensemble
Naess, Lars

Borodin, Alexander, 1833-1887

₍Prince Igor. Polovtsian Dance; arr. trumpet & brass ensemble₎
Polovtsian Dance from *Prince Igor*
(Polovtsiaanse dans from *Prince Igor*)
Mertens, Theo, 3)

₍Prince Igor. Polovtsian Dance; arr. trumpet & orchestra₎
Polovtsian Dance from *Prince Igor*
(Danse Polovtsienne from *Prince Igor*)
Méndez, Rafael, 20)

Bosanko, Ivor, 20th cent.

₍I Know He's Mine; arr. trumpet & band₎
I Know He's Mine
Thomas, Peggy Paton

Boulez, Pierre, 1925-

₍Éclat-Multiples, chamber ensemble (1970)₎
Éclat - Multiples
Chamber ensemble includes: alto flute, English horn, basset horn, trumpet, trombone, glockenspiel, vibraphone, tubular bells, piano, celesta, harp, cymbalum, mandolin, guitar, 10 violas & cello.
Cure, Antoine

₍Rituel in Memoriam Maderna, 8 chamber ensembles (1974)₎
Rituel in Memoriam Maderna
Cure, Antoine

Bowles, Paul, 1910-

₍Music for a Farce, clarinet, trumpet, percussion & piano, (1953)₎
Music for a Farce
¹Allegro rigoroso / ²Presto (Tempo di Tarantella) / ³Allegretto
(Tempo di Quickstep) / ⁴Allegro / ⁵Lento (Tempo di Valse) / ⁶Allegro
(Tempo di Marcia) / ⁷Presto / ⁸Allegretto (Molto staccato)
Crisara, Raymond, 5)
Mueller, Herbert

Bowman, Euday L., 1887-1949

₍12th Street Rag (1914); arr. trumpet quartet₎
12th Street Rag
Blackburn, Roger

Boyce, William, 1711-1779

₍Trumpet Tune, keyboard; arr. trumpet & organ (or harp)₎
Trumpet Tune
These may be two different works, and may be from Boyce's
collection of ten voluntaries.
André, Maurice, 84)
Deside

₍Voluntary, keyboard, C major; arr. trumpet & organ₎
Voluntary in C
¹Rather slow than fast / ²Brisk
This voluntary is the sixth in Boyce's collection of ten voluntaries.
Tarr, Edward, 41)

₍Voluntary, keyboard, D major; arr. trumpet & organ₎
Voluntary in D
The ten voluntaries of William Boyce have not been individually
identified for this index.
Bodenröder, Robert
Carroll, Edward, 6)
Güttler, Ludwig, 15)
Haas, Wolfgang
Loustalot, Alain
Rehm, Klaus
Rippas, Claude
Stringer, Alan, 3)
Tarr, Edward, 39)
Zapf, Gerd

Bozza, Eugène, 1905-
Bozza, Eugène Joseph

₍Badinage, trumpet & piano, (1950)₎
Badinage
(pour Trompette Ut ou Si♭ et Piano)
Hyatt, Jack
Stevens, Thomas, 6)

₍Caprice, trumpet & piano, op. 47, (1943)₎
Caprice
(pour Trompette Ut ou Si♭ et Piano)
Gardner, Ned
Head, Emerson
Hyatt, Jack
Lewis, E. Leonard
Plog, Anthony, 7)
Reinhart, Carole Dawn, 9)
Schwarz, Gerard, 12)
Stevens, Thomas, 6)

₍Lied, trumpet & piano₎
Lied
Stevens, Thomas, 6)

₍Rhapsodie, trumpet & piano, (1957); arr. trumpet & organ₎
Rhapsodie
(pour Trompette Ut ou Si et Piano)
Pliquett, Joachim

₍Rustiques, cornet (or trumpet) & piano, (1955)₎
Rustiques
(pour Cornet Si♭ ou Trompette Ut ou Si♭ et Piano)
Chunn, Michael
Haynie, John, 2)
Potpourri, 7)

Bradbury, William Batchelder, 1816-1868

₍Jesus Loves Me; arr. trumpet & orchestra₎
Jesus Loves Me
Driscoll, Phil

₍PLEASANT PASTURES; arr. trumpet & orchestra₎
Savior, Like a Shepherd, Lead Us
This hymn-tune is also known by the composer's name, BRADBURY.
Driscoll, Phil

₍Solid Rock; arr. trumpet & piano₎
The Solid Rock
(My hope is built on nothing less)
Blair, Stacy

Brade, William, 1560-1630

₁Paduanen und Galliarden (1614). Paduana, diverse instruments, No. 12, F major; arr. brass ensemble₁
Güttler, Ludwig, 9)

₁Paduanen und Galliarden... (1609). Canzon, diverse instruments, No. 16, G major₁
Canzon in G
Smithers, Don, 2)

Braga, António Correa
See: Correa Braga, António

Brahe, May H., 20th cent.

₁Bless this House, (1927); arr. trumpet quartet₁
Bless this House
Blackburn, Roger

Brahms, Johannes, 1833-1897

₁Lieder, op. 49. Wiegenlied, No. 4; arr. trumpet & organ₁
Wiegenlied, op. 49, no. 4
(Lullaby)
Grin, Freddy, 8)

₁Ungarische Tänze, piano, No. 5, g minor; arr. trumpet & orchestra₁
Ungarische Tänze g-moll, Nr. 5
(Hungarian Dance No. 5 in g minor)
(Danse hongroise en sol mineur, No. 5)
André, Maurice, 4)
Christensen, Ketil
Méndez, Rafael, 20), 24)

₁Ungarische Tänze, piano, No. 6, D major; arr. trumpet & orchestra₁
Ungarische Tänze D-dur, Nr. 6
(Hungarian Dance No. 6 in D major)
(Danse hongroise en re majeur, No. 6)
André, Maurice, 4)

₁Variations, theme by Handel, piano, op. 24, B♭; arr. orchestra₁
Variationen über eine Thema von Händel, op. 24
(Variations on a Theme by Handel, op. 24)
Arranged by Edmund Rubbra, this orchestration begins with a soloistic trumpet part.
Johnson, Gilbert, 4)

₁Walzer, piano, op. 39, (1-16?); arr. trumpet & harp₁
Valse
André, Maurice, 84)

Brandt, Vassily Gueorguyevitch, 1869-1923
Brandt, Willy

ₓConcerto, trumpet & piano, E♭ majorₓ
Concerto in E♭ major for Trumpet
[2]Andante
This excerpted work may actually be the middle section of the
Second Concertpiece, op. 12.
Polonsky, Naum E.[2]

ₓConcertpiece, trumpet & piano, No. 1, op. 11, f minorₓ
Erste Konzertstück F-moll, op. 11
(First Concertpiece in f minor, op. 11)
Dokshitser, Timofei, 23)
Ritter, David
Sommerhalder, Max
Wilder, Joseph B.

ₓConcertpiece, trumpet & piano, No. 2, op. 12, E♭ majorₓ
Zweite Konzertstück Es-dur, op. 12
(Second Concertpiece in E♭ major, op. 12)
Dokshitser, Timofei, 23)
Ots, Aavo
Sommerhalder, Max

Brant, Henry Dreyfus, 1913-

ₓConcerto, trumpet & chamber ensemble, (1941, rev. 1970)ₓ
Concerto for Trumpet and 9 Instruments
[1]Con brio / [2]Sostenuto / [3]Ritmico, ironico
Chamber ensemble includes: flute, 4 clarinets, 2 bass clarinets,
tuba & percussion.
Schwarz, Gerard, 10)

Bratton, John W., 1867-1947

ₓIsabelle; arr. cornet & brass ensembleₓ
Isabelle
Aquitaine Brass Ensemble

Braz, Dirceu, 20th cent.

ₓSuite Amazônica, trumpet/flügelhorn, guitar & percussionₓ
Suite Amazônica
Braz, Dirceu, 2)

Britten, Benjamin, 1913-1976
Lord Britten of Aldeburgh

ᵣFanfare for St. Edmundsbury, 3 trumpets (1959)ᵧ
Fanfare for St. Edmundsbury
Although parts are published in concert pitch in full score, each part may be performed on a different pitched natural trumpet: Trumpet 1 in D / Trumpet 2 in C / Trumpet 3 in F.
Giangiulio, Richard
Tarr, Edward, 34)
Wilbraham, John, 14)

Brixi, Franz Xaver, 1732-1771
Brixi, František Xaver

ᵣMotetto de nativitate Domini, mixed voices, 2 clarinets, 2 trumpets & stringsᵧ
Motetto de nativitate Domini
Buriánek, Jindřich

Broughton, 20th cent.

ᵣCountryside, trumpet & pianoᵧ
Countryside
Smith, Philip, 2)

Brown, Earle, 1926-

ᵣNovara, piano & chamber ensemble, (1962)ᵧ
Novara
Chamber ensemble includes: flute, trumpet, bass clarinet & string quartet.
Floore, John

Brown, Nacio, 1896-1964
Brown, Ignatio Herb

ᵣTemptation; arr. trumpet & instrumental ensembleᵧ
Temptation
Smith, Bramwell "Bram"

Brown, Newel Kay, 1932-

ᵣPastorale and Dance, trumpet & 4 instrumentsᵧ
Pastorale and Dance
Levy, Robert

ᵣPoetics, trumpet & piano (1970)ᵧ
Poetics
Levy, Robert

Brubeck, Dave, 1920-
Brubeck, David

[Blue Rondo a la Turc; arr. trumpet & brass ensemble]
Blue Rondo a la Turc
Based on the third movement of W.A. Mozart's *Sonata No. 11 in A major for Piano*, K. 331.
     Mertens, Theo, 5)

Bruch, Max, 1838-1920

[Concerto, violin & orchestra, no. 1, op. 26, g minor; arr. theme, cornet & band]
Theme from *Concerto for Violin*
     McCann, Phillip

Brün, Herbert, 1918-

[Gestures, chamber ensemble (1964)]
Gestures for 11 Instruments
Chamber ensemble includes: flute (piccolo), oboe (English horn), clarinet (bass clarinet), bassoon (contrabassoon), horn, trumpet, trombone, violin, viola, bass & percussion.
     Potpourri, 5)

Brunckhorst, Arnold Melchior, *d.* 1730

[Weihnachtsgeschichte, mixed voices & orchestra]
Die Weihnachtsgeschichte
     Maier, Hans Walter

Brüninghaus, Rainer, 20th cent.

[Continuum, trumpet, piano (synthesizer) & drums]
Continuum
     Stockhausen, Markus, 6)

[Stille, trumpet, piano (synthesizer) & drums]
Stille
     Stockhausen, Markus, 6)

Buchtel, Forrest Lawrence, 1899-
Buck, Lawrence
Lawrence, Victor

[Impromptu, trumpet & piano]
Impromptu
     Masters, Edward L.

Budd, Harold, 1936-

[New Work #5, trumpet & piano (1971)]
New Work #5
     Stevens, Thomas, 4)

Buesser, Henri-Paul
See: Büsser, Henri-Paul

Bull, Edvard Hagerup
See: Hagerup Bull, Edvard

Bull, John, *ca.* 1562-1628

ₜEnglish Dances (4), harpsichord; arr. trumpet & harpᵧ
Four English Dances
(Vier englische Tänze)
¹The Duchess of Brunswick's Toye / ²Country Dance / ³Courante
(Dr. Bull's Jewel) / ⁴Courante joyeuse
The "Courante joyeuse" of this arrangement also involves
percussion.
André, Maurice, 64)

Buonamente, Giovanni Battista, *ca.* 1590-1643

ₜCanzoni e Sonate (1636). Sonata, cornetto, viola & continuo, No. 5ᵧ
Sonata quinta a due
Smithers, Don, 1)

ₜCanzoni e Sonate (1636). Sonata, cornetto, violin & continuo, No. 4ᵧ
Sonata quarta a due
Smithers, Don, 1)

Buononcini, Giovanni
See: Bononcini, Giovanni

Burgon, Geoffrey, 1941-

ₜNunc dimittis, soprano (countertenor), trumpet & strings (1979)ᵧ
Nunc dimittis
Laird, Michael, 16)
Steele-Perkins, Crispian, 6)

Burke, James, 1923-1981

ₜAmorette, cornet & bandᵧ
Amorette
Burke, James, 5)

ₜDanza Allegra, cornet & bandᵧ
Danza Allegra
Burke, James, 5)
Reinhart, Carole Dawn, 11)

ₜHocus Polka, cornet & bandᵧ
Hocus Polka
Burke, James, 6)

⌜Jolene, cornet & piano⌝
Jolene
       Burke, James, 2)

⌜Joneta, cornet & band⌝
Joneta
       Burke, James, 2)

⌜Magic Trumpet, trumpet & piano⌝
The Magic Trumpet
       Nagel, Robert, 15)

Burkhard, Paul, 1911-1977

⌜Feuerwerk. O mein Papa!; arr. trumpet & orchestra⌝
O mein Papa! from *Fireworks*
       André, Maurice, 170)

Burrell, Mario, 20th cent.

⌜Moraima; arr. trumpet & orchestra⌝
Moraima
       Méndez, Rafael, 9), 24)

Bush (arr.), Irving, 20th cent.

⌜Trumpet and Drum 1976, trumpet, percussion, fender bass & electric guitar⌝
Trumpet and Drum 1976
    (American folksongs and Patriotic tunes)
       Bush, Irving

Büsser, Henri-Paul, 1872-1973

⌜Andante and Scherzo, trumpet & piano⌝
Andante et Scherzo
       Pliquett, Joachim

Buterne, Jean-Baptiste, 1650-1727

⌜Sonata, F major; arr. trumpet & organ⌝
Sonata in F major
       Braz, Dirceu, 4)

Buxtehude, Dietrich, 1637-1707

⌜Erschienen ist der herrlich Tag; arr. trumpet & organ⌝
Erschienen ist der herrlich Tag
       Basch, Wolfgang, 5)

⌜Ihr lieben Christen, freut euch nun. Fanfare and Chorus; arr. 3 trumpets, organ
& timpani⌝
Fanfare and Chorus from *Ihr lieben Christen, freut euch nun*
       Giangiulio, Richard

Byrd, William, 1543-1623

⌜Lullaby, voices & diverse instruments⌟
Lullaby, My Sweet Little Baby
Cook, Richard

Cabezón, Antonio de, 1510-1566

⌜Magnificat; arr. trumpet & organ⌟
Magnificat du quatrième ton
Hardy, Francis

Caldara, Antonio, *ca.* 1670-1736

⌜Sonata, 4 trumpets, timpani, strings & continuo, C major⌟
Sonata for 4 Trumpets, Timpani, Strings and Continuo
(Sonata à 4 trompettes, timbales, cordes et basse continue)
¹Allegro / ²Andante / ³Allegro (da capo)
André, Maurice, 79), 114)
Güttler, Ludwig, 1), 4)

Calleja, Gómez Rafael, 1874-1938
Callejo-Barrera

⌜Emigrantes. Granadinas (Farewell, My Granada); arr. trumpet & orchestra⌟
Farewell, My Granada
(Adios, Granada)
(Granadinas)
Hidalgo, José Luis
Méndez, Rafael, 2), 6), 9), 24)

Campbell, Thomas, 1777-1844

⌜SAGINA; arr. trumpet & orchestra⌟
And Can It Be that I Should Gain?
(Amazing Love!)
Nagel, Robert, 9)

Campion, Thomas, 1567-1620

⌜Never Weather-Beaten Sail; arr. cornetto & organ⌟
Never Weather-Beaten Sail
(Never weather-beaten saile more willing bent to shore)
Smithers, Don, 7)

Campo, Frank, 1927-
Campo, Frank Philip

⌜Commedie II, trumpet, piano & tape⌟
Commedie II for Trumpet, Piano and Tape
Plog, Anthony, 6)

₍Duet for Equal Trumpets, 2 trumpets, (1976)₎
Duet for Equal Trumpets
Plog, Anthony, 5)

₍Studies (2), trumpet & guitar₎
Two Studies for Trumpet and Guitar
Plog, Anthony, 4)

₍Times, trumpet, (1971)₎
Times
[1]Good Times (alla marcia) / [2]Hard Times (Interrupted Blues) /
[3]Time to Go
Stevens, Thomas, 1)

Campra, André, 1660-1744

₍Ballet des Ages, oboes, bassoon, trumpets, timpani & harpsichord, (1718)₎
Le Ballet des Ages
[1]Ouverture / [2]Air en rondeau / [3]Passepieds I & II / [4]Bransles I & II /
[5]Musettes I & II / [6]Courante / [7]Ritournelle / [8]Rigaudons I & II / [9]Airs
des Vendangeurs I & II / [10]Tambourin [11]Forlane / [12]Marche des
Masques
The "Ritournelle" involves solo trumpet with double-reed
ensemble, and the "Marche des Masques" includes three trumpets
and timpani with double-reed ensemble.
André, Maurice, 6)

₍Tancrede. Triumphal March, trumpet & strings₎
Triumphal March from *Tancrede*
Schwarz, Gerard, 2)

Capua, Eduardo di
See: di Capua, Eduardo

Carcasio, Giuseppe, *fl.* 1700

₍Sonata, 2 oboes, 2 trumpets & organ₎
Sonata d'organo con trombe ed oboe
(Sonata for Organ with 2 Trumpets and 2 Oboes)
Fink, Werner
Petit, Gilbert

₍Sonata, 2 oboes, 2 trumpets & organ; arr. 2 trumpets & organ₎
Sonata d'organo con trombe
(Sonata for 2 Trumpets and Organ)
Schultz, Erik, 9)

Carmichael, Hoagy, 1899-1981
Carmichael, Howard Hoagland

ₜStardust; arr. trumpet & orchestra (or combo)ₜ
Stardust
> Cowell, Johnny
> Smith, Bramwell "Bram"

Carmichael, Ralph R., 1927-

ₜAll My Life; arr. trumpet & orchestraₜ
All My Life
> Driscoll, Phil

ₜMy Friend and I; arr. trumpet & orchestraₜ
My Friend and I
> Driscoll, Phil

ₜSavior is Waiting; arr. trumpet & pianoₜ
The Savior is Waiting
> Blair, Stacy

Carr, Gordon, 1943-

ₜDialogue, trumpet & brass ensembleₜ
Dialogue for Trumpet and Brass
> Watson, James

Carradot, André, 20th cent.

ₜBallade, trumpet & orchestraₜ
Ballade pour Trompette
> André, Maurice, 5), 38), 66)

ₜGood Night Mister Johnny, trumpet & orchestraₜ
Good Night Mister Johnny
> André, Maurice, 5)

ₜKatrina, trumpet & orchestraₜ
Katrina
> André, Maurice, 5)

ₜKiss Me, trumpet & orchestraₜ
Kiss Me
> André, Maurice, 5)

ₜLiliana, trumpet & orchestraₜ
Liliana (bolero)
> André, Maurice, 5)

Carter, Elliott, 1908-
Carter, Elliott Cook

₍Canon, 3 equal instruments, (1971)₎
Canon for Three — In Memoriam Igor Stravinsky
Schwarz, Gerard, 10)
Stevens, Thomas, 4)

Cassella, Alfredo, 1883-1947

₍Serenata, clarinet, bassoon, trumpet, violin & cello, op. 46, (1927)₎
Serenata
Hopkins, Kenneth

Castello, Dario, 17th cent.

₍Sonatas, (1644). No. 6, violin, cornetto & continuo₎
Sonata No. 6 a 2 canti
The continuo instruments include trombone, cello and harpsichord or organ.
Dickey, Bruce

₍Sonatas, (1644). No. 13, violin, cornetto & continuo₎
Sonata No. 13 a 2 canti (in eco)
The continuo instruments include trombone, cello and harpsichord or organ.
Dickey, Bruce

₍Sonatas, (1644). No. 14, violin, cornetto & continuo₎
Sonata No. 14 a 2 canti
The continuo instruments include trombone, cello and harpsichord or organ.
Dickey, Bruce

Castérède, Jacques, 1926-

₍Sonatine, trumpet & piano, (1956)₎
Sonatine pour Trompette et Piano
Chunn, Michael

Catelinet, Philip B., 1905-
Catelinet, Philip Bramwell

₍Trumpet Tune, trumpet & organ₎
Trumpet Tune
Haas, Wolfgang

Cavalieri, Emilio de', *ca.* 1550-1602
Cavalieri, Emilio del

[Rappresentatione di anima e di corpo. (1600)]
La Rappresentatione di anima e di corpo
Once regarded as the first oratorio, this work is actually a morality play set to music.
Eichhorn, Holger

Cazzati, Maurizio, *ca.* 1620-1677
Cazzati, Mauritio

[Dances, cornetto, violin & continuo]
Balletto / Brando / Correnti a 3
Eichhorn, Holger

[Sonate a due istromenti..., op. 55, (1670). No. 1: cornetto (or violin) & continuo, d minor]
Sonata in d minor, "La Pellicana", op. 55, no. 1
[1]Largo, e vivace / [2]Grave / [3]Presto / [4]Prestissimo
Schwarz, Gerard, 17)

[Sonate a due istromenti..., op. 55, (1670). No. 1: cornetto (or violin) & continuo, d minor; arr. trumpet & organ]
Sonata in d minor, "La Pellicana", op. 55, no. 1
[1]Largo, e vivace / [2]Grave / [3]Presto / [4]Prestissimo
Touvron, Guy, 20)

[Sonate a due, tre, quattro, e cinque..., op. 35, (1665). No. 11: trumpet, strings & continuo, D major]
Sonata a 5, "La Bianchina", op. 35, no. 11
(Sonata [No. 2], "La Bianchina", op. 35, no. 11)
[1]Allegro / [2]Grave / [3]Allegro / [4]Vivace / [5]Vivace
André, Maurice, 79), 115)
Keavy, Stephen
Smithers, Don, 1)

Cellier, Alexandre, 1883-1968
Cellier, Alexandre-Eugène

[Variations, "Sing to the Lord a New Song", trumpet & organ]
Theme and Variations on Psalm 149, "Sing to the Lord a New Song"
Tarr, Edward, 5)

Cesare, Giovanni Martino, *ca.* 1590-1667

[Sonata, "La Augustana", cornetto, trombone & organ]
Sonata, "La Augustana"
Eichhorn, Holger

[Sonata, "La Famosa", cornetto, trombone & organ]
Sonata, "La Famosa"
Eichhorn, Holger

[Sonata, "La Fevice", cornetto, trombone & organ]
Sonata, "La Fevice"
Eichhorn, Holger

[Sonata, "La Foccarina", cornetto, trombone & organ]
Sonata, "La Foccarina"
Eichhorn, Holger

[Sonata, "La Gioia", cornetto, trombone & organ]
Sonata, "La Gioia"
Eichhorn, Holger

[Sonata, "La Giorgina", cornetto, trombone & organ]
Sonata, "La Giorgina"
Eichhorn, Holger

[Sonata, "La Hieronyma", cornetto, trombone & organ]
Sonata, "La Hieronyma"
Eichhorn, Holger

[Sonata, "La Massimiliana", cornetto, trombone & organ]
Sonata, "La Massimiliana"
Eichhorn, Holger

Chaikovskii, Piotr Il'yich
See: Tchaikovsky, Piotr Ilyitch

Chance, John Barnes, 1932-1972

[Credo, trumpet & piano, (1964)]
Credo
Amstutz, Keith
Hickman, David, 3)
Hyatt, Jack

Chardon, Yves, 1902-

[Sonata, trumpet & cello, op. 21]
Sonata for D-Trumpet and Cello, op. 21
Gardner, Ned

Charlier, Théo, 1868-1944

[Études Transcendantes (36), trumpet]
Trente-six Études Transcendantes pour Trompette
(36 Transcendental Etudes)
Baldwin, David

₍Solo de concours, trumpet & piano₎
Solo de concours
Schwarz, Gerard, 12)

Charpentier, Marc-Antoine, *ca.* 1645-1704

₍Te Deum. Air de trompettes, No. 2, trumpet(s) & chamber orchestra₎
Deuxième Air de trompettes from *Te Deum*
Coursier, Gérard
Soustrot, Bernard, 8)
Tarr, Edward, 18), 21)

₍Te Deum. Prélude, chamber orchestra₎
Prélude from *Te Deum*
(Marche de triomphe)
(Triumphmarsch)
André, Maurice, 12), 71)
Coursier, Gérard
Güttler, Ludwig, 13), 21)
Potpourri, 4), 13), 15)
Scherbaum, Adolf, 18), 25), 26), 34)
Soustrot, Bernard, 8)
Tarr, Edward, 21)

₍Te Deum. Prélude, chamber orchestra; arr. trumpet(s) & organ₎
Prélude from *Te Deum*
(Marche de triomphe)
(Triumphmarsch)
André, Maurice, 38), 40), 42), 44), 52), 67), 227)
Bernard, André, 9)
Blair, Stacy
Delmotte, Roger, 38)
Deside
Gabel, Bernard, 2)
Giangiulio, Richard
Potpourri, 43), 44)
Scherbaum, Adolf, 34)
Stringer, Alan, 3)

₍Te Deum. Te Deum laudamus, mixed voices & chamber orchestra₎
Te Deum laudamus from *Te Deum*
Coursier, Gérard

₍Te Deum, mixed voices & chamber orchestra₎
Te Deum
André, Maurice, 97)
Gabel, Bernard, 4)

Chávez, Carlos, 1899-1978
Chávez y Ramírez, Carlos (Antonio de Padua)

[Soli I, oboe, clarinet, bassoon & trumpet, (1933)]
Soli I
León, Felipe
Stevens, Thomas, 11)

[Soli IV, trumpet, horn & trombone, (1964)]
Soli IV
León, Felipe

Chaynes, Charles, 1925-

[Concerto, trumpet & orchestra, (1956)]
Concerto pour Trompette en Ut et Orchestre
(Concerto for C-Trumpet and Orchestra)
[1]Moderato - Allegro / [2]Adagio / [3]Final: Allegro giocoso
André, Maurice, 108)

Chebotaryan, Gayane Movsesovna, 1918-

[Prelude and Allegro, trumpet & piano]
Prelude and Allegro
Balyan, Yuri

Chen I-Haw

[Divertimento, trumpet & piano]
Divertimento
Yeh Shu-han

[Fantasy (theme from Chinese opera), trumpet & piano]
Fantasy sur un thème d'opéra Chinoise
(Fantasy on a Chinese opera theme)
Yeh Shu-han

Chichkov, Yuri Mikhailovich, 1929-

[Sonatina, trumpet & piano, G$\flat$ major]
Sonatina in G$\flat$ major for Trumpet and Piano
Usov, Yuri

Chitchian, Geguni Oganesovna, 1929-

[Prelude and Concert Scherzo, trumpet & piano]
Prelude and Concert Scherzo
Balyan, Yuri

Chopin, Frédéric François, 1810-1849
Chopin, Fryderyk Franciszek

⌜Etudes, piano, op. ?; arr. trumpet & piano⌟
Étude
Dokshitser, Timofei, 34)

⌜Etudes, piano, op. 10. No. 3: Tristesse, E major; arr. trumpet & ?⌟
Étude en mi majeur, "Tristesse", op. 10, no. 3
Scherbaum, Adolf, 34)

⌜Etudes, piano, op. 10. No. 3: Tristesse, E major; arr. trumpet & harp⌟
Étude en mi majeur, "Tristesse", op. 10, no. 3
André, Maurice, 84)

⌜Preludes, piano, op. 28. No. 4: e minor; arr. trumpet & piano⌟
Prélude en mi mineur, op. 28, no. 4
Dokshitser, Timofei, 34)

Chostakovitch, Dimitri
See: Shostakovich, Dmitri

Chou Wen-chung, 1923-

⌜Pien, chamber ensemble, (1966)⌟
Pien
Chamber ensemble includes: 2 flutes, oboe, clarinet, bassoon, horn, 2 trumpets, 2 trombones, piano & 4 percussion.
Anderson, Ronald, 1)

⌜Soliloquy of a Bhiksuñi, trumpet, brass & percussion, (1958)⌟
Soliloquy of a Bhiksuñi
Brass ensemble includes: 4 horns, 3 trombones & tuba.
Rapier, Leon, 3)
Stevens, Thomas, 4)

Cima, Gian Paolo, *b.* 1570?
Cima, Giovanni Paolo

⌜Sonata, cornetto, trombone & organ⌟
Sonata per cornetto e trombone
Eichhorn, Holger

Cimarosa, Domenico, 1749-1801

⌜Concerto, piano (oboe) & strings, C major. Introduction: Larghetto; arr. trumpet & organ⌟
Larghetto from *Oboe Concerto in C major*
André, Maurice, 39)

⌐Concerto, piano (oboe) & strings, C major. Introduction: Larghetto; arr. trumpet, organ, drums & string bass⌐
Mélodie
(Larghetto from *Oboe Concerto in C major*)
André, Maurice, 70)

⌐Concerto, piano (oboe) & strings, C major; arr. trumpet & orchestra⌐
Concerto in C major for Trumpet and Orchestra
[1]Introduction: Larghetto / [2]Allegro / [3]Siciliana / [4]Allegro giusto
André, Maurice, 41), 56), 227)

Clarke, Herbert Lincoln, 1867-1945

⌐Bride of the Waves, cornet & piano⌐
The Bride of the Waves (Polka Brillante)
Schwarz, Gerard, 19)

⌐Bride of the Waves, cornet & piano; arr. cornet & band⌐
The Bride of the Waves (Polka Brillante)
Clarke, Herbert L.

⌐Carnival of Venice, cornet & piano⌐
Carnival of Venice (Variations)
Smith, Leonard B.

⌐Carnival of Venice, cornet & piano; arr. cornet & orchestra⌐
Carnival of Venice (Variations)
Clarke, Herbert L.

⌐Carnival of Venice, cornet & piano; arr. cornet & wind ensemble⌐
Carnival of Venice (Variations)
Head, Emerson

⌐Cousins, cornet, trombone & piano⌐
Cousins
Impett, Jonathan
Schwarz, Gerard, 21)

⌐Débutante, cornet & piano⌐
The Débutante (Caprice Brillante)
(La Débutante)
Schwarz, Gerard, 19)
Sommerhalder, Max

⌐Débutante, cornet & piano; arr. cornet & band⌐
The Débutante (Caprice Brillante)
Clarke, Herbert L.

⌐Débutante, cornet & piano; arr. cornet & wind ensemble⌐
The Débutante (Caprice Brillante)
Marsalis, Wynton, 4)

[From the Shores of the Mighty Pacific, cornet & piano]
From the Shores of the Mighty Pacific (Rondo Caprice)
Schwarz, Gerard, 19)

[From the Shores of the Mighty Pacific, cornet & piano; arr. cornet & orchestra]
From the Shores of the Mighty Pacific (Rondo Caprice)
Clarke, Herbert L.

[Lake of Bays, cornet & piano; arr. cornet & chamber ensemble]
Lake of Bays (Concert Polka)
Schwarz, Gerard, 5)

[Maid of the Mist, cornet & piano]
The Maid of the Mist (Polka)
Schwarz, Gerard, 21)
Smith, Leonard B.

[Neptune's Court, cornet & piano; arr. cornet & chamber ensemble]
Neptune's Court
Schwarz, Gerard, 5)

[Norine, cornet & piano]
Norine (Waltz)
Haynie, John, 1)

[Showers of Gold, cornet & piano; arr. cornet & orchestra]
Showers of Gold (Scherzo)
Clarke, Herbert L.

[Side Partners, cornet, trombone (or 2 cornets) & piano; arr. cornet, baritone horn & chamber ensemble]
Side Partners
Schwarz, Gerard, 5)

[Sounds from the Hudson, cornet & piano]
Sounds from the Hudson (Valse Brillante)
Schwarz, Gerard, 19)

[Sounds from the Hudson, cornet & piano; arr. cornet & band]
Sounds from the Hudson (Valse Brillante)
Clarke, Herbert L.

[Sounds from the Hudson, cornet & piano; arr. cornet & wind ensemble]
Sounds from the Hudson (Valse Brillante)
Marsalis, Wynton, 4)

[Sounds from the Hudson, cornet & piano; arr. trumpet & piano]
Sounds from the Hudson (Valse Brillante)
Tobe, Yutaka

[Southern Cross, cornet & piano; arr. cornet & brass ensemble]
The Southern Cross (Romantique)
Caens, Thierry

[Southern Cross, cornet & piano; arr. cornet & chamber ensemble]
The Southern Cross (Romantique)
Schwarz, Gerard, 5)

[Southern Cross, cornet & piano; arr. cornet & orchestra]
The Southern Cross (Romantique)
Clarke, Herbert L.

[Stars in a Velvety Sky, cornet & piano]
Stars in a Velvety Sky (Polka Brillante)
Gardner, Ned
Haynie, John, 1)

[Stars in a Velvety Sky, cornet & piano; arr. cornet & band]
Stars in a Velvety Sky (Polka Brillante)
Clarke, Herbert L.

[Three Aces, cornet trio & band; arr. cornet trio & chamber ensemble]
Three Aces
Schwarz, Gerard, 5)

[Trixie Valse, cornet & piano]
Trixie Valse
Burke, James, 7)

[Twilight Dreams, cornet & piano]
Twilight Dreams (Waltz Intermezzo)
Burke, James, 7)
Schwarz, Gerard, 21)

[Veta, cornet & piano; arr. cornet & orchestra]
La Veta (Caprice)
Clarke, Herbert L.

Clarke, Jeremiah, *ca.* 1674-1707

[Airs; arr. trumpet, strings & continuo]
Ayres for the Theatre
a) Cebel / b) Trumpet Song (from *The Island Princess*) / c) Three
Minuets / d) Round-O (The Prince of Denmark's March) /
e) Serenade / f) Gigue
Steele-Perkins, Crispian, 5)

[King William's March, harpsichord; arr. trumpet & organ]
King William's March
Ghitalla, Armando, 5)
Laughton, Stuart

[Prince of Denmark's March, harpsichord, D major; arr. trumpet & band]
Rondeau: The Prince of Denmark's March
(Trumpet Voluntary)
Smith, Philip, 4)

ₜPrince of Denmark's March, harpsichord, D major; arr. trumpet & brass
  ensembleₜ
Rondeau: The Prince of Denmark's March
(Trumpet Voluntary)
>   André, Maurice, 173), 190), 193), 194), 197)
>   Canadian Brass, 5), 6)
>   Güttler, Ludwig, 9)
>   Potpourri, 1), 44)
>   Wilbraham, John, 17)

ₜPrince of Denmark's March, harpsichord, D major; arr. trumpet & instrumental
  accompanimentₜ
Rondeau: The Prince of Denmark's March
(Trumpet Voluntary)
>   Scherbaum, Adolf, 34)
>   Smith, Bramwell "Bram"

ₜPrince of Denmark's March, harpsichord, D major; arr. trumpet & organₜ
Rondeau: The Prince of Denmark's March
(Trumpet Voluntary)
>   André, Maurice, 40), 52), 67), 227)
>   Berinbaum, Martin
>   Bernard, André, 9)
>   Blair, Stacy
>   Bodenröder, Robert
>   Carroll, Edward, 6)
>   Chesnut, Walter
>   Delmotte, Roger, 38)
>   Deside
>   Ghitalla, Armando, 5)
>   Giangiulio, Richard
>   Grin, Freddy, 8), 9)
>   Kejmar, Miroslav, 1)
>   Laughton, Stuart
>   Lewark, Egbert
>   Lieberman, Harold J.
>   McGuffey, Patrick
>   Mertens, Theo, 2)
>   Potpourri, 43)
>   Rehm, Klaus
>   Scherbaum, Adolf, 32)
>   Stringer, Alan, 3)
>   Tarr, Edward, 41)
>   Tolley, Richard
>   Zapf, Gerd

ₜPrince of Denmark's March, harpsichord, D major; arr. trumpet & piano,
  B♭ majorₜ
Rondeau: The Prince of Denmark's March
(Trumpet Voluntary)
>   Ghitalla, Armando, 11)

[Prince of Denmark's March, harpsichord, D major; arr. trumpet & strings]
Rondeau: The Prince of Denmark's March
(Trumpet Voluntary)

This work is often attributed to Henry Purcell as *Trumpet Voluntary in D major*, and is catalogued by Franklin B. Zimmerman as a spurious attribution, S125. It originally appeared as a "Rondeau" from Jeremiah Clarke's *A Choice Collection of Ayres for the Harpsichord or Spinett*, (1700). It also appeared as the fourth movement of a *Suit de Clairque* found in four manuscript part books preserved in the British Museum. Though indexed separately, here, *The Prince of Denmark's March* (or *Trumpet Voluntary*) is often included in various arranged suites by Clarke or Purcell.

André, Maurice, 2), 73), 175), 214), 219)
Burns, Stephen
Carroll, Edward, 1)
Delmotte, Roger, 14), 19)
Geisler, Lloyd
Johnson, Gilbert, 3), 7)
Krauss, Sam
Potpourri, 4), 29), 32), 37), 46)
Reinhart, Carole Dawn, 4), 5)
Steele-Perkins, Crispian, 5)
Unidentified, Trumpet(s), 4)
Vaillant, Ludovic, 1), 3)
Voisin, Roger, 3)
Webb, Gordon, 7)
Wilbraham, John, 25), 30)
Wobisch, Helmut, 3)

[Prince of Denmark's March, harpsichord, D major; arr. trumpet trio & instrumental accompaniment]
Rondeau: The Prince of Denmark's March
(Trumpet Voluntary)
Victorian Trumpet Trio

[Prince of Denmark's March, harpsichord, D major; arr. trumpet, brass ensemble & organ]
Rondeau: The Prince of Denmark's March
(Trumpet Voluntary)
André, Maurice, 202)

[Shore's Trumpet, trumpet, strings & continuo]
Shore's Trumpet
Steele-Perkins, Crispian, 5)

[Suite, harpsichord; arr. trumpet & organ, D major]
English Suite in D major
> a) Trumpet Tune / b) Ayre / c) The Prince of Denmark's March
> The first and third movements are the famous pieces often attributed to Henry Purcell (Z. S124 & Z. S125). The second movement is a unique "air" not cited elsewhere in this index.
> **Tarr, Edward**, 41)

[Suite, trumpet, (2 oboes & bassoon), strings & continuo, D major]
Suite in D major for Trumpet, Strings and Continuo
> ¹Prelude: The Duke of Gloster's March / ²Minuet / ³Sybelle [Cebell] / ⁴Rondeau: The Prince of Denmark's March / ⁵Serenade [Andante] / ⁶Bourrée / ⁷Ecossaise / ⁸Hornpipe / ⁹Gigue
> This suite has been re-constructed based on authentic "part books" preserved in the British Museum. The oboe and bassoon parts are optional (in unison with strings); and the trumpet is tacet in the eighth movement.
> **André, Maurice**, 175)
> **Burns, Stephen**

[Suite, trumpet, (2 oboes & bassoon), strings & continuo, D major; arr. trumpet & organ]
Suite in D major for Trumpet, Strings and Continuo
> ¹Prelude: The Duke of Gloster's March / ²Minuet / ³Sybelle [Cebell] / ⁴Rondeau: The Prince of Denmark's March / ⁵Serenade [Andante] / ⁶Bourrée / ⁷Ecossaise / ⁸Hornpipe / ⁹Gigue
> Original harpsichord versions exist for the Prelude, Rondeau and Serenade. A separate score of the Sybelle exists as an "ode on the death of Henry Purcell". The other movements exist only in "part books" preserved in the British Museum. This suite was re-constructed from the part books for trumpet, strings and continuo; and then re-arranged for trumpet with keyboard accompaniment.
> **Haas, Wolfgang**
> **Hartog, Thomas**
> **Kejmar, Miroslav**, 1)
> **Wilbraham, John**, 3)
> **Zapf, Gerd**

[Suite, trumpet, (2 oboes & bassoon), strings & continuo, D major: Serenade; arr. trumpet & organ]
Serenade from *Suite in D major*
> **Ghitalla, Armando**, 5)
> **Laughton, Stuart**

[Trumpet Tune, harpsichord, C major; arr. trumpet & brass ensemble]
Trumpet Tune
> **André, Maurice**, 173), 190), 193), 194), 197)
> **Potpourri**, 1)
> **Wilbraham, John**, 17)

ₜTrumpet Tune, harpsichord, C major; arr. trumpet & harpᵣ
Trumpet Tune
André, Maurice, 84)

ₜTrumpet Tune, harpsichord, C major; arr. trumpet & organᵣ
Trumpet Tune
This *Trumpet Tune* is often attributed to Henry Purcell, and is catalogued by Franklin B. Zimmerman as a spurious attribution, S124. It has been identified on at least one recording as being from Clarke's *The Island Princess*. (Other arrangements of this tune are indexed separately, but without repeating this footnote.) This *Trumpet Tune* is often coupled with an *Air*, but not necessarily with the same "air" each time. (These "airs" are usually authentic works by Purcell, and are indexed separately.) This piece may also appear as part of an arranged "suite" and has been cited here even when included in various suites.

André, Maurice, 215)
Berinbaum, Martin
Blair, Stacy
Bouche
Braz, Dirceu, 1)
Carroll, Edward, 6)
Chesnut, Walter
Delmotte, Roger, 39)
Deside
Ghitalla, Armando, 5)
Grin, Freddy, 8), 9)
Güttler, Ludwig, 21)
McGuffey, Patrick
Mertens, Theo, 2)
Potpourri, 44)
Reinhart, Carole Dawn, 13)
Scherbaum, Adolf, 32)
Stringer, Alan, 3)
Tarr, Edward, 41)
Tolley, Richard
Tschotschev, Nicolai-Dimitrov
Urfer, Eric
Wilbraham, John, 24)

ₜTrumpet Tune, harpsichord, C major; arr. trumpet & pianoᵣ
Trumpet Tune
Hyatt, Jack
Schwarz, Gerard, 14)

ₜTrumpet Tune, harpsichord, C major; arr. trumpet & stringsᵣ
Trumpet Tune
Delmotte, Roger, 14)
Steele-Perkins, Crispian, 17)
Voisin, Roger, 3)

ₜTrumpet Tune, harpsichord, C major; arr. trumpet, brass ensemble & organ₎
Trumpet Tune
André, Maurice, 202)
Potpourri, 43)

ₜVoluntaries. Suite, harpsichord, D major; arr. trumpet & organ₎
Suite of Voluntaries in D major
The specific voluntaries in this suite have not been identified.
Rehm, Klaus

Clemens non Papa, Jacobus, *ca.* 1510-1556?
Clement, Jacobus

ₜMotet, "Vox in Rama audite est", mixed voices & instruments, (1549)₎
Vox in Rama audite est
Cook, Richard

Clérambault, Louis-Nicolas, 1676-1749

ₜSonata (Symphony), "La Magnifique", orchestra₎
Sonate, "La Magnifique"
(Symphonie VII, "La Magnifique")
Delmotte, Roger, 28)

Clergue, Jean, 1896-

ₜSarabande et Rigaudon, trumpet & piano₎
Sarabande et Rigaudon
Hyatt, Jack

Clérisse, Robert, 1899-1973

ₜThème Varié, cornet or trumpet & piano₎
Thème Varié
Crisara, Raymond, 6)

Coates, Eric, 1886-1957

ₜBy the Sleepy Lagoon, (1930); arr. trumpet & orchestra₎
Sleepy Lagoon (Valse Serenade)
Méndez, Rafael, 21)

Cochereau, Pierre, 1924-1984
Cochereau, Pierre Charles

ₜParaphrase de la Dédicace, mixed voices, brass, 6 timpani & 2 organs₎
Paraphrase de la Dédicace
Composed for the Eighth Centenary of Notre-Dame de Paris.
Brass includes 6 trumpets & 6 trombones.
André, Maurice, 186)

Code, Percy, 20th cent.

⌈Zelda; arr. cornet & brass ensemble⌉
Zelda
Caens, Thierry

Coelho, Manuel Rodrigues
See: Rodrigues Coelho, Manuel

Cole, Hugo, 1917-

⌈Hammersmith Galop, trumpet & piano⌉
The Hammersmith Galop
House, Lawrence

Colombier, Michel, 20th cent.

⌈Emmanuel; arr. trumpet & orchestra⌉
Emmanuel
Schultz, Erik, 8)

Concone, Giuseppe, 1801-1861
Concone, (Paolo) Giuseppe (Gioacchino)

⌈Lessons (50), voice & piano, op. 9. No. 27: Andantino; arr. trumpet & piano⌉
Andantino
Geyer, Charles

Confrey, Zez, 1895-1971
Confrey, Edward Elezear

⌈Kitten on the Keys, (1921); arr. trumpet & orchestra⌉
Kitten on the Keys
Méndez, Rafael, 29)

Connolly, Justin Riveagh, 1933-

⌈Tesserae D, trumpet & tape, (1971)⌉
Tesserae D
Wallace, John, 6)

Consonni, 20th cent.

⌈Sonata, trumpet & organ⌉
Sonata per tromba e organo
(In 4 tempi tratta da opera di Daniele Maffeis.)
Hunger, Helmut, 5)

Constant, Marius, 1925-

[Alleluias, trumpet & organ]
Alleluias pour trompette et orgue
Thibaud, Pierre, 2)

Cooper, John, *ca.* 1575-1626
Coperario, Giovanni
Coprario, Giovanni

[Fantasia, cornetti, shawms, sackbuts]
Fantasia a 5
Montesi, Robert, 3)

[Fantasia, no. 76; arr. 2 trumpets & 4 trombones]
Fantasia No. 76
André, Maurice, 176)

[Suite, cornetto & continuo]
Suite
¹Fantasia / ²Alman / ³Ayre
Smithers, Don, 1)

Cope, David Howell, 1941-

[Bright Angel, trumpet & tape]
Bright Angel
Stith, Marice, 8)

Coperario, Giovanni
See: Cooper, John

Copland, Aaron, 1900-

[Quiet City, English horn, trumpet & strings, (1940)]
Quiet City
Ghitalla, Armando, 4)
Glantz, Harry, 1)
Kuehn, David
Laird, Michael, 4)
Lang, William
Mear, Sidney, 1), 3)
Smith, Philip, 1)
Sullivan, William
Unidentified, Trumpet(s), 12)

Coprario, Giovanni
See: Cooper, John

Corbeil, Pierre de
See: Pierre de Corbeil

Cords, Gustav, 1870-1951

₍Fantasie de Concert, cornet & piano, e♭ minor₎
Fantasie de Concert in e♭ minor
Sommerhalder, Max

₍Romance, trumpet & piano₎
Romance
House, Lawrence

Corelli, Arcangelo, 1653-1713

₍Concerto, violin, 2 trumpets, strings & continuo, Anh. 13, D major₎
Concerto a quattro per Violino solo, due Trombe ò Violini e Basso, Anh. 13
[1]Allegro / [2]Grave [fehlt] / [3]Presto
Delmotte, Roger, 9), 23), 27), 40), 47)

₍Dances (3), 2 violins & continuo; arr. 2 trumpets & 4 trombones₎
Drei ländliche Tänze
(Suite of Dances)
[1]Allemanda / [2]Corrente / [3]Giga
The first dance = Sonata da camera, op. 4, no. 2 (second movement); the second and third dances = Sonata da camera, op. 4, no. 4 (second & fourth movements).
André, Maurice, 190), 197)

₍Dances (6), 2 violins & continuo; arr. 2 trumpets & 4 trombones₎
Suite of Dances
[1]Allemanda / [2]Grave / [3]Corrente / [4]Corrente / [5]Adagio / [6]Giga
The first three dances = Sonata da camera, op. 4, no. 2, movements 2-4; the last three dances = Sonata da camera, op. 4, no. 4, movements 2-4.
André, Maurice, 173)

₍Grave; arr. trumpet & organ₎
Grave
The source of this transcription has not been ascertained.
Bernard, André, 9), 11)
Erb, Helmut, 5)

₍Sonata, trumpet, 2 violins & continuo, WoO 4, D major₎
Sonata con tromba in D, WoO 4
[1]Adagio / [2]Allegro / [3]Grave / [4]Spiritoso et Adagio / [5]Allegro
Braz, Dirceu, 5)
Burns, Stephen
Cuvit, Michel
Fink, Werner
Hunger, Helmut, 3)

Immer, Friedemann, 9)
Keavy, Stephen
Schultz, Erik, 6)
Smithers, Don, 1)
Wobisch, Helmut, 3)
Yudashkin, Georgy

₍Sonata, trumpet, 2 violins & continuo, WoO 4, D major. 5. Allegro; arr. trumpet & piano, C major₎

Sonata con tromba in D, WoO 4
Nagel, Robert, 10)

₍Sonata, trumpet, 2 violins & continuo, WoO 4, D major; arr. trumpet & organ₎

Sonata con tromba in D, WoO 4
[1]Adagio (Lento) / [2]Allegro / [3]Grave / [4]Spiritoso et Adagio (Moderato) / [5]Allegro
Friedrich, Reinhold
Mertens, Theo, 4)
Scherbaum, Adolf, 29)
Schultz, Erik, 1)
Touvron, Guy, 12)

₍Sonate a violino solo, op. 5. No. 1, D major: Allemande; arr. trumpet, organ, drums & string bass₎

Allemande
André, Maurice, 70)

₍Sonate a violino solo, op. 5. No. 6, A major; arr. trumpet & organ₎

Sonata in A major
[1]Grave / [2]Allegro / [3]Allegro / [4]Adagio / [5]Allegro
The third movement is omitted from this arrangement.
Schultz, Erik, 2)

₍Sonate a violino solo, op. 5. No. 8, e minor; arr. trumpet & organ₎

Sonata in e minor
[1]Preludio (Largo) / [2]Allemanda (Allegro) / [3]Sarabanda (Largo) / [4]Giga (Allegro)
André, Maurice, 139)
Delmotte, Roger, 38)
Gabel, Bernard, 1), 5)
Rippas, Claude

₍Sonate a violino solo, op. 5. No. 8, e minor; arr. trumpet & piano, d minor₎

Sonata VIII
[1]Preludio (Largo) / [2]Allemanda (Allegro) / [3]Sarabanda (Largo) / [4]Giga (Allegro)
Ghitalla, Armando, 12)
Haynie, John, 1)
Smith, Leonard B.
Tobe, Yutaka

ₜSonate da camera, op. 4. No. 1, C major; arr. 2 trumpets, strings & continuo,
 B♭ majorₗ
Concertino in B♭ for 2 Trumpets, Strings and Basso continuo
[1]Preludio (Largo) / [2]Corrente (Allegro) / [3]Adagio / [4]Allemanda
(Presto)
>> **Delmotte, Roger,** 49)
>> **Potpourri,** 68)

Cornelius, Peter, 1824-1874
Cornelius, (Carl August) Peter

ₜWeihnachtslieder, op. 8, (1856). No. 3: Drei Kön'ge, soprano, trumpet & organₗ
"Drei Kön'ge wandern aus Morgenland", op. 8, no. 3
>> **Grin, Freddy,** 5)

Correa Braga, António, 17th cent.

ₜBatalha de 6° Tom; arr. trumpet & organₗ
Batalha de 6° Tom
>> **Hartog, Thomas**

Corrette, Michel, 1709-1795

ₜConcertos comiques. No. 3: "Margoton"; arr. trumpet, oboe, strings & continuoₗ
Concerto comique, "Margoton", No. 3
[1]Adagio / [2]Allegro / [3]Adagio / [4]Allegro
>> **André, Maurice,** 188)

ₜConcertos comiques. No. 7: "La Servante au bon Tabac"; arr. trumpet, flute,
 oboe, bassoon, horn, strings & continuoₗ
Concerto comique, "La Servante au bon Tabac", No. 7
[1]Allegro / [2]Adagio / [3]Allegro
>> **André, Maurice,** 188)

ₜConcertos comiques. No. 10: "Ma mie Margot"; arr. trumpet, flute, oboe,
 bassoon, horn & continuoₗ
Concerto comique, "Ma mie Margot", No. 10
[1]Allegro / [2]Adagio / [3]Allegro
>> **André, Maurice,** 188)

ₜConcertos comiques. No. 12: "La Découpure"; arr. trumpet, strings & continuoₗ
Concerto comique, "La Découpure", No. 12
[1]Allegro / [2]Adagio / [3]Allegro
>> **André, Maurice,** 188)

ₜDivertimenti, 2 trumpets, op. 7. No. 1, D majorₗ
Divertissement pour deux trompettes, op. 7, no. 1
[1]Ouverture - Canon / [2]March / [3](March) / [4]Minuet I / [5]Minuet II /
[6]Chaconne Comique
>> **André, Maurice,** 98[1])
>> **Touvron, Guy,** 16), 18)

₍Marche des gardes françaises, chamber orchestra₎
Marche des gardes françaises
Delmotte, Roger, 8)

₍Marche des gardes suisses, chamber orchestra₎
Marche des gardes suisses
Delmotte, Roger, 8)

₍Marche du Maréchal de Saxe, chamber orchestra, E♭ major₎
Marche du Maréchal de Saxe
Delmotte, Roger, 8)

₍Noël Allemande; arr. trumpet or corno da caccia & organ₎
Noël Allemande
Güttler, Ludwig, 15)

Costinescu, Gheorghe, 1934-

₍Jubilus, soprano, trumpet & organic percussion, (rev. 1984)₎
Jubilus
Hyatt, Jack

Cosyn, Benjamin, *ca.* 1570-1652

₍Suite Anglaise. Gaillarde; arr. trumpet & organ₎
Suite Anglaise
Potpourri, 44)

Couperin, François, 1668-1733
Couperin, François ("Le Grand")

₍Marche du régiment de Champagne, chamber orchestra₎
Marche du régiment de Champagne
Delmotte, Roger, 8)

₍Messe à l'usage des paroisses, organ, (1690). Excerpt; arr. trumpet & organ₎
Dialogue sur le trompette et la crumorne
([IV] Quatrième Couplet du Kyrie)
Hartog, Thomas[4]

₍Messe à l'usage des paroisses, organ, (1690). Excerpts; arr. trumpet & organ₎
Excerpts from *Messe à l'usage des paroisses*
[XI] Tierce en taille (6e Couplet du Gloria) / [XVII] Récit de cornet
(2e Couplet du Sanctus) / [XIX] Plein chant (1e Couplet de Agnus
Dei)
Tschotschev, Nicolai-Dimitrov

₍Nouveaux concerts, (1724). No. 9: harpsichord; arr. trumpet & organ₎
Neuvième Concert Intitulé, "Ritratto dell'Amore"
[1]Le Charme / [2]L'Enjouement / [3]Les Grâces, Courante françoise / [4]Le je-ne-scay-quoy / [5]La Vivacité / [6]La Noble Fierté, Sarabande / [7]La Douceur / [8]L'et Cœtera ou Menuets

Concerts royaux of 1722 includes four works for harpsichord (alternatively for violin, flute, oboe, cello and bassoon). The *Nouveaux concerts* of 1724 is a continuation of the *Concerts royaux*, but for unspecified instruments. (Thus, No. 9 is actually the fifth work of the second set.)
André, Maurice, 150)

₍Nouveaux concerts, (1724). No. 10: chamber orchestra₎
Concerts Royaux, No. 10
No. 10, here, is actually the sixth work of the 1724 set.
Delmotte, Roger, 11), 17)

₍Trio Sonata, "La Steinkerque", 2 violins & continuo; arr. 2 trumpets & organ₎
Trio Sonata, "La Steinkerque"
("La Steinquerque")
[1]Gayement / [2]Air / [3]Gravement / [4]Gayement
André, Maurice, 150)

Courbois, Philippe, *fl.* 1720

₍Air triomphal; arr. 2 trumpets & organ₎
Air triomphal
Loustalot, Alain

Cowell, Johnny, 1926-
Cowell, John Marwood

₍Butterscotch, trumpet & orchestra₎
Butterscotch
Cowell, Johnny

₍Lonely Trumpet, trumpet & orchestra₎
Lonely Trumpet
Cowell, Johnny

₍Roller Coaster, trumpet trio & orchestra₎
Roller Coaster
Cowell, Johnny

₍Sangre de Toro Bravo, trumpet & orchestra₎
Sangre de Toro Bravo
Cowell, Johnny

Croft, William, 1678-1727

ſShore's Tune, harpsichord; arr. trumpet & organꜣ
Shore's Tune
(Trumpet Tune)
> **Ghitalla, Armando, 5)**
> **Steele-Perkins, Crispian, 5)**

ſVoluntaries (12). No. 3, organ, D major; arr. trumpet & organꜣ
Voluntary in D
> **Carroll, Edward, 6)**

ſVoluntaries (12). No. 3, organ, D major; arr. 2 trumpets, timpani & organꜣ
Voluntary in D
> **Ghitalla, Armando, 5)**

Crüger, Johannes, 1598-1662

ſChrist lag in Todesbanden; 3 settings: solo trumpet / brass quartet / mixed voices & brassꜣ
Christ lag in Todesbanden
> **Thibaud, Pierre, 10)**

ſFröhlich soll mein Herze springen; arr. trumpet & brass ensembleꜣ
Fröhlich soll mein Herze springen
> **Güttler, Ludwig, 9)**

ſGelobet seist du, Jesu Christ; arr. trumpet & brass ensembleꜣ
Gelobet seist du, Jesu Christ
> **Güttler, Ludwig, 9)**

ſVom Himmel hoch; 2 settings: mixed voices & brass / mixed voices, 2 trumpets & stringsꜣ
Vom Himmel hoch
> **Thibaud, Pierre, 10)**

ſWie soll ich dich empfangen; arr. trumpet & brass ensembleꜣ
Wie soll ich dich empfangen
> **Güttler, Ludwig, 9)**

Crusell, Bernhard Henrik, 1775-1838

ſSinfonia Concertante, clarinet, horn, bassoon & chamber orchestraꜣ
Sinfonia Concertante in B♭, op. 3
The chamber orchestra includes trumpet.
> **Goethel, Siegfried**

Cuî, César Antonovich, 1835-1918
Kyui, Tsezar Antonovich

ſKaleidoscope, violin & piano, op. 50, (1893). No. 9: "Orientale"; arr. trumpet & violinsꜣ
Orientale, op. 50, no. 9
> **Dokshitser, Timofei, 14), 36), 38), 39)**

d'Andrieu, Jean-François
See: Dandrieu, Jean-François

d'Aquin, Claude
See: Daquin, Claude

Daetwyler, Jean, 1907-

ₜConcerto, trumpet & orchestraₗ
   Concerto for Trumpet and Orchestra
      Falentin, Paul, 4)

ₜConcerto, trumpet & organₗ
   Concerto for Organ and Trumpet
      Falentin, Paul, 4)

ₜNoël des Bergers, trumpet & organₗ
   Le Noël des Bergers
      Falentin, Paul, 5)

Damare, Eugène, 1840-1919

ₜCléopâtra; arr. cornet & brass ensembleₗ
   Cléopâtra
      Caens, Thierry

Dandrieu, Jean-François, *ca.* 1682-1738
d'Andrieu, Jean-François

ₜFanfares de Chantilly, trumpet & stringsₗ
   Fanfares de Chantilly
      Delmotte, Roger, 8), 26)

ₜSonata, d minor; arr. trumpet & organₗ
   Sonata in d minor
      ¹Allegro
      Potpourri, 44)

Danican-Philidor, Anne, 1681-1728

ₜSuite, oboe & continuo, No. 1, g minor; arr. trumpet & organₗ
   Suite No. 1 in g minor
      ¹Ouverture (Lentement-Vivement) / ²Le ballet / ³Bourrée /
      ⁴Sarabande / ⁵Gavotte / ⁶Les forgerons
         André, Maurice, 45), 55), 227)

Danican-Philidor (l'aîné), André, 1647-1730

ₜMarche des Boulonnais, instrumental ensembleₗ
   Marche des Boulonnais
      Delmotte, Roger, 8)

⌜Marche des Pompes Funèbres, instrumental ensemble⌝
Marche des Pompes Funèbres
Delmotte, Roger, 8)

⌜Mariage de la grosse Cathos, instrumental ensemble⌝
Le Mariage de la grosse Cathos
Delmotte, Roger, 11)

⌜Ordonnance de la compagnie des canonniers de la Rochelle, instrumental ensemble⌝
Ordonnance de la compagnie des canonniers de la Rochelle
Delmotte, Roger, 8)

Daniel-Lesur, Daniel Jean Yves
See: Lesur, Daniel

Daquin, Claude, 1694-1772
d'Aquin, Louis-Claude

⌜Livre de Noëls, organ, op. 2, (c. 1740). No. 10; arr. trumpet & organ⌝
Noël grand jeu et duo, Nr. 10
(Noël X)
Steele-Perkins, Crispian, 2)

⌜Livre de Noëls, organ, op. 2, (c. 1740). No. 12; arr. trumpet & organ⌝
Noël Suisse Nr. 12
(Noël XII)
Schultz, Erik, 3)

⌜Livre de Noëls, organ, op. 2, (c. 1740). No. 12; arr. 3 trumpets & organ⌝
Noël Suisse Nr. 12
(Noël XII)
Voisin, Roger, 5)

Darter, Thomas E., 1949-

⌜Sonatina, trumpet & piano⌝
Sonatina for Trumpet and Piano
(Three Aphorisms)
Stith, Marice, 4)

Darvas, Ferenc, 20th cent.

⌜Savannah, trumpet, vocal ensemble & orchestra⌝
Savannah
Geiger, György

Daser, Ludwig, *ca.* 1525-1589
Dasser, Ludwig
Dasserus, Ludovic

ₜMotet, "Fratres, sobrii estote", mixed voices, cornetto & serpentₜ
"Fratres, sobrii estote"
Renz, Albrecht, 4)

Dauverné, Georges-Auguste, 1799-1874
Dauverné, F.G.A.

ₜQuartet, 4 natural trumpets, no. 1, D major (1857)ₜ
Quator No. 1 en Ré majeur
(Quartet No. 1 in D major)
This quartet involves 4 natural trumpets in D.
Tarr, Edward, 34)

ₜQuartet, 4 natural trumpets, no. 6, C major (1857)ₜ
Quator No. 6 en Ut majeur
(Quartet No. 6 in C major)
This quartet involves 4 natural trumpets: one in E♭, one in D and two in C.
Tarr, Edward, 34)

da Viadana, Lodovico
See: Viadana, Lodovico Grossi da

Davidovsky, Mario, 1934-

ₜInflexions, chamber ensemble, (1965)ₜ
Inflexions
Chamber ensemble includes: 2 flutes, clarinet, trumpet, trombone, violin, viola, cello, bass, piano & 4 percussion.
Anderson, Ronald, 4)

Davies, Howard, 20th cent.

ₜWonder of His Grace; arr. trumpet & pianoₜ
The Wonder of His Grace
Thomas, Peggy Paton

Davies, Peter Maxwell
See: Maxwell Davies, Peter

de Barro, Joao
See: Vianna, C.A.

Debussy, Claude, 1862-1918
Debussy, Achille-Claude

ᵣMandoline, voice & piano, (1882); arr. trumpet & pianoᵣ
Mandoline
>> Schwarz, Gerard, 14)

ᵣPréludes, piano, Book 1, (1910). No. 8; arr. trumpet & pianoᵣ
Prélude No. 8, "La fille aux cheveux de lin"
(Prelude No. 8, "The girl with the flaxen hair")
>> **Malkov, Valentin**

ᵣValse (La plus que lente), piano, (1910); arr. trumpet & pianoᵣ
La plus que lente, valse pour piano
>> **Dokshitser, Timofei, 5), 9), 31), 35), 39)**

de' Cavalieri, Emilio
See: Cavalieri, Emilio de'

Dédé, Edmond, 1829-1903

ᵣMephisto Masqué, ophicleide; arr. euphonium & chamber ensembleᵣ
Mephisto Masqué
(Polka Fantastique)
>> **Schwarz, Gerard, 5)**

Dedrick, Arthur, 1915-

ᵣTune for Christopher, trumpet & pianoᵣ
A Tune for Christopher
>> **Crisara, Raymond, 6)**

Deering, Richard
See: Dering, Richard

de Falla, Manuel
See: Falla, Manuel de

Defaÿe, Jean-Michel, 1932-

ᵣFlashes (9), trumpet & brass ensemble, (1976)ᵣ
Neuf Flashes
Flash No. 1 / Flash No. 2 / Flash No. 3 / Flash No. 4 /
Flash No. 5 / Flash No. 6 / Flash No. 7 / Flash No. 8 / Flash No. 9
>> **André, Maurice, 157)**

ᵣKaléïdoscope, trumpet, brass ensemble & orchestraᵣ
Kaléïdoscope
>> **André, Maurice, 83)**

ᵣMélancolie, trumpet, organ, drums & string bassᵣ
Mélancolie
>> **André, Maurice, 70)**

ₜPrélude, trumpet & organ, (1976)ₙ
Prélude pour trompette et orgue
Pliquett, Joachim

Defaÿe, Jean-Michel (arr.), 1932-

ₜAmour de Moi; arr. trumpet, organ, drums & string bassₙ
L'Amour de Moi
André, Maurice, 69)

ₜFugatissimo, trumpet, organ, drums & string bassₙ
Fugatissimo
An arrangement of Bach's *Little Fugue in g minor*, S. 578.
André, Maurice, 70)

ₜGreensleeves; arr. trumpet, organ, drums & string bassₙ
Greensleeves
André, Maurice, 69)

ₜHop! Voila mon Echelle; arr. trumpet, organ, drums & string bassₙ
Hop! Voila mon Echelle
André, Maurice, 69)

ₜJ'ai du bon Tabac; arr. trumpet, organ, drums & string bassₙ
J'ai du bon Tabac
André, Maurice, 69)

ₜMère Michel; arr. trumpet, organ, drums & string bassₙ
La Mère Michel
André, Maurice, 69)

ₜPetit Quinquin; arr. trumpet, organ, drums & string bassₙ
Le Petit Quinquin
André, Maurice, 69)

ₜStille Nacht; arr. trumpet & organₙ
Stille Nacht
(Franz Gruber's "Silent Night" with obbligato)
André, Maurice, 69)

ₜSur un air de Bach, trumpet, organ, drums & string bassₙ
Sur un air de Bach
An arrangement of "Fugue" from Bach's *Prelude and Fugue XII in g minor*, S. 542.
André, Maurice, 70)

ₜSur un air de Corelli, trumpet, organ, drums & string bassₙ
Sur un air de Corelli
An arrangement of "Gavotte" from Corelli's *Sonata*, op.5, no. 10.
André, Maurice, 70)

de Fesch, Willem
See: Fesch, Willem de

de la Barre, Michel
See: Barre, Michel de la

Delalande, Michel-Richard, 1657-1726
Lalande, Michel-Richard de
Lande, Michel-Richard de la

ₜConcert de trompettes. No. 6: Air en écho (Fanfare) [532]; arr. trumpet & organ₁
Fanfare
(from *Concert de trompettes pour les festes sur le Canal de Versailles*)
Basch, Wolfgang, 11)

ₜConcert de trompettes. No. 6: Air en écho (Fanfare) [532]; arr. trumpet, oboes, strings & timpani₁
Air en écho
(from *Concert de trompettes pour les festes sur le Canal de Versailles*)
Delmotte, Roger, 23)

ₜConcert de trompettes; arr. trumpet, organ & timpani₁
Concert de trompettes pour les festes sur le Canal de Versailles (Suite)
[1]Symphonie du *Te Deum* [531] / [2]Air [164] / [3]Air [165] / [4]Menuet I [171] / [5]Menuet II [172] / [6]Air en écho (Fanfare) [532] / [7]Air gay [170?]
Touvron, Guy, 21)

ₜConcert de trompettes; orig. version: trumpets, oboes, bassoons & timpani₁
Concert de trompettes pour les festes sur le Canal de Versailles
[1]Premier air [164] / [2]Deuxième air mineur [165] / [3]Troisième air: Chaconne en écho [170] / [4]Quatrième air: Premier Menuet [171] / [5]Cinquième air: Deuxième Menuet [172] / [6]Sixième air: Air en écho (Fanfare) [532]
Some recordings may include the "Symphonie du *Te Deum*" [531] as the first movement (prior to [164]). Other recordings may exclude the sixth air [532].
André, Maurice, 101)
Delmotte, Roger, 17), 28), 29)
Scherbaum, Adolf, 11)
Tarr, Edward, 28)
Touvron, Guy, 11)

ₜSimphonies des Noëls. No. 1; arr. trumpets, trombones, organ & timpani₁
Premiere Simfonie des Noëls
[1](no title) [533] / [2]Premier Noël. Trio ou s'en vont ces gays Bergers [534a - 534b - 534a]
André, Maurice, 187)
Potpourri, 33), 43)

ₜSimphonies des Noëls. No. 2; arr. trumpets, trombones, organ & timpani₁
Deuxième Simfonie des Noëls
[1](no title) [535] / [2]Deuxième Noël. Ritournelle [536] / [3](Deuxième Noël). Une jeune pucelle [537] / [4](Deuxième Noël. Une jeune pucelle) Double [538] / [5]Troisième Noël. Laissez paître vos bestes [539]
André, Maurice, 187)

₍Simphonies des Noëls. No. 3; arr. trumpets, trombones, organ & timpani₎
Troisième Simfonie des Noëls
[1]Quatrième Noël [540] / [2](Quatrième Noël). Elle allait au Temple
[541] / [3](Quatrième Noël. Elle allait au Temple). Double [542] /
[4]Cinquième Noël. O ma voisine [543] / [5](Cinquième Noël. O ma
voisine). Double [544]
> **André, Maurice,** 187)
> **Potpourri,** 33)

₍Suite, strings & continuo, B♭ major; arr. trumpet, harpsichord & cello₎
Suite in B♭ major
[1]Menuet / [2]Air / [3]Menuet / [4]Air / [5]Air de paysan [360]
This recording has not been verified. If the "Air de paysan" is
from the ballet, *l'Inconnu*, it is originally in B♭ major.
> **Braz, Dirceu,** 5)

₍Symphonies pour les soupers du Roi. Excerpts₎
Symphonies pour les soupers du Roi (excerpts)
This album was not available for identification of movements.
> **André, Maurice,** 71)

₍Symphonies pour les soupers du Roi. Suite No. 4, (1727?)₎
Symphonies pour les soupers du Roi, Quatrième Suite (1727?)
Symphonies for the King's Dinners, Fourth Suite (1727?)
[1]Symphonie du *Te Deum* [531] / [2]Rondeau [455] / [3]Bourrée de
Cardenio [382] / [4]Gravement du *Ballet de l'Inconnu* [350] / [5]Menuet de
Cardenio [395] / [6]Grand air [481-482] / [7]Chœur Diane de *Palais de
Flore* [136]

The album notes refer to this *suite* as *No. 4*, but the movements
do not match those established by Sylvie Spycket in the **Catalogue
Thématique** included in *Notes et Références... de Delalande*
edited by Norbert Dufourcq. (The suites cited therein refer to
those compiled in 1703 and 1713/15; hence the above sequence of
movements may be according to a set of suites established in
1727.)
> **André, Maurice,** 12)

[Symphonies pour les soupers du Roi. Suite No. 4, (1736)]

Symphonies pour les soupers du Roi, Quatrième Suite (1736)

[1]Symphonie du *Te Deum* [531] / [2]Deuxième air du *Concert de trompettes pour les festes sur le Canal de Versailles* [165] / [3]Premier air du *Concert de trompettes* [164] / [4]Premier menu pour les trompettes (Quatrième air du *Concert de trompettes* [171] / [5]Deuxième menuet (Cinquième air du *Concert de trompettes* [172] / [6]Fanfare: Air en écho (Sixième air du *Concert de trompettes* [532] / [7]Air grave de *l'Amour fléchy* [218] / [8]Sarabande [461] / [9]Légèrement [434] / [10]Chantons ce héros: Gayement (*Ballet de la paix* [311] / [11]Sarabande de *Cardenio* {soprano solo} [409] / [12]Air du *Ballet de Mélicerte* [253] / [13]Musette du *Ballet de l'Inconnu* [358] / [14]Air de *Cardenio* [384] / [15]Rondeau de *Ballet Éléments* [423] / [16]Rondeau de *Cardenio* [422] / [17]Doucement et pesamment de *Cardenio* [404] / [18]La Pagode de *Cardenio* [406] / [19]Septième air du *Ballet de la Paix* [327] / [20]Chaconne en écho avec les Trompettes (Troisième air du *Concert de trompettes* [170]

From *Simphonies de M. De La Lande, Qu'il faisoit exécuter tous les 15 jours pendant le Souper de Louis XIV et Louis XV. Mises dans un nouvel ordre, et ses augmentations.* Recueillies en 1736. (Published in 1745)

Scherbaum, Adolf, 11)

[Symphonies pour les soupers du Roi. Suite No. 5: Caprice No. 2, 2 oboes, bassoon, strings & continuo, g minor]

Deuxième Fantaisie (Caprice)

("Caprice que le Roy demandoit souvent" from *Symphonies pour les soupers du Roi,* Cinquième Suite)

[1]Un peu lent [475] / [2]Vite [476] / [3]Doucement [477] / [4]Gracieusement [478] / [5]Gayement [479] / [6]Vivement [480]

The *Caprice No. 2* is included as movements 10 through 15 of the 20 movements from the *Suite No. 5.* (Even though this work does not include trumpets, it is indexed here for comparative identification.)

André, Maurice, 101)
Touvron, Guy, 11)

[Symphonies pour les soupers du Roi. Suite No. 6: Caprice No. 1, D major, (1727?); arr. 2 trumpets & organ]

Sixième Suite en Ré majeur, "Caprice de Villers-Cotterêts"

(Premier Caprice)

[1]Lent (Tous fièrement et détaché [493] - Plus doucement [494]) / [2]Gay (Tous Gracieusement [495]) / [3]Viste (Tous viste [496]) / [4]Vif [498] / [5]Récit en taille (Doucement [499]) / [6]Vivement [501]

The designation as *Suite No. 6* may come from the 1727 suites. This work is otherwise known as the *Premier Caprice* and is taken from *Symphonies pour les soupers du Roi,* Suite No. 7.

Loustalot, Alain

⌐Symphonies pour les soupers du Roi. Suite No. 7: Caprice No. 1, chamber
orchestra, D major¬
Premier Caprice
(Caprice de Villers-Cotterêts)
(from *Symphonies pour les soupers du Roi,* Septième Suite)
[1]Tous fièrement et détaché [493] / [2]Plus doucement [494] / [3]Tous
Gracieusement [495] / [4]Tous viste [496] / [5]Gracieusement sans lenteur
[497] / [6]Vif [498] / [7]Doucement [499] / [8]Violo seul ou hautbois [500] /
[9]Vivement [501]
> The *Caprice No. 1* consists of the last 9 of 21 movements from
> *Suite No. 7.* The instrumentation includes 2 oboes, bassoon, 2
> trumpets, timpani, strings & continuo.
>> **André, Maurice,** 47), 101)
>> **Potpourri,** 13), 15)
>> **Scherbaum, Adolf,** 18), 25)
>> **Touvron, Guy,** 11)

⌐Symphonies pour les soupers du Roi. Suite No. 12: Caprice No. 3, flutes, oboes,
bassoon, strings & continuo, D major¬
Troisième Caprice
(Symphonies pour les soupers du Roi, Douzième Suite)
[1]Premier air: Gracieusement [514] / [2]Deuxième air mineur [515] /
[3]Troisième air: Presto [516] / [4]Quatrième air: Gigue (Gracieusement)
[517] / [5]Cinquième air: Quatuor (Doucement) [518] / [6]Sixième air: Vif
[519]
> The *Caprice No. 3* is equal to the *Suite No. 12.* (Even though
> this work does not include trumpets, it is indexed here for
> comparative identification.)
>> **André, Maurice,** 101)
>> **Touvron, Guy,** 11)

⌐Symphonies pour les soupers du Roi. Suite, flute, oboes, bassoon, strings &
continuo¬
Symphonies pour les soupers du Roi (Suite)
(Symphonies for the King's Supper)
[1]Ouverture de la Première Suite [346-347] / [2]Troisième air de la
Première Suite [433] / [3]Air de Diane de *Palais de Flore* [136] / [4]Grand
air de la Cinquième Suite [481-482] / [5]Menuet (Septième air de
Cardenio) [395] / [6]Passepied de *l'Inconnu* [375] / [7]Rondeau-Sarabande
(Huitième air de la Cinquième Suite) [473] / [8]Air de *l'Inconnu* [350]
> Even though this suite does not include trumpets, it is indexed
> here for comparative identification. This suite does not match
> any of the suites cited by Sylvie Spycket in the **Catalogue
> Thématique** included in *Notes et Références... de Delalande*
> edited by Norbert Dufourcq.
>> **Delmotte, Roger,** 7), 26)

⌐Te Deum. Prelude, trumpet, strings & continuo; arr. trumpet & guitar¬
Prélude du *Te Deum*
> This arrangement has not been verified and may be taken from a
> work other than the *Te Deum.*
>> **Braz, Dirceu,** 2)

ₜTe Deum. Prelude, trumpet, strings & continuo; arr. trumpet & organ₎
Prélude du *Te Deum*
While the secular music of Delalande was catalogued numerically by movement themes by Sylvie Spycket, the religious music of Delalande was catalogued numerically by work by Marie Bert. Thus the *Te Deum* is numbered **68**.
Morisset, Michel

de Lassus, Roland
See: Lassus, Roland de

de la Vega, Aurelio, 1925-

ₜPara-Tangents, trumpet & tape, (1973)₎
Para-Tangents
Stevens, Thomas, 2), 5)

del Cavalieri, Emilio
See: Cavalieri, Emilio de'

del Encina, Juan
See: Encina, Juan del

Delerue, Georges, 1925-

ₜCérémonial, trumpet & brass ensemble, (1977)₎
Cérémonial
André, Maurice, 157)

ₜFanfares, trumpet & brass ensemble, (1977)₎
Fanfares pour tous les temps
(Fanfares for All Occasions)
[1]Pour un temps de danse / [2]Pour un temps de sérénité / [3]Pour un temps de fête / [4]Pour un temps de deuil / [5]Pour un temps de clarté / [6]Pour un temps de méditation / [7]Pour un temps de violence / [8]Pour un temps de plaintes / [9]Pour un temps de joie
André, Maurice, 157)

ₜRécit et Choral, trumpet & organ₎
Récit et Choral
Delmotte, Roger, 39)

Delibes, Léo, 1836-1891
Delibes, Clément-Philbert-Léo

ₜChanson Espagnole; arr. trumpet, orchestra & rhythm₎
Chanson Espagnole
André, Maurice, 4)

₍Filles de Cadiz; arr. trumpet & orchestra₎
Les filles de Cadiz
(The Maids of Cadiz)
> **Méndez, Rafael,** 21)

₍Lakmé, (1883). Chant de la clochette; arr. trumpet & orchestra₎
Bell Song from *Lakmé*
(Chant de la clochette)
(Scène et légende de la fille du paria)
(Aria, "Où va la jeune hindoue?")
> **André, Maurice,** 37), 161), 212)
> **Méndez, Rafael,** 2), 5), 10)

₍Sylvia, (1876). Excerpt; arr. trumpet, orchestra & rhythm₎
Sylvia cha cha cha
> **Andersen, Ole**

Dello Joio, Norman, 1913-

₍Sonata, trumpet & piano, (1980)₎
Sonata for Trumpet and Piano
> [1]Tema & Variations / [2]Andante, liberamente / [3]Allegro spumante
> Composition commissioned by the International Trumpet Guild.
> **Hickman, David,** 4)

Delmas, Marc-Jean-Baptiste, 1885-1931

₍Chorale and Variations, trumpet & piano₎
Chorale and Variations
> **Burkart, Richard**

de Luca, Severio, *fl.* 1690
Severo di Luca, (Antonio)

₍Aria, "Non posso disperar"; arr. trumpet & piano₎
Aria, "Non posso disperar"
> This aria is included as the third movement, "Andante", of an
> *Italian Suite* by various composers arranged by Bernard
> Fitzgerald.
> **Ghitalla, Armando,** 11)

Demantius, Christoph, 1567-1643
Demantius, Johannes Christoph

₍Diese Nacht hatt' ich ein' Traum, soprano, tenor, bass, recorder, cornetto &
trombone₎
Diese Nacht hatt' ich ein' Traum
> **Tarr, Edward,** 19)

₍Galliarde, No. 2, violin, 2 recorders, cornetto & trombone₎
Galliarde II
> **Tarr, Edward,** 10), 19)

[Herre, nun lässt du Diener in Frieden fahren, mixed voices, 2 flutes, cornetto, 3 trombones & continuo, (1610)]
Herre, nun lässt du Diener in Frieden fahren
Tarr, Edward, 19)

[Zart schönes Bild, soprano, tenor, bass, recorder, cornetto & trombone, (1615)]
Zart schönes Bild
Tarr, Edward, 19)

Dering, Richard, *ca.* 1580-1630
Deering, Richard

[Fantasia; arr. 2 trumpets & 4 trombones]
Fantasia
André, Maurice, 176)

Destouches, André Cardinal, 1672-1749

[Suite; arr. trumpet & organ, d minor]
Suite en ré mineur pour trompette et orgue
Morisset, Michel

de Vitry, Philippe
See: Vitry, Philippe de

Diabelli, Anton, 1781-1858

[Ceremonial Fanfares (2), trumpet ensemble]
Two Ceremonial Fanfares
Wallace, John, 5)

[Processional Fanfares (4), 6 trumpets & timpani]
Four Processional Fanfares
Eklund's Baroque Ensemble

di Capua, Eduardo, 1864-1917

[Aria, "O Sole mio", (1898); arr. cornet]
Aria, "O Sole mio"
Klochkov, Pavel, 5)

[Aria, "Why Am I So Madly in Love"; arr. cornet]
Aria, "Why Am I So Madly in Love"
Klochkov, Pavel, 5)

Diego de Conceiçao, Francisco, 17th cent.

[Mejo Registo, organ; arr. trumpet & organ]
Mejo Registo de Segundo Tom Acidental
Hartog, Thomas

Dietrich, Sixtus, *ca.* 1493-1548

ₜChrist is erstanden, soprano, cornetto & continuoₒ
Christ ist erstanden
The continuo instruments include: dulcian, viola da gamba &
lute. (There is also percussion added.)
Caudle, Theresa

di Lasso, Orlando
See: Lassus, Roland de

d'Indy, Vincent, 1851-1931

ₜSuite, 2 flutes, trumpet, strings, D major, op. 24ₒ
Suite en Ré majeur dans le style ancien, op. 24
(Suite in Olden Style, op. 24)
(Suite im alten Stil, op. 24)
[1]Prélude (Lent) / [2]Entrée (Gai et modéré) / [3]Sarabande (Lent) /
[4]Menuet (Animé) / [5]Ronde Française (Assez animé)
André, Maurice, 167)
Glantz, Harry, 4)

Dinicu, Grigoraş, 1889-1949

ₜHora Staccato, violin & piano, (1906); arr. trumpet & brass ensembleₒ
Hora Staccato
Originally composed by Grigoraş Dinicu, the 1930 copyright
indicates that Jascha Heifetz (1901-1987) should be mentioned
jointly on printed programs.
Geiger, György
Grin, Freddy, 2)

ₜHora Staccato, violin & piano, (1906); arr. trumpet & orchestraₒ
Hora Staccato
André, Maurice, 5), 7), 38), 66)
Méndez, Rafael, 17), 19), 22)

ₜHora Staccato, violin & piano, (1906); arr. trumpet & pianoₒ
Hora Staccato
Dokshitser, Timofei, 5), 7), 9), 35), 36), 38),
39)
Volle, Bjarne

Dlugoszewski, Lucia, 1931-

ₜSpace Is a Diamond, trumpet, (1970)ₒ
Space Is a Diamond
Schwarz, Gerard, 18)

Dobson, George, 20th cent.

ₜBlack Note Fantasy, trumpet trio & rhythmₜ
> Black Note Fantasy
>> **Victorian Trumpet Trio**

Dodge, Charles, 1942-
Dodge, Charles Malcolm

ₜExtensions, trumpet & tape, (1973)ₜ
> Extensions for Trumpet and Tape
>> **Anderson, Ronald,** 3)
>> **Stevens, Thomas,** 5)

Dokshitser, Timofei A., 1921-
Dokshitser, Timofei Alexandrovich

ₜArticulation on the Trumpet. Russianₜ
> Articulation on the Trumpet
>> **Dokshitser, Timofei,** 28)

Don Rong-Sheng, 20th cent.

ₜSpring Morning of Yang-Min Mountain; arr. trumpet & pianoₜ
> Spring Morning of Yang-Min Mountain
> (Clear Spring Morning)
>> **Yeh Shu-han**

Donaudy, Stefano, 1879-1925

ₜAria and Allegro; arr. trumpet & pianoₜ
> Aria and Allegro
>> [1]Aria, "Vaghissima sembianza" / [2]Allegro, "Ah, mai non cessate"
>> These vocal transcriptions may be taken from *Douze airs de style ancien*, or from any of six operas composed by Donaudy.
>>> **Nagel, Robert,** 15)
>>> **Ritter, David**
>>> **Tolley, Richard**

ₜAria I; arr. trumpet & pianoₜ
> Aria I
>> **Ghitalla, Armando,** 11)

ₜAria II; arr. trumpet & pianoₜ
> Aria II
>> **Ghitalla, Armando,** 11)

Donizetti, Gaetano, 1797-1848
Donizetti, (Domenico) Gaetano (Maria)

ₜDon Pasquale, (1843). Act I: Aria, "Quel guardo il cavaliere"; arr. trumpet & orchestraₗ
Aria, "Quel guardo il cavaliere" from *Don Pasquale*
André, Maurice, 37)

ₜL'elisir d'amore, (1832). Act II: Aria, "Una furtiva lagrima"; arr. trumpet & orchestraₗ
Aria, "Una furtiva lagrima" from *L'elisir d'amore*
André, Maurice, 37)

ₜLucia di Lammermoor, (1835). Act I: Aria, "Quando rapito in estasio"; arr. cornet & bandₗ
Aria, "Quando rapito in estasio"
McCann, Phillip

ₜTorquato Tasso, (1833). Aria, "Il L'udia"; arr. clapper shake key cornopean & pianoₗ
Aria, "Il L'udia" from *Torquato Tasso*
Impett, Jonathan

Donovan, Richard Frank, 1891-1970

ₜMusic for Six, chamber ensemble, (1961)ₗ
Music for Six
Chamber ensemble includes: oboe, clarinet, trumpet, violin, cello & piano.
Nagel, Robert, 3)

ₜSoundings, trumpet, bassoon & percussion, (c. 1956)ₗ
Soundings for Trumpet, Bassoon and Percussion
Nagel, Robert, 13)

Dornel, Louis-Antoine, *ca.* 1680-1756

ₜDialogue, Récit et Fugue sur les Trompettes, organ; arr. trumpet & organₗ
Dialogue, Récit et Fugue sur les Trompettes
[1]Vivement / [2]Fugue / [3]Gayement / [4]Trio (doucement) / [5]Récit
Scherbaum, Adolf, 17)

ₜFanfare, organ; arr. trumpet & organₗ
Fanfare
Morisset, Michel

Dowland, John, 1563-1626

ₜLacrimæ Pavin, "Flow, my tears", cornetto, organ, tenor violₗ
Lacrimæ Pavin, "Flow, my tears"
Smithers, Don, 7)

Dresher, Paul, 1951-

₍Channels Passing, chamber ensemble, (1981-82)₎
   Channels Passing
      (Study for Variations 1981-82)
         Chamber ensemble includes: flute, oboe, clarinet, trumpet,
         trombone, violin & cello.
            Pressley, Richard

Drigo, Riccardo, 1846-1930

₍Valse Bluette; arr. trumpet & orchestra₎
   Valse Bluette
            Méndez, Rafael, 17), 19)

Druckman, Jacob, 1928-

₍Incenters, chamber ensemble, (1968)₎
   Incenters
         Chamber ensemble includes: flute, oboe, clarinet, bassoon, horn,
         trumpet, trombone, violin, viola, cello, bass, piano/organ &
         percussion.
            Nagel, Robert, 20)

Dubois, Théodore, 1837-1924
   Dubois, François-Clément-Théodore

₍Grand Choeur, organ; arr. trumpet & organ?₎
   Grand Choeur
            Nystrom, Kaj

Dubrovay, László, 1943-

₍Concerto, trumpet & strings, No. 2, (1981)₎
   Concerto No. 2, for trumpet & 15 strings
            Geiger, György

Dufay, Guillaume, *ca.* 1400-1474

₍Fanfare, "Ad modum tubæ", 2 buisines₎
   Fanfare, "Ad modum tubæ"
      A buisine is a wooden trumpet.
            Laird, Michael, 1)

₍Missa, "Se la face ay pale", mixed voices, 2 cornetti, 2 trombones & viols₎
   Missa, "Se la face ay pale"
            Laird, Michael, 12)

Dugger, Edwin, 1940-

[Abwesenheiten und Wiedersehen, chamber ensemble (1971)]
Abwesenheiten und Wiedersehen
Chamber ensemble includes: flute (piccolo), clarinet, horn, trumpet, trombone, 2 violins, viola, cello & 2 percussion.
Metzger, Charles

[Intermezzi, chamber ensemble, (1969)]
Intermezzi
Chamber ensemble includes: flute, clarinet, trumpet, trombone, 2 violins, viola, cello, bass, piano (celesta) & 2 percussion.
Metzger, Charles

Dumage, Pierre, 1674-1751
Mage, Pierre du

[Livre d'orgue, I, (1708). No. 8: Grand-jeu; arr. trumpet & organ]
Grand-jeu from *Livre d'orgue*, I
Hartog, Thomas

Duning, George W., 1908-

[Cowboy. El Gitano, trumpet & orchestra]
El Gitano
Music for the film, *Cowboy*.
Méndez, Rafael, 25)

Dupuis, Thomas Sanders, 1733-1796

[Voluntaries (9), organ. No. 1, C major; arr. trumpet & organ]
Voluntary in C major
Carroll, Edward, 6)

Durante, Francesco, 1684-1755

[Danza, Danza, Fanciulla Gentile, voice & piano; arr. trumpet & piano]
Danza, Danza, Fanciulla Gentile
Included as the fourth movement of an *Italian Suite* (by various composers) arranged by Bernard Fitzgerald.
Ghitalla, Armando, 11)

[Magnificat, children's voices, mixed voices, chamber orchestra & trumpet ensemble]
Magnificat in B♭ major
Sauter, Hermann, 29)

Dvořáček, Jiří, 1928-

[Sonata, trumpet & piano, C major]
Sonáta pro trubku a klavír in do
(Sonata in C major for Trumpet and Piano)
Rejlek, Vladimir

Dvořák, Antonín, 1841-1904
Dvořák, Antonín Leopold

ₗHumoresque, piano (1884); arr. trumpet & pianoₗ
Humoresque
(Humoreske)
Christensen, Ketil

ₗSymphony No. 9, op. 95, (1893). 2: Largo (theme); arr. trumpet & organₗ
Largo
Grin, Freddy, 8)

ₗSymphony No. 9, op. 95, (1893). 2: Largo (theme); arr. trumpet, mixed voices & orchestraₗ
Largo
André, Maurice, 66), 206)

Dzhanibekov, Akhtinbek, 1934-

ₗRomance, trumpet & orchestraₗ
Romance for Trumpet with Orchestra
Shaltakbaev, Chorobek

Dzherbashyan, Stepan, 1917-

ₗScherzo, trumpet & piano, B♭ majorₗ
Scherzo in B♭ major
Usov, Yuri

Eben, Petr, 1929-

ₗDuets, 2 trumpets, (1956)ₗ
Dueta pro dvě trubky
(Duets for Two Trumpets)
Junek, Václav, 1)

ₗOkna, trumpet & organ, (1976)ₗ
Okna
(Windows — Movements for Trumpet and Organ after Marc Chagall)
¹Modré okno [Blue window]: Con moto / ²Zelené okno [Green window]: Andantino pastorale / ³Červené okno [Red window]: Risoluto e drammatico / ⁴Zlaté okno [Gold window]: Festivo
Groth, Konradin
Kejmar, Miroslav, 13)
Kozderka, Vladislav

Eccard, Johann, 1553-1611

ₗNun komm der Heiden Heiland, mixed voices & instrumental ensembleₗ
Nun komm der Heiden Heiland
Cook, Richard

ᵣVom Himmel hoch, mixed voices & instrumental ensembleᵣ
Vom Himmel hoch, da komm ich her
Stradner, Gerhard

ᵣVom Himmel hoch, mixed voices & instrumental ensemble; arr. trumpet & brass
ensembleᵣ
Vom Himmel hoch, da komm ich her
Güttler, Ludwig, 9)

Edelson, Edward, 1929-

ᵣAt Dusk, trumpet & pianoᵣ
At Dusk
House, Lawrence

Edwards, Alice, 20th cent.

ᵣConsecration; arr. trumpet & organᵣ
Consecration
Thomas, Peggy Paton

Egiazaryan, Grigory Egiazarovich, 1908-
Eghiazaryan, Grigor

ᵣDance, trumpet & pianoᵣ
Dance
Balyan, Yuri

Eisenach, Johann Jakob Löwe von
See: Löwe von Eisenach, Johann Jakob

Eisenhuet, Thomas, 1644-1702
Eisenhut, Thomas (Tobias)

ᵣHymni Ariosi, 2 sopranos, 2 trumpets, strings & continuo, op. 3, (1680)ᵣ
Hymni Ariosi, op. 3
Ave maris stella / Magna Pater Augustine
Quinque, Rolf, 4)

Eisler, Hannes, 1898-1962

ᵣNonet, chamber ensemble, no. 2ᵣ
Nonett Nr. 2
Chamber ensemble includes: flute, clarinet, bassoon, trumpet, 3
violins, bass & percussion.
Gass, Josef
Sommerhalder, Max

Elgar, Edward, 1857-1934
Elgar, Edward William

₍Salut d'amour, piano, op. 12, (1888); arr. trumpet & piano₎
Salut d'amour, op. 12
Christensen, Ketil

Ellington, Duke, 1899-1974
Ellington, Edward Kennedy

₍Caravan; arr. trumpet, orchestra & rhythm₎
Caravan
André, Maurice, 7)

Emmanuel, Maurice, 1862-1938
Emmanuel, (Marie François) Maurice

₍Sonata, cornet (trumpet) & piano, op. 29, (1936)₎
Sonate pour cornet
[1]Sarabande (Adagio) / [2]Allemande (Allegro moderato) / [3]Aria
(Tranquillo) / [4]Gigue (Vivo)
[Published in 1951.]
Hyatt, Jack

Encina, Juan del, 1468-1529

₍Motet, "Triste España sin ventura", mixed voices, cornetto, rauschpfeife,
trombone, crumhorn₎
Motet, "Triste España sin ventura"
Renz, Albrecht, 7)

Endler, Johann Samuel, 1694-1762

₍Concerto, trumpet, strings & continuo, F major₎
Concerto in F for Trumpet
This "concerto" is probably the *Sinfonia* in F major for clarino
cited in Don Smithers' *The Music & History of the Baroque
Trumpet before 1721*, p. 258.
Basch, Wolfgang, 9), 12)

₍Suite, 3 trumpets, strings & continuo, D major₎
Suite in D for 3 Trumpets
This "suite" is probably one of the 2 *Sinfonias* in D major for 3
trumpets cited in Don Smithers' *The Music & History of the
Baroque Trumpet before 1721*, p. 258.
Ullrich, Marc

Endresen, R.M., 20th cent.

₍Dancer, trumpet & piano₎
The Dancer
The Dancer is published by Rubank (but is not included in Endresen's *Indispensable Folio*).
House, Lawrence

₍Envoy, cornet (trumpet) & piano₎
The Envoy
The Envoy is the first solo in Endresen's *Indispensable Folio* published by Rubank (1940).
Burkart, Richard

₍Fox Hunt, cornet (trumpet) & piano₎
Fox Hunt
Fox Hunt is the third solo in Endresen's *Indispensable Folio* published by Rubank (1940).
Haynie, John, 1)

Endsley, Gerald, 20th cent.

₍Chant, trumpet, (1971)₎
Chant
Endsley, Gerald

Enesco, Georges, 1881-1955
Enescu, George

₍Légende, trumpet & piano, (*ca.* 1905)₎
Légende pour Trompette avec accompagnement de Piano
André, Maurice, 148)
Benedetti, Donald
Christensen, Ketil
Erb, Helmut, 4)
Gardner, Ned
Head, Emerson
Hyatt, Jack
Impett, Jonathan
Orvid, Georgy
Plog, Anthony, 7)
Roelant, Alain
Schwarz, Gerard, 12)
Smith, Philip, 2)
Thibaud, Pierre, 2)

Erb, Donald James, 1927-

₍Diversion, trumpet & percussion, (1966)₎
Diversion for Two (other than sex)
¹Allegro moderato / ²Adagio / ³Moderato
Murtha, Roger

Erickson, Robert, 1917-

ₜIdea of Order at Key West, soprano & chamber ensembleₜ
The Idea of Order at Key West
Chamber ensemble includes: flute, E♭-clarinet/bass clarinet, trumpet, viola & cello.
Burkhart, David

ₜKryl, solo trumpetₜ
Kryl
Plog, Anthony, 4)

ₜNight Music, trumpet & chamber ensembleₜ
Night Music
Chamber ensemble includes: flute, B♭-clarinet, E♭-clarinet/bass clarinet, trombone, 2 percussion, cello & 2 basses.
Burkhart, David

ₜOceans, trumpet & percussionₜ
Oceans
Logan, Jack

ₜPacific Sirens, chamber ensemble & electronic tapeₜ
Pacific Sirens
Chamber ensemble includes: flute, B♭-clarinet, E♭-clarinet/bass clarinet, horn, trumpet, trombone, 2 percussion, viola, cello & bass.
Burkhart, David

Ernst, David George, 1945-

ₜExit, trumpet & tapeₜ
Exit for Trumpet and Magnetic Tape
Logan, Jack

Eshpai, Andrei Yakovlevich, 1925-
Eshpay, Andrey Yakovlevich

ₜConcerto for Orchestra, trumpet, piano, vibraphone, bass & orchestra, (1967)ₜ
Concerto for Orchestra
(with solo trumpet, piano, vibraphone & double bass)
Dokshitser, Timofei, 29)
Maximenko, Anatoly, 1)

Fain, Sammy, 1902-
Feinberg, Sammy

ₜDear Hearts and Gentle People, (1949); arr. trumpet quartetₜ
Dear Hearts and Gentle People
Blackburn, Roger

Falik, Yuri, 1936-
Falik, Yury Alexandrovich

₍Concerto, chamber ensemble, (1966)₎
   Concerto for 7 Instruments
      (Skomorokhi [The jongleurs] or [The Jester])
         Chamber ensemble includes: flute, oboe, clarinet, bassoon, horn,
      trumpet & percussion.
                        Gorokhov, Vitaly
                        Maximenko, Anatoly, 3)

Falla, Manuel de, 1876-1946
Falla y Matheu, Manuel de

₍El Amor Brujo, (1914-15). Danza Ritual del Fuego; arr. trumpet & orchestra₎
   Danza Ritual del Fuego
      (Ritual Fire Dance)
                        André, Maurice, 4)
                        Méndez, Rafael, 15), 24)

₍El Amor Brujo, (1914-15). Danza Ritual del Fuego; arr. trumpet trio, bass
   clarinet & rhythm₎
      Danza Ritual del Fuego
         (Ritual Fire Dance)
                        Victorian Trumpet Trio

Fantini, Girolamo, *b. ca.* 1600

₍Balleto detto il Lunati, trumpet & bass, C major, (1638); arr. trumpet & organ₎
   Balleto detto il Lunati
         (Prima parte) / Seconda parte / Terza parte
                        Scherbaum, Adolf, 17)

₍Balletto detto il Ghisilieri, trumpet & bass, C major, (1638); arr. trumpet
   (muted) & trombone₎
      Balletto detto il Ghisilieri
                        Impett, Jonathan

₍Balletto detto lo Squilletti, trumpet & bass, C major, (1638); arr. trumpet &
   organ₎
      Balletto detto lo Squilletti
                        Keavy, Stephen
                        Riggione, Angelo

₍Brando del l'Albizi, trumpet & continuo, C major, (1638)₎
   Brando del l'Albizi
                        Keavy, Stephen

₍Brando detto il Baglioni, trumpet & bass, C major, (1638); arr. trumpet (muted)
   & trombone₎
      Brando detto il Baglioni
                        Impett, Jonathan

ᵣBrando detto il Bianchi, trumpet & bass, C major, (1638); arr. trumpet & organ₁
Brando detto il Bianchi
Prima parte / Seconda parte / Terza parte
Holy, Walter, 4)

ᵣBrando detto il Rucellai, trumpet & bass, C major, (1638); arr. trumpet & trombone₁
Brando detto il Rucellai
Impett, Jonathan

ᵣCapriccio detto del Carducci, trumpet & bass, C major, (1638)₁
Capriccio detto del Carducci
Holy, Walter, 4)
Riggione, Angelo

ᵣCapriccio detto del Gondi, trumpet & bass, C major, (1638)₁
Capriccio detto del Gondi
Holy, Walter, 4)
Riggione, Angelo

ᵣCapriccio detto il Caleppi, trumpet & bass, C major, (1638)₁
Capriccio detto il Caleppi
Riggione, Angelo

ᵣCapriccio detto il Visconti, trumpet & bass, C major, (1638)₁
Capriccio detto il Visconti
Riggione, Angelo

ᵣCapriccios (2), trumpet, C major, (1638); arr. trumpet & organ₁
Two Caprices
There are 6 pieces entitled *Chiamata di capriccio*, one piece entitled *Ritirata di capriccio*, and 5 other *Capriccios*. The 2 "Caprices" indexed here have not been specifically identified.
Morisset, Michel

ᵣChiamata di capriccio, trumpet, No. 3, C major, (1638); arr. 3 trumpets & timpani₁
Terza chiamata di capriccio
Voisin, Roger, 7)

ᵣChiamata di capriccio, trumpet, No. 6, C major, (1638); arr. 3 trumpets & timpani₁
Sesta chiamata di capriccio
Voisin, Roger, 7)

ᵣCorrente detta dello Staccoli, trumpet, C major, (1638); arr. trumpet & organ₁
Corrente detta dello Staccoli
Riggione, Angelo

ᵣCorrente detta la Schinchinelli, trumpet & bass, C major, (1638); arr. trumpet (muted) & trombone₁
Corrente detta la Schinchinelli
Impett, Jonathan

ₜCorrente, trumpet, C major, (1638); arr. trumpet & organₙ
Courante
(Corrente)
> There are 22 works entitled *Corrente* in the *Modo per Imparare a sonare di Tromba...*; this particular *Corrente* has not been specifically identified here.
> **Morisset, Michel**

ₜDances (5), trumpet, C major, (1638); arr. trumpet & organₙ
Five Dances
> Which dances are included has not been verified.
> **Sautter, Fred**

ₜEntrata Imperiale. No. 1: l'Imperiale, trumpet, C major, (1638); arr. 5 trumpets & timpaniₙ
l'Imperiale
(First Imperiale)
> **Tarr, Edward**, 20), 28)

ₜEntrata Imperiale, trumpet, C major, (1638); arr. 5 trumpets & timpaniₙ
Entrata Imperiale
¹l'Imperiale / ²Seconda Imperiale
> **Carroll, Edward**, 7), 9)

ₜSaltarello detto del Naldi, trumpet & organ, C major, (1638)ₙ
Saltarello detto del Naldi
> **Keavy, Stephen**
> **Riggione, Angelo**

ₜSarabanda detta del Zozzi, trumpet & organ, C major, (1638)ₙ
Sarabanda detta del Zozzi
> **Riggione, Angelo**

ₜSonata detta la Renuccini, trumpet & bass, C major, (1638); arr. trumpet & tromboneₙ
Sonata detta la Renuccini
> **Impett, Jonathan**

ₜSonata, trumpet & organ, no. 1, C major, (1638)ₙ

Prima Sonata di Tromba, et Organo insieme detta del Colloreto
(Sonata detta del Colloreto [No. 1])
> Allegro
> *Modo per Imparare a sonare DI TROMBA TANTO DI GUERRA Quanto Musicalmente in Organo, con Tromba Sordina, col Cimbalo, e ogn'altro istrumento.* (1638)
> > **André, Maurice**, 163)
> > **Carroll, Edward**, 7), 9)
> > **Chatel, Jean-Louis**
> > **Kejmar, Miroslav**, 1)
> > **Tarr, Edward**, 41)
> > **Ullrich, Marc**

[Sonata, trumpet & organ, no. 2, C major, (1638)]
Sonata detta del Gonzaga [No. 2]
Andante - Allegro - Andante
André, Maurice, 163)
Chatel, Jean-Louis
Kejmar, Miroslav, 1)
Tarr, Edward, 41)
Ullrich, Marc

[Sonata, trumpet & organ, no. 3, C major, (1638)]
Sonata detta del Niccolini [No. 3]
Andante - Allegro - Adagio
Güttler, Ludwig, 23)
Kejmar, Miroslav, 1)
Sautter, Fred
Tarr, Edward, 40)
Ullrich, Marc

[Sonata, trumpet & organ, no. 4, C major, (1638)]
Sonata detta del Saracinelli [No. 4]
Andante - Allegro - Presto - Andante
Kejmar, Miroslav, 1)

[Sonata, trumpet & organ, no. 5, C major, (1638)]
Sonata detta dell' Adimari [No. 5]
Andante - Presto - Adagio
Chatel, Jean-Louis
Kejmar, Miroslav, 1)
Ullrich, Marc

[Sonata, trumpet & organ, no. 6, C major, (1638)]
Sonata detta del Morone [No. 6]
Andante
Chatel, Jean-Louis
Kejmar, Miroslav, 1)
Sautter, Fred
Ullrich, Marc
Yudashkin, Georgy

[Sonata, trumpet & organ, no. 6, C major, (1638); arr. trumpet & harpsichord]
Sonata detta del Morone [No. 6]
Andante
Plog, Anthony, 6)

[Sonata, trumpet & organ, no. 7, C major, (1638)]
Sonata detta del Vitelli [No. 7]
Andante - Andante
Chatel, Jean-Louis
Kejmar, Miroslav, 1)
Tarr, Edward, 41)

[Sonata, trumpet & organ, no. 8, C major, (1638)]
Sonata detta del Nero [No. 8]
Andante - Allegro - Presto - Allegro - Presto - Adagio
André, Maurice, 163)
Braz, Dirceu, 3)
Chatel, Jean-Louis
Fink, Werner
Kejmar, Miroslav, 1)
Sautter, Fred
Scherbaum, Adolf, 17)
Tarr, Edward, 40)
Ullrich, Marc
Yudashkin, Georgy

[Sonata, trumpet & organ, no. 8, C major, (1638); arr. trumpet & piano, B♭ major]
Sonata detta del Nero [No. 8]
Maestoso - Allegretto - Maestoso
Nagel, Robert, 10)

[Sonata, 2 trumpets, (no. 6), C major, (1638)]
Sonata a due Trombe detta del Gucciardini
Delmotte, Roger, 23)
Holy, Walter, 4)
Keavy, Stephen
Smithers, Don, 7)

Fargason, Eddie, 20th cent.

[Jesus Shows Me the Way; arr. trumpet & piano]
Jesus Shows Me the Way
Blair, Stacy

Farnaby, Giles, *ca.* 1563-1640

[Almande, keyboard; arr. 2 trumpets & 4 trombones]
Almande
André, Maurice, 176)

[Maske, keyboard; arr. instrumental ensemble]
A maske
Smithers, Don, 2)

[Toye, keyboard; arr. brass ensemble]
A Toye
Wilbraham, John, 17)

Fasch, Carl Friedrich Christian, 1736-1800

₍Concerto, trumpet, oboe d'amore, violin, strings & continuo, E major₎
Triplekonzert E-dur für Trompete, Oboe d'amore, Violine,
Streicher und Basso continuo
Sauter, Hermann, 3)

Fasch, Johann Friedrich, 1688-1758

₍Concerto, trumpet, 2 oboes, strings & continuo, D major₎
Concerto a 8 in D major for Trumpet, 2 Oboes, Strings and
Continuo
[1]Allegro / [2]Largo / [3]Allegro (moderato)
**André, Maurice, 75), 81), 83[1]), 128), 149), 168),
169), 179), 217[1])**
Basch, Wolfgang, 3)
Bernard, André, 7)
Delmotte, Roger, 19)
Güttler, Ludwig, 3), 20[1]), 25)
Marsalis, Wynton, 2), 7)
Petz, Pál
Potpourri, 16), 21), 34), 35), 37), 40)
Reinhart, Carole Dawn, 3), 4)
Scherbaum, Adolf, 13), 19), 25)
Schetsche, Walter
Tamiya, Kenji
Tarr, Edward, 21)
Tasa, David
Ullrich, Marc
Wilbraham, John, 4), 5), 11), 15), 16)
Zickler, Heinz, 7)

Fauré, Gabriel, 1845-1924
Fauré, Gabriel Urbain

₍Sicilienne, cello & piano, op. 78, g minor, (1893); arr. trumpet & guitar₎
Sicilienne, op. 78
Méndez, Rafael, 14)

Fenigstein, Victor, 1924-

₍Passages, trumpet & strings₎
Passages for Trumpet and Strings
Millière, Gérard

Ferrabosco II, Alfonso, *ca.* 1578-1628

₍Alman; arr. 2 trumpets & 4 trombones₎
Alman
André, Maurice, 176)

₍Almande, No. 5; arr. 2 trumpets & 4 trombones₎
Almande No. 5
André, Maurice, 176)

₍Pavan; arr. 2 trumpets & 4 trombones₎
Pavan
André, Maurice, 176)

Fesch, Willem de, 1687-*ca.* 1757
Fesch, Wilhelm de

₍Concertos (8), op. 10, (1741). No. 7: flute, strings & continuo, D major; arr.
trumpet & strings, C major₎
Concerto in C major for Trumpet and Strings
[1]Vivace / [2]Larghetto / [3]Alla breve / [4]Minuetto / [5]Presto
The fifth movement is actually from *Concerto grosso in
B♭ major,* op. 3, no. 2.
André, Maurice, 137)

Festa, Costanzo, *ca.* 1490-1545

₍Madrigal, "Quando ritrova", 3 voices, cornetto & trombones₎
Madrigal, "Quando ritrova"
Unidentified, Trumpet(s), 1)

Fiala, George, 1922-

₍Concertino, piano, trumpet, timpani & strings₎
Concertino for Piano, Trumpet, Timpani & String Orchestra
LeComte, Jacques

Fibich, Zdenko, 1850-1900
Fibich, Zdeněk Antonín Václav

₍Poème, piano, op. 41, no. 6, (1894); arr. trumpet & orchestra₎
Poème, op. 41, no. 6
Scherbaum, Adolf, 34)

₍Poème, piano, op. 41, no. 14, (1894); arr. trumpet & piano₎
Poème, op. 41, no. 14
Dokshitser, Timofei, 5), 31)

Finck, Heinrich, *ca.* 1444-1527

₍Sauff aus und machs nit lang, cornetto, shawm, 2 sackbuts & tabor₎
Sauff aus und machs nit lang
Laird, Michael, 3)

Finger, Gottfried, *ca.* 1660-1730
Finger, Godfrey

[Sonata, trumpet, oboe & continuo, C major]
Sonata in C for Trumpet, Oboe and Continuo
[1](untitled) / [2](Adagio)-(Andante) / [3](untitled) / [4]Grave /
[5](untitled)
The second and fourth movements are oboe solos with continuo,
and the third movement is a trumpet solo with continuo.
Güttler, Ludwig, 8)
Steele-Perkins, Crispian, 5)

Fiocco, Joseph-Hector, 1703-1741

[Allegro, violin & piano, G major; arr. trumpet & organ]
Allegro in G major
Mertens, Theo, 2)

[Allegro, violin & piano, G major; arr. trumpet & piano, F major]
Allegro
Burkart, Richard
Nagel, Robert, 17)
Wilder, Joseph B.

[Andante; arr. trumpet & organ]
Andante
Stringer, Alan, 3)

[Missa Solemnis, soli, mixed voices & chamber orchestra, D major]
Missa Solemnis in D major
Solo voices include: soprano, countertenor, tenor & bass.
Chamber orchestra includes: 2 oboes, bassoon, 3 trumpets, 3
trombones, timpani, strings & continuo.
André, Maurice, 132)

Fischer, Johann Christian, 1733-1800

[Concerto, oboe & orchestra, C major; arr. trumpet & orchestra]
Konzert C-dur für Trompete und Orchester
André, Maurice, 73), 214), 165)

Fischer, Johann Kaspar Ferdinand, *ca.* 1670-1746

[Journal du Printemps, op. 1, (1695). Suite No. 1: Rigaudon, 2 trumpets, strings &
continuo]
Rigaudon from *Le Journal du Printemps*, op. 1, no. 1
Delmotte, Roger, 23)

[Journal du Printemps, op. 1, (1695). Suite No. 1:, 2 trumpets, strings & continuo]
Suite No. 1 from *Le Journal du Printemps*, op. 1
(Suite No. 1 from *The Springtime Journal*, op. 1)
Delmotte, Roger, 13)

₍Journal du Printemps, op. 1, (1695). Suite No. 8: 2 trumpets, strings & continuo₎
Suite No. 8 from *Le Journal du Printemps*, op. 1
(Suite No. 8 from *The Springtime Journal*, op. 1)
[1]Ouverture / [2]Entrée / [3]Canaries / [4]Gavotte en rondeau /
[5]Passepied / [6]Écho / [7]Menuet & Trio
> **Delmotte, Roger**, 13)
> **Voisin, Roger**, 7), 8)

Fitzgerald (arr.), Bernard, 1911-
Fitzgerald, Robert Bernard

₍English Suite; arr. trumpet & piano₎
English Suite for B♭ Trumpet and Piano
[1]Prelude ["Rule Britannia" — "British Grenadiers" by T. Arne] /
[2]Aria ["My Lovely Celia" by G. Munro] / [3]Pastoral ["Greensleeves"
(Anonymous)] / [4]Andante ["Polly Oliver" (Anonymous)] / [5]Finale
["Begone Dull Care" — "The Jolly Miller" (Anonymous)]
> **Haynie, John**, 2[1-2+4-5])
> **Masters, Edward L.**[1-3+5]
> **Ritter, David**[1-3+5]
> **Schwarz, Gerard**, 14[1+3])

₍Italian Suite; arr. trumpet & piano₎
Italian Suite for B♭ Trumpet and Piano
[1]Allegro [Aria, "Spesso vibra per suo gioco" by A. Scarlatti] /
[2]Allegretto [Aria, "Sebben, crudele" by A. Caldara] / [3]Andante [Aria,
"Non posso disperar" by S. De Luca] / [4]Danza [Aria, "Danza Danza,
Fanciulla Gentile" by F. Durante]
> **Ghitalla, Armando**, 11[1+3-4])

Fitzgerald, Bernard, 1911-
Fitzgerald, Robert Bernard

₍Concerto, trumpet & orchestra, a♭ minor, (1937); arr. trumpet & piano₎
Concerto in a♭ minor for Trumpet and Piano
[1]Lento espressivo, quasi fantasia / [2]Andante cantabile / [3]Scherzo and
Finale
The movements are published separately by Carl Fischer.
> **Smith, Leonard B.**[2]

₍Modern Suite, trumpet & piano, (1940)₎
Modern Suite for Trumpet and Piano
[1]Call / [2]Legend / [3]Frolic
The movements are published separately by Carl Fischer.
> **House, Lawrence**[1]
> **Masters, Edward L.**[2]
> **Nagel, Robert**, 15[3])
> **Reynolds, George**[1]
> **Tolley, Richard**[2]

Flemming, Hans Friedrich von, 18th cent.

[Teutsche Jäger. Jagdrufe, trumpet, 2 horns, 2 English horns, (1719)]
Jagdrufe aus *Der Teutsche Jäger*
(Hunting Call from *The German Hunter*)
Libiseller, Hansjörg

Flotow, Friedrich (Adolf Ferdinand) von, 1812-1883

[Martha, (1847). Aria, "M'appari tutt'amor"; arr. cornet & band]
Aria, "M'appari tutt'amor" from *Martha*
McCann, Phillip

Flyarkovsky, Aleksandr Georgievich, 1931-

[Humoresque, trumpet & piano, C major]
Humoresque in C major for Trumpet and Piano
Usov, Yuri

[Prelude, trumpet & piano, c minor]
Prelude in c minor for Trumpet and Piano
Usov, Yuri

Fontana, Giovanni Battista, *d. ca.* 1630

[Balletto e pass'e mezzo, solo instrument & continuo, (1641); ed. trumpet, harpsichord & bassoon]
Balletto e pass'e mezzo
Schwarz, Gerard, 17)

[Sonatas, (1641). No. 1: solo instrument & continuo; ed. trumpet, harpsichord & bassoon]
Sonata No. 1
These sonatas are from *Sonate a 1. 2. 3. per il violino, o cornetto, fagotto, chitarone, violoncino, o simile altro istrumento,* (1641).
Schwarz, Gerard, 9)

[Sonatas, (1641). No. 2: solo instrument & continuo; ed. trumpet, harpsichord & bassoon]
Sonata No. 2
Schwarz, Gerard, 9)

[Sonatas, (1641). No. 3: solo instrument & continuo; ed. trumpet, harpsichord & bassoon]
Sonata No. 3
Schwarz, Gerard, 9)

[Sonatas, (1641). No. 4: solo instrument & continuo; ed. trumpet, harpsichord & bassoon]
Sonata No. 4
Schwarz, Gerard, 9)

₍Sonatas, (1641). No. 5: solo instrument & continuo; ed. trumpet, harpsichord & bassoon₎
Sonata No. 5
Schwarz, Gerard, 9)

₍Sonatas, (1641). No. 6: solo instrument & continuo; ed. trumpet, harpsichord & bassoon₎
Sonata No. 6
Schwarz, Gerard, 9)

₍Sonatas, (1641). No. 10: solo instrument & continuo; ed. trumpet, harpsichord & bassoon₎
Sonata No. 10 in e minor
Schwarz, Gerard, 17)

₍Sonatas, (1641). No. 13: cornetto, violin & continuo₎
Sonata No. 13 a tre
Eichhorn, Holger

Fonville, John, 20th cent.

₍Afternoon with Anron at the Cafe, chamber ensemble, (1962)₎
An Afternoon with Anron at the Cafe
Chamber ensemble includes: flute, clarinet, trumpet, 2 trombones & percussion.
Sasaki, Ray

₍Proverbs/Converbs, chamber ensemble, (1984)₎
Proverbs/Converbs
Chamber ensemble includes: flute/piccolo/panpipes, clarinet/bass clarinet, trumpet, 2 trombones, didjeridu & percussion.
Sasaki, Ray

Förster, Anton, 20th cent.

₍Sonata, solo trumpet₎
Sonate für Trompete-solo
Luithle, Rainer

₍Trauermarsch, solo trumpet₎
Der Trauermarsch
Luithle, Rainer

Foster, Stephen, 1826-1864
Foster, Stephen Collins

₍Some folks; arr. mezzo-soprano, baritone, keyed bugle & piano₎
Some folks
Sheldon, Robert

Françaix, Jean, 1912-

₍Gay Paris, trumpet & wind ensemble₎
Le Gay Paris
> **Erb, Helmut, 3)**
> **Reinhart, Carole Dawn, 12)**

₍Sérénade, chamber orchestra, (1934)₎
Sérénade
> ¹Sérénade / ²Andantino con moto / ³Un poco allegretto / ⁴Vivace
> Chamber orchestra includes: flute, oboe, clarinet, bassoon, horn, trumpet, trombone & strings.
> **Lowrey, Alvin**

₍Sonatine, trumpet & piano, (1952)₎
Sonatine pour Trompette et Piano
> ¹Prélude (Allegretto) / ²Sarabande / ³Gigue
> **Hardenberger, Håkan**
> **Rippas, Claude**

Franceschini, Petronio, 1650?-1681

₍Sonata, recorder, trumpet, strings & continuo₎
Sonata a 7 for Recorder, Trumpet, Strings & Continuo
> This sonata may be an arrangement of the *Sonata in D major for 2 Trumpets.*
> **Soustrot, Bernard, 6)**

₍Sonata, 2 trumpets, strings & continuo, D major, (1680)₎
Sonata in D major for 2 Trumpets, Strings and Continuo
> (Suonata a 7 con due Trombe)
> ¹Grave / ²Allegro / ³Adagio / ⁴Allegro
> > **Cuvit, Michel**
> > **Güttler, Ludwig, 1)**
> > **Immer, Friedemann, 9)**
> > **Keavy, Stephen**
> > **Potpourri, 37)**
> > **Tarr, Edward, 21)**
> > **Touvron, Guy, 2)**
> > **Wallace, John, 4)**
> > **Wilbraham, John, 9)**

₍Sonata, 2 trumpets, strings & continuo, D major, (1680); arr. 2 trumpets & organ₎
Sonata in D major for 2 Trumpets and Organ
> (Suonata a 7 con due Trombe)
> ¹Grave / ²Allegro / ³Adagio / ⁴Allegro
> > **Schmidhäusler, Francis & René**

Franck, César, 1822-1890
Franck, César-Auguste-Jean-Guillaume-Hubert

[Panis Angelicus, tenor, cello, harp & organ, (1872); arr. trumpet & organ]
Panis Angelicus
("O Lord Most Holy")
Mertens, Theo, 2)

Franck, Melchior, *ca.* 1579-1639

[Neue Musicalische Intraden, (1608). No. 7: Intrada; arr. brass ensemble]
Intrada VII
André, Maurice, 98)

[Neue Pavanen, Galliarden und Intraden..., (1603). Pieces; arr. recorders, oboes, trumpets & trombones]
Partita in a minor for 5 and 6 voices
[1]Intrade / [2]Pavane / [3]Galliarde
Holy, Walter, 4)

[Sonatina, a minor; arr. trumpet & organ]
Sonatine en la mineur pour trompette et orgue
André, Maurice, 163)

Francœur, François, 1698-1787
Francœur, François (Le cadet)

[Gavotte; arr. Rondeau, trumpet & organ]
Rondeau in e minor
(arr. from a "Gavotte")
Braz, Dirceu, 3)

[Symphonies du Festin Royal, (1773). Suite No. 4, chamber orchestra]
Quatrième Suite de *Symphonies du Festin Royal*
[1]Ouverture [Francœur] / [2]Menuet gracieux [Rameau] / [3]Air gracieux [Grenier] / [4]Entrée de chasseurs [Dauvergne] / [5]Premier et deuxième Rondeau [Francœur] / [6]Rondeau gay [Francœur] / [7]Musette [Mondonville] / [8]Joyeux Rondeau [Mondonville] / [9]Premier et deuxième Menuet [Rebel & Francœur] / [10]Chaconne [Royer] / [11]Tambourin [Rameau]
> Jean-Philippe Rameau (1683-1764); Grenier (18th cent.); Antoine Dauvergne (1713-1797); Jean-Joseph Cassanéa de Mondonville (1711-1772); François Rebel (1701-1775); Jean-Nicolas-Pancrace Royer (1705-1755)
Scherbaum, Adolf, 18)

ₜSymphonies du Festin Royal, (1773). Suite No. 4, chamber orchestra: Excerptsₗ
Quatrième Suite de *Symphonies du Festin Royal*, (excerpts)
a) Menuet I [Rebel] & Menuet II [Francœur] / b) Entrée de chasseurs [Dauvergne] / c) Menuet gracieux [Rameau] / d) Air tendre [Francœur] / e) Air en rondeau [Francœur] / f) Musette [Mondonville] / g) Rondeau [Mondonville] / h) Rondeaux [Francœur] / i) Rondeau gay [Francœur]

> The movements included in the recordings by Maurice André and Adolf Scherbaum compare as follows: a=9; b=4; c=2; d=?; e=?; f=7; g=8; h=5; i=6
> **André, Maurice**, 121)

Fredrickson, Thomas, 1928-

ₜTriptych, oboe, trumpet, trombone & violaₗ
Triptych
Sasaki, Ray

Frescobaldi, Girolamo, 1583-1643

ₜCorrente (4); arr. trumpet & organₗ
Quatro Corrente
Sautter, Fred

ₜDances (4); arr. trumpet & harpₗ
Four Italian Dances
(Quatre danses italiennes / Vier italienische Tänze)
[1]Air detta la Frescobalda / [2]Gagliarda / [3]Corrente e Ciaccona / [4]Gagliarda
André, Maurice, 64)

ₜLibro delle Canzoni (1620). Selections; arr. cornetto & organₗ
Canzoni (1620)
Auswahl (Selections)
Pok, František, 1)

ₜPrimo libro delle canzoni..., (1628). Canzon seconda, canto solo & continuoₗ
Canzon seconda, violino solo, over cornetto (1628)
Canzona I (1966)

> This canzona is the first in the 1966 edition and was the second in the 1628 part-books, but was not included in the 1628 score or the 1634 edition. (This *Canzon seconda* is not the same as the *Canzona seconda detta la Bernardinia* nor is it the same as the *Canzona prima detta la Bonuisia*.
> **Schwarz, Gerard**, 9)

[Primo libro delle canzoni..., (1628). Canzona 1, canto solo & continuo]

Canzona prima, per canto solo, detta la Bonuisia

Canzona Prima (1628 score) = Canzon Terza (1634 part-books) = Canzon III (1966 edition). This canzona was not included in the 1628 part-books.

Eichhorn, Holger
Pok, František, 3)
Schwarz, Gerard, 9)

[Primo libro delle canzoni..., (1628). Canzona 2, canto solo & continuo]

Canzona seconda, per canto solo, detta la Bernardinia

Canzona Seconda (1628 score) = Canzon Prima (1628 part-books) = Canzon Terza (1634 part-books) = Canzon III (1966 edition)

Canihac, Jean-Pierre
Eichhorn, Holger
Schwarz, Gerard, 9)

[Primo libro delle canzoni..., (1628). Canzona 3, canto solo & continuo]

Canzona terza, per canto solo, detta la Lucchesina

Canzona Terza (1628 score) = Canzon Quarta (1628 part-books) = Canzon Seconda (1634 part-books) = Canzon IV (1966 edition)

Eichhorn, Holger
Schwarz, Gerard, 9)

[Primo libro delle canzoni..., (1628). Canzona 4, canto solo & continuo]

Canzona quarta, per canto solo, detta la Donatina

Canzona [quarta] (1628 score) = Canzon Terza (1628 part-books) = Canzon Quarta (1634 part-books) = Canzon V (1966 edition)

Schwarz, Gerard, 9)

[Primo libro delle canzoni..., (1628). Canzona 9, 2 canti & continuo]

Canzona 9, a due canti, detta la Gualterina

Laird, Michael, 1)

[Primo libro delle canzoni..., (1628). Canzona 10, 2 canti & continuo]

Canzona 10, a due canti, detta l'Henricuccia

Eichhorn, Holger
Loustalot, Alain

[Primo libro delle canzoni..., (1628). Canzona 12, 2 canti & continuo]

Canzona 12, a due canti, detta la Todeschina

Canihac, Jean-Pierre

[Primo libro delle canzoni..., (1628). Canzona 13, 2 canti & continuo]

Canzona 13, a due canti, detta la Bianchina

Canihac, Jean-Pierre

[Primo libro delle canzoni..., (1628). Canzona 19, canto, basso & continuo]

Canzona 19, a canto e basso, detta la Capriola

Eichhorn, Holger

⌜Primo libro delle canzoni..., (1628). Canzona 20, canto, basso & continuo⌝
Canzona 20, a canto e basso, detta la Lipparella
Eichhorn, Holger
Smithers, Don, 1)

⌜Primo libro delle canzoni..., (1628). Canzona 21, canto, basso & continuo⌝
Canzona 21, a canto e basso, detta la Tegrimuccia
Eichhorn, Holger

⌜Primo libro delle canzoni..., (1628). Canzona 22, canto, basso & continuo⌝
Canzona 22, a canto e basso, detta la Nicolina
Canihac, Jean-Pierre
Eichhorn, Holger

⌜Primo libro delle canzoni..., (1628). Canzona 26, canto, 2 bassi & continuo⌝
Canzona 26, a due bassi e canto, detta la Moricona
Canihac, Jean-Pierre
Eichhorn, Holger

⌜Primo libro delle canzoni..., (1628). Canzona 31, 2 canti, 2 bassi & continuo⌝
Canzona 31, a quattro, detta l'Arnolfina
Canihac, Jean-Pierre

⌜Primo libro delle canzoni..., (1628). Canzona 37, canto, alto, tenore, basso & continuo⌝
Canzona 37, a quattro, detta la Sardina
Canihac, Jean-Pierre

⌜Primo libro delle canzoni..., (1628). Canzona, canto solo & continuo; arr. cornetto, trombone & virginals⌝
Canzona a canto solo
This canzona is not specifically identified, but is probably one of the canzoni for "canto e basso" (No. 18-23).
Impett, Jonathan

Friboulet, Georges, 20th cent.

⌜Gaminerie, trumpet & piano, B♭ major, (1953)⌝
Gaminerie
House, Lawrence

⌜Gaminerie, trumpet & piano, B♭ major, (1953); arr. trumpet & organ⌝
Gaminerie
Braz, Dirceu, 4)

Friedman, Stanley, 1951-
Friedman, Stanley Arnold

⌜Antiphonia IV, 6 trumpets⌝
Antiphonia IV for Trumpet Sextet
First trumpet doubles on piccolo trumpet.
Giangiulio, Richard

ₜFanfare 1985, trumpet & horn, (1985)ₕ
Fanfare 1985
Giangiulio, Richard

ₜLaude, solo trumpetₕ
Laude
(Four Character Sketches for Solo Trumpet)
[1]Nocturne for St. Thomas / [2]Phantasie für der Wiz / [3]Berceuse for John Julius / [4]Rondo for Professor Nabob
Giangiulio, Richard

Fronmüller, Frieda, 1901-

ₜCantata, "Jerusalem, du hochgebaute Stadt", mixed voices, trumpet & trombonesₕ
Cantata, "Jerusalem, du hochgebaute Stadt"
Pfann, Karl

Frosini, Pietro, 1885-1951

ₜVariations, (Carnival of Venice); arr. trumpet & orchestraₕ
Carnival of Venice
This version of the "Carnival of Venice" variations is an orchestration of Arban's variations by Tutti Camarata after the late Italian cornetist, Pietro Frosini. (Arban's introductory section is omitted.)
Wilbraham, John, 24)

Frumerie, Gunnar de, 1908-1987
Frumerie, Per Gunnar Fredrik de

ₜMusik, piano & chamber ensemble, op. 75ₕ
Musik für Neun, op. 75
(Music for Nine, op. 75)
Schrello, Mark

Fux, Johann Joseph, 1660-1741

ₜCantata, "Plaudite, sonat tuba", tenor, trumpet & stringsₕ
Cantata, "Plaudite, sonat tuba"
Touvron, Guy, 15)

ₜConcentus musico-instrumentalis, op. 1, (1701). Serenada, 2 trumpets, 2 oboes, strings & continuoₕ
Serenada from *Concentus musico-instrumentalis*, op. 1
[1]Marche / [2]Guique / [3]Menuet / [4]Aria / [5]Intrada / [6]Rigadon / [7]Ciacona / [8]Guique / [9]Menuet / [10]Final
Delmotte, Roger, 23[5]), 25[3+7+9]), 48)
Voisin, Roger, 6), 8)

ₜSerenada, 3 trumpets, 2 oboes, strings & continuoₕ
Serenada a 8
Potpourri, 49), 50)

⌈Sonata, violin, cornetto, trombone & continuo⌉
Sonata a quattro
Potpourri, 49), 50)

⌈Suite, C major; arr. trumpet & piano⌉
Suite in C major
Hyatt, Jack

Gabaye, Pierre, 1930-

⌈Boutade, trumpet & piano, (1957)⌉
Boutade
Haynie, John, 2)
Lewis, E. Leonard
Ritter, David

⌈Boutade, trumpet & piano, (1957); arr. trumpet & brass ensemble⌉
Boutade
Mertens, Theo, 5)

⌈Feu d'Artifice, trumpet, strings & percussion, (1964); arr. trumpet & piano⌉
Feu d'Artifice
Amstutz, Keith

Gabe, Ralf, 1952-

⌈Air de Combattans, trumpet & synthesizer⌉
Air de Combattans
Braz, Dirceu, 2)

⌈Lyrisches Andante, trumpet & synthesizer⌉
Lyrisches Andante
Braz, Dirceu, 2)

Gabrieli, Andrea, *ca.* 1510-1586

⌈Ricercare del duodecimo tuono, four-part; arr. trumpet, horn & 2 trombones⌉
Ricercare del duodecimo tuono
Potpourri, 30)

⌈Ricercare del duodecimo tuono, four-part; arr. 3 trumpets & bass trumpet⌉
Ricercare del duodecimo tuono
Carroll, Edward, 10)

⌈Ricercare del sesto tuono, four-part; arr. trumpet, horn & 2 trombones⌉
Ricercare del sesto tuono
Potpourri, 30)

Gabrieli, Giovanni, 1555?-1612

ₜCanzoni e Sonate, (1615). No. 1: Canzona, five-part; arr. 4 trumpets, bass trumpet & organ₎
Canzona prima a 5
Carroll, Edward, 10)

ₜCanzoni e Sonate, (1615). No. 6: Canzona, seven-part; arr. 5 trumpets, 2 bass trumpets & organ₎
Canzon VI a 7
Carroll, Edward, 10)
Potpourri, 33)

ₜCanzoni e Sonate, (1615). No. 21: Sonata, 3 violins & continuo; arr. 3 trumpets, organ & bassoon₎
Sonata No. 21
(Sonata con tre violini overo altri instrumenti con il basso per l'organo)
Carroll, Edward, 7), 9)
Schwarz, Gerard, 20)

ₜMagnificat primi toni, mixed voices, 2 recorders, cornetto, 3 trombones, strings & continuo₎
Magnificat primi toni
Tarr, Edward, 20)

ₜMotet, "Quis est ist", mixed voices, 2 recorders, cornetto, 3 trombones, lute & organ₎
Motet, "Quis est ist"
Tarr, Edward, 20)

ₜSacrae symphoniae (1597). Sonata pian' e forte, cornetto, viola, 6 trombones; various arr.₎
Sonata pian' e forte
André, Maurice, 98)
Carroll, Edward, 7)
Geyer, Charles
Tarr, Edward, 20)
Wilbraham, John, 17)

Gabrielli, Domenico, 1651-1690

ₜSonata, trumpet, strings & continuo, (D. XI, 3), D major₎
Sonata a 6 for Trumpet, Strings and Continuo, [D. XI, 3]
[1]Largo - Presto / [2]Largo / [3]Presto e staccato
This sonata is No. 1 in the International Music edition (New York). The "D. XI" numbers refer to identification of the original manuscripts located in the Archives of the Basilica of San Petronio, Bologna.
André, Maurice, 79), 105)

ₜSonata, trumpet, strings & continuo, (D. XI, 3), D major; arr. trumpet & organ₎
Sonata in D major for Trumpet and Organ, [D. XI, 3]
[1]Largo - Presto / [2]Largo / [3]Presto e staccato
Haas, Wolfgang

[Sonata, trumpet, strings & continuo, (D. XI, 4), D major]
Sonata in D major for Trumpet, Strings and Continuo, [D. XI, 4]
[1]Grave - Allegro / [2]Grave / [3]Allegro
This sonata is No. 6 in the International Music edition (New York). It is No. 2 in the Musica Rara edition (London).
Wobisch, Helmut, 3)

[Sonata, trumpet, strings & continuo, (D. XI, 4), D major; arr. trumpet & organ]
Sonata in D major for Trumpet and Organ, [D. XI, 4]
[1]Grave - Allegro / [2]Grave / [3]Allegro
Delmotte, Roger, 39)

[Sonata, trumpet, strings & continuo, (D. XI, 5), D major]
Sonata a 4 e 5 con Tromba, [D. XI, 5]
(Sonata in D major for Trumpet, Strings and Continuo)
[1]Allegro / [2]Grave / [3]Presto / [4]Grave - Presto
This sonata is No. 2 in the International Music edition (New York).
André, Maurice, 79), 115)
Scherbaum, Adolf, 20)

[Sonata, trumpet, strings & continuo, (D. XI, 6), D major]
Sonata in D major for Trumpet, Strings and Continuo, [D. XI, 6]
[1]Allegro / [2]Largo / [3]Allegro / [4]Largo - Presto
This sonata is No. 5 in the International Music edition (New York). It is No. 4 in the Musica Rara edition (London).
André, Maurice, 50)
Cuvit, Michel
Immer, Friedemann, 9)
Potpourri, 37)
Schultz, Erik, 5)
Wobisch, Helmut, 6), 11)

[Sonata, trumpet, strings & continuo, (D. XI, 6), D major; arr. trumpet & harpsichord]
Sonata in D major for Trumpet and Harpsichord, [D. XI, 6]
[1]Allegro / [2]Largo / [3]Allegro / [4]Largo - Presto
Plog, Anthony, 6)

[Sonata, trumpet, strings & continuo, (D. XI, 6), D major; arr. trumpet & organ, C major]
Sonata in C major for Trumpet and Organ, [D. XI, 6]
[1]Allegro / [2]Largo / [3]Allegro / [4]Largo - Presto
Ode, James

[Sonata, trumpet, strings & continuo, (D. XI, 6), D major; arr. trumpet, organ & bassoon]
Sonata in D major for Trumpet and Continuo, [D. XI, 6]
[1]Allegro / [2]Largo / [3]Allegro / [4]Largo - Presto
Schultz, Erik, 1)

[Sonata, trumpet, strings & continuo, (D. XI, 7), D major]
Sonata in D major for Trumpet, Strings and Continuo, [D. XI, 7]
[1]Adagio - Allegro / [2]Adagio / [3]Presto
This sonata is No. 4 in the International Music edition (New York).
Immer, Friedemann, 9)

[Sonata, trumpet, strings & continuo, (D. XI, 8), D major]
Sonata a 6 in D major for Trumpet, Strings and Continuo, [D. XI, 8]
[1]Grave - Allegro / [2]Grave / [3]Allegro / [4]Grave - Presto
This sonata is No. 3 in the International Music edition (New York).
Smithers, Don, 5)

[Sonata, trumpet, strings & continuo, D major, (unidentified)]
Sonata a 6 in D major [unidentified]
Güttler, Ludwig, 8)

[Sonata, 2 trumpets, strings & continuo, D major]
Sonata in D major for 2 Trumpets, Strings and Continuo
Molénat, Claude

[Sonata, 2 trumpets, strings & continuo, D major; arr. 2 trumpets & organ]
Sonata per due Trombe e Organo
Schultz, Erik, 9)

[Sonata, 2 trumpets, strings & continuo, D major; arr. 2 trumpets & organ, C major]
Sonata in C major for 2 Trumpets and Organ
Waltzing, Gast

Gaburo, Kenneth, 1926-
Gaburo, Kenneth Louis

[Mouth-Piece, trumpet, (1965-70)]
Mouth-Piece
(Sextet for Solo Trumpet)
Logan, Jack

Gade, Jacob, 1879-1963

[Jalousie, (1925); arr. trumpet & instrumental ensemble]
Jalousie (Tango)
(Jealousy)
Andersen, Ole

[Jalousie, (1925); arr. trumpet & orchestra]
Jalousie (Tango)
(Jealousy)
Geiger, György
Méndez, Rafael, 27)

₍Jalousie, (1925); arr. trumpet & piano₎
   Jalousie
            Christensen, Ketil

Gagnebin, Henri, 1886-1977

₍Sonata da Chiesa per la Pasqua, trumpet & organ₎
   Sonata da Chiesa per la Pasqua
            André, Maurice, 164)

Gallois-Montbrun, Raymond, 1918-

₍Lied, trumpet & piano, (1950)₎
   Lied
            House, Lawrence

₍March, trumpet & piano, (1950)₎
   March
            House, Lawrence

₍Scherzo, trumpet & piano, (1950)₎
   Scherzo
            House, Lawrence

Gallus, Jacobus
See: Handl, Jacob

Ganne, Louis Gaston, 1862-1923
Ganne, (Gustave) Louis

₍Czarine; arr. flügelhorn & accordion band₎
   La czarine, mazurka
            André, Maurice, 61)

₍Saltimbanques, (1899). Theme; arr. flügelhorn & accordion band₎
   Les saltimbanques from *Les saltimbanques*
     ("The Acrobats")
            André, Maurice, 61)

Gascon, Celso, 20th cent.
₍Brave Matador, 3 trumpets & orchestra₎
   The Brave Matador
            Méndez, Rafael, 19)

Gaubert, Philippe, 1879-1941

₍Cantabile et Scherzetto, cornet & piano₎
   Cantabile et Scherzetto
     (pour Cornet à Pistons en Si♭ avec accompt de Piano)
     Performed on trumpet and piano
            Masters, Edward L.

Geissler, Fredrick, 1946-
Geissler, Fredrick Dietzmann

[Variations on a Modern American Trumpet Tune, trumpet & wind ensemble]
Variations on a Modern American Trumpet Tune
Stith, Marice, 1)

Geminiani, Francesco (Xaverio), 1687-1762

[Forêt enchantée, chamber orchestra, (c. 1756)]
La forêt enchantée
(The Enchanted Forest)
[1]Andante / [2]Allegro moderato / [3]Andante / [4]Allegro moderato /
[5]Andante / [6]Allegro moderato / [7]Andante spiritoso / [8]Adagio /
[9]Allegro / [10]Grave / [11]Allegro moderato / [12]Andante affettuoso /
[13]Allegro / [14]Allegro moderato / [15]Andante spiritoso / [16]Allegro assai /
[17]Andante / [18]Affettuoso / [19]Allegro / [20]Allegro moderato / [21]Andante /
[22]Allegro - Affettuoso - Allegro
Wind instruments included are 2 flutes and 2 horns. Trumpet
replaces one horn in movements 12 to 22.
André, Maurice, 130)

[Sonata, violin & continuo, No. 3; arr. trumpet & organ]
Sonata No. 3
Capouillez, Luc

Genzmer, Harald, 1909-

[Cantata, soprano, trumpet & strings]
Kantate (nach Whitman) für Sopran, Trompete und Streicher
Cantata (after Whitman) for Soprano, Trumpet and Strings
Reinhart, Carole Dawn, 8)

[Concerto, trumpet & orchestra, (1970)]
Konzert für Trompete und Orchester
(Concerto for Trumpet and Orchestra)
Reinhart, Carole Dawn, 8)
Tarr, Edward, 9)

[Concerto, trumpet & orchestra, (1970); arr. trumpet & piano]
Konzertantes Duo
Konzertantes Duo = piano reduction of *Trumpet Concerto*
Gardner, Ned

[Sonata, trumpet & organ, (1971)]
Sonate für Trompete und Orgel
[1][quarter = ca. 40] / [2]Allegro / [3]Choral: Tranquillo ("Aus tiefer Not
schrei' ich zu dir") / [4]Finale: Vivo
André, Maurice, 144)
Send, Peter

[Sonatina, trumpet & piano, (1965)]
Sonatine für Trompete und Klavier
[1]Allegro / [2]Andante tranquillo / [3]Saltarello: Allegro giocoso e molto vivace
Rippas, Claude

George, Earl, 1924-

[Tuckets and Sennets, trumpet and piano]
Tuckets and Sennets
Stith, Marice, 8)

Gershwin, George, 1898-1937

[American in Paris, (1928). Themes, orchestra; arr. trumpet & orchestra]
Themes from *An American in Paris*
André, Maurice, 170)

[Concerto, piano & orchestra, F major, (1925). Themes; arr. as Divertissement, trumpet & orchestra]
Divertissement
(Themes from Concerto in F major for Piano)
André, Maurice, 7)

[Porgy and Bess, (1935). Selections; arr. solo trumpet, solo horn, solo tuba & brass ensemble]
Selections from *Porgy and Bess*
Mertens, Theo, 3)

[Porgy and Bess, (1935). Summertime; arr. trumpet & orchestra]
Summertime from *Porgy and Bess*
André, Maurice, 7)

[Porgy and Bess, (1935). The Man I Love; arr. trumpet & orchestra]
The Man I Love from *Porgy and Bess*
André, Maurice, 7)

[Rhapsody in Blue, piano & jazz orchestra, (1924); arr. trumpet & orchestra]
Rhapsody in Blue
André, Maurice, 7)
Dokshitser, Timofei, 8), 37), 39)

[Rhapsody in Blue, piano & jazz orchestra, (1924); arr. trumpet & piano]
Rhapsody in Blue
Tarr, Edward, 6)

[Strike up the Band, (1927). Theme; arr. trumpet quartet]
Strike up the Band from *Strike up the Band*
Blackburn, Roger

Gervaise, Claude, *fl.* 1550

ₜDances (4), four-part; arr. trumpet & organ₁
Danceries de la Renaissance Française (4)
(Dances of the French Renaissance)
Unspecified dances.
Berinbaum, Martin

ₜDances (7), four-part. No. 7: Allemande; arr. trumpet & organ₁
Allemande
Blair, Stacy
Winslow, Richard

ₜDances (7), four-part; arr. brass ensemble₁
Danceries de la Renaissance Française (7)
(Dances of the French Renaissance)
[1]Pavane [Gervaise, 1555] / [2]Passamezzo [Gervaise, 1555] / [3]Gaillard [Gervaise, 1555] / [4]Basse Danse, "Celle qui m'a le nom d'amy donné" [Anonymous, 1547] / [5]Bransle de Bourgogne [Gervaise, 1556] / [6]Bransle de Champagne [Gervaise, 1555] / [7]Bransle d'Escosse [Estienne du Tertre, 1557]
André, Maurice, 98)

ₜDances (7), four-part; arr. trumpet & harp₁
Sept Danceries de la Renaissance Française
(Sieben französische Tänze)
(Seven Dances of the French Renaissance)
[1]Pavane [Gervaise] / [2]Gaillarde [Gervaise] / [3]Branle de Bourgogne [Anonymous] / [4]Branle de Champagne [Gervaise] / [5]Branle gai, "Que ie chatoulle ta fossette" [Anonymous] / [6]Branle simple [Anonymous [7]Allemande [Gervaise]
Dances numbered 1, 4, 5 & 7 also include percussion.
André, Maurice, 64), 227)

ₜDances (7), four-part; arr. trumpet & organ₁
Sept Danceries de la Renaissance Française
(Seven Dances of the French Renaissance)
[1]Pavane [Gervaise] / [2]Gaillarde [Gervaise] / [3]Branle de Bourgogne [Anonymous] / [4]Branle de Champagne [Gervaise] / [5]Branle gai, "Que ie chatoulle ta fossette" [Anonymous] / [6]Branle simple [Anonymous [7]Allemande [Gervaise]
Transcribed from *Danceries à 4 et 5 parties.* [6 vol.], published by Pierre Attaingnant, (1545-1556). Arranged for trumpet and organ by Marie-Claire Alain, (1970).
André, Maurice, 50), 118[1-2+7+3-6]**)**
Basch, Wolfgang, 5)
Bernard, André, 4)
Bouche
Gaudon, Jean-Jacques
Giangiulio, Richard
Pearson, Byron
Schultz, Erik, 10)
Touvron, Guy, 20)

Getchell (arr.), Robert, 20th cent.

⌐Baroque Suite; arr. trumpet & piano⌐
Baroque Suite
¹Sarabande [Tartini] / ²Rondeau [Buononcini]
Geyer, Charles

⌐Menuet and Ballo; arr. trumpet & piano⌐
Menuet and Ballo
¹Menuet [Hook] / ²Ballo [Steibelt]
Geyer, Charles

⌐Sarabande and Gigue; arr. trumpet & piano⌐
Sarabande and Gigue
¹Sarabande [Rameau] / ²Gigue [Pepusch]
Geyer, Charles

Getchell, Robert, 20th cent.

⌐Proclamation, Serenade and Frolic, trumpet & piano, (1976)⌐
Proclamation, Serenade and Frolic
Geyer, Charles

Giannini, Vittorio, 1903-1966

⌐Concerto, trumpet & orchestra, (1948); arr. trumpet & piano⌐
Concerto for Trumpet
¹Allegro energico / ²Andante sostenuto / ³Allegro
Burke, James, 7²)

Giazotto, Remo, 1910-

⌐Adagio, organ & strings, g minor, (1958); arr. trumpet & organ⌐
Adagio in g minor
(Célèbre Adagio)
An original composition by Remo Giazotto based on two thematic
drafts and one figured bass by Tomaso Albinoni. The Albinoni
thematic fragments are catalogued by Michael Talbot as
T. *Mi* 26.

**André, Maurice, 40), 42), 52), 67), 78), 178),
    227)**
Bernard, André, 9), 11)
Gräber, Wolfgang
Jorand, Jean-Claude
Mertens, Theo, 2)
Pearson, Byron
Potpourri, 36), 37)
Rausch, Heiner
Smedvig, Rolf
Tamiya, Kenji
Touvron, Guy, 9)

⌜Adagio, organ & strings, g minor, (1958); arr. trumpet, voices & orchestra⌝
Adagio in g minor
(Célèbre Adagio)
André, Maurice, 206)

Gideon, Miriam, 1906-

⌜Resounding Lyre, tenor & chamber ensemble⌝
The Resounding Lyre
Chamber ensemble includes: flute, oboe, bassoon, trumpet, violin, viola & cello.
Burns, Stephen

Gilardi, Gilardo, 1889-1963

⌜Concertino a Rafael Méndez, trumpet & orchestra⌝
Concertino a Rafael Méndez
Méndez, Rafael, 18)

Gilles, Jean, 1668-1705

⌜Te Deum laudamus, mixed voices, trumpet & strings⌝
Te Deum laudamus
Jeannoutot, Bernard

Gillet, Ernest, 1856-1940

⌜Loin du Bal, piano; arr. trumpet & instrumental ensemble⌝
Loin du Bal
Andersen, Ole

Giménez, Jerónimo, 1854-1923
Giménez y Bellido, Jerónimo

⌜Boda de Luis Alonso, (1897); arr. trumpet & orchestra⌝
La Boda de Luis Alonso, zarzuela
(The Wedding of Luis Alonso)
The album notes cite **G. Jiménez** as the composer, but most other sources provide the spelling as above. Another source spells both names with a **J.**
Méndez, Rafael, 16)

Giordani, Giuseppe, *ca.* 1753-1798

⌜Aria, "Caro mio ben"; arr. trumpet & organ⌝
Aria, "Caro mio ben"
Grin, Freddy, 8)

Glass, Philip, 1937-

ₜLiquid Days. Songs, voice & various chamber ensemblesₙ
Songs from Liquid Days
Wise, Wilmer

ₜPhotographer, violin, mixed voices & chamber ensembleₙ
The Photographer
Chamber ensemble includes: flute (saxophone), 2 horns, 2 trumpets, 2 trombones, keyboards (piano & bass synthesizer), electric organ & strings.
Soloff, Lew

Glazunov, Alexandre Konstantinovich, 1865-1936
Glazounov, Alexandre
Glasunow, Alexander

ₜAlbumblatt, trumpet & piano, (1899); arr. cornet & pianoₙ
Albumblatt
(Feuillet d'Album)
(Leaf from an Album)
Sommerhalder, Max

ₜAlbumblatt, trumpet & piano, (1899); arr. trumpet & orchestraₙ
Albumblatt
(Leaf from an Album)
Dokshitser, Timofei, 3), 12), 13), 37), 39)

ₜIn modo religioso, brass quartet, op. 38, (1892); arr. trumpet, organ & brass ensembleₙ
In modo religioso, op. 38
Grin, Freddy, 6)

Glickman, Loren, 20th cent.

ₜSection 8, trumpet(s)ₙ
Section 8
An eight-part composition for trumpet ensemble using a variety of trumpets recorded on multi-tracks by a single performer.
Lieberman, Harold J.

Glière, Reinhold Moritsevich, 1875-1956
Glier, Reyngol'd Moritsevich

ₜAndante avec variations, trumpet & piano, B♭ majorₙ
Andante avec variations in B♭
Sommerhalder, Max

ₜConcerto, coloratura & orchestra, op. 82, (1943); arr. trumpet & bandₙ
Concerto for Trumpet, op. 82
¹Andante / ²Allegro
Smith, Philip, 5)

[Concerto, coloratura & orchestra, op. 82, (1943); arr. trumpet & orchestra]
Concerto for Trumpet, op. 82
[1]Andante / [2]Allegro
Dokshitser, Timofei, 20)

[Concerto, coloratura & orchestra, op. 82, (1943); arr. trumpet & piano]
Concerto for Trumpet, op. 82
[1]Andante / [2]Allegro
Sveshnikov, Mikhail

[Pieces, op. 34, no. 21; arr. trumpet & piano]
Two Pieces, op. 34, no. 21
Meditation / Mazurka
Reynolds, George

Glindemann, Ib, 1934-
Glindemann, Ib Niels Carl

[Concerto, trumpet & orchestra, (1962)]
Concerto for Trumpet and Orchestra
[1]Allegro spagnuolo / [2]Andante con sentimento / [3]Allegro brillante
Hovaldt, Knud

Gluck, Christoph, 1714-1787
Gluck, Christoph Willibald Ritter von

[Airs (2); arr. trumpet & piano]
Two Classic Airs
Air No. 1 / Air No. 2
Burkart, Richard[1]

[Orfeo ed Euridice, (1762). Dance of the Blessed Spirits; arr. trumpet & orchestra]
Dance of the Blessed Spirits from *Orfeo ed Euridice*
Wilbraham, John, 24)

Gnattali, Radamés, 1906-

[Bossa Romantica, trumpet & guitar]
Bossa Romantica
Méndez, Rafael, 14)

Goedicke, Alexander Fedorovich, 1877-1957
Gödike, Alexander
Gedike, Alexandre Fyodorovich

[Concert Etude, trumpet & orchestra, op. 49, (1934); arr. cornet & band]
Concert Etude, op. 49
Haynie, John, 3)

ΓConcert Etude, trumpet & orchestra, op. 49, (1934); arr. trumpet & pianoꞁ
Concert Etude, op. 49
> Dokshitser, Timofei, 3), 5), 7), 27), 35)
> Gardner, Ned
> Haynie, John, 2)
> Ots, Aavo
> Reinhart, Carole Dawn, 9)
> Schwarz, Gerard, 15)
> Smith, Leonard B.
> Yeryomin, Sergei Nikolaivich

ΓConcerto, trumpet & orchestra, op. 41, b♭ minor, (1930)ꞁ
Concerto in b♭ minor for Trumpet and Orchestra, op. 41
Moderato sostenuto - Allegro con fuoco
> Dokshitser, Timofei, 6), 11), 30)

Goeyens, Alphonse, *d.* 1950

ΓAll' Antica, trumpet & pianoꞁ
All' Antica
> Amstutz, Keith
> Schwarz, Gerard, 16)

Goldman, Edwin Franko, 1878-1956

ΓIntroduction et Tarantella, trumpet & pianoꞁ
Introduction et Tarantella
> Benedetti, Donald

ΓScherzo, trumpet & bandꞁ
Scherzo
> Head, Emerson

Goller, Vinzenz, 1873-1953

ΓIte missa est, trumpet, organ & timpaniꞁ
Ite missa est
> Pohle, Wolfgang

ΓSursum corda, trumpet, organ & timpaniꞁ
Sursum corda
> Pohle, Wolfgang

Goltermann, Georg, 1824-1898
Goltermann, Georg Eduard

ΓAria, cello & piano; arr. trumpet & pianoꞁ
Aria
> Geyer, Charles

Goméz, Guillermo

₍Aires Andaluces; arr. trumpet & orchestra₎
Aires Andaluces
Composer = Carlos Gomes (1836-1896) ?
Méndez, Rafael, 12)

Gottlieb, Mikhail, 1907-1978

₍Theme with variations, trumpet & brass band₎
Theme with variations
Dokshitser, Timofei, 16), 20)

Gould, Morton, 1913-

₍Pavanne; arr. trumpet & orchestra₎
Pavanne
Hirt, Al

Gounod, Charles, 1818-1893
Gounod, Charles François

₍Ave Maria, voice & piano, (1859); arr. trumpet & organ₎
Ave Maria
An original melody by Charles Gounod superimposed on J.S. Bach's "Prelude No. 1" (S. 846) from *Das Wohltemperierte Klavier*, Book I.
André, Maurice, 39), 40), 42), 52), 67), 206), 207)
Bernard, André, 9)
Falentin, Paul, 5)
Hickman, David, 6)
Mertens, Theo, 2)
Schultz, Erik, 9)
Terracini, Paul

₍Ave Maria, voice & piano, (1859); arr. trumpet & strings₎
Ave Maria
Dokshitser, Timofei, 14), 36), 38), 39)
Méndez, Rafael, 16)

₍Faust, (1859). Aria, "Salut! Demeure chaste et pure"; arr. cornet & orchestra₎
Aria, "Salut! Demeure chaste et pure" from *Faust*
McCann, Phillip

₍Faust, (1859). Soldier's Chorus; arr. trumpet & orchestra₎
Soldier's Chorus from *Faust*
Ghitalla, Armando, 14)

₍Serenade, voice & piano, (1857); arr. trumpet & piano₎
Sérénade
Ots, Aavo

ₜSerenade, voice & piano, (1857); arr. trumpet & violin ensembleₙ
Sérénade
Dokshitser, Timofei, 14), 36), 38), 39)

Granados, Enrique, 1867-1916
Granados y Campiña, Enrique

ₜDanza Espagnole, op. 37, (1892). No. 5: Andaluza, piano; arr. trumpet & orchestraₙ
Andaluza from *Danza Espagnole*, op. 37
Méndez, Rafael, 15), 24)

ₜDanza Espagnole, op. 37, (1892). No. 5: Andaluza, piano; arr. trumpet & pianoₙ
Andaluza from *Danza Espagnole*, op. 37
Crisara, Raymond, 7)

Grandi, Alessandro, 1575-1630

ₜO beate Benedicte, countertenor, tenor & chamber ensembleₙ
O beate Benedicte
Chamber ensemble includes: cornetto, tenor sackbut, bass viol & organ.
Laird, Michael, 2)

Granier, Jules

ₜHosanna, mixed voices; arr. trumpet & organₙ
Hosanna
Stith, Marice, 9)

Graupner, Christoph, 1683-1760
Graupner, Johann Christoph

ₜConcerto, oboe & strings, G major; arr. trumpet & stringsₙ
Concerto in G major for Trumpet and Strings
[1]Vivace e ostenuto / [2]Andante / [3]Vivace e un poco allegro
André, Maurice, 137)

ₜConcerto, trumpet, strings & continuo, No. 1, D majorₙ
Konzert Nr. 1 D-dur für Trompete und Orchester
(Concerto No. 1 in D major for Trumpet, Strings and Continuo)
[1]Vivace / [2]Andante / [3]Allegro
Scherbaum, Adolf, 19), 25)
Smithers, Don, 11)

Green, George, 1930-
Green, George Clarence

[Triptych, trumpet]
Triptych for Trumpet Alone
[1]Preludio: Allegro marziale / [2]Aria: Tranquillo, ma con moto /
[3]Toccata: Allegro
Stith, Marice, 3)

Green, Johnny, 1908-
Green, John Waldo

[Body and Soul, (1930); arr. trumpet & orchestra]
Body and Soul
Méndez, Rafael, 21)

[Sing Me to Sleep; arr. trumpet & instrumental ensemble]
Sing Me to Sleep
Smith, Bramwell "Bram"

Greene, Maurice, 1696-1755

[Voluntary, keyboard, D major; arr. trumpet & organ]
Voluntary in D major
From *Ten Voluntarys for the Organ or Harpsichord Composed by
Dr. Green, Skinner, Stubely, James, Reading, Selby & Kuknan,*
(1767).
Carroll, Edward, 6)
Rippas, Claude
Tarr, Edward, 39)

Grieg, Edvard Hagerup, 1843-1907

[Lyrisches Stücke, piano, op. 43, (1886). No. 5: Liebeslied; arr. trumpet & harp]
Liebeslied aus *Lyrische Stücke*, op. 43
(Erotique de *Pièces Lyriques pour piano*, op. 43)
(Lyric Pieces for Piano, Book 3, op. 43)
André, Maurice, 84)

[Norwegian Folk Melodies, op. 66, (1896). Norwegian Folk Song; arr. trumpet &
piano]
Norwegian Folk Song
(Norske folkeviser)
Yeryomin, Sergei Nikolaivich

[Peer Gynt, (1874). Suite No. 2, op. 55, (rev. 1891): Solveig's Song; arr. trumpet
& brass ensemble]
Solvejgs Lied from *Peer Gynt*, Suite No. 2, op. 55
Mertens, Theo, 3)

[Peer Gynt, (1874). Suite No. 2, op. 55, (rev. 1891): Solveig's Song; arr. trumpet
& organ]
Solvejgs Lied from *Peer Gynt*, Suite No. 2, op. 55
Grin, Freddy, 8)

Groh, Johann, 1575?-1627
Ghro?, Johann

[Padoune und Galliard..., (1604). No. 1: Paduana; arr. trumpet & brass ensemble]
Paduana No. 1
Güttler, Ludwig, 9)

Gros, Sigismund, 18th cent.

[Concerto, trumpet & strings, D major]
Concerto in D major for Trumpet and Strings
Basch, Wolfgang, 6)

Gross, Walter, 1909-1967

[Tenderly; arr. trumpet & orchestra]
Tenderly
André, Maurice, 170)

[Tenderly; arr. trumpet & rhythm section]
Tenderly
Lieberman, Harold J.

Grossi, Andrea, 17th cent.

[Sonatas, op. 3, (1682). No. 10: trumpet, strings & continuo, D major]
Sonata a cinque in D major, op. 3, no. 10
[1]Vivace / [2]Adagio / [3]Grave / [4]Presto
Friedrich, Reinhold
Güttler, Ludwig, 3), 15), 19), 25)
Smithers, Don, 1)

[Sonatas, op. 3, (1682). No. 11: trumpet, strings & continuo, D major]
Sonata a cinque in D major, op. 3, no. 11
[1]Vivace / [2]Adagio / [3]Grave / [4]Allegro spiritoso
Güttler, Ludwig, 14), 21[2])
Smithers, Don, 4)

[Sonatas, op. 3, (1682). No. 12: trumpet, strings & continuo, D major]
Sonata a cinque in D major, op. 3, no. 12
[1]Grave / [2]Allegro / [3]Adagio / [4]Prestissimo / [5]Adagio / [6]Prestissimo
Smithers, Don, 5)

Grossi da Viadana, Lodovico
See: Viadana, Lodovico

Gruber, Franz Xaver, 1787-1863

ɾStille Nacht, (1818); arr. trumpet & organ˥
Stille Nacht, heilige Nacht
(Silent Night)

Grin, Freddy, 5)

ɾStille Nacht, (1818); arr. trumpet, children's voices & orchestra˥
Stille Nacht, heilige Nacht
(Silent Night)

André, Maurice, 166)

Grundman, Clare Ewing, 1913-

ɾConversation, cornet & piano, (1960)˥
Conversation for Cornet
Burkart, Richard
Haynie, John, 1)

Grusin, Dave, 1934-

ɾNew Hampshire Hornpipe; arr. trumpet & orchestra˥
New Hampshire Hornpipe
Schultz, Erik, 8)

ɾOn Golden Pond. Theme, "On Golden Pond"; arr. trumpet & orchestra˥
On Golden Pond from *On Golden Pond*
Schultz, Erik, 8)

ɾTootsie. Theme, "It Might Be You"; arr. trumpet & orchestra˥
It Might Be You from *Tootsie*
Schultz, Erik, 8)

Guerrero, Francisco, 1528-1599

ɾReyes siguen la estrella, mixed voices & instrumental ensemble˥
Los reyes siguen la estrella
Cook, Richard

ɾVirgen santa, el Rey del cielo, mixed voices & instrumental ensemble˥
Virgen santa, el Rey del cielo
Cook, Richard

Guilain, Jean Adam Guillaume, *fl.* 1720

ɾSuite. Plein jeu; arr. trumpet & organ˥
Suite im 1. Ton
Hartog, Thomas

Gullidge, Arthur, 20th cent.

ɾJubilate, trumpet & band˥
Jubilate
Reinhart, Carole Dawn, 10)

Gumbert, Ferdinand, 1818-1896

₍Cheerfulness, soprano, mezzo-soprano & piano, (*ca.* 1860); arr. cornet, trombone & piano₎
Cheerfulness
(Frohsinn)
Schwarz, Gerard, 21)

Guy, Nicholas, *d.* 1629

₍Almande No. 13; arr. 2 trumpets & 4 trombones₎
Almande No. 13
André, Maurice, 176)

Guy Ropartz, Joseph, 1864-1955
Ropartz, (Joseph) Guy (Marie)

₍Andante et Allegro, trumpet (or cornet) & piano₎
Andante et Allegro
Burke, James, 7)
Haynie, John, 1)
House, Lawrence
Schwarz, Gerard, 15)
Stevens, Thomas, 6)

Gwinner, Volker, 1912-

₍Variations (theme by Grieg), trumpet, organ & timpani₎
Variations on a theme by Grieg
Pohle, Wolfgang

Hackbarth, Glenn, 1949-

₍Double Concerto, trumpet, tuba & chamber ensemble, (1975)₎
Double Concerto for Trumpet and Tuba
Hickman, David, 5)

Hagerup Bull, Edvard, 1922-

₍Concerto, trumpet & orchestra, No. 1, (1950)₎
Concerto No. 1 for Trumpet and Orchestra
[1]Allegro moderato / [2]Adagietto / [3]Allegro molto moderato
Kvebaek, Harry

Haines, Edmund, 1914-1974

₍Concertino, flute, clarinet, horn, trumpet, violin, viola, cello & orchestra, (1959)₎
Concertino for Seven Solo Instruments and Orchestra
[1]Molto moderato - poco andante / [2]Allegro con fuoco - più andante / [3]Intermezzo: Andante espressivo / [4]Rondo: Vivace
Hood, Donald

Hamal, Henri, 1744-1820

ₜConcerto, oboe & strings, C major; arr. trumpet & strings, D majorₜ
Concerto in D major for Trumpet and Strings
¹Allegro / ²Largo / ³Allegro
André, Maurice, 35), 127)

Hamel, G., 20th cent.

ₜPerles de cristal; arr. cornet & brass ensembleₜ
Perles de cristal
(Pearls of Crystal)
Aquitaine Brass Ensemble

ₜPerles de cristal; arr. flügelhorn & accordion bandₜ
Perles de cristal
(Pearls of Crystal)
André, Maurice, 61)

Hamilton, Iain, 1922-
Hamilton, Iain Ellis

ₜScenes (5), trumpet & piano, (1966)ₜ
Five Scenes for Trumpet and Piano
¹Wild / ²Nocturnal / ³Declamato / ⁴Nocturnal / ⁵Brilliant
Stevens, Thomas, 1)
Wallace, John, 6)

Hammerschmidt, Andreas, *ca.* 1611-1675

ₜSonata super "Gelobet seist du Jesu Christ", alto, 2 trumpets, 4 trombones & continuoₜ
Sonata super "Gelobet seist du Jesu Christ"
Jones, Philip, 9)

ₜSonata super "Nun lob mein Seel den Herren", soprano, 2 trumpets, 4 trombones & continuoₜ
Sonata super "Nun lob mein Seel den Herren"
Jones, Philip, 9)

Handel, George Frideric, 1685-1759
Händel, Georg Friedrich
Hændel, George Frédéric

ₜAlcina, (1735), B. 102. Aria, "Verdi prati"; arr. trumpet & organₜ
Aria, "Verdi prati" from *Alcina*, B. 102
<In Chrysander's "Händel-Gesellschaft" edition, Vol. 86>
Chesnut, Walter

ₜAmadigi, (1715), B. 48. Excerpts: soprano, mezzo-soprano, oboe, trumpet & orchestraᵧ

Excerpts from *Amadigi*, B. 48
<In Chrysander's "Händel-Gesellschaft" edition, Vol. 62>
Tarr, Edward, 27)

ₜAnthem for the Foundling Hospital, mixed voices & orchestra, (1749), B. 146ᵧ

Anthem for the Foundling Hospital, B. 146
("Blessed are they that consider the poor")
<In Chrysander's "Händel-Gesellschaft" edition, Vol. 36>
Laird, Michael, 19)

ₜAria and Bourrée; arr. cornet & pianoᵧ

Aria and Bourrée
This Bernard Fitzgerald transcription includes: Aria, "In Jehovah's awful Sight" from *Deborah*, B. 94, and Bourrée from *Sonata in G major for Flute*, op. 1, no. 5, B. 67
Tolley, Richard

ₜAria and Bourrée; arr. trumpet & pianoᵧ

Aria and Bourrée
This Bernard Fitzgerald transcription includes: Aria, "In Jehovah's awful Sight" from *Deborah*, B. 94, and Bourrée from *Sonata in G major for Flute*, op. 1, no. 5, B. 67
Amstutz, Keith
Ritter, David

ₜAria en Bourrée; arr. trumpet & organᵧ

Aria en Bourrée
The source of this transcription has not been determined. (It could be the "Air" and "Bourrée" from the *Water Music*, "Suite in F major" or it could be Bernard Fitzgerald's transcription, "Aria and Bourrée".)
Grin, Freddy, 1)

ₜAtalanta, (1736), B. 107. Sinfonia, orchestra; arr. trumpet & organᵧ

Trumpet Overture from *Atalanta*, B. 107
<In Chrysander's "Händel-Gesellschaft" edition, Vol. 87>
Carroll, Edward, 12)

ₜBelshazzar, (1744), B. 137. Martial Symphony; arr. trumpet ensemble, organ, timpani & percussionᵧ

Martial Symphony from *Belshazzar*, B. 137
<In Chrysander's "Händel-Gesellschaft" edition, Vol. 19>
Carroll, Edward, 12)

ₜConcerti grossi (6), op. 3, (c. 1716-20), B. 53. No. 4, 2 oboes, strings & continuo, F major: Ouverture; arr. 2 trumpets & organᵧ

Ouverture from *Concerto Grosso*, op. 3, no. 4, B. 53/(4)
<In Chrysander's "Händel-Gesellschaft" edition, Vol. 21>
Loustalot, Alain

[Concertino; arr. trumpet & organ, F major]
Concertino in F major for Trumpet and Organ
Source of this transcription has not been determined.
Bouche

[Concerto; arr. trumpet & organ, B^b major]
Concerto in B^b major for Trumpet and Organ
from *Select Harmony* (?)
The exact source of this transcription has not been determined.
Could it be from *10 Select Voluntaries for the Organ or Harpsichord... by Mr Handel, Dr Green, etc.*, (London, c1780)?
Carroll, Edward, 12)

[Concerto, 2 horns, 2 oboes, strings & continuo, F major, (c. 1740-50), B. 164. Excerpts; arr. trumpet & organ]
Concerto in F major for Trumpet and Organ
[1]Ouverture / [2]Allegro / [3]Allegro ma non troppo
<In Chrysander's "Händel-Gesellschaft" edition, Vol. 47 & 48>
This transcription omits the last four of seven movements.
Schultz, Erik, 10)

[Concerto, 2 oboes, bassoon, 4 horns, 2 trumpets, drums, strings & continuo, D major, (c. 1748), B. 144]
Concerto in D major for 2 Trumpets and Orchestra
[1]Largo - Allegro [B. 144/(B)] / [2]Allegro [from B. 144/(A)]
<In Chrysander's "Händel-Gesellschaft" edition, Vol. 47>
Delmotte, Roger, 50)

[Concerto, 2 oboes, bassoon, 4 horns, 2 trumpets, drums, strings & continuo, D major, (c. 1748), B. 144/(B)]
Concerto in D major for 2 Oboes, Bassoon, 4 Horns, 2 Trumpets, Drums, Strings and Continuo
Largo - Allegro
<In Chrysander's "Händel-Gesellschaft" edition, Vol. 47>
Wilbraham, John, 26)

[Concertos (3), (c. 1705), B. 5. No. 1, oboe, strings & continuo, B^b major; arr. trumpet & organ]
Concerto B-dur
(Concerto in B^b major for Trumpet and Organ)
[1]Adagio / [2]Allegro / [3]Largo (Siciliana) / [4]Vivace
Smithers, Don, 7), 9)

[Concertos (3), (c. 1705), B. 5. No. 1, oboe, strings & continuo, B^b major; arr. trumpet, strings & continuo]
Concerto No. 1 in B^b major for Trumpet, Strings and Continuo
[1]Adagio / [2]Allegro / [3]Largo (Siciliana) / [4]Vivace
<In Chrysander's "Händel-Gesellschaft" edition, Vol. 21>
Some sources equate this concerto with Orchestral Concerto (or Concerto Grosso) No. 8.
André, Maurice, 18), 23), 31), 33), 63), 68)
Bernard, André, 5)
Potpourri, 15)

⌐Concertos (3), (c. 1705), B. 5. No. 2, oboe, strings & continuo, B♭ major; arr.
trumpet & organ⌐

Concerto en Si bémol
(Concerto in B♭ major for Trumpet and Organ)
[1]Vivace / [2]Allegro / [3]Andante / [4]Allegro
Gaudon, Jean-Jacques

⌐Concertos (3), (c. 1705), B. 5. No. 2, oboe, strings & continuo, B♭ major; arr.
trumpet, strings & continuo⌐

Concerto No. 2 in B♭ major for Trumpet, Strings and Continuo
[1]Vivace / [2]Allegro (Fuga) / [3]Andante / [4]Allegro
<In Chrysander's "Händel-Gesellschaft" edition, Vol. 21>
Some sources equate this concerto with Orchestral Concerto (or
Concerto Grosso) No. 9.
>
André, Maurice, 18), 23), 24), 26), 27), 28),
29), 33), 160)
Bernard, André, 5)
Potpourri, 15)

⌐Concertos (3), (c. 1705), B. 5. No. 3, oboe, strings & continuo, g minor; arr.
trumpet & organ⌐

Concerto in g minor
[1]Grave / [2]Allegro / [3]Largo (Sarabande) / [4]Allegro
>**André, Maurice**, 70)
Mertens, Theo, 4)

⌐Concertos (3), (c. 1705), B. 5. No. 3, oboe, strings & continuo, g minor; arr.
trumpet & piano, d minor⌐

Concerto for Trumpet with Piano Accompaniment
[1]Grave / [2]Allegro / [3]Largo (Sarabande) / [4]Allegro
>**Amstutz, Keith**
Burkart, Richard

⌐Concertos (3), (c. 1705), B. 5. No. 3, oboe, strings & continuo, g minor; arr.
trumpet, strings & continuo⌐

Concerto No. 3 in g minor for Trumpet, Strings and Continuo
[1]Grave / [2]Allegro / [3]Largo (Sarabande) / [4]Allegro
<In Chrysander's "Händel-Gesellschaft" edition, Vol. 21>
Some sources equate this concerto with Orchestral Concerto (or
Concerto Grosso) No. 10.
>**André, Maurice**, 18), 23), 28), 31), 73), 154),
169)
Bernard, André, 5)
Potpourri, 15)

⌐Coronation Anthems, mixed voices & orchestra, (1727), B. 78⌐

Coronation Anthems for George II, B. 78
<In Chrysander's "Händel-Gesellschaft" edition, Vol. 14>
>**Rudolf, Richard**

ₜDettingen Anthem, mixed voices & orchestra, D major, (1743), B. 133ₜ
Dettingen Anthem, B. 133
(Dettinger Anthem, "The King shall rejoice")
<In Chrysander's "Händel-Gesellschaft" edition, Vol. 36>
Laird, Michael, 10)

ₜDettingen Te Deum, soli, mixed voices & orchestra, D major, (1743), B. 134ₜ
Dettingen Te Deum, B. 134
(Dettinger Te Deum)
<In Chrysander's "Händel-Gesellschaft" edition, Vol. 25>
Orchestra includes oboes, trumpets, timpani & strings.
Basch, Wolfgang, 4)
Laird, Michael, 10)
Schneidewind, Helmut, 3)
Soustrot, Bernard, 2)

ₜFanfares and Voluntaries; arr. 2 trumpets, timpani, organ & bassoonₜ
Fanfares and Voluntaries
a) Fanfare in C major / b) Fanfare in D major from *Il Muzio Scevola* / c) Two Fanfares in D major from *Water Music* / d) Fanfare in D major from *Concerto for Horns, Strings and 2 Claviers* / e) Fanfare in C major from *Saul* / f) Voluntary in C major / g) Voluntary in D major
The source of the first fanfare has not been determined. The source of the "Voluntary in C major" is probably *Twelve Voluntaries and Fugues...*, B. ?25. And the the final voluntary is actually the second part of John Stanley's *Voluntary*, op. 6, no. 5.
Carroll, Edward, 6)

ₜFireworks Music, wind ensemble, D major, (1749), B. 145ₜ
Fireworks Music, B. 145
¹Ouverture (Adagio) / ²Allegro / ³Lentement / ⁴Bourrée / ⁵La Paix (Largo alla Siciliana) / ⁶La Réjouissance (Allegro) / ⁷Menuet I & II
<In Chrysander's "Händel-Gesellschaft" edition, Vol. 47>
Originally intended for 24 oboes, 12 bassoons, contrabassoon, 9 horns, 9 trumpets, side-drums & 3 pairs of timpani. (These recorded versions use the appropriate wind instruments, but with less doubling of parts.)
André, Maurice, 92)
Tarr, Edward, 33)

ₜFireworks Music, wind ensemble, D major, (1749), B. 145; arr. orchestraₜ
Fireworks Music, B. 145
¹Ouverture (Adagio) / ²Allegro / ³Lentement / ⁴Bourrée / ⁵La Paix (Largo alla Siciliana) / ⁶La Réjouissance (Allegro) / ⁷Menuet I & II
Quinque, Rolf, 1)
Tarr, Edward, 42)
Wilbraham, John, 26)

[Fireworks Music, wind ensemble, D major, (1749), B. 145; arr. trumpet, wind ensemble, organ & timpani]
Feux d'Artifice (version intégrale)
(Fireworks Music, B. 145)
[1]Ouverture (Lentement - Allegro - Lentement) / [2]Bourrée / [3]La Paix (Largo alla Siciliana) / [4]La Réjouissance (Allegro) / [5]Menuet I & II
André, Maurice, 189)

[Fireworks Music, wind ensemble, D major, (1749), B. 145: Excerpts; arr. trumpet ensemble, organ & timpani]
Music for Royal Fireworks
Carroll, Edward, 12)

[Fireworks Music, wind ensemble, D major, (1749), B. 145: Excerpts; arr. 2 trumpets & piano, A♭ major]
Two Pieces from *Music for the Royal Fireworks*, B. 145
I) La Paix / II) La Réjouissance
Nagel, Robert, 11)

[Fireworks Music, wind ensemble, D major, (1749), B. 145: La Réjouissance; arr. 2 trumpets & organ]
La Réjouissance from *Fireworks Music*, B. 145
André, Maurice, 39)
Waltzing, Gast

[Fireworks Music, wind ensemble, D major, (1749), B. 145: La Réjouissance; arr. 3 trumpets, organ & timpani]
La Réjouissance from *Fireworks Music*, B. 145
Giangiulio, Richard

[Fireworks Music, wind ensemble, D major, (1749), B. 145: Overture; arr. 2 trumpets, organ & timpani]
Concerto Royale
(Overture from *Fireworks Music*, B. 145)
Gabel, Bernard, 2)

[Floridante, (1721), B. 65. Marches (2); arr. trumpet ensemble, organ, timpani & percussion]
Two Marches from *Floridante*, B. 65
<In Chrysander's "Händel-Gesellschaft" edition, Vol. 65>
Carroll, Edward, 12)

[Gloria in excelsis Deo; arr. trumpet & organ]
Gloria in excelsis Deo
(Angels We Have Heard on High)
Attributed to Handel on various recordings and in various catalogues, this tune is a traditional anonymous French carol, "Gloria", with a trumpet obbligato presumably added by arranger Jean-Michel Defaye.
André, Maurice, 38), 40), 52), 67), 205), 206), 207)
Blair, Stacy

[Hercules (musical drama), (1744), B. 136. March, D major; arr. trumpet ensemble, organ, timpani & percussion]
March in D major from *Hercules*, B. 136
<In Chrysander's "Händel-Gesellschaft" edition, Vol. 4>
Carroll, Edward, 12)

[Hercules, (1744), B. 136. March, D major; arr. trumpet & organ]
March from *Hercules*, B. 136
<In Chrysander's "Händel-Gesellschaft" edition, Vol. 4>
Braz, Dirceu, 4)

[Italian Duets (2), 2 voices & continuo, (1708), B. 29; arr. trumpet & harp]
Duos I & II
<In Chrysander's "Händel-Gesellschaft" edition, Vol. 32>
The exact duets have not been determined, here, and may be from either of two other sets of Italian Duets: *13 Italian Duets*, B. 36, or *7 Italian Duets*, B. 129.
André, Maurice, 84)

[Joshua, (1747), B. 141. March; arr. trumpet & brass ensemble]
March II from *Joshua*, B. 141
<In Chrysander's "Händel-Gesellschaft" edition, Vol. 17>
Güttler, Ludwig, 9)

[Judas Maccabaeus, (1746), B. 139. Aria, "Sound an Alarm"; arr. trumpet & strings]
Aria, "Sound an Alarm" from *Judas Maccabaeus*, B. 139
<In Chrysander's "Händel-Gesellschaft" edition, Vol. 22>
Carroll, Edward, 4)

[Judas Maccabaeus, (1746), B. 139. Aria, "Tochter Zion, freue dich"; arr. trumpet & organ]
Aria, "Tochter Zion, freue dich" from *Judas Maccabaeus*, B. 139
<In Chrysander's "Händel-Gesellschaft" edition, Vol. 22>
Grin, Freddy, 8)

[Judas Maccabaeus, (1746), B. 139. Chorus, "See, the conqu'ring hero comes"; arr. 3 trumpets, organ & timpani]
Chorus, "See, the conqu'ring hero comes" from *Judas Maccabaeus*, B. 139
(Chorus, "Seht den Sieger ruhmgekrönt")
<In Chrysander's "Händel-Gesellschaft" edition, Vol. 22>
Läubin, Hannes, 2)

[Judas Maccabaeus, (1746), B. 139. Excerpts; arr. trumpet ensemble, organ, timpani & percussion]
Chorus and March from *Judas Maccabaeus*, B. 139
(Chorus, "See, the conqu'ring hero comes")
<In Chrysander's "Händel-Gesellschaft" edition, Vol. 22>
Carroll, Edward, 12)

[Judas Maccabaeus, (1746), B. 139. March; arr. trumpet & brass ensemble]
March II from *Judas Maccabaeus*, B. 139
<In Chrysander's "Händel-Gesellschaft" edition, Vol. 22>
Güttler, Ludwig, 9)

[L'Allegro, (1740), B. 124. Aria, "Or Let the Merry Bells Ring Round"; arr.
trumpet & orchestra]
Aria, "Or Let the Merry Bells Ring Round"
(from *l'Allegro, il Pensieroso ed il Moderato*, B. 124)
Carroll, Edward, 4)

[March; arr. trumpet & piano]
March
The source of this transcription has not been determined.
Schwarz, Gerard, 14)

[Messiah, (1741), B. 130]
Messiah, B. 130
<In Chrysander's "Händel-Gesellschaft" edition, Vol. 45>
Anderson, George
André, Maurice, 19)
Bravington, Eric
Dean, Allan, 10)
Goetting, Chandler
Herseth, Adolph, 2)
Johnson, Gilbert, 5)
Jones, Philip, 1)
Laird, Michael, 7)
Lang, William
Mason, David, 1)
Smith, James
Steele-Perkins, Crispian, 8), 12), 18)
Stringer, Alan, 5)
Unidentified, Trumpet(s), 18)
Vacchiano, William, 7)
Webb, Gordon, 3)
Weeks, Larry
Wilbraham, John, 2), 23)
Wobisch, Helmut, 15)

[Messiah, (1741), B. 130. Aria, "Rejoice greatly, O Daughter of Zion"; arr.
trumpet & orchestra]
Rejoice
(Aria, "Rejoice greatly, O Daughter of Zion" from *Messiah*, B. 130)
Cowell, Johnny

[Messiah, (1741), B. 130. Aria, "The Trumpet Shall Sound"; arr. trumpet & piano,
C major]
Aria, "The Trumpet Shall Sound" from *Messiah*, B. 130
In this abridged transcription, the bass voice part is incorporated
in the keyboard part.
Nagel, Robert, 10)

[Messiah, (1741), B. 130. Aria, "The Trumpet Shall Sound", bass, trumpet, oboes, strings & continuo]
Aria, "The Trumpet Shall Sound" from *Messiah*, B. 130
Reinhart, Carole Dawn, 2)

[Messiah, (1741), B. 130. Arias (2); arr. trumpet & organ]
Two Arias from *Messiah*, B. 130
a) He shall feed His flock [Version II] / b) Rejoice greatly, O daughter of Zion [Version I]
The organ plays the opening alto voice solo of "He shall feed His flock", and the trumpet enters at the soprano solo where the text is "Come unto Him, all ye that labour".
Schultz, Erik, 2)

[Messiah, (1741), B. 130. Arias; arr. trumpet & organ]
Arias from *Messiah*, B. 130
a) How beautiful are the feet of them that preach the gospel of peace [Version II] / b) Rejoice greatly, O daughter of Zion [Version II]
Schultz, Erik, 3)

[Messiah, (1741), B. 130. Chorus, "Hallelujah"; arr. trumpet, brass ensemble, organ & timpani]
Alleluia, extrait du *Messie*
(Hallelujah Chorus from *Messiah*, B. 130)
André, Maurice, 189), 198)
Potpourri, 43)

[Occasional (1746), B. 138. March; arr. trumpet & organ]
March from *Occasional Oratorio*, B. 138
<In Chrysander's "Händel-Gesellschaft" edition, Vol. 43>
Laughton, Stuart

[Ode for St. Cecilia's Day, (1739), B. 122. March, orchestra; arr. brass ensemble, organ & percussion]
A Trumpet Voluntary
(March from *Ode for St. Cecilia's Day*, B. 122)
<In Chrysander's "Händel-Gesellschaft" edition, Vol. 23>
Ghitalla, Armando, 5)

[Ode for St. Cecilia's Day, soprano, tenor, mixed voices, trumpet & strings, (1739), B. 122]
Ode for St. Cecilia's Day, B. 122
<In Chrysander's "Händel-Gesellschaft" edition, Vol. 23>
Mackintosh, Jack

[Ode for the Birthday of Queen Anne, (1713), B. 42. Aria, "Eternal Source of Light Divine"; arr. soprano, trumpet & organ]
Aria, "Eternal Source of Light Divine" from *Ode for the Birthday of Queen Anne*, B. 42
Laughton, Stuart

[Ode for the Birthday of Queen Anne, (1713), B. 42. Aria, "Eternal Source of Light Divine", soprano, trumpet, strings & continuo]
Aria, "Eternal Source of Light Divine" from *Ode for the Birthday of Queen Anne*, B. 42
<In Chrysander's "Händel-Gesellschaft" edition, Vol. 46a>
        Marsalis, Wynton, 2)
        Schwarz, Gerard, 4)

[Ode for the Birthday of Queen Anne, (1713), B. 42. Aria, "O jauchzet Gott"; arr. soprano, trumpet & organ]
Aria, "O jauchzet Gott" from *Ode for the Birthday of Queen Anne*
<In Chrysander's "Händel-Gesellschaft" edition, Vol. 46a>
        Schetsche, Walter

[Ode for the Birthday of Queen Anne, soli, mixed voices & orchestra, (1713), B. 42]
Ode for the Birthday of Queen Anne, B. 42
("Eternal Source of Light Divine")
<In Chrysander's "Händel-Gesellschaft" edition, Vol. 46a>
        Laird, Michael, 19)
        Rudolf, Richard

[Rinaldo, (1711), B. 37. Marcia; arr. trumpet & organ]
Marcia from *Rinaldo*, B. 37
<In Chrysander's "Händel-Gesellschaft" edition, Vol. 58>
        Laughton, Stuart

[Rinaldo, (1711), B. 37. Marcia; arr. trumpet ensemble, organ, timpani & percussion]
Grand March from *Rinaldo*, B. 37
<In Chrysander's "Händel-Gesellschaft" edition, Vol. 58>
        Carroll, Edward, 12)

[Samson, (1741-42), B. 131. Aria, "Let the Bright Seraphim"; arr. trumpet & organ]
Aria, "Let the Bright Seraphim" from *Samson*, B. 131
        Braz, Dirceu, 4)

[Samson, (1741-42), B. 131. Aria, "Let the Bright Seraphim"; arr. 2 trumpets & strings]
Aria, "Let the Bright Seraphim" from *Samson*, B. 131
        Carroll, Edward, 4)

[Samson, (1741-42), B. 131. Aria, "Let the Bright Seraphim", soprano, trumpet, strings & continuo]
Aria, "Let the Bright Seraphim" from *Samson*, B. 131
<In Chrysander's "Händel-Gesellschaft" edition, Vol. 10>
        Marsalis, Wynton, 2)
        Schwarz, Gerard, 4)
        Steele-Perkins, Crispian, 17)

[Samson, (1741-42), B. 131. Chorus, "Awake the trumpet's lofty sound"; arr. brass ensemble, organ, timpani & percussion]
Chorus, "Awake the Trumpet's Lofty Sound" from *Samson*, B. 131
Ghitalla, Armando, 5)

[Samson, (1741-42), B. 131. Chorus, "Awake the trumpet's lofty sound"; arr. 3 trumpets, organ & timpani]
Chorus, "Awake the trumpet's lofty sound" from *Samson*, B. 131
(Chor, "Erwacht der Trompeten stolzer Klang")
Läubin, Hannes, 2)

[Samson, (1741-42), B. 131. Chorus, "Let Their Celestial Concerts", mixed voices, oboe, trumpet & strings]
Chorus, "Let Their Celestial Concerts" from *Samson*, B. 131
Steele-Perkins, Crispian, 17)

[Saul, (1738), B. 116. Suite, orchestra]
Orchestral Suite from *Saul*, B. 116
(Saul Instrumentalsätze)
Sinfonia [I]: [no tempo marking] - Larghetto - Allegro - Andante larghetto / Sinfonia [II]: Andante allegro / Sinfonia [III]: Largo - Allegro / Sinfonia [IV]: Allegro / Dead March: Grave
<In Chrysander's "Händel-Gesellschaft" edition, Vol. 13>
Schneidewind, Helmut, 2)

[Serse (Xerxes), (1737-38), B. 115. Aria, "Ombra mai fù"; arr. trumpet & instrumental accompaniment]
Largo
(Aria, "Ombra mai fù" from *Xerxes*, B. 115)
Scherbaum, Adolf, 34)

[Serse (Xerxes), (1737-38), B. 115. Aria, "Ombra mai fù"; arr. trumpet & organ]
Largo
(Aria, "Ombra mai fù", from *Serse*, B. 115)
<In Chrysander's "Händel-Gesellschaft" edition, Vol. 92>
André, Maurice, 40), 42), 44), 52), 67), 206), 207), 227)
Blair, Stacy
Mertens, Theo, 4)

[Serse (Xerxes), (1737-38), B. 115. Aria, "Ombra mai fù"; arr. trumpet & strings]
Largo
(Aria, "Ombra mai fù", from *Serse*, B. 115)
<In Chrysander's "Händel-Gesellschaft" edition, Vol. 92>
Carroll, Edward, 4)

[Sinfonie diverse (8), B. 169. No. 7: March, trumpet, 4 oboes & bassoon, D major]
March für Trompete, 4 Oboen und Fagott
(No. 7 from *8 Sinfonie diverse*, B. 169)
<In Chrysander's "Händel-Gesellschaft" edition, Vol. 48>

₍Solomon, (1748), B. 142. Sinfonia, "Arrival of the Queen of Sheba"; arr. trumpet & orchestra₎
Arrival of the Queen of Sheba
(Sinfonia from *Solomon*, B. 142)
<In Chrysander's "Händel-Gesellschaft" edition, Vol. 26>
Wilbraham, John, 24)

₍Sonata, c minor; arr. trumpet & organ₎
Sonata in c minor for Trumpet and Organ
The exact source of this sonata has not been determined. It is likely op. 1, no. 8, for oboe.
Deside

₍Sonata, F major; arr. trumpet & organ₎
Sonata in F major for Trumpet and Organ
The exact source of this sonata has not been determined. It is likely op. 1, no. 12, for violin.
Capouillez, Luc

₍Sonata, viola da gamba & harpsichord, C major, (c. 1705), B. 7; arr. trumpet & organ₎
Sonata in C major for Trumpet and Organ
¹Adagio / ²Allegro
<In Chrysander's "Händel-Gesellschaft" edition, Vol. 48>
Scherbaum, Adolf, 29)

₍Sonata, 2 violins & continuo; arr. 2 trumpets & organ₎
Sonata for 2 Trumpets and Organ
Adagio / Allegro
The exact source of this trio sonata has not been determined. It is likely the third and fourth movements of Sonata No. 6 from *Sonates à deux Violons, deux hautbois ou deux Flûtes traversière et Basse Continue*, op. 2, (c. 1722).
Schultz, Erik, 9)

₍Sonatas ("Fitzwilliam"), B. 156. No. 3, recorder & continuo, d minor; arr. trumpet & orchestra₎
Concerto in d minor for Trumpet and Orchestra
¹Largo / ²Vivace / ³Furioso / ⁴Adagio / ⁵Alla breve
Although the *"Fitzwilliam" Sonatas for Treble Recorder and Cembalo* are not included in Chrysander's "Händel-Gesellschaft" edition, this *Sonata No. 3* appears in Vol. 27 as *Sonata in b minor for Flute and Continuo*, op. 1, no. 9, with two additional movements.
André, Maurice, 51), 67), 83), 126), 169), 216), 217)

₍Sonatas (15), op. 1, (c. 1722), B. 67. No. 3, violin & continuo, A major; arr. trumpet & organ₎
Sonata in A major for Trumpet and Organ
[1]Andante / [2]Allegro / [3]Adagio / [4]Allegro
<In Chrysander's "Händel-Gesellschaft" edition, Vol. 27>
The "adagio" of this transcription is actually the third movement from the *Sonata in g minor for Violin and Continuo*, op. 1, no. 10, arranged in f♯ minor.
André, Maurice, 76), 139)

₍Sonatas (15), op. 1, (c. 1722), B. 67. No. 3, violin & continuo, A major; arr. trumpet, organ, bass & drums₎
Sonata in A major
[1]Andante / [2]Allegro / [3]Adagio / [4]Allegro
Molénat, Claude

₍Sonatas (15), op. 1, (c. 1722), B. 67. No. 6, oboe & continuo, g minor; arr. trumpet & organ₎
Sonata in g minor for Trumpet and Organ
[1]Larghetto / [2]Allegro / [3]Adagio / [4]Allegro
<In Chrysander's "Händel-Gesellschaft" edition, Vol. 27>
André, Maurice, 45), 65)

₍Sonatas (15), op. 1, (c. 1722), B. 67. No. 8, oboe & continuo, c minor; arr. trumpet & organ₎
Sonata in c minor for Trumpet and Organ
[1][no tempo marking] / [2]Allegro / [3]Adagio / [4]Allegro
<In Chrysander's "Händel-Gesellschaft" edition, Vol. 27>
André, Maurice, 65)

₍Sonatas (15), op. 1, (c. 1722), B. 67. No. 8, oboe & continuo, c minor; arr. trumpet, harpsichord & bassoon₎
Sonata in c minor for Trumpet, Harpsichord and Bassoon
[1][no tempo marking] / [2]Allegro / [3]Adagio / [4]Allegro
<In Chrysander's "Händel-Gesellschaft" edition, Vol. 27>
André, Maurice, 197), 203)
Potpourri, 42)

₍Sonatas (15), op. 1, (c. 1722), B. 67. No. 10, violin & continuo, g minor; arr. trumpet & organ, f♯ minor₎
Sonata in f♯ minor for Trumpet and Organ
[1]Andante / [2]Allegro / [3]Adagio / [4][Allegro]
<In Chrysander's "Händel-Gesellschaft" edition, Vol. 27>
Tschotschev, Nicolai-Dimitrov

ₜSonatas (15), op. 1, (c. 1722), B. 67. No. 11, flute & continuo, F major; arr.
trumpet, strings & continuoₚ
Concerto in F major for Trumpet, Strings and Continuo
[1]Larghetto / [2]Allegro / [3]Siciliana / [4]Allegro
<In Chrysander's "Händel-Gesellschaft" edition, Vol. 27>
This "concerto" was originally a "sonata" for flute (op. 1, no. 11)
that was transcribed by Handel as a concerto for organ and
strings (op. 4, no. 5). The *Organ Concerto* may be found in
Chrysander's "Händel-Gesellschaft" edition, Vol. 28.
Sauter, Hermann, 25)

ₜSonatas (15), op. 1, (c. 1722), B. 67. No. 12, violin & continuo, F major; arr.
trumpet & organₚ
Sonata in F major for Trumpet and Organ
[1]Adagio / [2]Allegro / [3]Largo / [4]Allegro
<In Chrysander's "Händel-Gesellschaft" edition, Vol. 27>
André, Maurice, 76), 139), 156)
Groth, Konradin

ₜSonatas (15), op. 1, (c. 1722), B. 67. No. 12, violin & continuo, F major; arr.
trumpet & stringsₚ
Sonata in F major for Trumpet and Strings
[1]Adagio / [2]Allegro / [3]Largo / [4]Allegro
<In Chrysander's "Händel-Gesellschaft" edition, Vol. 27>
André, Maurice, 62), 227)

ₜSonatas (15), op. 1, (c. 1722), B. 67. No. 13, violin & continuo, D major:
Larghetto; arr. trumpet & violin ensembleₚ
Sonata in D major for Trumpet and Violin Ensemble
<In Chrysander's "Händel-Gesellschaft" edition, Vol. 27>
Dokshitser, Timofei, 14), 36), 38), 39)

ₜSonatas (15), op. 1, (c. 1722), B. 67. No. 15, violin & continuo, E major; arr.
trumpet & organₚ
Sonata in E major for Trumpet and Organ
[1]Adagio / [2]Allegro / [3]Largo / [4]Allegro
<In Chrysander's "Händel-Gesellschaft" edition, Vol. 27>
Mertens, Theo, 2)

ₜSonatas (15), op. 1, (c. 1722), B. 67. No. 15, violin & continuo, E major:
Excerpts; arr. trumpet & piano, E♭ majorₚ
Sonata in E♭ major for Trumpet and Piano
[1]Adagio / [2]Allegro
<In Chrysander's "Händel-Gesellschaft" edition, Vol. 27>
House, Lawrence
Tolley, Richard

ₜSonatas (9), op. 2, (c. 1722), B. 68. No. 3, 2 violins & continuo, B♭ major; arr. 3
trumpets & organₚ
Sonata in A♭ major for 3 Trumpets and Organ
[1][Andante] / [2]Allegro / [3][Larghetto] / [4]Allegro
<In Chrysander's "Händel-Gesellschaft" edition, Vol. 27>
Läubin, Hannes, 2)

[Suite, D major; arr. trumpet & organ]
Suite in D major
[1]Adagio / [2]Allegro leggero / [3]Adagio / [4]Allegro
This suite is of undetermined origin. However, the third movement (for organ alone) is from Handel's *Occasional Oratorio*, B. 138.

> Schultz, Erik, 4)

[Suite, trumpet, strings & continuo, [No. 1], D major, (1733)]
Suite in D major for Trumpet, Strings and Continuo (1733)
[1]Overture [Allegro] / [2][Gigue] Allegro / [3]Aire [Menuetto] / [4]Marche [Bourrée] / [5]March
Originally published in 1733 as *A Choice Sett of Aires, call'd HANDEL'S WATER PIECE.*
The instrumentation calls for 2 oboes and bassoon as optional.

> André, Maurice, 41), 44), 56), 67), 136), 168), 226), 227)
> Basch, Wolfgang, 3)
> Bernard, André, 5)
> Hunger, Helmut, 1)
> Reinhart, Carole Dawn, 1), 3), 4[1-4])
> Schwarz, Gerard, 4[1-4])
> Tarr, Edward, 21)

[Suite, trumpet, strings & continuo, [No. 1], D major, (1733); arr. trumpet & organ]
Suite in D major for Trumpet and Organ
[1]Overture [Allegro] / [2][Gigue] Allegro / [3]Aire [Menuetto] / [4]Marche [Bourrée] / [5]March

> Braz, Dirceu, 1)
> Chatel, Jean-Louis
> Gabel, Bernard, 1)
> Güttler, Ludwig, 6)
> Rippas, Claude
> Schultz, Erik, 1[1+3+2])
> Steele-Perkins, Crispian, 1[1+3]), 2)
> Tamiya, Kenji
> Tschotschev, Nicolai-Dimitrov
> Wilbraham, John, 3)

[Suite, trumpet, strings & continuo, [No. 2], D major]
Suite in D major for Trumpet and Strings, [No. 2]
[1]Allegro / [2]Rigaudon I & II / [3]Aria / [4]Anglaise I & II / [5]Sarabande / [6]Hornpipe I & II / [7]Menuet I & II / [8]Gigue - Duetto - Gigue
Manuscript located in the Archbishop's Library, Paderborn.

> Potpourri, 34), 35)
> Zickler, Heinz, 4)

ₜSuite, trumpet, strings & continuo, [No. 2], D major. Excerpts; arr. trumpet &
piano, B♭ majorₙ
Suite in B♭ major for Trumpet and Piano
(Anglaise, Minuet and Hornpipe)
Nagel, Robert, 10⁵⁺¹⁰⁺⁸)

ₜSuites de Pièces, (1718-20), B. 60. No. 5, harpsichord, E major: Air; arr. trumpet
& organₙ
Aria con variazioni from *Suite No. 5 for Harpsichord*
(Air, "Harmonious Blacksmith" [avec 5 Doubles])
(Air mit "Grobschmied-Variationen")
    <In Chrysander's "Händel-Gesellschaft" edition, Vol. 2>
Läubin, Hannes, 2)

ₜSuites de Pièces, (1718-20), B. 60. No. 5, harpsichord, E major: Air; arr. trumpet
& piano, F majorₙ
Aria con variazioni from *Suite No. 5 for Harpsichord*
(Air, "Harmonious Blacksmith" [avec 5 Doubles])
Haynie, John, 2)
Nagel, Robert, 16)

ₜUtrecht Te Deum and Jubilate, soli, mixed voices & chamber orchestra, (1713),
B. 41ₙ
Utrecht Te Deum and Jubilate, B. 41
    <In Chrysander's "Händel-Gesellschaft" edition, Vol. 31>
Immer, Friedemann, 17)

ₜVoluntaries and Fugues (12), (pub. c. 1780), B. ?25. No. 1, organ or harpsichord,
C major; arr. trumpet & organₙ
Voluntary No. 1 in C major
From *Twelve Voluntaries and Fugues for the Organ or
Harpsichord with Rules for tuning by the Celebrated Mr Handel,*
Book IV, c. 1780. [of dubious authenticity]
Haas, Wolfgang

ₜVoluntaries and Fugues (12), (pub. c. 1780), B. ?25. No. 2, organ or harpsichord,
C major; arr. trumpet & organₙ
Voluntary No. 2 in C major
a) Largo / b) Andante
Güttler, Ludwig, 2)

ₜVoluntaries and Fugues (12), (pub. c. 1780), B. ?25. No. 6, organ or harpsichord,
C major; arr. trumpet & organₙ
Voluntary No. 6 in C major
a) Adagio / b) [Allegro]
This voluntary is included in the Musica Rara edition of *Six
Voluntaries for Trumpet & Organ* (by Croft, Walond, Stubley,
Alcock, Handel & Dupuis) edited by Barry Cooper. The second
part of this voluntary is also included in the Brass Press edition of
A Suite of Trumpet Voluntaries by Handel & His Contemporaries
edited by Edward Tarr.
Tarr, Edward, 41)

ᵣWater Music, (1715), B. 50. Suite in F major: Air; arr. trumpet, organ, bass & drumsₗ
Aria from *Water Music*
(Air from "Suite in F major", B. 50)
André, Maurice, 70)

ᵣWater Music, (1715), B. 50. Suite in F major: Bourrée; arr. trumpet, organ, bass & drumsₗ
Bourrée from *Water Music*, Suite in F major
André, Maurice, 70)

ᵣWater Music, (1715/17), B. 50/55. Suites (3), chamber orchestraₗ
Water Music [complete]
(Suite in F major, B. 50)
(Suite in D major, B. 55/$^{1-5}$)
(Suite in G major / g minor, B. 55/$^{6-12}$)
SUITE IN F: ^{1}Overture [Grave - Allegro] / ^{2}Adagio e staccato / ^{3}[Allegro] / ^{4}Andante / ^{5}[Minuet] / ^{6}Air / ^{7}Minuet / ^{8}Bourrée / ^{9}Hornpipe / ^{10}[Andante] or [Allegro] / SUITE IN D: ^{1}[Overture] or [Allegro] / ^{2}Alla Hornpipe / ^{3}Minuet / ^{4}Lentement [Loure] / ^{5}Bourrée / SUITE IN G/g: ^{6}[Menuet] or [Sarabande] / ^{7}Rigaudon I / ^{8}Rigaudon II / ^{9}Menuet / ^{10}[Menuet II] / ^{11}[Gigue] / ^{12}[Gigue II]
<In Chrysander's "Händel-Gesellschaft" edition, Vol. 47>
Chamber orchestra for the *Suite in F* includes 2 oboes, bassoon, 2 horns, strings & harpsichord. The *Suite in D* includes, 2 oboes, bassoon, 2 horns, 2 trumpets, strings & harpsichord. The *Suite in G* includes 2 flutes, 2 oboes, strings & harpsichord.
Movements are numbered here according to A. Craig Bell's *Chronological Thematic Catalogue.* Various unspecified movement titles are taken directly from recordings. Actual recorded sequence of movements (and/or numerical designation) may not correspond to this listing. (Movements are listed in performance sequence under album listings.)
It should be noted that there are other recordings of "Water Music Suites" included in the album listings that are not indexed here since they are not performed by the artist under whose name they would appear (and include otherwise anonymous trumpeters). Furthermore, there are numerous recordings of the *Water Music* that have not been researched for this project.
André, Maurice, 89), 151)
Bodenröder, Robert
Hood, Boyde

₍Water Music, (1717), B. 50/55. Suite: excerpts; arr. trumpet, brass ensemble & organ₎
Suite en Fa
(extraits de "Water Music" et de Concerti Grossi)
(Excerpts from "Water Music", Suites in D & F)
[1]Andante [B. 55/(1)] / [2]Air [B. 50/(6)] / [3]Fanfares [B. 50/(7)] / [4]Bourrée [B. 50/(8)] / [5]Hornpipe [B. 55/(2)]
Although the title on the album indicates that this suite is in F major (and partly from concerti grossi), the first and last movements are from the "Suite in D" while the middle three movements are from the "Suite in F".
André, Maurice, 189)

₍Water Music, (1717), B. 55. Suite in D major; arr. trumpet & organ₎
Water Music, Suite in D major, B. 55
Güttler, Ludwig, 22)

₍Water Music, (1717), B. 55. Suite in D major: excerpts; arr. trumpet & organ₎
Water Music, Suite in D major, (excerpts), B. 55
Erb, Helmut, 5)

₍Water Music, (1717), B. 55. Suite in D major: excerpts; arr. trumpet ensemble, organ, timpani & percussion₎
Water Music, Suite in D major, (excerpts), B. 55
Carroll, Edward, 12)

₍Water Music, (1717), B. 55. Suite in D major: Hornpipe; arr. trumpet & organ₎
Hornpipe from *Water Music*, B. 55
Laughton, Stuart

₍Water Music, (1717), B. 55. Suite in G major: Rigaudon; arr. trumpet, organ, bass & drums₎
Rigaudon from *Water Music*, Suite in G major, B. 55
André, Maurice, 70)

Handl, Jacob, 1550-1591
Händl, Jacob
Hähnel, Jacob
Gallus, Jacobus

₍Alleluia, mixed voices, 2 trumpets, 2 trombones (& strings?)₎
Alleluia
Thibaud, Pierre, 10)

₍Duo Seraphim, mixed voices, 2 trumpets, 2 trombones (& strings?)₎
Duo Seraphim
Thibaud, Pierre, 10)

₍Haec est dies, mixed voices & instrumental ensemble₎
Haec est dies
Stradner, Gerhard

₍Laus et perennis Gloria, mixed voices, 2 trumpets, 2 trombones (& strings?)₎
Laus et perennis Gloria
Thibaud, Pierre, 10)

₍Pater noster qui es in coelis, mixed voices, trumpet & organ₎
Pater noster qui es in coelis
Krystek, Ulrich

₍Resonet in laudibus, mixed voices, cornetto, 3 trombones & strings₎
Resonet in laudibus
Stradner, Gerhard

Hansen, Thovald

₍Concert Waltz, cornet & piano₎
Koncert-Vals
(Concert Waltz)
Christensen, Ketil

₍Romance, cornet & piano₎
Romance
Christensen, Ketil

₍Scherzo, trumpet & piano₎
Scherzo
Christensen, Ketil

₍Sonata, cornet & piano, op. 18, (1903)₎
Sonata for Cornet and Piano, op. 18
Christensen, Ketil

Hanson, Raymond, 1913-

₍Concerto, trumpet & orchestra, (1952)₎
Concerto for Trumpet and Orchestra
[in one movement]
Robertson, John

Harbison, John H., 1938-

₍Confinement, chamber ensemble, (1965)₎
Confinement
Chamber ensemble includes: flute, oboe (English horn), clarinet (bass clarinet), alto saxophone, trumpet, trombone, violin, viola, cello, bass, piano & percussion.
Nagel, Robert, 20)

Harding, James, *d.* 1626

₍Almande; arr. 2 trumpets & 4 trombones₎
Almande
André, Maurice, 176)

Harrison, Lou, 1917-

 ⌐Mass, mixed voices, trumpet, harp & strings, (1939/54)⌐
Mass for Mixed Choir, Trumpet, Harp and Strings
Kutik, Ronald

Hartley, Walter S., 1927-
Hartley, Walter Sinclair

 ⌐Caprice, trumpet & piano⌐
Caprice
Levy, Robert

 ⌐Concertino, trumpet & wind ensemble⌐
Concertino for Trumpet and Wind Ensemble
Reese, Rebecca

 ⌐Sonatina, trumpet & piano, (1952)⌐
Sonatina for Trumpet and Piano
¹Allegro alla marcia / ²Adagio / ³Presto
There is also an orchestral version available on rental.
Ode, James

Hartmann, John, 19th cent.

 ⌐Facilita, cornet & piano⌐
Facilita
Published in 1932.
Chunn, Michael

 ⌐Fantasia Brilliante, "Rule Britannia", cornet & piano⌐
Fantasia Brilliante on the air "Rule Britannia"
Hardenberger, Håkan

Harut'unyan, Alexander Grigori
See: Arutiunian, Aleksandr Grigor'evich

Hastings, Thomas, 1784-1872

 ⌐TOPLADY; arr. trumpet & piano⌐
Rock of Ages
The hymn tune, TOPLADY, was composed by Thomas Hastings
for the hymn text by Augustus M. Toplady (1740-1778).
Reinhart, Carole Dawn, 13)

Haussmann, Valentin, *ca.* 1568-*ca.* 1614

 ⌐Dance; arr. instrumental ensemble⌐
Tantz
(Tanz)
Otto, Joachim

[Partita, 5 parts, G major; arr. recorders, trumpets & trombones]
Partita zu 5 Stimmen
(Partita a 5 in G major)
[1]Intrade / [2]Pavane / [3]Galliarde
Holy, Walter, 4)

Haydn, Franz Joseph, 1732-1809

[Concerto, oboe & orchestra, Hob. VIIg:C1, C major; arr. trumpet & orchestra]
Konzert für Trompete und Orchester C-dur
(Concerto in C major for Oboe and Orchestra, Hob. VIIg:C1)
[1]Allegro spiritoso / [2]Andante / [3]Rondo (Allegretto)
Attributed to F.J. Haydn, but of doubtful authenticity.
André, Maurice, 72), 75), 80), 162)

[Concerto, trumpet & orchestra, Hob. VIIe:1, E♭ major, (1796)]
Concert für Clarino in Es-dur
(Konzert für Trompete und Orchester Es-dur, Hob. VIIe:1)
(Concerto in E♭ major for Trumpet and Orchestra)
[1]Allegro / [2]Andante / [3]Finale: Allegro
André, Maurice, 20), 23), 24), 27), 28), 29),
32), 33), 34), 35[3]), 38[2-3]), 41), 42), 46), 54),
72), 75), 80), 96), 142), 169), 210), 213),
216), 218[3]), 226), 227)
Basch, Wolfgang, 13)
Berinbaum, Martin
Braeunig, Herbert
Calvayrac, Albert
Carroll, Edward, 2[3])
Delmotte, Roger, 10), 19), 23[3]), 27), 40), 50)
Dokshitser, Timofei, 1), 4), 6), 32)
Erb, Helmut, 4)
Eskdale, George, 1), 3[2-3])
Gleissle, Walter, 9), 10)
Grčar, Anton
Güttler, Ludwig, 5), 13[3]), 21[3])
Hardenberger, Håkan
Head, Emerson
Herseth, Adolph, 1)
Hirt, Al
Holler, Adolf
Hovaldt, Knud
Howarth, Elgar
Immer, Friedemann, 2)
Jeannoutot, Bernard
Krug, Willi, 4)
Lang, William
Longinotti, Paolo
Marsalis, Wynton, 1), 5)
Méndez, Rafael, 11)

Mertens, Theo, 7)
Potpourri, 1), 10), 12), 13), 15), 16), 20), 29),
34), 35), 37), 44³), 47)
Preis, Ivo
Reinhart, Carole Dawn, 3), 4)
Reyes, Arturo
Scherbaum, Adolf, 8), 15), 23), 25)
Schetsche, Walter
Schmidhäusler, Francis
Schneidewind, Helmut, 4)
Schwarz, Gerard, 6), 23)
Sevenstern, Harry
Smithers, Don, 8), 9)
Soustrot, Bernard, 1)
Steele-Perkins, Crispian, 13)
Stevens, Thomas, 14)
Stockhausen, Markus, 1)
Stringer, Alan, 1), 2), 4)
Thibaud, Pierre, 3), 4)
Tschotschev, Nicolai-Dimitrov
Voisin, Roger, 3), 13)
Wallace, John, 3)
Webb, Gordon, 6)
Wilbraham, John, 9), 25³)
Wobisch, Helmut, 4), 5), 9), 11), 13)

[Concerto, trumpet & orchestra, Hob. VIIe:1, E♭ major, (1796); arr. trumpet & band]

Concerto in E♭ major for Trumpet and Band, Hob. VIIe:1
^{1}Allegro / ^{2}Andante / ^{3}Finale: Allegro
Bilger, David$^{2-3}$
Haynie, John, 4)

[Concerto, trumpet & orchestra, Hob. VIIe:1, E♭ major, (1796); arr. trumpet & organ]

Concerto in E♭ major for Trumpet, Hob. VIIe:1
^{1}Allegro / ^{2}Andante / ^{3}Finale: Allegro
Bouche^2

[Concerto, trumpet & orchestra, Hob. VIIe:1, E♭ major, (1796); arr. trumpet & piano]

Concerto in E♭ major for Trumpet, Hob. VIIe:1
^{1}Allegro / ^{2}Andante / ^{3}Finale: Allegro
Ghitalla, Armando, 13$^{2-3}$**)**
Reinhart, Carole Dawn, 13^2**)**
Wilder, Joseph B.^{2}

Haydn, Michael, 1737-1806
Haydn, (Johann) Michael

⌈Serenade, P. 52, B♭ major, (ca. 1763-1770). Concerto, trumpet & orchestra, [No. 1], D major⌉

Konzert für Trompete und Orchester [Nr. 1] D-dur
(Concerto in D major for Trumpet and Orchestra)
[1]Adagio / [2]Allegro
The *Concerto in D major for Trumpet* consists of the third and fourth movements of the *Serenade in B♭ major*, P. 52, which was composed between 1763 and 1770.

> André, Maurice, 20), 23), 27), 31), 33), 34), 35[2]), 41), 44), 53), 67), 80), 104), 149), 168), 169), 216)
> Marsalis, Wynton, 6)
> Potpourri, 13)
> Scherbaum, Adolf, 2), 10), 13), 15), 25)
> Smithers, Don, 11)
> Vizzutti, Allen

⌈Sinfonia, P. 34, C major, (1763). Concerto, trumpet & orchestra, [No. 2], C major⌉

Konzert für Trompete und Orchester [Nr. 2] C-dur
(Concerto No. 2 in C major for Trumpet and Orchestra)
[1]Adagio / [2]Allegro molto
The *Concerto in C major for Trumpet* consists of the first two movements of the *Sinfonia in C major*, P. 34.

> Ghitalla, Armando, 4)
> Güttler, Ludwig, 3)
> Kejmar, Miroslav, 10)
> Potpourri, 10), 20)
> Schultz, Erik, 6)
> Smithers, Don, 8), 9)
> Soustrot, Bernard, 9)
> Steele-Perkins, Crispian, 13)

Hayman (arr.), Richard, 1920-
Hayman, Richard Warren Joseph

⌈Variations (Carnival of Venice); arr. trumpet & orchestra⌉
Carnival of Venice (Variations)
> Hirt, Al

Heifetz, Jascha, 1901-1987
See: Dinicu, Grigoraş

Heinichen, Johann David, 1683-1729

[Concerto, 2 horns, 2 flutes, 2 oboes, strings & continuo, F major]
Konzert für 2 Hörner, 2 Flöten, 2 Oboen, Streicher und Basso continuo F-dur
[no tempo marking] / [2]Andante / [3][no tempo marking]
This concerto for **horns** is indexed here since it is performed by trumpeters using modern *Corni da caccia* with valves. (This modern invention produces a very warm flügelhorn-type sound.)
Güttler, Ludwig, 27)

[Concerto, 2 horns, 2 flutes, 2 oboes, strings & continuo, F major; arr. 2 corni da caccia & organ]
Konzert für 2 Corni da caccia F-dur
Güttler, Ludwig, 15)

Heiss, John Carter, 1938-

[Inventions, Contours and Colors, chamber ensemble, (1973)]
Inventions, Contours and Colors
Chamber ensemble includes: flute, oboe, bassoon, horn, trumpet, trombone, tuba, violin, viola, cello & bass.
Ranger, Louis

Hellermann, William David, 1939-

[Passages 13 — The Fire, solo trumpet & tape, (1970-71)]
Passages 13 — The Fire
Schwarz, Gerard, 18)

Henderson, Robert, 1948-

[Variation Movements, solo trumpet, (1967)]
Variation Movements for Trumpet
[1]Theme / [2]Very fast / [3]Fast and marked / [4]Slow, in a lyric style / [5]Fast and rhythmic
Stevens, Thomas, 1)

Henneberg, Paul, 1863-1929

[Triplets of the Finest, cornet trio & piano, (ca. 1925)]
Triplets of the Finest — Concert Polka
Schwarz, Gerard, 21)

Henze, Hans Werner, 1926-

[Sonatina, solo trumpet, (1974)]
Sonatina for Solo Trumpet
[3 movements]
Stevens, Thomas, 5)
Wallace, John, 6)

Herbert, Victor, 1859-1924
Herbert, Victor August

[Babes in Toyland, (1903). March of the Toys; arr. 3 trumpets, clarinet & rhythm section]
March of the Toys from *Babes in Toyland*
Victorian Trumpet Trio

[Prince Ananias, (1894). Aria, "Ah! Cupid"; arr. cornet & orchestra]
Ah! Cupid from *Prince Ananias*
Clarke, Herbert L.

Herbst, Johann Andreas, 1588-1666

[Singt und klinget allzumal; arr. trumpet & brass ensemble]
Singt und klinget allzumal
Güttler, Ludwig, 9)

Herman, Jerry, 1933-

[Concerto, trumpet & orchestra; arr. trumpet & piano]
Concerto for Trumpet and Orchestra
Terracini, Paul

[Mame, (1966). Title song; arr. trumpet quartet]
"Mame" from *Mame*
Blackburn, Roger

Hermann (Monk of Salzburg), 14th cent.
Hermann der Mönch von Salzburg

[Das Nachthorn, medieval cornetto (tuohitorvi), triangle]
Das Nachthorn
Laird, Michael, 1)

[Der Trumpet, medieval cornetto (tuohitorvi), slide trumpet (tromba da tirarsi), shawm, tabor]
Der Trumpet
Laird, Michael, 1)

[Fanfare, "Untarn slaf tut den Sumer wol", clarion (posthorn)]
Fanfare, "Untarn slaf tut den Sumer wol"
Laird, Michael, 1)

Heron, Henry, 1730-1795

[Voluntary, keyboard, D major; arr. trumpet & organ]
Voluntary in D major
a) Andante / b) Allegro moderato
Zapf, Gerd

Hertel, Johann Wilhelm, 1727-1789

[Concerto, trumpet, oboe, strings & continuo, E♭ major]
Doppelkonzert für Trompete, Oboe, Streicher und Basso continuo Es-dur
[1]Allegro / [2]Arioso / [3]Allegro
Bibliothèque du Conservatoire royal de musique, Brussels: no. 7684 & no. 7685.

> **André, Maurice,** 63), 125)
> **Bernard, André,** 1)
> **Güttler, Ludwig,** 3)
> **Immer, Friedemann,** 12)
> **Potpourri,** 48)
> **Schultz, Erik,** 7)
> **Tarr, Edward,** 22)

[Concerto, trumpet, strings & continuo, [No. 1], E♭ major]
Konzert für Trompete, Streicher und Basso continuo Es-dur [Nr. 1]
[1]Allegro / [2]Larghetto / [3]Vivace
Bibliothèque du Conservatoire royal de musique, Brussels: no. 5565.

> **André, Maurice,** 35[2]), 44), 51), 67), 125)
> **Güttler, Ludwig,** 3), 25)

[Concerto, trumpet, strings & continuo, [No. 2], E♭ major]
Konzert für Trompete, Streicher und Basso continuo Es-dur [Nr. 2]
[1]Allegro mà moderatamente / [2]Largo / [3]Allegro
Bibliothèque du Conservatoire royal de musique, Brussels: no. 5566.

> **André, Maurice,** 160)
> **Schultz, Erik,** 5)

[Concerto, trumpet, strings & continuo, [No. 3], D major]
Konzert für Trompete, Streicher und Basso continuo D-dur [Nr. 3]
[1]Allegro / [2]Largo / [3]Vivace
Bibliothèque du Conservatoire royal de musique, Brussels: no. 5567.

> **André, Maurice,** 160)
> **Basch, Wolfgang,** 6)
> **Hardenberger, Håkan**

[Concerto, trumpet, 2 oboes & 2 bassoons, D major]
Concerto a cinque per il tromba, due oboi e due fagotti in Re maggiore
[1]Allegro / [2]Cantabile / [3]Plaisanterie - Duetto - Plaisanterie /
[4]Menuet - Trio - Menuet
Bibliothèque du Conservatoire royal de musique, Brussels.
            André, Maurice, 125)
            Basch, Wolfgang, 6)
            Läubin, Hannes, 1)
            Potpourri, 34), 35)
            Schwarz, Gerard, 8)
            Wilbraham, John, 4), 5), 15)
            Zickler, Heinz, 7)

[Partita, organ, No. 2, F major; arr. trumpet & organ]
Partita No. 2 in F major
[1]Allegro / [2]Largo / [3]Vivace
            André, Maurice, 163)

[Sinfonie, 8 timpani, 2 oboes, 2 trumpets & strings, C major]
Sinfonie C-dur
(Concerto for Timpani and Orchestra)
Although this work appears on an album listed under Guy Touvron, the trumpeters are unidentified members of the RSO Berlin.
            Touvron, Guy, 19)

Heyne, Joe
[Petite Waltz; arr. trumpet & instrumental ensemble]
The Petite Waltz
            Andersen, Ole

Hibbard, William, 1939-
Hibbard, William Alden

[Ménage, soprano, trumpet & violin, (1974)]
Ménage
            Dean, Allan, 3)

Hidalgo, José Luis, 20th cent.
[Andalucia Beat, trumpet & instrumental ensemble]
Andalucia Beat
            Hidalgo, José Luis

[Atencion, trumpet & instrumental ensemble]
Atencion
            Hidalgo, José Luis

ɪEmbrujo de Trompeta, trumpet & instrumental ensembleɪ
Embrujo de Trompeta
Hidalgo, José Luis

ɪEternamente, trumpet & instrumental ensembleɪ
Eternamente
Hidalgo, José Luis

ɪNuria, trumpet & instrumental ensembleɪ
Nuria
Hidalgo, José Luis

ɪSonida Granada, trumpet & instrumental ensembleɪ
Sonida Granada
Hidalgo, José Luis

Hiller, Lejaren, 1924-

ɪComputer Cantata, soprano & chamber ensemble, (1963)ɪ
Computer Cantata
[1]Prolog to Strophe I — Strophe I / [2]Prolog to Strophe II —
Strophe II / [3]Prolog to Strophe III — Strophe III — Epilog to
Strophe III / [4]Strophe IV — Epilog to Strophe IV / [5]Strophe V —
Epilog to Strophe V

Chamber ensemble includes: flute, bass clarinet, horn, trumpet,
guitar, theremin, violin, viola & 10 percussion.

Composed in collaboration with Robert Baker using MUSICOMP
(an expandible set of programs for composition) written in
SCATRE (an IBM-7094 assembly language) and partly in
FORTRAN. The texts, in approximations of spoken English, were
generated by Professors Hultzén, Allen and Miron of the
University of Illinois.
Bastin, Ernie

Hindemith, Paul, 1895-1963

ɪConcert Music, piano, 2 harps & brass, op. 49, (1930)ɪ
Konzertmusik für Klavier, Blechbläser und Harfen, op. 49
(Concert Music for Piano, Brass and 2 Harps, op. 49)
Mičaník, Jaroslav

ɪConcerto, trumpet, bassoon & string orchestra, (1949)ɪ
Konzert für Trompete in B und Fagott mit Streichorchester
(Concerto for Trumpet in B^b and Bassoon with String Orchestra)
[1]Allegro spiritoso / [2]Molto adagio / [3]Vivace
Guarneri, Mario
Haug, Edward

ɪKleine Kammermusik, chamber ensemble, op. 24, no. 1, (1922)ɪ
Kleine Kammermusik, op. 24, Nr. 1
Chamber ensemble includes: flute, clarinet, bassoon, trumpet,
percussion, piano, 2 violins, viola, cello & bass.
Haug, Edward

₍Pieces (3), clarinet, trumpet, violin, bass & piano, (1925)₎
Drei Stücke für 5 Instrumente
(Three Pieces for 5 Instruments)
McNab, Malcolm

₍Septet, chamber ensemble, (1948)₎
Septett für Bläser
(Septet for Winds)
Chamber ensemble includes: flute, oboe, clarinet, bass clarinet, bassoon, horn & trumpet.
Junek, Václav, 3)

₍Sonata, trumpet & piano, (1939)₎
Sonate für Trompete in B und Klavier
(Sonata for Trumpet in B♭ and Piano)
[1]Mit Kraft / [2]Mässig bewegt / [3]Trauermusik: Sehr langsam — Alle Menschen müssen sterben

> **André, Maurice, 148)**
> **Benedetti, Donald**
> **Dokshitser, Timofei, 17)**
> **Gardner, Ned**
> **Ghitalla, Armando, 13[2])**
> **Hyatt, Jack**
> **Johnson, Gilbert, 6)**
> **Junek, Václav, 5)**
> **Kvebaek, Harry**
> **Lösch, Reinhold**
> **Malkov, Valentin**
> **Orvid, Georgy**
> **Plog, Anthony, 4)**
> **Potpourri, 39)**
> **Reinhart, Carole Dawn, 9)**
> **Sevenstern, Harry**
> **Stevens, Thomas, 4), 13)**
> **Stith, Marice, 5)**
> **Tarr, Edward, 6)**
> **Wilson, Alex**

Hingeston, John, *d.* 1688
Hingston, John

₍Fantasia, cornetto, trombone & organ; arr. trumpet, trombone & organ₎
Fantasy in F major for Trumpet, Bass Trombone and Organ
Yudashkin, Georgy

₍Fantasia, 2 cornetti, trombone & organ; arr. trumpet & organ₎
Fantasia for Trumpet and Organ
Rausch, Heiner

₍Fantasia, 2 cornetti, trombone & organ; arr. 1 cornetto, trombone, organ & viola da gamba₎
Fantasia
(Fantasia for 2 cornetts and sagbut with ye organ)
¹Fantasia / ²Almande / ³Ayre
Smithers, Don, 1)

₍Fantasia, 2 cornetti, trombone & organ; arr. 2 trumpets & organ₎
Fantasia for 2 Trumpets and Organ
¹Fantasia / ²Almande / ³Ayre
Pohle, Wolfgang

₍Fantasia, 2 cornetti, trombone & organ; arr. 2 trumpets, trombone & organ₎
Fantasy in F major for 2 Trumpets, Bass Trombone and Organ
Yudashkin, Georgy

Hoch, Theodore, 1842-1906

₍Chants d'Oiseaux de la Forêt de Thuringe, cornet, piano & harp, op. 22₎
Chants d'Oiseaux de la Forêt de Thuringe, op. 22
Sommerhalder, Max

₍Fantasia, "Pearls of the Ocean", cornet with unidentified accompaniment, op. 19₎
Fantasia, "Pearls of the Ocean", op. 19
("Une Perle de l'Océan")
Lemos, Alexandre Vasilievich

Hoffman, Edward, 20th cent.

₍Miniatures (4), solo trumpet, (ca. 1973)₎
Four Miniatures
[four movements]
Hickman, David, 2)

Hofmann, Wolfgang, 1922-

₍Concerto Gregorianico, trumpet & strings₎
Concerto Gregorianico für Trompete und Streicher
Quinque, Rolf, 5)

Höhne, Carl, 19th cent.
Höncke, Karl

₍Slavische Fantasie, cornet & piano, (1899)₎
Slavische Fantasie
Schwarz, Gerard, 19)

₍Slavische Fantasie, cornet & piano, (1899); arr. trumpet & brass ensemble₎
Slavische Fantasie
Mertens, Theo, 3)

Holborne, Anthony, *d.* 1602

[Pavans, Galliards, Almains..., (1599). Selections; arr. instrumental ensemble]
Pavans, Galliards, Almains, and other short aeirs...
[20]Galliard / [39]Pavan / [42]Galliard / [49]Pavana ploravit / [50]Sic semper soleo / [59]The Choise / [60]The Honie-Suckle / [61]Wanton / [63]The Fairie-round / [65]Heigh ho holiday
Montesi, Robert, 3)

Holland, Jack, 1926-

[Scales (major & minor, just intonation), trumpet]
Major & minor scales with Just Intonation
Holland, Jack

Holloway, Joseph, 19th cent.
Holloway, John

[Wood Up Quickstep, 2 keyed bugles & band, (1835); arr. B$^\flat$-cornet, E$^\flat$-cornet & band]
The Wood Up Quickstep
Broiles, Melvin

[Wood Up Quickstep, 2 keyed bugles & band, (1835); arr. E$^\flat$-keyed-bugle, 5-keyed flute, 5-keyed clarinet & strings]
Wood Up Quick Step
Dudgeon, Ralph

Holmboe, Vagn, 1909-

[Chamber Concertos (13). No. 11: trumpet, 2 horns & strings, op. 44, (1948)]
Concerto No. 11 for Trumpet Solo, Two Horns and String Orchestra, op. 44
[1]Largo — Allegro con fuoco / [2]Poco lento / [3]Allegretto ma vivace
Nagel, Robert, 12)

[Triade, trumpet & organ, op. 123, (1975)]
Triade für Trompete und Orgel, op. 123
Tarr, Edward, 5)

Holmes, Paul W., 1923-

[Sonata, trumpet & piano, (1962)]
Sonata for Trumpet and Piano
[3 movements]
Burkart, Richard[1]
Ghitalla, Armando, 13[3])

Homilius, Gottfried August, 1714-1785

₍Chorale Prelude, "Durch Adams Fall", organ; arr. trumpet & organ₎
Chorale Prelude, "Durch Adams Fall ist ganz verderbt"
Rhoten, Bruce
Tarr, Edward, 8)
Touvron, Guy, 20)
Voisin, Roger, 2)

₍Chorale Prelude, "Komm, Heiliger Geist", organ; arr. trumpet & organ₎
Chorale Prelude, "Komm, Heiliger Geist, Herre Gott"
Rausch, Heiner
Rhoten, Bruce
Tarr, Edward, 8)

₍Chorale Prelude, "O Heiliger Geist", organ; arr. trumpet & organ₎
Chorale Prelude, "O Heiliger Geist, kehr bei uns ein"
Rhoten, Bruce
Tarr, Edward, 8)

Höncke, Karl
See: Höhne, Carl

Honegger, Arthur, 1892-1955

₍Intrada, trumpet & piano, (1947)₎
Intrada pour Trompette en ut et Piano
André, Maurice, 148)
Gardner, Ned
Hardenberger, Håkan
Hyatt, Jack
Lewis, E. Leonard
Malkov, Valentin
Reinhart, Carole Dawn, 9)
Schwarz, Gerard, 12)
Stith, Marice, 5)

₍Oratorio, "Le Roi David", soli, mixed voices & chamber orchestra, (1921)₎
Oratorio, "Le Roi David"
("King David")
Chamber orchestra includes: 2 flutes (piccolo), oboe (English horn), 2 clarinets (bass clarinet), bassoon, horn, 2 trumpets, trombone, cello, bass, timpani, celesta, piano, organ & 2 percussion.
Longinotti, Paolo
Thibaud, Pierre, 9)

₍Symphony, strings & trumpet, No. 2, (1941)₎
Deuxième Symphonie, pour cordes et trompette ad libitum
(Symphony No. 2 for Strings and [optional] Trumpet)
[1]Molto moderato — Allegro / [2]Adagio mesto / [3]Vivace, non troppo
Lagorce, Marcel

Hook, James, 1746-1827

₍Menuet; arr. trumpet & piano₎
Menuet
    Included as the first part of a transcription by Robert Getchell,
    "Menuet and Ballo". (The "Ballo" is by Daniel Steibelt.)
        Geyer, Charles

Horlick, Harry, 20th cent.

₍Black Eyes, (1926); arr. trumpet & instrumental ensemble₎
Dark Eyes
    (Black Eyes)
            Smith, Bramwell "Bram"

₍Black Eyes, (1926); arr. trumpet & orchestra₎
Dark Eyes
    (Black Eyes)
            Méndez, Rafael, 17), 19)

Hotteterre, Jacques, 1674-1763
Hotteterre, Jacques-Martin (le Romain)

₍Sonata, flute & continuo, C major; arr. trumpet & organ₎
Sonata in C major
            Braz, Dirceu, 1)

Hovhaness, Alan, 1911-
Hovhaness, Alan Scott

₍Cantata, "Avak, the Healer", soprano, trumpet & chamber orchestra, op. 65,
    (1945, rev. 1946)₎
Cantata, "Avak, the Healer", op. 65
            Rapier, Leon, 6)
            Stevens, Thomas, 10)

₍Concerto, "Khaldis", piano, 4 trumpets & percussion, op. 91, (1951)₎
Khaldis
    (Concerto for Piano, 4 Trumpets and Percussion)
        [1]Overture / [2]Transmutation / [3]Three Tones / [4]Adoration (Bhajana) /
        [5]Jhala with Drum / [6]Processional / [7]Finale
            Glantz, Harry, 2), 5)

₍Concerto, "Return and Rebuild the Desolate Places", trumpet & wind orchestra,
    op. 213, (1944, rev. 1965)₎
Return and Rebuild the Desolate Places
    (Concerto for Trumpet)
        [1]Prelude (netori) / [2]Hymn (The Chalice of Holiness - Wings of
        Compassion - The Triumph of Faith)
            Schwarz, Gerard, 13)

₍Etchmiadzin, op. 62, (1946). Intermezzo: Prayer of Saint Gregory, trumpet & strings, op. 62b₎
Prayer of Saint Gregory
Stevens, Thomas, 10)
Unidentified, Trumpet(s), 20)

₍Etchmiadzin, op. 62, (1946). Intermezzo: Prayer of Saint Gregory, trumpet & strings, op. 62b; arr. trumpet & organ₎
Prayer of Saint Gregory
Blair, Stacy
Chesnut, Walter
McGuffey, Patrick
Pearson, Byron
Plog, Anthony, 2)
Willwerth, Paul

₍Etchmiadzin, op. 62, (1946). Intermezzo: Prayer of Saint Gregory, trumpet & strings, op. 62b; arr. trumpet & piano₎
Prayer of Saint Gregory
Haynie, John, 1)

₍Haroutiun, trumpet & strings, op. 71, (1948); arr. trumpet & organ₎
Haroutiun (Resurrection), op. 71
[1]Aria / [2]Fugue
Ode, James

₍Holy City, trumpet, harp, strings & percussion, op. 218, (1967)₎
The Holy City, op. 218
Howarth, Elgar

₍Is There Survival, op. 59, (1949). Suite, chamber ensemble₎
Ballet Suite, "Is There Survival?"
(Alternate title = "King Vahaken")
[1]Overture / [2]Canon / [3]Canon / [4]Aria / [5]Fugue / [6]Fantasy / [7]Double Canon
Chamber ensemble includes: 4 clarinets, saxophone, 4 trumpets & 3 percussion.
Glantz, Harry, 6)

₍Sonata, trumpet & organ, op. 200, (1962)₎
Sonata for Trumpet and Organ, op. 200
[1]Senza Misura / [2]Senza Misura / [3]Senza Misura
Plog, Anthony, 5[1])
Stith, Marice, 6)

₍Symphonies. No. 6: "Celestial Gate", chamber orchestra, op. 173, (1959)₎
Symphony No. 6, "Celestial Gate"
Chamber orchestra includes: flute, oboe, clarinet, bassoon, horn, trumpet, timpani, chimes, harp & strings.
Unidentified, Trumpet(s), 20)

[Symphonies. No. 9: "Saint Vartan", chamber ensembles, op. 80, (1950)]
Symphony No. 9, "Saint Vartan", op. 80
[1]Yerk / [2]Tapor / [3]Aria / [4]Aria / [5]Aria / [6]Bar / [7]Tapor / [8]Bar / [9]Bar / [10]Estampie / [11]Bar / [12]Bar / [13]Aria / [14]Lament, "Death of Vartan" [15]Estampie / [16]Yerk (To Sensual Love) / [17]Aria (To Sacred Love) / [18]Estampie / [19]Bar / [20]Aria / [21]Bar / [22]Bar / [23]Bar / [24]Estampie
Each movement features a different ensemble combination. Instruments included are: alto saxophone, horn, 4 trumpets, piano, percussion & strings.
Weis, Theodore, 3)

[Symphonies. No. 24: "Majnun Symphony", tenor, mixed voices, trumpet, violin & orchestra, op. 273, (1973)]
Symphony No. 24, "Majnun Symphony"
Wilbraham, John, 29)

Hubay, Jenö, 1858-1937
Huber, Eugen

[Hejre Kati, violin & orchestra, op. 32; arr. trumpet & orchestra]
Hejre Kati
Geiger, György
Méndez, Rafael, 17), 19)

Hubbell, Harriss, 20th cent.

[Spring is Never Ending, cornet & band]
Spring is Never Ending
Burke, James, 2)

Hubeau, Jean, 1917-

[Sonata, trumpet & piano, (1943)]
Sonate pour trompette chromatique et piano
[1]Sarabande: Andante con moto / [2]Intermède: Allegro con brio / [3]Spiritual: Andante molto calmo (Tempo di Blues)
André, Maurice, 148)
Erb, Helmut, 4)
Potpourri, 28)
Roelant, Alain
Terracini, Paul

Hüe, Georges, 1858-1948
Hüe, Georges-Adolphe

[Solo de concert, cornet & piano]
Solo de concert
(Premier Solo de Cornet à Pistons avec accompagnement de Piano)
Reynolds, George

Hummel, Bertold, 1925-
Hummel, Berthold

[Invocationes, trumpet & organ, op. 68]
Invocationes, op. 68
Erb, Helmut, 2)

[Sonatina, trumpet & piano, (1965)]
Sonatine für Trompete und Klavier
[1]Bewegt (Moved) / [2]Langsame Achtel (Slow quavers) / [3]Rondo:
Ziemlich lebhaft (Rather lively)
Darling, James

Hummel, Johann Nepomuk, 1778-1837

[Adagio, Thema und Variationen, oboe & orchestra, op. 102, (c. 1824); arr.
trumpet & orchestra]
Adagio, Thema und Variationen, op. 102
(Introduction, Theme and Variations, op. 102)
[1]Adagio / [2]Allegretto - Calando
André, Maurice, 81), 160), 208)

[Concerto, trumpet & orchestra, E major, (1803)]
Konzert für Trompete und Orchester E-dur
(Concerto a Tromba principale)
[1]Allegro con Spirito / [2]Andante / [3]Rondo
**André, Maurice, 35[2]), 81), 112), 155), 168),
208), 213)**
Basch, Wolfgang, 6)
Ghitalla, Armando, 2)
Groot, Willem (Wim)
Güttler, Ludwig, 21[3]), 26)
Hardenberger, Håkan
Potpourri, 16)
Schwarz, Gerard, 6)
Tarr, Edward, 22)
Touvron, Guy, 1)
Wilbraham, John, 4), 7), 15)

[Concerto, trumpet & orchestra, E major, (1803); arr. trumpet & band, E♭ major]
Concerto in E♭ major for Trumpet and Band
[1]Allegro con Spirito / [2]Andante / [3]Rondo
Reese, Rebecca

⌈Concerto, trumpet & orchestra, E major, (1803); arr. trumpet & orchestra,
  E♭ major⌉
Konzert für Trompete und Orchester Es-dur
(Concerto a Tromba principale)
[1]Allegro con Spirito / [2]Andante / [3]Rondo
> André, Maurice, 38[2-3]), 60), 119), 210)
> Berinbaum, Martin
> Bernard, André, 1)
> Cuvit, Michel
> Dokshitser, Timofei, 4), 26), 32)
> Head, Emerson
> Lang, William
> Marsalis, Wynton, 1), 7)
> Potpourri, 12), 15), 29)
> Quinque, Rolf, 6)
> Reinhart, Carole Dawn, 1), 3), 4), 5[1]), 7[3])
> Thibaud, Pierre, 4)
> Tschotschev, Nicolai-Dimitrov
> Wallace, John, 5)
> Webb, Gordon, 5)

⌈Concerto, trumpet & orchestra, E major, (1803); arr. trumpet & piano, E♭ major⌉
Concerto in E♭ major for Trumpet
[1]Allegro con Spirito / [2]Andante / [3]Rondo
> Nagel, Robert, 17[3])
> Reynolds, George[3]

⌈Septet, "Grand Military", chamber ensemble, op. 114, C major⌉
Septett op. 114 C-dur, Militär-Septett
(Grand Military Septet in C major, op. 114)
Chamber ensemble includes: flute, clarinet, trumpet, violin, cello,
bass & piano.
> Schmidt, Ingus

Humphries, John, *ca.* 1707-*ca.* 1740

⌈Concerto, trumpet, strings & continuo, op. 2, no. 12, D major⌉
Concerto in D major for Trumpet, Strings and Continuo, op. 2, no. 12
> Steele-Perkins, Crispian, 13)

Hurník, Ilja, 1922-

⌈Abenteuer einer Kapelle, speaker & chamber ensemble⌉
Abenteuer einer Kapelle
Chamber ensemble includes: flute, clarinet, bassoon, trumpet,
trombone, violin, bass, guitar, harp & percussion.
> Schmid, Bernhard, 13)

Iannaconne, Anthony J., 1943-

ₜSonatina, trumpet & tubaₗ
Sonatina for Trumpet and Tuba
Eggers, Carter

Ibert, Jacques, 1890-1962
Ibert, Jacques François Antoine

ₜConcertino da Camera, saxophone & chamber ensemble, (1935)ₗ
Concertino da Camera
Chamber ensemble includes a woodwind quintet (flute, oboe, clarinet, bassoon & horn), trumpet, and a string quartet (2 violins, viola & cello).
Davidson, Louis

ₜDivertissement, chamber orchestra, (1930)ₗ
Divertissement pour orchestre de chambre
Suite from incidental music for *Le Chapeau de paille d'Italie*.
Johnson, Gilbert, 1)

ₜEntr'acte, flute & guitar, (1935); arr. trumpet & guitarₗ
Entr'acte
Méndez, Rafael, 14)

ₜImpromptu, trumpet & piano, (1951)ₗ
Impromptu pour trompette en ut et piano
Christensen, Ketil
Darling, James
Hyatt, Jack
Malkov, Valentin
Schwarz, Gerard, 12)
Stevens, Thomas, 6)

ₜSuite Symphonique, "Paris", chamber orchestra, (1930-32)ₗ
Suite Symphonique, "Paris"
[1]Le Métro / [2]Faubourgs / [3]La Mosquée de Paris / [4]Restaurant au Bois de Boulogne / [5]Le Paquebot "Ile-de-France" / [6]Parade Foraine
Suite from incidental music for *Donogoo*.
Chamber orchestra includes: flute, oboe, clarinet, bassoon, horn, trumpet, trombone & strings.
Lowrey, Alvin

Indy, Vincent d'
See: d'Indy, Vincent

Irons, Earl D., 1891-1967

ₜCedar Vale, trumpet & pianoₗ
Cedar Vale
Amstutz, Keith

ᵣEchoes from the Painted Desert, cornet & pianoᵣ
Echoes from the Painted Desert
Amstutz, Keith

ᵣEmerald Isle, trumpet & pianoᵣ
Emerald Isle
Amstutz, Keith

ᵣFleur de Lis, cornet & pianoᵣ
Fleur de Lis
Amstutz, Keith

ᵣSong of the Pines, cornet & pianoᵣ
Song of the Pines
Haynie, John, 1)

Isaac, Heinrich, *ca.* 1450-1517

ᵣA la bataglia, instrumental ensembleᵣ
A la bataglia
Laird, Michael, 13)
Montesi, Robert, 6)

ᵣCommunio, "Ecce virgo concipiet", mixed voices, cornetto, tenor cornetto, sackbut, dulcianᵣ
Communio: "Ecce virgo concipiet"
Renz, Albrecht, 4)

ᵣIn meinem Sinn, cornetto, 2 shawms, 3 sackbutsᵣ
In meinem Sinn
Montesi, Robert, 2)

ᵣIntroitus, "Rorate cœli", mixed voices, cornetto, tenor cornetto, sackbut, dulcianᵣ
Introitus: "Rorate cœli"
Renz, Albrecht, 4)

ᵣLa Mi La Sol, cornetto, 2 shawms, 3 sackbutsᵣ
La Mi La Sol
Montesi, Robert, 2)

ᵣMotet, "Imperii proceres", mixed voices, cornetto, recorder, fiedel, trombone, crumhornᵣ
"Imperii proceres"
Renz, Albrecht, 7)

ᵣMotet, "Quis dabit capiti meo aquam?", mixed voices, cornetto, tenor cornetto, sackbut, dulcianᵣ
"Quis dabit capiti meo aquam laurus impetu?"
Renz, Albrecht, 7)

Isakova, Aida Petrovna, 1940-
₍Concerto, trumpet, piano & orchestra₎
Concerto for Trumpet, Piano and Orchestra
Klushkin, Yuri

Israel, Brian, 1951-1986
₍Dance Variations, solo trumpet, (1973-74)₎
Dance Variations
Stith, Marice, 4)

Ives, Charles Edward, 1874-1954
₍All the way around and back, chamber ensemble, (1906)₎
Scherzo, "All the Way Around and Back"
Chamber ensemble includes: clarinet (flute), bugle, violin, bells
& piano.
Prokopov, Vyacheslav

₍From the Steeples and the Mountains, trumpet, trombone & bells, (1901)₎
From the Steeples and the Mountains
The trumpet and trombone parts are doubled.
Kuehn, David

₍Over the Pavements, chamber ensemble, (1906-13)₎
Scherzo, "Over the Pavements"
Chamber ensemble includes: piccolo, clarinet, bassoon, trumpet, 3
trombones, percussion & piano (4 hands).
Crisara, Raymond, 9)
Prokopov, Vyacheslav
Unidentified, Trumpet(s), 2)

₍The Unanswered Question, orchestra, (1906)₎
The Unanswered Question
Crisara, Raymond, 9)
Herseth, Adolph, 5)
Vacchiano, William, 6)
Voisin, Roger, 12)

₍Tone Roads, no. 3, chamber orchestra, (1915)₎
Tone Roads, No. 3
Chamber orchestra includes: flute, clarinet, trumpet, trombone,
chimes, piano & strings.
Unidentified, Trumpet(s), 2)

₍Variations on America, organ, (1891?); arr. orchestra₎
Variations on "America"
Arranged by William Schuman
Herseth, Adolph, 5)
Rapier, Leon, 4)

Jacchini, Giuseppe Maria, *ca.* 1663-1727
Iacchini, Giuseppe Maria

[Sinfonia, trumpet, strings & continuo, D major, (1690)]
Sinfonia con Tromba in re maggiore
Archives of the Basilica of San Petronio, Bologna. D. XII, 5
Hunger, Helmut, 1)

[Sonata, trumpet, strings & continuo, D major]
Sonata con Tromba in re maggiore
¹Allegro / ²Presto / ³Maestoso
Archives of the Basilica of San Petronio, Bologna. D. XII, 6
Hunger, Helmut, 3)

[Sonata, 2 trumpets, strings & continuo, D major]
Sonata con due Trombe in re maggiore
There are 3 compositions by Jacchini for 2 trumpets: *Sonata con Trombe*, (1695); *Sinfonia con due Trombe* [D. XII, 7]; *Sonata con due Trombe*, op. 5, no. 1. (It has not been determined which of these has been recorded here: Bernard Soustrot's recording includes two of these.)
Molénat, Claude
Soustrot, Bernard, 7)
Wobisch, Helmut, 6)

[Trattenimenti per camera... op. 5, (1703). No. 5: Sonata, trumpet, violins, cello & continuo, D major]
Sonata con Tromba sola, Violini e Violoncelle obligato in re maggiore, op. 5, no. 5
¹Allegro / ²Grave - Allegro - Adagio / ³Allegro
from *Trattenimenti per camera a 3, 4, 5, e 6 Strumenti con alcune a una e due Trombe*, Opus V. (The sections of the second movement are sometimes listed as separate movements.)
André, Maurice, 177)
Haas, Wolfgang
Scherbaum, Adolf, 20)
Smithers, Don, 4)
Vaillant, Ludovic, 6)

Jackson, Nicholas, 1934-

[Suite on the Magnificat, mixed voices, trumpet & organ]
Suite on the "Magnificat"
Murphy, Maurice

Jacob, Gordon, 1895-1984
Jacob, Gordon Percival Septimus

[Music for a Festival, brass soli & band]
Music for a Festival
¹Intrada / ²Overture / ³Round / ⁴Air / ⁵Interlude / ⁶March / ⁷Sarabande / ⁸Scherzo / ⁹Madrigal / ¹⁰Minuet & Trio / ¹¹Finale
Potpourri, 7)

Jacobi, Christian August, 1688-1725?

[Cantata, "Der Himmel steht uns wieder offen", tenor, mixed voices, 2 trumpets]
Cantata, "Der Himmel steht uns wieder offen"
Güttler, Ludwig, 10)

Jacoby, Don, 20th cent.

[Carnival Variations, 3 trumpets & concert band]
Carnival Variations
Garside, Derek M.
Jacoby, Don

[Jacob Jones, trumpet & dance band]
Jacob Jones
Jacoby, Don

[Trumpeter's Soliloquy, trumpet & dance band]
Trumpeter's Soliloquy
Jacoby, Don

James, Woodrow, 1936-

[Elegy, trumpet & piano]
Elegy
Amstutz, Keith

Janáček, Leoš, 1854-1928

[Capriccio, piano (left hand) & chamber wind ensemble, (1926)]
Capriccio for Piano (left hand) and Wind Instruments
[1]Allegro / [2]Adagio / [3]Allegretto / [4]Andante
Chamber wind ensemble includes: flute (piccolo), 2 trumpets, 3 trombones & tuba.
Crisara, Raymond, 3)
Horák, Jiří, 4)
Lisý, Rudolf
Popov, Sergei, 3)

Jarre, Maurice, 1924-
Jarre, Maurice Alexis

[Doctor Zhivago, (1965). Lara's Theme; arr. trumpet & orchestra]
Lara's Theme
(from music for the film, *Doctor Zhivago*)
Méndez, Rafael, 16)

Jeanjean, Paul, 1874-1928

[Capriccioso, cornet & piano, (1924)]
Capriccioso
Haynie, John, 1)

Jelić, Vincenz, 1596-*ca.* 1636
Jelich, Vincenzo

ₜParnassia militia concertuum, op. 1, (1622). Ricercar, trumpet & trombone, f minorₙ
Ricercar in f minor
Holy, Walter, 4)

Jiménez, Gerónimo
See: Giménez, Jerónimo

Johann Ernst von Sachsen-Weimar, 1696-1715
Johann Ernst (Prince of Sachsen-Weimar)

ₜSonata, trumpet, strings & continuo, D majorₙ
Sonate D-dur für Trompete, Streicher und Basso continuo
Güttler, Ludwig, 21^5), 26)

Johnson, Francis, 19th cent.

ₜBugle Quick Step, keyed bugle & orchestra, (ca. 1825)ₙ
The Bugle Quick Step
Dudgeon, Ralph

ₜColonel C.G. Child's Parade March, keyed bugle & orchestra, (1826)ₙ
Colonel C.G. Child's Parade March
Dudgeon, Ralph

Johnson, Robert, *ca.* 1583-1633

ₜAlmande, no. 7; arr. 2 trumpets & 4 trombonesₙ
Almande No. 7
André, Maurice, 176)

Jolivet, André, 1905-1974

ₜAir de bravoure, trumpet & piano, (1953)ₙ
Air de bravoure
Piano accompaniment is optional.
Christensen, Ketil
Darling, James
Gardner, Ned
Schwarz, Gerard, 12)
Stith, Marice, 5)

ₜArioso Barocco, trumpet & organ, (1969)ₙ
Arioso Barocco pour trompette et orgue
André, Maurice, 144), 145)
Perinelli, René

ſConcertino, trumpet, piano & strings, (1948)]
Concertino pour trompette, orchestre à cordes et piano
In one movement: Allegro - Allegro molto - Meno vivo...
> **André, Maurice,** 82), 103), 145)
> **Delmotte, Roger,** 18)
> **Marsalis, Wynton,** 3)
> **Thibaud, Pierre,** 4)

ſConcerto, trumpet & chamber ensemble, no. 2, (1954)]
Deuxième Concerto pour Trompette
(Second Concerto for Trumpet)
[1]Mesto / [2]Grave / [3]Giocoso
The *Concertino for Trumpet, Piano and Strings* is apparently considered as "Concerto No. 1".
The instrumentation for the chamber ensemble of this "second concerto" is: 2 flutes (piccolo), clarinet, English horn, alto saxophone, tenor saxophone, contrabassoon, trombone, percussion, harp, piano & bass.
> **André, Maurice,** 35[3]), 82), 103), 145)
> **Delmotte, Roger,** 4), 21)
> **Marsalis, Wynton,** 3), 7)
> **Potpourri,** 68)

ſHeptade, trumpet & percussion, (1971)]
Heptade pour trompette et percussion
[1]Allegro / [2]Vivo / [3]Cantante / [4]Veemente / [5]Maestoso / [6]Sempre stringendo / [7]Vivo e ritmico
> **André, Maurice,** 145)

ſRhapsodie, chamber ensemble, (1957)]
Rhapsodie à 7
Chamber ensemble includes: clarinet, bassoon, cornet, trombone, violin, bass & percussion.
> **Delmotte, Roger,** 6)
> **Perinelli, René**
> **Volodin, Lev**

ſSuite Delphique, chamber ensemble, (1942)]
Suite Delphique
Chamber ensemble includes: flute, oboe, clarinet, 2 horns, trumpet, trombone, ondes Martinot, harp, timpani & percussion.
> **Delmotte, Roger,** 5)

Jonasson, Emanuel

ſKuckuckswalzer; arr. flügelhorn & accordion band]
Kuckuckswalzer
> **André, Maurice,** 61)

Jones, Jeffrey, 1944-

₍Ambiance, soprano & chamber ensemble, (1968-69)₎
Ambiance
Chamber ensemble includes: flute (piccolo), oboe (English horn),
bassoon, horn, trumpet, trombone, violin, cello, piano (celeste),
harpsichord, harp & percussion.
Dean, Allan, 6)

Joplin, Scott, 1868-1917

₍Pleasant Moments, piano, (1909); arr. cornet & ragtime ensemble₎
Pleasant Moments
Schwarz, Gerard, 5)

Jørgensen, A., 20th cent.

₍Caprice Orientale, trumpet & piano₎
Caprice Orientale
Christensen, Ketil

Josquin des Préz, *ca.* 1440-1521
Despres, Josquin
Despret, Josquin
Desprez, Josquin

₍Bernardina, cornetto, dulcian & trombone₎
La Bernardina
Laird, Michael, 13)

₍Déploration sur la mort de Johan Okeghem, soli, mixed voices, cornetto muto, 2
trombones & pommer₎
Déploration sur la mort de Johan Okeghem
(Lament on the Death of Ockeghem)
Hagge, Detlef

₍Fanfare, "Vive le roi", four-part instrumental ensemble, (1498); arr. brass
ensemble₎
Royal Fanfare for the Consecration of Louis XII
("Vive le roy")
André, Maurice, 98)

₍Fanfare, "Vive le roi", four-part instrumental ensemble, (1498); arr. brass
quintet₎
Royal Fanfare for the Consecration of Louis XII
("Vive le roy")
Canadian Brass, 1)

₍Fanfare, "Vive le roi", four-part instrumental ensemble, (1498); arr. cornetto,
shawm & 2 trombones₎
Royal Fanfare for the Consecration of Louis XII
("Vive le roy")
Laird, Michael, 13)

Joy, Edward

₍At Peace with God; arr. trumpet & piano₎
At Peace with God
Thomas, Peggy Paton

Kagel, Mauricio, 1931-
Kagel, Maurizio Raúl

₍Acusta, experimental sound producers & loud speakers₎
Acusta
Tarr, Edward, 16)

₍Atem, 1 wind instrument, (1969/70)₎
Atem, für einem Bläser
(Breath, for a wind-musician)
Tarr, Edward, 29)

₍Morceau de concours, trumpet(s), (1968-70)₎
Morceau de concours
Solo trumpeter plays C-trumpet, piccolo trumpet, Baroque trumpet, tromba da tirarsi, cornetto, Nafir, Kindertrompete & Muschelhorn.
Tarr, Edward, 29)

₍Schall, flute, trumpet, trombone, guitar, percussion & chamber ensemble₎
Der Schall
(Sound)
Five soloists with ensemble of 54 instruments.
Tarr, Edward, 14)

₍1898, children's voices & chamber ensemble, (1973)₎
1898
Chamber ensemble includes: trumpet, horn, trombone, tuba, harp, piano, percussion, violin, viola, cello & bass.
Bauer, Adam

Kalsons, Romualds, 1936-

₍Concerto grosso, trumpet, horn & orchestra₎
Concerto Grosso for Trumpet, Horn and Symphony Orchestra
Klishans, Yanis

Kaminski, Joseph, 1903-1972

₍Concertino, trumpet & orchestra, (1941)₎
Concertino for Trumpet
[1]"Un poco Vivaldi" (Allegramente) / [2]Improvisazione (Vivace, ironico) / [3]Tarantella (Presto)
A piano reduction by the composer was published in 1952 by Israeli Music Publications. The first movement is a parody in C major of Vivaldi's *Concerto in a minor for Violin*, R. 356.
Tarr, Edward, 9)

Karayev, Kara Abdul'faz-oglï, 1918-1982
Kareva, Kara Abdulfaz-ogly

⌐Piece, trumpet & piano⌐
Piece
Ots, Aavo

Karg-Elert, Sigfrid, 1877-1933

⌐Sinfonische Kanzone, op. 85, (1910). No. 1: Kanzone und Tokkata, organ; arr. trumpet & organ⌐
Kanzone und Tokkata, op. 85, nr. 1
Rhoten, Bruce

Kaufmann, Armin, 1902-1980

⌐Music, trumpet & orchestra, op. 38, (1948)⌐
Musik für Trompete und Streichorchester, op. 38
[1]Allegro molto / [2]Andante con Var. / [3]Allegro
A piano reduction by the composer was published in 1953 by Ars Viva.
Wobisch, Helmut, 10)

Kaufmann, Georg Friedrich, 1679-1735

⌐Chorale Prelude, "Ach Gott, von Himmel sieh Darein", oboe & organ; arr. trumpet & organ⌐
Chorale Prelude, "Ach Gott, von Himmel sieh Darein"
Erb, Helmut, 2)
Touvron, Guy, 20)

⌐Chorale Prelude, "Gelobet seist du, Jesu Christ", oboe & organ; arr. trumpet & organ⌐
Chorale Prelude, "Gelobet seist du, Jesu Christ"
Erb, Helmut, 2)

⌐Chorale Prelude, "Herr Christ, der einig Gottes Sohn", oboe & organ; arr. trumpet & organ⌐
Chorale Prelude, "Herr Christ, der einig Gottes Sohn"
Falentin, Paul, 5)

⌐Chorale Prelude, "Herr Gott, dich loben alle wir", oboe & organ; arr. trumpet & organ⌐
Chorale Prelude, "Herr Gott, dich loben alle wir"
Touvron, Guy, 20)

⌐Chorale Prelude, "Wie schön leuchtet der Morgenstern", oboe & organ; arr. trumpet & organ⌐
Chorale Prelude, "Wie schön leuchtet der Morgenstern"
Erb, Helmut, 2)
Falentin, Paul, 5)
Güttler, Ludwig, 24)

Kay, Ulysses Simpson, 1917-

ıFanfares (3), trumpet quartet, (1942)ı
Three Fanfares
Giangiulio, Richard

Kazaryan, Y.

ıSonata, trumpet & pianoı
Sonata for Trumpet and Piano
Balyan, Yuri

Keller, Max, 1770-1855

ıProcessional Fanfares (6), 6 trumpets, timpani & organı
Six Processional Fanfares
Eklund's Baroque Ensemble

Kelterborn, Rudolf, 1931-

ıMusik, piano & 8 wind instruments, (1970)ı
Musik für Klavier und 8 Bläser
The wind ensemble includes: flute, oboe, 2 clarinets, bassoon, horn, trumpet & trombone.
Scholz, Walter

Kennan, Kent, 1913-
Kennan, Kent Wheeler

ıPieces (3), orchestra, (1936)ı
Three Pieces for Orchestra
[1]Promenade / [2]Nocturne [viola solo & orchestra] / [3]Il Campo dei Fiori [trumpet solo & orchestra]
Austin, James

ıSonata, trumpet & piano, (1956)ı
Sonata for Trumpet and Piano
[1]With strength and vigor / [2]Rather slowly and with freedom / [3]Moderately fast, with energy
> **Amstutz, Keith**[1]
> **Darling, James**
> **Head, Emerson**
> **Hickman, David,** 4)
> **Malkov, Valentin**
> **Masters, Edward L.**[1]
> **Stith, Marice,** 3)

Kennedy

ıGloria, trumpet & organı
Gloria
Pliquett, Joachim

Kern, Jerome (David), 1885-1945

[Show Boat, (1927). Ol' Man River; arr. trumpet & orchestra]
Ol' Man River from *Show Boat*
André, Maurice, 66)

Kerzinger, August, 17th cent.

[Sonata, trumpet, brass & orchestra]
Sonata a 9
Güttler, Ludwig, 1), 4)

Khachaturian, Aram Il'yich, 1903-1978

[Gayaneh, (1942). Sabre Dance; arr. trumpet & brass ensemble]
Sabre Dance from *Gayaneh*
The ballet, *Gayaneh* is sometimes spelled: *Gayane* or *Gayne*.
Grin, Freddy, 2)
Mertens, Theo, 1)

[Gayaneh, (1942). Sabre Dance; arr. trumpet & orchestra]
Sabre Danse from *Gayaneh*
André, Maurice, 4)

[Gayaneh, (1942). Sabre Dance; arr. trumpet trio, clarinet & rhythm]
Sabre Dance from *Gayaneh*
Victorian Trumpet Trio

Khamidi, Latif Abdulaevich, 1906-1983

[Scherzo, trumpet & orchestra]
Scherzo for Trumpet and Orchestra
Klushkin, Yuri

Klein, John M., 1915-

[Lament, trumpet & piano, (1954)]
Lament
Haynie, John, 2)

Knapp, Phoebe Palmer, 1839-1908

[Open the Gates of the Temple; arr. trumpet & organ]
Open the Gates of the Temple
Stith, Marice, 9)
Tolley, Richard

Knight, Morris H., 1933-

[Assortments No. 1, clarinet, trumpet & violin]
Assortments No. 1 for Clarinet, Trumpet and Violin
Greenho, David

Kobekin, Vladimir, 1947-

ɼSymphony, trumpet, bassoon, piano & orchestraɹ
Symphony
Ikov, Andrei

Koenig, Heinrich, 19th cent.

ɼPost Horn Galop; arr. posthorn & pianoɹ
Post Horn Galop
Impett, Jonathan

ɼPost Horn Galop; arr. trumpet trio, clarinet & rhythmɹ
Post Horn Galop
Victorian Trumpet Trio

Koetsier, Jan, 1911-

ɼConcerto, trumpet, trombone & orchestra, (1965)ɹ
Konzert für Trompete, Posaune und Orchester
Wilbraham, John, 10)

ɼSonatina, trumpet & piano, (1970)ɹ
Sonatina per Tromba e Pianoforte
[1]Larghetto con variazioni: a) Allegretto; b) Allegramente; c) Allegro assai, Tempo primo / [2]Rondo (Allegro)
Rippas, Claude

Kondo, Jo, 1947-

ɼAir I, amplified piano & trumpetɹ
Air I for Amplified Piano with Trumpet
Soken, Hosei

Korn, Peter Jona, 1922-

ɼConcerto, trumpet & orchestra, op. 67ɹ
Concerto for Trumpet and Orchestra, op. 67
Reinhart, Carole Dawn, 6)

ɼMorgenmusik, trumpet & strings, op. 54ɹ
Morgenmusik, op. 54
Quinque, Rolf, 5)

Korngold, Erich Wolfgang, 1897-1957

ɼLove for Love, (1947); arr. trumpet & orchestraɹ
Love for Love
Méndez, Rafael, 4)

Kosaku, Yamada, 1886-1965

₍Akatombo; arr. trumpet & piano₎
Akatombo
(Red Dragonfly)
Dokshitser, Timofei, 19)

₍Kono Michi; arr. trumpet & piano₎
Kono Michi
(This Pathway)
Dokshitser, Timofei, 19)

₍Machibooke; arr. trumpet & piano₎
Machibooke
(Waiting Hopelessly)
Dokshitser, Timofei, 19)

Kosma, Joseph, 1905-1969

₍Autumn Leaves, (1946); arr. flügelhorn, drums, guitar & electric organ₎
Autumn Leaves
Lieberman, Harold J.

₍Autumn Leaves, (1946); arr. trumpet & orchestra₎
Les feuilles mortes
(The Autumn Leaves)
This music was inspired by Jacques Prévert's poem, "Les feuilles mortes", and was originally used in the French film, *Les portes de la nuit*, (1946). English lyrics were added by Johnny Mercer and used in the American film, *Autumn Leaves*, (1956).
André, Maurice, 7), 170)

Koutník, Tomáš Norbert, 1698-1775

₍Regina cœli, mixed voices, 2 trumpets, strings & continuo₎
Regina cœli
Buriánek, Jindřich

Koželuch, Leopold Antonín, 1747-1818

₍Sinfonia concertante, piano, mandolin, trumpet, bass & orchestra, E♭ major₎
Sinfonia concertante Es-dur
Erb, Helmut, 1)
Goethel, Siegfried
Leroy, Jean-Paul

Kraft, William, 1923-

₍Encounters III, trumpet & percussion, (1971)₎
Encounters III
¹Strategy / ²Truce of God / ³Tactics
Encounters I is for solo percussion, and *Encounters II* is for solo tuba.
Stevens, Thomas, 1), 16)

Krämer, Leo, 1944-

₍Veni creator spiritus, 2 trumpets, 3 trombones & organ₎
Veni creator spiritus
Grin, Freddy, 4)

Krapf, Gerhard, 1924-

₍Easter Salutation, "Christ Is Risen", mixed voices, 2 trumpets & 2 trombones, (1980)₎
Easter Salutation, "Christ Is Risen"
Pier, Fordyce

Krasotov, Alexandra, 1936-

₍Concert-Symphony, trumpet & orchestra₎
Concert-Symphony for Trumpet and Orchestra
Dokshitser, Timofei, 21), 25)

Krebs, Johann Ludwig, 1713-1780

₍Chorale Prelude, "Ach Gott! erhör mein Seufzen", trumpet & organ₎
Chorale Prelude, "Ach Gott! erhör mein Seufzen"
Delmotte, Roger, 39)

₍Chorale Prelude, "Es ist gewisslich an der Zeit", trumpet & organ₎
Chorale Prelude, "Es ist gewisslich an der Zeit"
André, Maurice, 77), 131)
Güttler, Ludwig, 6), 22)
Hartog, Thomas
Tarr, Edward, 8)

₍Chorale Prelude, "Gott der Vater wohn' uns bei", trumpet & organ₎
Chorale Prelude, "Gott der Vater wohn' uns bei"
André, Maurice, 77), 131)
Tarr, Edward, 8), 40)

₍Chorale Prelude, "Herzlich lieb' hab' ich dich, o Herr", trumpet & organ₎
Chorale Prelude, "Herzlich lieb' hab' ich dich, o Herr"
André, Maurice, 77), 131)
Güttler, Ludwig, 6), 22)
Tarr, Edward, 8)

ₜChorale Prelude, "Herzlich tut mich verlangen", trumpet & organ₁
Chorale Prelude, "Herzlich tut mich verlangen"
Held, Friedrich

ₜChorale Prelude, "In allen meinen Taten", trumpet & organ₁
Chorale Prelude, "In allen meinen Taten"
André, Maurice, 40), 55)
Haas, Wolfgang
Potpourri, 35)
Rehm, Klaus
Spindler, Josef, 4)
Tarr, Edward, 8), 40)
Touvron, Guy, 12)

ₜChorale Prelude, "Jesus meine Freude", trumpet & organ₁
Chorale Prelude, "Jesus meine Freude"
André, Maurice, 40), 55)

ₜChorale Prelude, "Komm', heiliger Geist, Herre Gott", trumpet & organ₁
Chorale Prelude, "Komm', heiliger Geist, Herre Gott"
Tarr, Edward, 41)

ₜChorale Prelude, "Liebster Jesu, wir sind hier", trumpet & organ₁
Chorale Prelude, "Liebster Jesu, wir sind hier"
André, Maurice, 77), 131)
Bernard, André, 4)
Hartog, Thomas

ₜChorale Prelude, "Wachet auf, ruft uns die Stimme", trumpet & organ₁
Chorale Prelude, "Wachet auf, ruft uns die Stimme"
There are three settings by Krebs for this chorale prelude. They are specified on the recordings by Edward Tarr, but the other recordings have not been specifically identified.
André, Maurice, 131), 215)
Bernard, André, 4)
Braz, Dirceu, 2)
Chesnut, Walter
Erb, Helmut, 2)
Güttler, Ludwig, 24)
Hartog, Thomas
Laughton, Stuart
Potpourri, 35)
Rehm, Klaus
Spindler, Josef, 4)
Tarr, Edward, 8), 39), 41)
Voisin, Roger, 2)

ₜChorale Prelude, "Was mein Gott will, das g'scheh' allzeit", trumpet & organ₁
Chorale Prelude, "Was mein Gott will, das g'scheh' allzeit"
André, Maurice, 77), 131)

₍Chorale Preludes, trumpet & organ, {unspecified}₎
Two Chorale Preludes
Send, Peter

₍Fantasia, oboe & organ, f minor; arr. trumpet & orchestra₎
Fantasia in f minor
André, Maurice, 73), 214), 165)

₍Fantasia, trumpet & organ, C major₎
Fantasie C-dur
(Fantasia in C major)
Tarr, Edward, 8)
Touvron, Guy, 12)

Kreisler, Fritz, 1875-1962

₍Caprice Viennois, violin & piano, op. 2; arr. trumpet & orchestra₎
Caprice Viennois
André, Maurice, 4)

₍Liebesfreud, violin & piano; arr. trumpet & brass ensemble₎
Liebesfreud
Grin, Freddy, 2)

₍Liebesfreud, violin & piano; arr. trumpet & piano₎
Liebesfreud
Christensen, Ketil
Dokshitser, Timofei, 5), 7), 9), 31), 35), 36), 38), 39)

₍Liebesleid, violin & piano; arr. trumpet & piano₎
Liebesleid
Christensen, Ketil
Dokshitser, Timofei, 5), 7), 9), 31), 35), 36), 38), 39)

₍Schön Rosmarin, violin & piano; arr. trumpet & brass ensemble₎
Schön Rosmarin
Grin, Freddy, 2)

₍Schön Rosmarin, violin & piano; arr. trumpet & piano₎
Schön Rosmarin
Dokshitser, Timofei, 5), 7), 9), 31), 35), 36), 38), 39)

Kreutzenhoff, Johannes, 15th cent.-16th cent.

₍Frisch und frölich wölln wir leben, cornetto, alto shawm, tenor crumhorn, bass sackbut₎
Frisch und frölich wölln wir leben
Laird, Michael, 3)

Krieger, Johann Philipp, 1649-1725
Kriegher, Giovanni Filippo

₍Cephalus und Procris, (1689). Allegro; arr. trumpet & piano₎
Allegro from *Procris*
This "allegro" is included as the second part of a transcription by
Bernard Fitzgerald: *Aria and Allegro*. The "aria" is by Antonio F.
Tenaglia, (1685-1750).
Ghitalla, Armando, 11)
Haynie, John, 2)

Krol, Bernhard, 1920-

₍Cantata, "Wort-Gottes", baritone, mixed voices, 3 trumpets, 4 trombones &
organ, op. 68₎
Wort-Gottes-Kantate, op. 68
Wolf, Hans, 13)

₍Fantasia notturna, trumpet & organ, op. 54₎
Fantasia notturna, op. 54
Tamiya, Kenji

₍Krönungsfantasie, trumpet, trombone & organ, op. 76₎
Krönungsfantasie nach Monteverdi, op. 76
Tamiya, Kenji

₍Variations, (theme from Bach's Magnificat), trumpet & orchestra, op. 40, (1965)₎
Magnificat-Variationen für Bachtrompete und Streichorchester, op. 40
(Variations sur le "Magnificat" de Bach, op. 40)
Based on the aria, "Quia fecit mihi magna".
André, Maurice, 146)

Kryl, Bohumir, 1874-1961

₍Josephine, cornet & piano, (1909); arr. cornet & chamber ensemble₎
Josephine
Schwarz, Gerard, 5)

Kryukov, Vladimir Nikolayevich, 1902-1960

₍Concerto-Poem in C major, trumpet & orchestra, op. 59, (1955)₎
Concerto-Poem in C major, op. 59
(Kontsert-Poema, op. 59)
Dokshitser, Timofei, 33)

Kubik, Gail Thompson, 1914-1984

₍Symphony Concertante, trumpet, viola, piano & orchestra, (1952)₎
Symphony Concertante
[1]Fast, vigorously / [2]Quietly / [3]Fast, with energy
Haneuse, Arthur

Küffner, Joseph, 19th cent.

ₜPolonaise, keyed bugle, clarinet, flute & chamber ensemble, (1823)ₜ
Polonaise pour le cor de signal-à-clef
Dudgeon, Ralph

Kugelmann, Johann, *ca.* 1495-1542

ₜNun lob' mein Seel' den Herren, (1540); arr. brass ensembleₜ
Nun lob' mein Seel' den Herren
André, Maurice, 98)

Kümmerlin, Ludwig, 1936-

ₜDialogue d'amour, trumpet & organₜ
Dialogue d'amour
Braz, Dirceu, 1)

Kupferman, Meyer, 1926-

ₜInfinities No. 22, trumpet & piano, (1968)ₜ
Infinities No. 22 for Trumpet and Piano
Nagel, Robert, 21)

ₜThree Ideas, trumpet & piano, (1967)ₜ
Three Ideas
Levy, Robert
Stevens, Thomas, 5)

Kurz, Siegfried, 1930-

ₜConcerto, trumpet & string orchestra, op. 23ₜ
Konzert für Trompete und Streichorchester, op. 23
Erb, Helmut, 3)
Stephan, Wolfgang

Kuzhamyarov, Kuddus Khodzhamyarovich, 1918-

ₜConcerto, trumpet & orchestraₜ
Concerto for Trumpet and Orchestra
Klushkin, Yuri

Kvandal, Johan, 1919-
Kvandal Johansen, David Johan

ₜO Domine Deus, soprano, trumpet & organ (?), op. 26, no. 2ₜ
O Domine Deus, op. 26, no. 2
This work may be for organ alone.
Nystrom, Kaj

Labole, P.N.

₍Pinson et Fauvette; arr. 2 cornets & brass ensemble₎
  Pinson et Fauvette
                    Aquitaine Brass Ensemble

Lalande, Michel-Richard de
See: Delalande, Michel-Richard

Lambro, Phillip, 1935-

₍Trumpet Voluntary, solo trumpet, (c. 1977)₎
  Trumpet Voluntary
    From music for the film, *Mineral King*
        Plog, Anthony, 6)

Lampl, Carl G., 1898-1962

₍Thoughtless, (1948); arr. trumpet & orchestra₎
  Thoughtless
                    Méndez, Rafael, 4)

Landowski, Marcel, 1915-
Landowski, Marcel François Paul

₍Au bout de Chagrin, trumpet, orchestra & electronic elements, (c. 1976)₎
  Au bout de Chagrin, une fenêtre ouverte
    (Concerto pour trompette, orchestre et éléments électroacoustiques)
      ¹Cantiques d'un soir / ²Chant pour une feuille morte / ³Cortège
        André, Maurice, 159)

₍Cahier pour Quatre Jours, trumpet & organ, (c. 1976)₎
  Cahier pour Quatre Jours
    (Quatre Pièces pour Trompette et Orgue)
      ¹Jour du secret intérieur / ²Jour de quête de soi / ³Jour des regrets et
    des pardons / ⁴Jour de joie
        André, Maurice, 159¹⁻⁴)

Lane, 20th cent.

₍Song, cornet & piano₎
  Song for Cornet and Piano
        Smith, Philip, 2)

Lang, 20th cent.

₍Trumpet and Drum, trumpet, drum & band₎
  Trumpet and Drum
                    Crisara, Raymond, 10)

Langford, Gordon, 1930-

₍Rhapsody, cornet & brass band₎
Rhapsody for Cornet and Brass Band
Watson, James

Langlais, Jean, 1907-
Langlais, Jean-François

₍Chorale Prelude, "O, dass doch bald dein Feuer brennte", trumpet & organ₎
Chorale Prelude, "O, dass doch bald dein Feuer brennte"
Güttler, Ludwig, 22)

₍Chorale Preludes (7), trumpet & keyboard instrument, (1972)₎
Sept Chorals pour trompette ou flûte ou hautbois avec
accompagnement d'orgue ou de piano ou de clavecin
[1]Aus tiefer Not schrei' ich zu dir / [2]Ein' feste Burg ist unser Gott /
[3]Vater unser im Himmelreich / [4]Psalm 140: Herr, schütze mich, behüte
mein Leben / [5]In dulci jubilo / [6]Jesu, meine Freude / [7]Lobe den
Herren, den mächtigen König der Ehren
Translations: [1]In deep distress I cry to Thee / [2]A mighty fortress
is our God / [3]Our Father who art in Heaven / [4]Lord, protect me,
guard my life / [5]In dulci jubilo / [6]Jesus, my Joy / [7]Praise to the
Lord, the Almighty King of Honor
André, Maurice, 164[5-6+3+2])
Blair, Stacy[6+5+2]
Delmotte, Roger, 44[1+3-4])
Grin, Freddy, 3[1-7]), 5[5+7])
Güttler, Ludwig, 22[6-7])
Pearson, Byron[1-2]
Willwerth, Paul[1+4+7]

₍Mass, "Salve Regina", baritone, mixed voices & brass ensemble₎
Messe "Salve Regina"
Delmotte, Roger, 44)

₍Pastorale and Rondo, 2 trumpets & organ₎
Pastorale et Rondo
(Pastorale und Rondo)
Haas, Wolfgang

₍Pièce, trumpet & keyboard instrument, (1972)₎
Pièce pour Trompette (ou hautbois ou flûte) avec
accompagnement d'orgue, de piano ou de clavecin
[1]Introduction: Allegro / [2]Andante / [3]Final: Allegro
Grin, Freddy, 3)

₍Psaume Solennel. No. 3, "Laudate Dominum de coelis", baritone, mixed voices &
brass ensemble₎
Psaume Solennel No. 3, "Laudate Dominum de coelis"
Delmotte, Roger, 44)

⌜Sonatina, trumpet, keyboard instrument, (1976)⌝
Sonatine pour Trompette avec accompagnement de piano, clavecin ou orgue (sans mixtures)
[1]Allegro / [2]Andantino / [3]Mouvement perpétuel: Allegro vivo
A footnote on the published music indicates that the solo part may be performed by flute, oboe or violin.
André, Maurice, 164)
Grin, Freddy, 3)
Murphy, Maurice
Pearson, Byron

Langworthy

⌜Heavenly Gales; arr. trumpet & piano⌝
Heavenly Gales
Smith, Philip, 2)

Lara, Agustín, 1900-1969

⌜Granada, (1932); arr. trumpet & orchestra⌝
Granada
André, Maurice, 7), 170)
Hidalgo, José Luis
Unidentified, Trumpet(s), 3)

Lara, Maria Teresa, 20th cent.

⌜Valencia; arr. trumpet & orchestra⌝
Valencia
Méndez, Rafael, 12)

Lassus, Roland de, 1532-1594
Lasso, Orlando di
Lassus, Orlandus

⌜Madrigals; Suite, arr. instrumental ensemble⌝
A Suite of Madrigals
[1]Hor che la nuova / [2]Chichilichi! Cucurucu! / [3]Echo — Valle profunda / [4]Passan vostri triomphi
Montesi, Robert, 6)

⌜Motet, "Gloria patri", mixed voices & instrumental ensemble⌝
Motet, "Gloria patri"
Renz, Albrecht, 4)

⌜Sacræ Lectiones ex propheta Job, mixed voices & instrumental ensemble⌝
Sacræ Lectiones ex propheta Job
(Lamentations of Job)
Pok, František, 6)

[Weihnachtsmesse, No. 3. Offertorium, mixed voices & instrumental ensemble]
Tui sunt cœli
(Offertorium d. Dritte Weihnachtsmesse)
Renz, Albrecht, 4)
Stradner, Gerhard

Latham, William P., 1917-
Latham, William Peters

[Suite, trumpet & orchestra, (1952?); arr. trumpet & band]
Suite for Trumpet and Band
[1]Prelude: Marziale / [2]Air: Andante sostenuto / [3]Dance: Presto
Haynie, John, 5)

[Suite, trumpet & orchestra, (1952?); arr. trumpet & piano]
Suite for Trumpet and Orchestra
[1]Prelude: Marziale / [2]Air: Andante sostenuto / [3]Dance: Presto
Piano reduction published in 1955.
Burkart, Richard[2-3]
Masters, Edward L.
Nagel, Robert, 17)

Lazari, Ferdinando Antonio, 1678-1754
Lazzari, Fra. Ferdinando Antonio

[Sonata, 2 trumpet & strings, D major]
Sonata a 6 con 2 Trombe e Stromenti
Touvron, Guy, 2)

Lazarof, Henri, 1932-

[Concertazioni, trumpet/flügelhorn, chamber ensemble & tape, (1973)]
Concertazioni, for solo trumpet, 6 instruments, and 4-channel tape amp.
The tape consists of pre-recorded trumpets and flügelhorns on 4 channels.
The chamber ensemble includes: flute/alto flute, clarinet/bass clarinet, horn, cello, harp & vibraphone.
Stevens, Thomas, 2), 5)

[Spectrum, trumpet/flügelhorn, orchestra & tape, (1973)]
Spectrum for Solo Trumpet, Orchestra and Tape
2 movements
The tape consists of pre-recorded trumpets on 4 channels.
Stevens, Thomas, 3)

Leduc, Jacques, 1932-

[Comptines, trumpet & piano, op. 44]
Comptines, op. 44
Phillippe, André

228

Leetherland, Thomas, 16th cent.-17th cent.

[Pavan; arr. 2 trumpets & 4 trombones]
Pavan
André, Maurice, 176)

Leffloth, Johann Matthäus, 1705-1731

[Concerto, flute or violin & harpsichord, D major; arr. trumpet & organ]
Konzert D-dur für Flöte oder Violine und Cembalo
[1]Andante / [2]Allegro / [3]Adagio / [4]Bourrée en rondeau
André, Maurice, 55)

Legrand, Michel, 1932-

[Cave se rebiffe. Cavatine; arr. cornet & orchestra]
Cavatine from *Le Cave se rebiffe*
André, Maurice, 207)

[Umbrellas of Cherbourg, (1964). Theme; arr. trumpet, mixed voices & orchestra]
Theme from *The Umbrellas of Cherbourg*
André, Maurice, 66)

Legrenzi, Giovanni, 1626-1690

[Sonata, "La Buscha", 2 cornetti, strings & continuo, op. 8; arr. 2 trumpets, strings & continuo]
Sonata a 6 per due cornetti, "La Buscha", op. 8
Güttler, Ludwig, 8)
Petit, Gilbert
Schmidhäusler, Francis & René
Voisin, Roger, 5), 8)

Lehár, Franz, 1870-1948
Lehár, Ferencz

[Land des Lächelns, (1929). Aria, "Dein ist mein ganzes Herz"; arr. trumpet & orchestra]
Yours is My Heart Alone from *The Land of Smiles*
(Aria of Prince Sou-Chong, "Dein ist mein ganzes Herz", from *Das Land des Lächelns*)
André, Maurice, 161), 212)

Leidzén, Erik, 1894-1962

[Happy All the Day; arr. trumpet & band]
Happy All the Day
(A Happy Day)
Reinhart, Carole Dawn, 10)

₍Happy All the Day; arr. trumpet & piano₎
Happy All the Day
(A Happy Day)
Thomas, Peggy Paton
Tobe, Yutaka

₍Songs in the Heart; arr. cornet & band₎
Songs in the Heart
Smith, Philip, 4)

₍Songs in the Heart; arr. trumpet & piano₎
Songs in the Heart
Thomas, Peggy Paton

₍Tucker, trumpet & band₎
Tucker
Reinhart, Carole Dawn, 10)

₍Wondrous Day; arr. cornet & band₎
Wondrous Day
Smith, Philip, 3)

Leighton, Kenneth, 1929-1988

₍Easter Sequence, treble voice, tenor, mixed voices & trumpet, op. 55, (1968)₎
An Easter Sequence, op. 55
Wiggans, Brian

Lemmel

₍Turn Your Eyes Upon Jesus; arr. trumpet & organ₎
Turn Your Eyes Upon Jesus
Reinhart, Carole Dawn, 13)

Lemmens, Jaak Nikolaas, 1823-1881
Lemmens, Jacques Nicolas

₍Fanfare, trumpet, organ & brass ensemble, D major₎
Fanfare in D major
Grin, Freddy, 9)

Lennon, John, 1940-
See: Rifkin, Joshua

Leoncavallo, Ruggero, 1857-1919

₍Pagliacci, (1892). Aria, "Vesti la giubba"; arr. trumpet & orchestra₎
Aria, "Vesti la giubba" from *I Pagliacci*
Méndez, Rafael, 9)

Leonchik, Svetlana Gavrilovna, 1939-

⌈Concerto, trumpet & orchestra, d minor, (1964)⌉
Concerto in d minor for Trumpet and Orchestra
Maximenko, Anatoly, 5)

Lesur, Daniel, 1908-
Daniel-Lesur, Daniel Jean Yves

⌈Aubade, trumpet & piano, 1953⌉
Aubade
Nagel, Robert, 15)
Ode, James

Levy, Jules, 1838-1903

⌈Grand Russian Fantasia, cornet & piano⌉
Grand Russian Fantasia
Haynie, John, 1)

⌈Grand Russian Fantasia, cornet & piano; arr. cornet & orchestra⌉
Grand Russian Fantasia
Clarke, Herbert L.

⌈Grand Russian Fantasia, cornet & piano; arr. cornet & wind ensemble⌉
Grand Russian Fantasia
Marsalis, Wynton, 4), 7)

Lévy, Roland Alexis Manuel
See: Roland-Manuel, Alexis

Lewis, Robert Hall, 1926-

⌈Monophony VII, solo trumpet, 1972⌉
Monophony VII
[1]Senza misura / [2]Andante moderato / [3]Senza misura quasi cadenza /
[4]Allegretto
Stevens, Thomas, 4)

Lieberman, Harold J., 1931-

⌈Fanfare, 8 trumpets⌉
Fanfare for 8 Trumpets
Lieberman, Harold J.

Lincke, Paul, 1866-1946
Lincke, (Carl Emil) Paul

⌈Komm, Karlineken; arr. flügelhorn & accordion band⌉
Komm, Karlineken
André, Maurice, 61)

231

Lindenfeld, Harris, 1945-
Lindenfeld, Harris Nelson

₍Combinations 1, trumpet & piano₎
Combinations 1 — The Last Gold of the Perished Stars
Stith, Marice, 4)

Lister, Mosie, 20th cent.

₍He Has Surely Borne Our Sorrows, mixed voices; arr. trumpet & orchestra₎
He Has Surely Borne Our Sorrows
Nagel, Robert, 9)

Liszt, Franz, 1811-1886
Liszt, Ferencz

₍Nocturnes (3), op. 62. No. 3: "Liebesträume", piano; arr. trumpet & harp₎
Nocturne, "Liebesträume", op. 62, no. 3
("Rêve d'amour")
André, Maurice, 84)

Llewellyn, Edward B., 1879-1936

₍My Regards, cornet & piano₎
My Regards, Waltz
Published in 1940
Gardner, Ned
Smith, Leonard B.

Lloyd Webber, Andrew, 1948-

₍Jesus Christ Superstar, (1970). Song, "I don't know how to love Him"; arr. trumpet & brass ensemble₎
"I don't know how to love Him" from *Jesus Christ Superstar*
Mertens, Theo, 1)

Lœillet, Jacques, 1685-1748
Lœillet, Jacob

₍Concerto, flute, strings & continuo, D major; arr. trumpet & string orchestra₎
Concerto en ré majeur pour trompette et orchestre à cordes
¹Allegro / ²Grave / ³Allegro
[Priestman: XVIII]
André, Maurice, 137)

₍Concerto, oboe, strings & continuo, E♭ major; arr. trumpet & string orchestra₎
Concerto en mi bémol majeur pour trompette et orchestre à cordes
¹Largo e puntato / ²Allegro / ³Largo - Vivace
[Priestman: XVII]
André, Maurice, 127)

Lœillet, Jean-Baptiste, 1688-*ca.* 1720
Lœillet de Gant, Jean-Baptiste
L'Œillet de Gant, Jean-Baptiste

[Sonatas, op. 3. No. 11, alto recorder & continuo, A major; arr. trumpet & organ,
F major]
Sonata in A major, op. 3, no. 11
[1]Largo / [2]Allemanda (Vivace) / [3]Gavotta (poco Allegro) /
[4]Sarabanda / [5]Siciliana (Affettuoso e poco largo) / [6]Giga (Vivace)
[Priestman: III, 11]
Braz, Dirceu, 5)

[Sonatas, op. 3. No. 11, alto recorder & continuo, A major; arr. trumpet & organ,
G major]
Sonata in A major, op. 3, no. 11
[1]Largo / [2]Allemanda (Vivace) / [3]Gavotta (poco Allegro) /
[4]Sarabanda / [5]Siciliana (Affettuoso e poco largo) / [6]Giga (Vivace)
[Priestman: III, 11] The fourth movement is omitted from this
arrangement.
André, Maurice, 45), 59)

[Sonatas, op. 3. No. 5, alto recorder & continuo, c minor; arr. trumpet & organ,
a minor]
Sonata in c minor, op. 3, no. 5
[1]Largo / [2]Allegro / [3]Menuet en rondeau / [4]Adagio / [5]Giga
[Priestman: III, 5]
André, Maurice, 59)

[Sonatas, op. 5. No. 1, flute, oboe (or violin) & continuo, e minor; arr. trumpet &
guitar]
Suite in e minor
[1]Allemande (Lente) / [2]Allegro / [3]Sarabande (Lente) / [4]Gavotte /
[5]Gigue
[Priestman: V, 1]
Braz, Dirceu, 2)

[Sonatas, op. 5. No. 1, flute, oboe (or violin) & continuo, e minor; arr. trumpet,
harpsichord & bassoon]
Trio Sonata in e minor, op. 5, no. 1
[1]Allemande (Lente) / [2]Allegro / [3]Sarabande (Lente) / [4]Gavotte /
[5]Gigue
[Priestman: V, 1]
André, Maurice, 203)

Lœillet, Jean-Baptiste, 1680-1730
Loeillet of London, John
Lœillet de Londres, Jean-Baptiste

ₜSonatas, op. 1. No. 2, 2 flutes & continuo, G major; arr. trumpet & organ₎
Sonata in G major, op. 1, no. 2
[1]Andante / [2]Allegro / [3]Andante / [4]Allegro
[Priestman: IX, 2]

                 André, Maurice, 141)
                 Güttler, Ludwig, 21), 24)
                 Kejmar, Miroslav, 1)
                 Pliquett, Joachim
                 Rapier, Leon, 1)
                 Tamiya, Kenji

ₜSonatas, op. 2. No. 1, 2 violins & continuo, B♭ major; arr. trumpet & organ₎
Sonata I in B♭ major
Allegro
[Priestman: X, 1]

                 Mertens, Theo, 4)

ₜSonatas, op. 2. No. 7, 2 violins & continuo, E major; arr. trumpet & organ₎
Sonata II in E major
Vivace
[Priestman: X, 7]

                 Mertens, Theo, 4)

ₜSonatas, op. 3. Nos. 1, 4, 10: flute or recorder & continuo, C major; arr. trumpet & organ₎
Sonata in C major
[1]Adagio [first movement of No. 1] / [2]Allegro [second movement of No. 10] / [3]Largo [first movement of No. 4] / [4]Allegro [second movement of No. 1]
[Priestman: VIII, 1, 4, 10]

                 André, Maurice, 50), 77), 131)
                 Gräber, Wolfgang
                 Güttler, Ludwig, 4), 6), 21), 22)

Lohmann, G.

ₜBayrische Polka; arr. trumpet & brass ensemble₎
Bayrische Polka
                 Grin, Freddy, 2)

London, Edwin, 1929-

ₜPsalm of These Days III, chamber ensemble₎
Psalm of These Days III
Chamber ensemble includes: flute, clarinet, trumpet, trombone, tuba, viola, bass, piano & percussion. (There are also incidental vocal parts sung by the instrumentalists.)
                 Sasaki, Ray

López, Miguel, 1669-1723

₍Cancion a la Sta. Imogen de Montserrat, mixed voices & chamber orchestra₎
Cancion a la Sta. Imogen de Montserrat
Espigoli, Jaume

₍Salve Regina, mixed voices & chamber orchestra₎
Salve Regina
Espigoli, Jaume

₍Villancico a la Natividad, mixed voices & chamber orchestra₎
Villancico a la Natividad
Espigoli, Jaume

Lortzing, Albert, 1801-1851
Lortzing, Gustav Albert

₍Theme and Variations, trumpet & orchestra, b♭ minor₎
Theme and Variations in b♭ minor for Trumpet and Orchestra
Hunger, Helmut, 1)

Loucheur, Raymond, 1899-1979

₍Concertino, trumpet & clarinet sextet₎
Concertino pour Trompette et Sextuor de Clarinettes
Ménardi, Louis

Louiguy, Louis Guglielmi, 1916-
Guglielmi, Luis

₍La vie en rose; arr. trumpet & orchestra₎
La vie en rose
Original French lyrics by Edith Piaf. Later English lyrics were authored by Mack David.
André, Maurice, 170)
Méndez, Rafael, 13)

Lovelock, William, 1899-

₍Concerto, trumpet & orchestra, 1970₎
Concerto for Trumpet and Orchestra
¹Allegro / ²Moderato / ³Allegro
Robertson, John

Löwe von Eisenach, Johann Jacob, 1629-1703

₍Sonaten, Canzonen und Capriccen..., (1664). No. 16: Capriccio, 2 trumpets & continuo, C major₎
Capriccio a due clarini [XVI]
Jones, Philip, 9)
Pohle, Wolfgang
Rehm, Klaus
Scherbaum, Adolf, 29)

₍Sonaten, Canzonen und Capriccen..., (1664). No. 17: Capriccio, 2 trumpets & continuo, C major₎
Capriccio secunda a due clarini [XVII]
Jones, Philip, 9)
Pohle, Wolfgang
Rehm, Klaus
Scherbaum, Adolf, 29)

Luca, Severio de
See: de Luca, Severio

Lully, Jean-Baptiste, 1632-1687

₍Airs pour le carrousel de Monseigneur, 4 trumpets, 3 oboes, bassoon & timpani, LWV 72, (1686)₎
Airs pour le carrousel de Monseigneur, LWV 72
(Fanfares pour le carrousel de Monseigneur, LWV 72)
(Airs de trompettes, hautbois et timbales)
(Carrousel Music)
¹Prélude du Carrousel / ²Menuet / ³Gigue / ⁴Gavotte pour les trompettes et hautbois
     André, Maurice, 6), 12), 98)
     Delmotte, Roger, 7), 17), 23), 25), 26), 28)
     Potpourri, 15)
     Scherbaum, Adolf, 18)
     Tarr, Edward, 28), 33)
     Voisin, Roger, 7)

₍Airs pour le carrousel de Monseigneur, 4 trumpets, 3 oboes, bassoon & timpani, LWV 72, (1686). Prélude; arr. 2 trumpets, oboe & organ₎
Prélude from *Les Airs de Trompettes, Timbales et Hautbois*
(Prélude from *Fanfares pour le carrousel de Monseigneur*, LWV 72)
     André, Maurice, 39)

₍Airs pour Madame la Dauphine, LWV 70, (1685). No. 1, Pavane, trumpet & strings₎
Pavane from *Airs pour Madame la Dauphine*, LWV 70
     Delmotte, Roger, 25), 26)

₍Airs pour Madame la Dauphine, LWV 70, (1685). Suite, orchestra₎
Airs pour Madame la Dauphine, LWV 70
(Plusieurs pièces de symphonie)
(Noce de Village)
¹Pavane / ²Gigue / ³Menuet / ⁴Menuet / ⁵Chaconne pour Madame la Princesse de Conty / ⁶Passepied / ⁷Passepied
     Delmotte, Roger, 11), 17)

₍Alceste, LWV 50, (1674). Suite, trumpets & strings₎
Suite from *Alceste*, LWV 50
(or *Le Triomphe d'Alcide*, LWV 50)
     Delmotte, Roger, 29)

[Amadis, LWV 63, (1684). Excerpts, C major; arr. 2 trumpets & piano, A♭ major]
Three Duets from *Amadis de Gaules*, LWV 63
[22]Marche pour le Combat de la Barrière / [23]Premier Air des Combattants / [24]Second Air (des Combattants)
Nagel, Robert, 11)

[Amadis, LWV 63, (1684). No. 23: Premier Air des Combattants, trumpet & strings]
Soldier' Air from *Amadis*, LWV 63
Delmotte, Roger, 23)

[Amadis, LWV 63, (1684). Suite, orchestra]
Suite from *Amadis*, LWV 63
[1]Ouverture / [4]Premier Air / [5]Second Air: Gigue / [11]Rondeau / [22]Marche pour le Combat de la Barrière / [23]Premier Air des Combattants / [24]Second Air (des Combattants) / [33] pour les Démons et les Monstres / [67]Chaconne
Tarr, Edward, 36), 38)

[Amadis, LWV 63, (1684). Suite, trumpet & orchestra]
Suite from *Amadis de Gaule*, LWV 63
The movements of this suite have not been ascertained.
André, Maurice, 91)

[Bellerophon, LWV 57, (1679). No. 69: Fanfare, 2 trumpets & strings]
Fanfare from *Bellerophon*, LWV 57
Delmotte, Roger, 23)

[Bourgeois Gentilhomme, LWV 43, (1670)]
Le Bourgeois Gentilhomme, LWV 43
There are 41 selections in this complete ballet.
Delmotte, Roger, 12)

[Bourgeois Gentilhomme, LWV 43, (1670). Menuet, trumpet & strings]
Menuet from *Le Bourgeois Gentilhomme*, LWV 43
Delmotte, Roger, 25)

[Bruits de trompettes. Selections, trumpets & strings]
Bruits de trompettes
[1]Ouverture from *Te Deum*, LWV 55 / [2]Marche from *Thesée*, LWV 51/30 / [3]Air de trompette, LWV 75/48 / [4]La descente de Mars from *Thesée*, LWV 51/5, [+ unidentified theme] / [5]Second Air from *Thesée*, LWV 51/79 / [6]Second Air from *Bellerophon*, LWV 57/69 / [7]Bruit de trompettes from *Proserpine*, LWV 58/4 / [8]Premier Air from *Proserpine*, LWV 58/44 / [9]Deuxième Air from *Proserpine*, LWV 58/47 / [10]Second Air from *Amadis*, LWV 63/24, [+ Air from *Isis*, LWV 54/12] / [11]Premier Air des Combattants from *Amadis*, LWV 63/23 / [12]Prelude de trompettes from *Le Divertissement Royal*, LWV 42/32 / [13]Prelude from *Proserpine*, LWV 58/82
While there are only 13 movements listed on the album, there are 15 thematic sections.
Delmotte, Roger, 43)

ₜHercule amoureux, LWV 17, (1662)ₗ
Hercule amoureux, LWV 17
There are 41 selections in the incidental music for this drama.
(This album probably consists of excerpts).
Delmotte, Roger, 14)

ₜHercule amoureux, LWV 17, (1662). Menuet, trumpet & stringsₗ
Menuet from *Hercule amoureux*, LWV 17
Delmotte, Roger, 25)

ₜMarche des forçats des galères turques, trumpet & stringsₗ
Marche des forçats des galères turques
(March of the Turkish galley convicts)
This work is not catalogued by Herbert Schneider in
*Chronologisch-Thematisches Verzeichnis sämmtlicher Werke von
Jean-Baptiste Lully.*
Delmotte, Roger, 8)

ₜMarche du Régiment de Turenne, orchestraₗ
Marche du Régiment de Turenne
(March of the Turenne Regiment)
This work is not catalogued by Herbert Schneider in
*Chronologisch-Thematisches Verzeichnis sämmtlicher Werke von
Jean-Baptiste Lully.*
Delmotte, Roger, 7), 28)

ₜMarches et Batteries de tambour, LWV 44, (1670). No. 2: Marche du régiment du
Roy, trumpet & stringsₗ
Marche du régiment du Roy, LWV 44
Delmotte, Roger, 8)

ₜPremière Marche des Mousquetaires, oboes, bassoon & trumpets, LWV 10, (1658)ₗ
Première Marche des Mousquetaires, LWV 10
(March of the Grey Musketeers)
Delmotte, Roger, 7)

ₜSymphonies de la chambre du Roi. Marche Gay, D major; arr. trumpet & piano,
C majorₗ

Marche Gay from *Symphonies for the King's Bed Chamber*
Although there are 14 sections (movements) entitled
"Symphonie" included in *Trios de la chambre du Roi*, LWV 35,
the theme for this march is not indexed by Herbert Schneider in
his *Chronologisch-Thematisches Verzeichnis sämmtlicher Werke
von Jean-Baptiste Lully.* (LWV 35 is alternately titled *Trios pour
le coucher du Roi.*)
Nagel, Robert, 10)

⌜Symphonies pour les couchers du Roi. Excerpts, trumpet & strings⌝
Symphonies pour les couchers du Roi
Although there are 14 selections (movements) entitled
"Symphonie" included in *Trios de la chambre du Roi*, LWV 35,
the themes for these excerpts are not indexed by Herbert
Schneider in his *Chronologisch-Thematisches Verzeichnis
sämmtlicher Werke von Jean-Baptiste Lully*. (LWV 35 is
alternately titled *Trios pour le coucher du Roi*.)
Delmotte, Roger, 17), 23), 25), 26)

⌜Thesée, LWV 51, (1675). No. 30, La Marche, trumpet & strings⌝
Marche Royale from *Thesée*, LWV 51
Delmotte, Roger, 8), 26)

⌜Thesée, LWV 51, (1675). No. 30, La Marche, trumpet & strings; arr. trumpet,
organ & brass ensemble⌝
Marche Royale from *Thesée*, LWV 51
André, Maurice, 187)
Potpourri, 35), 43), 44)

⌜Xerxes, LWV 12, (1660). Suite; arr. oboes, bassoon, trumpets, timpani &
harpsichord⌝
Le Ballet de Xerxes (Suite), LWV 12
[1]Ouverture / [8]Entrée [Menuet] / [2]Entrée [Bourrée] / [14]Gavotte en
Rondeau / [10]Troisième Air [Marche] / [9]Second Air [Gavotte]
From an anthology of 300 suites for oboe ensembles collated by
Anne Danican Philidor. (Trumpets perform only in the final two
selections.)
André, Maurice, 6)

Lupo, Thomas, *d.* 1628

⌜Almande; arr. 2 trumpets & 4 trombones⌝
Almande
André, Maurice, 176)

⌜Fantasia, cornetti, shawms & sackbuts⌝
Fantasia a 6
Montesi, Robert, 3)

Lust, L.

⌜Quadrille des Lanciers; arr. cornet & brass ensemble⌝
Quadrille des Lanciers
[1]Les tiroirs / [2]Les lignes / [3]Les moulinets / [4]Les visites / [5]Les lanciers
Aquitaine Brass Ensemble

Luther, Martin, 1483-1546

⌜Chorale, "Ein' feste Burg"; arr. 2 trumpets & 2 trombones⌝
A Mighty Fortress Is Our God
(Ein' feste Burg ist unser Gott)
Voisin, Roger, 2)

ₗEIN' FESTE BURG; arr. trumpet & orchestra⌉
A Mighty Fortress Is Our God
(EIN' FESTE BURG)
Driscoll, Phil

ₗNon moriar, sed vivam; arr. mixed voices, trumpet & organ⌉
Non moriar, sed vivam
Krystek, Ulrich

MacDougall, Robert, 1941-

ₗAnacoluthon: A Confluence, chamber ensemble, (1972)⌉
Anacoluthon: A Confluence
Chamber ensemble includes: flute, oboe, clarinet, trumpet, violin, viola & cello.
Dean, Allan, 2)

MacDowell, Edward Alexander, 1860-1908

ₗWoodland Sketches, piano, op. 51, (1896). No. 1: To a Wild Rose; arr. trumpet & piano⌉
To a Wild Rose
House, Lawrence

Machaut, Guillaume de, *ca.* 1300-1377
Machault, Guillaume de
Machaud, Guillaume de
Guillelmus de Mascaudio

ₗMesse Nostre Dame, mixed voices & instrumental ensemble⌉
Messe Nostre Dame
(Notre Dame Mass)
Neunhoeffer, Frieder
Renz, Albrecht, 1), 3)

ₗMotet, "O livoris feritas", 2 countertenors & instrumental ensemble⌉
Motet, "O livoris feritas"
Neunhoeffer, Frieder

ₗMotet, "Trop plus est belle que biaute", contralto, tenor, recorder, cornetto, organ & fiddle⌉
Motet, "Trop plus est belle que biaute"
Otten, Kees

MacMurrough, Dermot, 19th cent.-20th cent.

ₗMacushla, voice; arr. cornet & band⌉
Macushla
McCann, Phillip

Maderna, Bruno, 1920-1973

ₒSerenata, chamber ensemble, no. 2, (1954)₇
Serenata No. 2
Chamber ensemble includes: flute/piccolo, clarinet, bass clarinet, horn, trumpet, piano, harp, percussion, violin, viola & bass.
Jones, Philip, 11)

Mailman, Martin, 1932-

ₒConcertino, trumpet & band, op. 31, (1965)₇
Concertino for Trumpet and Band, op. 31
¹Allegro / ²Adagio / ³Vivace
Thunderburke, Mike

ₒConcertino, trumpet & band, op. 31, (1965); arr. trumpet & piano₇
Concertino for Trumpet and Band, op. 31
¹Allegro / ²Adagio / ³Vivace
Amstutz, Keith¹

Mainerio, Giorgio, *ca.* 1535-1582
Maynerius, Giorgio

ₒPass'e mezzo della Paganina; arr. instrumental ensemble₇
Pass'e mezzo della Paganina
Instrumental ensemble includes: recorder, rauschpfeiffen, 2 cornetti, 4 sackbuts, regal & percussion.
Laird, Michael, 2)

ₒSchiarazula Marazula; arr. cittern or instrumental ensemble₇
Schiarazula Marazula
Instrumental ensemble includes: cornetto, rauschpfeife, crumhorn, pommer, tenor gamba, bass gamba & hand clapping.
Laird, Michael, 2)
Otto, Joachim

ₒZanetta; arr. instrumental ensemble₇
La Zanetta
Instrumental ensemble includes: tenor cornetto, tenor sackbut, shawm, dulcian & percussion.
Laird, Michael, 2)

Maire, Jean, 1902-

ₒCoq et Frelon, trumpet & piano₇
Coq et Frelon
Chunn, Michael

Malotte, Albert Hay, 1895-1964

ₒLord's Prayer, voice & piano, (1935); arr. trumpet & orchestra₇
The Lord's Prayer
Méndez, Rafael, 16)

ₜLord's Prayer, voice & piano, (1935); arr. trumpet & organₜ
The Lord's Prayer
Blair, Stacy
Hickman, David, 6)
Stith, Marice, 9)
Tolley, Richard

Malvezzi, Cristofano, 1547-1599

ₜMadrigal, "Dal vago e bel sereno", mixed voices & instrumental ensembleₜ
Madrigal, "Dal vago e bel sereno"
Unidentified, Trumpet(s), 1)

ₜMadrigal, "O fortunato giorno", mixed voices & instrumental ensembleₜ
Madrigal, "O fortunato giorno"
Unidentified, Trumpet(s), 1)

ₜMadrigal, "O qual risplende nube", mixed voices & instrumental ensembleₜ
Madrigal, "O qual risplende nube"
Unidentified, Trumpet(s), 1)

ₜSinfonia, instrumental ensembleₜ
Sinfonia
Unidentified, Trumpet(s), 1)

Mancini, Francesco, 1672-1737

ₜGl'amanti generosi, (1705). Sinfonia, chamber orchestraₜ
Sinfonia from *Gl'Amanti Generosi*
Keavy, Stephen

Manfredini, Francesco (Onofrio), 1684-1762

ₜConcerto, 2 trumpets, strings & continuo, D majorₜ
Concerto per due Trombe con orchestra d'archi, clavicembalo e organo
¹Allegro / ²Largo / ³Allegro
Delmotte, Roger, 45), 49)
Güttler, Ludwig, 14)
Hunger, Helmut, 3)
Immeı, Friedemann, 9)
Molénat, Claude
Petit, Gilbert
Potpourri, 10), 21), 34), 35), 65)
Voisin, Roger, 4), 8)
Wobisch, Helmut, 4), 11)

ₜConcerto, 2 trumpets, strings & continuo, D major; arr. 2 trumpets & organₜ
Concerto per due Trombe e Organo
¹Allegro / ²Largo / ³Allegro
Pearson, Byron
Schmidhäusler, Francis & René
Waltzing, Gast

Mangione, Chuck, 1940-
Mangione, Charles Frank

ₜGato triste; arr. trumpet & brass ensembleₜ
El gato triste
Geiger, György

Manichicourt, Pierre de
See: Pierre de Manchicourt

Manneke, Daan, 1939-
Manneke, Daniël

ₜDiaphony for Geoffrey, trumpet, horn, trombone & piano, (1973)ₜ
Diaphony for Geoffrey
Ros, Ad

Manning, 20th cent.
ₜCarnival in Venice, trumpet & orchestra, (1948)ₜ
A Carnival in Venice
Méndez, Rafael, 1)

Marcello, Alessandro, 1684-1750
Stinfalico, Eterio

ₜConcerto, oboe, strings & continuo, d minor, (1717 or 1718). Adagio; arr. trumpet, organ, bass & drums, c minorₜ
Adieu à Venise
(Adagio from *Concerto in c minor for Oboe, Strings and Continuo*)
André, Maurice, 70)

ₜConcerto, oboe, strings & continuo, d minor, (1717 or 1718). Final; arr. trumpet, organ, bass & drums, c minorₜ
Final from *Concerto in c minor for Oboe, Strings and Continuo*
André, Maurice, 70)

ₜConcerto, oboe, strings & continuo, d minor, (1717 or 1718); arr. trumpet & brass ensembleₜ
Konzert D-moll für Trompete und Posaunenchor
¹Andante e spiccato / ²Adagio / ³Presto
Michel, Jean-François

ₜConcerto, oboe, strings & continuo, d minor, (1717 or 1718); arr. trumpet, strings
& continuo, c minorₜ
Concerto in c minor for Trumpet, Strings and Continuo
[1]Andante e spiccato / [2]Adagio / [3]Presto
Formerly attributed to Benedetto Marcello, this concerto is the
second from a set of ten concerti a cinque by various composers
published in Amsterdam *ca.* 1717.
André, Maurice, 38), 41), 54), 67), 226), 227)

Marcello, Benedetto, 1686-1739

ₜAllegro; arr. trumpet & organ, B♭ majorₜ
Allegro in B♭ major
Original key and source of this transcription are unknown.
Mertens, Theo, 2)

ₜLargo and Allegretto, flute & continuo; arr. trumpet, harpsichord & bassoonₜ
Largo and Allegretto
Largo / Allegretto
Original key and source of this transcription are unknown.
André, Maurice, 194), 197), 203)
Potpourri, 44)

ₜLargo and Allegro, flute & continuo; arr. trumpet & pianoₜ
Largo and Allegro
Largo (in d minor) / Allegro (in F major)
Original key and source of this transcription are unknown.
Geyer, Charles

ₜSonata; arr. trumpet & organₜ
Sonata for Trumpet and Organ
Original key and source of this transcription are unknown.
Terracini, Paul

ₜSuonate (12), op. 2, (1712). No. 2, recorder & continuo, c♯ minor; arr. trumpet
& stringsₜ
Sonata in c♯ for Trumpet and Strings, op. 2, no. 2
[1]Adagio / [2]Allegro / [3]Largo / [4]Allegro
Published as "Opus 2" in 1712, and published as "Opus 1" in
1732.
Zapf, Gerd

ₜSuonate (12), op. 2, (1712). No. 5, flute & continuo, G major; arr. trumpet &
organₜ
Sonata in G major for Trumpet and Organ, op. 2, no. 5
[1]Largo / [2]Allegro / [3]Adagio / [4]Allegro
Published as "Opus 2" in 1712, and published as "Opus 1" in
1732.
André, Maurice, 45), 55)

ₜSuonate (12), op. 2, (1712). No. 11, flute & continuo, d minor; arr. trumpet & stringsₗ
Sonata in d minor for Trumpet and Strings, op. 2, no. 11
Published as "Opus 2" in 1712, and published as "Opus 1" in 1732.
Kejmar, Miroslav, 11)

Marchat, L., 20th cent.

ₜÀ Cœur Joie; arr. trumpet & orchestraₗ
À Cœur Joie
André, Maurice, 207)

Marchetti, Filippo D., 1831-1902

ₜFascination; arr. trumpet & orchestraₗ
Fascination
Méndez, Rafael, 9)

Marini, Biagio, *ca.* 1587-1663

ₜAffetti musicali, op. 1. Sonata, "La Ponte", violin & continuo; arr. trumpet & organₗ
Sonata, "La Ponte", op. 1
Touvron, Guy, 20)

ₜAria, "La Soranza", violin, cornetto, trombone, cello & keyboard instrumentₗ
Aria a 3, "La Soranza"
Dickey, Bruce

ₜArie, madrigali et corenti..., op. 8, (1629). Romanesca, violin & continuo; arr. trumpet, bassoon & harpsichordₗ
Romanesca for Trumpet and Continuo
Schwarz, Gerard, 17)

ₜBalletto and Correnti, violin, cornetto, dulcian, chitarrone & organₗ
Balletto and Correnti a 3
Eichhorn, Holger

ₜBrando, "Il Boncio", violin, cornetto, trombone, cello & keyboard instrumentₗ
Brando a 2, "Il Boncio"
Dickey, Bruce

ₜCorente, "La Martia", violin, cornetto, trombone, cello & keyboard instrumentₗ
Corente a 3, "La Martia"
Dickey, Bruce

ₜDiversi generi di Sonate..., op. 22, (1655). No. 2: Sonata, violin, cornetto & continuoₗ
Sonata seconda a 2, op. 22
Dickey, Bruce

⌈Diversi generi di Sonate..., op. 22, (1655). No. 3: Sonata, violin, cornetto, trombone, cello & keyboard instrument⌉
Sonata terza per sonar variato, op. 22
Dickey, Bruce

⌈Diversi generi di Sonate..., op. 22, (1655). Sonata, violin, unspecified bass instrument & continuo; arr. trumpet, bassoon & harpshichord⌉
Sonata in d minor for Trumpet, Bassoon and Harpsichord
Schwarz, Gerard, 17)

⌈Passacaglio, cornetto, violin, dulcian, chitarrone & organ⌉
Passacaglio a 3
Eichhorn, Holger

⌈Sinfonia, "La Martinenga", violin, cornetto, trombone, cello & keyboard instrument⌉
Sinfonia a 2, "La Martinenga"
Dickey, Bruce

⌈Sinfonia, "La Orlandia", violin, cornetto, trombone, cello & keyboard instrument⌉
Sinfonia, "La Orlandia"
Dickey, Bruce

⌈Sonata, "La Foscarina"; arr. cornetto, trombone & organ⌉
Sonata, "La Foscarina"
Eichhorn, Holger

⌈Sonatas. No. 1, cornetto, violin, dulcian, chittarone & organ⌉
Sonata prima a 3, Sopra fuggi dolente core
Eichhorn, Holger

⌈Sonatas. No. 2, cornetto, violin, dulcian, chittarone & organ⌉
Sonata seconda a 3
Eichhorn, Holger

⌈Sonatas. No. 3, violin, recorder, cornetto, organ & harpsichord⌉
Sonata terza a 3
Eichhorn, Holger

Marquina, Pascual, 20th cent.

⌈España Cañi; arr. 3 trumpets & orchestra⌉
España Cañi
(Por la España Cañi)
Méndez, Rafael, 12), 24)

Marshall, C.

⌈I Hear You Calling Me; arr. cornet & organ⌉
I Hear You Calling Me
McCann, Phillip

Martá, István, 1952-

ₜJ. M. WYX Meets Romeo & Juliet, chamber ensembleₜ
J. M. WYX Meets Romeo & Juliet
Chamber ensemble includes: recorder, trumpet, cello, hurdy-gurdy & harpsichord.
Geiger, György

Marteau, Henri, 1874-1934

ₜMorceau vivant, trumpet & pianoₜ
Morceau vivant
Crisara, Raymond, 7)

Martin, Frank, 1890-1974

ₜConcerto, 7 wind instruments, timpani, percussion & strings, (1949)ₜ
Concerto for Seven Wind Instruments, Timpani, Percussion and String Orchestra
[1]Allegro / [2]Adagietto / [3]Allegro vivace
Wind instrument soloists include: flute, oboe, clarinet, bassoon, horn, trumpet, trombone.
Herseth, Adolph, 6)

Martín y Coll, Antonio, *d. ca.* 1734

ₜPiezas de clarines (4), organ; arr. trumpet & organₜ
Quatro piezas de clarines
[1]Entrada de Clarines antes de tocar Canciones (despacio) / [2]Canción de Clarin, con eco (a discretion) / [3]Otra canción (se de tocar grave) / [4]Corriente; Corneta
Scherbaum, Adolf, 17)

Martini, Giovanni Battista, 1706-1784

ₜElevazione, organ, E major; arr. trumpet & organₜ
Elevazione
André, Maurice, 134), 218)

ₜLargo, organ, E major; arr. trumpet & organₜ
Largo
André, Maurice, 134), 218)
Basch, Wolfgang, 5)
Thomas, Peggy Paton

ₜSonata al' Postcommunio, organ, D major; arr. trumpet & organₜ
Sonata al' Postcommunio
[1]Introduction (Moderato) / [2]Allegro
André, Maurice, 134), 218)

[Sonata al' Postcommunio, organ, D major; arr. trumpet, organ, bass & drums]
Sonata al' Postcommunio
[1]Introduction (Moderato) / [2]Allegro
Molénat, Claude

[Toccata, organ, D major; arr. trumpet & orchestra]
Toccata
Geiger, György

[Toccata, organ, D major; arr. trumpet & organ]
Toccata
André, Maurice, 35), 134), 218)
Basch, Wolfgang, 5)
Capouillez, Luc
Carroll, Edward, 10)
Thomas, Peggy Paton
Tolley, Richard
Winslow, Richard

[Toccata, organ, D major; arr. trumpet, organ, bass & drums]
Toccata
Molénat, Claude

Martini, J.P.S., 1741-1816
Martini, Jean Paul Égide
Martini, Johann Paul Aegidius
Martini, Giovanni Paolo (Il Tedesco)
Schwarzendorf, Johann Paul

[Air, "Plaisir d'amour"; arr. trumpet & harp]
Air, "Plaisir d'amour"
This composer's true surname was originally Schwarzendorf.
André, Maurice, 84)

Martinů, Bohuslav, 1890-1959
Martinů, Bohuslav Jan

[Ballet, "La Révue de cuisine", chamber ensemble, (1927)]
Kuchyňská revue
(Ballet, "La Révue de cuisine")
Chamber ensemble includes: clarinet, bassoon, trumpet, violin, cello & piano.
Junek, Václav, 6)

[Cantata, "Prophecy of Isaiah", soli, male voices, trumpet, viola, piano & timpani, (1959)]
Cantata, "Prophecy of Isaiah"
("Prophétie d'Isaie")
("Izaiášovo proroctví")
Junek, Václav, 4)

ㄷKhorovody, chamber ensemble, (1930)ㄱ
Khorovody
(Les rondes)
Chamber ensemble includes: oboe, clarinet, bassoon, trumpet, 2 violins & piano.
Krylov, Gleb

ㄷSonatina, trumpet & piano, (1956)ㄱ
Sonatine pour Trompette et Piano
Dokshitser, Timofei, 17)
Hunger, Helmut, 4)
Potpourri, 39)
Rippas, Claude
Roelant, Alain
Sveshnikov, Mikhail
Tarr, Edward, 6)

Martirano, Salvatore, 1927-

ㄷO, O, O, O, That Shakespeherian Rag, mixed voices & chamber ensemble, (1958)ㄱ
O, O, O, O, That Shakespeherian Rag
Chamber ensemble includes: clarinet, saxophone, trumpet, trombone, bass & percussion.
Mills, Fred

Mas, Jacques, 20th cent.

ㄷPavane, cornet & pianoㄱ
Pavane
Christensen, Ketil

Mascagni, Pietro, 1863-1945

ㄷCavalleria Rusticana, (1890). Intermezzo; arr. cornet & bandㄱ
Intermezzo from *Cavalleria Rusticana*
McCann, Phillip

Mason, Lowell, 1792-1872

ㄷHAMBURG; arr. trumpet & orchestraㄱ
When I Survey the Wondrous Cross
Driscoll, Phil

ㄷNearer, my God, to Thee; arr. cornet, trombone & pianoㄱ
Nearer, my God, to Thee
Potpourri, 8)

ㄷNearer, my God, to Thee; arr. trumpet & organㄱ
Nearer, my God, to Thee
Grin, Freddy, 8)

Massenet, Jules, 1842-1912
Massenet, Jules-Émile-Frédéric

₍Pièces de genre (10), piano, op. 10, (1866). No. 5: Élégie; arr. trumpet & organ₎
Élégie, op. 10, no. 5
Mertens, Theo, 4)

₍Thaïs, (1894). Méditation, violin & orchestra; arr. trumpet & piano₎
Méditation from *Thaïs*
Christensen, Ketil

₍Thaïs, (1894). Méditation, violin & orchestra; arr. trumpet, mixed voices & orchestra₎
Méditation from *Thaïs*
André, Maurice, 66)

Matěj, Josef, 1922-
Matěj, Jožka

₍Concerto, trumpet & orchestra₎
Koncert pro trubku a orchestr
(Concerto for Trumpet and Orchestra)
Kejmar, Miroslav, 9)

₍Concerto, trumpet, horn, trombone & chamber orchestra₎
Trojkonzert pro Trubku, Lesní roh a Pozoun, s pruvodem komorního orchestru
(Triple Concerto for Trumpet, Horn and Trombone with Chamber Orchestra)
Kejmar, Miroslav, 3)

Matteis, Nicola, *d. ca.* 1707

₍Concerto, 3 trumpets, flute(s), violin(s) & continuo₎
Concerto di Trombe a tre Trombette con violini e flauti
[1]Allegro / [2]Aria (Adagio) / [3]Aria
Keavy, Stephen

Maury, Jacques-Hippolyte, 1834-1881

₍Solo de concours, cornet & piano, no. 1₎
Premier Solo de Concours
Chunn, Michael

Maxwell Davies, Peter, 1934-

₍Frammenti di Leopardi, soprano, contralto & chamber ensemble, (1961)₎
Frammenti di Leopardi
(Leopardi fragments)
  Chamber ensemble includes: flute/piccolo, oboe, clarinet, bassoon, trumpet, trombone, harp & cello.
Jones, Philip, 2)

[Sonata, trumpet & piano, (1955)]
Sonata for Trumpet and Piano
[1]Allegro moderato / [2]Lento / [3]Allegro vivo
Though composed in 1955, this sonata was not published until 1969.
> Hardenberger, Håkan
> Schwarz, Gerard, 18)
> Stevens, Thomas, 9)

Maybrick, Michael
See: Adams, Stephen

Mayer, William R., 1925-

[Concerto Piece, trumpet & piano, (1959)]
Concerto Piece for Trumpet and Piano
> Levy, Robert

Mays, Walter A., 1941-

[Concerto, alto saxophone & chamber ensemble, (1974)]
Concerto for Alto Saxophone and Chamber Ensemble
Three movements
Chamber ensemble includes: oboe, clarinet, bassoon, trumpet, trombone, 2 violins, viola, cello, bass, electronic organ, piano/celesta & percussion.
> Potpourri, 6)

Mazzaferrata, Giovanni Battista, *d.* 1691

[Sonatas, op. 5, (1674). No. 7: violin, cornetto & continuo]
Sonata Settima a 3
> Eichhorn, Holger

McAfee, Cleland B., 1866-1944

[Near to the Heart of God; arr. trumpet & orchestra]
Near to the Heart of God
(There is a place of quiet rest near to the Heart of God)
> Driscoll, Phil

McCartney, Paul, 1942-
See: Rifkin, Joshua

McHugh, Jimmy, 1894-1969
McHugh, James Francis

[On the Sunny Side of the Street; arr. trumpet & orchestra]
On the Sunny Side of the Street
> Méndez, Rafael, 21)

McKay, George Frederick, 1899-1970

ₜConcert Solo Suite. Tumblers, cornet & pianoₙ
Tumblers from *Concert Solo Suite for Young Players*
Tolley, Richard

McKee, William, 20th cent.

ₜEpisodes (2), trumpet, horn, piano & tapeₙ
Episodes I & II
Henderson, Douglas

McPhee, Colin, 1900-1964
McPhee, Colin Carhart

ₜConcerto, piano & wind octet, (1928)ₙ
Concerto for Piano with Wind Octet Accompaniment
¹Allegretto / ²Chorale / ³Coda
Wind octet includes: piccolo, flute, oboe, clarinet, bassoon, horn, trumpet & trombone.
Unidentified, Trumpet(s), 6), 7)

Melani, Alessandro, 1639-1703

ₜCantata, "All'armi, pensieri", soprano, trumpet & continuoₙ
Cantata, "All'armi, pensieri"
Basch, Wolfgang, 2)
Carroll, Edward, 8), 9)
Ferry, Dennis

ₜSinfonia, trumpet, 2 violin & continuoₙ
Sinfonia a cinque
Ferry, Dennis

Mendelssohn, Felix, 1809-1847
Mendelssohn-Bartholdy, Jakob Ludwig Felix

ₜConcerto, violin & orchestra, op. 64, e minor, (1844). Themes; arr. trumpet & orchestraₙ
Mendelssohn Concerto
Abridged arrangement of themes from all three movements in one continuous movement. Published in 1948.
Méndez, Rafael, 2), 5), 10)

ₜConcerto, violin & orchestra, op. 64, e minor, (1844). 2: Andante (theme) ; arr. cornet & bandₙ
Theme from *Concerto for Violin in e minor*
McCann, Phillip

ₜElijah, op. 70, (1846). Aria, "If with all your hearts"; arr. trumpet & organₙ
Aria, "If with all your hearts" from *Elijah*, op. 70
Stith, Marice, 9)

ₜElijah, op. 70, (1846). Aria, "If with all your hearts"; arr. trumpet & pianoₜ
Aria, "If with all your hearts" from *Elijah*, op. 70
Crisara, Raymond, 7)

ₜLieder ohne Worte, piano, op. 53, (1841). No. 2: Allegro non troppo, E♭ major; arr. trumpet & pianoₜ
Lieder ohne Worte, Nr. 20
(Song without Words, op. 53, no. 2)
Dokshitser, Timofei, 2)

ₜLieder ohne Worte, piano, op. 53, (1841). No. 4: Adagio, F major; arr. trumpet & pianoₜ
Lieder ohne Worte, Nr. 22
(Song without Words, op. 53, no. 4)
Dokshitser, Timofei, 2)

ₜLieder ohne Worte, piano, op. 62, (1844). No. 1: Andante espressivo, G major; arr. trumpet & pianoₜ
Lieder ohne Worte, Nr. 25
(Song without Words, op. 62, no. 1)
Dokshitser, Timofei, 2)

ₜLieder ohne Worte, piano, op. 62, (1844). No. 6: Allegretto grazioso, A major; arr. trumpet & pianoₜ
Lieder ohne Worte, "Frühlingslied", Nr. 30
(Song without Words, "Spring Song", op. 62, no. 6)
Dokshitser, Timofei, 2), 27)

ₜSommernachtstraum, op. 61, (1842). No. 9: Hochzeitsmarsch; arr. 3 trumpets, timpani & organₜ
Wedding March from *A Midsummer Night's Dream*, op. 61, no. 9
(Hochzeitsmarsch aus *Ein Sommernachtstraum*)
Giangiulio, Richard

Méndez, Rafael, 1906-1981

ₜAnniversary Polka, trumpet & orchestraₜ
Anniversary Polka
Méndez, Rafael, 13)

ₜBullfighter's Prayer, trumpet & orchestraₜ
Bullfighter's Prayer
SEE: Plegaria Taurina

ₜBurrito Ruso, trumpet & orchestra, (1968)ₜ
El Burrito Ruso
(The Little Russian Donkey)
Méndez, Rafael, 15)

ₜThe Tre-Méndez Polka, trumpet trio & orchestra, (1957)ₗ
The Tre-Méndez Polka
With a correctly placed accent, this title is a play on words.
Méndez, Rafael, 19)

ₜValse Suriano, trumpet & orchestra, (1954)ₗ
Valse Suriano
Méndez, Rafael, 11)

ₜVirgen de la Macarena; arr. trumpet & orchestraₗ
La Virgen de la Macarena
This work, often attributed to Rafael Méndez, is originally by
Bernardino Monterde. (Various arrangments are indexed under
Monterde.)

Mendigaliev, Nagim, 1921-

ₜSuite, trumpet & pianoₗ
Suite for Trumpet and Piano
Klushkin, Yuri

Mendizábal, Pedro, 20th cent.

ₜGranito de Arena; arr. trumpet & orchestraₗ
Granito de Arena
Méndez, Rafael, 12), 24)

Métra, Olivier, 1830-1889
Métra, Jules-Louis-Olivier

ₜRoses; arr. cornet & brass ensembleₗ
Les Roses
Aquitaine Brass Ensemble

Meulemans, Arthur, 1884-1966

ₜConcerto, organ, trumpet, horn & tromboneₗ
Concerto for Grand Organ, Trumpet, Horn and Trombone
Unidentified, Trumpet(s), 19)

Meyer, Ernst Hermann, 1905-

ₜConcerto grosso, 2 trumpets, trombone, timpani & strings, (1966)ₗ
Concerto Grosso für zwei Trompeten, Tenorposaune, Pauken und Streichorchester (mit Solo-Violine)
[1]Poco adagio: Allegro assai moderato / [2]Lento / [3]Allegretto assai
tranquillo
Krug, Willi, 2)

Miaskovsky, Nicolai Yakovlevich, 1881-1950

[Yellowed Leaves, piano, op. 31, no. 1; arr. trumpet & piano]
Yellowed Leaves, op. 31, no. 1
Dokshitser, Timofei, 7), 9), 35)

[Yellowed Leaves, piano, op. 31, no. 6; arr. trumpet & piano]
Yellowed Leaves, op. 31, no. 6
Dokshitser, Timofei, 9)

Mihalovici, Marcel, 1898-1985

[Meditation, trumpet & piano, (1959)]
Meditation
House, Lawrence

[Scherzo-Valse, trumpet & piano, (1959)]
Scherzo-Valse
Hyatt, Jack

Mikhailov, Giovanni, 1938-

[Partita, "Inspiratsii", 3 trumpets, percussion, organ & bass, op. 9]
Partita, "Inspiratsii", op. 9
Unidentified, Trumpet(s), 16)

Milán, Luis de, *ca.* 1500-*ca.* 1561

[Pavanes (3); arr. trumpet & organ]
Trois Pavanes
Deside

Miles, C. Austin, 1868-1946

[In the Garden, (1912); arr. trumpet & orchestra]
In the Garden
(I Come to the Garden Alone)
Driscoll, Phil

[In the Garden, (1912); arr. trumpet & piano]
In the Garden
(I Come to the Garden Alone)
Blair, Stacy

Milhaud, Darius, 1892-1974

[Aspen-Sérénade, chamber ensemble, (1957)]
Aspen-Sérénade
[1]Animé / [2]Souple et Printanier / [3]Paisible / [4]Energique / [5]Nerveux et Coloré
Chamber ensemble includes: flute, oboe, clarinet, bassoon, trumpet, violin, viola, cello & bass.
Thibaud, Pierre, 1)

ᵣCréation du Monde, chamber orchestra, (1923)₁
La Création du Monde
Chamber orchestra includes: 2 flutes, oboe, 2 clarinets, bassoon, saxophone, horn, 2 trumpets, trombone, piano, percussion & strings.
> **Clift, Dennis**
> **Dean, Allan,** 5)

Molter, Johann Melchior, 1696-1765

ᵣConcerto, trumpet, strings & continuo, [no. 1], D major, MWV IV, 12₁
Konzert D-dur für Trompete, Streicher und Basso continuo, MWV IV, 12
¹Allegro / ²Adagio / ³Allegro
This concerto is indicated *Conc 5* on the original manuscript and is numbered **ms 303** in the Badische Landesbibliothek.
> **Basch, Wolfgang,** 12)
> **Bernard, André,** 7)
> **Güttler, Ludwig,** 5), 21)
> **Hickman, David,** 1)
> **Sauter, Hermann,** 1)
> **Schultz, Erik,** 6)
> **Smithers, Don,** 8)

ᵣConcerto, trumpet, strings & continuo, [no. 2], D major, MWV IV, 13₁
Konzert D-dur für Trompete, Streicher und Basso continuo, MWV IV, 13
¹Andante / ²Adagio / ³Allegro
This concerto is indicated *Conc 33* on the original manuscript and is numbered **ms 331** in the Badische Landesbibliothek.
> **André, Maurice,** 140), 208), 209)
> **Ghitalla, Armando,** 2)
> **Hickman, David,** 1)
> **Kejmar, Miroslav,** 2)
> **Marsalis, Wynton,** 2)
> **Soustrot, Bernard,** 9)
> **Ullrich, Marc**

ᵣConcerto, trumpet, strings & continuo, [no. 3], D major, MWV IV, 14₁
Konzert D-dur für Trompete, Streicher und Basso continuo, MWV IV, 14
¹[Allegro] / ²Andante Cantabile / ³[Allegro]
This concerto is indicated *Conc 35* on the original manuscript and is numbered **ms 333** in the Badische Landesbibliothek.
> **André, Maurice,** 140), 208)
> **Basch, Wolfgang,** 9)
> **Schultz, Erik,** 5)

₍Concerto, 2 trumpets, strings & continuo, D major, MWV IV, 7; arr. 2 trumpets & organ₎
Konzert D-dur für 2 Trompeten, Streicher und Basso continuo, MWV IV, 7
This concerto is numbered **ms 308** in the Badische Landesbibliothek.
Pohle, Wolfgang

₍Concerto, 2 trumpets, strings & continuo, D major, MWV IV, 10₎
Konzert D-dur für 2 Trompeten, Streicher und Basso continuo, MWV IV, 10
This concerto is numbered **ms 329** in the Badische Landesbibliothek.
Ullrich, Marc

₍Concerto, 2 trumpets, strings & continuo, D major, MWV IV, 11₎
Konzert D-dur für 2 Trompeten, Streicher und Basso continuo, MWV IV, 11
[1]Allegro / [2]Andante / [3]Allegro
This concerto is numbered **ms 330** in the Badische Landesbibliothek.
André, Maurice, 140), 208)
Sauter, Hermann, 3)
Touvron, Guy, 9)
Ullrich, Marc

₍Sinfonia concertante, chamber ensemble, D major, MWV VIII, 2₎
Sinfonia concertante, MWV VIII, 2
[1]Allegro / [2]Largo / [3]Marche / [4]Alla Breve / [5]Vivace ò tempo di Menuet
Chamber ensemble includes: trumpet, 2 oboes, 2 horns & bassoon.
Tarr, Edward, 28)

₍Symphonie, 4 horns (4 trumpets), C major, ms 667₎
Symphonie in C-dur für 4 Hörner (oder Trompeten) in 5 Satzen, ms 667
[1]Allegro / [2]Menuet / [3]Allegro / [4]Allegro / [5]Allegro
Schwarz, Gerard, 20)

Monhardt, Maurice, 1929-
₍So Soft the Silver Sound and Clear, trumpet & piano, (1976)₎
So Soft the Silver Sound and Clear
Geyer, Charles

Montbrun, Raymond Gallois
See: Gallois-Montbrun, Raymond

Montéclair, Michel Pignolet de, 1667-1737

[Cantata, "Le Retour de la paix", soprano, trumpet, strings & continuo]
Cantata, "Le Retour de la paix"
Delmotte, Roger, 32)

Monterde, Bernardino Bautista, 20th cent.

[Virgen de la Macarena; various arr. trumpet & instrumental accompaniment]
La Virgen de la Macarena
This work is often attributed to Rafael Méndez due to the popularity of his published arrangement.
Canadian Brass, 1)
Geiger, György
Ghitalla, Armando, 15), 16)
Hidalgo, José Luis
Hirt, Al
Lewis, E. Leonard
Lieberman, Harold J.
Méndez, Rafael, 2), 7), 12), 24)
Terracini, Paul
Unidentified, Trumpet(s), 3)

Monteverdi, Claudio, 1567-1643
Monteverdi, Claudio Giovanni Antonio

[Fanfare — Sinfonia da Guerra]
Fanfare — Sinfonia da Guerra
SEE: Ritorno d'Ulisse in Patria.

[Madrigali, Libro X, (1632). Et è pur dunque vero, soprano, cornetto & continuo]
Et è pur dunque vero
from "Scherzi Musicali" (Madrigali, Libro X)
Impett, Jonathan

[Magnificat]
Magnificat
SEE: Vespers.

[Motet, "Ave maris stella"]
Motet, "Ave maris stella"
SEE: Vespers.

[Orfeo, (1607). Excerpts, soli, mixed voices & instrumental ensemble]
l'Orfeo (excerpts)
Potpourri, 47)

[Orfeo, (1607). Toccata, 5 trumpets & timpani]
Toccata from *l'Orfeo*
Wallace, John, 4)

[Orfeo, (1607). Toccata, 5 trumpets & tımpani; arr. brass ensemble]
Toccata from *l'Orfeo*
> **Grin, Freddy,** 4)
> **Güttler, Ludwig,** 23)
> **Laird, Michael,** 1)
> **Unidentified, Trumpet(s),** 1)

[Orfeo, (1607). Toccata, 5 trumpets & timpani; arr. 3 trumpets, 2 bass trumpets & timpani]
Toccata from *l'Orfeo*
> **Carroll, Edward,** 7), 9)

[Orfeo, soli, mixed voices & instrumental ensemble, (1607)]
l'Orfeo
> **Tarr, Edward,** 32)

[Ritorno d'Ulisse in Patria, (1641). Fanfare, "Sinfonia da Guerra"; arr. 2 trumpets, timpani & strings]
Fanfare — Sinfonia da Guerra
> **Voisin, Roger,** 7), 8)

[Vespers, (1610). No. 12: Motet, "Ave maris stella", mixed voices & instrumental ensemble]
Motet, "Ave maris stella"
> **Tarr, Edward,** 20)

[Vespers, (1610). No. 13: Magnificat, soli, mixed voices & instrumental ensemble]
Magnificat
> **Tarr, Edward,** 43)

[Vespers, soli, mixed voices & instrumental ensemble, (1610)]
Vesperæ della Beatæ Mariæ Virginis
(Vespro della Beata Vergine)
> **Laird, Michael,** 14)
> **Tarr, Edward,** 30), 45)

Monti, Vittorio, 1868-1922

[Czardas, violin & piano; arr. trumpet & orchestra]
Czardas
> **Méndez, Rafael,** 2), 6), 10)
> **Volle, Bjarne**

[Czardas, violin & piano; arr. trumpet & piano]
Czardas
> **Andersen, Ole**
> **Christensen, Ketil**

Moody, May Whittle, 1870-1963

[MOMENT BY MOMENT; arr. trumpet & orchestra]
Dying with Jesus
> **Nagel, Robert,** 9)

Morales, Cristóbal de, *ca.* 1500-1553

ᵣMagnificat, male voices & instrumental ensembleᵣ
Magnificat
Male voices include: 3 countertenors, 4 tenors & 4 basses.
Instrumental ensemble includes: cornetti, sackbuts & pommer.
Laird, Michael, 9)

ᵣMotet, "Jubilate Deo omnis terra", male voices & instrumental ensembleᵣ
Motet, "Jubilate Deo omnis terra"
Male voices include: 3 countertenors, 4 tenors & 4 basses.
Instrumental ensemble includes: cornetti, sackbuts & pommer.
Laird, Michael, 9)

Morceau, V., 20th cent.

ᵣBe Bop 1900; arr. flügelhorn & accordion bandᵣ
Be Bop 1900
André, Maurice, 61)

Morin, Jean-Baptiste, 1677-1754

ᵣChasse du cerf, (1708). Overture, trumpet, strings & continuoᵣ
Overture from *La chasse du cerf*
(Overture from *The Deer Hunt*)
Delmotte, Roger, 23)

ᵣChasse du cerf, (1708). Suite des Fanfares, oboe, trumpet, strings & continuoᵣ
Die Hirschjagd
(Suite des Fanfares from *La chasse du cerf*)
Libiseller, Hansjörg

ᵣChasse du cerf, soli, mixed voices & chamber orchestra, (1708)ᵣ
La chasse du cerf
(The Deer Hunt)
Delmotte, Roger, 22)

Moritz von Hessen, 1572-1632
Moritz (Landgraf von Hessen)

ᵣAventuroso piu d'altro terreno, soprano, tenor, bass, recorder & cornettoᵣ
Aventuroso piu d'altro terreno
Tarr, Edward, 19)

ᵣFuga a 4; arr. recorder, 2 pommers, 2 cornetti, 5 trombones & 5 violas da gambaᵣ
Fuga a 4
Tarr, Edward, 19)

ᵣGagliarda Brusvicese, recorder, 2 pommers, 2 cornetti, 5 trombones & 5 violas da gambaᵣ
Gagliarda Brusvicese
Tarr, Edward, 19)

[Gagliarda del Sopradetto, recorder, 2 pommers, 2 cornetti, 5 trombones & 5 violas da gamba]
Gagliarda del Sopradetto
Tarr, Edward, 19)

[Pavana del Francisco Segario, recorder, 2 pommers, 2 cornetti, 5 trombones & 5 violas da gamba]
Pavana del Francisco Segario
Tarr, Edward, 19)

[Pavana del povero soldato, recorder, 2 pommers, 2 cornetti, 5 trombones & 5 violas da gamba]
Pavana del povero soldato
Tarr, Edward, 19)

Morley, Thomas, 1557-1602

[Canzonet, "La Caccia", cornetto & tenor viol]
Canzonet, "La Caccia"
Smithers, Don, 7)

[Canzonet, "La Sampogna", cornetto & tenor viol]
Canzonet, "La Sampogna"
Smithers, Don, 7)

Morrill, Dexter G., 1938-

[Studies, trumpet & computer, (1974-75)]
Studies for Trumpet and Computer
Stith, Marice, 4)

Morrisey, John J., 1906-
Morrisey, John Joseph

[Soliloquy, trumpet & band, (1954); arr. trumpet & piano]
Soliloquy for Trumpet
Stith, Marice, 5)

Morrison, George, 1891-1974

[Lullaby, violin & piano; arr. cornet, trombone & chamber ensemble]
Lullaby
Schwarz, Gerard, 5)

Morton, Robert, *ca.* 1430-*ca.* 1476

[L'omme armé, soli, mixed voices & instrumental ensemble]
L'omme armé
Thibaud, Pierre, 14)

Moryl, Richard, 1929-

ₜSalvos, solo trumpet, (1969)ⱼ
Salvos
Schwarz, Gerard, 10)

Mösl

ₜAufzuge (6); arr. trumpet, organ & timpaniⱼ
Aufzuge (6)
? Mosel, Ignaz Franz von, 1772-1844.
Pohle, Wolfgang

Mouret, Jean Joseph, 1682-1738

ₜJeux Olimpiques, chamber orchestraⱼ
Les Jeux Olimpiques
(The Olympic Games)
¹Les jeux olimpiques / ²Les amans ignorans / ³Panurge / ⁴L'isle du divorce / ⁵La foire des fées / ⁶L'amante difficile / ⁷Les paysans de qualité / ⁸L'empereur dans la lune
Garreau, André

ₜSarabande; arr. trumpet & organⱼ
Sarabande
Source: undetermined.
Delmotte, Roger, 38)

ₜSuites de Simphonies, (1729). Excerpts; arr. trumpet & organⱼ
Simphonies de Fanfares
(Suites de Simphonies)
¹Rondeau from *Première Suite* / ²Air from *Seconde Suite*
Hunger, Helmut, 5)

ₜSuites de Simphonies, (1729). No. 1: Fanfares. Rondeau; arr. trumpet(s), (timpani) & organⱼ
Rondeau from *Première Suite de Simphonies*
These albums include arrangements for 1, 2 or 3 trumpets with organ and optional timpani.
Bernard, André, 9)
Blair, Stacy
Carroll, Edward, 10)
Hunger, Helmut, 5)
Mertens, Theo, 4)
Potpourri, 32)

₁Suites de Simphonies, (1729). No. 1: Fanfares, oboes, bassoons, trumpets, timpani & strings, D major₁

Première Suite de Simphonies
(Fanfares pour les trompettes, timbales, violons et hautbois)
¹Rondeau / ²Gracieusement, sans lenteur / ³[Allegro] / ⁴Gay
André, Maurice, 12), 15), 47), 71), 91), 178)
Delmotte, Roger, 7), 17), 28)
Potpourri, 4¹), 36), 37)
Scherbaum, Adolf, 11), 23)
Schwarz, Gerard, 2¹)

₁Suites de Simphonies, (1729). No. 1: Fanfares, oboes, bassoons, trumpets, timpani & strings, D major; arr. trumpet(s), timpani & organ₁

Première Suite de Simphonies
(Fanfares pour les trompettes, timbales, violons et hautbois)
¹Rondeau / ²Gracieusement / ³[Allegro] / ⁴Gay
André, Maurice, 150)
Berinbaum, Martin
Bouche
Chesnut, Walter¹⁻³
Giangiulio, Richard
Held, Friedrich
Morisset, Michel
Touvron, Guy, 18), 21)

₁Suites de Simphonies, (1729). No. 1: Fanfares, oboes, bassoons, trumpets, timpani & strings, D major; arr. trumpet, brass ensemble, timpani & organ₁

Première Suite de Simphonies
(Fanfares pour les trompettes, timbales, violons et hautbois)
¹Rondeau / ²Gracieusement / ³[Tambourin] / ⁴Gay
André, Maurice, 187)
Potpourri, 35), 43), 44)

₁Suites de Simphonies, (1729). No. 2: oboes, horns & strings, F major₁

Seconde Suite de Simphonies
(Suite pour des Violons, des Hautbois, et des Cors de chasse)
¹Air, ou Prélude / ²Allegro, "La Chasse" / ³Air I & II /
⁴Gavotte I & II / ⁵Fanfare & Air / ⁶Menuet I & II / ⁷Allegro [second movement, reprise]
The *Seconde Suite de Simphonies* does not include trumpets, but is indexed here for clarity of identification.
André, Maurice, 12), 15), 71), 91)
Scherbaum, Adolf, 11)

Mouton, Jean, *ca.* 1459-1522

₁Noe, noe, psallite noe, soli, mixed voices & instrumental ensemble₁

Noe, noe, psallite noe
Cook, Richard

ᵣNon nobis domine, mixed voices & instrumental ensembleᵣ
Non nobis domine, non nobis
Instrumental ensemble includes: recorder, cornetto, tenor fiedel,
trombone & bass crumhorn.
Renz, Albrecht, 7)

Mozart, Leopold, 1719-1787
Mozart, (Johann Georg) Leopold

ᵣConcerto, trumpet, 2 horns, strings & harpsichord, D major, (1762)ᵣ
Konzert D-dur für Trompete, 2 Hörner, Streicher und Cembalo
¹Adagio / ²Allegro moderato
This concerto is actually taken from the *Serenade in D major.*
      André, Maurice, 60), 72), 149), 168), 169),
           197), 200), 216), 219)
      Basch, Wolfgang, 13)
      Bernard, André, 10)
      Cuvit, Michel
      Delmotte, Roger, 10), 19), 24), 49)
      Frei, Marcel
      Güttler, Ludwig, 4), 5)
      Holy, Walter, 8), 10)
      Krug, Willi, 4)
      Marsalis, Wynton, 1)
      Mertens, Theo, 7)
      Nagel, Robert, 16)
      Potpourri, 12), 13), 36), 37)
      Preis, Ivo
      Quinque, Rolf, 8)
      Reinhart, Carole Dawn, 3), 4)
      Scherbaum, Adolf, 10), 15), 22), 25)
      Schultz, Erik, 6)
      Smithers, Don, 8), 9)
      Tarr, Edward, 22)
      Thibaud, Pierre, 3)
      Touvron, Guy, 8)
      Wilbraham, John, 4), 7), 15)
      Wobisch, Helmut, 4)
      Zapf, Gerd

ᵣConcerto, trumpet, 2 horns, strings & harpsichord, D major, (1762); arr. trumpet
& piano, B♭ majorᵣ
Concerto in B♭ for Trumpet and Piano
¹Adagio / ²Allegro moderato
Nagel, Robert, 16)

ᵣSerenade, trumpet, trombone & strings, D majorᵣ
Serenade D-dur für Trompete, Posaune und Streicher
The first three movements include a soloistic part for trombone,
and the last two movements are known as Leopold Mozart's
Concerto for Trumpet in D major.
Touvron, Guy, 17)

[Sinfonia di Camera, horn, strings & continuo, D major]
Sinfonia di Camera
Performed on a twentieth century valved "Clarinhorn"
Streitwieser, Franz Xaver

[Suite, piano, F major; arr. trumpet & organ]
Suite in F major
Braz, Dirceu, 3)

Mozart, Wolfgang Amadeus, 1756-1791
Mozart, (Johann Chrysostom) Wolfgang Amadeus

[Allegretto; arr. trumpet & piano]
Allegretto
Source of transcription is undetermined.
Crisara, Raymond, 7)

[Ave verum, mixed voices & orchestra, K. 618, (1791); arr. trumpet & orchestra]
Ave verum, K. 618
Andersen, Ole

[Concerto, oboe & orchestra, C major, K. 285d, (1777); arr. trumpet & orchestra]
Concerto in C major for Trumpet and Orchestra
(Konzert C-dur für Oboe und Orchester, K. 285d)
[1]Allegro aperto / [2]Adagio non troppo / [3]Rondo (Allegretto)
Mozart transcribed this *Concerto in C major for Oboe* for flute
in D major in 1778. The flute concerto is catalogued by Köchel as
K. 314.
André, Maurice, 72), 75), 162)

[Divertimento, 2 flutes, 5 trumpets & timpani, no. 5, C major, K. 187, (1773)]
Divertimento No. 5 in C major, K. 187
[1]Allegro moderato / [2]Menuetto / [3]Adagio / [4]Menuetto / [5]Allegro /
[6]Allegro moderato / [7]Allegro molto / [8]Allegro non troppo
Movements 1-5 are now attributed to Josef Starzer. Movements
6-8 are now attributed to Christoph Gluck. (Edward Tarr's
recording indexed, here, includes only the movements by Starzer
and is, therefore, cross-referenced to the original title, *Musica da
camera molto particulare* under Starzer.) Starzer's original version
is scored for 2 chalumeaux rather than 2 flutes. Both versions
include 3 trumpets in C and 2 trumpets in D.
Horák, Jiří, 5)
Pollin, Pierre
Spindler, Josef, 2)
Tarr, Edward, 34)
Vaillant, Ludovic, 7)
Wilbraham, John, 14), 17)

₍Divertimento, 2 flutes, 5 trumpets & timpani, no. 6, C major, K. 188, (1776)₎

Divertimento No. 6 in C major, K. 188
[1]Andante / [2]Allegro / [3]Menuetto / [4]Andante / [5]Menuetto / [6][sans tempo marking]
This serenade includes 3 trumpets in C & 2 trumpets in D.
Horák, Jiří, 3)
Pollin, Pierre
Spindler, Josef, 2)
Tarr, Edward, 28)
Vaillant, Ludovic, 7)

₍Duos (12), 2 horns, K. 487, (1786); arr. 2 trumpets₎

Duos für Bläser, K. 487
[1]Allegro / [2]Menuetto (Allegretto) / [3]Andante / [4]Polonaise / [5]Larghetto / [6]Menuetto / [7]Adagio / [8]Allegro / [9]Menuetto / [10]Andante / [11]Menuetto / [12]Allegro
Pohle, Wolfgang[1+8-10]

₍Entführung aus dem Serail, K. 384, (1782). Act II, No. 11, Aria, "Martern aller Arten"; arr. trumpet & orchestra₎

Aria, "Martern aller Arten" aus *Die Entführung aus dem Serail*, K. 384
(Aria of Constance from *The Abduction from the Seraglio,* K. 384)
André, Maurice, 37), 161)

₍Exultate, Jubilate, K. 165, (1773). Alleluia, soprano & orchestra; arr. trumpet & orchestra₎

Alleluia from *Exultate, Jubilate,* K. 165
Wilbraham, John, 24)

₍Exultate, Jubilate, K. 165, (1773). Alleluia, soprano & orchestra; arr. trumpet & organ₎

Alleluia from *Exultate, Jubilate,* K. 165
André, Maurice, 40), 52), 67), 227)
Schultz, Erik, 3)

₍Minuet; arr. trumpet & orchestra₎

Minuet
Source of transcription is undetermined.
Méndez, Rafael, 18)

₍Serenade, "Posthorn", orchestra, no. 9, D major, K. 320, (1779)₎
Serenade No. 9 in D major, "Posthorn", K. 320
[1]Adagio maestoso - Allegro con spirito / [2]Menuetto (Allegretto) /
[3]Concertante (Andante grazioso) / [4]Rondeau (Allegro ma non
troppo) / [5]Andantino / [6]Menuetto / [7]Finale (Presto)
Orchestration includes: 2 flutes, 2 oboes, 2 bassoons, 2 horns,
posthorn, 2 trumpets, timpani & strings. (The solo posthorn
appears only in the sixth movement.)
Adelstein, Bernard
Benzinger, Karl
Blee, Eugene
Laird, Michael, 20)
Nowicki, August
Voisin, Roger, 13)

₍Sonata, piano, no. 11, A major, K. 331, (1778). Rondo alla turca; arr. trumpet &
brass ensemble₎
Turkish March, K. 331
Grin, Freddy, 2)

₍Sonata, piano, no. 11, A major, K. 331, (1778). Rondo alla turca; arr. trumpet &
orchestra₎
Rondo alla turca, K. 331
André, Maurice, 4)

₍Sonata, piano, no. 11, A major, K. 331, (1778). Rondo alla turca; arr. trumpet
trio, clarinet & rhythm instruments₎
Rondo alla Turka, K. 331
Victorian Trumpet Trio

₍Sonata, piano, no. 15, C major, K. 545, (1788). Allegro; arr. trumpet trio,
clarinet & rhythm instruments₎
Sonata in C major, K. 545
Paraphrase and elaboration of the first movement.
Victorian Trumpet Trio

₍Zauberflöte, K. 620, (1791). Act I, No. 4, Aria, "O zittre nicht"; arr. trumpet &
orchestra₎
Aria der Köningen der Nacht, "O zittre nicht, mein lieber Sohn", aus *Die Zauberflöte*, K. 620
(Aria of the Queen of the Night, from *The Magic Flute*, K. 620)
Wilbraham, John, 24)

₍Zauberflöte, K. 620, (1791). Act II, Aria, "Ach, ich fühl's"; arr. trumpet &
orchestra₎
Aria, "Ach, ich fühl's" aus *Die Zauberflöte*, K. 620
(Pamina's aria from *The Magic Flute*, Act II)
André, Maurice, 37)

₍Zauberflöte, K. 620, (1791). Act II, No. 10, Aria, "O Isis und Osiris"; arr. trumpet & piano₎
Aria, "O Isis und Osiris" from *Die Zauberflöte*, K. 620
(Aria from *The Magic Flute*, K. 620)
Schwarz, Gerard, 14)

₍Zauberflöte, K. 620, (1791). Act II, No. 14, Aria, "Der Hölle Rache"; arr. trumpet & orchestra₎
Aria der Köningen der Nacht, "Der Hölle Rache kocht in meinem Herzen", aus *Die Zauberflöte*, K. 620
(Aria of the Queen of the Night, from *The Magic Flute*, K. 620)
André, Maurice, 37), 161), 218)
Wilbraham, John, 24)

Mudge, Richard, 1718-1763

₍Concerto, trumpet, strings & continuo, D major₎
Concerto in D major for Trumpet, Strings and Basso continuo
¹Vivace / ²Allegro / ³Larghetto andante
André, Maurice, 175)

Munro, George, 1680-1731

₍My Lovely Cecilia; arr. trumpet & piano₎
My Lovely Cecilia
Included as the second movement in Bernard Fitzgerald's *English Suite*, a transcription for trumpet and piano.
Masters, Edward L.
Ritter, David

Murov, Askold Federovich, 1928-

₍Stereophonia (Variations and Dithyramb), solo trumpet₎
Stereophonia (Variations and Dithyramb)
Gorokhov, Vitaly

Mussorgsky, Modest Petrovich, 1839-1881
Moussorgski, Modeste

₍Pictures at an Exhibition, piano, (1874). Promenade; arr. trumpet & piano₎
Promenade from *Pictures at an Exhibition*
Stith, Marice, 5)

Nagel (arr.), Robert E., 1924-

₍American Folk Hymns; arr. trumpet trio₎
American Folk Hymns
Nagel, Robert, 9)

₍Chorales for Trumpets; arr. trumpet trio₎
Chorales for Trumpets
Nagel, Robert, 9)

[Christmas Trumpets; arr. trumpet trio]
Christmas Trumpets
Nagel, Robert, 9)

[Easter Trumpets; arr. trumpet trio]
Easter Trumpets
Nagel, Robert, 9)

[My Wonderful Lord (Medley); arr. trumpet & orchestra]
My Wonderful Lord (Medley)
Nagel, Robert, 9)

[Trumpets of Thanksgiving; arr. trumpet trio]
Trumpets of Thanksgiving
Nagel, Robert, 9)

Nagel, Robert E., 1924-

[Brass Trio, trumpet, horn & trombone, no. 2]
Brass Trio No. 2
Giangiulio, Richard

[Concerto, trumpet & strings, op. 8, (1951)]
Concerto for Trumpet and Strings, op. 8
¹Moderate / ²Slow / ³Fast
Blee, Eugene

[Trumpet Processional, trumpet & organ (piano), (1961)]
Trumpet Processional
Nagel, Robert, 17)

Nardini, Pietro, 1722-1793

[Adagio cantabile; arr. trumpet & organ]
Adagio cantabile
Mertens, Theo, 4)

Nazareth, Ernesto, 1863-1934
Nazaré, Ernesto Júlio de

[Cavaquinho; arr. trumpet & orchestra]
Cavaquinho (samba)
André, Maurice, 5)

Nelhýbel, Václav, 1919-

[Golden Concerto, trumpet & piano, (1960)]
Golden Concerto (on a twelve tone row)
Ode, James

Neruda, Johann Baptist Georg, *ca.* 1707-1780
Neruda, Jan Křtitel Jiří

₍Concerto, corno da caccia & orchestra, E♭ major; arr. "modern clarinhorn" & orchestra₎
Konzert Es-dur für Corno da caccia und Orchester
¹Allegro / ²Largo / ³Vivace
The *clarinhorn* is a modern instrument with valves.
Streitwieser, Franz Xaver

₍Concerto, corno da caccia & orchestra, E♭ major; arr. "modern corno da caccia" & orchestra₎
Konzert Es-dur für Corno da caccia und Orchester
¹Allegro / ²Largo / ³Vivace
The original *corno da caccia* was a valveless horn. This recording involves a modern instrument with valves.
Güttler, Ludwig, 27)

₍Concerto, corno da caccia & orchestra, E♭ major; arr. trumpet & orchestra₎
Konzert Es-dur für Corno da caccia und Orchester
¹Allegro / ²Largo / ³Vivace
> **André, Maurice, 119)**
> **Basch, Wolfgang, 9), 12)**
> **Erb, Helmut, 3)**
> **Güttler, Ludwig, 3), 7)**
> **Hickman, David, 2)**
> **Lang, William**
> **Rejlek, Vladimir**
> **Steele-Perkins, Crispian, 13)**
> **Svejkovský, Josef**
> **Wallace, John, 5)**

₍Concerto, corno da caccia & orchestra, E♭ major; arr. trumpet & organ₎
Konzert Es-dur für Corno da caccia und Orchester
¹Allegro / ²Largo / ³Vivace
> **McGuffey, Patrick**
> **Schultz, Erik, 2)**

Nessler, Viktor E., 1841-1890
Nessler, Viktor Ernst

₍Trompeter von Säckingen, (1884). Behüt' dich Gott; arr. trumpet & band₎
Behüt' dich Gott from *Der Trompeter von Säckingen*
Reinhart, Carole Dawn, 10)

₍Trompeter von Säckingen, (1884). Behüt' dich Gott; arr. trumpet & organ₎
Behüt' dich Gott from *Der Trompeter von Säckingen*
Grin, Freddy, 8)

Nesterov, Arkadi Aleksandrovich, 1918-

ſConcerto, trumpet & orchestra, op. 42, c minorꞁ
Concerto in c minor for Trumpet and Orchestra, op. 42
Dokshitser, Timofei, 13), 37)

Nestico, Sammy, 1924-
Nestico, Samuel L.

ſPortrait of a Trumpet, trumpet & pianoꞁ
Portrait of a Trumpet
Crisara, Raymond, 8)

Neukomm, Sigismund Ritter von, 1778-1858

ſFanfares (3), 4 trumpetsꞁ
Three Fanfares for 4 Trumpets
Voisin, Roger, 6)

Nicolai, Philipp, 1556-1608

ſHow Brightly Shines the Morning Star; arr. 2 trumpets, organ & bassoonꞁ
How Brightly Shines the Morning Star
(Wie schön leuchtet der Morgenstern)
Voisin, Roger, 2)

Niedermeyer, Louis, 1802-1861
Niedermeyer, Abraham Louis

ſStradella, (1837). Aria, "Pieta Signore"; arr. trumpet & organꞁ
Aria, "Pieta Signore" from *Stradella*
This aria from the opera about Stradella's life is often incorrectly
attributed to Stradella, himself.
Schultz, Erik, 3)

Niehaus, Manfred, 1933-

ſConnections, chamber ensembleꞁ
Connections
Chamber ensemble includes: trumpet, bassoon (& accordion),
saxophone (& viola), zither, bass & percussion.
Schoof, Manfred

ſImitation, voice & chamber ensembleꞁ
Imitation
Chamber ensemble includes: clarinet, trumpet, trombone, violin,
guitar, piano/organ & percussion.
The title of this work may actually be *Initiation*.
Stockhausen, Markus, 2)

Niles, John Jacob, 1892-1980

[Black is the Color of My True Love's Hair; arr. trumpet & piano]
Black is the Color of My True Love's Hair
Haynie, John, 2)

Nuckolls, Lawrence, 1951-

[Chaconne, trumpet & organ]
Chaconne
Pearson, Byron

Nurimov, Char, 1941-

[Concerto, trumpet & orchestra]
Concerto for Trumpet and Orchestra
Maximenko, Anatoly, 4)

Nye, F.A.

[Penobscot Park March. Excerpt; arr. solo cornet]
Penobscot Park March [excerpt]
Demonstration performance of excerpted cornet part.
Voisin, Roger, 13)

Obrecht, Jakob, *ca.* 1450-1505

[Ein fröhlich wesen, countertenor, tenor, baritone, cornetto, 2 sackbuts & bass dulcian]
Ein fröhlich wesen
Laird, Michael, 13)

[Magnificat, soli, mixed voices & instrumental ensemble]
Magnificat
Cook, Richard

[Tsaat een meskin was junck, cornetto, shawm & 2 trombones]
Tsaat een meskin was junck
Laird, Michael, 13)

O'Brien, Eugene, 1945-

[Embarking for Cythera, chamber ensemble, (1978)]
Embarking for Cythera
Chamber ensemble includes: flute, clarinet, bassoon, trumpet, harp, piano/electric organ, violin & cello.
Dolce, Christine

Ockeghem, Johannes, *ca.* 1410-1497
Okeghem, Johannes

[Missa pro defunctis, male voices, cornetto, 2 trombones & pommer]
Missa pro defunctis
The male voices include: 3 countertenors, 3 tenors & 3 basses.
Hagge, Detlef

Offenbach, Jacques, 1819-1880

[Contes d'Hoffmann, (1880). Act II: Aria, "Les oiseaux dans la charmille"; arr. trumpet, mixed voices & orchestra]
Aria, "Les oiseaux dans la charmille" from *Les Contes d'Hoffmann*
(Doll Song from *The Tales of Hoffmann*)
André, Maurice, 37)

[Contes d'Hoffmann, (1880). Act III: Barcarolle; arr. trumpet & orchestra]
Barcarolle from *Les Contes d'Hoffmann*
(Barcarole from *Tales of Hoffmann*)
Scherbaum, Adolf, 34)

[Contes d'Hoffmann, (1880). Act III: Barcarolle; arr. trumpet & organ]
Barcarolle from *Les Contes d'Hoffmann*
(Barcarole from *Tales of Hoffmann*)
Grin, Freddy, 8)

[Périchole, (1868). Lettre de la Périchole; arr. cornet & brass ensemble]
Lettre de la Périchole from *La Périchole*
Caens, Thierry

Ohana, Maurice, 1914-

[Mass, soli, mixed voices & instrumental ensemble, (1976-77)]
Messe
Instrumental ensemble includes: flute or oboe, clarinet, bassoon, trumpet, trombone & organ.
Caens, Thierry

Olbrisch, Franz Martin, 1952-

[Epigenese, flute, saxophone, trumpet, cello, piano & percussion]
Epigenese
Kierski, Eckhard

Olsen, Ole, 1850-1927

[Fantasy, cornet & brass ensemble]
Fantasy for E♭-cornet and brass ensemble
Naess, Lars

Ortiz, Diego, *ca.* 1510-*ca.* 1570

⌐Recercada Segunda; arr. trumpet & organ⌐
Recercada Segunda
Hardy, Francis

Österreich, Georg, 1664-1735

⌐Aria, "Ach Herr, wie sind meiner Feinde so viel", tenor, trumpet & orchestra⌐
Aria, "Ach Herr, wie sind meiner Feinde so viel"
Touvron, Guy, 16)

Ott, Lorenz Justinian, 1748-1805
Ott, Lucianus Justinianus

⌐Aufzüge (3), 8 trumpets & timpani⌐
Drei Aufzüge
Immer, Friedemann, 18)
Tarr, Edward, 28)

Otto, Luigi, *fl. ca.* 1750

⌐Concerto, trumpet & orchestra, E♭ major⌐
Concerto in E♭ major for Trumpet and Orchestra
¹Allegro moderato / ²Adagio / ³Rondo
André, Maurice, 62)

Otto, Valerius, 1579-*ca.* 1612

⌐Paduanen, Galliarden, Intraden und Currenten, (1611). No. 1: Intrada, E♭ major; arr. trumpet & brass ensemble⌐
Intrada No. 1 in E♭ major
Güttler, Ludwig, 9), 21)

Overton, Hall, 1920-1972
Overton, Hall Franklin

⌐Pulsations, chamber ensemble, (1972)⌐
Pulsations
Chamber ensemble includes: flute, clarinet, bassoon, horn, trumpet, trombone, violin, cello, bass, piano & percussion.
Stubbs, James

Ovunts, Gagic, 1930-

⌐Pieces (2), trumpet & piano⌐
Two Pieces for Trumpet and Piano
¹Tema (Theme) / ²Ritmika (Rhythmics)
Krivosheyev, Yuri

Pachelbel, Johann, 1653-1706

₍Canon, strings & continuo, D major; arr. trumpet & strings₎
Canon in D major
(Kanon D-dur)
Touvron, Guy, 9)

₍Canon, strings & continuo, D major; arr. 3 trumpets & strings₎
Canon in D major for 3 Trumpets & Strings
(Kanon D-dur)
Marsalis, Wynton, 6), 7)

₍Chorale prelude, "Vater unser im Himmelreich"; arr. trumpet & organ₎
Vater unser im Himmelreich
Delmotte, Roger, 39)
Potpourri, 44)

₍Chorale prelude, "Was Gott tut, das ist wohlgetan"; arr. trumpet & organ₎
Was Gott tut, das ist wohlgetan
Laughton, Stuart

Padilla, José, 1889-1960

₍Princesita; arr. trumpet & orchestra₎
Princesita
(Litte Princess)
Méndez, Rafael, 15)

₍Relicario; arr. trumpet trio, clarinet, piano & drums₎
El Relicario
Victorian Trumpet Trio

Paganini, Niccolò, 1782-1840

₍Moto perpetuo, violin & orchestra, op. 11, (c. 1830); arr. cornet & wind ensemble₎
Moto perpetuo, op. 11
(Perpetual Motion)
Marsalis, Wynton, 4)

₍Moto perpetuo, violin & orchestra, op. 11, (c. 1830); arr. trumpet & orchestra₎
Moto perpetuo, op. 11
(Perpetual Motion)
Méndez, Rafael, 9), 24)

Paisner, Ben, 1912-

₍Prelude to a Mood, trumpet & piano, (1948)₎
Prelude to a Mood
Reynolds, George

Pakhmutova, Alexandra Nikolayevna, 1929-

[Concerto, trumpet & orchestra, e♭ minor, (1955)]
Concerto in e♭ minor for Trumpet and Orchestra
In one movement: Andante-Allegro-Adagio-Allegro-Maestoso
Revised by the composer in 1978. Piano reduction of revised
version published in 1979 by Musika (State Publisher of the
U.S.S.R.); piano reduction of original version published in 1964
by Leeds Music of New York.
>   **Dokshitser, Timofei,** 8)
>   **Popov, Sergei,** 5)

Pallavicino, Carlo, *d.* 1688
Pallavicini, Carlo

[Diocletiano, (1674). Sinfonia, chamber orchestra]
Sinfonia from *Il Diocletiano*
The *New Groves* suggests that the oft cited birthyear of 1630 is
doubtful, and that Pallavicino may have been born around 1640.
>   **Keavy, Stephen**
>   **Molénat, Claude**

Palmer, Robert, 1915-
Palmer, Robert Moffett

[Sonata, trumpet & piano]
Sonata for Trumpet and Piano
>   **Stith, Marice,** 7)

Panella, Manuel, *b.* 1880

[Gato Montes; arr. trumpet & orchestra]
El Gato Montes
>   **Méndez, Rafael,** 12)

Parkins, William

[Lover of the Lord; arr. trumpet & band]
Lover of the Lord
>   **Reinhart, Carole Dawn,** 10)

Parry, Hubert, 1848-1918
Parry, (Charles) Hubert (Hastings)

[Jerusalem, unison voices & orchestra, (1916); arr. trumpet & organ]
Jerusalem
>   **Grin, Freddy,** 8)

Parsons, Robert, *ca.* 1530-1570

[Trumpetts, instrumental ensemble]
Trumpetts
Instrumental ensemble may include: recorders, crumhorns, bass sordune, racket, tenor curtal, shawm, cornetti, sackbuts & strings.
Smithers, Don, 2)

Partch, Harry, 1901-1974

[Ulysses Departs from the Edge of the World, speaker, saxophone, trumpet & Partch instruments, (1955)]
Ulysses Departs from the Edge of the World
Logan, Jack

Pascal, Claude, 1921-
Pascal, Claude René Georges

[Capriccio, trumpet & piano, (1953)]
Capriccio
Ode, James
Schwarz, Gerard, 12)

Pauer, Jiří, 1919-

[Concerto, trumpet & orchestra, (1972)]
Koncert pro Trubku a Orchestr
(Concerto per Tromba e Orchestra)
[1]Presto rabbioso / [2]Andante / [3]Allegro
Piano reduction published in 1975 by Panton.
Sejpal, Stanislav

[Trompetina, trumpet & piano]
Trompetina
Dokshitser, Timofei, 17)
Kejmar, Miroslav, 7)

Pearson (arr.), Leslie, 1931-

[Elizabethan Fantasy; arr. trumpet & organ]
An Elizabethan Fantasy
Wilbraham, John, 3)

[Mediaevel Pageant; arr. trumpet & organ]
Mediaevel Pageant
Wilbraham, John, 3)

Peerson, Martin, *ca.* 1572-1651

[Blow out the trumpet, mixed voices & instrumental ensemble]
Blow out the trumpet
Davenport, LaNoue

Peeters, Flor, 1903-1986

⌐Sonata, trumpet & piano, op. 51, (1961)¬
Sonata for Trumpet and Piano, op. 51
¹Allegro / ²Aria (Adagio) / ³Finale (Toccata)
Head, Emerson

⌐Sonata, trumpet & piano, op. 51, (1961). Aria¬
Aria from *Sonata for Trumpet and Piano*, op. 51
Performed on flügelhorn and organ.
Tolley, Richard

⌐Sonata, trumpet & piano, op. 51, (1961). Toccata¬
Toccata from *Sonata for Trumpet and Piano*, op. 51
Performed on cornet and piano.
Tolley, Richard

Pelz, William, 20th cent.

⌐Country Dance, trumpet & piano, (1952)¬
Country Dance
Burkart, Richard

⌐Enchanted Swing, cornet & piano, (1952)¬
The Enchanted Swing
Tolley, Richard

Pennequin, J.G., 20th cent.

⌐Morceau de concert, cornet & piano, (1907)¬
Morceau de concert
Christensen, Ketil

Pepusch, Johann Christoph, 1667-1752

⌐Gigue; arr. trumpet & piano¬
Gigue
Geyer, Charles

⌐Sonata, recorder & continuo, c minor; arr. trumpet & organ¬
Sonata in c minor
¹Adagio / ²Allegro / ³Largo / ⁴Allegro
André, Maurice, 59)

Pergolesi, Giovanni Battista, 1710-1736

⌐Nina; arr. trumpet & piano¬
Nina
Schwarz, Gerard, 14)

Pérotin, *ca.* 1180-1236
Perotinus Magnus
Pérotinus le Grand

₍Alleluja Nativitas, mixed voices & instrumental ensemble₎
Allcluja Nativitas
Otten, Kees
Renz, Albrecht, 2)

₍Sederunt principes, mixed voices & instrumental ensemble₎
Sederunt principes
Renz, Albrecht, 1), 2), 3)

₍Viderunt omnes fines terræ, mixed voices & instrumental ensemble₎
Viderunt omnes fines terræ
Renz, Albrecht, 1), 2)

Persichetti, Vincent, 1915-1987

₍Hollow Men, trumpet & strings, op. 25, (1944)₎
The Hollow Men, op. 25
Inspired by T.S. Eliot's poem, "The Hollow Men".
Baker, Sidney
Parker, R. Ted

₍Hollow Men, trumpet & strings, op. 25, (1944); arr. trumpet & organ₎
The Hollow Men, op. 25
Keyboard reduction by the composer was published by
Elkan-Vogel in 1948.
Plog, Anthony, 2)
Stith, Marice, 6)

₍Hollow Men, trumpet & strings, op. 25, (1944); arr. trumpet & piano₎
The Hollow Men, op. 25
Keyboard reduction by the composer was published by
Elkan-Vogel in 1948.
Levy, Robert

₍Parable XIV, solo trumpet, (c. 1975)₎
Parable XIV for Solo Trumpet
Giangiulio, Richard

Perti, Giacomo Antonio, 1661-1756

₍Sinfonia avanti la Serenata, trumpet, strings & continuo, D major₎
Sinfonia avanti la Serenata
¹Grave - Allegro / ²Grave - Allegro
Smithers, Don, 5)

₍Sonata, 4 trumpets, strings & continuo, D major₎
Sonata a 4 Trombe
¹Andante / ²Presto / ³Adagio / ⁴Allegro
Touvron, Guy, 2)
Wobisch, Helmut, 3)

Pesente, Martino, *ca.* 1600-*ca.* 1648

[Gagliarda, cornetto, spinet & viol]
    Gagliarda
        Otten, Kees

Peskin, Vladimir Amenevich, 1906-

[Nocturne and Scherzo, trumpet & brass band]
    Nocturne and Scherzo
        Dokshitser, Timofei, 15), 20)

[Prelude, trumpet & piano, E$^\flat$ major, (1957)]
    Prelude in E$^\flat$ major for Trumpet and Piano
        Sveshnikov, Mikhail

[Scherzo, trumpet & piano]
    Scherzo for Trumpet and Piano
        Dokshitser, Timofei, 5), 7), 27), 35)

Peterson, John Willard, 1921-

[So Send I You, (1954); arr. trumpet & band]
    So Send I You
        Reinhart, Carole Dawn, 10)

[So Send I You, (1954); arr. trumpet & piano]
    So Send I You
        Reinhart, Carole Dawn, 13)

Petit, Alexandre Sylvain, 1864-1925

[Fête Militaire; arr. cornet & band]
    Fête Militaire
        André, Maurice, 120), 212)

[Goutte d'eau; arr. cornet & band]
    Goutte d'eau
        André, Maurice, 120), 212)

[Goutte d'eau; arr. cornet & brass ensemble]
    Goutte d'eau
        Caens, Thierry

[Gouttes d'eaux. Excerpt, cornet]
    Gouttes d'eaux (Polka)
      (Drops of Water)
        Short excerpt performed on unaccompanied cornet as a demonstration piece.
        Voisin, Roger, 13)

₍Madeleine; arr. cornet & band₎
Madeleine
André, Maurice, 120), 212)

₍Myrto Polka; arr. cornet & band₎
Myrto Polka
André, Maurice, 120), 212)

₍Myrto Polka; arr. trumpet & orchestra₎
Myrto Polka
André, Maurice, 7)

Petrassi, Goffredo, 1904-

₍Fanfare, 3 trumpets, (1944, rev. 1976)₎
Fanfare for 3 Trumpets
Plog, Anthony, 4)

Petrov, Valery, 1929-

₍Suite, trumpet & brass band₎
Suite for Trumpet and Brass Band
Dokshitser, Timofei, 20)

₍Suite, trumpet & orchestra, no. 2₎
Second Suite for Trumpet and Orchestra
[1]Good Morning / [2]By the Lake / [3]Stroll / [4]In the Mountains / [5]Playful Game
Dokshitser, Timofei, 24)

Petterson, Svante, 20th cent.

₍Summer Night of Gotland; arr. trumpet & instrumental ensemble₎
Summer Night of Gotland
Andersen, Ole

Peuerl, Paul, 1570-*ca.* 1625
Peyerl, Paul
Bäuerl, Paul

₍Neue Paduanen..., (1611). Partita, d minor; arr. recorders, oboes, trumpets & trombones₎
Partita a 4 in d minor
[1]Pavane / [2]Intrade / [3]Deutscher Tanz / [4]Galliarde / [5]Deutscher Tanz
Holy, Walter, 4)

Pezel, Johann Christoph, 1639-1694
Pezelius

₍Bicinia Variorum Instrumentorum, (1675). No. 61: Sonatina, 2 cornetti &
continuo, (No. 1), a minor₎
Sonatina a due cornetti, BVI 61
> The specific instruments used for these sonatinas are not
> differentiated in this index, but may ascertained by referring to
> the album listings. The continuo instruments may be any
> combination of harpsichord or organ and bassoon, trombone or
> cello.
>> **Schwarz, Gerard**, 20)
>> **Yudashkin, Georgy**

₍Bicinia Variorum Instrumentorum, (1675). No. 62: Sonatina, 2 cornetti &
continuo, (No. 2), a minor₎
Sonatina a due cornetti, BVI 62
>> **Carroll, Edward**, 11)
>> **Schwarz, Gerard**, 20)
>> **Touvron, Guy**, 21)
>> **Yudashkin, Georgy**

₍Bicinia Variorum Instrumentorum, (1675). No. 63: Sonatina, 2 cornetti &
continuo, (No. 3), a minor₎
Sonatina a due cornetti, BVI 63
>> **Pohle, Wolfgang**

₍Bicinia Variorum Instrumentorum, (1675). No. 64: Sonatina, 2 cornetti &
continuo, (No. 4), a minor₎
Sonatina a due cornetti, BVI 64
>> **Pohle, Wolfgang**

₍Bicinia Variorum Instrumentorum, (1675). No. 65: Sonatina, 2 cornetti &
continuo, (No. 5), C major₎
Sonatina a due cornetti, BVI 65
>> **Carroll, Edward**, 11)
>> **Schwarz, Gerard**, 20)
>> **Touvron, Guy**, 21)

₍Bicinia Variorum Instrumentorum, (1675). No. 66: Sonatina, 2 cornetti &
continuo, (No. 6), C major₎
Sonatina a due cornetti, BVI 66
>> **Schwarz, Gerard**, 20)

₍Bicinia Variorum Instrumentorum, (1675). No. 67: Sonatina, 2 cornetti &
continuo, (No. 7), C major₎
Sonatina a due cornetti, BVI 67
>> **Pohle, Wolfgang**

₍Bicinia Variorum Instrumentorum, (1675). No. 69: Sonatina, 2 trumpets & continuo, (No. 1), C major₎
Sonatina a due clarini, BVI 69
Güttler, Ludwig, 15)
Immer, Friedemann, 18)
Tarr, Edward, 40)
Touvron, Guy, 21)

₍Bicinia Variorum Instrumentorum, (1675). No. 70: Sonatina, 2 trumpets & continuo, (No. 2), C major₎
Sonatina a due clarini, BVI 70
Tarr, Edward, 40)

₍Bicinia Variorum Instrumentorum, (1675). No. 71: Sonatina, 2 trumpets & continuo, (No. 3), C major₎
Sonatina a due clarini, BVI 71
Fink, Werner
Jones, Philip, 9)
Tarr, Edward, 40)

₍Bicinia Variorum Instrumentorum, (1675). No. 72: Sonatina, 2 trumpets & continuo, (No. 4), C major₎
Sonatina a due clarini, BVI 72
Tarr, Edward, 41)
Touvron, Guy, 21)

₍Bicinia Variorum Instrumentorum, (1675). No. 73: Sonatina, 2 trumpets & continuo, (No. 5), C major₎
Sonatina a due clarini, BVI 73
Güttler, Ludwig, 15)
Immer, Friedemann, 18)
Tarr, Edward, 41)

₍Bicinia Variorum Instrumentorum, (1675). No. 74: Sonatina, 2 trumpets & continuo, (No. 6), C major₎
Sonatina a due clarini, BVI 74
Jones, Philip, 9)
Tarr, Edward, 40)

₍Bicinia Variorum Instrumentorum, (1675). No. 75: Sonatina, trumpet, bassoon & continuo, (No. 1), C major₎
Sonatina a due, per clarino e fagotto, BVI 75
Schultz, Erik, 7)
Tarr, Edward, 39)

₍Fünff-stimmigte blasende Music, (1685). Suite, 2 cornetti & 3 trombones₎
Suite from *Fünff-stimmigte blasende Music*
[1]Intrade [FBM 59] / [2]Allemande [FBM 60] / [3]Courente [FBM 61] / [4]Bal [FBM 62] / [5]Sarabande [FBM 63] / [6]Gigue [FBM 64]
There are numerous recordings by modern brass quintets of pieces from *Fünff-stimmigte blasende Music*. However, only the performances involving **cornetti** are indexed here.
Tarr, Edward, 10)

ₜHora Decima Musicorum Lipsiensium, (1670). No. 1: Sonata, 2 cornetti &
3 trombones₎
Sonata, HDM 1
> There are numerous recordings by modern brass quintets of
> sonatas from *Hora Decima*. However, only the performances
> involving **cornetti** are indexed here.
>
> **Steinkopf, Otto**

ₜHora Decima Musicorum Lipsiensium, (1670). No. 30: Sonata, 2 cornetti &
3 trombones; arr. 2 trumpets, 2 oboes & strings₎
Sonata, HDM 30
> **Voisin, Roger,** 7)

ₜHora Decima Musicorum Lipsiensium, (1670). No. 39: Sonata, 2 cornetti &
3 trombones₎
Sonata, HDM 39
> **Steinkopf, Otto**

Philidor, Anne Danican
See: Danican-Philidor, Anne

Philidor (l'aîné), André Danican
See: Danican-Philidor (l'aîné), André

Philipps, Thomas, 19th cent.

ₜLast Bugle, (c. 1822); arr. tenor, keyed bugle, flute, clarinet & strings₎
The Last Bugle
> **Dudgeon, Ralph**

Phillips, Burrill, 1907-1988

ₜCanzona III, reader & chamber ensemble, (1964)₎
Canzona III
> Chamber ensemble includes: flute, clarinet, trumpet, violin, cello,
> piano & percussion.
>
> **Romm, Ronald**

Picchi, Giovanni, *fl. ca.* 1615

ₜCanzoni da sonar..., (1625). No. 3, violin, cornetto & continuo₎
Canzon terza a 2
> Continuo instruments include: harpsichord (organ), trombone &
> cello.
>
> **Dickey, Bruce**

ₜCanzoni da sonar..., (1625). No. 9, cornetto, violin, recorder & continuo₎
Canzona nona a 3
> Continuo instruments include: harpsichord & chitarrone.
>
> **Eichhorn, Holger**

ₜCanzoni da sonar..., (1625). No. 12, violin, cornetto, trombone, cello & continuoₜ
 Canzon duodecima a 4
   Dickey, Bruce

ₜToccata, violin, cornetto & continuoₜ
 Toccata
   Continuo instruments include: harpsichord (organ), trombone &
   cello.
   Dickey, Bruce

Pierre de Corbeil, *d.* 1222

ₜConcordi lætitia; arr. mixed voices, brass & stringsₜ
 Concordi lætitia
   Thibaud, Pierre, 10)

Pierre de Manchicourt, *ca.* 1510-1564

ₜBicinia gallica et latina, (1545). Bicinium, "Amour", alto cornetto & tenor
cornettoₜ
 Bicinium, "Amour"
   Laird, Michael, 1)

Pilss, Karl, 1902-1949

ₜSonata, trumpet & piano, (1935)ₜ
 Sonate für Trompete und Klavier
   [1]Allegro appassionato / [2]Adagio, molto cantabile / [3]Allegro agitato
   Reinhart, Carole Dawn, 9)

ₜSonata, trumpet & piano, (1935). Adagio; arr. trumpet & organₜ
 Adagio from *Sonata for Trumpet and Piano*
   Tolley, Richard

Pinkham, Daniel, 1923-
Pinkham, Daniel Rogers

ₜOther voices of the trumpet, trumpet & organ, (1971)ₜ
 The other voices of the trumpet
   Pearson, Byron

Planel, Robert, 1908-

ₜConcerto, trumpet & strings, (1966)ₜ
 Concerto pour Trompette et Orchestre à Cordes
   [1]Largement / [2]Lent et trés calme / [3]Vivace, gai et léger
   André, Maurice, 147)

Platti, Giovanni Benedetto, *ca.* 1700-1763

₍Suite, violin & continuo, A major; arr. trumpet & organ₎
Suite in A major
(Suite A-dur für Violine und Cembalo)
¹Andante / ²Allegro / ³Adagio / ⁴Presto
André, Maurice, 55)

Plau, Arild, 1920-

₍Preludes (4), trumpet & piano₎
Four Preludes for Trumpet and Piano
Naess, Lars

Pleskow, Raoul, 1931-

₍Movement for 9 Players, chamber ensemble, (1967)₎
Movement for 9 Players
Chamber ensemble includes: flute, clarinet, trumpet, violin, cello, bass, piano, piano/celeste & percussion.
Dean, Allan, 1)

Plog, Anthony, 1947-

₍Animal Ditties, narrator, trumpet & piano, (1978)₎
Animal Ditties for Narrator, Trumpet & Piano
¹The Turtle / ²The Python / ³Hyena / ⁴Hog
Text by Ogden Nash.
Plog, Anthony, 6)

₍Animal Ditties, narrator, trumpet & piano, no. 2, (1983)₎
Animal Ditties 2, for Narrator, Trumpet & Piano
¹The Canary / ²The Chipmunk / ³The Ostrich / ⁴The Elk
Text by Ogden Nash.
Plog, Anthony, 4)

₍Concert Duets (10), 2 trumpets, (1980)₎
Concert Duets
¹Fanfare / ²Pastorale / ³Scherzo / ⁴Dialogue / ⁵Textures / ⁶Toccata / ⁷Take A Train / ⁸Statements / ⁹Song / ¹⁰Abstractions
Giangiulio, Richard¹⁻⁴

₍Fanfare, 2 trumpets, (1977)₎
Fanfare for Two Trumpets
Included in a collection of trumpet duets published by Wimbledon: Contemporary Music for Two Trumpets.
Pearson, Byron
Plog, Anthony, 5)

₍Scenes (2), soprano, trumpet & organ, (c. 1974)₎
Two Scenes for Soprano, Trumpet and Organ
Text by Daveda Lamont. "The Hills of Morning": (In the west...;
In the east...).
Plog, Anthony, 2)

Plotnikov, Boris

₍And for Me Comes Spring; arr. cornet & accompaniment₎
And for Me Comes Spring
Klochkov, Pavel, 4)

₍Fragrance of Lilacs; arr. cornet & accompaniment₎
The Fragrance of Lilacs
Klochkov, Pavel, 4)

Podkovirov, Petr Petrovich, 1910-

₍Sonata, trumpet & piano₎
Sonata for Trumpet and Piano
Volkov, Vitaly

Poglietti, Alessandro, *d.* 1683

₍Ballet, 4 trumpets & strings, C major₎
Ballet C-dur für 4 Trompeten und Streicher
Ullrich, Marc

₍Sonata, recorder, cornetto, bassoon & continuo, C major₎
Sonata a 3
Continuo instruments include: organ & viola da gamba.
Pok, František, 5)

₍Sonata, recorder, cornetto, bassoon & continuo, C major; arr. flute, trumpet, bassoon & continuo₎
Sonate C-dur für Flöte, Trompete, Fagott und Basso continuo
Continuo instruments include: harpsichord & cello.
Yudashkın, Georgy

₍Sonata, 2 trumpets, strings & continuo, C major₎
Sonate C-dur für 2 Trompeten, Streicher und Basso continuo
Scherbaum, Adolf, 16)

Poliakin, F.
See: Polnarioff, Kurt

Polnarioff, Kurt, 1917-1958
Nero, Paul

₍Canari, violin & piano; arr. trumpet & instrumental ensemble₎
The Hot Canary
(Le canari)
> Although both albums listed here attribute this composition to F. Poliakin, the actual composer was violinist Kurt Polnarioff who used the pseudonym, Paul Nero. Maynard Ferguson also recorded this work with the Stan Kenton Orchestra in the early 1950's on a 78-rpm disc (Capitol: 7-1713). On Ferguson's recording, the composition is attributed correctly to Paul Nero.
> **Andersen, Ole**

₍Canari, violin & piano; arr. trumpet & orchestra₎
Le canari
André, Maurice, 4)

Ponce, Manuel Maria, 1882-1948

₍Estrellita; arr. trumpet & orchestra₎
Estrellita
Hidalgo, José Luis
Méndez, Rafael, 19)

Ponchielli, Amilcare, 1834-1886

₍Gioconda, (1876). Aria, "Cielo e mar"; arr. trumpet & orchestra₎
Aria, "Cielo e mar" from *La Gioconda*
André, Maurice, 37)

₍Gioconda, (1876). Dance of the Hours; arr. trumpet & orchestra₎
Dance of the Hours from *La Gioconda*
Méndez, Rafael, 10), 24)

Poot, Marcel, 1901-

₍Etude de concert, trumpet & piano, (1933)₎
Etude de concert
Haynie, John, 2)
Roelant, Alain

₍Humoresque, trumpet & piano, (1958)₎
Humoresque
House, Lawrence

Popov, Gavriil Nikolayevich, 1904-1972

₍Chamber Symphony, chamber ensemble, op. 2, C major₎
Chamber Symphony in C major for 7 Instruments, op. 2
Chamber ensemble includes: flute (piccolo), clarinet, bassoon, trumpet, violin, cello & bass.
Popov, Sergei, 2)

Porret, Julien, 1896-

꜀Esquisses (6), trumpet & piano, (1953)꜒
Six Esquisses
(Six Sketches)
Reynolds, George

꜀Esquisses (6), trumpet & piano, (1953). No. 1꜒
Esquisses No. 1
Schwarz, Gerard, 14)

Porrino, Eino, 1910-1959
Porrino, Ennio

꜀Concertino, trumpet & orchestra, (1934)꜒
Concertino for Trumpet and Orchestra
Hunger, Helmut, 1)

꜀Concertino, trumpet & orchestra, (1934); arr. cornet & piano꜒
Concertino
Tolley, Richard

Post, Michael, 20th cent.

꜀Greatest American Hero. Theme; arr. trumpet & orchestra꜒
Theme from *The Greatest American Hero*
This film music is credited to Michael Post and Stephen Geyer.
(Stephen Geyer may be the lyricist for the songs.)
Schultz, Erik, 8)

Poulenc, Francis, 1899-1963
Poulenc, Francis Jean Marcel

꜀Cantata, "Le bal masqué", baritone voice, cornet, piano & chamber orchestra, (1932)꜒
Le bal masqué
Delmotte, Roger, 1), 51)
Ménardi, Louis

꜀Sonata, horn, trumpet & trombone, (1922)꜒
Sonate pour Cor, Trompette et Trombone
[1]Allegro moderato / [2]Andante / [3]Rondeau
Glantz, Harry, 7)
Ménardi, Louis
Potpourri, 30)
Stevens, Thomas, 6)
Wilbraham, John, 21)

₍Suite Française, chamber wind ensemble, (1935)₎
Suite Française
(Dances by Claude Gervaise)
[1]Bransle de Bourgogne / [2]Pavane / [3]Petite Marche Militaire / [4]Complainte / [5]Bransle de Champagne / [6]Sicilienne / [7]Carillon
Chamber wind ensemble includes: 2 oboes, 2 bassoons, 2 trumpets, 3 trombones & percussion.
André, Maurice, 172)

Powell, Mel, 1923-
Powell, Melvin

₍Divertimento, flute, oboe, clarinet, bassoon & trumpet, (1956)₎
Divertimento for Five Winds
[1]Allegro cantabile / [2]Presto / [3]Largo / [4]Vivo
Karpilovsky, Murray

Powell, Morgan E., 1938-

₍Alone, solo trumpet, (1973)₎
Alone
Potpourri, 66)

₍Duet V, flute/piccolo, clarinet/bass clarinet, trumpet & 2 trombones, (1984)₎
Duet V
Five musicians.
Sasaki, Ray

₍Fine Tuning, clarinet, trumpet & percussion, (1981)₎
Fine Tuning
Sasaki, Ray

Prætorius, Michael, *ca.* 1571-1621
Praetorius = Schultheiss

₍Chorale, "Vom Himmel hoch, da komm ich her"; arr. mixed voices, 2 trumpets, 2 trombones & strings₎
Chorale, "Vom Himmel hoch, da komm ich her"
Thibaud, Pierre, 10)

₍Es ist ein Ros' entsprungen; arr. children's voices, trumpet & orchestra₎
Es ist ein Ros' entsprungen
("Lo, how a rose e'er blooming")
André, Maurice, 166)

₍Musæ Sioniæ IV, (1607). Lobt Gott ihr Christen alle gleich; arr. 4 sackbuts₎
Lobt Gott ihr Christen alle gleich
(Lobt Gott, ihr Christen allzugleich)
The four trombones are: soprano, alto, tenor & bass.
Laird, Michael, 1)

⌐Quem pastores laudavere, mixed voices & instrumental ensemble⌐

Quem pastores laudavere
Instrumental ensemble may include: recorders, crumhorns, flutes, dulcian, cornetto, sackbut, violas da gamba & lute.
Cook, Richard

⌐Terpsichore, (1612). Suite; arr. instrumental ensemble⌐

A Suite of Dances
[1]Passameze pour les cornetz / [2]Galliarde de Monsieur Wustrow / Galliarde de la guerre / [3]Pavane de Spaigne / [4]La bourrée / [5]Courrant de la Royne / [6]Passameze - Galliarde
Instrumental ensemble may include: recorders, flute or rauschpfeiefe, crumhorns, shawms, rackett or dulcian, cornetti, sackbuts, percussion, harpsichord or organ & bass viola da gamba.
Montesi, Robert, 6)

⌐Terpsichore, (1612). Suite; arr. trumpet, harp & percussion⌐

Sieben deutsche Tänze
(Seven German Dances)
[1]Branle gay / [2]Spagnoletta / [3]Volte du tambour / [4]Ballet de Praetorius / [5]Courant de Perichou / [6]Courante / [7]Bransle de Village
André, Maurice, 64)

⌐Wie schön leuchtet der Morgenstern, mixed voices & instrumental ensemble⌐

Wie schön leuchtet der Morgenstern
Instrumental ensemble may include: recorders, crumhorns, flutes, dulcian, cornetto, sackbut, violas da gamba & lute.
Cook, Richard

Prentzl, 17th cent.
Prentzel

⌐Sonata, trumpet, bassoon & continuo, C major⌐

Sonata a 2 instromenti, Trombetta è Fagotto, con basso continuo
[1]Andante / [2]Andante arioso / [3]Allegro - Allegro
Tarr, Edward, 39)

Pres, Josquin Des
See: Josquin des Préz

Presser, William H., 1916-
Presser, William Henry

⌐Suite, solo trumpet, (1967)⌐

Suite for Trumpet
[1]Adagio / [2]Adagio - Allegro / [3]Allegro vivo
Hickman, David, 3)

Prin, Jean Baptiste, 1669-*ca.* 1742

₍Echo der Psyche; arr. trumpet, organ & timpani₎
    Das Echo der Psyche
        Potpourri, 48)
        Touvron, Guy, 16), 18), 19)

Prioli, Giovanni, *ca.* 1575-1629

₍Canzoni. No. 1; arr. 3 cornetti, tenor cornetto, organ, 4 sackbuts, regal & strings₎
    Canzona prima a 12
        Laird, Michael, 2)

Prokofiev, Sergei (Sergeyevich), 1891-1953
Prokofieff, Serge

₍Lieutenant Kije, symphonic suite, op. 60, (1934). Part III: The Wedding of Kije,
theme; arr. trumpet & piano₎
    Kije's Wedding
        This transcription for trumpet and piano was published by
        Edition Musicus in 1944.
        Nagel, Robert, 15)

Puccini, Giacomo, 1858-1924
Puccini, Giacomo (Antonia Domenico Michele Secondo Maria)

₍Bohème, (1896). Act I: Aria, "Che gelida manina"; arr. cornet & band₎
    Aria, "Che gelida manina", from *La Bohème*
        McCann, Phillip

₍Bohème, (1896). Act I: Aria, "Che gelida manina"; arr. trumpet & orchestra₎
    Aria, "Che gelida manina", from *La Bohème*
        André, Maurice, 37)
        Ghitalla, Armando, 14)

₍Bohème, (1896). Act II: Musetta's Waltz, "Quando me'n vo"; arr. trumpet &
orchestra₎
    Musetta from *La Bohème*
        Méndez, Rafael, 20)

₍Madame Butterfly, (1904). Act II: Aria, "Un bel di, vedremo"; arr. trumpet &
orchestra₎
    Aria, "Un bel di, vedremo" from *Madame Butterfly*
        Méndez, Rafael, 21)

₍Tosca, (1900). Act III: Aria, "E lucevan le stelle"; arr. trumpet & orchestra₎
    Aria, "E lucevan le stelle", from *Tosca*
        Méndez, Rafael, 9)

Purcell, Daniel, *ca.* 1660-1717

[Indian Queen, (1695). Act V: excerpts, trumpet, strings & continuo]
Sonata (Masque)
(Symphony - [Adagio] - Trumpet Air)
This music, composed by Daniel Purcell, was added to Henry Purcell's *Indian Queen*, Z. 630, and is included here (with authentic movements by Henry Purcell) in a suite of "Incidental Music to *The Indian Queen*"
Steele-Perkins, Crispian, 5)

[Indian Queen, (1695). Act V: Trumpet Air, trumpet, strings & continuo, C major]
Trumpet Air
This "air", composed by Daniel Purcell, was added to Henry Purcell's *Indian Queen*, Z. 630, and is often erroneously attributed to Henry Purcell.
Marsalis, Wynton, 2)

[Indian Queen, (1695). Act V: Trumpet Air, trumpet, strings & continuo, C major; arr. trumpet & piano, B♭ major]
Trumpet Air
Nagel, Robert, 10)

[Indian Queen, (1695). Act V: Trumpet Air, trumpet, strings & continuo, C major; arr. trumpet, brass ensemble & organ]
Fanfare
(Trumpet Air)
André, Maurice, 202)

[Sonata, recorder & harpsichord, F major; arr. trumpet & organ]
Sonata in F major
[1]Andante cantabile / [2]Moderato / [3]Allegro / [4]Adagio / [5]Allegretto
André, Maurice, 150)

[Sonata, trumpet, strings & continuo, C major; arr. trumpet & organ]
Sonata in C major for Trumpet and Strings
[1]Allegro / [2]Adagio / [3]Allegro
Braz, Dirceu, 3)
Hunger, Helmut, 5)

[Sonata, trumpet, strings & continuo, D major; arr. trumpet & organ]
Sonata in D major for Trumpet and Strings
[1]Allegro / [2]Adagio / [3]Allegro
Braz, Dirceu, 3)
Hunger, Helmut, 5)

[Trumpet Tune; arr. trumpet & organ]
Trumpet Tune
This "trumpet tune", attributed to Daniel Purcell on the slipcover of the album, may be the same as the one often attributed to Henry Purcell and catalogued spuriously by Zimmermann as Z. S124. It is most likely Jeremiah Clarke's *Trumpet Tune*.
Grin, Freddy, 9)

Purcell, Henry, 1659-1695

[Abdelazer, Z. 570, (1695). Hornpipe, strings, B♭ major; arr. trumpet & organ]

Hornpipe from *Abdelazer, (or the Moor's Revenge)*, Z. 570/(8)
(Hornpipe for Harpsichord, Z. T683)
Zapf, Gerd

[Abdelazer, Z. 570, (1695). Jig, strings, g minor; arr. trumpet & organ]

Jig from *Abdelazer, (or the Moor's Revenge)*, Z. 570/(7)
(Jig for Harpsichord, Z. T686)
(Aria)
André, Maurice, 141)

[Abdelazer, Z. 570, (1695). Jig, strings, g minor; arr. trumpet & strings]

Jig from *Abdelazer, (or the Moor's Revenge)*, Z. 570/(7)
(Jig for Harpsichord, Z. T686)
(Sicilienne)
André, Maurice, 184), 193), 197)

[Air, harpsichord, G major, Z. 641; arr. cornetto & organ]

Air, Z. 641
(Ayre)
Smithers, Don, 7)

[Bonduca, Z. 574, (1695). Excerpts, soli, mixed voices, 2 flutes, 2 oboes, trumpet, strings & continuo]

Bonduca, (or the British Heroine), Z. 574
(Ayres for the Theatre)
1) Overture [Grave - Canzona - Adagio] / 4) Air / 5) Hornpipe / 6) Air / 7) Hornpipe / 8) Air / 9) Minuet / 10) Jack, thou'rt a toper / 11a) Prelude / 11b) Hear us, great Rugwith / 12) Hear, ye gods of Britain / 13a) Symphony / 13b) Sing ye Druids all / 14) Divine Andate / 15a) Symphony / 15b) To arms / 16a) Prelude / 16b) Britons strike home / 17a) O lead me to some peaceful gloom / 17b) There let me soothe
Laird, Michael, 17)
Steele-Perkins, Crispian, 11)

[Bonduca, Z. 574, (1695). Song-tune, strings, C major; arr. 2 trumpets, trombone, timpani, percussion & organ]

Song-tune from *Bonduca (or the British Heroine)*, Z. 574/(3)
(Trumpet Tune)
Ghitalla, Armando, 5)

[Dido and Aeneas, Z. 626, (1689?). Act I: Triumphing Dance, strings, C major; arr. trumpet & organ]

Triumphing Dance from *Dido and Aeneas*, Z. 626/(13)
Zapf, Gerd

₍Don Quixote, Z. 578, (1694). Excerpts, soli, chamber orchestra & continuo₎
The Comical History of Don Quixote, Z. 578
Overture [Z. 770] / 1a) Sing all ye muses / 2) When the world first knew creation / 3a) Let the dreadful engines of eternal will / 4a) Prelude / 4b) With this sacred charming wand / 6a) Since times are so bad / 6b) Ambition's a trade / 7a) Prelude / 7b) Genius of England / 7c) Then follow, brave boys / 8) Lads and Lasses / 9a) From rosy bow'rs / 9b) Or if more influencing / 9c) Ah! 'tis in vain / 9d) Bleak winds in tempests blow / 9e) No, no, I'll straight run mad
Chamber orchestra includes: trumpet, strings & continuo. (Trumpet is included only in sections 7a, 7b & 7c.)
Laird, Michael, 18)

₍Duke of Gloucester's Birthday Ode, Z. 342, (1695). Aria, "Sound the Trumpet", countertenor, trumpet, strings & continuo; arr. soprano, trumpet & organ₎
Aria, "Sound the Trumpet", from *The Duke of Gloucester's Birthday Ode*, Z. 342/(6)
(Fifth Song with Trumpet)
Endsley, Gerald

₍Duke of Gloucester's Birthday Ode, Z. 342, (1695). Aria, "Sound the Trumpet", soprano, trumpet, strings & continuo₎
Aria, "Sound the Trumpet", from *The Duke of Gloucester's Birthday Ode*, Z. 342/(6)
(Ode, "Who can from joy refrain?")
Marsalis, Wynton, 2)

₍Duke of Gloucester's Birthday Ode, Z. 342, (1695). Chaconne, trumpet, 2 oboes, strings & continuo, C major₎
Chaconne from *The Duke of Gloucester's Birthday Ode*, Z. 342/(7)
Marsalis, Wynton, 2)

₍Duke of Gloucester's Birthday Ode, Z. 342, (1695). Symphony, trumpet, 2 oboes, strings & continuo, C major₎
Overture from *The Duke of Gloucester's Birthday Ode*, Z. 342/(1)
(Symphony [Grave - Canzona - Adagio])
This overture (or symphony) is also used as the Overture (in D major) to *Timon of Athens*, Z. 632. The first first two sections were transcribed by Purcell for harpsichord as an "Overture in D major", Z. T691. This work has also been published recently by Musica Rara as *Trumpet Sonata No. 2 in D major* edited by Edward Tarr (and includes the "air" [or march] that follows the three sections of the overture in Z. 632).
Voisin, Roger, 5), 8)

₍Fairy Queen, soli, mixed voices, chamber orchestra & continuo, Z. 629, (1692)₎
The Fairy Queen, Z. 629
(based on Shakespeare's *Midsummer-Night's Dream*)
  Chamber orchestra includes: 2 flutes, 2 oboes, 2 trumpets, timpani, strings & continuo.
  Jackson, Harold
  Nashan, Rudolph

₍Fairy Queen, Z. 629, (1692). Act I: Overture & Canzona, 2 trumpets, strings & continuo, D major₎
Overture and Canzona from *The Fairy Queen*, Z. 629/(3a,b)
  André, Maurice, 184), 193), 197)

₍Fairy Queen, Z. 629, (1692). Act I: Overture & Canzona, 2 trumpets, strings & continuo, D major; arr. trumpet, brass ensemble & organ₎
Overture and Canzona from *The Fairy Queen*, Z. 629/(3a,b)
  André, Maurice, 202)
  Potpourri, 43)

₍Fairy Queen, Z. 629, (1692). Act I: Overture & Canzona, 2 trumpets, strings & continuo, D major; arr. 2 trumpets & organ₎
Overture and Canzona from *The Fairy Queen*, Z. 629/(3a,b)
  Loustalot, Alain

₍Fairy Queen, Z. 629, (1692). Act II: Echo, trumpet, strings & continuo, C major₎
Echo from *The Fairy Queen*, Z. 629/(8c)
  Steele-Perkins, Crispian, 5)

₍Fairy Queen, Z. 629, (1692). Act IV: Symphony, 2 trumpets, timpani & strings, D major₎
Symphony from *The Fairy Queen*, Z. 629/(27)
("Sonata while the sun rises")
  a) Symphony [Grave] / b) Canzona / c) [Largo] / d) Allegro / e) [Adagio] / f) Allegro [*d*) - *da capo*]
  Voisin, Roger, 7), 8)

₍Fairy Queen, Z. 629, (1692). Act V: Aria, "Thus the gloomy world at first began to shine", alto, trumpet, 2 violins & continuo; arr. soprano, trumpet & organ₎
Aria, "Thus the gloomy world at first began to shine" from *The Fairy Queen*, Z. 629/(43)
  Schetsche, Walter

₍Funeral Music for Queen Mary II, Z. 860, (1692). March: 2 trumpets & 2 trombones; arr. trumpet & strings₎
Funeral Music for Queen Mary II, Z. 860
(March)
  André, Maurice, 218)

ₜGordian Knot Unty'd, Z. 597, (1691). Minuet, strings, D major; arr. trumpet &
organ]

Minuet from *The Gordian Knot Unty'd*, Z. 597/(8)
This minuet originally appeared as a ritornello in Purcell's *From
hardy times*, Z. 325/(7), [1683].
Zapf, Gerd

ₜGround in Gamut, harpsichord, G major, Z. 645; arr. trumpet, brass ensemble &
organ]

Ground in Gamut, Z. 645
André, Maurice, 202)

ₜIndian Queen, Z. 630, (1695?). Act III: Trumpet Overture, trumpet & strings,
D major]

Trumpet Overture from *The Indian Queen*, Z. 630/(16)
(Grave - Canzona - Adagio)
Some of these recordings may not include all three sections of the
overture.
Delmotte, Roger, 19)
Fink, Werner
Marsalis, Wynton, 2)
Potpourri, 37), 42), 46)
Smithers, Don, 4)
Vaillant, Ludovic, 1), 3)
Voisin, Roger, 5), 8)

ₜIndian Queen, Z. 630, (1695?). Act III: Trumpet Overture, trumpet & strings,
D major; arr. trumpet & organ]

Trumpet Overture from *The Indian Queen*, Z. 630/(16)
(Moderato - Canzona - Largo)
Some of these arrangements may not include all three sections of
the overture.
André, Maurice, 141)
Haas, Wolfgang
Zapf, Gerd

ₜIndian Queen, Z. 630, (1695?). Act III: Trumpet Overture, trumpet & strings,
D major; arr. trumpet & piano, D♭ major]

Trumpet Overture from *The Indian Queen*, Z. 630/(16a,b)
(Allegro - Canzona)
Nagel, Robert, 11)

ₜIndian Queen, Z. 630, (1695?). Act III: Trumpet Overture, trumpet & strings,
D major; arr. trumpet, brass ensemble & organ]

Trumpet Overture from *The Indian Queen*, Z. 630/(16a)
(March I)
André, Maurice, 202)

[Indian Queen, Z. 630, (1695?). Act V: Air, strings, d minor; arr. trumpet & organ]

Air from *The Indian Queen*, Z. 630/(22)
(Air in d minor for Harpsichord, Z. T675)
> **Haas, Wolfgang**
> **Scherbaum, Adolf**, 32)
> **Schultz, Erik**, 10)
> **Wilbraham, John**, 24)

[Indian Queen, Z. 630, (1695?). Act V: Air, strings, d minor; arr. trumpet & strings]

Air from *The Indian Queen*, Z. 630/(22)
(Air in d minor for Harpsichord, Z. T675)
> **Steele-Perkins, Crispian**, 17)
> **Voisin, Roger**, 3)

[Indian Queen, Z. 630, (1695?). Incidental music, chamber orchestra]

Incidental Music to *The Indian Queen*, Z. 630
16) Trumpet Overture [Grave - Canzona] / 20) Fourth Act tune [strings] / Act V) Symphony [Daniel Purcell] / 22) Air [strings] / 5) Symphony [a) Grave - b) Canzona - c) Adagio - b) Canzona - d) Allegro]
Chamber orchestra includes: 2 flutes, 2 oboes, 2 trumpets, timpani, strings & continuo.
Daniel Purcell composed music for Act V
[*see also:* Daniel PURCELL].
> **Steele-Perkins, Crispian**, 5)

[Indian Queen, Z. 630, (1695?). Prologue (Act I): Trumpet Tune, trumpet & strings, C major]

Trumpet Tune from *The Indian Queen*, Z. 630/(4a)
(Trumpet Tune in C major for Harpsichord, Z. T698)
(Trumpet Air)
(Entrada)
> **André, Maurice**, 184), 193), 197)
> **Marsalis, Wynton**, 2)
> **Steele-Perkins, Crispian**, 5)

[Indian Queen, Z. 630, (1695?). Prologue (Act I): Trumpet Tune, trumpet & strings, C major; arr. brass & percussion]

Trumpet Tune from *The Indian Queen*, Z. 630/(4a)
(Trumpet Tune in C major for Harpsichord, Z. T698)
(Fanfare in C major)
> **Ghitalla, Armando**, 5)

ₜIndian Queen, Z. 630, (1695?). Prologue (Act I): Trumpet Tune, trumpet & strings, C major; arr. trumpet & organ⌉

Trumpet Tune from *The Indian Queen*, Z. 630/(4a)
(Trumpet Tune in C major for Harpsichord, Z. T698)
André, Maurice, 141)
Carroll, Edward, 6)
Scherbaum, Adolf, 17)
Schultz, Erik, 3)
Touvron, Guy, 21)
Wilbraham, John, 24)

ₜIndian Queen, Z. 630, (1695?). Prologue (Act I): Trumpet Tune, trumpet & strings, C major; arr. trumpet, brass ensemble & organ⌉

Trumpet Tune from *The Indian Queen*, Z. 630/(4a)
(Trumpet Tune in C major for Harpsichord, Z. T698)
(Entrée)
André, Maurice, 202)

ₜIndian Queen, Z. 630, (1695?). Prologue (Act I): Trumpet Tune, trumpet & strings, C major; arr. 2 trumpets & organ⌉

Trumpet Tune from *The Indian Queen*, Z. 630/(4a)
(Trumpet Tune in C major for Harpsichord, Z. T698)
Loustalot, Alain

ₜKing Arthur, Z. 628, (1691). Act V: Trumpet Tune, strings, C major; arr. trumpet & organ⌉

Air from *King Arthur, (or the British Worthy)*, Z. 628/(40)
(Fifth act tune [Trumpet tune])
This tune serves as the central part of an arrangement, "Prélude et Air". The "prelude" (an alto aria from *Yorkshire Feast Song*, Z. 333) is arranged for brass ensemble alone. [The arrangement, then, is: Z. 333/(13) - Z. 628/(40) - Z. 333/(13).]
André, Maurice, 202)

ₜKing Arthur, Z. 628, (1691). Excerpts (5), orchestra⌉

Suite from *King Arthur, (or the British Worthy)*, Z. 628
Tarr, Edward, 35)

ₜKing Arthur, Z. 628, (1691). Excerpts, orchestra⌉

Suite from *King Arthur, (or the British Worthy)*, Z. 628
1) Chaconne / 4) Overture [Grave - Canzona] / 11) First Act tune [Air] / 17b) Hornpipe / 18) Second Act tune [Hornpipe II] / 31) Fourth Act tune [Trumpet Tune] / 33) Symphony / Appendix 2) Song Tune ["Round thy coasts"] / 40) Fifth Act tune [Trumpet Tune] / Song Tune [*da capo*]
Tarr, Edward, 38)

ₜKing Arthur, Z. 628, (1691). Excerpts, trumpet, strings & continuo⌉

Fifth Act Tunes from *King Arthur, (or the British Worthy)*, Z. 628
31) Trumpet Tune / 33) Symphony / 34) Song tune ("Round thy coasts") / 40) Trumpet Tune
Steele-Perkins, Crispian, 5)

[Libertine, Z. 600, (1692). Act V: Aria, "To arms, heroic prince", soprano, trumpet & continuo]
Aria, "To arms, heroic prince" from *The Libertine, or the Libertine Destroyed*, Z. 600
Impett, Jonathan

[March, harpsichord, C major, Z. 647, (1689); arr. trumpet & organ]
March, Z. 647
(Lesson)
> **Gabel, Bernard**, 2)
> **Scherbaum, Adolf**, 17), 29)

[March, harpsichord, C major, Z. 648, (1689); arr. trumpet & organ]
March, Z. 648
(Marche)
> **Gabel, Bernard**, 2)
> **Scherbaum, Adolf**, 29)

[Married Beau, Z. 603, (1694). Excerpts, strings; arr. trumpet & organ]
Air, Hornpipe and March from *The Married Beau, (or the Curious Impertinent)*, Z. 603
Zapf, Gerd

[Married Beau, Z. 603, (1694). March, strings, C major; arr. trumpet & organ]
March from *The Married Beau, (or the Curious Impertinent)*, Z. 603/(8)
(Marche de la Suite, "Le Marié galant")
(March in C major for Harpsichord, Z. T687)
> **André, Maurice**, 141)
> **Scherbaum, Adolf**, 17)
> **Touvron, Guy**, 21)
> **Wilbraham, John**, 24)

[Married Beau, Z. 603, (1694). March, strings, C major; arr. trumpet & strings]
March from *The Married Beau, (or the Curious Impertinent)*, Z. 603/(8)
(Marche de la Suite, "Le Marié galant")
(March in C major for Harpsichord, Z. T687)
> **André, Maurice**, 184), 193), 197)

[Married Beau, Z. 603, (1694). March, strings, C major; arr. trumpet, brass ensemble & organ]
March from *The Married Beau, (or the Curious Impertinent)*, Z. 603/(8)
(Marche de la Suite, "Le Marié galant")
(March in C major for Harpsichord, Z. T687)
> **André, Maurice**, 202)

₍Minuet, harpsichord, a minor, Z. 649, (1689); arr. trumpet, brass ensemble & organ₎

Minuet, Z. 649
(Menuet)

André, Maurice, 202)

₍Minuet, harpsichord, a minor, Z. 650, (1689); arr. trumpet & organ₎

Minuet, Z. 650

Scherbaum, Adolf, 29)

₍Ode for Queen Mary's Birthday, soli, mixed voices, chamber orchestra & continuo, Z. 323, (1694)₎

Ode for Queen Mary's Birthday, Z. 323
(Ode, "Come ye sons of art away")
Chamber orchestra includes: 2 oboes, trumpet, timpani, strings & continuo.

Laird, Michael, 11)

₍Ode for Queen Mary's Birthday, Z. 323, (1694). Aria, "Sound the trumpet", 2 altos (countertenors) & continuo, D major; arr. 2 trumpets & organ₎

Duet Aria, "Sound the trumpet" from *Ode for Queen Mary's Birthday,* Z. 323/(3)
(Ode, "Come ye sons of art away")

Läubin, Hannes, 2)

₍Ode for Queen Mary's Birthday, Z. 323, (1694). Prelude, oboe, strings & continuo, D major; arr. trumpet, brass ensemble & organ₎

Prelude from *Ode for Queen Mary's Birthday,* Z. 323/(2a)
(Prelude from the Ode, "Come ye sons of art away")
(Air grandiose)

André, Maurice, 202)

₍Ode for St. Cecilia's Day, soli, mixed voices, chamber orchestra & continuo, Z. 328, (1692)₎

Ode for St. Cecilia's Day, Z. 328
(Ode, "Hail, Bright Cecilia")
Chamber orchestra includes: recorder, 2 flutes, 2 oboes, 2 trumpets, timpani, strings & continuo.

Eskdale, George, 5)
Steele-Perkins, Crispian, 7)
Wilbraham, John, 20)

₍Ode for St. Cecilia's Day, Z. 328, (1692). Overture, trumpet, strings & continuo₎

Overture from *Ode for St. Cecilia's Day,* Z. 328/(1)
(Grave - Canzona)

Steele-Perkins, Crispian, 5)

₍Prophetess, Z. 627, (1690). Act IV: Aria, "Sound, Fame, thy brazen trumpet", alto, trumpet & continuo, D major; arr. soprano, trumpet & organ₎

Aria, "Sound, Fame, thy brazen trumpet", from *The Prophetess, (or the History of Dioclesian),* Z. 627/(22)
(A Song with Trumpet)

Endsley, Gerald

[Prophetess, Z. 627, (1690). Act IV: Trumpet Tune, 2 trumpets & continuo, D major; arr. trumpet & organ]

Trumpet Tune from *The Prophetess, (or the History of Dioclesian)*, Z. 627/(21)
(Trumpet Tune in C major for Harpsichord, Z. T697)
Gabel, Bernard, 2)

[Prophetess, Z. 627, (1690). Act IV: Trumpet Tune, 2 trumpets & continuo, D major; arr. trumpet & strings]

Trumpet Tune from *The Prophetess, (or the History of Dioclesian)*, Z. 627/(21)
(Trumpet Tune in C major for Harpsichord, Z. T697)
Voisin, Roger, 5), 8)

[Prophetess, Z. 627, (1690). Act IV: Trumpet Tune, 2 trumpets & continuo, D major; arr. 2 trumpets & piano, B♭ major]

Trumpet Tune from *The Prophetess, (or the History of Dioclesian)*, Z. 627/(21)
(Trumpet Tune in C major for Harpsichord, Z. T697)
Nagel, Robert, 10)

[Rigadoon, harpsichord, C major, Z. 653, (1689); arr. trumpet & organ]

Rigadoon, Z. 653
(Rigaudon)
Gabel, Bernard, 2)
Touvron, Guy, 21)

[Rigadoon, keyboard instrument, d minor, Z. D227; arr. trumpet & organ]

Rigadoon, Z. D227
Touvron, Guy, 21)

[Sefauchi's Farewell, harpsichord, d minor, Z. 656, (1689); arr. trumpet & organ]

Sefauchi's Farewell, Z. 656
André, Maurice, 202)

[Sonata, trumpet & strings, D major, Z. 850, (?1694); arr. 2 solo trumpets & brass ensemble]

Sonata in D major, Z. 850
[Allegro] / [Adagio] / [Presto]
Canadian Brass, 2), 7)

[Sonata, trumpet & strings, D major, Z. 850, (1694?)]

Sonata in D major for Trumpet and Strings, Z. 850
[Allegro] / [Adagio] / [Presto]
This sonata is assumed to have been the overture to the missing ode, *The Light of the World*, Z. 330.
André, Maurice, 73), 169)
Basch, Wolfgang, 3)
Bernard, André, 3), 11)
Burns, Stephen
Cooper, Grant
Delmotte, Roger, 19), 31)
Egan, Dennis

Erb, Helmut, 6)
Gorokhov, Vitaly
Mertens, Theo, 7)
Potpourri, 9), 21), 34), 35), 37), 40)
Reinhart, Carole Dawn, 1), 3), 4)
Steele-Perkins, Crispian, 5)
Tarr, Edward, 18)
Voisin, Roger, 3)
Wallace, John, 4)
Wobisch, Helmut, 3)
Zickler, Heinz, 9)

[Sonata, trumpet & strings, D major, Z. 850, (1694?); arr. trumpet & organ]
Sonata in D major for Trumpet and Strings, Z. 850
[1][Allegro] / [2]Adagio / [3][Presto]
André, Maurice, 154)
Bouche
Delmotte, Roger, 38)
Erb, Helmut, 2)
Gabel, Bernard, 5)
Güttler, Ludwig, 6), 21)
Lieberman, Harold J.
McGuffey, Patrick
Morisset, Michel
Schultz, Erik, 2)
Stringer, Alan, 3)
Tamiya, Kenji
Touvron, Guy, 12)

[Sonata, trumpet & strings, D major, Z. 850, (1694?); arr. trumpet & piano]
Sonata in D major for Trumpet and Strings, Z. 850
[1][Allegro] / [2]Adagio / [3][Presto]
Ghitalla, Armando, 12)
Hyatt, Jack

[Sonata, trumpet, strings & continuo, [No. 2], D major]
Trumpet Sonata No. 2
[1]Overture [a) Grave - b) Allegro - c) Adagio] / [2]March [Allegro]
This sonata, edited by Edward Tarr, is extracted from *Timon of Athens*, Z. 632. The first movement was also used as the overture to *The Duke of Gloucester's Birthday Ode*, Z. 342. Further, the first two sections of the first movement were transcribed by Purcell for harpsichord, Z. T691. (Other arrangements may be cited under *Timon of Athens* or *The Duke of Gloucester's Birthday Ode*.)
André, Maurice, 169)
Hunger, Helmut, 1)

[Sonata, trumpet, strings & continuo, [No. 2], D major; arr. trumpet & organ]
Trumpet Sonata No. 2
[1]Overture [a) Grave - b) Allegro - c) Adagio] / [2]March [Allegro]
André, Maurice, 154)

ₗSong Tune, harpsichord, C major, Z. T694, (1689); arr. trumpet & organ⌐
Song Tune in C major for Harpsichord, Z. T694
Scherbaum, Adolf, 17), 29)

ₗSuite, harpsichord, C major, Z. 665, (1689). Almand; arr. trumpet & organ⌐
Almand from *Suite in C major for Harpsichord,* Z. 665/(2)
(Air)
Gabel, Bernard, 2)
Scherbaum, Adolf, 29)

ₗSuite, harpsichord, C major, Z. 665, (1689). Almand; arr. trumpet, brass
ensemble & organ⌐
Almand from *Suite in C major for Harpsichord,* Z. 665/(2)
Air (Andantino)
André, Maurice, 202)

ₗSuite, harpsichord, C major, Z. 666, (1689). Prelude; arr. trumpet, brass
ensemble & organ⌐
Prelude from *Suite in C major for Harpsichord,* Z. 666/(1)
This suite is indicated as "No. 5" on the album as it is the fifth
suite included in the Purcell Society Edition. It is, however, the
seventh of ten suites for harpsichord catalogued by Zimmerman
(**Z. 660-669**).
André, Maurice, 202)

ₗSuite, harpsichord, C major, Z. 666, (1689). Prelude; arr. 2 trumpets & organ⌐
Prelude from *Suite in C major for Harpsichord,* Z. 666/(1)
Loustalot, Alain

ₗSuite, harpsichord, F major, Z. 669, (1689). Minuet; arr. trumpet & organ⌐
Minuet from *Suite in F major for Harpsichord,* Z. 669/(4)
André, Maurice, 141)

ₗSuite, harpsichord, G major, Z. 660. Saraband; arr. trumpet & strings⌐
Saraband from *Suite in G major for Harpsichord,* Z. 660/(4)
(Menuet)
André, Maurice, 184), 193), 197)

ₗTe Deum and Jubilate, soli, mixed voices, 2 trumpets, strings & continuo,
D major, Z. 232, (1694)⌐
Te Deum and Jubilate, Z. 232
[1]Te Deum Laudamus ("The Song of St. Ambrose") / [2]Jubilate Deo
(Psalm 100:1-5)
Jones, Philip, 7)

ₗTimon of Athens, Z. 632, (1694?). Canzona, trumpet & strings, D major; arr. 2
trumpets, trombone & strings⌐
Canzona from *Timon of Athens, the Man-Hater,* Z. 632/(1b)
Included as part of the final movement of "Suite de Danses".
André, Maurice, 184), 193), 197)

⌜Timon of Athens, Z. 632, (1694?). Chorus, "Who can resist", mixed voices & strings, d minor; arr. trumpet & organ⌝
Chorus from *Timon of Athens, the Man-Hater*, Z. 632/(15)
(New Minuet in d minor for Harpsichord, Z. T689)
André, Maurice, 141)

⌜Timon of Athens, Z. 632, (1694?). Chorus, "Who can resist", mixed voices & strings, d minor; arr. trumpet, brass ensemble & organ⌝
Chorus from *Timon of Athens, the Man-Hater*, Z. 632/(15)
(New Minuet in d minor for Harpsichord, Z. T689)
André, Maurice, 202)

⌜Timon of Athens, Z. 632, (1694?). Excerpts, trumpet, strings & continuo⌝
Timon of Athens, the Man-Hater, Z. 632
(Ayres for the Theatre)
  1) Overture [Grave - Canzona - Adagio] / 20) Curtain tune
  Steele-Perkins, Crispian, 11)

⌜Timon of Athens, Z. 632, (1694?). Overture & Canzona, trumpet & strings, D major; arr. trumpet, brass ensemble & organ⌝
Overture and Canzona from *Timon of Athens, the Man-Hater*, Z. 632/(1a,b)
(Overture in D major for Harpsichord, Z. T691)
  Included as a part of an arranged suite given the title, "Ouverture Solennelle".
  André, Maurice, 202)
  Potpourri, 43)

⌜Trumpet Minuet, keyboard instrument, C major, Z. D230; arr. trumpet & organ⌝
Trumpet Minuet, Z. D230
  Touvron, Guy, 21)

⌜Trumpet Tune, "Cibell", harpsichord, C major, Z. T678, (1689?); arr. trumpet & brass ensemble⌝
Trumpet Tune, "Cibell", Z. T678
  André, Maurice, 173), 190), 193), 194), 197)
  Potpourri, 1)

⌜Trumpet Tune, "Cibell", harpsichord, C major, Z. T678, (1689?); arr. trumpet & organ⌝
Trumpet Tune, "Cibell", Z. T678
  Gabel, Bernard, 2)
  Ghitalla, Armando, 5)
  Scherbaum, Adolf, 29)
  Smithers, Don, 7)
  Touvron, Guy, 21)

⌜Trumpet Tune, "Cibell", harpsichord, C major, Z. T678, (1689?); arr. trumpet & strings⌝
Trumpet Tune, "Cibell", Z. T678
  Steele-Perkins, Crispian, 5)
  Voisin, Roger, 5), 8)

[Trumpet Tune, "Cibell", harpsichord, C major, Z. T678, (1689?); arr. trumpet, brass ensemble & organ]
Trumpet Tune, "Cibell", Z. T678
André, Maurice, 202)
Potpourri, 43)

[Trumpet Tune, "Cibell", harpsichord, C major, Z. T678, (1689?); arr. 2 trumpets & organ]
Trumpet Tune, "Cibell", Z. T678
Loustalot, Alain

[Trumpet Tune, harpsichord or organ, C major, Z. S124]
Trumpet Tune in C major, Z. S124
See: CLARKE, Jeremiah: Trumpet Tune.

[Trumpet Voluntary, harpsichord or organ, D major, Z. S125]
Trumpet Voluntary in D major, Z. S125
(The Prince of Denmark's March)
See: CLARKE, Jeremiah: Prince of Denmark's March.

[Voluntary on the 100th Psalm, organ, A major, Z. 721; arr. trumpet(s) & strings]
Voluntary on the 100th Psalm, Z. 721
(Voluntary on the doxology)
Delmotte, Roger, 14)

[Voluntary, organ, C major, Z. D241]
Voluntary in C major, Z. D241
See: BARRETT, John: Voluntary in C major.

[Voluntary, organ, C major, Z. 717; arr. trumpet & organ]
Voluntary in C major, Z. 717
Gabel, Bernard, 2)

[Yorkshire Feast Song, Z. 333, (1690). Aria, "Sound, trumpet, sound", alto, strings & continuo, D major; arr. brass ensemble]
Aria and Ritornello from *The Yorkshire Feast Song,* Z. 333/(13)
This alto aria and its attached ritornello for 2 trumpets and strings is arranged for brass as the opening and closing parts of a "Prélude et Air". The central "air" of this arrangement (for trumpet and organ) from *King Arthur,* Z. 628, is indexed separately.
André, Maurice, 202)

[Yorkshire Feast Song, Z. 333, (1690). Symphony, 2 trumpets & strings, D major]
Symphony from *The Yorkshire Feast Song,* Z. 333/(1)
(Grave - Canzona)
Voisin, Roger, 5), 8)

Putsché, Thomas, 1929-1983

₍Cat and the Moon, soprano, tenor, bass & chamber ensemble, (1957)₎
The Cat and the Moon
Chamber ensemble includes: flute, oboe, clarinet, bassoon, horn, trumpet, trombone, 2 violins, 2 violas, cello, bass, harp & percussion.
Miller, Rodney

Pyle, Francis Johnson, 1901-

₍Concerto, trumpet & wind ensemble, (c. 1966)₎
Concerto for Trumpet and Wind Ensemble
[no tempo marking] / [2]Andante / [3]Finale: Presto
Weast, Robert[2-3]

Querfurth, Franz, 18th cent.

₍Concerto, trumpet, strings, bassoon & continuo, E♭ major₎
Konzert Es-dur für Trompete, Streicher, Fagott und Basso continuo
[1]Allegro / [2]Adagio / [3]Presto
Güttler, Ludwig, 26)
Kejmar, Miroslav, 2)
Smithers, Don, 11)

Rabe, Folke, 1935-
Rabe, Folke Alvar Harald Reinhold

₍Shazam, solo trumpet₎
Shazam
Hardenberger, Håkan

Rachmaninov, Sergei Vasilievich, 1873-1943
Rachmaninoff, Sergej
Rakhmaninov, Sergey Vasil'yevich

₍Lieder, op. 34, (1912). No. 14: Vocalise; arr. trumpet & piano₎
Vocalise, op. 34, no. 14
Dokshitser, Timofei, 5), 7), 9), 31), 35), 38), 39)

Rakov, Nikolai Petrovich, 1908-

₍Melody, trumpet & piano, f minor₎
Melody in f minor
Usov, Yuri

₍Rondo-Tarantella, trumpet & piano, B♭ major₎
Rondo-Tarantella in B♭ major
Usov, Yuri

Raksin, David, 1912-

₍Laura, (1944). Theme song; arr. trumpet & orchestra₎
"Laura" from *Laura*
Méndez, Rafael, 20)

Rameau, Jean-Philippe, 1683-1764

₍Fêtes d'Hébé, (1739). Suite, chamber orchestra₎
Les Fêtes d'Hébé
(Divertissement)
¹Ouverture / ²Menuets / ³Entrée et Loure / ⁴Gavottes / ⁵Musette,
Tambourin et Contredanse
Chamber orchestra includes: 2 flutes, (2 piccolos), 2 oboes,
bassoon, 2 horns, trumpet, timpani & strings.
Lowrey, Alvin

₍Sarabande; arr. trumpet & piano₎
Sarabande
Geyer, Charles

₍Suite, trumpet & strings, D major₎
Suite pour trompettes et cordes en D majeur
Delmotte, Roger, 42)

₍Tambourin, chamber orchestra₎
Tambourin
Delmotte, Roger, 25), 46)

Ramírez, "Ram", 1913-
Ramírez, Roger

₍Malagueña Salerosa, trumpet & guitar₎
Malagueña Salerosa
Méndez, Rafael, 14), 18)

Rance, 20th cent.

₍Reason, cornet & band₎
The Reason
Smith, Philip, 4)

Randall, J.K., 1929-
Randall, James Kirtland

₍Improvisation, soprano & chamber ensemble, (1960)₎
Improvisation on a poem by e.e. cummings
Chamber ensemble includes: clarinet, saxophone, trumpet, piano
& guitar.
Anderson, Ronald, 5)

Raselius, Andreas, *ca.* 1563-1602

ₜNun komm der Heiden Heiland; arr. trumpet & brass ensembleₗ
Nun komm der Heiden Heiland
Güttler, Ludwig, 9)

ₜNun komm der Heiden Heiland, soli, mixed voices & instrumental ensembleₗ
Nun komm der Heiden Heiland
Instrumental ensemble may include: recorders, crumhorns, flutes, dulcian, cornetto, sackbut, viola da gamba & lute.
Cook, Richard

Rathgeber, Johann Valentin, 1682-1750

ₜChelys sonora excitans spiritum musicorum..., op. 6, (1728). No. 15: Concerto, 2 trumpets, 2 violins & continuo, E♭ majorₗ
Concerto in E♭ major, op. 6, no. 15
[1]Allegro / [2]Adagio / [3]Allegro
Schwarz, Gerard, 20)

ₜChelys sonora excitans spiritum musicorum..., op. 6, (1728). No. 19: Concerto, trumpet, strings & continuo, C majorₗ
Concerto in C major for Trumpet, Strings and Continuo, op. 6, no. 19
Sauter, Hermann, 3)

Rautavaara, Einojuhani (Eino), 1928-

ₜTarantará, solo trumpet, (1976)ₗ
Tarantará
Wallace, John, 6)

Ravel, Maurice, 1875-1937
Ravel, (Joseph) Maurice

ₜHabañera, 2 pianos, (1895); arr. trumpet & pianoₗ
Habañera
Dokshitser, Timofei, 5), 7), 9), 31), 34), 35), 36), 38), 39)

ₜPavane pour une infante defunt, piano, (1899); arr. trumpet & pianoₗ
Pavane
(Pavane pour une infante defunt)
House, Lawrence

ₜPièce en forme de habañera, voice & piano, (1907); arr. trumpet & guitarₗ
Pièce en forme de habañera
Méndez, Rafael, 14)

Reed, Alfred, 1921-

₍Ceremony of Flourishes, cornet trio & band₎
Ceremony of Flourishes
Lowrey, Alvin

₍Ode, trumpet & band, (1956)₎
Ode for Trumpet
Head, Emerson
Jacoby, Don

Reger, Max, 1873-1916

Reger, (Johann Baptist Joseph) Maximilian

₍Romanze, violin & piano, G major, (1902); arr. trumpet & piano₎
Romance in G major
(Romanze)
Christensen, Ketil

Reiche, Johann Gottfried, 1667-1734

₍Fanfare, "Abblasen", trumpet, (1727)₎
Fanfare, "Abblasen"
This fanfare is taken from Elias Gottlieb Haussmann's famous
portrait of Gottfried Reiche.
Carroll, Edward, 11)
Haas, Wolfgang
Smithers, Don, 6)

₍Fanfare, "Abblasen", 2 trumpets in unison, (1727)₎
Fanfare, "Abblasen"
Canadian Brass, 5), 6)

₍Quatricinia, (1696). No. 1: Sonatina, cornetto & 3 trombones₎
Sonatina No. 1
There are numerous brass ensemble recordings of the sonatinas
from *Vier und zwantzig Neue Quatricinia*; however, only the
performances involving cornetto are indexed in this discography.
Tarr, Edward, 10)

₍Quatricinia, (1696). No. 24: Sonatina, cornetto & 3 trombones₎
Sonatina No. 24, "Allein Gott in der Höh sei Ehr"
Tarr, Edward, 10)

Reinhart, Carole Dawn, 1941-

Reinhart(-Stoppacher), Carole Dawn

₍Dedication, trumpet & band₎
Dedication
Reinhart, Carole Dawn, 10)

Rentaro, Taki, 1879-1903

ɾMoon above Castle Ruins; arr. trumpet & pianoɿ
Kojo No Tsuki
(The Moon above Castle Ruins)
Dokshitser, Timofei, 19)

ɾYoimachigusa; arr. trumpet & pianoɿ
Yoimachigusa
"Yoimachigusa" is a Japanese name for a particular flower.
Dokshitser, Timofei, 19)

Resinarius, Balthasar, *ca.* 1485-1544
Hartzer, Balthasar

ɾNun komm der Heiden Heiland, soli, mixed voices & instrumental ensembleɿ
Nun komm der Heiden Heiland
Instrumental ensemble may include: recorders, crumhorns, flutes, dulcian, cornetto, sackbut, viola da gamba & lute.
Cook, Richard

Respighi, Ottorino, 1879-1936

ɾPini di Roma, (1924). Pini presso una Catacomba: excerpt, solo trumpetɿ
Off-stage solo from *Pines of Rome*
Demonstration *sans* orchestra.
Voisin, Roger, 13)

Reutter, Karl Georg von, 1708-1772
Reutter, (Johann Adam Joseph Karl) Georg von

ɾConcerto, trumpet, strings & continuo, D major, no. 2ɿ
Konzert D-dur für Trompete, Streicher und Basso continuo, Nr. 2
Basch, Wolfgang, 13)

ɾServizio di Tavola, 2 oboes, 4 trumpets, timpani & stringsɿ
Servizio di Tavola
Zickler, Heinz, 6)

Revueltas, Silvestre, 1899-1940

ɾHomenaje a Federico García Lorca, chamber ensemble, (1935)ɿ
Homenaje a Federico García Lorca
(Hommage to Federico García Lorca)
Chamber ensemble includes: piccolo, E♭-clarinet, 2 trumpets, trombone, tuba, percussion, piano, 2 violins & bass.
Crisara, Raymond, 4)
Reyes, Arturo

ₜLittle Serious Pieces (2), chamber ensemble, (1957)ᵣ
Dos Piezas Serias
(Two Little Serious Pieces)
¹First Little Serious Piece [fiesta time] / ²Second Little Serious Piece [siesta time]
Chamber ensemble includes: piccolo, oboe, clarinet, trumpet & baritone saxophone.
Crisara, Raymond, 4)
Stevens, Thomas, 11)

ₜOcho por Radio, chamber ensemble, (1933)ᵣ
Ocho por Radio
(Eight for Radio)
Chamber ensemble includes: clarinet, bassoon, trumpet, percussion, 2 violins, cello & bass.
Potpourri, 31)

ₜSonetos (3), chamber ensembleᵣ
Tres Sonetos
Chamber ensemble includes: 2 clarinets, bassoon, horn, 2 trumpets, tuba, percussion & piano.
Crisara, Raymond, 4)

Reynaud, J.
ₜMerle et Pinson; arr. 2 cornet soli & brass ensembleᵣ
Merle et Pinson
Aquitaine Brass Ensemble

Reynolds, Roger, 1934-
ₜ"...the serpent snapping eye", trumpet, percussion, piano & tapeᵣ
"...the serpent snapping eye"
Harkins, Edwin

ₜQuick Are the Mouths of Earth, 3 flutes, oboe, trumpet, 2 trombones, 3 cellos, piano & percussion, (1965)ᵣ
Quick Are the Mouths of Earth
Nagel, Robert, 18)

Reynolds, Verne, 1926-
ₜFantasy Etudes, trumpet & pianoᵣ
Fantasy Etudes
Thibaud, Pierre, 2)

ₜMusic, 5 trumpets, (1955)ᵣ
Music for 5 Trumpets
¹Fanfare / ²Chorale / ³Finale
Plog, Anthony, 5)

₍Signals, solo trumpet, solo tuba, 5 trumpets & 5 horns, (1976)₎
Signals
Stevens, Thomas, 8)

Rhodes, Phillip, 1940-

₍Divertimento, chamber orchestra, (1971)₎
Divertimento for Small Orchestra
Chamber orchestra includes: flute/piccolo, bassoon, horn, trumpet & strings.
Potpourri, 6)

Rice-Brown-Daniels
Rice, Seymour
Brown, Albert
Daniels, Charles N.

₍You Tell Me Your Dream; arr. trumpet quartet₎
You Tell Me Your Dream, I'll Tell You Mine
Blackburn, Roger

Richard, Raymond, 20th cent.

₍Air Varié, trumpet & orchestra₎
Air Varié
Maurice André collaborated in the composition of these variations.
André, Maurice, 5)

Richter, Franz Xaver, 1709-1789

₍Concerto, trumpet, strings & continuo, D major₎
Konzert D-dur für Trompete, Streichorchester und Basso continuo
¹Allegro moderato / ²Andante / ³Allegro
André, Maurice, 20), 24), 27), 29)
Preis, Ivo
Quinque, Rolf, 3), 6), 7)
Smithers, Don, 11)

₍Concerto, trumpet, strings & continuo, D major. Moderato; arr. trumpet & piano₎
Moderato from *Concerto in D for Trumpet*
Arranged for B♭-trumpet down an octave (in the original key).
Nagel, Robert, 11)

Riedl, Bartholomäus, *fl. ca.* 1685

₍Aufzug, 4 trumpets & timpani₎
Ein schöner Aufzug, und noch ganz ney
("A beautiful procession, and completely new")
Tarr, Edward, 34)

ₜAufzuge (4), 8 trumpets & timpaniₙ
Vier Aufzuge
Immer, Friedemann, 18)

Rifkin, Joshua, 1944-

ₜCantata, "Last Night I Said", tenor, mixed voices & chamber orchestra, MBE 58,000ₙ
Cantata for the Third Saturday after Shea Stadium, "Last Night I Said", MBE 58,000
[1]Chorus, "Last night I said" — "Please, Please Me" / [2]Recitative, "In they came jorking" — Aria, "When I was younger" - "Help!" / [3]Chorale: "You know, if you break my heart" "I'll Be Back"
A arrangement of Beatles songs (by John Lennon and Paul McCartney) in the style of a Baroque cantata. The chamber orchestra includes: oboes, bassoon, trumpets, timpani, strings & continuo.
Nagel, Robert, 6)

ₜRoyale Beatleworks Musick, chamber orchestra, MBE 1963ₙ
The Royale Beatleworks Musicke, MBE 1963
[1]Overture: "I Want to Hold Your Hand" — "You're Going to Lose that Girl" / [2]Réjouissance: "I'll Cry Instead" / [3]La Paix: "Things We Said Today" / [4]L'Amour s'en cach "You've got to Hide Your Love Away" / [5]Les Plaisirs: "Ticket to Ride"
An orchestral arrangement in the Baroque style of songs by John Lennon and Paul McCartney. The chamber orchestra includes: flutes, oboes, bassoon, trumpets, strings & continuo.
Nagel, Robert, 6)

Riisager, Knudåge, 1897-1974

ₜConcertino, trumpet & strings, op. 29, (1935)ₙ
Concertino per tromba e strumenti ad arco, op. 29
[1]Allegretto / [2]Andante semplice / [3]Rondo vivace
Christensen, Ketil
Johnson, Gilbert, 2)

ₜConcertino, trumpet & strings, op. 29, (1935); arr. trumpet & pianoₙ
Concertino per tromba e strumenti ad arco, op. 29
[1]Allegretto / [2]Andante semplice / [3]Rondo vivace
Amstutz, Keith

Rimbault, Stephen F., 19th cent.

ₜBugle Horn, tenor, keyed bugle & instrumental ensembleₙ
The Bugle Horn
Dudgeon, Ralph

Rimsky-Korsakov, Nikolai Andreyevich, 1844-1908

₍Capriccio Espagnol, op. 34, (1887). Excerpt, trumpet₎
Excerpt from *Capriccio Espagnol*, op. 34
This demonstration album presents this excerpt *sans* orchestra.
Voisin, Roger, 13)

₍Capriccio Espagnol, op. 34, (1887); arr. chamber ensemble₎
Capriccio Espagnol
This arrangement by Easley Blackwood is for: flute, clarinet, bassoon, horn, trumpet, violin, cello, bass & piano.
Vosburgh, George

₍Coq d'Or, (1906-1907). Excerpt: Fanfare, trumpet₎
Fanfare from *Le Coq d'Or*
This demonstration album presents the trumpet call *sans* orchestra.
Voisin, Roger, 13)

₍Coq d'Or, (1906-1907). Excerpt: Fanfares₎
Fanfares from *Le Coq d'Or*
This demonstration album presents the fanfares with trumpet alone, and then with full orchestra.
Geisler, Lloyd

₍Tsar Saltan, op. 57, (1899-1900). Flight of the Bumblebee; arr. brass quintet₎
The Flight of the Bumblebee
This arrangement features both trumpeters and the tubist of the brass quintet.
Canadian Brass, 4), 6)

₍Tsar Saltan, op. 57, (1899-1900). Flight of the Bumblebee; arr. cornet & wind ensemble₎
The Flight of the Bumblebee
Marsalis, Wynton, 4), 7)

₍Tsar Saltan, op. 57, (1899-1900). Flight of the Bumblebee; arr. trumpet & orchestra₎
The Flight of the Bumblebee
(Le Vol du Bourdon)
André, Maurice, 5), 7), 38), 66)
Méndez, Rafael, 19), 22)

₍Tsar Saltan, op. 57, (1899-1900). Flight of the Bumblebee; arr. trumpet & piano₎
The Flight of the Bumblebee
Christensen, Ketil
Dokshitser, Timofei, 3), 7), 9), 35), 36), 38), 39)

Rivier, Jean, 1896-

ₜAria, trumpet & organₜ
Aria
> Bernard, André, 6)
> Delmotte, Roger, 39)
> Pliquett, Joachim
> Send, Peter

ₜConcerto, saxophone, trumpet & strings, (1955)ₜ
Concerto pour saxophone alto, trompette et orchestre à cordes
¹Allegro burlesco / ²Adagio / ³Vivacissimo
> Delmotte, Roger, 33)
> Send, Peter

Robbins, Geoffrey, 20th cent.

ₜMont Saint-Michel, trumpet & piano, (1954)ₜ
Mont Saint-Michel
> Haynie, John, 2)

ₜMont Saint-Michel, trumpet & piano, (1954); arr. trumpet & organₜ
Mont Saint-Michel
> Tolley, Richard

Rodgers, Richard, 1902-1979
Rodgers, Richard Charles

ₜOklahoma, (1943). I Cain't Say No; arr. trumpet quartetₜ
"I Cain't Say No" from *Oklahoma*
> Blackburn, Roger

ₜPal Joey, (1940). Bewitched, Bothered and Bewildered; arr. trumpet & orchestraₜ
"Bewitched, Bothered and Bewildered" from *Pal Joey*
> Méndez, Rafael, 20)

ₜSound of Music, (1959). Theme song; arr. solo horn, solo trumpet & brass
ensembleₜ
"The Sound of Music" from *The Sound of Music*
> Mertens, Theo, 1)

ₜSound of Music, (1959). Theme song; arr. trumpet quartetₜ
"The Sound of Music" from *The Sound of Music*
> Blackburn, Roger

Rodrigo, Joaquín, 1901-

ₜConcierto de Aranjuez, guitar & orchestra, (1939); arr. trumpet & brass ensembleₜ
Adagio from *Concierto de Aranjuez*
> Mertens, Theo, 5)

ﺭConcierto de Aranjuez, guitar & orchestra, (1939); arr. trumpet, mixed voices & orchestraﺮ
Adagio from *Concierto de Aranjuez*
André, Maurice, 66)

Rodrigues Coelho, Manuel, 1583-*ca.* 1635
Coelho, Manuel Rodrigues

ﺭFlores de musica, (1620). Verses (3); arr. trumpet & organﺮ
Trois versets du cinquième ton
(Three Verses on the Fifth Tone)
Delmotte, Roger, 38)

Rodriguez, Robert Xavier, 1946-

ﺭMy Lady Carey's Dompe, trumpet, horn & piano/harpsichordﺮ
My Lady Carey's Dompe
[1]My Lady Carey's Dompe / [2]When Griping Grief... / [3]O Play Me Some... / [4]Then Music With...
Giangiulio, Richard

Rogers-Lyons-Yosco, 20th cent.

ﺭSpaghetti Rag; arr. trumpet quartetﺮ
Spaghetti Rag
Blackburn, Roger

Rogers, Walter B., 1865-1939

ﺭVolunteer, cornet & bandﺮ
The Volunteer
Burke, James, 2)

Roland-Manuel, Alexis, 1891-1966
Lévy, Roland Alexis Manuel

ﺭSuite dans le gout Espagnol, oboe, bassoon, trumpet & harpsichord, (1933)ﺮ
Suite dans le gout Espagnol
Delmotte, Roger, 41)

Rollin, Robert, 1947-
Rollin, Robert Leon

ﺭReflections on Ruin By the Sea, trumpet & pianoﺮ
Reflections on Ruin By the Sea
Stith, Marice, 7)

Roman, Johann Helmich, 1694-1758

ﺭSuite, chamber orchestra, no. 2; arr. trumpet & organﺮ
Suite No. 2
Stringer, Alan, 3)

Romanino, Giuseppe, 18th cent.

ᵣConcerto, trumpet, strings & continuo, D majorᵣ
Concerto di Tromba
Fink, Werner

Root, George F., 1820-1895

ᵣJesus Loves the Little Children; arr. trumpet & pianoᵣ
Medley (with variations)
Medley uses the traditional tune,"Tramp, Tramp", and George F.
Root's children's hymn, "Jesus Loves the Little Children".
Reinhart, Carole Dawn, 13)

Ropartz, Joseph Guy
See: Guy Ropartz, Joseph

Rosas, Juventino, 1868-1894

ᵣSobre las Olas, (1891); arr. trumpet & orchestraᵣ
Over the Waves
(Sobre las Olas)
Méndez, Rafael, 3), 10)

Rosenberg, Voldemar
See: Wal-Berg

Rosenmüller, Johann, *ca.* 1619-1684
Rosenmiller, Giovanni

ᵣLaudate Pueri Dominum, soli, mixed voices & trumpetᵣ
Laudate Pueri Dominum
Immer, Friedemann, 8)

ᵣMissa brevis, soli, mixed voices & trumpetᵣ
Missa brevis
Immer, Friedemann, 8)

Rosier, Carl, 1640-1725

ᵣSonata, trumpet, oboes, strings & continuoᵣ
Sonata for Trumpet, Oboes and Strings
Marinus, Jan

ᵣSonata, trumpet, strings & continuo, C majorᵣ
Sonata in C major for Trumpet, Strings and Continuo
Sequence number is unspecified.
Hunger, Helmut, 1)

ₜSonatas. No. 1, trumpet, strings & continuoₙ
Sonata No. 1 for Trumpet, Strings and Continuo
These numbered sonatas may be transcriptions from *Quatorze Sonates pour les Violons et le Hautbois à 6 Parties.*
Haas, Wolfgang

ₜSonatas. No. 4, trumpet, strings & continuoₙ
Sonata No. 4 for Trumpet, Strings and Continuo
Soustrot, Bernard, 9)

ₜSonatas. No. 5, trumpet, strings & continuoₙ
Sonata No. 5 for Trumpet, Strings and Continuo
Haas, Wolfgang

ₜSonatas. No. 7, trumpet, strings & continuoₙ
Sonata No. 7 for Trumpet, Strings and Continuo
Haas, Wolfgang

ₜSonatas. No. 11, trumpet, strings & continuoₙ
Sonata No. 11 for Trumpet, Strings and Continuo
Haas, Wolfgang

Rossini, Gioacchino, 1792-1868
Rossini, Gioacchino Antonio

ₜBarber of Seville, (1816). Aria (?); arr. trumpet & harpₙ
Aria from *Il Barbiere di Siviglia*
André, Maurice, 84)

ₜBarber of Seville, (1816). Cavatine d'Almaviva; arr. trumpet & orchestraₙ
Aria, "Ecce ridente in cielo" from *Il Barbiere di Siviglia*
(Cavatine de Conte)
André, Maurice, 161)

ₜBarber of Seville, (1816). Cavatine de Figaro; arr. trumpet & orchestraₙ
Aria, "Largo al factotum" from *Il Barbiere di Siviglia*
Ghitalla, Armando, 14)
Méndez, Rafael, 13), 24)

ₜBarber of Seville, (1816). Cavatine de Rosine; arr. trumpet & orchestraₙ
Aria, "Una voce poco fa" from *Il Barbiere di Siviglia*
André, Maurice, 161), 206), 207)
Méndez, Rafael, 15)

ₜDonna del lago, (1819). Rondo d'Elena; arr. trumpet & brass ensembleₙ
Aria, "Tanti affetti in tal momento" from *La donna del lago*
Brass-zination

ₜSemiramide, (1823). Act I: Aria, "Bel raggio lusinghier"; arr. trumpet & orchestraₙ
Aria, "Bel raggio lusinghier" from *Semiramide*
André, Maurice, 37)

[Soirées musicales, (c. 1830-35). No. 8: Arietta, tenor & piano; arr. trumpet & orchestra]
La Danza, (Tarentelle napolitaine)
(Arietta, "Già la luna è in mezzo al mare")
André, Maurice, 4)
Geiger, György

[William Tell, (1829). Overture; arr. brass quintet & percussion]
William Tell Overture
(Overture to *Guglielmo Tell*)
This arrangement features both trumpet players as soloists.
Dallas Brass

Rosso, 20th cent.

[Il silenzio, trumpet & orchestra]
Il silenzio
André, Maurice, 170)

Rota, Nino, 1911-1979
Rota Rinaldi, Nino

[Romeo and Juliette, (1968). Love Theme; arr. trumpet & orchestra]
Love Theme from *Romeo and Juliet*
Méndez, Rafael, 16)

[Strada, (1954). Love Theme; arr. trumpet & orchestra]
Love Theme from *La Strada*
André, Maurice, 170)

Rouse, Christopher, 1949-

[Subjectives VIII, solo trumpet, (1972-73)]
Subjectives VIII
Stith, Marice, 4)

Rubinstein, Anton Grigorievich, 1829-1894
Rubinshteyn, Anton Grigor'yevich

[Démon, (1871). Aria, "Still night, warm night"; arr. cornet & accompaniment]
"Still night, warm night" from *Le Démon*
Klochkov, Pavel, 1)

[Melody, piano, op. 3, no. 1, F major, (1852); arr. trumpet & piano]
Melody in F major, op. 3, no. 1
Dokshitser, Timofei, 9), 36), 38), 39)

[Romance, "Desire", piano; arr. cornet & accompaniment]
Romance, "Desire"
Lemos, Alexandre Vasilievich

Rueff, Jeanine, 1922-

ₜSonatina, trumpet & piano, (1957)ₗ
Sonatine pour Trompette et Piano
[1]Allegro risoluto / [2]Andante sostenuto / [3]Presto
Dokshitser, Timofei, 17)
Rippas, Claude

Ruggles, Carl (Sprague), 1876-1971
Sprague, Charles

ₜAngels, 6 trumpets, (1922); arr. 4 trumpets, 4 trombones, (1939)ₗ
Angels
Performed with 4 trumpets, 3 trombones & tuba.
Kuehn, David

Ryu, Khirota

ₜHamachidori; arr. trumpet & pianoₗ
Hamachidori
This Japanese composer's name may actually be Hirota Ryotaro
(1892-1952). The Japanese word, **Hamachidori**, is the name of a
kind of bird.
Dokshitser, Timofei, 19)

Sabarich, Raymond, 1909-1966

ₜAubade, solo trumpetₗ
Aubade
Potpourri, 28)

ₜEtudes (10), trumpet, (1954)ₗ
Dix Études
Ménardi, Louis

ₜLamento, solo trumpetₗ
Lamento
A co-author of this work is Rolland.
Potpourri, 28)

Saeverud, Harald, 1897-
Saeverud, Harald Sigurd Johan

ₜTromba Solo, solo trumpet, (1970)ₗ
Tromba Solo
Kvebaek, Harry

St. Preux

ₜConcerto, voice & orchestra; arr. trumpet & brass ensembleₗ
Concerto pour une voix
Mertens, Theo, 1)

Saint-Saëns, Camille, 1835-1921
Saint-Saëns, Charles Camille

[Carnaval des Animaux, (1886). No. 13: Le cygne; arr. trumpet & organ]
The Swan from *The Carnival of the Animals*
(Le Cygne de *Le Carnaval des Animaux*)
Grin, Freddy, 8)

[Carnaval des Animaux, (1886). No. 13: Le cygne; arr. trumpet & piano]
The Swan from *The Carnival of the Animals*
(Le Cygne de *Le Carnaval des Animaux*)
Wilder, Joseph B.

[Samson et Delila, op. 47, (1877). Aria, "Amour viens aider ma faiblesse"; arr. trumpet & piano]
Aria, "Amour viens aider ma faiblesse" de *Samson et Delila*
Reynolds, George

[Septet, trumpet, piano, string quartet & bass, op. 65, E^b major, (1880)]
Septuor en mi bémol majeur, op. 65
[1]Préambule (Allegro moderato) / [2]Menuet (Tempo di minuetto moderato) / [3]Intermède (Andante) / [4]Gavotte et Final (Allegro non troppo)
André, Maurice, 49)
Delmotte, Roger, 36)
Glantz, Harry, 4), 7)
Lagorce, Antoine
Margolin, Veniamin
Unidentified, Trumpet(s), 11)

Sanders, Robert L., 1906-1974
Sanders, Robert Levine

[Square Dance, trumpet & piano, (1959)]
Square Dance
Burkart, Richard
Crisara, Raymond, 8)

Sanz, Gaspar, 17th cent.-18th cent.

[Spanish Dances (5), guitar; arr. trumpet & harp]
Five Spanish Dances
[1]Rurejo / [2]Paradetas / [3]Matachin / [4]Zarabanda / [5]Españoleta
Percussion is added to the first two dances.
André, Maurice, 64)

Sapieyevski, Jerzy, 1945-

[Mercury Concerto, trumpet & chamber ensemble]
Mercury Concerto
Chamber ensemble includes: piccolo, flute, oboe, clarinet, bassoon, contrabassoon & horn.
Ghitalla, Armando, 1)

Sarasate, Pablo de, 1844-1908
Sarasate (y Navascuéz), Pablo (Martín Melitón) de

[Spanische Tänze, violin & piano, op. 21, (1878). No. 1: Malagueña; arr. trumpet & orchestra]
Malagueña, op. 21, no. 1
Méndez, Rafael, 15)

[Spanische Tänze, violin & piano, op. 23, (1880). No. 2: Zapateado; arr. trumpet & orchestra]
Zapateado, op. 23, no. 2
Méndez, Rafael, 18)

[Zigeunerweisen, violin & piano, op. 20, (1878). No. 1; arr. trumpet & orchestra]
Zigeunerweisen, op. 20, no. 1
(Gypsy Airs)
Méndez, Rafael, 2), 8)

[Zigeunerweisen, violin & piano, op. 20, (1878). No. 1; arr. trumpet & piano]
Zigeunerweisen, op. 20, no. 1
(Gypsy Airs)
Dokshitser, Timofei, 5), 7), 9), 31), 35), 36), 38), 39)

Sartorio, Antonio, 1630-1680

[l'Adelaide, (1672). Sinfonia, 2 trumpets, strings & continuo]
Sinfonia from *l'Adelaide*
Tarr, Edward, 27)

Sarvil

[Noël de petits santons; arr. children's voices, trumpet & orchestra]
Noël de petits santons
André, Maurice, 166)

Satic, Erik, 1866-1925
Satie, Erik Alfred Leslie

[Carillon, 2 trumpets, (1921)]
Carillon
(Sonnerie pour réveiller le roi des singes)
For awakening the good fat monkey king (Who always sleeps with one eye open)
Giangiulio, Richard
Thibaud, Pierre, 11)

[Gymnopédies (3), piano, (1888). No. 3; arr. trumpet & orchestra]
Gymnopédie No. 3
Cowell, Johnny

Scarlatti, Alessandro, 1660-1725
Scarlatti, (Pietro) Alessandro (Gaspare)

⌈Arias (7), soprano, trumpet & continuo⌉
Arie con Tromba Sola
[1]Si suoni la tromba / [2]In terra la guerra / [3]Con voce festiva / [4]Rompe sprezza / [5]Si riscaldi il Tebro / [6]Mio tesoro / [7]Farò la vendetta

      Basch, Wolfgang, 2[1-7])
      Carroll, Edward, 8[4+6]), 9[4+6])
      Ferry, Dennis[1-7]
      Impett, Jonathan[1]
      Schetsche, Walter[2-3+6-7]

⌈Arias. "Gia il sole dal Gange", tenor, trumpet, strings & continuo⌉
Aria, "Gia il sole dal Gange"
    Mantovani, Alberto

⌈Arias. "Nacqui donna ma", alto, trumpet, strings & continuo⌉
Concert Aria, "Nacqui donna ma"
    Touvron, Guy, 16)

⌈Arias. "Sento nel core"; arr. trumpet & piano⌉
Aria, "Sento nel core"
    Schwarz, Gerard, 14)

⌈Arias. "Spesso vibra per suo gioco"; arr. trumpet & piano⌉
Allegro
(Aria, "Spesso vibra per suo gioco")
This aria is included as the first movement of Bernard Fitzgerald's transcription, *Italian Suite,* (with four selections by different composers).
    Ghitalla, Armando, 11)

⌈Cantata, "Su le sponde del Tebro", soprano, trumpet, strings & continuo⌉
Cantata, "Su le sponde del Tebro"
    André, Maurice, 48)
    Bauer, Willibald, 2)
    Carroll, Edward, 8), 9)
    Ghitalla, Armando, 3)
    Güttler, Ludwig, 20)
    Potpourri, 18)
    Rudolf, Richard
    Scherbaum, Adolf, 21)
    Schwarz, Gerard, 4)
    Touvron, Guy, 15)
    Wobisch, Helmut, 7), 8[1-2])

⌈Exultate Deo, mixed voices, brass & strings⌉
Exultate Deo
    Thibaud, Pierre, 10)

⌈Serenatas. "Endimione e Cintia", soprano, trumpet, strings & continuo, (1705)⌉
"Endimione e Cintia"
    Thibaud, Pierre, 5)

[Serenatas. "Endimione e Cintia", soprano, trumpet, strings & continuo, (1705). Excerpts]

Excerpts from "Endimione e Cintia"
[1]Aria, "Mi sembra di sognar" / [2]Recitative, "Vaga Cintia, adorata anima mia" / [3]Aria, "Se geloso e il mio core"
> **Hickman, David,** 2[2-3])
> **Scherbaum, Adolf,** 21[1-3])
> **Schwarz, Gerard,** 3[3])

[Serenatas. "Endimione e Cintia", soprano, trumpet, strings & continuo, (1705). Excerpts; arr. soprano, trumpet & organ]

Excerpts from "Endimione e Cintia"
[1]Aria, "Mi sembra di sognar" / [2]Recitative, "Vaga Cintia, adorata anima mia" / [3]Aria, "Se geloso e il mio core"
> **Basch, Wolfgang,** 2[1])
> **Haas, Wolfgang**[1-3]
> **Laughton, Stuart**[2-3]
> **Touvron, Guy,** 16[3])

[Serenatas. "Venere e Adone: Il giardino d'amore", (c. 1700-05). Sinfonia; arr. trumpet & organ]

Sinfonia from *Il Giardino di amore*
> **Tamiya, Kenji**
> **Tschotschev, Nicolai-Dimitrov**

[Serenatas. "Venere e Adone: Il giardino d'amore", soprano, alto, trumpet, strings & continuo, (1705)]

Serenata, "Il Giardino di amore"
> **Quinque, Rolf,** 2)

[Sinfonias (12), chamber orchestra, (1715). No. 2: flute, trumpet, strings & continuo, D major]

Sinfonia Seconda Concertata con li ripieni
(Concerto grosso No. 2 in D major for Flute, Trumpet, Strings and Continuo)
[1]Spiritoso / [2]Adagio / [3]Allegro / [4]Adagio - Presto
> **André, Maurice,** 13), 21), 25), 178)
> **Couëffé, Yves**
> **Jackson, Harold**
> **Potpourri,** 36), 37)
> **Schmid, Bernhard,** 12)
> **Soustrot, Bernard,** 5)
> **Voisin, Roger,** 6), 8)

[Sinfonias (12), chamber orchestra, (1715). No. 2: flute, trumpet, strings & continuo, D major; arr. recorder, trumpet, strings & continuo]

Sinfonia Seconda Concertata con li ripieni
(Concerto grosso No. 2 in D major for Flute, Trumpet, Strings and Continuo)
[1]Spiritoso / [2]Adagio / [3]Allegro / [4]Adagio - Presto
> **Soustrot, Bernard,** 6)

ₑToccatas, keyboard instrument. No. 7: D major; arr. 2 trumpets, organ &
timpaniₑ
Toccata in D major, No. 7
Läubin, Hannes, 2)

Scarlatti, Domenico, 1685-1757
Scarlatti, (Giuseppe) Domenico

ₑStabat Mater, 10 voices, brass, strings & continuoₑ
Stabat Mater
Potpourri, 18)

Schafer, R. Murray, 1933-
Schafer, Raymond Murray

ₑArcana, soprano & chamber ensemble, (1972)ₑ
Arcana
Chamber ensemble includes: flute, clarinet, trumpet, trombone,
violin, cello, bass, harp, piano/organ & percussion.
Chenette, Stephen

Scheidt, Samuel, 1587-1654

ₑCorrento, 2 trumpets & 3 trombonesₑ
Corrento
2 natural trumpets & 3 sackbuts
Potpourri, 67)

ₑCourant Dolorosa, cornetto, 3 trombones & continuoₑ
Courant Dolorosa a 4
Tarr, Edward, 10)

ₑPaduan, cornetto, 3 trombones & continuoₑ
Paduan a 4
Tarr, Edward, 10)

ₑPaduana, galliarda, couranta..., (1621). Canzona, 4 cornetti; arr. 4 trumpetsₑ
Canzon cornetto a 4
Jones, Philip
Potpourri, 29)
Schwarz, Gerard, 20)
Tarr, Edward, 3)

Schein, Johann Hermann, 1586-1630

ₑ"Vom Himmel hoch, da komm ich her"; arr. trumpet & brass ensembleₑ
"Vom Himmel hoch, da komm ich her"
Güttler, Ludwig, 9)

Schertzinger, Victor, 1890-1941

[Marcheta; arr. trumpet & studio orchestra]
Marcheta
Jacoby, Don

Schickele, Peter, 1935-

[Knight of the Burning Pestle, (1974). Songs, soli & chamber ensemble]
Songs from *The Knight of the Burning Pestle*
[1]For Love Hath Tossed Me / [2]Nose, Nose, Jolly Red Nose / [3]Tell Me Dearest, What Is Love? / [4]A Man's Seed / [5]As You Came from Walsingham / [6]My Mother Told Me Not to Worry / [7]For Now the Fragrant Flowers / [8]Come, All Ye Whose Loves / [9]Better Music Ne'er Was Known

Vocal soli are: soprano, alto, tenor & baritone. (The composer also vocalizes.)

Chamber ensemble includes: recorder, clarinet, bassoon, trumpet, trombone, violin, bass, drums & harpsichord. (The recorder & bassoon parts are covered by the same musician.)

SEE also: Bach, P.D.Q.
Mase, Raymond

Schickhardt, Johann Christian, *ca.* 1682-1762

[Hamburger Suite, oboe & continuo, op. 2, no. 1; arr. trumpet & organ]
Hamburger Suite, op. 2, no. 1
[1]Adagio / [2]Allegro / [3]Adagio / [4]Vivace / [5]Allegro / [6]Largo / [7]Allegro (Giga)
Hartog, Thomas

[Piece, recorder solo, op. 17, no. 12; arr. trumpet]
Stück für Trompete solo, op. 17, Nr. 12
(Piece for Trumpet Solo)
(Pièce pour trompette solo)
André, Maurice, 39)

Schilling, Hans Ludwig, 1927-

[Canzona, "Christ ist erstanden", trumpet & organ, (1967)]
Canzona über "Christ ist erstanden"
Bodenröder, Robert
Pearson, Byron
Pliquett, Joachim
Rhoten, Bruce

[Chorale Preludes. No. 1: "Adeste fideles", trumpet & organ]
Chorale Prelude No. 1, "Adeste fideles"
Lewark, Egbert

Schmelzer, Johann Heinrich, *ca.* 1622-1680
Schmeltzer, Johann Heinrich
Schmelzer von Ehrenruef

[Balletto à Cavallo, (1667). Airs, 12 trumpets, 2 timpani, 2 flutes, 5 oboes, 2 bassoons & strings]
Arie par il Balletto à Cavallo
[1]Sinfonia (Allegro) / [2]Corrente (Grave) per l'Intrada di S.M.C. & di tutti i Cavaglieri / [3]Eco / [4](Corrente *da capo*) / [5]Battaglia / [6]Gavotte / [7]Giga (Allegro) per Entrata de i Saltatori, er per molto altre figure / [8]Follia (Allegro) per nuovo ingresso de i Saltatori & altre operazioni de Cavalli / [9]Allemanda (Grave e Maestoso) per gl'intrecci e figure di passegio grave introdotto di S.M.C. e Cavaglieri / [10]Sarabanda per termine del Balletto / [11]Ritirata
Tarr, Edward, 28)

[Balletto à Cavallo, (1667). Excerpts (3), 6 trumpets & timpani]
Drei Stücke zum Pferdeballett
[1]Corrente / [3]Follia / [5]Sarabanda
Idinger, Matthias

[Balletto à Cavallo, (1667). Excerpts, 6 trumpets & timpani]
Balletto à Cavallo
[1]Corrente / [2]Giga / [3]Follia / [4]Allemanda / [5]Sarabanda
Smithers, Don, 10)

[Sacro Profanus concentus musicus..., (1662). No. 2a: Sonata, cornetto, 3 trombones, strings & continuo]
Sonata 2a
Tarr, Edward, 10)

[Sonata con arie, 3 trumpets, timpani, strings & continuo, C major]
Sonata con arie zu der kaiserlichen Serenade
Tarr, Edward, 27)

[Sonata per Chiesa et Camera, 5 trumpets, strings & continuo, C major]
Sonata per Chiesa et Camera
Scherbaum, Adolf, 16)

[Sonata, "La Carolietta", cornetto, trombone, violin & dulcian, G major]
Sonata a 4, "La Carolietta"
("La Carioletta"?)
Potpourri, 49), 64)

[Sonata, trumpet, bassoon, strings & continuo, C major]
Sonata a 5
[1]Allegro moderato / [2]Adagio / [3]Allegro / [4]Adagio / [5]Presto / [6]Moderato
Potpourri, 42), 49), 64)
Smithers, Don, 4)

[Sonata, trumpet, trombone, violin & continuo, C major]
Sonata a 3
Potpourri, 49), 64)

[Sonatas. No. 1, 2 trumpets, strings & continuo, C major]
Sonata I a 8
Potpourri, 49), 64)

[Sonatas. No. 2, cornetto, 3 trombones, strings & continuo, C major]
Sonata II a 8
(Sonata II a due Chori)
Potpourri, 49), 64)

[Sonatas. No. 12, 2 cornetti, 2 trumpets, 3 trombones & continuo, C major]
Sonata a 7
(Sonata XII)
Spindler, Günter

Schmidt, Eric, 1907-
Schmid, Erich

[Rhapsodia Sacra, trumpet & organ]
Rhapsodia Sacra
Chatel, Jean-Louis

Schmidt, Ole, 1928-

[Pièce Concertante, trumpet, trombone & chamber orchestra, op. 19, (1956)]
Pièce Concertante for Trumpet and Trombone, op. 19
Chamber orchestra includes: piano, celeste, harp, percussion & strings.
Hovaldt, Knud

Schmidt, William, 1926-
Schmidt, William Joseph

[Concertino, 2 trumpets & organ]
Concertino for Two Trumpets and Organ
Plog, Anthony, 10)

[Concerto, trumpet, piano & chamber orchestra, (1980)]
Double Concerto for Trumpet and Piano
Andante-Allegro — Adagio — Allegro con moto
Plog, Anthony, 11)

[Sonata, trumpet & piano]
Sonata for Trumpet and Piano
Plog, Anthony, 10)

[Variants with Solo Cadenzas, 4 trumpets]
Variants with Solo Cadenzas
Plog, Anthony, 10)

[Variations, "The Turkish Lady", trumpet & piano]
Variations on a Whaling Song
("The Turkish Lady")
Plog, Anthony, 9)

Schneider, Willy, 1907-1983

[Sonatina, trumpet & piano, (1956)]
Sonatine für Trompete und Klavier
[1]Allegro moderato / [2]Andante sostenuto / [3]Un poco allegro
Rippas, Claude

Schnitke, Alfred, 1934-
Schnittke, Alfred Garrievich

[Suite in Old Style, violin & piano, C major; arr. trumpet & piano]
Suite in Old Style
Kafelnikov, Vladimir

Schönberg, Arnold (Franz Walter), 1874-1951

[Nachtwandler, soprano, flute/(piccolo), trumpet, percussion & piano, (1901)]
Nachtwandler
Scholz, Walter
Snell, Howard

Schostakowitsch, Dimitri
See: Shostakovich, Dmitri

Schubert, Franz, 1797-1828
Schubert, Franz Peter

[Ellens Gesänge (3), op. 56, D 837-839, (1825). No. 3: Ave Maria, D 839; arr. cornet & organ]
Ave Maria
(Ellens Gesang, op. 56, no. 3)
McCann, Phillip

[Ellens Gesänge (3), op. 56, D 837-839, (1825). No. 3: Ave Maria, D 839; arr. trumpet & orchestra]
Ave Maria
(Ellens Gesang, op. 56, no. 3)
André, Maurice, 170)
Méndez, Rafael, 13)

[Ellens Gesänge (3), op. 56, D 837-839, (1825). No. 3: Ave Maria, D 839; arr.
trumpet & organ]
Ave Maria
(Ellens Gesang, op. 56, no. 3)
>>> André, Maurice, 38), 39), 40), 42), 52), 67),
>>> 205), 206), 207), 227)
>>> Bernard, André, 9)
>>> Falentin, Paul, 5)
>>> Gabel, Bernard, 2)
>>> Mertens, Theo, 4)
>>> Terracini, Paul
>>> Volle, Bjarne
>>> Wilbraham, John, 24)

[Ellens Gesänge (3), op. 56, D 837-839, (1825). No. 3: Ave Maria, D 839; arr.
trumpet & piano]
Ave Maria
(Ellens Gesang, op. 56, no. 3)
>>> Ots, Aavo

[Gebet, mixed voices & piano, D 815, (1824); arr. trumpet & organ]
Gebet
Preghiera (Prayer)
>>> Mertens, Theo, 2)

[Lieder. Allmacht, D 852, (1825); arr. trumpet & organ]
Die Allmacht
>>> Gabel, Bernard, 2)

[Lieder. Du bist die Ruh', D 776, (1823); arr. trumpet & piano]
Du bist die Ruh'
("My Sweet Repose")
>>> House, Lawrence

[Lieder. Pilgrim, D 794, (1823); arr. trumpet & organ]
Der Pilgrim
>>> Gabel, Bernard, 2)

[Schwanengesang, voice & piano, op. ph., D 957. No. 4: Ständchen; arr.
flügelhorn & orchestra]
Serenade
(Ständchen aus *Schwanengesang*)
(Sérénade de *Chant du Cygne*)
>>> André, Maurice, 4)

[Schwanengesang, voice & piano, op. ph., D 957. No. 4: Ständchen; arr. trumpet
& instrumental accompaniment]
Serenade
>>> Hidalgo, José Luis
>>> Scherbaum, Adolf, 34)

₍Schwanengesang, voice & piano, op. ph., D 957. No. 4: Ständchen; arr. trumpet & orchestra₎
Schubert's Serenade
Méndez, Rafael, 16)

₍Schwanengesang, voice & piano, op. ph., D 957. No. 4: Ständchen; arr. trumpet & organ₎
Serenade
Mertens, Theo, 4)

₍Schwanengesang, voice & piano, op. ph., D 957. No. 12: Am Meer; arr. trumpet & organ₎
Am Meer aus *Schwanengesang*
Gabel, Bernard, 2)

₍Schwanengesang, voice & piano, op. ph., D 957. No. 13: Der Doppelgänger; arr. trumpet & organ₎
Der Doppelgänger aus *Schwanengesang*
Gabel, Bernard, 2)

₍Winterreise, voice & piano, op. 89, D 911, (1827). No. 5: Der Lindenbaum; arr. trumpet & organ₎
Der Lindenbaum aus *Die Winterrreise*, op. 89
Scherbaum, Adolf, 34)

₍Winterreise, voice & piano, op. 89, D 911, (1827). No. 6: Wasserflut; arr. trumpet & organ₎
Wasserflut aus *Die Winterreise*, op. 89
Gabel, Bernard, 2)

Schuler

₍Overshadowed; arr. trumpet & orchestra₎
Overshadowed
Driscoll, Phil

Schultz, Erik, 1952-

₍Improvisation, solo trumpet₎
Improvisation
Schultz, Erik, 10)

Schumann, Robert, 1810-1856
Schumann, Robert Alexander

₍Album für die Jungen, piano, op. 68, (1848). No. 8: Wilder Reiter, a minor; arr. 3 trumpets & band₎
Trumpets Wild
Butterfield, Billy

ₜKinderszenen, piano, op. 15, (1838). No. 7: Träumerei; arr. trumpet & harpₗ
Träumerei aus *Kinderszenen*, op. 15, no. 7
(Rêverie de *Scènes d'enfants*)
André, Maurice, 84)

ₜKinderszenen, piano, op. 15, (1838). No. 7: Träumerei; arr. trumpet &
instrumental accompanimentₗ
Träumerei aus *Kinderszenen*, op. 15, no. 7
(Rêverie de *Scènes d'enfants*)
Mertens, Theo, 5)

Schütz, Heinrich, 1585-1672

ₜGeistliche Chormusik. SWV 269-397: Motets (29), soli, mixed voices &
instrumental ensembleₗ
Geistliche Chormusik, SWV 369-397
Some of these motets include 2 trumpets & 4 trombones.
Ellinghaus, Wolfram

ₜSymphoniæ sacræ I, (1629). SWV 257-276: soli, mixed voices & instrumental
ensembleₗ
Simphoniæ sacræ I, SWV 257-276
Tamiya, Kenji

ₜSymphoniæ sacræ II, (1647). SWV 344: Concerto No. 4, "Meine Seele erhebt den
Herren", soprano & instrumental ensembleₗ
Concerto No. 4, "Meine Seele erhebt den Herren", SWV 344
Instrumental ensemble includes: 2 recorders, 2 oboes, 2 cornetti, 2
trumpets, 2 trombones, 2 violins & continuo.
Tarr, Edward, 4)

ₜSymphoniæ sacræ II, (1647). SWV 350: Concerto No. 10, "Lobet den Herrn in
seinem Heiligtum", tenor & instrumental ensembleₗ
Concerto No. 10, "Lobet den Herrn in seinem Heiligtum", SWV 350
Instrumental ensemble includes: 2 recorders, 2 oboes, 2 cornetti, 2
trombones & continuo.
Tarr, Edward, 4)

ₜSymphoniæ sacræ II, (1647). SWV 359: Concerto No. 19, "Der Herr ist mein
Licht", 2 tenors, 2 cornetti, 2 violins & continuoₗ
Concerto No. 19, "Der Herr ist mein Licht", SWV 359
Tarr, Edward, 4)

ₜWeihnachts-Oratorium, soli, children's voices & instrumental ensemble, SWV 435ₗ
Christmas Oratorio, SWV 435
(Historia von der freudenreichen Geburt Jesu Christ)
Holy, Walter, 5)

Schwaen, Kurt, 1909-

[Concertino Apollineo, piano & chamber ensemble]
Concertino Apollineo
Chamber ensemble includes: flute, oboe, English horn, bass clarinet, bassoon, horn & trumpet.
Potpourri, 19)

[Ostinati (3), trumpet & piano]
Drei Ostinati für Trompete und Klavier
Potpourri, 19)

Schwartz, Elliott, 1936-

[Cycles and Gongs, trumpet, organ & tape]
Cycles and Gongs
Dean, Allan, 9)

[Essays, trumpet & trombone]
Essays for Trumpet and Trombone
Patti, Douglas

Schwartzkopff, Theodorus, 1659-1732
Schwartzkopf, Theodor

[Suite, 2 oboes, bassoon, trumpet, strings & continuo, C major]
Suite in C major
(Ouvertüre)
[1]Ouvertüre / [2]Bourrée / [3]Menuet / [4]Chaconne / [5]Gigue
Güttler, Ludwig, 26)

Scott, Raymond, 1910-

[Toy Trumpet; arr. trumpet & band]
The Toy Trumpet
Head, Emerson

[Toy Trumpet; arr. trumpet & orchestra]
The Toy Trumpet
Hirt, Al

Scriabin, Alexander, 1872-1915
Skriabine, Alexandre
Skryabin, Aleksandre Nikolayevich

[Symphonies. No. 4, "Poem of Ecstasy", op. 54, (1905-1907)]
Poem of Ecstasy, op. 54
(Symphony No. 4, "Poem of Ecstasy")
(Symphony No. 4, "Le poème de l'extase")
Although this "symphonic tone-poem" is **not** a "concerto for trumpet", the first trumpet part is considered soloistic enough to include the player's name on the record jacket. (There are actually 4 trumpets in the orchestration.)
Giangiulio, Richard
Margolin, Veniamin
Mills, Fred
Popov, Sergei, 4)
Vacchiano, William, 3)
Volodin, Lev

Seiti, Okano

[Furusato; arr. trumpet & piano]
Furusato
(Native Land)
This Japanese composer actually may be Okano Teiichi, (1878-1941).
Dokshitser, Timofei, 19)

Selig, Robert Leigh, 1939-1984

[Mirage, trumpet & strings, (1968)]
Mirage
Ghitalla, Armando, 4)

Selma y Salaverde, Bartolomé de
See: Bartolomeo, Padre Francesco

Semenoff, Ivan K., 1917-1972
Semenov, Ivan K.

[Tender Sonia, trumpet & piano]
The Tender Sonia
Ode, James

Semler-Collery, Jules, 1902-

[Evocation et Scherzetto, trumpet & piano, (1971)]
Evocation et Scherzetto
Gardner, Ned

Senaillé, Jean Baptiste, *ca.* 1688-1730
Senallié, Jean Baptiste
Senaillier, Jean Baptiste

[Sonata, violin & continuo, no. 5, d minor. Allegro spiritoso; arr. trumpet & organ]
Sonata No. 5 in d minor
André, Maurice, 40), 52), 67)

Senée, Henri, 19th cent.-20th cent.

[Concertino, cornet & orchestra; arr. trumpet & piano]
Concertino pour cornet à pistons en si♭
(avec accompagnement d'orchestre ou de piano)
[1]Introduction (Allegro moderato) / [2]Romance (Andante) / [3]Ballet
(Allegro moderato)
Reynolds, George
Schwarz, Gerard, 12)

Senfl, Ludwig, *ca.* 1486-*ca.* 1543

[Ach Elslein, liebes Elselein, soli & instrumental ensemble]
Ach Elslein, liebes Elselein
Vocal soloists are countertenor, tenor & bass. Instrumental
ensemble includes: crumhorns, alto shawm, cornetto, alto and
tenor sackbuts & 2 lutes.
Laird, Michael, 3)

[Carmen-Lamentatio, cornetto, pommer & 2 trombones]
Carmen-Lamentatio
Renz, Albrecht, 4)

[Carmen, cornetto, pommer & 2 trombones, d minor]
Carmen in re
Renz, Albrecht, 4)

[Das Gläut zu Speyer, countertenor, tenor, bass, cornetto & 2 sackbuts]
Das Gläut zu Speyer
Laird, Michael, 3)

[Gottes Namen fahren wir, tenor, bass, cornetto, alto sackbut & bass shawm]
Gottes Namen fahren wir
Laird, Michael, 3)

[Ich weiss nit, was er ihr verhiess, soli & instrumental ensemble]
Ich weiss nit, was er ihr verhiess
Vocal soloists are tenor & bass. Instrumental ensemble includes:
tenor dulcian, cornetto, tenor and bass sackbuts, bass viol & lute.
Laird, Michael, 3)
Smithers, Don, 12)

[Missa ferialis, mixed voices & instrumental ensemble]
Missa ferialis
Instrumental ensemble includes: cornetto, alto and tenor trombones & alto crumhorn.
Renz, Albrecht, 4)

[Missa Paschalis, mixed voices & instrumental ensemble]
Missa Paschalis
(Easter Mass)
Instrumental ensemble may include: recorders, crumhorns, cornetto, shawm, 3 sackbuts, bass viol & organ.
Montesi, Robert, 5)

[Mit Lust tritt ich an diesen Tanz, soli & instrumental ensemble]
Mit Lust tritt ich an diesen Tanz
Vocal soloists are countertenor, tenor & bass. Instrumental ensemble includes: crumhorns, cornetto, alto and bass sackbuts, bass shawm, lute & regal.
Laird, Michael, 3)

[Was wird es doch, soli & instrumental ensemble]
Was wird es doch
Vocal soloists are countertenor, tenor & bass. Instrumental ensemble includes: descant recorder, soprano crumhorn, alto shawm, tenor recorder, bass crumhorn, cornetto, tenor and bass sackbuts, 2 lutes & organ (regal).
Laird, Michael, 3)

Sessions, Roger, 1896-1985
Sessions, Roger Huntington

[Concertino, chamber orchestra, (1972)]
Concertino for Chamber Orchestra
Chamber orchestra includes: flute/piccolo, oboe/English horn, clarinet/bass clarinet, bassoon/contrabassoon, 2 horns, trumpet, trombone, percussion, piano & strings.
Miller, Rodney

Shadwell, Nancy, 20th cent.

[Theme and Variations, solo trumpet, (1977)]
Theme and Variations
Endsley, Gerald

Shakhov, Ilya, 1925-

[Romantic Concerto, trumpet & orchestra, d minor, (1955)]
Romantic Concerto in d minor for Trumpet and Orchestra
Dokshitser, Timofei, 22)

Shapero, Harold, 1920-
Shapero, Harold Samuel

₁Sonata, trumpet & piano, (1956)₁
Sonata for Trumpet and Piano
Stith, Marice, 7)

Shapey, Ralph, 1921-

₁Concertante, trumpet & chamber ensemble, no. 1₁
Concertante No. 1 for Trumpet and 10 Players
Prologue / ¹Variations / ²Song / ³Rondo / Epilogue
Chamber ensemble includes: flute (alto flute/piccolo), oboe
(English horn), clarinet (E♭-clarinet/bass clarinet), 2 bassoons,
horn, viola, cello & percussion.
Potpourri, 38)

Shchedrin, Rodion Konstantinovich, 1932-

₁In the Style of Albéniz, trumpet & piano₁
In the Style of Albéniz
Dokshitser, Timofei, 9), 39)

Shchelokov, Vyacheslav Ivanovich, 1904-
Shelokov, Vyacheslav
Shchelukov, Vyacheslav

₁Ballada, trumpet & piano, (1960)₁
Ballada
Ots, Aavo

₁Concerto, "Children's", trumpet & piano₁
Concerto, "Children's"
Ots, Aavo

₁Etude, trumpet & piano, E♭ major, (1957)₁
Etude in E♭ major
Polonsky, Naum E.

₁Legend, trumpet & piano, (1960)₁
Legend
House, Lawrence
Masters, Edward L.

₁Scherzo, trumpet & piano, (1960)₁
Scherzo
House, Lawrence
Masters, Edward L.

Sheppard, Franklin L, 1852-1930

[TERRA BEATA; arr. trumpet & orchestra]
This Is My Father's World
Driscoll, Phil

Sherwin, William F., 1826-1888

[Sound the Battle Cry; arr. trumpet & band]
Sound the Battle Cry
Blair, Stacy

[Sound the Battle Cry; arr. trumpet & orchestra]
Sound the Battle Cry
Driscoll, Phil

[Sound the Battle Cry; arr. trumpet & piano]
Sound the Battle Cry
Reinhart, Carole Dawn, 13)

Shiao Wei-Chen, 20th cent.

[Enchantment of the Mongolian Lark, trumpet & piano]
Enchantment of the Mongolian Lark
(Sing, the beautiful lark)
Shinjian folk song.
Yeh Shu-han

[How Can I Forget Her, trumpet & piano]
How Can I Forget Her
Literal translation of the Chinese title: "How can I don't miss her".
Yeh Shu-han

[Lullaby, trumpet & piano]
Lullaby
(The Lullaby Song)
Yeh Shu-han

[Memories of Paris, trumpet & piano]
Memories of Paris
(Parisian Reminiscence)
Yeh Shu-han

[Variation, "Great Wall", trumpet & piano]
Variation, "Great Wall"
(Song of the Great Wall)
Yeh Shu-han

[Variation, "Words of the West Wind", trumpet & piano]
Variation, "Words of the West Wind"
(Voice of the Western Wind)
Yeh Shu-han

Shire, David, 1937-

ₜHindenburg, (1975). Main Title, trumpet & orchestraₜ
Main Title from *The Hindenburg*
Motion picture sound track.
Stevens, Thomas, 15)

Shore, John, *ca.* 1662-1752

ₜPrince Eugene's March, trumpet, strings & continuoₜ
Prince Eugene's March
Steele-Perkins, Crispian, 5)

ₜTrumpett, trumpet, strings & continuoₜ
Trumpett
Steele-Perkins, Crispian, 5)

Shostakovich, Dmitri Dmitrievich, 1906-1975
Schostakovitsch, Dimitri
Chostakovitch, Dimitri

ₜConcerto, piano, trumpet & strings, op. 35, c minor, (1933)ₜ
Concerto No. 1 in c minor for Piano, Trumpet and Strings, op. 35
[1]Allegro moderato / [2]Lento / [3]Moderato / [4]Allegro brio
André, Maurice, 129)
Bauer, Willibald, 5)
Burns, Stephen
Glantz, Harry, 3)
Jones, Philip, 4)
Kafelnikov, Vladimir
Kejmar, Miroslav, 4)
Klein, Manny
Korolev, Alexandre
Popov, Sergei, 1)
Schnackenberg, Friedemann
Senior, Rodney
Thompson, James
Vacchiano, William, 1), 5)
Vaillant, Ludovic, 5)
Volovnik, Iosif
Wesenigk, Fritz
Wilbraham, John, 8)

ₜFantistic Dances (3), piano, op. 5, (1922); arr. trumpet & pianoₜ
Three Fantastic Dances, op. 5
Dokshitser, Timofei, 7), 9), 35), 39)

Shreffler, Ted, 20th cent.

ɾHomophonium I, solo trumpet & 4 trumpetsɹ
Homophonium I
The 4 ensemble trumpets may be "live" or "pre-recorded" in actual performance.
Parker, Craig B.

Shtegman, Igor, 1932-

ɾParaphrase of Porgy and Bess, harp, trumpet, 2 horns, trombone & tubaɹ
Paraphrase of Gershwin's *Porgy and Bess*
Paniotov, Kharlampi

Shteiman
See: Steiman, S.

Shteynberg
See: Steinberg, M.

Sibelius, Jean, 1865-1957
Sibelius, Johann Julius Christian

ɾFINLANDIA; arr. trumpet & studio orchestraɹ
Be Still, My Soul
This hymn-tune is adapted from Sibelius' symphonic tone-poem, "Finlandia", op. 26, (1900).
Nagel, Robert, 9)

Sidelnikov, Nikolai, 1930-
Sidel'nikov, Nikolay Nikolayevich

ɾConcerto, "Russian Tales", chamber ensemble, (1968)ɹ
Concerto for 12 Soloists, "Russkiye skazki"
("Russian Tales")
Trumpet is included as one of the 12 solo instruments.
Prokopov, Vyacheslav

Silverman, Faye-Ellen, 1947-

ɾPassing Fancies, chamber ensembleɹ
Passing Fancies
Chamber ensemble includes: flute/piccolo, oboe, clarinet/bass clarinet, bassoon, horn, trumpet, trombone, timpani/percussion, 2 violins, viola, cello & bass.
Potpourri, 38)

Simon, Frank, 1889-1967

ₐWillow Echoes, cornet & piano, (1920)₎
Willow Echoes
          Burke, James, 7)
          Gardner, Ned
          Schwarz, Gerard, 19)
          Smith, Leonard B.
          Tobe, Yutaka

Simpson, Thomas, 1582-*ca.* 1630

ₐIntrada; arr. 2 trumpets & 4 trombones₎
Intrada
          André, Maurice, 176)

Sjøberg, C.L.

ₐTonerna, trumpet & piano₎
Tonerna
          Carl Sjøberg (1861-1900) or Svante Leonard Sjøberg (1873-1935)?
          Christensen, Ketil

Skillings, Otis, 1935-

ₐNow Walk with God, mixed voices; arr. trumpet & studio orchestra₎
Now Walk with God
          Nagel, Robert, 9)

Skryabin, Aleksandre
See: Scriabin, Alexander

Smetana, Bedřich, 1824-1884

ₐBartered Bride, (1866). Dance of the Comedians; arr. trumpet & orchestra₎
Dance of the Comedians from *The Bartered Bride*
          Méndez, Rafael, 20)

Smirnova Solodchenkova, Tatiana Georgievna, 1940-

ₐSonata-Ballada, trumpet & piano₎
Sonata-Ballada
          Usov, Yuri

Smith, Clay, 1878-1930

ₐCascades, cornet, trombone & piano, (c. 1904)₎
The Cascades - Polka Brillante
          Schwarz, Gerard, 21)

Smith, Leonard B., 1915-
Smith, Leonard Bingley

₍Picnic Time, cornet (trumpet) & piano₎
Picnic Time
Amstutz, Keith

₍Vignette, cornet & piano, (1940)₎
Vignette
Smith, Leonard B.

Smith, Walter M., 1891-1937

₍Three Kings, cornet trio & band, (1932); arr. cornet trio & chamber ensemble₎
Three Kings
Schwarz, Gerard, 5)

Sokol, Thomas, 1929-

₍Sonatina, trumpet & piano₎
Sonatina
Stith, Marice, 4)

Soler, (Padre) Antonio, 1729-1783
Soler Ramos, Antonio Francisco Javier José

₍Minué, D major; arr. trumpet & organ₎
Minué in D major
Tarr, Edward, 7)

Somers, Harry S., 1925-
Somers, Harry Stewart

₍Gloria, tenor, mixed voices, 2 trumpets & organ, (1964)₎
Gloria
Umbrico, Joseph

Sommerfeldt, Øistein, 1919-

₍Divertimento, solo trumpet, op. 21₎
Divertimento for Trumpet Solo, op. 21
Kvebaek, Harry

₍Elegy, trumpet & organ, op. 27₎
Elegy, op. 27
Nystrom, Kaj

Southers, Leroy W., 1941-
Southers, Leroy William

₍Evolutions, trumpet & organ₎
Evolutions
Plog, Anthony, 2)

ᵣSpheres (3), trumpet, bassoon & pianoᵣ
Three Spheres
Sphere I / Sphere II / Sphere III
Plog, Anthony, 5)

Speer, Daniel, 1636-1707

ᵣGrund-richtiger... Unterricht der musikalischen Kunst, (1697). Intrade, 2 cornetti, trombone & continuo, C major; arr. 2 trumpets, trombone & positive organ, B♭ majorᵣ
Intrade
(Intrada in B♭ major)
Holy, Walter, 4)

ᵣNeugebachene Taffel-Schnitz, (1685). Aufzugsmusiken (2), 6 trumpets & timpaniᵣ
Zwei Aufzuge
Idinger, Matthias
Immer, Friedemann, 18)

ᵣNeugebachene Taffel-Schnitz, (1685). Aufzugsmusiken (3), 6 trumpets & timpani; arr. 3 trumpets, 3 trombones & timpaniᵣ
Fanfares (3)
(Drei Aufzuge)
Jones, Philip, 9)

ᵣNeugebachene Taffel-Schnitz, (1685). Sonata, trumpet & 3 trombonesᵣ
Sonate für Trompete und 3 Posaunen
Eklund's Baroque Ensemble
Idinger, Matthias
Immer, Friedemann, 18)

ᵣNeugebachene Taffel-Schnitz, (1685). Sonata, trumpet, 3 trombones & continuo, C majorᵣ
Sonate für Trompete, 3 Posaunen und Continuo
Jones, Philip, 9)

ᵣSonata, cornetto & 3 trombonesᵣ
Sonate für Zink und 3 Posaunen
Immer, Friedemann, 18)
Stradner, Gerhard

ᵣSonata, 2 trumpets, 3 trombones & continuoᵣ
Sonate für 2 Trompeten, 3 Posaunen und Orgel
Potpourri, 30)

ᵣSonatas (2), 2 cornetti & 3 trombonesᵣ
Zwei Sonaten für 2 Zinken und 3 Posaunen
Immer, Friedemann, 18)

ᵣSonatas. No. 28: 2 trumpets & 3 trombonesᵣ
Sonate Nr. 28 a 5
Eklund's Baroque Ensemble

Sperger, Johann Matthias, 1750-1812

ɾConcerto, corno da caccia, strings & continuo, D majorɿ
Konzert D-dur für Corno da caccia
This concerto is intended for a valveless instrument. The instrument used for this recording is a modern valved "corno da caccia".
Güttler, Ludwig, 20²)

ɾConcerto, corno da caccia, strings & continuo, D major; arr. "clarinhorn", strings & continuoɿ
Konzert D-dur für Corno da caccia
Streitwieser, Franz Xaver

ɾConcerto, corno da caccia, strings & continuo, no. 2, D majorɿ
Konzert D-dur für Corno da caccia, Nr. 2
This concerto is intended for a valveless instrument. The instrument used for this recording is a modern valved "corno da caccia".
Güttler, Ludwig, 21)

ɾConcerto, trumpet, strings & continuo, no. 2, D majorɿ
Konzert D-dur für Trompete, Nr. 2
Potpourri, 20), 40)

Stachowicz, Damian, 1658-1699

ɾConcerto, "Veni Consolator", soprano, trumpet & organɿ
Veni Consolator
(Concerto a 2)
Haas, Wolfgang
Schetsche, Walter

Staden, Johann, 1581-1634

ɾAufzug, cornetto & 3 pommersɿ
Aufzug
Although this work is included on an album listed under Edward Tarr, the cornetto player is Albrecht Renz.
Tarr, Edward, 10)

Staigers, Del, 1899-1950
Staigers, Charles Delaware

ɾVariations (Carnival of Venice), cornet & band, (1928); arr. cornet & brass bandɿ
Carnival of Venice, Fantasia Brillante
McCann, Phillip

[Variations (Carnival of Venice), cornet & band, (1928); arr. cornet & piano]
Carnival of Venice, Fantasia Brillante
The piano reduction was published in 1928 as "Carnival of Venice, Fantasia Brillante", Solo for B♭ Cornet (Trumpet), Baritone, (or Euphonium) or E♭ Alto Saxophone.
Haynie, John, 1)
Lieberman, Harold J.

[Variations (Carnival of Venice), cornet & band, (1928); arr. trumpet & brass ensemble]
Carnival of Venice, Fantasia Brillante
Canadian Brass, 4), 6)

[Variations (Carnival of Venice), cornet & band, (1928); arr. trumpet & instrumental accompaniment]
Carnival of Venice, Fantasia Brillante
Andersen, Ole

[Variations (Carnival of Venice), cornet & band, (1928); arr. trumpet & piano]
Carnival of Venice, Fantasia Brillante
Christensen, Ketil

[Variations (Carnival of Venice), cornet & band, (1928); arr. trumpet & wind ensemble]
Carnival of Venice, Fantasia Brillante
Head, Emerson

Stamitz, Johann Wenzel Anton, 1717-1757

[Concerto, trumpet & orchestra, D major]
Konzert D-dur für Trompete und Orchester
Hardenberger, Håkan

Stanley, John, 1712-1786

[Solos (6), flute, violin or harpsichord, op. 4, (1745). No. 5, D major; arr. trumpet & organ]
Solo in D major, op. 4, no. 5
[1]Adagio / [2]Allegro / Adagio (op. 4, no. 4) / [3]Gigg
Schultz, Erik, 4)

[Voluntaries (10), organ, op. 5, (1748). No. 1, C major; arr. trumpet & organ]
Voluntary in C major, op. 5, no. 1
a) Adagio (Diapasons) / b) Andante (Trumpet) / c) Slow (Swell) / d) Allegro (Ecchos)
Rhoten, Bruce
Steele-Perkins, Crispian, 15)

[Voluntaries (10), organ, op. 5, (1748). No. 5, D major; arr. trumpet & organ]
Voluntary in D major, op. 5, no. 5
a) Slow (Diapasons) / b) Allegro (Trumpet)
Steele-Perkins, Crispian, 15)
Stringer, Alan, 3)

ₜVoluntaries (10), organ, op. 5, (1748). No. 7, g minor; arr. cornetto & organₜ

Voluntary in g minor, op. 5, no. 7
a) Adagio (Diapasons) / b) Allegro (Cornet)
Steele-Perkins, Crispian, 15)

ₜVoluntaries (10), organ, op. 5, (1748). No. 8, d minor: Adagio; arr. trumpet & organₜ

Voluntary in d minor, op. 5, no. 8b
Included as the third section of "A Trumpet Voluntary" that combines sections from four different voluntaries.
Scherbaum, Adolf, 17)

ₜVoluntaries (10), organ, op. 5, (1748). No. 8, d minor: Allegro; arr. trumpet & organₜ

Voluntary in d minor, op. 5, no. 8a
Included as the third section of a "Voluntary in d" combined with op. 6, no. 1.
Steele-Perkins, Crispian, 15)

ₜVoluntaries (10), organ, op. 6, (1752). No. 1, d minor; arr. trumpet & organₜ

Voluntary in d minor, op. 6, no. 1
a) Siciliano (Swell) / b) Andante (Eccho)
Included as the first two sections of a "Voluntary in d" combined with the first section of op. 5, no. 8.
Steele-Perkins, Crispian, 15)

ₜVoluntaries (10), organ, op. 6, (1752). No. 5, D major: Andante Largo; arr. trumpet & organₜ

Voluntary in D major, op. 6, no. 5b
(Trumpet Voluntary)
(Trumpet Tune)

> **André, Maurice**, 40), 52), 67), 227)
> **Blair, Stacy**
> **Braz, Dirceu**, 4)
> **Carroll, Edward**, 6)
> **Mertens, Theo**, 2)
> **Potpourri**, 1)
> **Scherbaum, Adolf**, 17)
> **Steele-Perkins, Crispian**, 15)
> **Wilbraham, John**, 24)

ₜVoluntaries (10), organ, op. 6, (1752). No. 5, D major: Andante Largo; arr. trumpet & stringsₜ

Voluntary in D major, op. 6, no. 5b
(Trumpet Voluntary in D major)
(Trumpet Tune in D major)

> **Burns, Stephen**
> **Sauter, Hermann**, 25)
> **Voisin, Roger**, 5), 8)
> **Wobisch, Helmut**, 3)

[Voluntaries (10), organ, op. 6, (1752). No. 5, d minor/D major; arr. trumpet & organ]
Voluntary in d/D, op. 6, no. 5
a) Adagio (Diapasons) / b) Andante Largo (Trumpet) / c) Moderato (Swell)
Rhoten, Bruce

[Voluntaries (10), organ, op. 6, (1752). No. 5, d minor/D major: excerpts; arr. trumpet & organ]
Voluntary in d/D, op. 6, no. 5a/b
a) Adagio (Diapasons) / b) Andante Largo (Trumpet)
Smithers, Don, 7)
Tarr, Edward, 39)

[Voluntaries (10), organ, op. 6, (1752). No. 6, D major; arr. trumpet & organ]
Voluntary in D major, op. 6, no. 6
a) Adagio (Diapasons) / b) Andante (Trumpet) / c) Adagio
(Swell) / d) Allegro moderato (Ecchos)
André, Maurice, 163)
Carroll, Edward, 6)

[Voluntaries (10), organ, op. 6, (1752). No. 6, D major: excerpts; arr. trumpet & organ]
Voluntary in D major, op. 6, no. 6a/b
a) Adagio (Diapasons) / b) Andante (Trumpet)
Included as the second and third sections of a "Voluntary in D"
combined with op. 6, no. 5b as the first part.
Steele-Perkins, Crispian, 15)

[Voluntaries (10), organ, op. 7, (1754). No. 5, D major: Vivace; arr. trumpet & organ]
Voluntary in D major, op. 7, no. 5b
Scherbaum, Adolf, 17)
Steele-Perkins, Crispian, 15)
Tarr, Edward, 39)

[Voluntaries (10), organ, op. 7, (1754). No. 6, F major; arr. flügelhorn & organ]
Voluntary in F major, op. 7, no. 6
a) Andante (Diapasons) / b) Vivace (Corno or Diapasons)
Steele-Perkins, Crispian, 15)

[Voluntaries (10), organ, op. 7, (1754). No. 9, G major: Largo staccato; arr. trumpet & organ]
Voluntary in G major, op. 7, no. 9a
Scherbaum, Adolf, 29)

ₜVoluntaries, organ, opus unspecified; arr. trumpet & organₙ
Voluntary
(Trumpet Voluntary or Trumpet Tune)
These voluntaries were not specifically identified by opus and have not been further researched. (Most of these are likely the "Voluntary in D major", op. 6, no. 5b.)
> **Bodenröder, Robert**
> **Chesnut, Walter**
> **Deside**
> **Wilbraham, John**, 3)

Stanley, Leo, 20th cent.

ₜHuntsmen, posthorn & bandₙ
The Huntsmen
> **Head, Emerson**

Starer, Robert, 1924-

ₜConcerto, clarinet, trumpet, trombone & strings, (1954)ₙ
Concerto a tre
> **Schwarz, Gerard**, 11)

Starzer, Joseph, *ca.* 1726-1787

ₜMusica da camera, 2 chalumeaux, 5 trumpets & timpani, C majorₙ
Musica da camera molto particulare
[1]Allegro moderato / [2]Menuetto / [3]Adagio / [4]Menuetto / [5]Allegro
This work, along with 3 additional movements transcribed from Gluck's opera, *Paride ed Elena*, has formerly been attributed to W.A. Mozart as *Divertimento No. 5 in C major*, K. 187. (Mozart replaced the chalumeaux with flutes.)
For additional listings, *see:* Mozart, W.A.
> **Tarr, Edward**, 34)

Stauffer, Eric, 1921-

ₜFantasie, trumpet & organ, (1971)ₙ
Fantasie
> **Haas, Wolfgang**

Stebbins, Goerge C., 1846-1945

ₜADELAIDE, (1907); arr. flügelhorn & pianoₙ
Have Thine Own Way, Lord
> **Thomas, Peggy Paton**

Steibelt, Daniel, 1765-1823

₍Ballo; arr. trumpet & piano₎
Ballo
>> Included as the second part of a transcription by Robert Getchell, "Menuet and Ballo". (The menuet is by James Hook.)
>> **Geyer, Charles**

Steiman, S.
Shteiman, S.

₍Corner; arr. cornet with accompaniment₎
"Corner", Romance
>> **Klochkov, Pavel, 3)**

Steinberg, M.
Shteinberg, M.

₍Troika; arr. cornet with accompaniment₎
"Troika", Gypsy Romance
>> **Klochkov, Pavel, 3)**

Steiner-Kimmel, Michael, 1957-

₍Pieces (2), 2 trumpets₎
Two Short Pieces for 2 Trumpets
>> **Cesare, James**

Stevens, Halsey, 1908-

₍Sonata, trumpet & piano, (1959)₎
Sonata for Trumpet and Piano
>> [1]Allegro moderato / [2]Adagio tenero / [3]Allegro
>> **Darling, James**
>> **Hickman, David, 3)**
>> **Plog, Anthony, 4)**
>> **Stith, Marice, 3)**

Stevens, Thomas, 1938-

₍Moudon Fanfares, 2 solo trumpets & 2 trumpet quintets, (1979)₎
The Moudon Fanfares for Twelve Trumpets
>> [1]Fanfare Deux à Dix / [2]Fanfare *BIM* / [3]Fanfare Tranquille / [4]Fanfare Clifford / [5]Fanfare Epilogue Deux à Dix
>> **Giangiulio, Richard**

₍New Carnival of Venice, 4 trumpets & piano, (1985)₎
A New Carnival of Venice
>> **Stevens, Thomas, 9)**

ᵣVariations on Clifford Intervals, trumpet, vibraphone & bass, (1983)₁
Variations on Clifford Intervals
(after jazz solos by Clifford Brown)
Stevens, Thomas, 9)

Stith, Marice W., 1926-

ᵣMy Hand in God's, trumpet & organ₁
My Hand in God's
Stith, Marice, 9)

Stockhausen, Karlheinz, 1928-

ᵣDonnerstag aus Licht, soli, mixed voices, orchestra & electronics, (1977-80)₁
Donnerstag aus Licht
(Opera in 3 acts: "Thursday from Light")
Stockhausen, Markus, 5)

ᵣEnsemble, chamber ensemble, (1967)₁
Ensemble
Chamber ensemble includes: flute, oboe, clarinet, bassoon, horn, trumpet, trombone, violin, cello, bass, percussion & electric organ.
Twelve additional composers were involved in the creation of this work: Tomás Marco, Avo Somer, Nicolaus Huber, Róbert Wittinger, John McGuire, Peter Farmer, Gregory Biss, Jürgen Beurle, Mesias Maiguashca, Jorge Peixinho, Rolf Gehlhaar and Johannes Fritsch.
Jurča, Vladimir

ᵣKontra-Punkte, chamber ensemble, (1952-53)₁
Kontra-Punkte
Chamber ensemble includes: flute, clarinet, bass clarinet, bassoon, trumpet, trombone, violin, cello, harp & piano.
Miller, John

ᵣOberlippentanz, solo trumpet₁
Oberlippentanz
Stockhausen, Markus, 1)

ᵣSirius, soprano, bass, trumpet, bass clarinet & electronics, (1975-77)₁
Sirius
Stockhausen, Markus, 3)

ₜSternklang, 5 chamber groups, (1969-71)ₜ
Sternklang
("Star Sound", Park Music for 5 Groups)
Group I: synthesizer, viola with synthesizer, bassoon with synthesizer & electric organ with synthesizer.
Group II: soprano, trombone with synthesizer, bass & electronium with synthesizer.
Group III: mezzo-soprano, 2 tenors & trombone with synthesizer.
Group IV: violin with synthesizer, clarinet with synthesizer, electric organ with synthesizer & cello with synthesizer.
Group V: trumpet with synthesizer, clarinet with synthesizer, recorder/alto voice & recorder/bass voice.
Stockhausen, Markus, 4)

ₜStop, 6 chamber groups, (1973 version)ₜ
Stop
Group I: oboe, piano & electric organ.
Group II: trumpet, cello & electronium.
Group III: bass clarinet, electric cello & percussion.
Group IV: English horn, bassoon & synthesizer.
Group V: clarinet, trombone, violin & harp.
Group VI: flute, horn & electric bassoon/alto saxophone/synthesizer.
Miller, John

ₜYlem, chamber orchestra, (1973 version)ₜ
Ylem
Chamber orchestra includes: flute, oboe, English horn, clarinet, bass clarinet, electric saxophone/synthesizer, bassoon, horn, trumpet, trombone, violin, cello, electric cello, harp, piano, electric organ, synthesizer, electronium, vibraphon & tamtam.
Miller, John

Stockmeier, Wolfgang, 1931-

ₜPieces (2), trumpet & organₜ
Zwei Stücke für Trompete und Orgel
¹Präludium / ²Elegie
Rhoten, Bruce

Stoltzer, Thomas, *ca.* 1482-1526
Stolczer, Thomas

ₜOcto tonorum melodiae. Melodia 8, pommer, cornetto, trombone, viola da gamba & luteₜ
Melodia 8 (hypomixolydisch)
Caudle, Theresa

Stölzel, Gottfried Heinrich, 1690-1749
Stoelzel, Gottfried Heinrich
Stöltzel, Gottfried Heinrich

[Aria, "Bist du bei mir"; arr. cornet & piano]
Bist du bei mir
Formerly attributed to J.S. Bach, S. 508.
Masters, Edward L.

[Aria, "Bist du bei mir"; arr. trumpet & orchestra]
Bist du bei mir
Formerly attributed to J.S. Bach, S. 508.
André, Maurice, 85), 153, 215))

[Aria, "Bist du bei mir"; arr. trumpet & organ]
Bist du bei mir
Formerly attributed to J.S. Bach, S. 508.
Braz, Dirceu, 1)
Chesnut, Walter
Hunger, Helmut, 5)
Smithers, Don, 6)

[Aria, "Bist du bei mir"; arr. trumpet & piano]
Bist du bei mir
Formerly attributed to J.S. Bach, S. 508.
Amstutz, Keith
House, Lawrence
Schwarz, Gerard, 14)

[Concerto grosso, D major]
Concerto a quattro cori
(Concerto grosso in D major for 6 Trumpets)
[1]Allegro / [2]Adagio / [3]Allegro
This concerto grosso is for 4 groups plus timpani and continuo.
I: 3 trumpets; II: 3 trumpets; III: flute, 3 oboes & bassoon;
IV: strings.
André, Maurice, 47), 143), 168), 169), 216)
Delmotte, Roger, 15), 23), 49)
Holy, Walter, 7), 8)
Potpourri, 21), 34), 35), 44)
Zickler, Heinz, 7)

[Concerto, oboe, strings & continuo, D major; arr. trumpet & strings]
Konzert D-dur für Trompete und Streichorchester
[1]Allegro / [2]Andante / [3]Allegro
André, Maurice, 22), 28), 31), 117), 169), 191),
193), 194), 197)
Bernard, André, 3)
Petz, Pál
Potpourri, 44)

ɾConcertos, Concertino & Sonata; arr. trumpet, strings & harpsichordɹ
Concertos pour Trompette
This index entry refers to an album that has not been researched.
It contains: concerti in B♭, C & D; a concertino in e minor; and a
sonata in D.
Soustrot, Bernard, 3)

ɾSonata, oboe(?) & continuo, D major; arr. trumpet & stringsɹ
Sonate D-dur für Trompete und Streicher
[1]Andante / [2]Allegro / [3]Adagio / [4]Vivace
André, Maurice, 36), 41), 63)

Störl, Johann Georg Christian, 1675-1719

ɾSonata, cornetto & 3 trombones, (c. 1696)ɹ
Sonate für Zink und drei Posaunen
Idinger, Matthias

Stradella, Alessandro, 1644-1682

ɾAria, "Pieta Signore"ɹ
Aria, "Pieta Signore"
See: Niedermeyer, Louis.

ɾSerenata, "Il Barcheggio", [Part I], (1681). Sinfonia, trumpet, strings & continuo,
D majorɹ
Sinfonia avanti "Il Barcheggio", [Part I]
[1]Spiritosa, e staccata / [2][Allegretto - Corrente] / [3]Canzona /
[4][Allegro]
> **Hunger, Helmut,** 3)
> **Immer, Friedemann,** 11)
> **Kejmar, Miroslav,** 11)
> **Tarr, Edward,** 31)
> **Voisin, Roger,** 6), 8)

ɾSerenata, "Il Barcheggio", [Part I], (1681). Sinfonia, trumpet, strings & continuo,
D major; arr. trumpet, flute, oboe, violin & continuoɹ
Sinfonia avanti "Il Barcheggio", [Part I]
[1]Spiritosa, e staccata / [2][Allegretto - Corrente] / [3]Canzona /
[4][Allegro]
> **Güttler, Ludwig,** 8)

ɾSerenata, "Il Barcheggio", [Part II], (1681). Sinfonia, trumpet, 2 violins &
continuo, D majorɹ
Sinfonia avanti "Il Barcheggio", [Part II]
[1][Allegro] / [2][Andante / [3][Allegro] / [4][Allegro]
Immer, Friedemann, 9)

ɾSerenata, "Il Barcheggio", [Part II], (1681). Sinfonia, trumpet, 2 violins &
continuo, D major; arr. trumpet, flute, oboe, violin & continuoɹ
Sinfonia avanti "Il Barcheggio", [Part II]
[1][Allegro] / [2][Andante / [3][Allegro] / [4][Allegro]
Güttler, Ludwig, 14)

[Sonata; arr. trumpet & organ]
Sonata de concert
Delmotte, Roger, 38)
Potpourri, 43)

[Sonata, trumpet, strings & continuo, D major]
Sonata a otto Viole con una Tromba
(Sinfonia in D major for Trumpet and Double String Orchestra)
[1][Allegro] or [Andante mosso] / [2]Aria / [3][Canzona] or [Allegro non troppo] / [4]Aria
Battagliola, Anania
Immer, Friedemann, 11)
Keavy, Stephen
Potpourri, 35)
Sauter, Hermann, 28)
Scherbaum, Adolf, 19), 25)
Tarr, Edward, 1), 31)
Voisin, Roger, 7), 8)

[Sonata, 2 cornetti, 2 violins & continuo, D major]
Sonata a quattro
[1]Allegro / [2]Andante / [3]Presto
This sonata is a "mini concerto grosso" with two groups of instruments. The 2 cornetti are supported by organ & trombone, and the 2 violins are supported by harpsichord & cello.
Immer, Friedemann, 11)
Tarr, Edward, 1), 31)

Strauss, Richard, 1864-1949
Strauss, Richard Georg

[Lieder, op. 10. No. 8: Allerseelen, voice & piano; arr. cornet & piano]
Allerseelen, op. 10, no. 8
Tolley, Richard

[Stimmungsbilder, piano, op. 9, (1882-1884). No. 2: An einsamer Quelle; arr. trumpet & piano]
An einsamer Quelle from *Stimmungsbilder*, op. 9
(Beside the Spring)
Dokshitser, Timofei, 31)

Stravinsky, Igor Fyodorovich, 1882-1971
Strawinsky, Igor Fjodorovitch

[Concertino, string quartet, (1920); arr. chamber ensemble, (1952)]
Concertino for 12 Instruments
Chamber ensemble includes: flute, oboe, English horn, clarinet, 2 bassoons, 2 trumpets, 2 trombones, violin & cello.
Ghitalla, Armando, 7)
Vasse, Claude

 ₍Fanfare for a New Theatre, 2 trumpets, (1964)₎
Fanfare for a New Theatre
                    Heinrich, Robert (+ Robert Nagel)
                    Hoffman, Edward (+ James Thompson)
                    Logan, Jack (+ Ronald Modell)
                    Stevens, Thomas, 4) (+ Mario Guarneri)
                    Watson, James (+ Paul Archibald)

 ₍Histoire du Soldat, (1918). Suite, violin & chamber ensemble₎
l'Histoire du Soldat, Suite
(A Soldier's Tale)
   ¹The Soldier's March / ²Soldier at the Brook / ³Pastorale / ⁴The Royal
March / ⁵The Little Concerto / ⁶Three Dances: (Tango, Waltz,
Ragtime) / ⁷The Devil's Dance / ⁸Chorale / ⁹Triumphal March of the
Devil
   In addition to the solo violin, the ensemble includes: clarinet,
   bassoon, cornet (or trumpet), trombone, bass & percussion. (The
   suite does not include narration.)
                    Brady, Charles
                    Clift, Dennis
                    Cuvit, Michel
                    Foriscot, J.
                    Foveau, Eugène
                    Herseth, Adolph, 4)
                    Jandorf, D.
                    Longinotti, Paolo
                    Mills, Fred
                    Nagel, Robert, 1)
                    Plog, Anthony, 8)
                    Spindler, Josef, 1)
                    Voisin, Roger, 10)
                    Volodin, Lev
                    Vosburgh, George
                    Weis, Theodore, 5)

 ₍Histoire du Soldat, 3 narrators, solo violin & chamber ensemble, (1918). English₎
A Soldier's Tale
(l'Histoire du Soldat)
   Chamber ensemble includes: clarinet, bassoon, cornet (or
   trumpet), trombone, bass & percussion.
                    Ghitalla, Armando, 9)
                    Unidentified, Trumpet(s), 22)
                    Walton, Richard
                    Weis, Theodore, 4)

₍Histoire du Soldat, 3 narrators, solo violin & chamber ensemble, (1918). French₎
l'Histoire du Soldat
Chamber ensemble includes: clarinet, bassoon, cornet (or trumpet), trombone, bass & percussion.
>André, Maurice, 181)
>Cuvit, Michel
>Delmotte, Roger, 35)
>Ghitalla, Armando, 8)
>Weis, Theodore, 4)

₍Histoire du Soldat, 3 narrators, solo violin & chamber ensemble, (1918). German₎
Die Geschichte vom Soldat
(l'Histoire du Soldat)
Chamber ensemble includes: clarinet, bassoon, cornet (or trumpet), trombone, bass & percussion.
>Ghitalla, Armando, 6)

₍Octet, chamber ensemble, (1922-23)₎
Octet for Wind Instruments
¹Sinfonia / ²Tema con variazioni / ³Finale
Chamber ensemble includes: flute, clarinet, 2 bassoons, 2 trumpets & 2 trombones.
>Cuvit, Michel
>Ghitalla, Armando, 7)
>Mager, Georges
>Margolin, Veniamin
>Mičaník, Jaroslav
>Nagel, Robert, 1), 4)
>Prokopov, Vyacheslav
>Watson, James

₍Petrouchka, (1911). Danse de la Ballerina, cornet & snare drum; arr. trumpet & piano₎
Dance of the Ballerina from *Petrouchka*
>Schwarz, Gerard, 16)

₍Petrouchka, (1911). Danse de la Ballerina, cornet & snare drum; excerpt, solo trumpet₎
Danse de la Ballerina from *Petrouchka*
>Voisin, Roger, 13)

₍Ragtime, chamber ensemble, (1918)₎
Ragtime for 11 Instruments
Chamber ensemble includes: cimbalom, flute/piccolo, clarinet/E♭-clarinet, horn, trumpet, trombone, percussion, 2 violins, viola & bass.
>Adelbrecht, Henri, 3)
>Ghitalla, Armando, 7)

┌Renard, soli & chamber ensemble, (1916-17)┐
Renard
> (Histoire burlesque chantée et jouée)
> Vocal soloists are: 2 tenors, baritone & bass.
> Chamber ensemble includes: flute/piccolo, oboe/English horn, clarinet/E^b-clarinet, bassoon, 2 horns, trumpet, timpani, 2 percussion, 2 violins, viola, cello & bass.
> **Adelbrecht, Henri,** 3)

Stubley, Simon, 18th cent.

┌Voluntaries (10), (c. 1767). No. 3b: organ or harpsichord, C major; arr. trumpet & organ┐
Voluntary in C major
> The source for this voluntary is *Ten Voluntaries for the Organ or Harpsichord Composed by Dr Green / Skinner / Stubley / James / Reading / Selby & Kuknan,* (c. 1767).
> This voluntary is included as the second section of Edward Tarr's "Suite of Trumpet Voluntaries by Handel & His Contemporaries" [published by The Brass Press]. It is also included in the Musica Rara collection, "Six Voluntaries for Trumpet & Organ" edited by Barry Cooper. (The Musica Rara edition includes the slow introductory part of the voluntary.)
> **Carroll, Edward,** 6)
> **Güttler, Ludwig,** 2)
> **Haas, Wolfgang**
> **Tarr, Edward,** 41)

Subotnick, Morton, 1933-

┌After the Butterfly, trumpet, chamber ensemble & "ghost" electronics, (1979)┐
After the Butterfly
> [1]Cocoon / [2]Butterfly / [3]After the Butterfly
> Chamber ensemble includes: 2 clarinets, 2 trombones, 2 celli & percussion.
> **Guarneri, Mario**

Sullivan, Arthur Seymour, 1842-1900

┌Lost Chord, (1877); arr. trumpet & orchestra┐
The Lost Chord
> **Hirt, Al**

Sulpizi, Fernando, 1936-

┌Suite Trovadorica, "Les Jongleurs", trumpet & piano, op. 16┐
Suite Trovadorica, "Les Jongleurs", op. 16
> **Gardner, Ned**

Sumner, John B., 1838-1918

ₜChild of the King; arr. flügelhorn/trumpet & organ₁
Child of the King
Tolley, Richard

Surinach, Carlos, 1915-

ₜRitmo Jondo, trumpet, clarinet, xylophone & percussion, (1952)₁
Ritmo Jondo
Potpourri, 31)

Susato, Tielman, *ca.* 1500-*ca.* 1561

ₜDanserye, (1551). Dances (12), instrumental ensemble₁
Twelve Dances
(from *Danserye, Het derde Musyck boexken*)
[1]La Mourisque / [2]Branle Quatre Bransles / [3]Ronde & Salterelle /
[4]Ronde mon amy / [5]Allemaigne & Recoupe / [6]Pavane Mille regretz /
[7]Basse Danse Bergeret sans roch & Reprise / [8]Danse du Roy / [9]Ronde /
[10]Passe et Medio & Reprise le pingue / [11]Ronde / [12]Pavane La Bataille
Instrumental ensemble includes: recorders, crumhorns, dulcian,
rackett, cornetti, sackbuts, strings, lute, regal & harpsichord.
Percussion parts have also been added according to examples
prescribed by Thoinot Arbeau in *Orchésographie*, 1589.
Smithers, Don, 3)

ₜDanserye, (1551). Dances (7), instrumental ensemble₁
Suite of Dances
(from *Danserye, Het derde Musyck boexken*)
[1]Basse danse, "La mourisque" / [2]Branle & "Fagot" / [3]Two Rondes /
[4]Basse danse & Reprise / [5]Allemaingne & Recoupe / [6]Pavane, "Mille
regretz" / [7]Pavane, "La batille"
Instrumental ensemble includes: recorders, crumhorns, schryari,
shawms, cornetto, sackbuts, strings, portative organ, regal,
harpsichord & percussion.
Montesi, Robert, 4)

ₜDanserye, (1551). Suite; arr. trumpet, organ & brass ensemble₁
Suite from *Het Derde Musyck Boexken*
[1]Rondo / [2]Pavane / [3]Saltarello
Grin, Freddy, 9)

Suter, Hermann, 1870-1926

ₜFanfares et Pastorales, trumpet, 2 horns & trombone, (1965)₁
Fanfares et Pastorales
Jones, Philip, 6)

Svirsky, Rudolf, 1918-

₍Scherzo, trumpet & piano, g minor₎
Scherzo in g minor
Usov, Yuri

Sweelinck, Jan Pieterszoon, 1562-1621

₍Flemish Dances (4); arr. trumpet & harp₎
Four Flemish Dances
(Vier flämische Tänze)
¹Ballo del Granduca / ²Courante / ³Volte / ⁴Pavane
The first dance is arranged for trumpet, harp & percussion.
André, Maurice, 64)

Symonds, Norman A., 1920-
Symonds, Norman Alec

₍Nameless Hour, flügelhorn & orchestra, (1966)₎
The Nameless Hour
Stone, Fred

Tabourot, Jehan
See: Arbeau, Thoinot

Tadasi, Yananda, 1885-1959
Tadashi, Yanada (Yanaida)

₍Jogashima No Ame; arr. trumpet & piano₎
Jogashima No Ame
(Rain on Jogashima)
Dokshitser, Timofei, 19)

Tadasuke, Ono, 1895-1930

₍Hana; arr. trumpet & piano₎
Hana
(Flower)
Dokshitser, Timofei, 19)

Tag, Christian Gotthilf, 1735-1811

₍Chorale Prelude, "Befiehl du deine Wege"; arr. trumpet & organ₎
Chorale Prelude, "Befiehl du deine Wege"
Erb, Helmut, 2)

₍Chorale Prelude, "Nun danket alle Gott"; arr. trumpet & organ₎
Chorale Prelude, "Nun danket alle Gott"
Hartog, Thomas
Tarr, Edward, 8)

 ₍Chorale Prelude, "Nun freut euch, lieben Christen g'mein"; arr. trumpet & organ₎
Chorale Prelude, "Nun freut euch, lieben Christen g'mein"
Tarr, Edward, 8)

Tal, Josef, 1910-

 ₍Shape, mezzo-soprano & chamber ensemble, (1975)₎
Shape
Chamber ensemble may include: flute/piccolo, oboe/English horn, clarinet/bass clarinet, bassoon/contrabassoon, 3 horns, 2 trumpets, trombone, tuba, 2 percussion, harp, piano, piano/celeste, 2 violins, viola, cello, bass & tape.
Perry, Brian

Tamberg, Eino Martinovich, 1930-

 ₍Concerto, trumpet & orchestra, op. 42, (1972)₎
Konsert trompetile ja orkestrile, op. 42
(Concerto for Trumpet and Orchestra, op. 42)
Dokshitser, Timofei, 10), 13), 37)

Tarr (arr.), Edward H., 1936-
Tarr, Edward Hankins

 ₍Voluntaries; arr. Suite, trumpet & organ₎
A Suite of Trumpet Voluntaries in C major
[1]Adagio [Stanley, op. 7, no. 5(a)] / [2]Allegro [Stubley] / [3]Allegro [Handel, B. ?25] / [4]Rather slow than fast [Boyce] / [5]Brisk [Boyce]
These individual voluntaries are also cross-referenced under each composer's name.
Edward Tarr has edited and/or arranged many other individual works.
Tarr, Edward, 41)

Tárrega, Francisco, 1852-1909
Tárrega y Eixea, Francisco

 ₍Recuerdos de la Alhambra; arr. trumpet & instrumental accompaniment₎
Recuerdos de la Alhambra
Hidalgo, José Luis

Tartini, Giuseppe, 1692-1770

 ₍Adagio Cantabile; arr. trumpet & organ₎
Adagio Cantabile
Mertens, Theo, 2)

 ₍Concerto, violin, strings & continuo, E major; arr. trumpet & band, D major₎
Concerto in D major for Trumpet and Band
[1]Allegro / [2]Andante / [3]Allegro grazioso
Chunn, Michael

₍Concerto, violin, strings & continuo, E major; arr. trumpet & organ, D major₎
Concerto en ré majeur pour trompette et orgue
[1]Allegro / [2]Andante / [3]Allegro grazioso
Gaudon, Jean-Jacques
Schultz, Erik, 4)
Volle, Bjarne

₍Concerto, violin, strings & continuo, E major; arr. trumpet & strings, D major₎
Concerto en ré majeur pour trompette et orchestre
[1]Allegro / [2]Andante / [3]Allegro grazioso
André, Maurice, 38), 41), 56), 67), 74), 83),
117), 154), 169), 217), 227)
Bernard, André, 8)
Dassé, Jean-Luc
Dokshitser, Timofei, 4), 14), 36)
Soustrot, Bernard, 6)

₍Sonata, violin & continuo. Sarabande; arr. trumpet & piano₎
Sarabande
This sarabande from an unidentified violin sonata is included in a
"Baroque Suite" arranged and edited by Robert Getchell.
Geyer, Charles

Tchaikovsky, Piotr Ilyitch, 1840-1893
Tchaikovski, Pyotr Ilyich
Tschaikowsky, Peter Iljitsch
Chaikovskii, Piotr Il'yich

₍Serenade for Strings, op. 48, (1880). Waltz; arr. trumpet & orchestra₎
Waltz from *Serenade for Strings*, op. 48
Méndez, Rafael, 21)

₍Songs (6), op. 16, (1872). No. 1: Berceuse; arr. trumpet & violin ensemble₎
Berceuse, op. 16, no. 1
("Kolïbel'naya pesnya")
Dokshitser, Timofei, 14), 36), 38), 39)

₍Songs (6), op. 63, (1887). No. 2: I Opened the Window; arr. cornet₎
"I Opened the Window"
("Rastvoril ya okno")
Klochkov, Pavel, 2)

₍Songs (6), op. 65, (1888). No. 1: Where, where did you go; arr. cornet₎
"Where, where did you go"
(Sérénade, "Où vas-tu?")
Klochkov, Pavel, 1)

₍Songs (12), op. 60, (1886). No. 8: Forgive; arr. cornet₎
"Forgive, Heavenly Creature"
("Prosti")
Klochkov, Pavel, 2)

ₜSwan Lake, op. 20, (1875). Neapolitan Dance; arr. trumpet & pianoₒ
Napolitana
Tobe, Yutaka

ₜSwan Lake, op. 20, (1875). Neapolitan Dance, cornet (trumpet) & orchestraₒ
Neapolitan Dance from *Swan Lake*, op. 20
Dokshitser, Timofei, 12), 36), 37), 38), 39)
Ots, Aavo

ₜSymphony, no. 5, e minor, op. 64, (1888). Excerptₒ
Excerpt from *Symphony No. 5 in e minor*, op. 64
This short excerpt is performed on trumpet alone and in orchestral context.
Geisler, Lloyd

Teiichi, Okano
See: Seiti, Okano

Telemann, Georg Philipp, 1681-1767

ₜCantata, "Allein Gott in der Hoh' sei Ehr' ", bass, mixed voices & orchestra, (1750-51)ₒ
Kantata, "Allein Gott in der Hoh' sei Ehr' "
One bass aria is with solo trumpet.
André, Maurice, 122)

ₜConcerto, corno da caccia, oboe, strings & continuo, D major, <Kross: Hr. D>ₒ
Konzert D-dur für Corno da caccia, Orchester und Generalbass
¹Vivace / ²Largo / ³Allegro
This performance is with a "modern valved corno da caccia".
(The oboe part is in unison with the violin.)
Güttler, Ludwig, 27)

ₜConcerto, flute, strings & continuo, G major, <Kross: Fl. G (2)>; arr. trumpet, strings & continuoₒ
Konzert G-dur für Flöte, Streicher und Generalbass
¹Allegro, ma non troppo / ²Adagio, sempre piano [Andante] / ³Allegro
André, Maurice, 18), 28), 87), 158), 169), 214)

ₜConcerto, oboe, strings & continuo, c minor, <Kross: Ob. c (2)>; arr. trumpet, strings & continuoₒ
Konzert c-moll für Oboe, Streicher und Generalbass
¹[Grave] / ²Allegro / ³Andante / ⁴Vivace
André, Maurice, 18), 24), 27), 29), 36), 226)

ₜConcerto, oboe, strings & continuo, e minor, <Kross: Ob. e>; arr. trumpet & organₒ
Concerto en mi mineur pour Trompette et Orgue
¹Andante / ²Allegro molto / ³Largo / ⁴Allegro
Gaudon, Jean-Jacques

[Concerto, oboe, strings & continuo, e minor, <Kross: Ob. e>; arr. trumpet, strings & continuo]
Konzert e-moll für Oboe, Streicher und Generalbass
[1]Andante / [2]Allegro molto / [3]Largo / [4]Allegro
> André, Maurice, 18), 28), 87), 158), 169), 214)
> Potpourri, 44)
> Soustrot, Bernard, 4)

[Concerto, oboe, strings & continuo, E$\flat$ major; arr. trumpet, strings & continuo]
Konzert Es-dur für Oboe, Streicher und Generalbass
[1]Allegro / [2]Largo / [3]Allegro
> Soustrot, Bernard, 4)

[Concerto, oboe, strings & continuo, f minor, <Kross: Ob. f (1)>; arr. trumpet, strings & continuo]
Konzert f-moll für Oboe, Streicher und Generalbass
[1]Allegro / [2]Largo e piano / [3]Vivace
> André, Maurice, 54), 67), 197), 200)
> Hardy, Francis
> Potpourri, 42)
> Schultz, Erik, 8), 10)

[Concerto, oboe, 2 violins & continuo, D major, <Kross: Ob. D>; arr. trumpet, 2 oboes & continuo]
Konzert D-dur für Oboe, Streicher und Generalbass
(Concerto in D major for Trumpet, 2 Oboes and Continuo)
[1][Lento] / [2]Vivace / [3]Adagio / [4]Scherzando
> André, Maurice, 36)

[Concerto, trumpet, 2 oboes & continuo, D major]
Konzert D-dur für Trompete, 2 Oboen und Continuo
[1]Largo / [2]Vivace / [3]Siciliano / [4]Vivace
Since this concerto is really chamber music, it is not catalogued by Kross.
> André, Maurice, 44), 53), 116), 149), 169), 227)
> Bernard, André, 7)
> Güttler, Ludwig, 8)
> Hardenberger, Håkan
> Läubin, Hannes, 1)
> Potpourri, 21), 34), 35)
> Scherbaum, Adolf, 7)
> Schwarz, Gerard, 8)
> Touvron, Guy, 3)
> Voisin, Roger, 4), 8)
> Zickler, Heinz, 9)

[Concerto, trumpet, 2 oboes & continuo, D major. Largo; arr. trumpet & piano, A$\flat$ major]
Largo from *Concerto in D major for Trumpet, 2 Oboes and Continuo*
> Nagel, Robert, 11)

[Concerto, trumpet, 2 oboes, strings & continuo, D major,
  <Kross: 2 Ob. + Trp. D>]
Konzert D-dur für Trompete, 2 Oboen, Streicher und Basso Continuo
[Allegro] / [2]Grave - Aria - Grave / [3][Vivace]
> André, Maurice, 10), 51), 87), 113)
> Basch, Wolfgang, 12)
> Bernard, André, 7)
> Hardenberger, Håkan
> Holy, Walter, 8)
> Potpourri, 40), 42)
> Quinque, Rolf, 6)
> Schneidewind, Helmut, 6)
> Steele-Perkins, Crispian, 13)
> Touvron, Guy, 3)
> Wilbraham, John, 4), 5), 11)

[Concerto, trumpet, 2 oboes, strings & continuo, D major,
  <Kross: 2 Ob. + Trp. D>; arr. trumpet & organ]
Concerto in D major for Trumpet and Organ
[Allegro] / [2]Grave - Aria - Grave / [3][Vivace]
> Willwerth, Paul

[Concerto, trumpet, 2 violins & continuo, D major, <Kross: Trp. D>]
Konzert D-dur für Trompete, Streicher und Generalbass
[1]Adagio / [2]Allegro / [3]Grave / [4]Allegro
> Adelbrecht, Henri, 2)
> André, Maurice, 27), 41), 46), 60), 73), 87),
>   111), 135), 154), 169), 206[1]), 207[1]), 210),
>   213), 219)
> Basch, Wolfgang, 9), 13)
> Bernard, André, 2), 3)
> Blair, Stacy
> Calvayrac, Albert
> Cooper, Grant
> Erb, Helmut, 6)
> Fink, Werner
> Güttler, Ludwig, 7), 13[1-2]), 21[1])
> Hardenberger, Håkan
> Hickman, David, 1)
> Holy, Walter, 7)
> Immer, Friedemann, 7)
> Kejmar, Miroslav, 10)
> Krug, Willi, 1), 4)
> Mertens, Theo, 4[4]), 7)
> Potpourri, 12), 14), 20), 21), 34), 35), 42), 45)
> Preis, Ivo
> Quinque, Rolf, 5), 7)
> Reinhart, Carole Dawn, 3), 4)
> Sauter, Hermann, 25)
> Scherbaum, Adolf, 14), 15), 22), 28)
> Schetsche, Walter

Schneidewind, Helmut, 6), 9)
Schultz, Erik, 5)
Schwarz, Gerard, 7)
Smithers, Don, 4)
Soustrot, Bernard, 9)
Steele-Perkins, Crispian, 2)
Tarr, Edward, 9)
Thibaud, Pierre, 3), 4)
Touvron, Guy, 3)
Tschotschev, Nicolai-Dimitrov
Voisin, Roger, 5), 8)
Wilbraham, John, 9)
Zickler, Heinz, 9), 10)

ₜConcerto, trumpet, 2 violins & continuo, D major, <Kross: Trp. D>; arr.
trumpet & organ₎

Konzert D-dur für Trompete, Streicher und Generalbass
(Concerto in D major for Trumpet and Organ)
[1]Adagio / [2]Allegro / [3]Grave / [4]Allegro
Gabel, Bernard, 5)
Zapf, Gerd

ₜConcerto, unspecified, D major; arr. trumpet & organ₎

Concerto in D major for Trumpet and Organ
This arrangement has not been verified and may be the standard
Concerto in D major for Trumpet, Strings and Continuo.
Gaudon, Jean-Jacques

ₜConcerto, viola, strings & continuo, G major, <Kross: Va. G>; arr. trumpet,
strings & continuo, E♭ major₎

Konzert G-dur für Viola, Streicher und Generalbass
(Concerto in E♭ major for Trumpet, Strings and Continuo)
[1]Largo / [2]Allegro / [3]Andante / [4]Presto
André, Maurice, 137)

ₜConcerto, violin, strings & continuo, B♭ major, <Kross: V. B (1)>; arr. trumpet,
strings & continuo₎

Konzert B-dur für Violine, Streicher und Generalbass
[1]Allegro / [2]Adagio / [3]Allegro
Kejmar, Miroslav, 5)
Soustrot, Bernard, 4)

ₜConcerto, violin, trumpet, cello, strings & continuo, D major,
<Kross: V. + Vc. D>₎

Konzert D-dur für Violine und Violoncelle, Orchester und Generalbass
(Concerto in D major for Violin concertato, Trumpet, Cello obbligato,
Strings & Continuo)
[1]Vivace / [2]Adagio / [3]Allegro
Johnson, Gilbert, 8)
Kejmar, Miroslav, 5)
Sauter, Hermann, 25)
Schneidewind, Helmut, 9), 12)

₍Concerto, 2 flutes, strings & continuo, a minor, <Kross: 2 Fl. a>; arr. 2 trumpets & strings₎

Divertissement pour deux Trompettes
(Konzert a-moll für 2 Flöten, Streicher und Generalbass)
²Vistement / ³Largement / ⁴Vivement
This "Divertissement" is listed in numerous catalogues as having the tonality of **D major**, but, is, in reality, in **a minor**. (The first movement, Gravement, is not included in this arrangement.)
André, Maurice, 173), 184), 193), 197)

₍Concerto, 2 flutes, strings & continuo, B♭ major, <Kross: 2 Fl. B>; arr. 2 trumpets, strings & continuo₎

Konzert B-dur für 2 Flöten, Streicher und Generalbass
¹Grave / ²Vivace / ³Tendrement / ⁴Gayment
Soustrot, Bernard, 4)

₍Concerto, 3 oboes, 3 violins, strings & continuo, B♭ major; arr. 3 trumpets, strings & continuo₎

Konzert B-dur für 3 Oboen und 3 Violinen
¹Allegro / ²Largo / ³Allegro
Not catalogued by Kross.
Marsalis, Wynton, 6)

₍Concerto, 3 trumpets, 2 oboes, timpani, strings & continuo, D major, <Kross: 3 Trp. D (1)>₎

Konzert D-dur für 3 Clarinen, Orchester und Generalbass
¹Intrada / ²Allegro / ³Largo / ⁴Vivace
André, Maurice, 10), 119), 143), 168)
Bauer, Willibald, 3)
Delmotte, Roger, 15), 23²⁺⁴), 49)
Güttler, Ludwig, 1)
Hardenberger, Håkan
Holy, Walter, 8)
Immer, Friedemann, 7)
Johnson, Gilbert, 8)
Kejmar, Miroslav, 5)
Potpourri, 34), 35), 68)
Sauter, Hermann, 3)
Schneidewind, Helmut, 11)
Statter, Arthur
Touvron, Guy, 3)
Ullrich, Marc
Weis, Theodore, 1)

₍Concerto, 3 trumpets, 2 oboes, timpani, strings & continuo, D major, <Kross: 3 Trp. D (2)>₎

Konzert D-dur für 3 Clarinen, Orchester und Generalbass [Nr. 2]
¹Largo / ²Allegro / ³Adagio / ⁴Presto
Immer, Friedemann, 1)
Marsalis, Wynton, 6)
Sauter, Hermann, 1)

[Deutsche Psalmen. Psalm 100, "Jauchzet dem Herrn, alle Welt", bass, trumpet, strings & continuo]

Psalm 100, "Jauchzet dem Herrn, alle Welt"
Sauter, Hermann, 2)
Touvron, Guy, 16)

[Deutsche Psalmen. Psalm 111, "Ich danke dem Herrn von ganzem Herzen", soli, mixed voices & chamber orchestra]

Psalm 111, "Ich danke dem Herrn von ganzem Herzen"
Chamber orchestra includes: solo recorder, solo oboe & solo trumpet with strings & continuo.
Sauter, Hermann, 2)

[Deutsche Psalmen. Psalm 111: Aria, "Er sendet eine Erlösung", bass, trumpet, strings & continuo]

Aria, "Er sendet eine Erlösung" from *Psalm 111*
Reinhart, Carole Dawn, 2)

[Deutsche Psalmen. Psalm 111: Aria, "Ich danke dem Herrn", soprano, trumpet, strings & continuo]

Aria, "Ich danke dem Herrn" from *Psalm 111*
Reinhart, Carole Dawn, 2)

[Deutsche Psalmen. Psalm 117, "Lobet den Herrn, alle Heiden", soprano, alto, 3 trumpets, timpani, strings & continuo]

Psalm 117, "Lobet den Herrn, alle Heiden"
Sauter, Hermann, 2)

[Essercizii musici, (1739-40). No. 2: Trio 1, recorder, oboe & continuo, c minor, TWV 42: c 1; arr. trumpet, oboe & strings]

Triosonate Nr. 1 c-moll
(Concerto en do mineur pour Trompette, Oboe et Orchestre)
[1]Largo / [2]Vivace / [3]Andante / [4]Allegro
André, Maurice, 126), 169), 216)
Kejmar, Miroslav, 5)

[Essercizii musici, (1739-40). No. 9: Solo 5, oboe & continuo, B^b major, TWV 41: B 6; arr. trumpet, harpsichord & bassoon]

Sonate B-dur
(Sonata in B^b major)
[1]Adagio / [2]Allegro / [3]Cantabile / [4]Vivace
Smedvig, Rolf

[Essercizii musici, (1739-40). No. 24: Trio 12, oboe, harpsichord obbligato & continuo, E^b major, TWV 42: Es 3; arr. trumpet & organ]

Triosonate Nr. 12 Es-dur
(Trio Sonata No. 12 in E^b major)
Carroll, Edward, 11)

₍Essercizii musici, (1739-40). No. 24: Trio 12, oboe, harpsichord obbligato & continuo, E♭ major, TWV 42: Es 3; arr. trumpet, harpsichord & bassoon₎
Triosonate Nr. 12 Es-dur
(Trio Sonata No. 12 in E♭ major)
André, Maurice, 203)

₍Fugierende und verändernde Choräle, (1735). Prelude 20: "Herr Jesu Christ, dich zu uns wend' ", TWV 31:40; arr. trumpet (or corno da caccia) & organ₎
Choralvorspiele, "Herr Jesu Christ, dich zu uns wend' "
Güttler, Ludwig, 15), 21)

₍Fugierende und verändernde Choräle, (1735). Prelude 21: "Gott der Vater wohn uns bei", TWV 31:42; arr. trumpet & organ₎
Choralvorspiele, "Gott der Vater wohn uns bei"
Güttler, Ludwig, 24)

₍Getreue Music-Meister, (1728). No. 18: Air, trumpet & continuo, C major, TWV 41: C 1; arr. 2 trumpets & organ₎
Overture from *Der getreue Musikmeister*
(Air de trompette)
Ghitalla, Armando, 5)

₍Getreue Music-Meister, (1728). No. 18: Air, trumpet & continuo, C major, TWV 41: C 1; perf. natural trumpet, harpsichord & trombone₎
Air de trompette
Tarr, Edward, 12), 40)

₍Getreue Music-Meister, (1728). No. 18: Air, trumpet & continuo, C major, TWV 41: C 1; perf. trumpet & harpsichord₎
Air de trompette
Plog, Anthony, 6)

₍Getreue Music-Meister, (1728). No. 18: Air, trumpet & continuo, C major, TWV 41: C 1; perf. trumpet & organ₎
Air de trompette
Basch, Wolfgang, 5)
Chesnut, Walter
Lewark, Egbert
McGuffey, Patrick

₍Getreue Music-Meister, (1728). No. 18: Air, trumpet & continuo, C major, TWV 41: C 1; perf. trumpet, harpsichord & bassoon₎
Air de trompette
Schwarz, Gerard, 17)

₍Getreue Music-Meister, (1728). No. 18: Air, trumpet & continuo, C major, TWV 41: C 1; perf. trumpet, organ & bassoon₎
Air de trompette
Fink, Werner

ₜGetreue Music-Meister, (1728). No. 50: Sonata, oboe & continuo, a minor,
TWV 41: a 3; arr. trumpet & organ₁
Sonate a-moll
(Sonata in a minor)
[1]Siciliana / [2]Spirituoso / [3]Andante / [4]Vivace
André, Maurice, 163)
Deside

ₜHeilig, Heilig, mixed voices, trumpet & orchestra, (1747)₁
Heilig, Heilig
(Sanctus)
André, Maurice, 122)

ₜHeldenmusik, (1728). Marches (12), solo instrument & continuo,
TWV Anh. 41: 1-12; arr. trumpet & harpsichord₁
Heldenmusik, bestehend aus 12 Märschen
(Musique héroïque ou XII Marches)
(Heroic Music [12 Heroic Marches])
[1]Maestoso (La Majesté : Honor) / [2]Grazioso (La Grâce : Charm) /
[3]Con bravura (La Vaillance : Bravery) / [4]Tranquillo (La Tranquillité :
Quietness) / [5]Bellicoso (L'Armement : Vigor) / [6]Amore (L'Amour :
Love) / [7]Sostenuto (La Vigilance : Vigilance) / [8]Giocoso (La
Gaillardise : Playfulness) / [9]Con dolcezza (La Douceur : Gentleness) /
[10]Con delicatezza (La Générosité : Generosity) / [11]Risoluto
(L'Espérance : Hope) / [12]Con spirito (La Réjouissance : Joy)
Plog, Anthony, 6)

ₜHeldenmusik, (1728). Marches (12), solo instrument & continuo,
TWV Anh. 41: 1-12; arr. trumpet & organ₁
Heldenmusik, bestehend aus 12 Märschen
(Musique héroïque ou XII Marches)
(Heroic Music [12 Heroic Marches])
[1]Maestoso (La Majesté : Honor) / [2]Grazioso (La Grâce : Charm) /
[3]Con bravura (La Vaillance : Bravery) / [4]Tranquillo (La Tranquillité :
Quietness) / [5]Bellicoso (L'Armement : Vigor) / [6]Amore (L'Amour :
Love) / [7]Sostenuto (La Vigilance : Vigilance) / [8]Giocoso (La
Gaillardise : Playfulness) / [9]Con dolcezza (La Douceur : Gentleness) /
[10]Con delicatezza (La Générosité : Generosity) / [11]Risoluto
(L'Espérance : Hope) / [12]Con spirito (La Réjouissance : Joy)
André, Maurice, 77), 156)
Basch, Wolfgang, 5), 11)
Berinbaum, Martin
Capouillez, Luc
Carroll, Edward, 11)
Gabel, Bernard, 1)
Giangiulio, Richard
Grin, Freddy, 1)
Hartog, Thomas
Hickman, David, 6)
Lewark, Egbert

Pliquett, Joachim
Sautter, Fred
Send, Peter
Spindler, Günter
Steele-Perkins, Crispian, 2)
Touvron, Guy, 12)

₍Heldenmusik, (1728). Marches (12), solo instrument & continuo,
TWV Anh. 41: 1-12; arr. trumpet & piano₎
Two Pieces from *Heroic Music*
[11]Andante (L'Espérance : Hope) / [6]Allegro (La Gaillardise :
Playfulness)
Nagel, Robert, 10)

₍Heldenmusik, (1728). Marches (12), solo instrument & continuo,
TWV Anh. 41: 1-12; arr. trumpet, harpsichord & bassoon₎
Heldenmusik, bestehend aus 12 Märschen
(Musique héroïque ou XII Marches)
(Heroic Music [12 Heroic Marches])
[1]Maestoso (La Majesté : Honor) / [2]Grazioso (La Grâce : Charm) /
[3]Con bravura (La Vaillance : Bravery) / [4]Tranquillo (La Tranquillité :
Quietness) / [5]Bellicoso (L'Armement : Vigor) / [6]Amore (L'Amour :
Love) / [7]Sostenuto (La Vigilance : Vigilance) / [8]Giocoso (La
Gaillardise : Playfulness) / [9]Con dolcezza (La Douceur : Gentleness) /
[10]Con delicatezza (La Générosité : Generosity) / [11]Risoluto
(L'Espérance : Hope) / [12]Con spirito (La Réjouissance : Joy)
Smedvig, Rolf

₍Heldenmusik, (1728). Marches (12), solo instrument & continuo,
TWV Anh. 41: 1-12; arr. 2 trumpets, timpani, percussion & organ₎
Heldenmusik, bestehend aus 12 Märschen
(Musique héroïque ou XII Marches)
(Heroic Music [12 Heroic Marches])
[1]Maestoso (La Majesté : Honor) / [2]Grazioso (La Grâce : Charm) /
[3]Con bravura (La Vaillance : Bravery) / [4]Tranquillo (La Tranquillité :
Quietness) / [5]Bellicoso (L'Armement : Vigor) / [6]Amore (L'Amour :
Love) / [7]Sostenuto (La Vigilance : Vigilance) / [8]Giocoso (La
Gaillardise : Playfulness) / [9]Con dolcezza (La Douceur : Gentleness) /
[10]Con delicatezza (La Générosité : Generosity) / [11]Risoluto
(L'Espérance : Hope) / [12]Con spirito (La Réjouissance : Joy)
Ghitalla, Armando, 5)

[Heldenmusik, (1728). Marches (12), solo instrument & continuo,
TWV Anh. 41:1-12; Suite, arr. trumpet & organ]

Suite Héroïque

[2]La Grâce / *Grave / [3]La Vaillance / *Dolce / [4]La Tranquillité /
*Aria / [9]La Douceur / *Minuet / [10]La Générosité / *Loure / [1]La
Majesté

*Movements added from other sources: Grave from
Klavierfantasie, TWV 33:9; Dolce from *Klavierfantasie*,
TWV 33:28; Loure from *Ouverture à la Polonaise in d minor*,
TWV 32:2. (Source of the Aria and Minuet have not been
determined.)

        Schultz, Erik, 4)

[Kleine Kammermusik, (1716). Partia, violin (or flute or oboe) & continuo,
B♭ major, TWV 41: B 1; arr. trumpet, organ & bassoon]

Suite for Trumpet, Organ and Bassoon

(Partia B-dur für Violine oder Querflöte oder Oboe und Generalbass)
[1]Aria 1: Presto / [2]Aria 2: Dolce / [3]Aria 4: Largo / [4]Aria 5: [Vivace] /
[5]Aria 6: Allegro

An introductory movement and the third aria are omitted from
this arrangement. (*Die kleine Kammermusik* was published as
Kleine Cammer-Music in 1716, and as *La Petite Musique de
Chambre* in 1728.)

        Schultz, Erik, 1)

[Sonata, trumpet, strings & continuo, D major]

Sonate D-dur für Trompete, Streicher und Basso continuo

[1]Spirituoso / [2]Largo / [3]Vivace

Original manuscript is located in the Hochschulbibliothek of
Darmstadt.

        Erb, Helmut, 6)
        Hunger, Helmut, 1)
        Potpourri, 15)
        Scherbaum, Adolf, 19), 25)

[Sonata, trumpet, strings & continuo, D major; arr. trumpet & orchestra]

Sonate de concert en Ré majeur

(Sonate D-dur für Trompete, Streicher und Basso continuo)
[1]Modéré et gracieux / [2]Largo / [3]Vivace

Original manuscript is located in the Hochschulbibliothek of
Darmstadt.

This sonata is an authentic work for trumpet, but this
arrangement by Fernand Oubradous adds melodic passages not
suitable for the originally intended natural trumpet.

        André, Maurice, 22), 28), 31), 33), 135), 169),
           210), 213)
        Bernard, André, 10)
        Potpourri, 36), 37)
        Soustrot, Bernard, 6)
        Touvron, Guy, 1)
        Wilbraham, John, 13)

[Sonata, trumpet, strings & continuo, D major; arr. trumpet & organ]
Sonate de concert en Ré majeur
(Sonate D-dur für Trompete, Streicher und Basso continuo)
[1]Modéré et gracieux / [2]Largo / [3]Vivace
Gaudon, Jean-Jacques

[Sonata, unspecified, D major; arr. trumpet & organ]
Sonata in D major
Morisset, Michel

[Sonata, violin (or oboe) & continuo, c minor, TWV 41: c 6; arr. trumpet, harpsichord & bassoon]
Sonate c-moll
(Sonata in c minor)
[1]Affettuoso / [2]Andante e staccato / [3]Largo / [4]Allegro / [5]Grave / [6]Allegro cantabile
André, Maurice, 203)
Smedvig, Rolf

[Sonate metodiche, (1728). No. 1: Sonata, violin (or flute) & continuo, g minor, TWV 41: g 3; arr. trumpet & organ]
Sonate g-moll
(Sonata in g minor)
[1]Adagio / [2]Vivace / [3]Grave / [4]Allegro
Carroll, Edward, 11)

[Sonate metodiche, (1728). No. 4: Sonata, violin (or flute) & continuo, D major, TWV 41: D 3; Presto, arr. trumpet & piano, B♭ major]
Presto from *Sonata in B♭ major*
Amstutz, Keith
Schwarz, Gerard, 15)

[Sonaten im Kanon, (1738). No. 1: 2 flutes (or 2 violins or 2 violas da gamba); arr. flute & trumpet]
Canonic Sonata No. 1
[1]Vivace / [2]Adagio / [3]Allegro
Plog, Anthony, 7)

[Suites, orchestra. TWV 55: D 7, trumpet & strings, D major]
Ouverture D-dur
(Suite in D major [No. 18])
[1]Ouverture / [2]Air / [3]Rigaudon / [4]Plainte / [5]Furies (Très viste) / [6]Loure / [7]Trezza / [8]Minuet I & II
André, Maurice, 196)
Basch, Wolfgang, 7)
Potpourri, 42), 44)

[Suites, orchestra. TWV 55: D 8, trumpet & strings, D major]
Ouverture D-dur
(Suite in D major [No. 19])
[1]Ouverture / [2]March(e) / [3]Minuet I & II / [4]Aria / [5]La Réjouissance / [6]Sarabande / [7]Gigue / [8]Passapied I & II / [9]Rondeau
Basch, Wolfgang, 7)

[Suites, orchestra. TWV 55: D 15, 3 oboes & strings, D major; arr. 3 trumpets & strings]
Ouverture D-dur
(Suite in D major [No. 26])
[1]Ouverture / [2]Prélude / [3]Gigue / [4]Minuet I & II / [5]Harlequinade / [6]Loure / [7]Rondeau / [8]Réjouissance
Basch, Wolfgang, 7)

[Suites, orchestra. TWV 55: D 17, 2 trumpets & strings, D major]
Ouverture D-dur
(Suite in D major [No. 28])
[1]Ouverture / [2]Les Janissaires / [3]Minuet I & II / [4]Espagniole / [5]Carillon / [6]à la Trompette / [7]Bourrée
Basch, Wolfgang, 7)

[Suites, orchestra. TWV 55: D 18, 2 trumpets, timpani & strings, D major]
Ouverture D-dur
(Suite in D major [No. 29])
[1]Ouverture / [2]Minuet I & II / [3]Gavotte (en Rondeau) / [4]Passacaille / [5]Air (Lentement) / [6]Les Postillons / [7]Fanfare (Très Vite)
Immer, Friedemann, 7)

[Suites, orchestra. TWV 55: D 19, 2 horns & strings, D major; arr. 2 trumpets & strings]
Ouverture D-dur
(Suite in D major [No. 30])
[1]Ouverture / [2]Bourrée / [3]Loure / [4]Rondeau (Légèrement) / [5]Écossaise / [6]Menuet (& Trio) / [7]Gigue
Güttler, Ludwig, 7)

[Suites, orchestra. TWV 55: D 22, 3 trumpets, timpani & strings, D major]
Ouverture, jointes d'une Suite tragi-comique
(Suite in D major [No. 33])
[1]Ouverture / [2]Le Petite-Maître / [3]Le Podagre (Loure) / [4]Remède expérimente: La Poste et la Dance (Menuet en Rondeau) / [5]L'Hypochondre (Sarabande - Gigue) / [6]Remède: Souffrance héroïque (Marche) / [7]Remède: Petite-maison (Furies)
Ullrich, Marc

[Tafelmusik II, (1733). No. 1, Ouverture, trumpet, oboe, strings & continuo, D major, TWV 55: D 1]
Ouverture D-dur für Oboe, Trompete, Streicher und Basso continuo
[1]Ouverture (Lentement - Vite) / [2]Air I (Tempo giusto) / [3]Air II (Vivace) / [4]Air III (Presto) / [5]Air IV (Allegro)
André, Maurice, 14), 221), 224)
Gabel, Bernard, 3)
Tarr, Edward, 11)

₍Tafelmusik II, (1733). No. 6, Conclusion, trumpet, oboe, strings & continuo, D major, TWV 55: D 1₎
Conclusion D-dur für Oboe, Trompete, Streicher und Basso continuo
Allegro - Adagio - Allegro
> **André, Maurice**, 221), 224)
> **Gabel, Bernard**, 3)
> **Tarr, Edward**, 11)

₍Tafelmusik III, (1733). No. 3, Concerto, 2 horns, strings & continuo, E♭ major, TWV 55: Es; arr. 2 trumpets, strings & continuo₎
Concerto in E♭ major for 2 Trumpets, Strings and Continuo
[1]Maestoso / [2]Allegro / [3]Grave / [4]Vivace
> **Hardenberger, Håkan**

₍Tafelmusik III, (1733). No. 5, Sonata, oboe & continuo, g minor, TWV 41: g 6; arr. trumpet & organ₎
Sonate g-moll
(Sonata in g minor)
[1]Largo / [2]Presto / [3]Tempo giusto / [4]Andante / [5]Allegro
> **André, Maurice**, 35), 131)

Tellamel, H., 20th cent.
₍Corso blanc; arr. flügelhorn & accordion band₎
Le corso blanc
> **André, Maurice**, 61)

Tenaglia, Antonio Francesco, *ca.* 1615-*ca.* 1661
₍Aria; arr. trumpet & piano₎
Aria
This aria is published as part of a transcription by Bernard Fitzgerald, *Aria and Allegro*. (The allegro is by Johann Philipp Krieger.)
> **Ghitalla, Armando**, 11)
> **Haynie, John**, 2)

Tessarini, Carlo, *ca.* 1690-1766
₍Sonata, flute & continuo, D major; arr. trumpet & orgue₎
Sonata en ré majeur pour trompette et orgue
[1]Allegro / [2]Adagio / [3]Allegro
> **Gaudon, Jean-Jacques**
> **Mertens, Theo**, 4)
> **Touvron, Guy**, 20)

₍Sonata, flute & continuo, D major; arr. trumpet & piano₎
Sonata en ré majeur pour trompette et piano
[1]Allegro / [2]Adagio / [3]Allegro
> **Lewis, E. Leonard**

ₗSonata, flute & continuo, D major; arr. trumpet & stringsₗ
Sonata en ré majeur pour trompette et cordes
[1]Allegro / [2]Adagio / [3]Allegro
>**André, Maurice,** 126)
>**Güttler, Ludwig,** 14), 21)
>**Kejmar, Miroslav,** 11)

Thilde, Jean, 20th cent.

ₗSérénade fantasque, solo trumpetₗ
Sérénade fantasque
>**Potpourri,** 28)

ₗSicilienne et tambourin, solo trumpetₗ
Sicilienne et tambourin
>**Potpourri,** 28)

Thomas, Stanley, 20th cent.

ₗTorero, trumpet & pianoₗ
El Torero
>**Burkart, Richard**

Thomé, Francis, 1850-1909
Thomé, François Luc Joseph

ₗFantaisie, cornet & piano, (1902)ₗ
Fantaisie pour Cornet à Pistons avec accompagnement de Piano
>**Sommerhalder, Max**

Thompson, Wayne, 20th cent.

ₗAlways On My Mind; arr. trumpet & orchestraₗ
Always On My Mind
>Other names associated in the authorship of this song are Mark
>James & Johnny Christopher.
>**Schultz, Erik,** 8)

Thomson, Virgil, 1896-

ₗAt the Beach, trumpet (cornet) & piano, (1949)ₗ
At the Beach — Concert Waltz
>Derived from a 1929 set of waltzes, *Le Bains-Bar*, for violin and
>piano by Virgil Thomson.
>**Schwarz, Gerard,** 19)

ₗSonata da chiesa, chamber ensemble, (1926)ₗ
Sonata da chiesa
>[1]Chorale / [2]Tango / [3]Fugue
>Chamber ensemble includes: viola, E♭-clarinet, D-trumpet,
>F-horn & B♭-tenor trombone.
>**Mills, Fred**

Thorne, Francis, 1922-
Thorne, Francis Burritt

[Set Pieces (7), chamber ensemble, (1967)]
Seven Set Pieces for 13 Players
[1]Grotesque I (Andante maestoso - Allegretto misterioso) / [2]Romance (Adagietto) / [3]Jam Session I (Presto vivace) / [4]Grotesque II (Allegretto) / [5]Choral Prelude (Adagio semplice) / [6]Jam Session II (Allegro fuoco) / [7]Finale (Andante - Presto)
Chamber ensemble includes: clarinet, bass clarinet, bassoon, contrabassoon, 2 trumpets, trombone, 2 violas, bass, piano/celeste & 2 percussion.
Miller, Rodney

Tisné, Antoine, 1932-

[Héraldiques, trumpet & piano, (1975)]
Héraldiques
Hardenberger, Håkan
Thibaud, Pierre, 2)

Tjeknavorian, Loris, 1937-

[Symphonies. No. 1: "Requiem for the massacred", trumpet, celeste & percussion ensemble, op. 20]
Symphony No. 1, "Requiem for the massacred", op. 20
Wallace, John, 2)

Tolar, Pater A., 17th cent.

[Sonata, 4 trumpets, 4 trombones, strings & continuo, C major, (c. 1660)]
Sonata für 4 Trompeten, 4 Posaunen, Fagott, Streicher und Continuo
[1]Allegro / [2]Presto / [3]Presto
Two of the 4 trumpet parts were originally for cornetto.
Pater A. Tolar = Jan Křtitel (Johann Baptiste) Tolar ?
Scherbaum, Adolf, 16), 22), 23)

Tolley, Richard, 20th cent.

[Meditation, solo trumpet]
Meditation
Tolley, Richard

Tomasi, Henri, 1901-1971

[Concerto, trumpet & orchestra, (1948)]
Concerto pour Trompette et Orchestre
[1]Vif / [2]Nocturne (Andante) / [3]Final (Allegro vivo)
André, Maurice, 108)
Marsalis, Wynton, 3)

₍Concerto, trumpet & orchestra, (1948); arr. trumpet & band₎
Concerto for Trumpet and Band
¹Vif / ²Nocturne (Andante) / ³Final (Allegro vivo)
Smith, Philip, 5)

₍Semaine Sainte à Cuzco, trumpet/piccolo trumpet, timpani, 2 harps & strings, (1964); arr. trumpet/piccolo trumpet & organ₎
Semaine Sainte à Cuzco
(Procession du Vendredi Saint)
André, Maurice, 144)
Pearson, Byron

₍Suite, 3 trumpets, (1964)₎
Suite for Three Trumpets
¹Havanaise / ²Lento Egeen / ³Danse Bolivienne
Giangiulio, Richard

₍Triptyque, trumpet & piano, (1957)₎
Triptyque
¹Scherzo / ²Largo / ³Saltarelle
Stevens, Thomas, 6)

₍Variationes Gregoriennes, trumpet & organ, (1964)₎
Variationes Gregoriennes
Pliquett, Joachim

Torelli, Giuseppe, 1658-1709

₍Concerto, trumpet, strings & continuo, [Roger 188:6], D major₎
Concerto in D major for Trumpet, Strings and Continuo, [Roger 188:6]
¹Allegro / ²Adagio - Presto - Adagio / ³Allegro
Originally published in 1713 by Estienne Roger (Amsterdam) in Collection No. 188 as "Concerto VI" from *Concerts à 5 6 7 instruments...*, along with concertos by other composers. Torelli's authorship of this concerto is disputable.

               André, Maurice, 22), 27), 28), 31), 41), 46), 83), 135), 169), 174), 177), 210), 216), 217), 222), 224), 225)
               Bernard, André, 3)
               Dassé, Jean-Luc
               Delmotte, Roger, 16), 27), 47), 50)
               Hunger, Helmut, 3)
               Potpourri, 21), 34), 35), 65), 68)
               Quinque, Rolf, 6)
               Scherbaum, Adolf, 20)
               Smithers, Don, 5)
               Steele-Perkins, Crispian, 13)
               Thibaud, Pierre, 3)
               Voisin, Roger, 6)

₍Concerto, trumpet, strings & continuo, [Roger 188:6], D major; arr. trumpet & organ₎
Concerto in D major for Trumpet and Organ
¹Allegro / ²Adagio - Presto - Adagio / ³Allegro
Gabel, Bernard, 5)
Grin, Freddy, 1)
Lieberman, Harold J.
Schultz, Erik, 10)

₍Concerto, trumpet, strings & continuo, [Roger 188:6], D major: Allegro; arr. trumpet & piano, C major₎
Allegro from *Concerto for Trumpet and Strings*
Nagel, Robert, 10)

₍Sinfonias, Sonatas & Concertos. G. 1: Sonata, trumpet, strings & continuo, D major, (1690)₎
Sonata a 5 con Tromba
(Sonata in D major for Trumpet, Strings and Continuo, G. 1)
¹[Andante] - Adagio / ²[Allegro] / ³Grave / ⁴[Allegro]
Burns, Stephen
Erb, Helmut, 5)
Güttler, Ludwig, 3), 19), 21¹), 25)
Kejmar, Miroslav, 11)
Orvid, Georgy
Quinque, Rolf, 5)
Reinhart, Carole Dawn, 3)
Schwarz, Gerard, 7)
Smithers, Don, 5)
Spindler, Josef, 5)
Tarr, Edward, 21)
Vizzutti, Allen
Wobisch, Helmut, 6)
Zapf, Gerd

₍Sinfonias, Sonatas & Concertos. G. 2-3: Concerto, trumpet, strings & continuo, D major; arr.₎
Concerto en ré majeur pour trompette, orchestre à cordes et continuo, G. 2-3
¹(Allegro) [G.2a] / ²Adagio [G.3a] / ³Allegro (molto) [G.3b] / ⁴Grave [G.3c] - Allegro [G.3d] - Adagio [G.3e] / ⁵Allegro [G.2c=G.1d]
This 1962 arrangement by Jean-François Paillard combines Geigling 2 and Geigling 3. The first and last movements are the first and last movements from G. 2; and movements 2-4 are the first three movements of G. 3. (The second movement of G. 2 is omitted, and the final movement of G. 3 is omitted.) It should also be noted that the final movement of G. 2-3 (the final movement of G. 2) is the same as the final movement of G. 1.
André, Maurice, 90), 222), 224)
Dassé, Jean-Luc
Scherbaum, Adolf, 19), 25)

₍Sinfonias, Sonatas & Concertos. G. 3: Sinfonia, trumpet, strings & continuo, D major₎
Sinfonia a 5 con Tromba
(Sinfonia in D major for Trumpet, Strings and Continuo, G. 3)
(Sonata in D major for Trumpet, Strings and Continuo, G. 3)
[1]Adagio - Allegro / [2]Grave - Allegro - Adagio / [3]Allegro
This work is designated as a "sinfonia" in Franz Giegling's *Torelli Werkverzeichnis*. According to notes by Edward Tarr for the Musica Rara edition, the title of "Sonata a 5 con Tromba" appeared on the original trumpet part. To add to the confusion, the Musica Rara edition is entitled "Sinfonia in D, (G.3)" on the cover, but "Sonata in D, (G.3)" on all the instrumental parts.
> **Marsalis, Wynton**, 2)
> **Unidentified, Trumpet(s)**, 24)

₍Sinfonias, Sonatas & Concertos. G. 5: Sonata, trumpet, strings & continuo, D major₎
Sonata a 5 con Tromba
(Sonata in D major for Trumpet, Strings and Continuo, G. 5)
[1]Adagio (Grave) / [2]Allegro e staccato / [3]Adagio (Grave) / [4]Allegro
> **Dassé, Jean-Luc**

₍Sinfonias, Sonatas & Concertos. G. 6: Sonata, trumpet, strings & continuo, D major₎
Sonata a 5 con Tromba
(Sonata in D major for Trumpet, Strings and Continuo, G. 6)
[1]Vivace / [2]Adagio - Largo - Adagio / [3]Allegro come stà
> **Immer, Friedemann**, 9)
> **Scherbaum, Adolf**, 21)

₍Sinfonias, Sonatas & Concertos. G. 6: Sonata, trumpet, strings & continuo, D major; arr. trumpet & piano, B♭ major₎
Sonata a 5 con Tromba
(Sonata in B♭ major for Trumpet and Piano, G. 6)
[1]Allegro / [2](Adagio - Largo - Adagio) / [3]Allegro
The "tacet" second movement is omitted from this arrangement.
> **Nagel, Robert**, 11[1+3])

₍Sinfonias, Sonatas & Concertos. G. 7: Sonata, trumpet, strings & continuo, D major₎
Sonata a 5 con Tromba
(Sonata in D major for Trumpet, Strings and Continuo, G. 7)
[1]Grave - Allegro / [2]Grave (Adagio) / [3]Allegro / [4]Grave - Allegro
> **Berinbaum, Martin**
> **Güttler, Ludwig**, 14)
> **Marsalis, Wynton**, 2)
> **Potpourri**, 40), 42), 46)
> **Scherbaum, Adolf**, 21)
> **Schneidewind, Helmut**, 9)
> **Smithers, Don**, 4)
> **Spindler, Josef**, 5)

[Sinfonias, Sonatas & Concertos. G. 8: Sinfonia, trumpet, strings & continuo, D major]
Sinfonia con Tromba
(Sinfonia in D major, G. 8)
[1]Allegro / [2]Adagio / [3]Allegro / [4]Allegro [non troppo]
Güttler, Ludwig, 24)
Smithers, Don, 5)
Voisin, Roger, 4)

[Sinfonias, Sonatas & Concertos. G. 8: Sinfonia, trumpet, strings & continuo, D major; arr. trumpet & organ]
Sinfonia con Tromba
(Sinfonia in D major, G. 8)
[1]Allegro / [2]Adagio / [3]Allegro / [4]Allegro [non troppo]
Pearson, Byron
Schultz, Erik, 4)
Stith, Marice, 6)

[Sinfonias, Sonatas & Concertos. G. 9: Sinfonia, trumpet, strings & continuo, D major]
Sinfonia con Tromba
(Sinfonia in D major, G. 9)
[1]Allegro / [2]Adagio / [3]Prestissimo (-Adagio) / [4]Allegro
Potpourri, 34), 35), 65)
Smithers, Don, 5)
Zickler, Heinz, 9)

[Sinfonias, Sonatas & Concertos. G. 11: Sonata, trumpet, strings & continuo, D major]
Sonata a 5 con Tromba
(Sonata in D major for Trumpet, Strings and Continuo, G. 11)
[1]Allegro / [2]Adagio / [3]Presto / [4][Allegro]
Battagliola, Anania
Scherbaum, Adolf, 21)

[Sinfonias, Sonatas & Concertos. G. 18: Concerto, 2 trumpets, strings & continuo, D major]
Concerto con [due] Trombe
(Concerto in D major for 2 Trumpets, Strings and Continuo, G. 18)
[1]Largo assai / [2][Allegro] / [3]Adagio e staccato / [4][Allegro] - Adagio - [Allegro]
Battagliola, Anania
Scherbaum, Adolf, 21)
Wobisch, Helmut, 4)

ₜSinfonias, Sonatas & Concertos. G. 20: Sinfonia, 2 trumpets, strings & continuo,
D majorₙ
Sinfonia con due Trombe
(Sinfonia in D major, G. 20)
[1][Allegro] / [2]Adagio - Largo e staccato / [3]Allegro / [4]Aria
Battagliola, Anania
Scherbaum, Adolf, 22)
Unidentified, Trumpet(s), 24)
Wobisch, Helmut, 6), 11)

ₜSinfonias, Sonatas & Concertos. G. 23: Sinfonia, 2 trumpets, strings & continuo,
D majorₙ
Sinfonia
(Sinfonia con due Trombe, G. 23)
[1][Allegro] / [2]Largo - Allegro - Adagio / [3][Allegro]
Scherbaum, Adolf, 20)

ₜSinfonias, Sonatas & Concertos. G. 26: Sinfonia, 2 trumpets, 2 oboes, strings &
continuo, D majorₙ
Sinfonia
(Sinfonia con due Trombe e due Oboi, G. 26)
[1][Allegro] / [2]Adagio e staccato / [3]Presto
Battagliola, Anania
Unidentified, Trumpet(s), 24)

ₜSinfonias, Sonatas & Concertos. G. 29: Sinfonia, 2 trumpets, 2 oboes, strings &
continuo, D majorₙ
Sinfonia con Trombe e Oboi
(Sinfonia in D major, G. 29)
[1]Adagio e staccato / [2]Allegro (-Adagio e staccato) / [3]Allegro /
[4]Adagio / [5]Allegro
André, Maurice, 90)

ₜSinfonias, Sonatas & Concertos. G. 30: Sinfonia, 2 trumpets, 2 oboes, strings &
continuo, D majorₙ
Sinfonia con Oboi, Trombe e Violini
(Sinfonia in D major, G. 30)
[1][Allegro] / [2]Largo / [3][Allegro]
Wobisch, Helmut, 6)

ₜSinfonias, Sonatas & Concertos. G. 31: Sinfonia, 2 trumpets, 2 oboes,
(trombone), 4 solo violins, strings & continuo, D majorₙ
Sinfonia con Trombe e Oboi
(Sinfonia in D major, G. 31)
[1][Allegro] / [2]Adagio e spiccato - Andante / [3]Allegro (-adagio) /
[4]Allegro
André, Maurice, 90)

ₜSinfonias, Sonatas & Concertos. G. 32: Concerto, 2 trumpets, 2 oboes, strings & continuo, D majorₜ

Concerto a due Chori, G. 32
[1][Largo] / [2]Allegro / [3]Largo - Allegro / [4][Aria (allegro)] / [5][Menuet]
The strings are divided into two choirs: 2 oboes play with Choir I, and 2 trumpets play with Choir II.
André, Maurice, 105)
Scherbaum, Adolf, 20)

ₜSinfonias, Sonatas & Concertos. G. 33: Sinfonia, 4 trumpets, 4 oboes, (2 bassoons), (trombone), timpani, strings & continuo, C majorₜ

Sinfonia in C major, G. 33
[1][Allegro] / [2]Adagio / [3][Allegro]
André, Maurice, 47), 143)
Touvron, Guy, 2)
Ullrich, Marc
Unidentified, Trumpet(s), 24)
Vaillant, Ludovic, 6)
Wallace, John, 4)
Wobisch, Helmut, 3)

ₜSinfonias, Sonatas & Concertos. G. 165: Sonata, trumpet, strings & continuo, D majorₜ

Sonata a cinque
(Sonata in D major for Trumpet, Strings and Continuo, G. 165)
[1]Allegro / [2]Largo / [3]Allegro
Güttler, Ludwig, 14)
Immer, Friedemann, 9)
Wobisch, Helmut, 3)

ₜSinfonias, Sonatas & Concertos. G. 168: Concerto, 2 trumpets, strings & continuo, D majorₜ

Concerto in D major for 2 Trumpets, Strings and Continuo, G. 168
Güttler, Ludwig, 7)

ₜWorks, trumpet(s), strings & continuo, <undetermined Giegling catalogue numbers>ₜ

Sinfonias, Sonatas, Concertos.... G. ?
Any of these works could also be the "Estienne Roger" concerto (*sans* Geigling number).
Basch, Wolfgang, 3)
Bernard, André, 10)
Blair, Stacy
Cuvit, Michel
Friedrich, Reinhold
Krug, Willi, 3), 4)
Molénat, Claude
Novikov, Vadim
Potpourri, 36), 37)
Schneidewind, Helmut, 12)
Wilbraham, John, 9)

ᵣWorks, trumpet(s), strings & continuo, <undetermined Giegling catalogue numbers>; arr. trumpet(s) & organ⌐

Sinfonias, Sonatas, Concertos.... G. ?
Any of these works could also be the "Estienne Roger" concerto (*sans* Geigling number).
> **Bodenröder, Robert**
> **Gaudon, Jean-Jacques**
> **Hardy, Francis**
> **McGuffey, Patrick**
> **Morisset, Michel**
> **Volle, Bjarne**

Trabaci, Giovanni Maria, *ca.* 1575-1647

ᵣGalliarde, keyboard instrument; arr. trumpet & organ⌐
Gaillarde
(Galliarde)
> **Morisset, Michel**

Trotsyuk, Bogdan Jakoblevich, 1931-
Trozjuk, Bogdan

ᵣConcert-Symphony, trumpet & orchestra⌐
Concert-Symphony for Trumpet and Orchestra
(Symphonic Concerto)
> **Dokshitser, Timofei, 25)**

Truax, Bert, 1954-

ᵣAdagio and Allegro, 3 piccolo trumpets, (1979)⌐
Adagio and Allegro
[1]Adagio (slow fugue) / [2]Allegro (theme and variations)
> **Giangiulio, Richard**

ᵣFanfare, 3 trumpets, organ & timpani⌐
Fanfare for 3 Trumpets, Organ and Timpani
> **Giangiulio, Richard**

Tschaikowsky, Peter Iljitsch
See: Tchaikovsky, Piotr Ilyitch

Tubin, Eduard, 1905-1982

ᵣAve Maria, contralto, baritone, mixed voices, trumpet, piano/organ & percussion, (1952)⌐
Ave Maria
> **Hardenberger, Håkan**

ᵣRequiem for Fallen Soldiers, contralto, baritone, mixed voices, trumpet, piano/organ & percussion, (1979)⌐
Requiem for Fallen Soldiers
> **Hardenberger, Håkan**

[Retreating Soldiers' Song, contralto, baritone, mixed voices, trumpet, piano/organ
& percussion, (1969)]
The Retreating Soldiers' Song
Hardenberger, Håkan

Tull, Fisher, 1934-
Tull, Fisher Aubrey

[Bagatelles (3), trumpet & piano]
Three Bagatelles
Plog, Anthony, 7)

[Concerto, trumpet & orchestra, no. 2]
Concerto No. 2 for Trumpet and Orchestra
Severinsen, Carl "Doc"

[Profiles, solo trumpet]
Profiles for Solo Trumpet
Plog, Anthony, 4)

Turrin, Joseph, 1947-
Turrin, Joseph Edigio

[Caprice, trumpet & piano]
Caprice
Hickman, David, 4)
Smith, Philip, 2)

[Elegy, trumpet & piano]
Elegy
Smith, Philip, 2)

Tuthill, Burnet, 1888-
Tuthill, Burnet Corwin

[Scherzo, cornet & piano, op. 10, (1948)]
Scherzo, op. 10
Tolley, Richard

Tyler, 20th cent.
[Java; arr. trumpet & orchestra]
Java
Hirt, Al

Tyzik, Jeff
See: Vizzutti, Allen

Uccellini, Marco, *ca.* 1603-1680

₍Sonata, cornetto, violin, recorder & continuo, no. 12₎
Sonata Duodecima a 4
> Continuo instruments include: organ & chitaronne.
> **Eichhorn, Holger**

Udbye, Martin Andreas, 1820-1889

₍Adagio, E♭ major; arr. trumpet & brass ensemble₎
Adagio in E♭ major for Trumpet and Brass Ensemble
> **Naess, Lars**

Udow, Michael, 1949-
Udow, Michael William

₍Dancing Hands, chamber ensemble, (1984)₎
Dancing Hands
> Music originally composed for a documentary film, *Dancing Hands: the Visual Art of Rita Blitt*. Chamber ensemble includes: flute/piccolo, clarinet/bass clarinet, trumpet, 2 trombones & percussion.
> **Sasaki, Ray**

Urovsky, Vladimir
See: Yurovsky, Vladimir

Vačkář, Dalibor Cyril, 1906-1984
Vačář, Dalibor

₍Jazz Concerto, trumpet, piano, bass & drums₎
Jazz Concerto
> **Kejmar, Miroslav, 6)**

Vainberg, Moisei Samuilovich, 1919-

₍Concerto, trumpet & orchestra, op. 94, B♭ major, (1970)₎
Concerto in B♭ for Trumpet and Orchestra, op. 94
> [1]Etude (Allegro molto) / [2]Episode (Andante) / [3]Fanfare (Andante - Allegro)
> **Dokshitser, Timofei, 8), 33)**

Valente, Antonio, *fl.* 1578
Valente, Antonio ("il Cieco")

₍Ballo del' Intorcia; arr. 2 trumpets & organ₎
Lo Ballo del' Intorcia
> Source?: *Intavolatura de cimbalo... libro primo*, (1576).
> or *Versi spirituali sopra tutti le note...*, (1580).
> **Pearson, Byron**

Valentine, Robert, *ca.* 1680-*ca.* 1735
Valentini, Roberto
Valentino, Roberto

[Sonata, flute, oboe or violin & continuo, d minor; arr. trumpet & organ]
Sonata in d minor
(Sonate en ré mineur pour Trompette & Piano ou Orgue)
[1]Adagio / [2]Allegro / [3]Adagio / [4]Allegro
This arrangement is published by Billaudot. It is also included as the first sonata in the Nagels Musik-Archiv series Nr. 149: *Drei Sonaten für Blockflöte (Querflöte) und Basso continuo.* (In this latter publication, it is suggested that these sonatas are from Valentino's op. 2, but are otherwise unspecified.)
Basch, Wolfgang, 2)
Hardy, Francis
Kejmar, Miroslav, 1)

[Sonata, flute, oboe or violin & continuo, d minor; arr. trumpet, harpsichord & bassoon]
Sonata in d minor
(Sonate en ré mineur pour Trompette & Piano ou Orgue)
[1]Adagio / [2]Allegro / [3]Adagio / [4]Allegro
Fink, Werner

[Sonata, flute, oboe or violin & continuo, F major; arr. trumpet & organ]
Sonata in F major
(Sonate en Fa majeur pour Trompette & Piano ou Orgue)
[1]Grave / [2]Allegro / [3]Andante / [4]Allegro
This arrangement is published by Billaudot. It is also included as the third sonata in the Nagels Musik-Archiv series Nr. 149: *Drei Sonaten für Blockflöte (Querflöte) und Basso continuo.* (In this latter publication, it is suggested that these sonatas are from Valentino's op. 2, but are otherwise unspecified.)
Güttler, Ludwig, 24)

[Sonatas, recorder & continuo, op. 2, (1708). No. 10, C major, (1708); arr. trumpet & harpsichord]
Sonata in C major, op. 2, no. 10
[1]Adagio / [2]Allegro / [3]Adagio / [4]Giga
André, Maurice, 203)

[Sonatas, recorder & continuo, op. 2, (1708). No. 10, C major, (1708); arr. trumpet & organ]
Sonata in C major, op. 2, no. 10
[1]Adagio / [2]Allegro / [3]Adagio / [4]Giga
André, Maurice, 77), 156)

[Sonatas, recorder & continuo, op. 2, (1708). No. 10, C major, (1708); arr. trumpet, organ & bassoon]
Sonata in C major, op. 2, no. 10
[1]Adagio / [2]Allegro / [3]Adagio / [4]Giga
Carroll, Edward, 10)

Valentini, Giuseppe, *ca.* 1680-*ca.* 1759

[Concerto, oboe, strings & continuo, no. 4, C major; arr. trumpet, strings & continuo]
Concerto in C major
[1]Allegro / [2]Largo / [3]Allegro e spiccato
André, Maurice, 127)

Valverde, Joaquín, 1846-1910

[Clavelitos; arr. trumpet & orchestra]
Clavelitos
This work may have been composed by Joaquín Valverde's son, Joaquín ("Quinito") Valverde, 1875-1918.
Méndez, Rafael, 9), 24)

van Appledorn, Mary Jeanne, 1927-

[Concerto, trumpet/flügelhorn & orchestra, (1960); arr. trumpet/flügelhorn & band]
Concerto for Trumpet and Concert Band
[1]Fast and spirited / [2]Broad and slow - Fast - Broad and slow / [3]Fast and brisk
Transcribed for band by Mark Rogers.
Birch, Robert

[Missa Brevis, trumpet & organ, (1987)]
Missa Brevis
Birch, Robert

Varèse, Edgar, 1883-1965
Varèse, Edgard Victor Achille Charles

[Ecuatorial, bass & chamber ensemble, (1934)]
Ecuatorial
Chamber ensemble includes: 4 trumpets, 4 trombones, piano, organ, 2 ondes Martenot & 5 percussion.
Dean, Allan, 4)

[Hyperprism, chamber ensemble, (1923)]
Hyperprism
Chamber ensemble includes: flute, clarinet, 3 horns, 2 trumpets, 2 trombones & 16 percussion.
Delmotte, Roger, 2)

[Intégrales, chamber ensemble, (1925)]
Intégrales
Chamber ensemble includes: 2 piccolos, oboe, E$^\flat$-clarinet, horn, 2 trumpets, trombone, bass trombone, contrabass trombone & 4 percussion.
Dean, Allan, 4)
Delmotte, Roger, 2)
Ghitalla, Armando, 10)

₍Octandre, chamber ensemble, (1924)₎
Octandre
Chamber ensemble includes: flute/piccolo, oboe, clarinet/bass clarinet, bassoon, horn, trumpet, trombone & bass.
Dean, Allan, 4)
Delmotte, Roger, 2)
Ghitalla, Armando, 10)

₍Offrandes, soprano & chamber orchestra, (1921)₎
Offrandes
Chamber orchestra includes: piccolo, flute, oboe, clarinet, bassoon, horn, trumpet, trombone, harp, strings & 6 percussion.
Dean, Allan, 4)

Vasilenko, Sergei Nikiforovich, 1872-1956

₍Concerto, trumpet & orchestra, op. 113, c minor, (1945)₎
Concerto in c minor for Trumpet and Orchestra, op. 113
¹Allegro drammatico / ²Molto sostenuto, quasi adagio / ³Finale: Allegro vivace
Dokshitser, Timofei, 6), 11), 30)

Vecchi, Orazio Tiberio, 1550-1605
Vecchi, Horatio

₍Saltavan ninfe, instrumental ensemble₎
Saltavan ninfe
Instrumental ensemble may include recorders, crumhorns, bass sordune, racket, tenor curtal, shawm, cornetti, sackbuts, and/or strings.
Smithers, Don, 2)

Vega, Aurelio de la
See: de la Vega, Aurelio

Vejvanovský, Pavel Josef, *ca.* 1639-1693
Weiwanowski, Paul Joseph
Weywanowsky, Paul Joseph
Wegwanowskij, Paulo Josepho

₍Balletti pro tabula, 2 trumpets, strings & continuo, C major, (1670)₎
Balletti pro tabula
Breitenbacher: XIV/180.
Schneidewind, Helmut, 8), 10)
Wilbraham, John, 6)

₍Intrada con altre ariæ, 3 piffari, bassoon, 2 trumpets, strings & continuo, C major, (1679); arr. 2 flutes, 2 trumpets, strings & continuo₎
Intrada con altre ariæ
Breitenbacher: XIV/92.
Schneidewind, Helmut, 8)

₍Intrada, 2 trumpets, strings & continuo, C major, (1683)₎

Intrada in C major
Breitenbacher: XIV/124.
> **Smithers, Don,** 4)

₍Serenada, 2 trumpets, strings & continuo, C major, (1670)₎

Serenada in C major
¹[Andante] / ²Grave / ³Sarabanda / ⁴Presto - Adagio - Allegro /
⁵Conclusion
Breitenbacher: XIV/91.
> **Horák, Jiří,** 2)
> **Kejmar, Miroslav,** 12)

₍Serenada, 5 trumpets, strings & continuo, C major, (1691)₎

Serenada in C major
¹Ingressus / ²Sarabanda / ³Gavotte / ⁴Minuett / ⁵Gigue
Breitenbacher: XIV/45. [There is a discrepancy of dates provided
within the **Musica Antiqua Bohemica** publication of the score for
this *Serenada*; the Editor's Notes following the preface indicate
the date of publication as 1691 while the date shown at the top of
the first page of the score is 1679. Perhaps this serenade was
composed as early as 1679 and not published until 1691. Also, the
fifth trumpet part would appear to be intended for trombone.]
> **Horák, Jiří,** 1)
> **Kejmar, Miroslav,** 12)
> **Smithers, Don,** 10)

₍Serenada, 5 trumpets, timpani, strings & continuo, C major, (1680)₎
Breitenbacher: XIV/98.
> **Horák, Jiří,** 2)

₍Sonata "Ittalica", 3 trumpets, 2 cornetti, strings & continuo, C major₎

Sonata "Ittalica" a 12 in C major
¹Adagio / ²Tardé / ³Adagio / ⁴Tardé / ⁵Canzon (Presto)
> **Güttler, Ludwig,** 1)
> **Pok, František,** 5)
> **Smithers, Don,** 10)

₍Sonata "Ittalica", 3 trumpets, 2 cornetti, strings & continuo, C major; arr. 5
trumpets, strings & continuo₎

Sonata "Ittalica" a 12 in C major
¹Adagio / ²Tardé / ³Adagio / ⁴Tardé / ⁵Canzon (Presto)
> **Scherbaum, Adolf,** 16), 23)

₍Sonata "Natalis", 2 trumpets, strings & continuo, C major₎

Sonata "Natalis" a 8 in C major
Breitenbacher: IV/202.
> **Horák, Jiří,** 1)
> **Wilbraham, John,** 6)

₍Sonata "Tribus Quadrantibus", trumpet, violin, trombone & continuo, C major₎

Sonata "Tribus Quadrantibus" a 3 in C major
> **Wilbraham, John,** 6)

[Sonata "Venatoria", 2 trumpets, strings & continuo, D major, (1684)]
Sonata "Venatoria" a 5 in D major
[Andante] - [Allegro] - [Andante]
Breitenbacher: IV/199.
Horák, Jiří, 1)
Kejmar, Miroslav, 12)

[Sonata "Vespertina", 2 trumpets, 3 trombones, strings & continuo, C major, (1665)]
Sonata "Vespertina" a 8 in C major
[Allegro] - [Presto] - [Allegro]
Breitenbacher: IV/201.
Horák, Jiří, 1)
Kejmar, Miroslav, 12)

[Sonata, trumpet, strings & continuo, g minor]
Sonata a 4 in g minor for Trumpet, Strings and Continuo
(Sonata be mollis)
[Moderato] - [Grave] - [Allegro] - [Andante] - [Allegro] - [Andante]
[Moderato]
Breitenbacher: IV/43 (no date).
Güttler, Ludwig, 2)
Horák, Jiří, 1)
Kejmar, Miroslav, 12)
Rausch, Heiner
Scherbaum, Adolf, 29), 32)
Soustrot, Bernard, 9)

[Sonata, trumpet, trombone, strings & continuo, C major]
Sonata a 5 in C major for Trumpet, Alto Trombone, Strings and Continuo
Breitenbacher: IV/70 (no date).
Scherbaum, Adolf, 16)

[Sonata, 2 recorders, 2 trumpets, 3 trombones & continuo, no. 12]
Sonata No. 12 a 7
The actual identity of this sonata has not been ascertained. It may be an arrangement of the *Sonata "Vespertina"* for 2 violins, 2 trumpets, 3 trombones and continuo.
Schneidewind, Helmut, 8), 9)

[Sonata, 2 trumpets, strings & continuo, C major]
Sonata a 7 in C major for 2 Trumpets, Strings and Continuo
Horák, Jiří, 2)

[Sonata, 2 trumpets, strings & continuo, D major]
Sonata a 5 in D major for 2 Trumpets, Strings and Continuo
Horák, Jiří, 1)
Kejmar, Miroslav, 12)

ɾSonata, 2 trumpets, 2 trombones, strings & continuo, C major, (1666)ᒾ
Sonata a 10 in C major for 2 Trumpets, 2 Trombones, Strings and Continuo
Breitenbacher: IV/198.
Horák, Jiří, 2)

ɾSuite, B♭ major; arr. trumpet & organᒾ
Suite in B♭ major for Trumpet and Organ
¹Allemande / ²Courante / ³Sarabande / ⁴Canario
Braz, Dirceu, 3)

Veracini, Francesco Maria, 1690-1768

ɾConcerto, flute or violin, strings & continuo, e minor; arr. trumpet, strings & continuoᒾ
Concerto in e minor
¹Allegro / ²Gavotte / ³Gigue
André, Maurice, 83), 126), 217), 218)

Verdi, Giuseppe, 1813-1901
Verdi, Giuseppe Fortunino Francesco

ɾAïda, (1871). Aria, "Celeste Aïda"; arr. cornet, harp & orchestraᒾ
Aria, "Celeste Aïda" from *Aïda*
McCann, Phillip

ɾAïda, (1871). Duet, "La fatal pietra"; arr. cornet, trombone & bandᒾ
Duet, "The Fatal Stone", from *Aïda*
Potpourri, 8)

ɾAïda, (1871). Triumphal March; arr. trumpet & orchestraᒾ
Triumphal March from *Aïda*
André, Maurice, 170)

ɾNabucco, (1842). Slave's Chorus, "Va pensiero sul'ali dorate"; arr. trumpet & instrumental accompanimentᒾ
Sklavenchor from *Nabucco*
Scherbaum, Adolf, 34)

ɾRigoletto, (1851). Act III: Aria, "La donna è mobile"; arr. trumpet & orchestraᒾ
Aria, "La donna è mobile" from *Rigoletto*
André, Maurice, 37)

ɾRigoletto, (1851). Act IV: Aria, "Caro nome"; arr. trumpet & orchestraᒾ
Aria, "Caro nome" from *Rigoletto*
Méndez, Rafael, 19)

ɾRigoletto, (1851). Quartet, "Bella figlia dell'amore"; arr. trumpet & orchestraᒾ
Quartet, "Bella figlia dell'amore" from *Rigoletto*
Ghitalla, Armando, 14)

[Traviata, (1853). Aria, "Sempre libera"; arr. trumpet & brass ensemble]
Aria, "Sempre libera" from *La Traviata*
Canadian Brass, 4)

Viadana, Lodovico (da), *ca.* 1560-1627
Grossi da Viadana, Lodovico

[Sinfonie musicali, (1610). Canzon, "La Padovana", instrumental ensemble]
Canzon a 8, "La Padovana"
Instrumental ensemble includes: cornetti, sackbuts, schryari, shawms, recorders, portative organ & viols.
Montesi, Robert, 4)

Vianna, C.A., 20th cent.

[Carinhoso; arr. trumpet & guitar]
Carinhoso
In addition to C.A. Vianna, two other names are cited as co-producers of this work: Joao de Barro & Pedro Berrios (Vianna/de Barro/Berrios).
Méndez, Rafael, 14)

Victoria, Tomás Luis de, 1548-1611

[Motet, "O magnum mysterium", mixed voices & instrumental ensemble]
O magnum mysterium
Cook, Richard
Stradner, Gerhard

Vierdank, Johann, *ca.* 1605-1646
Vierdanck, Johann
Vierdank, John

[Capriccio, 2 cornetti, (1640); arr. 2 trumpets]
Capriccio a 2 Cornetti
Geyer, Charles

Vierne, Louis, 1870-1937

[Marche triomphale, trumpet, organ, brass ensemble & timpani, op. 46, (1921)]
Marche triomphale pour le Centenaire de Napoléon I, op. 46
André, Maurice, 186)
Potpourri, 41)

Villa-Lobos, Heitor, 1887-1959

[Bachianas Brasileiras. No. 5: soprano & 8 celli, (1938-1945); arr. trumpet & guitar]
Bachiana Brasileira No. 5
Braz, Dirceu, 5)
Schultz, Erik, 8)

ₜSuite, voice & violin, (1923). Sertaneja; arr. trumpet & guitarₗ
Sertaneja from *Suíte para canto e violino*
Braz, Dirceu, 5)

Vincent, Thomas, *ca.* 1720-1783

ₜSonata, solo instrument & continuo, op. 1, D major, (1748); arr. trumpet & organₗ
Sonata in D major
¹Andante / ²Allegro / ³Siciliana / ⁴Minuet
from *Six Solos for a Hautboy, German Flute, Violin, or Harpsichord, with a Thorough Bass*, op. 1, (1748).
André, Maurice, 163)

Vinci, Leonardo, *ca.* 1690-1730

ₜDidone abbandonata, (1726). Sinfonia, 2 trumpets & chamber orchestra, F majorₗ
Sinfonia in F major from *Didone abbandonata*
Allegro - Largo - Allegro
Kejmar, Miroslav, 14)

ₜSonata, flute & continuo, D major. Excerpts; arr. trumpet & organₗ
Sonata in D major
Allegro / Allegro
from *12 Solos for flute or violin and basso continuo...*, (c. 1746).
Mertens, Theo, 2)

Vitali, Tomaso Antonio, 1663-1745

ₜSinfonia, 2 oboes, 2 trumpets, strings & continuoₗ
Sinfonia pour 2 trompettes, 2 hautbois, cordes et basse continue
Allegro - Grave - Presto - Grave - Allegro
André, Maurice, 79), 115)

Vitry, Philippe de, 1291-1361
Vitriaco, Philippus de

ₜMotet, "Tribum que non abhorruit", mixed voices & instrumental ensembleₗ
Motet, "Tribum que non abhorruit"
Renz, Albrecht, 6)

Vivaldi, Antonio, 1678-1741
Vivaldi, Antonio Lucio

ₜAllegros, D major & a minor; arr. trumpet & harpₗ
Allegros pour trompette et harpe
[These transcribed movements are not clearly identified.]
André, Maurice, 84)

[Concerto, cello, strings & continuo, c minor, RV 401; arr. trumpet & strings]
Concerto en ut mineur pour trompette et cordes
[1]Allegro non molto / [2]Adagio / [3]Allegro molto
Ryom: RV 401 = Pincherle: P. 434 = Fanna: F. III/1 = Rinaldi: op. 20, no. 3.
[The *Bielefelder Katalog* indicates that only the fourth movement is transcribed; however, this concerto has only three movements.]
Touvron, Guy, 5)

[Concerto, diverse instruments, strings & continuo, C major, RV 555]
Concerto in C major for Diverse Instruments
[1]Allegro / [2]Largo à piacimento / [3]Allegro
Ryom: RV 555 = Pincherle: P. 87 = Fanna: F. XII/23 = Rinaldi: op. 53, no. 3.
Diverse instruments include: 2 recorders, oboe, 2 salmoè, (2) violins & 2 harpsichords. [This recording uses 2 flutes, oboe, English horn, solo violin & 2 harpsichords with 2 trumpets added for the third movement.]
Spindler, Josef, 3)

[Concerto, diverse instruments, strings & continuo, C major, RV 556]
Concerto "per la Solennità di San Lorenzo"
[1]Largo / [2]Allegro molto / [3]Largo e cantabile / [4][Allegro]
Ryom: RV 556 = Pincherle: P. 84 = Fanna: F. XII/14 = Rinaldi: op. 53, no. 2.
Originally designated for 2 solo violins, 2 recorders, 2 oboes, 2 trumpets, bassoon, strings & continuo; this version utilizes flute, oboe, bassoon, 2 trumpets, solo cello, harp, organ, harpsichord & strings.
André, Maurice, 124)
Haas, Rudolf

[Concerto, diverse instruments, strings & continuo, C major, RV 558]
Concerto in C major for Diverse Instruments
[1]Allegro molto / [2]Andante molto / [3]Allegro
Ryom: RV 558 = Pincherle: P. 16 = Fanna: XII/37 = Rinaldi: op. 64, no. 6.
Diverse instruments include: 2 recorders, 2 theorbos, 2 mandolins, 2 salmoè, 2 violins (tromba marina) & cello. [Flutes may be substituted for recorders; harps for theorbos; bass oboe for salmo; and trumpets for trombe marina.]
Haas, Rudolf
Vacchiano, William, 4)

[Concerto, flute, strings & continuo, G major, RV 436; arr. trumpet & organ]
Concerto en sol majeur pour trompette et orgue
[1]Allegro / [2]Largo / [3]Allegro
Ryom: RV 436 = Pincherle: P. 140 = Fanna: F. VI/8 = Rinaldi: op. 44, no. 21.
Jorand, Jean-Claude

ᵣConcerto, oboe, strings & continuo, D major, RV 453; arr. trumpet & stringsᵢ
Concerto en ré majeur pour trompette et cordes
[1]Allegro / [2]Largo / [3]Allegro
Ryom: RV 453 = Pincherle: P. 187 = Fanna: F. VII/10
Touvron, Guy, 5)

ᵣConcerto, oboe, strings & continuo, op. 7, no. 1, B♭ major, RV 465, (1716); arr.
trumpet, strings & continuoᵢ
Concerto en si bémol majeur pour trompette et orchestre à cordes
[1]Allegro / [2]Adagio / [3]Allegro
Ryom: RV 465 = Pincherle: P. 331 = Fanna: F. VII/14 =
Rinaldi: op. 7, no. 1.
> **André, Maurice**, 127)
> **Kejmar, Miroslav**, 11)
> **Touvron, Guy**, 5)

ᵣConcerto, oboe, violin, strings & continuo, B♭ major, RV 548; arr. trumpet & organᵢ
Concerto en si bémol majeur pour trompette et orgue
[1][Allegro] / [2]Largo / [3]Allegro ·
Ryom: RV 548 = Pincherle: P. 406 = Fanna: F. XII/16 =
Rinaldi: op. 52.
[There is also a version for 2 violins, RV 764.]
> **Hardy, Francis**
> **Jorand, Jean-Claude**
> **Willwerth, Paul**

ᵣConcerto, oboe, violin, strings & continuo, B♭ major, RV 548; arr. trumpet, violin, strings & continuoᵢ
Concerto en si bémol majeur pour trompette, violon et orchestre à cordes
[1][Allegro] / [2]Largo / [3]Allegro
Ryom: RV 548 = Pincherle: P. 406 = Fanna: F. XII/16 =
Rinaldi: op. 52.
[There is also a version for 2 violins, RV 764.]
> **André, Maurice**, 36), 48), 158), 135), 169),
> 200), 210), 214), 216)
> **Bernard, André**, 8)
> **Touvron, Guy**, 5)

ᵣConcerto, oboe, violin, strings & continuo, B♭ major, RV 548: Largo; arr.
trumpet, oboe & organᵢ
Largo from *Concerto in B♭ major for Oboe and Violin*, RV 548
André, Maurice, 39)

ₜConcerto, 2 corni da caccia, strings & continuo, F major, RV 538/RV 539; arr. 2 trumpets, strings & continuo, E♭ majorₗ

Concerto in E♭ major for 2 Trumpets

[1]Allegro moderato [first movement of RV 538] / [2]Larghetto [second movement of RV 539] / [3]Allegro [third movement of RV 539]
Ryom: RV 538 = Pincherle: P. 320 = Fanna: F. X/1 = Rinaldi: op. 47, no. 5.
Ryom: RV 539 = Pincherle: P. 321 = Fanna: F. X/2 = Rinaldi: op. 47, no. 6.

Battagliola, Anania
Hausdoerfer, Fred
Voisin, Roger, 4), 8)

ₜConcerto, 2 corni da caccia, strings & continuo, F major, RV 539ₗ

Concerto per 2 Corni da Caccia

[1]Allegro / [2]Larghetto / [3]Allegro
Ryom: RV 539 = Pincherle: P. 321 = Fanna: F. X/2 = Rinaldi: op. 47, no. 6.
[This version utilizes "modern corni da caccia" with valves.]
Guttler, Ludwig, 20)

ₜConcerto, 2 oboes, strings & continuo, C major, RV 534; arr. oboe, trumpet, strings & continuoₗ

Concerto en ut majeur pour hautbois, trompette, orchestre à cordes et basso continue

[1]Allegro / [2]Largo / [3]Allegro
Ryom: RV 534 = Pincherle: P. 85 = Fanna: F. VII/3 = Rinaldi: op. 53, no. 1.

André, Maurice, 47)

ₜConcerto, 2 oboes, strings & continuo, d minor, RV 535; arr. trumpet, oboe & stringsₗ

Concerto en ré mineur pour trompette, hautbois et orchestre à cordes

[1]Largo / [2]Allegro / [3]Largo / [4]Allegro molto
Ryom: RV 535 = Pincherle: P. 302 = Fanna: F. VII/9 = Rinaldi: op. 42, no. 2.

André, Maurice, 47)

[Concerto, 2 trumpets, strings & continuo, C major, RV 537]

Concerto con 2 Trombe
[1]Allegro / [2]Largo / [3][Allegro]
Ryom: RV 537 = Pincherle: P. 75 = Fanna: F. IX/1 = Rinaldi:
op. 46, no. 1.

          Adelbrecht, Henri, 4), 5), 6), 7)
          André, Maurice, 3), 9), 15), 22), 27), 28), 29),
              30), 31), 33), 35[1]), 36), 41), 74), 77), 86),
              102), 117), 131), 169), 178), 206[1]), 207[1]),
              215), 218), 219), 226), 227)
          Biessecker, Friedhelm
          Calvayrac, Albert
          Carroll, Edward, 1[1])
          Cuvit, Michel
          Delmotte, Roger, 9), 27), 37), 46), 47), 50)
          Doets, Jas
          Güttler, Ludwig, 3), 19), 21[1])
          Hausdoerfer, Fred
          Hunger, Helmut, 3)
          Jones, Philip, 3)
          Laird, Michael, 5), 6)
          Marsalis, Wynton, 6), 7)
          Nagel, Robert, 14)
          Orvid, Georgy
          Petit, Gilbert
          Potpourri, 14), 15), 21), 29), 34), 35), 36), 37),
              65), 68)
          Scherbaum, Adolf, 19), 22), 23), 24), 25), 26)
          Schetsche, Walter
          Schmidhäusler, Francis & René
          Schultz, Erik, 9)
          Schwarz, Gerard, 7)
          Soustrot, Bernard, 7)
          Steele-Perkins, Crispian, 2), 19)
          Thompson, James
          Touvron, Guy, 7), 18)
          Voisin, Roger, 3)
          Wallace, John, 4)
          Wilbraham, John, 6), 11), 12), 18), 19)
          Wobisch, Helmut, 3), 14)
          Zapf, Gerd
          Zickler, Heinz, 8[1]), 9)

[Concerto, 2 trumpets, strings & continuo, C major, RV 537; arr. 2 trumpets & organ]

Concerto in C major for 2 Trumpets and Organ
[1]Allegro / [2]Largo / [3][Allegro]
Ryom: RV 537 = Pincherle: P. 75 = Fanna: F. IX/1 = Rinaldi:
op. 46, no. 1.
          Waltzing, Gast

ₗConcerto, 2 trumpets, violin, strings & continuo, D major, RV 781ₗ
Concerto in D major for 2 Trumpets, Violin, Strings and Basso continuo
[1]Allegro / [2]Grave / [3]Allegro
Ryom: RV 781 = Pincherle: P. 210 = Fanna: F. XII/50.
[This concerto is also designated for 2 oboes as RV 563.]
Laird, Michael, 21)

ₗGloria, soli, mixed voices, oboe, trumpet, strings & continuo, D major, RV 589ₗ
Gloria in D major
Greffin, Jean Jacques
Tarr, Edward, 13)

ₗJuditha Triumphans, RV 644, (1716). Aria del Vagante; arr. trumpet & pianoₗ
Allegro
(Aria del Vagante from *Juditha Triumphans*)
Nagel, Robert, 16)

ₗSonata, oboe & continuo, c minor, RV 53; arr. trumpet & organₗ
Sonata per Oboe Solo
[1]Adagio / [2]Allegro / [3]Andante / [4]Allegro
Ryom: RV 53 = Pincherle: p. 6, no. 3 = Fanna: F. XV/2.
André, Maurice, 65)

ₗSonata, violin & continuo, D major, RV 10; arr. Concerto, trumpet & stringsₗ
Concerto en ré majeur pour trompette et cordes
[1]Allegro / [2]Allegro / [3]Adagio / [4]Allegro
Ryom: RV 10 = Pincherle: p. 5, no. 10 = Fanna: F. XIII/6
[The first movement is omitted from this arrangement.]
André, Maurice, 3), 86), 126)

ₗSonatas, op. 2, (1709). No. 4, violin & continuo, F major, RV 20; arr. Concerto, trumpet & organ, A♭ majorₗ
Concerto en la bémol pour trompette et orgue
[1]Andante / [2]Allemanda (Allegro) / [3]Sarabanda (Andante) / [4]Corrente (Presto)
Ryom: RV 20 = Pincherle: p. 2, no. 4 = Fanna: F. XIII/32 = Rinaldi: op. 2, no. 4.
[The first movement is omitted from this arrangement.]
Jorand, Jean-Claude

₍Sonatas, op. 2, (1709). No. 4, violin & continuo, F major, RV 20; arr. Concerto, trumpet & strings, A♭ major₎

Concerto en la bémol pour trompette et orchestre à cordes
[1]Andante / [2]Allemanda (Allegro) / [3]Sarabanda (Andante) / [4]Corrente (Presto)
Ryom: RV 20 = Pincherle: p. 2, no. 4 = Fanna: F. XIII/32 = Rinaldi: op. 2, no. 4.
[The first movement is omitted from this arrangement.]
>> **André, Maurice,** 3), 60), 74), 83[2]), 86), 117), 168), 169), 184), 193), 197), 210), 213), 217[2])
>> **Bernard, André,** 8), 10)
>> **Blair, Stacy**
>> **Potpourri,** 36), 37)
>> **Touvron, Guy,** 5)

₍Sonatas, op. 2, (1709). No. 4, violin & continuo, F major, RV 20: Presto; arr. Concerto, trumpet & organ, A♭ major₎

Concerto en la bémol pour trompette et orgue
Ryom: RV 20 = Pincherle: p. 2, no. 4 = Fanna: F. XIII/32 = Rinaldi: op. 2, no. 4.
>> **Laughton, Stuart**

₍Sonatas, op. 5, (1716). No. 5, 2 violins & continuo, B♭ major, RV 76; arr. 2 trumpets & organ₎

Sonate à trois en si bémol majeur pour deux trompettes et orgue, op. 5, no. 17
(Trio Sonata in B♭, op. 5, no. 5)
[1]Preludio (Andante) / [2]Allemanda (Allegro) / [3]Corrente (Allegro)
Ryom: RV 76 = Pincherle: p. 3, no. 7 = Fanna: F. XIII/45 = Rinaldi: op. 5, no. 5.
There are 12 sonatas in *Opus 2* and 6 sonatas in *Opus 5*. The original publication of *Opus 5* included the alternative title, *Parte Seconde del Opera Seconda*. Therefore, *Opus 5, No. 5 = Opus 2, No. 17*, and is often indicated *Opus 5, No. 17*.
>> **André, Maurice,** 150)

₍Sonatas, op. 13, (1737). No. 6, flute (oboe or violin) & continuo, g minor, RV 58; arr. Concerto, trumpet & band₎

Concerto in g minor for Trumpet and Band
[1]Vivace / [2]Allabreve (Fuga da Capella) / [3]Largo / [4]Allegro ma non presto
Ryom: RV 58 = Pincherle: p. 4, no. 4 = Fanna: F. XVI/10 = Rinaldi: op. 13, no. 6.
The title of this collection was *Il Pastor Fido, Sonates, pour La Musette, Viele, Flûte, Hautbois, Violin, avec la Basse Continüe...*, op. 13.
[The second movement is omitted from this arrangement.]
>> **Stith, Marice,** 2)

[Sonatas, op. 13, (1737). No. 6, flute (oboe or violin) & continuo, g minor, RV 58; arr. Concerto, trumpet & organ]
Concert en sol mineur pour trompette et piano ou orgue
[1]Vivace / [2]Allabreve (Fuga da Capella) / [3]Largo / [4]Allegro ma non presto
Ryom: RV 58 = Pincherle: p. 4, no. 4 = Fanna: F. XVI/10 = Rinaldi: op. 13, no. 6.
The title of this collection was *Il Pastor Fido, Sonates, pour La Musette, Viele, Flûte, Hautbois, Violin, avec la Basse Continüe...,* op. 13.
[The second movement is omitted from this arrangement.]
André, Maurice, 45), 65)
Bernard, André, 4), 11)
Jorand, Jean-Claude

[Sonatas, op. 13, (1737). No. 6, flute (oboe or violin) & continuo, g minor, RV 58; arr. Concerto, trumpet & strings]
Concert en sol mineur pour trompette et orchestre à cordes
[1]Vivace / [2]Allabreve (Fuga da Capella) / [3]Largo / [4]Allegro ma non presto
Ryom: RV 58 = Pincherle: p. 4, no. 4 = Fanna: F. XVI/10 = Rinaldi: op. 13, no. 6.
The title of this collection was *Il Pastor Fido, Sonates, pour La Musette, Viele, Flûte, Hautbois, Violin, avec la Basse Continüe...,* op. 13.
[The second movement is omitted from this arrangement.]
André, Maurice, 3), 83[3]), 86), 126), 217[3])
Bernard, André, 8)
Kejmar, Miroslav, 11)
Touvron, Guy, 5)

Vivarino, Innocentio, *ca.* 1575-1626

[Motettenbuch I, (1620). No. 1: Sonata, cornetto, trombone & organ]
Sonata No. 1
Eichhorn, Holger

[Motettenbuch I, (1620). No. 2: Sonata, cornetto, trombone & organ]
Sonata No. 2
Eichhorn, Holger

[Motettenbuch I, (1620). No. 3: Sonata, cornetto, trombone & organ]
Sonata No. 3
Eichhorn, Holger

Viviani, Giovanni Buonaventura, 1638-*ca.* 1692

[Sinfonie, Arie, Capricci..., op. 4, (1678). Sonata, trumpet & continuo (harpsichord), no. 2, C major]
Sonata seconda per trombetta sola
[1][Allegro] / [2][Allegro] / [3]Adagio / [4]Aria / [5]Presto
Plog, Anthony, 7)

[Sinfonie, Arie, Capricci..., op. 4, (1678). Sonata, trumpet & continuo (organ), no. 1, C major]
Sonata prima per trombetta sola
[1][Andante] / [2][Allegro] / [3][Presto] / [4][Allegro] / [5][Adagio]
    André, Maurice, 22), 28), 29), 33), 118)
    Berinbaum, Martin
    Bernard, André, 4), 11)
    Capouillez, Luc
    Carroll, Edward, 7), 9)
    Chatel, Jean-Louis
    Erb, Helmut, 5)
    Fink, Werner
    Gaudon, Jean-Jacques
    Gräber, Wolfgang
    Groth, Konradin
    Güttler, Ludwig, 22)
    Haas, Wolfgang
    Keavy, Stephen
    Rehm, Klaus
    Riggione, Angelo
    Sautter, Fred
    Scherbaum, Adolf, 29), 32)
    Schultz, Erik, 1)
    Smithers, Don, 1)
    Stringer, Alan, 3)
    Tarr, Edward, 40)
    Thomas, Peggy Paton
    Touvron, Guy, 20)
    Ullrich, Marc
    Wilbraham, John, 9)
    Yudashkin, Georgy

[Sinfonie, Arie, Capricci..., op. 4, (1678). Sonata, trumpet & continuo (organ), no. 2, C major]
Sonata seconda per trombetta sola
[1][Allegro] / [2][Allegro] / [3]Adagio / [4]Aria / [5]Presto
    André, Maurice, 27), 118)
    Bernard, André, 4)
    Carroll, Edward, 7), 9)
    Chesnut, Walter
    Fink, Werner
    Güttler, Ludwig, 2)
    Immer, Friedemann, 9)
    Rehm, Klaus
    Riggione, Angelo
    Sautter, Fred
    Scherbaum, Adolf, 17), 32)

Schultz, Erik, 1)
Smithers, Don, 1)
Tamiya, Kenji
Tarr, Edward, 40)
Ullrich, Marc
Wilbraham, John, 9)

[Sinfonie, Arie, Capricci..., op. 4, (1678). Sonata, trumpet & continuo, no. 1, C major; arr. trumpet & organ, D major]
Sonata prima per trombetta sola
[1][Andante] / [2][Allegro] / [3][Presto] / [4][Allegro] / [5][Adagio]
Wilbraham, John, 9)

[Sinfonie, Arie, Capricci..., op. 4, (1678). Sonata, trumpet & continuo, no. 2, C major; arr. trumpet & organ, D major]
Sonata seconda per trombetta sola
[1][Allegro] / [2][Allegro] / [3]Adagio / [4]Aria / [5]Presto
Wilbraham, John, 9)

Vizzutti, Allen, 1952-

[Adventures, piccolo trumpet & strings]
Adventures for Piccolo Trumpet and Strings
Vizzutti, Allen

[Andante and Capriccio, trumpet & strings]
Andante and Capriccio
Vizzutti, Allen

[Concerto, trumpet & orchestra]
Concerto for Trumpet and Orchestra
3 movements
Jeff Tyzik collaborated in composing this concerto.
Severinsen, Carl "Doc"

von Reutter, Karl Georg
See: Reutter, Karl Georg von

von Weber, Carl Maria
See: Weber, Carl Maria von

Vrijens, Gé, 20th cent.

[Gastronomy, trumpet & brass ensemble]
Gastronomy
Grin, Freddy, 2)

[Progressitive, trumpet & brass ensemble]
Progressitive
Grin, Freddy, 2)

Vrijens (arr.), Gé, 20th cent.

ᵣNational Hymn, "Wilhelmus"; arr. trumpet, organ & brass ensembleᵤ
National Hymn, "Wilhelmus"
Grin, Freddy, 9)

Vulpius, Melchior, *ca.* 1570-1615

ᵣEs ist ein Ros' entsprungen; arr. trumpet & brass ensembleᵤ
Es ist ein Ros' entsprungen
Güttler, Ludwig, 9)

Wade, John Francis, *ca.* 1711-1786

ᵣAdeste fidelis; arr. children's voices, trumpet & orchestraᵤ
Adeste fidelis
(O Come, All Ye Faithful)
André, Maurice, 166)

Wagenseil, Georg Christoph, 1715-1777

ᵣSymphony, 2 oboes, 2 trumpets, timpani, strings & continuo, D majorᵤ
Symphony in D major
Spindler, Josef, 6)

Wagner, Richard, 1813-1883
Wagner, (Wilhelm) Richard

ᵣLohengrin, (1850). Wedding March; arr. trumpet & organᵤ
Wedding March from *Lohengrin*
Giangiulio, Richard

Waignien, André, 1941-

ᵣMouvements (3), trumpet & pianoᵤ
Trois Mouvements
(Three Movements)
Phillippe, André

Wal-Berg, 1910-
Rosenberg, Voldemar

ᵣConcerto, trumpet & orchestra, g minor, (1948)ᵤ
Concerto in g minor for Trumpet and Orchestra
[1]Allegretto moderato giocoso / [2]Andante cantabile / [3]Vivo con brio
Wal-Berg is a pseudonym for Voldemar Rosenberg.
Erb, Helmut, 3)

Wallace, John, 20th cent.

ᵣRhapsody, trumpet & double bassᵤ
Rhapsody
Wallace, John, 6)

Walond, William, *ca.* 1725-1770

ᵣVoluntary, organ, D major; arr. trumpet & organᵣ
Voluntary in D major
This voluntary may be the fourth of *Ten Voluntaries for the Organ or Harpsichord*, op. 2, (1758).
Sautter, Fred

ᵣVoluntary, organ, no. 3; arr. trumpet & organᵣ
Voluntary No. 3
This voluntary may be the third of *Ten Voluntaries for the Organ or Harpsichord*, op. 2, (1758).
Basch, Wolfgang, 5)

Walters (arr.), Harold L., 1918-

ᵣHigh Society; arr. clarinet, saxophone, trumpet, trombone & concert bandᵣ
High Society
(We're Gonna Be in High Society)
Butterfield, Billy

Walther, Johann Gottfried, 1684-1748

ᵣConcerto del Sigr. Blamr, organ; arr. trumpet & organᵣ
Concerto del Sigr. Blamr
¹Adagio / ²Andante allegro / ³Pastorella
André, Maurice, 59)

ᵣConcerto del Sigr. Meck, organ; arr. trumpet & organᵣ
Concerto del Sigr. Meck
Winslow, Richard

ᵣConcerto, organ, G major; arr. trumpet & organᵣ
Concerto in G major
¹Adagio / ²Largo / ³Vivace / ⁴Aria / ⁵Vivace
André, Maurice, 134)
Basch, Wolfgang, 11)

ᵣEin' feste Burg ist unser Gott, organ; arr. trumpet & organᵣ
Ein' feste Burg ist unser Gott
Braz, Dirceu, 4)

ᵣJoseph, lieber Joseph mein, soli, mixed voices & instrumental ensembleᵣ
Joseph, lieber Joseph mein
Cook, Richard

Walton, William, 1902-1983
Walton, William Turner

[Façade, reciter & chamber ensemble, op. 10, (1922)]
Façade — An Entertainment
Originally composed in 1922 as musical settings for poetry by
Dame Edith Sitwell, there have been versions for five different
media: reciter and chamber ensemble, ballet, suites for orchestra,
various individual arrangements and simple recitations. With
twenty-one different poems, there have also been a variety of
selected settings arranged in suites (plus a separate opening
"fanfare"). Basically, the various suites with reciter and chamber
ensemble have been indexed together. Where ascertained, the
specific settings have been included in the **Album** listings.
Chamber ensemble includes: flute, clarinet, saxophone, trumpet,
2 cellos & percussion.
> **Broiles, Melvin**
> **Crisara, Raymond**, 1)
> **Evans, Laurie**
> **Izan, Bernard**
> **Johnson, Gilbert**, 1)
> **Mason, David**, 3), 5)
> **Mueller, Herbert**[1-8+10-21]
> **Roberts, Standish**
> **Weis, Theodore**, 2)
> **Wilbraham, John**, 1)

[Henry V, op. 47, (1944). Touch Her Soft Lips and Part; arr. cornet, organ &
band]
Touch Her Soft Lips and Part from *Henry V*
Originally composed as music for the film, *Henry V*, this song has
been arranged for a variety of different media, including for
mixed voices and orchestra.
> **Read, David**

Watts, John, 1930-1982

[Elegy to Chimney, trumpet & tape/synthesizer, (1972)]
Elegy to Chimney: In Memoriam
> **Levy, Robert**

Wayne, Mabel, 1904-

[In a Little Spanish Town, (1926); arr. trumpet & orchestra]
In a Little Spanish Town
Lyricists for this popular song were Sam M. Lewis and Joe
Young.
> **Méndez, Rafael**, 29)

Weast, Robert, 20th cent.

ₜSonata, trumpet & piano, (1969)ₙ
Sonata for Trumpet and Piano
¹Vigorously / ²Slowly / ³Allegro
Weast, Robert

Webb, George James, 1803-1887

ₜWEBB, (1930); arr. trumpet & pianoₙ
Stand Up for Jesus
Reinhart, Carole Dawn, 13)

Webber, Andrew Lloyd
See: Lloyd Webber, Andrew

Webber, Lloyd, 20th cent.

ₜSonata, trumpet & piano, F majorₙ
Sonata in F major for Trumpet and Piano
This "Lloyd Webber" may actually be William Southcombe Lloyd Webber (1914-1982). And the work listed as "sonata" in the **Music Minus One** brochure may actually be Lloyd Webber's *"Suite" in F major for Trumpet and Piano*, (1952).
Ghitalla, Armando, 12)

Weber, Alain, 1930-

ₜSonatine Breve, trumpet & piano, (1958)ₙ
Sonatine Breve
Hyatt, Jack

Weber, Carl Maria von, 1786-1826

ₜMarcia Vivace, 10 trumpets, J. 288ₙ
Marcia Vivace for 10 Trumpets, J. 288
Wallace, John, 5)

Weber, Friedrich Dionys, 1766-1842

ₜVariations, trumpet & orchestra, F majorₙ
Variations in F major for Trumpet and Orchestra
Wallace, John, 5)

Weill, Kurt, 1900-1950
Weill, Kurt Julian

⌜Dreigroschenoper, (1928). Suite, chamber ensemble⌝
Suite from The Threepenny Opera
(Kleine Dreigroschenmusik)
Chamber ensemble includes: 2 flutes (piccolo), oboe, 2 clarinets, 2 bassoons, saxophone, horn, 2 trumpets, trombone, tuba, piano, 2 violins, cello, bass, guitar (banjo), bandoneon & 2 percussion.
Dean, Allan, 5)

Weinberg, Henry, 1931-

⌜Cantus Commemorabilis I, chamber ensemble, (1966)⌝
Cantus Commemorabilis I
Chamber ensemble includes: flute, oboe, clarinet, horn, trumpet, trombone, violin, cello, bass, piano & percussion.
Miller, Rodney

Weiner, Stanley Milton, 1925-

⌜Fantasies. No. 1, trumpet & organ, op. 57⌝
Phantasy Nr. 1, op. 57
Tarr, Edward, 5)

⌜Fantasies. No. 2, 2 trumpets & organ, op. 113, (1982)⌝
Phantasy Nr. 2 für 2 Trompeten und Orgel, op. 113
Haas, Wolfgang
Tarr, Edward, 44)

Weinzweig, John Jacob, 1913-

⌜Divertimenti. No. 5, trumpet, trombone & wind ensemble, (1961)⌝
Divertimento No. 5
Chevanelle, Serge

Weisgall, Hugo David, 1912-

⌜Stronger, soprano & piano, (1952); arr. soprano & chamber ensemble, (1955)⌝
The Stronger
Chamber ensemble includes: 2 saxophones, trumpet, violin, viola, cello, bass & piano.
Anderson, Ronald, 2)

Wenrich, Percy, 1887-1952

⌜Moonlight Bay, (1912); arr. trumpet quartet⌝
Moonlight Bay
Blackburn, Roger

Werner, Fritz, 1898-1977
Werner, Fritz Eugen Heinrich

ₜDuo, trumpet & organ, op. 53ⱼ
Duo für Trompete und Orgel, op. 53
Haas, Wolfgang
Tarr, Edward, 5)

ₜSuite Concertante, trumpet, antique cymbals, timpani & strings, op. 48, (1969)ⱼ
Suite Concertante pour trompette, orchestre à cordes, crotales et timbales, op. 48
¹Allegro giocoso / ²Andante sostenuto / ³Allegro vivace / ⁴Lento molto expressivo / ⁵Allegro quasi presto
André, Maurice, 146)

Wernicke, Isreal Gottlieb, 1755-1836

ₜCanon in ostinato über B-A-C-H, trumpet, horn & 2 trombonesⱼ
Canon in ostinato über B-A-C-H
Christiansen, Jan

White, William, *ca.* 1585-*ca.* 1667

ₜFantasia; arr. trumpet trioⱼ
Fantasia
Included in David Baldwin's arrangement, "Consort Music".
Carroll, Edward, 10)

Whitney, Maurice C., 1909-
Whitney, Maurice Cary

ₜConcertino, trumpet & band, (1959); arr. trumpet & pianoⱼ
Concertino for Trumpet (and Band)
¹Allegro non troppo / ²Lento / ³Allegro scherzando
Crisara, Raymond, 7²)
Schwarz, Gerard, 16³)

Whittenberg, Charles, 1927-1984

ₜPolyphony, solo trumpet, (1965)ⱼ
Polyphony
Schwarz, Gerard, 10)

Wilbye, John, 1574-1638
Willoughbye, John

ₜMadrigals; arr. trumpet trioⱼ
Two Madrigals
"So Light is Love" / "What Shall I Doe"
Included in David Baldwin's arrangement, "Consort Music".
Carroll, Edward, 10)

Wilder, Alec, 1907-1980
Wilder, Alexander Lafayette Chew

₍Sonata, trumpet & piano, (1963)₎
Sonata for Trumpet and Piano
[1]Slow (Recitatif) / [2]Bright, and Lyrical / [3]Slow (Soliloquy) /
[4]Rhythmic (Duologue)
Wilder, Joseph B.

₍Song for a Friend, trumpet & piano₎
A Song for a Friend
Levy, Robert

₍Suite, trumpet & marimba, (1977)₎
Suite for Trumpet and Marimba
Levy, Robert

₍Suite, trumpet & piano, (1969)₎
Suite for Trumpet and Piano
Levy, Robert

Willard, arr., 20th cent.

₍O STORE GUD; arr. trumpet & piano₎
O Mighty God, When I Behold the Wonder
(How Great Thou Art)
The hymn text for this Swedish folk melody was by Carl Boberg,
(1886). It was translated to English and arranged with four-part
harmony by Stuart K. Hine, (1949).
Reinhart, Carole Dawn, 13)

Williams, Ernest S., 1882-1947

₍Concerto, trumpet & piano, no. 4, (1937)₎
Fourth Concerto for Trumpet
[1]Allegro con spirito / [2]Andante mesto / [3]Allegro commodo
Burke, James, 7[1])

₍Little Classics, cornet (or trumpet) & piano, (1946)₎
Little Classics
[1]Concertone / [2]Sarabande and Bourrie / [3]Osseo Fantasia / [4]Wyalusing
Polka / [5]Winema Waltz / [6]Mitena Gavotte / [7]Wanatuska March /
[8]Chemung Rondino / [9]Chenango Schottisch / [10]Temecu Waltz / [11]The
Adirondacks Polka / [12]The Catskills Polka
Autrey, Byron L.[5+6+9+8+7+12]

₍Little Classics, cornet (or trumpet) & piano, (1946). No. 6: Mitena₎
Mitena (Gavotte)
Haynie, John, 1)

₍Sonata, trumpet & piano, (1942)₎
Sonata for Trumpet and Piano
Burke, James, 7)

Williams, Grace (Mary), 1906-1977

ₐConcerto, trumpet & orchestra, (1963)ₐ
Concerto for Trumpet and Orchestra
Snell, Howard

Williams, J. Clifton, 1923-1976
Williams, James Clifton

ₐDramatic Essay, trumpet & band, (1958)ₐ
Dramatic Essay
Head, Emerson
Jacoby, Don

Willis, Richard, 19th cent.

ₐVariations, "Yankee Doodle", fife, keyed bugle & instrumental ensemble, (c. 1820)ₐ
Yankee Doodle Variations
Dudgeon, Ralph

Willson, Meredith, 1902-1984
Willson, (Robert) Meredith

ₐMusic Man, (1957). Medley; arr. trumpet quartetₐ
Goodnight My Someone / Seventy-six Trombones
Jacoby, Don

Willwerth, Paul, 20th cent.

ₐLegacy, trumpet & organₐ
Legacy
Willwerth, Paul

Wilson, George Balch, 1927-

ₐConcatenations, chamber ensemble, (1969)ₐ
Concatenations
Chamber ensemble includes: flute, clarinet, bass clarinet, horn, trumpet, trombone, violin, cello, bass & percussion.
Ferrantino, Kenneth

Wilson, Olly, 1937-
Wilson, Olly Woodrow

ₐPiece for Four, flute, trumpet, piano & bass, (1966)ₐ
Piece for Four
Young, Gene

Windsor

[Alpine Echoes, cornet & band]
Alpine Echoes
McCann, Phillip

Wolf, Peter, 20th cent.

[Serenade, trumpet & instrumental ensemble]
Serenade
Geiger, György

Wolff, Christian, 1934-

[Edges, trumpet, violin, percussion & bass, (1968)]
Edges
Edges was composed for any combination of musicians.
Wallace, John, 6)

Wolpe, Stefan, 1902-1972

[Piece, trumpet & chamber ensemble, (1971)]
Piece for Solo Trumpet and 7 Instruments
Chamber ensemble includes: clarinet, bassoon, horn, 2 violins, cello & bass.
Guarneri, Mario

[Quartet, trumpet, tenor saxophone, percussion & piano, (1950)]
Quartet
[1]Sostenuto / [2]Con moto
Dean, Allan, 6)
Nagel, Robert, 7)

[Solo Piece, solo trumpet, (1966)]
Solo Piece for Trumpet
[1]Graceful, talking / [2]Not too big, intimate
The first movement is designated for trumpet in C, and the second movement is designated for trumpet in F Alto. (But a footnote suggests that both movements may be played on a trumpet in B♭.)
Levy, Robert
Schwarz, Gerard, 10)
Wallace, John, 6)

Wood, Haydn, 1882-1959

[Brown Bird Singing; arr. cornet & organ]
A Brown Bird Singing
McCann, Phillip

Wood, Samuel Balmforth, 1896-

₍D.M.G., cornet & brass band, (1967)₎
Cornet Solo, "D.M.G."
The title of this solo comes from the initials of the soloist, Derek M. Garside.
Garside, Derek M.

Wright, Denis, 1895-1967

₍Trio Concerto, cornet, trombone, euphonium & brass band, (1967)₎
Trio Concerto
¹Prelude / ²Elegy / ³Finale
Garside, Derek M.

Wrubel, Allie, 1905-1973

₍Zip-a-Dee Doo-Dah, (1945); arr. trumpet quartet₎
Zip-a-Dee Doo-Dah
Blackburn, Roger

Wuensch, Gerhard J., 1925-
Wuensch, Gerhard Joseph

₍Suite, trumpet & organ, op. 40, (1972)₎
Suite for Trumpet and Organ, op. 40
¹Alla breve / ²Perpetuum Mobile / ³Dirge / ⁴Rondo
Chatel, Jean-Louis
Plog, Anthony, 2)

Wyner, Yehudi, 1929-

₍Serenade, flute, horn, trumpet, trombone, viola, cello & piano, (1958)₎
Serenade for 7 Instruments
¹Nocturne I / ²Toccata / ³Capriccio - Aria / ⁴Nocturne II
Nagel, Robert, 5)

Yanchenko, Oleg Grigorevich, 1939-

₍Concerto grosso, 4 trumpets, timpani & organ₎
Concerto Grosso for 4 Trumpets, Timpani and Organ
Volodin, Lev

Yeh Shu-han, 1957-

₍Hand in Hand, trumpet & piano₎
Hand in Hand, fantasy
Based on a Shinjian folksong.
Yeh Shu-han

Yon, Pietro Alessandro, 1886-1943

[Gesù Bambino, organ, (1917); arr. trumpet & organ]
Gesù Bambino
Stith, Marice, 9)

Yosinao, Nakata, 1923-

[Memories of Summer; arr. trumpet & piano]
Natsu No Omoide
(Memories of Summer)
Dokshitser, Timofei, 19)

[Walking through town in the snowfall; arr. trumpet & piano]
Yuki No Furu Machio
(Walking through town in the snowfall)
Dokshitser, Timofei, 19)

Youmans, Vincent, 1898-1946
Youmans, Vincent Millie

[I Know that You Know, (1926); arr. trumpet & orchestra]
I Know that You Know
Méndez, Rafael, 28)

[Tea for Two, (1924); arr. trumpet & orchestra]
Tea for Two
Méndez, Rafael, 28)

Young, Gordon Ellsworth, 1919-

[Contempora Suite, trumpet & piano, (1956)]
Contempora Suite
[1]Prelude / [2][Air] / [3]Sarabande / [4]Gigue
Amstutz, Keith[3-4]
Ritter, David
Schwarz, Gerard, 14[1])

Young, Victor, 1900-1956

[Around the World in 80 Days, (1956). Theme song; arr. trumpet & orchestra]
"Around the World in 80 Days" from *Around the World in 80 Days*
Méndez, Rafael, 13)

[I Don't Stand a Ghost of a Chance with You; arr. trumpet & orchestra]
I Don't Stand a Ghost of a Chance with You
Méndez, Rafael, 21)

Yttrehus, Rolv, 1926-
[Sextet, horn, trumpet, violin, piano, bass & percussion, (1969-70)]
Sextet
Potpourri, 5)

Yurovsky, Vladimir Mikhailovich, 1915-
Urovsky, Vladimir

[Dance, trumpet & piano]
Dance
Dokshitser, Timofei, 5), 27)

Zatin, Anatoly, 1954-
[Concerto, horn, trumpet, piano & orchestra]
Concerto for Horn, Trumpet and Piano with Orchestra
Dokshitser, Timofei, 22)

Zbinden, Julien-François, 1917-
[Concertino, trumpet, strings & drum, op. 6, (1946)]
Concertino pour Trompette, Orchestre à cordes et Tambour, op. 6 [1]Allegro / [2]Trés lent / [3]Presto
André, Maurice, 147)

[Dialogues, trumpet & organ, op. 50]
Dialogues, op. 50
André, Maurice, 164)

Zelenka, Johann Dismas, 1679-1745
Zelenka, Jan Dismas

[Capriccen. No. 5, 2 corni da caccia & instrumental ensemble, G major: 4. Furibondo (Presto assai)]
Capriccio No. 5 in G major
Güttler, Ludwig, 20)

[Cavalry Fanfares. No. 5, trumpet ensemble]
Cavalry Fanfare No. 5
Smithers, Don, 10)

[Fanfare, 4 trumpets & timpani]
Fanfare
from *Jezdecké fanfáry del Sig. Zelenka*
Tarr, Edward, 28)

Zhubanova, Gaziza Akhmetovna, 1928-
[Canzonetta, trumpet & orchestra]
Canzonetta
Klushkin, Yuri

⌐Humoresque, trumpet & orchestra⌐
Humoresque
Klushkin, Yuri

Zipoli, Domenico, 1688-1726

⌐Pastorale; arr. trumpet & organ⌐
Pastorale
Basch, Wolfgang, 5)

⌐Suite, 3 trumpets & strings, F major⌐
Suite in F major
André, Maurice, 74), 153), 209²)

Zipp, Friedrich, 1914-
Zipp, Friedrich Otto Gottfried

⌐Chorale Prelude, "Nun freut euch, lieben Christen gmein", trumpet & organ⌐
Chorale Prelude, "Nun freut euch, lieben Christen gmein"
Lewark, Egbert

Zonn, Paul, 1938-

⌐Gemini Fantasy, trumpet, tuba, viola, bass, piano & percussion⌐
Gemini Fantasy
Sasaki, Ray

Zundel, John, 1815-1882

⌐"Wat de toekomst brenge moge"; arr. trumpet, organ & brass ensemble⌐
"Wat de toekomst brenge moge"
Grin, Freddy, 9)

Accordion
[includes bandoneon]

Aussem, Peter
see: Schoof, Manfred

Jolles, Jerome
see: Dean, Allan, 5)

Alto (voice)
[includes contralto (and may include
some cross-referenced countertenor)]

Anderson, Cynthia
see: Geyer, Charles

Baker, Janet
see: Jones, Philip, 1), 3)
see: Laird, Michael, 15)
see: Tarr, Edward, 24), 25), 26)
see: Wilbraham, John, 22)

Bence, Margarethe
see: Gleissle, Walter, 8), 11)
see: Unidentified, Trumpet(s),
23)
see: Zickler, Heinz, 2)

Beutler, Ann
see: Levy, Robert

Bloss, Susan
see: Geyer, Charles

Bornemann, Eva
see: Köpp, Rudolf

Bratschke, Detlef
see: Potpourri, 61)

Brett, Charles
see: Laird, Michael, 14)
see: Steele-Perkins, Crispian,
16)

Bright, Matthew
see: Laird, Michael, 7)

Brunssen, Karen
see: Geyer, Charles

Bumbry, Grace
see: Stringer, Alan, 5)

Bunshaft, Gillian
see: Potpourri, 66)

Cable, Margaret
see: Jones, Philip, 9)

Casoni, Bianca Maria
see: André, Maurice, 11)

Charney, Miriam
see: Cook, Richard

Chedel, Arlette
see: Adelbrecht, Henri, 3)

Cockerham, Michael
see: Laird, Michael, 7)

Cohen, Beth
see: Cook, Richard

Coles, Marilyn
see: Potpourri, 66)

Collard, Jeanine
see: André, Maurice, 71)
see: Greffin, Jean Jacques
see: Thibaud, Pierre, 9)

Conrad, Margrit
see: Tarr, Edward, 32)

Cooke, Jonathan
see: Laird, Michael, 7)

Deckert, Patricia
see: Geyer, Charles

Denley, Catherine
see: Steele-Perkins, Crispian,
12)

Eder, Claudia
see: Soustrot, Bernard, 8)

Stein, Andreas
see: Potpourri, 22)

Stevens, Pauline
see: Jones, Philip, 2)

Stumpf, Michael
see: Potpourri, 60)

Sydney, Lorna
see: Stracker, Wilhelm

Tate, Virginia
see: Geyer, Charles

Taylor, David
see: Laird, Michael, 7)

Terbeek, Dale
see: Geyer, Charles

Tipping, Christopher
see: Laird, Michael, 10)

Toepper, Hertha
see: Gleissle, Walter, 2), 3)

Töpper, Hertha
see: Gleissle, Walter, 3)
see: Scherbaum, Adolf, 9)
see: Tarr, Edward, 15)
see: Unidentified, Trumpet(s), 8)

Watkinson, Carolyn
see: Immer, Friedemann, 6)
see: Laird, Michael, 7)
see: Potpourri, 25)
see: Sauter, Hermann, 17)
see: Touvron, Guy, 10)
see: Wolf, Hans, 4), 9)

Watts, Helen
see: André, Maurice, 16)
see: Groot, Willem (Wim)
see: Lang, William
see: McGregor, Rob Roy, 1), 2), 3), 4), 5)
see: Miller, Rodney
see: Sauter, Hermann, 9), 10), 11), 23), 24), 35)
see: Schmid, Bernhard, 2), 5), 6), 7)
see: Spindler, Josef, 10)
see: Unidentified, Trumpet(s), 18)
see: Wolf, Hans, 3), 4), 5), 6), 7)

Wilke, Elisabeth
see: Güttler, Ludwig, 20)

Winslow, Sandra
see: Potpourri, 66)

Wolf-Matthäus, Lotte
see: Holy, Walter, 1)
see: Zeh, Karl Heinz

Bagpipe
[includes bladderpipes & cornemuse]

Casier, Robert
see: André, Maurice, 6)

Eisenstadt, Maurice
see: Platt, Seymour

Gruskin, Shelley
see: Potpourri, 67)

Malgoire, Jean-Claude
see: André, Maurice, 6)

Munrow, David
see: Laird, Michael, 1)

Pok, František
see: Pok, František, 4)

Tyler, James
see: Laird, Michael, 1)

van der Beek, Andrew
see: Laird, Michael, 1)

Balalaika

Zolotareff, Peter
see: Platt, Seymour

Banjo

Berliner, Jay
see: Dean, Allan, 5)

Baritone (Euphonium)

Cottle, Andrew
see: Chunn, Michael

Lewis, Wayne
see: Butterfield, Billy

Matthessen, Jozef
see: Mertens, Theo, 1)

Orosz, Josef
see: Ghitalla, Armando, 14)
see: Voisin, Roger, 13)

Richards, Robert
see: Garside, Derek M.

Schwarz, Gerard
see: Schwarz, Gerard, 5)

Smith, Roger M.
see: Burke, James, 5), 6)

Swallow, John
see: Schwarz, Gerard, 5)

Waters, David
see: Schwarz, Gerard, 13)

Wiley, Hunter
see: Butterfield, Billy

Baritone (voice)

Abdoun, Georges
see: André, Maurice, 97), 186)

Abel, Bruce
see: Schmitt, Siegfried

Baker, Mark
see: Cook, Richard

Bär, Olaf
see: Steele-Perkins, Crispian, 4)

Bauer, Gustav
see: Pok, František, 4)

Benoit, Jean-Christophe
see: Ménardi, Louis

Berman, Karel
see: Junek, Václav, 4)

Bernac, Pierre
see: Delmotte, Roger, 1), 51)

Bevan, Maurice
see: Eskdale, George, 5)
see: Jones, Philip, 7)
see: Laird, Michael, 12)
see: Renz, Albrecht, 1)
see: Rudolf, Richard

Brown, Greg
see: Levy, Robert

Bruce, Neely
see: Levy, Robert

Burrows, Arthur
see: Davenport, LaNoue
see: Montesi, Robert, 1), 2), 5)

Fischer-Dieskau, Dietrich
see: Tarr, Edward, 18)

Frisch, Richard
see: Stubbs, James

Geier, Ulf
see: Soustrot, Bernard, 8)

Germain, Pierre
see: Jeannoutot, Bernard

Giraud, Patrick
see: Delmotte, Roger, 44)

Gray, Alexander
see: Umbrico, Joseph

Guinn, Leslie
see: Dean, Allan, 10)
see: Sheldon, Robert

Huttenlocher, Philippe
see: Adelbrecht, Henri, 3)
see: Gabel, Bernard, 4)
see: Tarr, Edward, 30), 32), 43)

Illavsky, Ladislav
see: Pok, František, 4)

Klein, Karl Heinz
see: Smithers, Don, 12)

Krol, Rafael
see: Wolf, Hans, 13)

Kuehn, Robert
see: Mase, Raymond
see: Montesi, Robert, 2)

Kunz, Laszlo
see: Pok, František, 4)

Mason, Patrick
see: Potpourri, 6)

Maurane, Camille
see: André, Maurice, 78)
see: Delmotte, Roger, 29)

McDaniel, Barry
see: Tarr, Edward, 19)

Metcalf, William
see: Romm, Ronald

Myers, Gordon
see: Montesi, Robert, 1), 2), 5)

Ocker, Claus
see: Steinkopf, Otto

Patrick, Julian
see: Anderson, Ronald, 2)
see: Schwarz, Gerard, 11)

Pfeiffer, Thomas
see: Maier, Hans Walter

Prey, Hermann
see: Eichhorn, Holger
see: Tarr, Edward, 18)

Pruvost, Jacques
see: Jeannoutot, Bernard

Roberts, Stephen
see: Wilbraham, John, 23)

Rovetta, Teodor
see: Battagliola, Anania

Rydell, Roland
see: Hardenberger, Håkan

Schickele, Peter
see: Mase, Raymond

Schöne, Wolfgang
see: McGregor, Rob Roy, 6)

Shaw, Geoffrey
see: Jones, Philip, 2)
see: Laird, Michael, 3), 12), 13)

Tripp, Alva
see: Montesi, Robert, 1), 2)

van Egmond, Max
see: Tarr, Edward, 45)

Varcoe, Stephen
see: Steele-Perkins, Crispian, 7)

Warfield, William
see: Johnson, Gilbert, 5)
see: Vacchiano, William, 7)

Weller, Lawrence
see: Miller, Rodney

Widmer, Kurt
see: Scholz, Walter

Bass clarinet
[cross-referenced under clarinet]

Bloom, Arthur
see: Nagel, Robert, 18), 20)

Blustine, Allen
see: Anderson, Ronald, 3)
see: Dean, Allan, 6), 7)

Buxbaum, Merritt
see: Stevens, Thomas, 2), 5)

Crowley, Charles
see: Victorian Trumpet Trio

Dailey, Dwight
see: Henderson, Douglas

Davis, Stanley
see: Miller, Rodney
see: Perry, Brian

DeRoche, Don
see: Potpourri, 5)

Devendra, Anand
see: Anderson, Ronald, 6)

DeWar, Ron
see: Ferrantino, Kenneth

Fallows, Roger
see: Miller, John

Gizard, Michel
see: André, Maurice, 120)

Hambleton, Hale
see: Wilbraham, John, 1)

Hambleton, Wilfred
see: Jones, Philip, 11)

Hotz, Kurt
see: Adelbrecht, Henri, 1)

Howard, Alexander
see: Burke, James, 6)

Howes, Peter
see: Izan, Bernard

Howland, Paul E.
see: Burke, James, 5), 6)

Jewett, Thomas
see: Bastin, Ernie

Kalina, David
see: Geisler, Lloyd

King, Thea
see: Mason, David, 5)

Leclerc, Jean-Claude
see: André, Maurice, 120)

Leeson, Daniel
see: Schwarz, Gerard, 13)

Montaigne, Louis
see: Delmotte, Roger, 2)
see: Thibaud, Pierre, 1)

Pay, Antony
see: Evans, Laurie

Pons, André
see: Thibaud, Pierre, 9)

Post, Jean
see: Thibaud, Pierre, 9)

Richman, Boomie
see: Butterfield, Billy

Russo, Charles
see: Crisara, Raymond, 1)
see: Weis, Theodore, 2)

Rybín, Alois
see: Junek, Václav, 3)

Sasaki, David
see: Sasaki, Ray

Savage, Temple
see: Mason, David, 3)

Smylie, Dennis
see: Anderson, Ronald, 6)

Sparnaay, Harry
see: Floore, John

Stephens, Suzanne
see: Stockhausen, Markus, 3)

Sukhalenak, Victor
see: Dokshitser, Timofei, 16)

Trier, Stephen
see: Jones, Philip, 11)
see: Webb, Gordon, 2)

Wächter, Heinz
see: Potpourri, 19)

Warren, John
see: Potpourri, 38)

Webner, Erich
see: Rudolf, Richard

Wohlmacher, William
see: Burkhart, David

Yeh, John Bruce
see: Potpourri, 38)

Bass trombone
[cross-referenced under trombone]

Biddlecome, Robert E.
see: Dean, Allan, 4)

Bobowski, Wolfgang
see: Eichhorn, Holger

Buchanan, James
see: Schwarz, Gerard, 13)

Carlsson, Lars-Göran
see: Eklund's Baroque Ensemble

Christen, Jo-Ann
see: Schwarz, Gerard, 13)

Cravens, Terry
see: Plog, Anthony, 9), 11)

Federowitz, Kurt
see: Potpourri, 47)
see: Tarr, Edward, 3), 10), 28),
32)

Geyer, Wilfried
see: Eichhorn, Holger

Girard, Pierre
see: André, Maurice, 120)

Hallberg, Gordon
see: Ghitalla, Armando, 7)

Henry, Martin
see: Brass-zination

Kahlenbach, Hermann Josef
see: Wolf, Hans, 4), 6), 7)

Kohlert, Walfried
see: Hagge, Detlef

Lister, Richard A.
see: Immer, Friedemann, 18)
see: Tarr, Edward, 3)

Menken, Julien
see: Ghitalla, Armando, 10)

Miller, Donald
see: Kuehn, David

Mosheimer, Herbert
see: Idinger, Matthias

Orosz, Josef
see: Voisin, Roger, 13)

Perkins, Geoffrey
see: Watson, James

Posten, Robert
see: Ghitalla, Armando, 1)

Poulet, Bernard
see: Aquitaine Brass Ensemble

Pritchard, John G.
see: Webb, Gordon, 2)

Raph, Alan
see: Wise, Wilmer

Reynolds, Jeffrey
see: Stevens, Thomas, 4)

Rückert, Hans
see: Potpourri, 24), 25)

Taylor, David
see: Carroll, Edward, 7)

Venglovsky, Victor
see: Yudashkin, Georgy

Votava, Josef
see: Kejmar, Miroslav, 13)

Waters, David
see: Schwarz, Gerard, 13)

Wenth, Andreas
see: Spindler, Josef, 7)

Wright, Robert
see: Nagel, Robert, 18)

Bass trumpet
[cross-referenced under trumpet]

Deck, Warren
see: Carroll, Edward, 10)
see: Potpourri, 33)

Finn, Kenneth
see: Carroll, Edward, 12)

Langlitz, David
see: Carroll, Edward, 7), 9)

Mueller, Thomas
  see: Carroll, Edward, 7), 9)

Orosz, Josef
  see: Voisin, Roger, 13)

Taylor, Jonathan
  see: Carroll, Edward, 10)
  see: Potpourri, 33)

Basset horn
[cross-referenced under clarinet]

Damiens, Alain
  see: Cure, Antoine

Bassoon
[may include Baroque bassoon]

Allard, Maurice
  see: André, Maurice, 63), 68), 172)
  see: Delmotte, Roger, 1), 6), 7), 26), 32), 41)
  see: Mule, Marcel
  see: Scherbaum, Adolf, 13)
  see: Touvron, Guy, 7)

Allard, Raymond
  see: Mager, Georges
  see: Voisin, Roger, 10)

Angerhoefer, Günther
  see: Haas, Rudolf

Anton, Herbert
  see: André, Maurice, 138)
  see: Scherbaum, Adolf, 5), 31)

Aussem, Peter
  see: Schoof, Manfred

Bar-Lev, Assaf
  see: Touvron, Guy, 10)

Bauch, Ethan
  see: Carroll, Edward, 4)

Bayens, Eddy
  see: Lowrey, Alvin

Beauchamp, Martha
  see: Birch, Robert

Beck
  see: Schneidewind, Helmut, 2)

Berdie, Serge
  see: André, Maurice, 92)

Berkenstock, James
  see: Miller, Rodney
  see: Perry, Brian

Bevers, Michael
  see: Dolce, Christine

Böcker, Helmut
  see: Tarr, Edward, 39)

Boden, Claus Frithjof
  see: Basch, Wolfgang, 1)

Bond, Daniel
  see: Immer, Friedemann, 14)
  see: Laird, Michael, 7)
  see: Potpourri, 59), 60), 61)

Bossart, David
  see: Schwarz, Gerard, 13)

Breidenthal, David
  see: Guarneri, Mario
  see: Plog, Anthony, 9)

Brightman, Kay
  see: Stevens, Thomas, 11)

Brusen, Peter
  see: Potpourri, 38)

Bülow, Martin
  see: Zeh, Karl Heinz

Buschmann, Eberhard
  see: Goethel, Siegfried

Camden, Archie
  see: Clift, Dennis

Carbonelli, Joan
  see: Espigoli, Jaume

Carl, Christoph
  see: Immer, Friedemann, 6)
  see: Läubin, Hannes, 5), 7), 8)
  see: Schmid, Bernhard, 9)

428

Carmen, Elias
see: Karpilovsky, Murray
see: Potpourri, 31)

Carroll, David
see: Berinbaum, Martin

Cermak, Leo
see: Rudolf, Richard

Checchia, Anthony
see: Broiles, Melvin
see: Nagel, Robert, 14)

Christlieb, Don
see: Brady, Charles

Cran, John
see: Webb, Gordon, 5)

D'Attilio, Lawrence
see: Rapier, Leon, 4)

Delage, Michel
see: André, Maurice, 92), 188)

Delage, R.
see: André, Maurice, 89)

Deutcher, Sylvia
see: Nagel, Robert, 1), 13)

Dherin
see: Foveau, Eugène

Dibner, Steven
see: Carroll, Edward, 7), 9),
10), 11)

Dicker, Michael
see: Potpourri, 6)

Droulez, Raymond
see: André, Maurice, 92)

Duhamel, Hervé
see: André, Maurice, 120)

Dvořák, Karl
see: Scherbaum, Adolf, 36)

Eck, Michel
see: André, Maurice, 92)

Eichenberger, André
see: Adelbrecht, Henri, 3)

Elliot, Willard
see: Herseth, Adolph, 1), 4), 6)
see: Vosburgh, George

Elliott, Vernon
see: Clift, Dennis

Estill, Cynthia
see: McGuffey, Patrick

Etherton, Howard
see: Jones, Philip, 5)
see: Wilbraham, John, 20), 23)

Etzold, Kurt
see: Friedrich, Reinhold
see: Immer, Friedemann, 5), 6)
see: Läubin, Hannes, 6)
see: McGregor, Rob Roy, 1),
2), 4), 6)
see: Miller, Rodney
see: Potpourri, 25)
see: Sauter, Hermann, 12), 13),
17), 35)
see: Schmid, Bernhard, 4), 5),
6), 7), 8), 9), 10), 11)
see: Unidentified, Trumpet(s),
5)
see: Wolf, Hans, 5), 6), 7), 8),
9), 10), 11), 12)

Fain, Alexandre
see: Yudashkin, Georgy

Faisandier, Gérard
see: André, Maurice, 172)

Ferrel, Scott
see: Smithers, Don, 13)

Feves, Julie
see: Schwarz, Gerard, 9)

Fleischmann, Otto
see: Bryant, Ralph, 1)
see: Holy, Walter, 9)
see: Potpourri, 49), 50), 51),
52), 55), 56), 57), 64)
see: Rudolf, Richard
see: Spindler, Josef, 8), 10),
11), 12)

Formáček, Jiří
see: Horák, Jiří, 4), 5)
see: Junek, Václav, 6)

Franquet, J.M.
see: Foriscot, J.

Franse, Stephen
see: Schultz, Erik, 1)

Fustin, Claude
see: André, Maurice, 160)

Garfield, Bernard
see: Ghitalla, Armando, 10)
see: Wilson, Alex

Gatt, Martin
see: Jones, Philip, 3)
see: Laird, Michael, 15)
see: Wilbraham, John, 26), 27)

Glickman, Loren
see: Burke, James, 5), 6)
see: Nagel, Robert, 1), 4)
see: Schwarz, Gerard, 3), 6), 7)
see: Weis, Theodore, 1)

Godburn, Dennis
see: Holmgren, Fred

Gode, Jürgen
see: Tarr, Edward, 4)
see: Wolf, Hans, 1)
see: Zickler, Heinz, 3)

Goldstein, Lauren
see: Burns, Stephen

Goodman, Alan
see: Stevens, Thomas, 12)

Gottling, Philip
see: Potpourri, 38)

Hara, László
see: Petz, Pál

Hartmann, Karl-Otto
see: André, Maurice, 16)
see: Goethel, Siegfried

Heilmann, Herbert
see: Gass, Josef

Helaerts, Henri
see: André, Maurice, 181)
see: Cuvit, Michel
see: Longinotti, Paolo

Henker, Fritz
see: Bauer, Willibald, 1)
see: Scherbaum, Adolf, 7), 9), 10)

Hennige, Albert
see: Ellinghaus, Wolfram

Herder, Hermann
see: Sauter, Hermann, 14), 15), 16), 17), 18)

Herman, František
see: Kejmar, Miroslav, 8)

Hindell, Leonard
see: Schwarz, Gerard, 20)

Hongne, Paul
see: André, Maurice, 12), 89), 92), 94), 95), 116), 122), 124), 125), 149), 151), 152), 169), 172)
see: Gleissle, Walter, 3), 6), 7)
see: Thibaud, Pierre, 1), 9)
see: Vaillant, Ludovic, 4)

Horák, Vilém
see: Pok, František, 5)

Howard, David
see: Schultz, Erik, 7)

Jacques, André
see: Potpourri, 48)

James, Cecil
see: Jackson, Harold
see: Scherbaum, Adolf, 3)
see: Webb, Gordon, 1)

Jenny, Florenz
see: Adelbrecht, Henri, 1)

Jung, Helman
see: André, Maurice, 142)
see: Potpourri, 2)

Kennedy, Valentine
see: Webb, Gordon, 2)

Kilburn, Nicholas
see: Blee, Eugene
see: Chevanelle, Serge
see: LeComte, Jacques

Klepac, Rudolf
see: André, Maurice, 25)

Klier, Günter
see: Güttler, Ludwig, 12), 19), 20), 21)

Kolbinger, Karl
see: André, Maurice, 17), 26), 93)
see: Bauer, Willibald, 4)
see: Potpourri, 11)
see: Scherbaum, Adolf, 9)
see: Thibaud, Pierre, 7), 8)

Krasavin, Sergei
see: Ikov, Andrei
see: Maximenko, Anatoly, 3)

Krenn, Walter
see: Rudolf, Richard

Kühl, Detlef
see: André, Maurice, 17), 25)
see: Bauer, Willibald, 3)

Kurpekov, Y.
see: Popov, Sergei, 3)

Lamothe, Jean-Marie
see: Vasse, Claude

Lang, Martin
see: Köpp, Rudolf

Lange, Hansjürg
see: Laird, Michael, 17), 19)

Laptev, I.
see: Volodin, Lev

Laroque, Jean-Pierre
see: Bernard, André, 7)
see: Caens, Thierry
see: Thibaud, Pierre, 14)

Lawson, Richard
see: Anderson, Ronald, 6)

Leihenseder, Paul Gerhard
see: Schmid, Bernhard, 3)
see: Wolf, Hans, 3)

Lemke, Hans
see: André, Maurice, 180), 199)

Levesley, Neil
see: Webb, Gordon, 2), 4)

Levin, Philip
see: Holmgren, Fred
see: Immer, Friedemann, 13)

Liebscher, Wolfgang
see: Haas, Rudolf

Lipp, Charles
see: Potpourri, 5)

Lohrer, Klaus J.
see: Junge, Harald

Longazo, George
see: Geisler, Lloyd

Louchez, Jean
see: André, Maurice, 92)

Luzin, Vladimir
see: Gorokhov, Vitaly

MacCourt, Donald
see: Anderson, Ronald, 1), 6)
see: Burns, Stephen
see: Dean, Allan, 4), 5), 6), 8)
see: Ferrantino, Kenneth
see: Nagel, Robert, 2), 19), 20)
see: Ranger, Louis
see: Schwarz, Gerard, 8), 13)

Mantels, Hans
see: Sauter, Hermann, 4), 5), 6), 7), 8), 9), 10), 11), 35)

Martanovic, Jan
see: Jurča, Vladimir

Mauruschat, Peter
see: Bodenröder, Robert
see: Bryant, Ralph, 2)
see: Potpourri, 22)
see: Tarr, Edward, 28)

Rabot, André
see: Delmotte, Roger, 2)

Rinderspacher, Alfred
see: Erb, Helmut, 6)

Rolleri, Marc
see: André, Maurice, 120)

Rönnebeck, Tore
see: Schrello, Mark

Roscher, Matthias
see: Basch, Wolfgang, 6)

Ruckteschler, Holger
see: Sauter, Hermann, 2)

Ruggiero, Matthew
see: Ghitalla, Armando, 7)

Sagarman, Daniel
see: Broiles, Melvin

Salomons, Louis
see: León, Felipe

Sato, Atsuko
see: Burns, Stephen
see: Gould, Mark

Sax, Manfred
see: Potpourri, 48)

Schiffl, Anton
see: Fink, Werner

Schmitt, Emil
see: Potpourri, 34), 35)
see: Sauter, Hermann, 26)
see: Zickler, Heinz, 7)

Schneebeli, David
see: Sommerhalder, Max

Schoenbach, Sol
see: Johnson, Gilbert, 1)
see: Krauss, Sam

Schottstädt, Rainer
see: Läubin, Hannes, 4)
see: Sauter, Hermann, 1)

Schulze, Gerd
see: Güttler, Ludwig, 26)

Scribner, William
see: Haneuse, Arthur
see: Schwarz, Gerard, 8), 13)

Segal, C.
see: Jandorf, D.

Seidl, Jiří
see: Kejmar, Miroslav, 5)

Seith, Rudolf
see: Tarr, Edward, 23), 24),
25), 26), 27)

Sennedat, André
see: André, Maurice, 6), 160),
194), 197), 203)
see: Potpourri, 42), 44)
see: Scherbaum, Adolf, 11), 23)

Sharrow, Leonard
see: Crisara, Raymond, 9)
see: Davidson, Louis
see: Schwarz, Gerard, 17)

Sheen, Graham
see: Bernard, André, 12)
see: Hardenberger, Håkan
see: Laird, Michael, 15), 21),
22)
see: Watson, James

Shubin, Matthew
see: Carroll, Edward, 6)

Slanička, Josef
see: Mičaník, Jaroslav

Sokolov, Alexander
see: Margolin, Veniamin

Steinbrecher, Karl
see: Zickler, Heinz, 2)

Steinkopf, Otto
see: Tarr, Edward, 11)

Stiedl, Hermann
see: Spindler, Josef, 2)

Stiftner, Walter
see: Eichhorn, Holger
see: Immer, Friedemann, 3)
see: Potpourri, 62), 63)
see: Tarr, Edward, 12), 13), 17)

Stiftner, William
see: Immer, Friedemann, 14)

Swillens, Arnold
see: Sevenstern, Harry

Taylor, Jane
see: Dean, Allan, 1)
see: Mase, Raymond

Thieme, Erich
see: Schneidewind, Helmut, 13)

Thompson, Robin
see: Miller, John
see: Stockhausen, Markus, 4)

Thunemann, Klaus
see: André, Maurice, 16), 196)
see: Läubin, Hannes, 8)
see: Sauter, Hermann, 14), 16)
see: Touvron, Guy, 14)
see: Wolf, Hans, 7), 8), 11),
12)

Tobias, Norman
see: Umbrico, Joseph

Topol, A.
see: Krylov, Gleb

Trier, Collins
see: Potpourri, 38)

Troog, Henning
see: André, Maurice, 192)

Turković, Milan
see: Bryant, Ralph, 2), 3), 4),
5)
see: Immer, Friedemann, 14),
15), 16)
see: Potpourri, 49), 50), 53),
54), 58), 59), 60), 61), 62),
63), 64)
see: Spindler, Josef, 10), 13),
14), 15), 16)

Turnovsky, Stepan
see: Immer, Friedemann, 17)

Ullery, Charles
see: Potpourri, 6)

Vacek, Karel
see: Junek, Václav, 3), 5)

Vaněk, Lumir
see: Kejmar, Miroslav, 13)

Ventulett, Karl
see: Basch, Wolfgang, 6)

Vlasenko, Vladimir
see: Popov, Sergei, 2)

Vogel, Howard
see: Broiles, Melvin

Vorlíček, M.
see: Mičaník, Jaroslav

Wallez, Amaury
see: André, Maurice, 44), 53),
92), 125), 151), 227)
see: Ménardi, Louis
see: Touvron, Guy, 11)
see: Unidentified, Trumpet(s),
15)
see: Wilbraham, John, 21)

Walt, Sherman
see: Ghitalla, Armando, 6), 7),
8), 9)
see: Smedvig, Rolf

Ward, Jeremy
see: Laird, Michael, 7), 19)

Warnock, Felix
see: Immer, Friedemann, 4)
see: Laird, Michael, 7)

Waterhouse, William
see: Clift, Dennis
see: Jones, Philip, 2)
see: Laird, Michael, 11)
see: Miller, John

Watts, Andrew
see: Keavy, Stephen
see: Steele-Perkins, Crispian,
16), 18)

Weihs, Karl
see: André, Maurice, 201)

Weisberg, Arthur
see: Nagel, Robert, 4)

Werke, Eberhard
see: Ellinghaus, Wolfram

Wetherill, John
see: Vasse, Claude

Winter, Horst
see: Braeunig, Herbert
see: Schmid, Bernhard, 13)
see: Tasa, David

Wolfson, Ken
see: Plog, Anthony, 5)

Young, Jean
see: Ghitalla, Armando, 1)

Zirkuli, Bernadette
see: Dean, Allan, 5)

Zuckerman, George
see: Hopkins, Kenneth

Bass (string bass / double bass)
[Violone is cross-referenced here]

Akahashi, Akira
see: Touvron, Guy, 19)

Amaro, Jimmy
see: Mills, Fred

Amherst, Nigel
see: Clift, Dennis

Andreyev, Leopold
see: Dokshitser, Timofei, 29)
see: Popov, Sergei, 2)

Azarkhin, Rodion
see: Maximenko, Anatoly, 1)

Baines, Francis
see: Laird, Michael, 11), 14),
17), 19)
see: Wilbraham, John, 23)

Barthélémy, Ennemond
see: Thibaud, Pierre, 9)

Beal, John
see: Mase, Raymond
see: Wise, Wilmer

Beers, Adrian
see: Jones, Philip, 1), 11)

Berg, Christian
see: Immer, Friedemann, 3)

Bertz, Harro
see: Immer, Friedemann, 5), 6)
see: Läubin, Hannes, 3), 4), 5)
see: Miller, Rodney
see: Potpourri, 25)
see: Sauter, Hermann, 21), 22)
see: Schmid, Bernhard, 4), 5),
6), 8), 9)
see: Wolf, Hans, 11), 12)

Beyer, Achim
see: Güttler, Ludwig, 4), 8),
14)

Botwright, Valerie
see: Steele-Perkins, Crispian,
16), 18)

Boussagol
see: Foveau, Eugène

Braun, Heinrich
see: Goetting, Chandler

Brehm, Alvin
see: Anderson, Ronald, 4)
see: Dean, Allan, 1), 4), 5), 7)
see: Miller, Rodney
see: Schwarz, Gerard, 3)

Breuer, Paul
see: Schneidewind, Helmut, 7)
see: Tarr, Edward, 35), 37), 38)

Brichet, André
see: André, Maurice, 120)

Brookes, Oliver
see: Laird, Michael, 1), 2)
see: Smithers, Don, 3)

Buccarella, Lucio
see: Adelbrecht, Henri, 6), 7)
see: Touvron, Guy, 14)

Buchanan, James
see: Schwarz, Gerard, 13)

Cazauran, Jacques
see: André, Maurice, 49)
see: Delmotte, Roger, 2)
see: Lagorce, Antoine
see: Thibaud, Pierre, 1)

Chickering, Robert
see: Miller, Rodney

Cliquennois, Pierre
see: André, Maurice, 120)

Colonna, Leonardo
see: André, Maurice, 130)
see: Leroy, Jean-Paul

Courtney, Neil
see: Geisler, Lloyd

Cruft, Eugene
see: Clift, Dennis

Davis, Carolyn
see: Gould, Mark

Dean, Roger
see: Wallace, John, 6)

Degen, Rudolf
see: Eichhorn, Holger

Deloria, Deborah
see: Pressley, Richard

Dembowski, Drew
see: Plog, Anthony, 11)

Deppe, Chris
see: Plog, Anthony, 11)

Duft, Herbert
see: André, Maurice, 17)
see: Lachenmeir, Paul
see: Potpourri, 11)
see: Thibaud, Pierre, 7), 8)

Fichtner, Jürgen
see: Potpourri, 22)

Fink, Claus
see: Ellinghaus, Wolfram

Franklin, Brian
see: Immer, Friedemann, 11)

Fredrickson, Richard
see: Berinbaum, Martin
see: Schwarz, Gerard, 6)

Fredrickson, Thomas
see: Ferrantino, Kenneth
see: Sasaki, Ray

Freeman, A.
see: Haug, Edward

Frei, Rudolf
see: Adelbrecht, Henri, 1)

Fricker, Kenneth
see: Montesi, Robert, 1)

Fryba, Hans
see: Longinotti, Paolo

Gammie, Ian
see: Keavy, Stephen

Gartiser, Peter
see: Sauter, Hermann, 24)

Gegin, A.
see: Volodin, Lev

Geller, Michael
see: Perry, Brian

Goldman, Alan
see: Potpourri, 5)

Goldman, Allen
see: Logan, Jack

Gradmann, Dietrich
see: Sauter, Hermann, 2)

Granier, Gérard
see: André, Maurice, 152)

Gräser, Manfred
see: McGregor, Rob Roy, 2), 5)
see: Sauter, Hermann, 4), 6),
   7), 8), 9), 10), 11), 12),
   13), 15), 16), 19), 20), 23),
   24), 35)
see: Schmid, Bernhard, 2), 3),
   4)
see: Tarr, Edward, 11)
see: Unidentified, Trumpet(s),
   5)
see: Wolf, Hans, 3)
see: Zickler, Heinz, 2)

Gräser, Martin
see: Sauter, Hermann, 14)

Grauer, Jay
see: Stevens, Thomas, 10)

Graves, Mel
see: Burkhart, David

Greco, Costantino
see: Thompson, James

Grey, John
see: Wilbraham, John, 20), 22)

Grodner
see: Davidson, Louis

Guastafeste, Joseph
see: Geyer, Charles
see: Herseth, Adolph, 4)
see: Vosburgh, George

Gut, Joachim
see: André, Maurice, 181)
see: Cuvit, Michel

Höbarth, Hermann
see: Tarr, Edward, 45)

Höger, Franz
see: Bauer, Willibald, 4)

Honeyman, John
see: Webb, Gordon, 1)

Hörtnagel, Georg
see: André, Maurice, 93)
see: Gleissle, Walter, 11)
see: Tarr, Edward, 4)
see: Zickler, Heinz, 1)

Hruza, Eduard
see: Bryant, Ralph, 1), 3), 4),
   5)
see: Holy, Walter, 9)
see: Immer, Friedemann, 14),
   15), 16), 17)
see: Potpourri, 49), 50), 51),
   52), 53), 54), 55), 56), 57),
   58), 59), 60), 61), 62), 63),
   64)
see: Spindler, Josef, 7), 8), 9),
   10), 11), 12), 13), 14), 15),
   16)
see: Tarr, Edward, 45)

Illek, Karol
see: Jurča, Vladimir

Jamitz, R.
see: Jandorf, D.

Jerling, Frank
see: Holy, Walter, 2)

Johansson, Jan
see: Eklund's Baroque Ensemble

Karr, Garry
see: McNab, Malcolm

Kelley, Richard
see: Brady, Charles

Kiblböck, Ludwig
see: André, Maurice, 17)

Kierdorf, Theo
see: Schoof, Manfred

Klaus, Günter
see: Erb, Helmut, 1)

Klein, Martin
see: Sauter, Hermann, 27)

Knussen, Stuart
see: Clift, Dennis

Koch, Hans
see: Hagge, Detlef

Komachkov, Rifat
see: Volodin, Lev

Körfer, Klaus
see: Immer, Friedemann, 11)

Kotsaftis, Ted
see: Butterfield, Billy

Kremsa, Edgar
see: Adelbrecht, Henri, 3)

Krüger, Günter
see: Zickler, Heinz, 3)

Kuchelmeister, Klaus
see: Potpourri, 2)

Kulowitch, John T.
see: Miller, Rodney

Kurbatov, Mikhail
see: Margolin, Veniamin

Langille, James
see: Dudgeon, Ralph

Lau, Ulrich
see: Sauter, Hermann, 5), 6), 35)

Lemon, J. Karla
see: Burkhart, David

Lessing, Alfred
see: Steinkopf, Otto
see: Tarr, Edward, 10)

Levine, Jeffrey
see: Dean, Allan, 8)
see: Nagel, Robert, 18), 19), 20)

Levine, Julius
see: Broiles, Melvin
see: Ghitalla, Armando, 10)
see: Nagel, Robert, 1)

Lieberman, Barry
see: Stevens, Thomas, 9)

Locher, Albert Michael
see: Läubin, Hannes, 3)
see: Schmid, Bernhard, 8)

Lockwood, Willy
see: Molénat, Claude

Logerot, Gaston
see: Delmotte, Roger, 6), 35), 36)

Lom, Thomas
see: Immer, Friedemann, 5), 6)
see: Läubin, Hannes, 6)
see: McGregor, Rob Roy, 1), 2), 3), 4), 5), 6)
see: Miller, Rodney
see: Potpourri, 25)
see: Sauter, Hermann, 14), 15), 16), 17), 18), 20), 21), 22)
see: Schmid, Bernhard, 5), 6), 7), 8), 9)
see: Wolf, Hans, 2), 3), 5), 6), 7), 8), 9), 10), 11), 12)

MacNamara, Amanda
see: Laird, Michael, 8)
see: Steele-Perkins, Crispian, 7), 10), 16), 18)

Marcellin, Francis
see: Potpourri, 47)
see: Tarr, Edward, 32)

Marck, Peter
see: Lowrey, Alvin

Marjoram, Keith
see: Laird, Michael, 7), 8)

Martin, Thomas
see: Laird, Michael, 15)
see: Steele-Perkins, Crispian, 14)

McCarthy, Peter
see: Laird, Michael, 7)

Meares, Edward
see: Schwarz, Gerard, 1)

Merrett, James W.
see: Jones, Philip, 9), 10)
see: Mason, David, 1)

Meuter, Walter
see: André, Maurice, 192)
see: Goethel, Siegfried

Minkler, Mark
see: Potpourri, 6)

Modell, Carl
see: Haug, Edward

Moleux, Georges
see: Voisin, Roger, 10)

Monohan, Thomas
see: Chenette, Stephen

Morneweg, Emil
see: Tarr, Edward, 19), 20), 23), 24), 25), 26)

Mosher, Skip
see: Stevens, Thomas, 2)

Navone, Toni
see: Metzger, Charles

Neidlinger, Buell
see: McNab, Malcolm

Nitsche, Peter
see: Schmid, Bernhard, 7)
see: Wolf, Hans, 10)

Nossek, Wilhelm
see: André, Maurice, 16)

Nothdorf, Georg
see: Bauer, Adam
see: Scherbaum, Adolf, 21)
see: Schmidt, Ingus

Oboda, Jaroslav
see: Pok, František, 2)

Ortner, Franz
see: Scherbaum, Adolf, 9)

Paer, Lewis
see: Burns, Stephen

Palma, Donald
see: Carroll, Edward, 8), 9)
see: Dean, Allan, 3)
see: Ranger, Louis
see: Stubbs, James

Pap, Nicholas
see: Immer, Friedemann, 14)
see: Potpourri, 61), 63)

Pedersen, Guy
see: André, Maurice, 8), 69), 70)

Pimenov, Y.
see: Volodin, Lev

Pirker, Firmin
see: Rudolf, Richard

Planyavsky, Alfred
see: Eichhorn, Holger

Portnoi, Henry
see: Ghitalla, Armando, 6), 7), 8), 9)

Pošta, František
see: Pok, František, 5)

Primetens, Edmond
see: André, Maurice, 82)

Quarrington, Joel
see: Mills, Fred
see: Schultz, Erik, 8)

Ranney, Susan
see: Hood, Boyde
see: Plog, Anthony, 8)
see: Stevens, Thomas, 10)

Richter, Hans
see: Gass, Josef

Riedel, Georg
see: Potpourri, 3)

Rizzoli, Oscar
see: Dassé, Jean-Luc

Ros, Pere
see: Immer, Friedemann, 3)

Rühm, Otto
see: Spindler, Josef, 1)
see: Wobisch, Helmut, 2)

Sala, F.
see: Foriscot, J.

Schlegel, Rudolf
see: Bodenröder, Robert

Schlender, Dietrich
see: Basch, Wolfgang, 1)

Schuster, Frits
see: Reinhart, Carole Dawn, 2)

Wehrli, Walter
see: Sommerhalder, Max

Widmer, Fritz
see: Touvron, Guy, 10)

Willens, Michael
see: Holmgren, Fred
see: Immer, Friedemann, 13)

Winkler, Dieter
see: Preis, Ivo

Witte, Friedrich
see: Groth, Konradin

Wolfe, Lawrence
see: Potpourri, 38)

Wöllert, Heinz
see: Zeh, Karl Heinz

Woodrow, Anthony
see: Bryant, Ralph, 2), 4), 5)
see: Groot, Willem (Wim)
see: Immer, Friedemann, 14)
see: Potpourri, 51), 52), 57),
58), 59), 60), 63)
see: Rippas, Claude
see: Smithers, Don, 13), 14),
15)
see: Spindler, Josef, 11), 13),
14), 15)

Zimmermann, Claus
see: Friedrich, Reinhold
see: Läubin, Hannes, 4), 5), 6),
7), 8)
see: Schmid, Bernhard, 10), 11)
see: Send, Peter

Zimmermann, Jack
see: Smith, Bramwell "Bram"

Bass (voice)
[may include baritone &
bass-baritone]

Abdoun, Georges
see: Jeannoutot, Bernard
see: Thibaud, Pierre, 14)

Abel, Bruce
see: Sauter, Hermann, 2)

Adam, Theo
see: Eichhorn, Holger
see: Tarr, Edward, 35)
see: Thibaud, Pierre, 7)
see: Unidentified, Trumpet(s),
9)

Alan, Hervey
see: Egan, Dennis

Anderson, Norman
see: Sauter, Hermann, 19)

Anthony, Trevor
see: Jackson, Harold

Bär, Olaf
see: Güttler, Ludwig, 20)

Barron, David
see: Potpourri, 66)

Bastin, Jules
see: Adelbrecht, Henri, 3)
see: André, Maurice, 132)

Baumann, Ludwig
see: Immer, Friedemann, 17)

Beavan, Nigel
see: Laird, Michael, 11)

Berberian, Ara
see: Broiles, Melvin

Berg, Arthur
see: Geyer, Charles

Bettens, Ethienne
see: Potpourri, 18)

Bevan, Maurice
see: Laird, Michael, 11)

Billing, Hans-Alderich
see: Stockhausen, Markus, 4)

Brannigan, Owen
see: Bravington, Eric

Brett, Richard
see: Laird, Michael, 7)

Bröcheler, John
see: Soustrot, Bernard, 2)

Brodard, Michel
  see: Touvron, Guy, 10)

Brown, Mark
  see: Hagge, Detlef
  see: Laird, Michael, 9)

Carmeli, Boris
  see: Stockhausen, Markus, 3)

Caruso, Daniel
  see: Montesi, Robert, 1)

Černy, Miroslav
  see: Pok, František, 6)

Charlesworth, Stephen
  see: Steele-Perkins, Crispian,
    16)

Clary, Robert
  see: Stevens, Thomas, 15)

Crass, Franz
  see: André, Maurice, 17), 19)
  see: Schneidewind, Helmut, 3)
  see: Tarr, Edward, 19), 23)

Degerman, Johannes
  see: Potpourri, 3)

Donat, Peter
  see: Stevens, Thomas, 15)

Engen, Kieth
  see: Scherbaum, Adolf, 9)
  see: Unidentified, Trumpet(s),
    8)

Estes, Simon
  see: Goetting, Chandler
  see: Vasse, Claude

Etheridge, Brian
  see: Hagge, Detlef
  see: Laird, Michael, 9)

Finkel, Klaus
  see: Soustrot, Bernard, 8)

Fischer-Dieskau, Dietrich
  see: Lachenmeir, Paul
  see: Laird, Michael, 15)
  see: Potpourri, 11)
  see: Scherbaum, Adolf, 9)
  see: Tarr, Edward, 15)
  see: Thibaud, Pierre, 7)
  see: Unidentified, Trumpet(s),
    8)

Fissore, Enrico
  see: Tarr, Edward, 30), 43)

Frost, John
  see: Eskdale, George, 5)
  see: Unidentified, Trumpet(s),
    1)

George, Michael
  see: Laird, Michael, 9)
  see: Steele-Perkins, Crispian,
    12)

Gerihsen, Franz
  see: Läubin, Hannes, 3)

Grant, Joe
  see: Potpourri, 66)

Günther, Horst
  see: Zeyer, Adam

Gutstein, Ernst
  see: Eichhorn, Holger

Hale, Robert
  see: Steele-Perkins, Crispian,
    18)

Hall, Peter
  see: Laird, Michael, 7)

Handlos, Franz
  see: Pok, František, 4)

Hanson, Richard
  see: Potpourri, 66)

Hartinger, Albert
  see: Immer, Friedemann, 15)

Hartmann, Rudolf A.
  see: Pfann, Karl

Hayes, Marvin
  see: Montesi, Robert, 2), 5)

Heldwein, Walter
  see: Immer, Friedemann, 5), 6),
    14), 15)
  see: Läubin, Hannes, 5), 6)
  see: McGregor, Rob Roy, 2), 3)
  see: Potpourri, 23), 24)
  see: Schmid, Bernhard, 4)
  see: Send, Peter
  see: Wolf, Hans, 4), 5), 6), 8),
    9), 11), 12)

Hemsley, Thomas
  see: Jackson, Harold

Herincx, Raimond
  see: Jones, Philip, 1)

Hillebrand, Nikolaus
  see: Tarr, Edward, 17)

Hines, Jerome
  see: Mason, David, 1)

Holl, Robert
  see: Güttler, Ludwig, 28)
  see: Immer, Friedemann, 14),
    15), 17)
  see: Potpourri, 62)

Hoover, John
  see: Cook, Richard

Horvath, Jeffrey
  see: Geyer, Charles

Howell, Gwynne
  see: Herseth, Adolph, 2)
  see: Wilbraham, John, 2)

Howlett, Neil
  see: Jones, Philip, 5)

Hudemann, Hans-Olaf
  see: Zeh, Karl Heinz

Huttenlocher, Philippe
  see: Adelbrecht, Henri, 3)
  see: Bryant, Ralph, 4), 5)
  see: Gabel, Bernard, 4)
  see: Immer, Friedemann, 6)
  see: Läubin, Hannes, 3), 5), 7),
    8)
  see: McGregor, Rob Roy, 4), 5)
  see: Miller, Rodney
  see: Potpourri, 24), 25), 59),
    62)
  see: Sauter, Hermann, 21)
  see: Schmid, Bernhard, 5), 6),
    7), 8), 9), 10)
  see: Send, Peter
  see: Wolf, Hans, 2), 3), 7), 10),
    11)

Hynninen, Jorma
  see: Reinhart, Carole Dawn, 2)

Illerhaus, Edmund
  see: Sauter, Hermann, 26)

Jarvis, Jan
  see: Geyer, Charles

Kalaš, Karel
  see: Pok, František, 5)

Kastler, Karl
  see: Pok, František, 4)

Kelch, Franz
  see: Gleissle, Walter, 2), 3), 4),
    8)

Keyte, Christopher
  see: Laird, Michael, 17)

Kinz, Hanns-Friedrich
  see: Sauter, Hermann, 16)

Kitely, Murray
  see: Potpourri, 66)

Knapp, Peter
  see: Laird, Michael, 14)

Kraus, Philip
  see: Geyer, Charles

Krause, Tom
  see: André, Maurice, 16)

Kunz, Hanns-Friedrich
see: Potpourri, 24)
see: Sauter, Hermann, 4), 7), 9)
see: Schmid, Bernhard, 4)
see: Spindler, Josef, 15)

Kunz, Roland
see: Köpp, Rudolf

Lackner, Herbert
see: Eichhorn, Holger

Lagger, Oscar
see: Tarr, Edward, 43)

Larson, Phil
see: Potpourri, 66)

Lewis, Brayton
see: Davenport, LaNoue
see: Montesi, Robert, 1), 2), 5)

Liendo, Pedro
see: Pok, František, 4)

Littasy, Georg
see: André, Maurice, 11)

Lloyd, Robert
see: Laird, Michael, 11)

Loomis, James
see: Potpourri, 18)

Lopes, José Oliveira
see: Gabel, Bernard, 4)

Lorenz, Siegfried
see: Güttler, Ludwig, 16)
see: Potpourri, 60)

Loup, François
see: Tarr, Edward, 30), 32), 43)

MacDaniel, Berry
see: André, Maurice, 94)

Mack, James
see: Miller, Rodney

Malaguti, Laerte
see: Zickler, Heinz, 6)

Mars, Jacques
see: André, Maurice, 97)

McDaniel, Barry
see: André, Maurice, 122)
see: Lagorce, Marcel

McIntyre, Donald
see: Webb, Gordon, 3)

Mielke, Gerrit
see: Immer, Friedemann, 8)

Milligan, James
see: Anderson, George

Müller, Carl-Heinz
see: Zeh, Karl Heinz

Müller-Heuser, Franz
see: Tarr, Edward, 19)

Neunhoeffer, Frieder
see: Renz, Albrecht, 4), 5), 6), 7)

Nimsgern, Siegmund
see: Basch, Wolfgang, 4)
see: Bryant, Ralph, 3)
see: McGregor, Rob Roy, 1), 5), 6)
see: Potpourri, 22), 24), 53)
see: Sauter, Hermann, 5), 6), 8), 13), 35)
see: Spindler, Josef, 13)

Noble, John
see: Laird, Michael, 14)

Noguera, Louis
see: Coursier, Gérard

Nott, David
see: Montesi, Robert, 1)

Obermayer, Ernst
see: Renz, Albrecht, 4), 5), 6), 7)

Ocker, Claus
see: Holy, Walter, 5)

Opalach, Jan
see: Holmgren, Fred

Paul, Thomas
see: Dean, Allan, 4)
see: Smith, James

Pearce, Michael
see: Laird, Michael, 10)

Pernerstorfer, Alois
see: Stracker, Wilhelm

Pietzsch, Walter
see: Potpourri, 19)

Pinzarrone, Joe
see: Potpourri, 66)

Poellein, John
see: Potpourri, 66)

Polster, Hermann Christian
see: Güttler, Ludwig, 16)

Pommerien, Wilhelm
see: Ellinghaus, Wolfram
see: Tarr, Edward, 4)

Possemeyer, Berthold
see: Basch, Wolfgang, 1)

Prey, Hermann
see: Bauer, Willibald, 4)

Ramey, Samuel
see: Weeks, Larry

Reinhart, Gregory
see: Steele-Perkins, Crispian, 8)

Reischl, Erwin
see: Tasa, David

Rippon, Michael
see: Wilbraham, John, 20)

Robinson, Scott
see: Cook, Richard

Roles, Kenneth
see: Laird, Michael, 7)

Rowe, Timothy
see: Laird, Michael, 7)

Rudolf, Homer
see: Potpourri, 66)

Russell, Bruce
see: Laird, Michael, 7)

Schaible, Ulrich
see: Unidentified, Trumpet(s), 23)

Scheibner, Andreas
see: Güttler, Ludwig, 17)

Schmidt, Andreas
see: Friedrich, Reinhold
see: Schmid, Bernhard, 10), 11)

Schneider, Heinrich
see: Stradner, Gerhard

Schöne, Wolfgang
see: Immer, Friedemann, 5)
see: McGregor, Rob Roy, 3)
see: Miller, Rodney
see: Potpourri, 23), 24)
see: Sauter, Hermann, 5), 7),
9), 10), 11), 12), 14), 15),
16), 17), 18), 19), 20), 21),
22), 23), 30), 33), 35)
see: Schmid, Bernhard, 2), 3),
4), 5), 8)
see: Wolf, Hans, 4), 6), 7), 8),
9), 10)

Schopper, Michael
see: Smithers, Don, 13)

Schramm, Ernst Gerald
see: Touvron, Guy, 16)

Schultze, Andrew Walker
see: Holmgren, Fred

Shaw, Geoffrey
see: Laird, Michael, 11)

Shirley-Quirk, John
see: Lang, William
see: Wilbraham, John, 20), 22)

Sotin, Hans
see: Tarr, Edward, 24), 25), 26)

Spitzer, Leopold
see: Eichhorn, Holger

Stalman, Roger
see: Unidentified, Trumpet(s), 18)

Stämpfli, Jakob
see: André, Maurice, 99), 100),
106), 107), 110), 123), 138)
see: Gleissle, Walter, 7)
see: Holy, Walter, 1), 3)
see: Potpourri, 2)
see: Tarr, Edward, 32)
see: Unidentified, Trumpet(s),
13), 15)
see: Zickler, Heinz, 1), 3)

Standen, Richard
see: Wobisch, Helmut, 15)

Stewart, Charles
see: Steele-Perkins, Crispian,
16)

Stuart, Richard
see: Steele-Perkins, Crispian,
16)

Swenson, Peter
see: Geyer, Charles

Tadeo, Giorgio
see: Battagliola, Anania

Thomas, David
see: Hagge, Detlef
see: Laird, Michael, 7), 9), 18),
19)
see: Potpourri, 67)
see: Steele-Perkins, Crispian,
7), 16)

Thomaschke, Thomas
see: Potpourri, 63)

Thurman, Leon
see: Potpourri, 66)

Tibbetts, Paul
see: Nashan, Rudolph

Tüller, Niklaus
see: McGregor, Rob Roy, 2)
see: Potpourri, 23), 24)
see: Sauter, Hermann, 15), 16),
17), 20), 24), 31)
see: Unidentified, Trumpet(s),
5)
see: Wolf, Hans, 3)

Upham, John
see: Montesi, Robert, 2)

van der Kamp, Harry
see: Immer, Friedemann, 10)
see: Tamiya, Kenji

van der Meer, Ruud
see: Bryant, Ralph, 4)
see: Potpourri, 54), 55), 56),
57), 58), 59), 60), 61)
see: Spindler, Josef, 14), 15),
16)

van Egmond, Max
see: Bryant, Ralph, 1), 2), 3),
4), 5)
see: Groot, Willem (Wim)
see: Immer, Friedemann, 14)
see: Potpourri, 51), 52), 53),
57), 58), 59), 60), 61), 63)
see: Smithers, Don, 14), 15)
see: Spindler, Josef, 7), 10),
11), 12), 13), 14)

Varcoe, Stephen
see: Laird, Michael, 10)

Vetter, Michael
see: Stockhausen, Markus, 4)

Villisech, Jacques
see: Spindler, Josef, 7)
see: Tarr, Edward, 45)

Vinický, Vratislav
see: Pok, František, 6)

Visser, Lieuwe
see: Spindler, Josef, 16)

Vogt, Richard
see: Montesi, Robert, 1), 2)

Voketaitis, Arnold
see: Herseth, Adolph, 4)

Walker, William
see: Geyer, Charles

Wallington, Lawrence
see: Steele-Perkins, Crispian,
16)

Ward, David
see: Stringer, Alan, 5)

Warrington, Peter
see: Cook, Richard

Wenk, Erich
see: André, Maurice, 99), 100)
see: Gleissle, Walter, 5), 6), 7), 11)
see: Unidentified, Trumpet(s), 14), 15)
see: Wolf, Hans, 1)
see: Zickler, Heinz, 1), 2)

Winner, Siegfried
see: Renz, Albrecht, 4), 5), 6), 7)

Wollitz, Eduard
see: Holy, Walter, 2)

Wyatt, Walker
see: Potpourri, 52)

Wyrick, Warren
see: Montesi, Robert, 2)

Celesta

Beaufort, Raphaël
see: Thibaud, Pierre, 9)

Cobb, John
see: Miller, Rodney

Kalish, Gilbert
see: Dean, Allan, 6)

Karis, Aleck
see: Anderson, Ronald, 6)
see: Dean, Allan, 3)

Kokhanova, Elena
see: Dokshitser, Timofei, 12)

Masselos, William
see: Glantz, Harry, 6)

Massey, Michael
see: Lowrey, Alvin

Miller, Mayne
see: Blee, Eugene

Noble, R.
see: Wallace, John, 2)

Petrescu, Christian
see: Cure, Antoine

Rzewski, Frederic
see: Dean, Allan, 1), 6)

Sampen, Marilyn
see: Potpourri, 6)

Swan, Andrea
see: Perry, Brian

Tartak, Marvin
see: Metzger, Charles

Wong, Shirley
see: Logan, Jack

Woollen, Russell
see: Geisler, Lloyd

Cello

Abramowitz, Jonathan
see: Anderson, Ronald, 2)

Adcock, Robert
see: Stevens, Thomas, 10)

Aichinger, Wolfgang
see: Immer, Friedemann, 14), 17)
see: Potpourri, 63)

Aisslinger, Andreas
see: Sauter, Hermann, 27)

Albin, Roger
see: Jones, Philip, 8)

Alexander, Fred
see: Izan, Bernard

Altwegg, Raffaele
see: Jones, Philip, 6)

Anastasio, R.
see: Haug, Edward

Apostle, Anne
see: Tarr, Edward, 41)

Arico, Fortunato
  see: Anderson, Ronald, 4)
  see: Gould, Mark
  see: Immer, Friedemann, 13)

Auburn, Valerie
  see: Roberts, Standish

Aubut, Alain
  see: Thompson, James

Bach, Timothy
  see: Plog, Anthony, 11)

Baines, Francis
  see: Eskdale, George, 5)

Banks, Elaine Scott
  see: Potpourri, 38)

Barab, Seymour
  see: Jones, Philip, 11)

Barchet, Siegfried
  see: André, Maurice, 16)
  see: Longinotti, Paolo
  see: Scherbaum, Adolf, 5)

Bartholemew, Alan K.
  see: Guarneri, Mario

Bartlett, Eric
  see: Burns, Stephen

Basseux, Pierre
  see: Nagel, Robert, 3)

Bauer, Alwin
  see: André, Maurice, 192)

Baumann, Jörg
  see: Groth, Konradin

Beckedorf, Horst
  see: Bodenröder, Robert
  see: Tarr, Edward, 35), 37)
  see: Zickler, Heinz, 1)

Becker, Manfred
  see: Basch, Wolfgang, 1)

Beinl, Ludwig
  see: Wobisch, Helmut, 2)

Bernhardt, Wolfgang
  see: Gass, Josef

Besnard, Guy
  see: André, Maurice, 152)

Bethge, Dietrick
  see: Steele-Perkins, Crispian, 14)

Bex, Robert
  see: Lagorce, Antoine

Bills, Jean
  see: McGuffey, Patrick

Bineau, Normand
  see: Lowrey, Alvin

Bischof, Joachim
  see: Haas, Rudolf

Blees, Thomas
  see: Holy, Walter, 2)
  see: Schneidewind, Helmut, 11)
  see: Schoof, Manfred
  see: Tarr, Edward, 36)
  see: Wolf, Hans, 1)
  see: Zickler, Heinz, 2), 3)

Bogatin, Barbara
  see: Gould, Mark
  see: Immer, Friedemann, 13)

Bogner, Wolfgang
  see: Adelbrecht, Henri, 1)

Borwitzky, Ottomar
  see: Groth, Konradin

Bosbach, Philipp
  see: Immer, Friedemann, 11)

Bottermund, H.
  see: Spörri, Paul

Brachmann, Dieter
  see: Sauter, Hermann, 13), 35)

Brancaleon, R.
  see: Battagliola, Anania

Brennand, Charles
  see: Mills, Fred

Brindel, Jill
  see: Perry, Brian

Brion, Claude
  see: Scherbaum, Adolf, 20)

Bruni, Franca
  see: Dassé, Jean-Luc

Buck, Peter
  see: Schmid, Bernhard, 6)
  see: Schneidewind, Helmut, 13)

Buhl, Reinhard
  see: Bauer, Willibald, 4)

Buhl, Reinhold Johannes
  see: Tarr, Edward, 35), 36), 37)
  see: Zickler, Heinz, 4)

Bunting, Christopher
  see: Webb, Gordon, 7)

Bylsma, Anner
  see: André, Maurice, 221), 222),
    223), 224), 225)
  see: Bryant, Ralph, 2), 4), 5)
  see: Groot, Willem (Wim)
  see: Immer, Friedemann, 14)
  see: Laird, Michael, 5)
  see: Potpourri, 51), 52), 57),
    58), 59), 60)
  see: Rippas, Claude
  see: Smithers, Don, 13), 14),
    15)
  see: Spindler, Josef, 11), 13),
    14), 15)

Cameron, Alexander
  see: Webb, Gordon, 2), 4)

Canselosi, Robert
  see: Dudgeon, Ralph

Cassoli, Max
  see: André, Maurice, 130)

Caudle, Mark
  see: Keavy, Stephen
  see: Laird, Michael, 7)
  see: Steele-Perkins, Crispian,
    10)

Chiampan, Gianni
  see: André, Maurice, 130)

Christie, James
  see: Webb, Gordon, 1)

Clark, Raymond
  see: Jackson, Harold
  see: Mason, David, 1)

Clarke, Jennifer Ward
  see: Laird, Michael, 8)

Coe, Jane
  see: Keavy, Stephen

Coin, Christophe
  see: Immer, Friedemann, 15),
    16)

Coppock, Bruce
  see: Dean, Allan, 2)

Cordier, Robert
  see: Ménardi, Louis

Courmont, Alain
  see: André, Maurice, 152), 211),
    215)

Cruthirds, Harold
  see: McGuffey, Patrick

Custer, Stephen
  see: Guarneri, Mario

Dam, Peter
  see: Touvron, Guy, 19)

Davis, Douglas
  see: Hood, Boyde
  see: Schwarz, Gerard, 1)

Demenga, Thomas
  see: Sommerhalder, Max

Dickinson, Lynn
  see: Immer, Friedemann, 3)

Diesselhorst, Jan
  see: Tasa, David

Dillner, C.
  see: Haas, Rudolf

Döcke, Gisela
  see: Preis, Ivo

Donderer, Erwin
  see: Touvron, Guy, 19)

Koster, Dijck
  see: Bryant, Ralph, 2)
  see: Potpourri, 51), 52), 57), 58)
  see: Smithers, Don, 13), 14), 15)
  see: Spindler, Josef, 11), 13), 14), 15)

Kouguell, Alexander
  see: Broiles, Melvin
  see: Heinrich, Robert

Kraemer, Nicholas
  see: Wilbraham, John, 2)

Kreger, James
  see: Berinbaum, Martin

Krosnick, Joel
  see: Anderson, Ronald, 4)
  see: Potpourri, 38)
  see: Young, Gene

Kubizek, Elli
  see: Spindler, Josef, 10)

Kuijken, Wieland
  see: Rippas, Claude

Kvalbein, Aage
  see: Christiansen, Jan

Lamothe, Claude
  see: Thompson, James

Lasher, Anita
  see: Steele-Perkins, Crispian, 14)

Lasker, Anita
  see: Wilbraham, John, 27)

Laurie, Ronald
  see: Schultz, Erik, 8)
  see: Umbrico, Joseph

Legbandt, Phyllis
  see: Greenho, David

Lehwalder, Julie
  see: Steele-Perkins, Crispian, 16), 18)

Lenske, Larry
  see: Miller, Rodney

Leonhard, Ronald
  see: Stevens, Thomas, 12)

Leopold, Rudolf
  see: Immer, Friedemann, 16)

Lesser, Laurence
  see: Schwarz, Gerard, 3)

Lessing, Alfred
  see: Tarr, Edward, 10)

Linnebach, Günther
  see: Gleissle, Walter, 1)

Little, Dane Richards
  see: Guarneri, Mario

Lodeon, Frederic
  see: André, Maurice, 167)

Loyevsky, Yuri
  see: Dokshitser, Timofei, 12)

Lupu, Dan
  see: Hunger, Helmut, 4)

Lutzke, Myron
  see: Carroll, Edward, 8), 9)

Ma, Yo-Yo
  see: Marsalis, Wynton, 5)

Malitz, Roger
  see: Miller, Rodney

Mandalka, Rudolf
  see: Bodenröder, Robert
  see: Potpourri, 22)
  see: Tarr, Edward, 35), 37), 38)

Manescu, Cristina
  see: Braz, Dirceu, 5)

Mantel, Gerhard
  see: Sauter, Hermann, 17)
  see: Schmid, Bernhard, 5), 6), 7), 8)
  see: Wolf, Hans, 10)

Marchesini, Michel
  see: Thibaud, Pierre, 9)

Neuman, Maxine
see: Mase, Raymond

Nothas, Walter
see: Goetting, Chandler

Novotný, Karel
see: André, Maurice, 220)

Oliver, Nils
see: Schwarz, Gerard, 1)

Olofsson, Ake
see: Schrello, Mark

Orton, Stephen
see: Wilbraham, John, 27)

Ostertag, Martin
see: Potpourri, 25)
see: Schmid, Bernhard, 9)
see: Wolf, Hans, 9), 11), 12)

Palm, Siegfried
see: Bauer, Adam

Pank, Siegfried
see: Güttler, Ludwig, 4), 8)

Parnas, Leslie
see: Nagel, Robert, 2)

Paternoster, Vito
see: Touvron, Guy, 14)

Petkov, Georgi
see: Touvron, Guy, 19)

Pini, Anthony
see: Jones, Philip, 8)
see: Mason, David, 3)

Pleeth, Anthony
see: Laird, Michael, 5), 7), 8),
19)

Plümacher, Hans
see: Tarr, Edward, 23), 24),
25), 26)

Pocaterra, Antonio
see: Tarr, Edward, 1)

Pople, Ross
see: Wilbraham, John, 1)

Poppen, Irmgard
see: Tarr, Edward, 18)

Posegga, Wilhelm
see: Bauer, Willibald, 5)

Rácz, Zoltan
see: Immer, Friedemann, 3)

Radunskaya, Ami
see: Burkhart, David

Raiskin, Boris
see: Yudashkin, Georgy

Reculard, Mireille
see: Delmotte, Roger, 32)

Reher, Kurt
see: Stevens, Thomas, 13)

Rehm, Uwe-Peter
see: Zeh, Karl Heinz

Rénard, M.
see: Thibaud, Pierre, 1)

Reuter, Johannes
see: Kierski, Eckhard

Richards, Bernard
see: Clift, Dennis
see: Webb, Gordon, 1)

Robbins, Alice
see: Dickey, Bruce

Robinson, Michael
see: Miller, John
see: Stockhausen, Markus, 4)

Rose, Leonard
see: Vacchiano, William, 2)

Rossi, Gilbert
see: Adelbrecht, Henri, 3)

Rostropovitch, Mstislav
see: André, Maurice, 82)

Rothmuller, Daniel
see: Guarneri, Mario
see: Stevens, Thomas, 2), 5)

Ruijsenaars, Harro
see: Floore, John

Sádlo, Miloš
see: Junek, Václav, 6)

Schäfer, Herbert
see: Gleissle, Walter, 8), 11)

Schenkman, Peter
see: Schultz, Erik, 8)

Schijfes, Lidewij
see: Bryant, Ralph, 4), 5)
see: Potpourri, 61), 63)
see: Smithers, Don, 15)

Schneider, Ansgar
see: Läubin, Hannes, 3)

Schneider, Jean
see: Broiles, Melvin
see: Nagel, Robert, 14)

Schneller, Wilhelm
see: André, Maurice, 93)

Schober, Andrea
see: Schultz, Erik, 5)

Schrecker, Bruno
see: Groot, Willem (Wim)

Schulz, Friedemann
see: Sauter, Hermann, 19), 20), 21), 22)

Schwebsch, Wolfgang
see: André, Maurice, 16)

Schweitzer, Ray
see: Karpilovsky, Murray

Sedo, Luis
see: Espigoli, Jaume

Seemann, Irmingard
see: Scherbaum, Adolf, 21), 32)

Sekreve, Henk
see: Reinhart, Carole Dawn, 2)

Shapiro, Harvey
see: Broiles, Melvin
see: Crisara, Raymond, 1)

Sherman, Hannah
see: Nashan, Rudolph

Sherry, Fred
see: Berinbaum, Martin
see: Burns, Stephen
see: Dean, Allan, 1), 4), 5), 6), 7), 8)
see: Ferrantino, Kenneth
see: Nagel, Robert, 18)
see: Ranger, Louis
see: Romm, Ronald

Shinebourne, John
see: Mackintosh, Jack

Shulman, Alan
see: Crisara, Raymond, 1)
see: Wallace, John, 3)

Shuttleworth, Anna
see: Eskdale, George, 5)
see: Jones, Philip, 7)

Silpigni, Salvatore
see: Greenho, David

Simek, Peter
see: Sauter, Hermann, 6), 35)

Simon, Victor
see: Popov, Sergei, 2)

Simpson, Derek
see: Clift, Dennis

Slowik, Kenneth
see: Holmgren, Fred

Solow, Jeffrey
see: Schwarz, Gerard, 3)

Sommer, F.
see: Scherbaum, Adolf, 35)

Spengler, Hans
see: André, Maurice, 171)
see: Gleissle, Walter, 1)

Starck, Claude
see: Scherbaum, Adolf, 6), 24)

Stella, Pietro
see: Touvron, Guy, 14)

Storck, Klaus
see: Tarr, Edward, 17)

Strano, Francesco
see: Touvron, Guy, 14)

Strauch, Pierre
see: Cure, Antoine
see: Vasse, Claude

Štros, Jan
see: Horák, Jiří, 5)

Stross, H.
see: Haug, Edward

Sylvester, Robert
see: Nagel, Robert, 3)

Tachezi, Herwig
see: Immer, Friedemann, 17)

Tannenberger, František
see: Jurča, Vladimir

Taylor, Muriel
see: Clift, Dennis

Tekula, Joseph
see: Murtha, Roger

Terebesi, György
see: Quinque, Rolf, 7)

Teulières
see: Perinelli, René

Teutsch, Götz
see: Groth, Konradin

Thomas, Ronald
see: Hoffman, Edward

Thorn, D.
see: Wilbraham, John, 30)

Thorner, Madeline
see: Steele-Perkins, Crispian, 18)

Tortelier, Paul
see: Mule, Marcel

Tournus, Michel
see: André, Maurice, 49)
see: Thibaud, Pierre, 1)

Towb, Suki
see: Steele-Perkins, Crispian, 16)

Trauer, Stefan
see: Friedrich, Reinhold
see: Läubin, Hannes, 4), 5), 6), 7), 8)
see: Schmid, Bernhard, 10), 11)
see: Send, Peter

Trexler, Peter
see: Friedrich, Reinhold

Trotta, Joseph
see: Espigoli, Jaume

Tunnell, Charles
see: Marsalis, Wynton, 2)
see: Mason, David, 5)
see: Steele-Perkins, Crispian, 14)

Tunnicliffe, Richard
see: Steele-Perkins, Crispian, 16)

Uhl, Oswald
see: André, Maurice, 17)
see: Scherbaum, Adolf, 9)

Ulsamer, Josef
see: Tarr, Edward, 12)

Vanderkooi, David
see: Hood, Donald

van der Meer, Richte
see: Immer, Friedemann, 14)
see: Potpourri, 57), 58), 59), 60), 63)
see: Rippas, Claude
see: Smithers, Don, 14)
see: Spindler, Josef, 13)

van Kampen, Christopher
see: Evans, Laurie
see: Miller, John

Varah, James
see: Potpourri, 6)

Varga, Laszlo
see: Vacchiano, William, 4)

457

Chalumeau
[cross-referenced under clarinet]

Erig, Richard
see: Pok, František, 4)

Fest, Frithjof
see: Tarr, Edward, 12)

Hofer, Heinz
see: Tarr, Edward, 34)

Stalder, Hans Rudolf
see: Tarr, Edward, 34)

Steinkopf, Otto
see: Tarr, Edward, 12)

Clapper shake key cornopean

Impett, Jonathan
see: Impett, Jonathan

Clarinet
[includes all ranges of clarinets plus basset horn & chalumeau]

Abato, James
see: Butterfield, Billy

Abato, Vincent J.
see: Burke, James, 5), 6)

Agogue, René
see: André, Maurice, 120)

Allard, Joseph
see: Burke, James, 5), 6)

Andresen, Erik
see: Christiansen, Jan

Atkins, David
see: Plog, Anthony, 9), 11)
see: Stevens, Thomas, 11)

Bagdasarian, Rafael
see: Dokshitser, Timofei, 12)

Bass, Marilyn
see: Miller, Rodney

Bezruchenko, Valery
see: Margolin, Veniamin

Bibbins, Frealon
see: Haug, Edward

Blackwell, Virgil
see: Ranger, Louis
see: Romm, Ronald
see: Schwarz, Gerard, 13)

Blaha, František
see: Rejlek, Vladimir

Blayman, Herbert
see: Burke, James, 5), 6)

Bloch, Kalman
see: Heinrich, Robert
see: Nagel, Robert, 4)

Bloom, Arthur
see: Dean, Allan, 1), 4), 5), 6)
see: Mills, Fred
see: Nagel, Robert, 18), 19), 20)
see: Romm, Ronald

Blustine, Allen
see: Anderson, Ronald, 3), 4), 5)
see: Dean, Allan, 2), 6), 7), 8)
see: Patti, Douglas
see: Stubbs, James

Bockman, Sigurd
see: Burke, James, 5), 6)

Bonaventure, Michel
see: André, Maurice, 120)

Bonifert, Andreas
see: Bernard, André, 2)

Bornier, Francis
see: André, Maurice, 120)

Boutard, André
see: André, Maurice, 172)
see: Delmotte, Roger, 6)
see: Ménardi, Louis

Bright, Ernest
see: Burke, James, 5), 6)

Brody, Clark
see: Herseth, Adolph, 4), 6)

Brymer, Jack
  see: Jackson, Harold
  see: Wilbraham, John, 1), 30)
  see: Wobisch, Helmut, 14)

Bunke, Jerome
  see: Dean, Allan, 9)

Bureš, Juraj
  see: Jurča, Vladimir

Buxbaum, Merritt
  see: Stevens, Thomas, 2), 5)

Campbell, James
  see: Mills, Fred

Cardillo, Pasquale
  see: Ghitalla, Armando, 14)

Chiapelli, Michel
  see: André, Maurice, 120)

Cohen, Frank
  see: Schwarz, Gerard, 13)

Colonico, Robert
  see: Metzger, Charles

Coste, René
  see: André, Maurice, 120)

Crowley, Charles
  see: Victorian Trumpet Trio

Dailey, Dwight
  see: Henderson, Douglas

Damiens, Alain
  see: Cure, Antoine
  see: Vasse, Claude

D'Antonio, Roy
  see: Brady, Charles

Davies, Hugh
  see: Stockhausen, Markus, 4)

Davis, Stanley
  see: Miller, Rodney
  see: Perry, Brian

de Kant, Ronald
  see: Hopkins, Kenneth

Delattre, Michel
  see: André, Maurice, 120)

Delécluse, Ulysse
  see: André, Maurice, 181)

de Peyer, Gervase
  see: Clift, Dennis
  see: Jones, Philip, 2)
  see: Potpourri, 16)
  see: Schwarz, Gerard, 3)

Deplus, Guy
  see: Caens, Thierry
  see: Delmotte, Roger, 2)

DeRoche, Don
  see: Potpourri, 5)

Desurmont, Claude
  see: André, Maurice, 49)

Devendra, Anand
  see: Anderson, Ronald, 6)

DeWar, Ron
  see: Ferrantino, Kenneth

d'Hondt, Jos
  see: Sevenstern, Harry

Diestel, Werner
  see: Schmidt, Ingus

Dillies, Philippe
  see: André, Maurice, 120)

Dlouhý, Karel
  see: Horák, Jiří, 4), 5)
  see: Junek, Václav, 6)

Dort, Gérard
  see: André, Maurice, 120)

Dovillez, Patrick
  see: André, Maurice, 120)

Drucker, Stanley
  see: Jandorf, D.

Eichler, Rolf
  see: Spindler, Josef, 2), 3)

Erezeo, Francis
  see: André, Maurice, 120)

Erig, Richard
  see: Pok, František, 4)

Estrin, Harvey
  see: Crisara, Raymond, 2)

Fadle, Jorg
  see: Potpourri, 48)

Fallows, Roger
  see: Miller, John

Fest, Frithjof
  see: Tarr, Edward, 12)

Flores, Anastasio
  see: León, Felipe

Gabai, Maurice
  see: Wilbraham, John, 21)

Galaup, André
  see: André, Maurice, 120)

Gallodoro, Alfred
  see: Burke, James, 5), 6)

Geisser, Hermut
  see: Stockhausen, Markus, 2)

Gerard, Guy
  see: Potpourri, 48)

Gigliotti, Anthony
  see: Johnson, Gilbert, 1)
  see: Krauss, Sam

Gizard, Michel
  see: André, Maurice, 120)

Glantz, Fred
  see: Glantz, Harry, 6)

Glassman, Karl
  see: Glantz, Harry, 6)

Glazer, David
  see: Mueller, Herbert

Gluzman, Mikhail
  see: Gorokhov, Vitaly

Gmür, Rolf
  see: Sommerhalder, Max

Godeau
  see: Foveau, Eugène

Goldstein, William
  see: Murtha, Roger

Hambleton, Hale
  see: Wilbraham, John, 1)

Hambleton, Wilfred
  see: Jones, Philip, 11)

Hepp, Heinz
  see: Schmid, Bernhard, 13)

Hill, James
  see: Ghitalla, Armando, 1)

Hill, Robert
  see: Dolce, Christine

Hill, Tom
  see: Hoffman, Edward

Hilton, Janet
  see: Wallace, John, 1)

Himmler, Hans
  see: Gass, Josef

Hofer, Heinz
  see: Tarr, Edward, 34)

Hoffman, Robert
  see: Burke, James, 5), 6)

Hoogstoel, Leon
  see: Longinotti, Paolo

Hotz, Kurt
  see: Adelbrecht, Henri, 1)

Howard, Alexander
  see: Burke, James, 6)

Howes, Peter
  see: Izan, Bernard

Howland, Paul E.
  see: Burke, James, 5), 6)
  see: Heinrich, Robert

Hudelson, Charles
  see: Lowrey, Alvin

Izmailov, Mikhail
  see: Margolin, Veniamin

461

Janda, Miroslav
  see: Mičaník, Jaroslav

Jewett, Thomas
  see: Bastin, Ernie

Jindra, Oldřich
  see: Buriánek, Jindřich

Jones, James
  see: Potpourri, 6)

Kalina, David
  see: Geisler, Lloyd

Kasper, Michel
  see: André, Maurice, 120)

King, Thea
  see: Jones, Philip, 11)
  see: Mason, David, 5)

Kirkbride, Jerry
  see: Dean, Allan, 1)

Klein, Franz
  see: André, Maurice, 179)

Klink, Albert
  see: Burke, James, 5), 6)

Klöcker, Dieter
  see: Bernard, André, 2)
  see: Goethel, Siegfried

Kopecký, Miloš
  see: Horák, Jiří, 5)
  see: Junek, Václav, 3), 5)

Kreiselman, Jack
  see: Anderson, Ronald, 1)
  see: Heinrich, Robert

Labe, Russell
  see: Reese, Rebecca

Lancelot, Jacques
  see: Thibaud, Pierre, 1)

Leclerc, Jean-Claude
  see: André, Maurice, 120)

Lecoules, Claude
  see: André, Maurice, 120)

Leeson, Daniel
  see: Schwarz, Gerard, 13)

Lefebvre, Pierre
  see: Delmotte, Roger, 35)

Legbandt, Rolf
  see: Greenho, David

Lemser, Hans
  see: Scholz, Walter

Lerner, Jeffrey
  see: Weast, Robert

Lethiec
  see: Perinelli, René

Lewis, Walter
  see: Jones, Philip, 11)

Lherondeau, Roland
  see: André, Maurice, 88)

Listokin, Robert
  see: Nagel, Robert, 3)

Livingston, James
  see: Rapier, Leon, 4)

Löchner, Hans-Detlef
  see: Güttler, Ludwig, 20)

Loeb, Alfred
  see: Mase, Raymond

London, Larry
  see: Burkhart, David

Lytell, Jimmy
  see: Butterfield, Billy

Madrick, Steve
  see: Butterfield, Billy

Manners, Artie
  see: Butterfield, Billy

Marcellus, Robert
  see: Blee, Eugene

Marques, Jean-Marie
  see: André, Maurice, 120)

Mauldin, Bonnie
  see: Birch, Robert

McCartney, Stanley
  see: Chenette, Stephen
  see: Chevanelle, Serge
  see: LeComte, Jacques

McGinnis, Robert
  see: Butterfield, Billy

Michaels, Jost
  see: André, Maurice, 20)
  see: Scherbaum, Adolf, 8)

Mikhailov, L.
  see: Maximenko, Anatoly, 2)

Moinet, Philippe
  see: André, Maurice, 120)

Mondello, Toots
  see: Butterfield, Billy

Montaigne, Louis
  see: Delmotte, Roger, 2)
  see: Thibaud, Pierre, 1)

Montoni, Bruno
  see: André, Maurice, 120)

Moore, Ronald
  see: Webb, Gordon, 2)

Morf, Antony
  see: Adelbrecht, Henri, 3)
  see: Cuvit, Michel

Mozgovenko, I.
  see: Volodin, Lev

Myasnikov, Edward
  see: Prokopov, Vyacheslav

Naulais, Marcel
  see: Delmotte, Roger, 2)

Nilsson, Ulf
  see: Schrello, Mark

Nuixa, Jean-Jacques
  see: André, Maurice, 120)

O'Brien, Don
  see: Metzger, Charles

Oein, Theodore
  see: Potpourri, 38)

Oppenheim, David
  see: Nagel, Robert, 1), 4)

Osseck, William
  see: Mear, Sidney, 1)

Pages, Jean
  see: André, Maurice, 120)

Pañella, Julio
  see: Foriscot, J.

Papeghin, Bernard
  see: André, Maurice, 120)

Paschek, Joseph
  see: Scholz, Walter

Pay, Antony
  see: Evans, Laurie
  see: Miller, John
  see: Watson, James

Plesnicar, Paula
  see: Schwarz, Gerard, 13)

Poiret, Christian
  see: André, Maurice, 120)

Polatschek, Victor
  see: Voisin, Roger, 10)

Pons, André
  see: Thibaud, Pierre, 9)

Portal, Michael
  see: Wilbraham, John, 21)

Portnoy, Bernard
  see: Burke, James, 5), 6)
  see: Davidson, Louis
  see: Glantz, Harry, 6)
  see: Potpourri, 31)

Post, Jean
  see: Thibaud, Pierre, 9)

Powell, William Edward
  see: Guarneri, Mario

Prinz, Alfred
  see: Spindler, Josef, 1)

Puddy, Keith
  see: Howarth, Elgar

Quemard, Olivier
see: André, Maurice, 120)

Rabbai, Joseph
see: Schwarz, Gerard, 11), 13)

Ricci, Paul
see: Burke, James, 5), 6)
see: Butterfield, Billy

Rice, Al
see: Parker, Craig B.

Richman, Boomie
see: Butterfield, Billy

Roginsky, Isaac
see: Popov, Sergei, 5)

Rohrig, James D.
see: Guarneri, Mario

Rosé, Alfred
see: Rudolf, Richard

Ross, Ben
see: Butterfield, Billy

Russo, Charles
see: Broiles, Melvin
see: Burke, James, 5), 6)
see: Crisara, Raymond, 1)
see: Heinrich, Robert
see: Schwarz, Gerard, 6)
see: Weis, Theodore, 2)

Rybín, Alois
see: Horák, Jiří, 4)
see: Junek, Václav, 3)

Sasaki, David
see: Sasaki, Ray

Sauze, Marcel
see: André, Maurice, 88)

Savage, Temple
see: Mason, David, 3)

Schmidt, André
see: André, Maurice, 120)

Schöbinger, Adolf
see: Spindler, Josef, 2), 3)

Schönhofer, Richard
see: Rudolf, Richard

Schultz, John
see: Schwarz, Gerard, 13)

Sefsik, Stephen
see: McGuffey, Patrick

Sereque, Christopher
see: Pressley, Richard

Shapiro, Wallace
see: Burke, James, 5), 6)
see: Ghitalla, Armando, 10)

Shifrin, David
see: Haneuse, Arthur
see: Plog, Anthony, 8)

Silfies, George
see: Crisara, Raymond, 3)

Simenauer, Peter
see: Mills, Fred

Smylie, Dennis
see: Anderson, Ronald, 6)

Sokolov, Vladimir
see: Maximenko, Anatoly, 3)
see: Volodin, Lev

Sparnaay, Harry
see: Floore, John

Spear, Julian
see: McNab, Malcolm
see: Plog, Anthony, 9)

Stalder, Hans Rudolf
see: Adelbrecht, Henri, 1)
see: Schneidewind, Helmut, 12)
see: Tarr, Edward, 34)

Steinkopf, Otto
see: Tarr, Edward, 12)

Štengl, Jiří
see: Kejmar, Miroslav, 13)
see: Mičaník, Jaroslav

Stephens, Suzanne
see: Stockhausen, Markus, 3),
4)

Zukovsky, Michele
see: Guarneri, Mario
see: Stevens, Thomas, 14)

Clavichord

Hogwood, Christopher
see: Laird, Michael, 1)

Lester, Harold
see: Potpourri, 67)

Miedema, Barbara
see: Otten, Kees

Contrabassoon
[cross-referenced under bassoon]

Berkenstock, James
see: Miller, Rodney
see: Perry, Brian

Delage, Michel
see: André, Maurice, 92)

Fleischmann, Otto
see: Rudolf, Richard

Kennedy, Valentine
see: Webb, Gordon, 2)

Lawson, Richard
see: Anderson, Ronald, 6)

Lipp, Charles
see: Potpourri, 5)

Longazo, George
see: Geisler, Lloyd

MacCourt, Donald
see: Schwarz, Gerard, 13)

McKay, James
see: Miller, Rodney

Schoenbach, Sol
see: Johnson, Gilbert, 1)

Young, Jean
see: Ghitalla, Armando, 1)

Contralto
[cross-referenced under alto (voice)]

Baker, Janet
see: Jones, Philip, 3)

Bence, Margarethe
see: Unidentified, Trumpet(s), 23)

Bumbry, Grace
see: Stringer, Alan, 5)

Casoni, Bianca Maria
see: André, Maurice, 11)

Collard, Jeanine
see: André, Maurice, 71)
see: Thibaud, Pierre, 9)

Conrad, Margrit
see: Tarr, Edward, 32)

Fischer, Lore
see: Zeyer, Adam

Gohl, Verena
see: Potpourri, 18)

Green, Elvira
see: Dean, Allan, 10)

Höffgen, Marga
see: André, Maurice, 19)

Hoffman, Grace
see: Mason, David, 1)

Kippersluys, Will
see: Otten, Kees

Kopleff, Florence
see: Broiles, Melvin
see: Smith, James

Lensky, Margaret
see: Potpourri, 18)

Lipton, Martha
see: Johnson, Gilbert, 5)

Lisken, Emmy
see: Lagorce, Marcel
see: Schneidewind, Helmut, 3)

Lundin, Kerstin
see: Hardenberger, Håkan

Merriman, Nan
see: Wobisch, Helmut, 15)

Minetto, Maria
see: Potpourri, 18)

Minty, Shirley
see: Laird, Michael, 19)

Palmateer, Mary
see: Anderson, George

Phillips, Rosemary
see: Jones, Philip, 2)

Procter, Norma
see: Bravington, Eric
see: Wilbraham, John, 23)

Reynolds, Anna
see: Webb, Gordon, 3)
see: Wilbraham, John, 2)

Rideout, Patricia
see: Umbrico, Joseph

Schwarz, Hanna
see: Goetting, Chandler

Stevens, Pauline
see: Jones, Philip, 2)

Watkinson, Carolyn
see: Laird, Michael, 7)

Watts, Helen
see: André, Maurice, 16)
see: Lang, William
see: Unidentified, Trumpet(s),
18)

Cornet
[cross-referenced under trumpet]

Amstutz, Keith
see: Amstutz, Keith

André, Maurice
see: André, Maurice, 8), 88),
120), 212)

Autrey, Byron L.
see: Autrey, Byron L.

Boone, Dalvin
see: Lowrey, Alvin

Brady, Charles
see: Brady, Charles

Broiles, Melvin
see: Broiles, Melvin

Brönimann, Walter
see: McCann, Phillip

Bruneau, Michel
see: André, Maurice, 120)

Burke, James
see: Broiles, Melvin
see: Burke, James, 2), 4), 5),
6), 7), 8)

Burri, Mario
see: McCann, Phillip

Caens, Thierry
see: Caens, Thierry

Christensen, Ketil
see: Christensen, Ketil

Chunn, Michael
see: Chunn, Michael

Clarke, Herbert L.
see: Clarke, Herbert L.

Clift, Dennis
see: Clift, Dennis

Cronshaw, Brian
see: Garside, Derek M.

Cuvit, Michel
see: Cuvit, Michel

Dean, Allan
see: Schwarz, Gerard, 5), 21)

Delmotte, Roger
see: Delmotte, Roger, 1), 6),
51)

Dion, Jean-François
see: Aquitaine Brass Ensemble

Reichen, Roland
see: McCann, Phillip

Riva, Bruno
see: Aquitaine Brass Ensemble

Schrello, Marc
see: Potpourri, 3)

Schultz, Erik
see: Schultz, Erik, 8)

Schüpbach, Susanne
see: McCann, Phillip

Schwarz, Gerard
see: Schwarz, Gerard, 5), 19), 21)

Smith, Leonard B.
see: Smith, Leonard B.

Smith, Philip
see: Smith, Philip, 3), 4)

Sommerhalder, Max
see: Sommerhalder, Max

Stucki, Jacqueline
see: McCann, Phillip

Tolley, Richard
see: Tolley, Richard

Urfer, Eric
see: Urfer, Eric

Voisin, Roger
see: Voisin, Roger, 13)

von Kaenel, Andreas
see: McCann, Phillip

Walton, Richard
see: Walton, Richard

Watson, James
see: Watson, James

Weis, Theodore
see: Weis, Theodore, 5)

Cornetto (Zink)

Berger, Sven
see: Otten, Kees

Brandes, Lothar
see: Tarr, Edward, 4), 10), 18)

Bryant, Ralph
see: Bryant, Ralph, 1), 3), 4), 5)
see: Immer, Friedemann, 18)
see: Potpourri, 52), 53), 56), 57), 59), 62), 63)

Canihac, Jean-Pierre
see: Canihac, Jean-Pierre

Caudle, Theresa
see: Caudle, Theresa

Cook, Richard
see: Cook, Richard

Davenport, LaNoue
see: Davenport, LaNoue
see: Montesi, Robert, 6)

Dickey, Bruce
see: Canihac, Jean-Pierre
see: Dickey, Bruce

Eichhorn, Holger
see: Eichhorn, Holger
see: Potpourri, 47)
see: Tarr, Edward, 1), 31), 32)

Hagge, Detlef
see: Hagge, Detlef

Immer, Friedemann
see: Immer, Friedemann, 11), 18)

Impett, Jonathan
see: Impett, Jonathan

Laird, Michael
see: Laird, Michael, 1), 2), 3), 9), 12), 13), 14)
see: Potpourri, 67)
see: Smithers, Don, 3)

Lumsden, Alan
see: Laird, Michael, 1), 2), 12)

Montesi, Robert
  see: Montesi, Robert, 1), 2), 3),
      4), 5), 6)

Neugebauer, Willi
  see: Tarr, Edward, 19)

Neunhoeffer, Frieder
  see: Neunhoeffer, Frieder

Otten, Kees
  see: Otten, Kees

Otto, Joachim
  see: Otto, Joachim

Owen, Peter
  see: Smithers, Don, 2)

Pok, František
  see: Pok, František, 1), 2), 3),
      4), 5), 6)

Renz, Albrecht
  see: Renz, Albrecht, 1), 2), 3),
      4), 5), 6), 7)
  see: Steinkopf, Otto
  see: Tarr, Edward, 10), 45)

Schmid, Bernhard
  see: Potpourri, 26)
  see: Schmid, Bernhard, 5), 6),
      7)

Schmidt, Kurt
  see: Tarr, Edward, 19)

Smithers, Don
  see: Montesi, Robert, 3), 4)
  see: Potpourri, 49), 50), 64),
      67)
  see: Smithers, Don, 1), 2), 3),
      6), 7), 12)

Steele-Perkins, Crispian
  see: Steele-Perkins, Crispian,
      15)

Steinkopf, Otto
  see: Steinkopf, Otto

Stradner, Gerhard
  see: Idinger, Matthias
  see: Stradner, Gerhard
  see: Tarr, Edward, 45)

Tarr, Edward
  see: Potpourri, 2), 47)
  see: Tarr, Edward, 1), 4), 7),
      10), 18), 19), 20), 29), 31),
      32), 45)

Thibaud, Pierre
  see: Thibaud, Pierre, 14)

Voisin, Roger
  see: Voisin, Roger, 13)

Westermann, Hans Peter
  see: Immer, Friedemann, 11)

Whiting, Graham
  see: Laird, Michael, 2)

Wilson, Ian
  see: Laird, Michael, 1), 2), 9),
      14)

Countertenor

Boggis, Peter
  see: Jackson, Harold

Bohn, William
  see: Montesi, Robert, 1), 2)

Bowman, James
  see: Hagge, Detlef
  see: Laird, Michael, 2), 3), 9),
      11), 12), 13), 17), 18), 19)
  see: Neunhoeffer, Frieder
  see: Steele-Perkins, Crispian,
      6), 8)

Breitschopf, Hans
  see: Pok, František, 4)

Brett, Charles
  see: Laird, Michael, 11), 12)
  see: Steele-Perkins, Crispian,
      6), 16), 18)

Burgess, Grayston
  see: Unidentified, Trumpet(s),
      1)

Chance, Michael
  see: Steele-Perkins, Crispian,
      16)

Clarkson, Julian
  see: Steele-Perkins, Crispian,
    16)

Deller, Alfred
  see: Eskdale, George, 5)
  see: Jones, Philip, 7)
  see: Pok, František, 1), 3)
  see: Renz, Albrecht, 1)
  see: Rudolf, Richard

Deller, Mark
  see: Rudolf, Richard

Devos, Louis
  see: André, Maurice, 132)

Dooley, Jeffrey
  see: Holmgren, Fred

Esswood, Paul
  see: Eichhorn, Holger
  see: Hagge, Detlef
  see: Jones, Philip, 1)
  see: Laird, Michael, 9)
  see: Wilbraham, John, 20), 23)

Farber, Jesse
  see: Montesi, Robert, 2)

Ferrante, John
  see: Montesi, Robert, 5)
  see: Platt, Seymour

Gall, Jeffrey
  see: Dean, Allan, 10)

Giles, Andrew
  see: Laird, Michael, 11)

Girod, Vincent
  see: Tarr, Edward, 32)

Gordon, Brian
  see: Steele-Perkins, Crispian,
    16)

James, David
  see: Laird, Michael, 11)
  see: Steele-Perkins, Crispian,
    12)

Jordan, Paul
  see: Montesi, Robert, 1)

Lesueur, Jean-Jacques
  see: André, Maurice, 186)

Mallabrera, André
  see: André, Maurice, 97)

McLain, Jerry
  see: Montesi, Robert, 2)

Meurant, André
  see: Jeannoutot, Bernard

Minter, Drew
  see: Holmgren, Fred

Murphy, Earnest
  see: Davenport, LaNoue
  see: Montesi, Robert, 5)

Oberlin, Russell
  see: Montesi, Robert, 1)
  see: Vacchiano, William, 7)

Orgis, Emil
  see: Stradner, Gerhard

Rice, Daniel
  see: Montesi, Robert, 1), 2)

Sage, J.
  see: Thibaud, Pierre, 14)

Salmon, Peter
  see: Eskdale, George, 5)

Skinner, John York
  see: Laird, Michael, 11)

Smith, Kevin
  see: Hagge, Detlef
  see: Laird, Michael, 9)

Smith, Peter
  see: Montesi, Robert, 1), 2)

Stafford, Ashley
  see: Steele-Perkins, Crispian,
    16)

Sutcliffe, Tom
  see: Neunhoeffer, Frieder

Swansborough, Wilfred
  see: Steele-Perkins, Crispian,
    16)

Tatnell, Roland
see: Wilbraham, John, 20), 23)

Terbeek, Dale
see: Geyer, Charles

Vandersteene, Zeger
see: Pok, František, 4)

White, Robert
see: Montesi, Robert, 1), 2)

Whitworth, John
see: Jackson, Harold

Williams, John
see: Gabel, Bernard, 4)

Zaepffel, Alain
see: Güttler, Ludwig, 13)

Courtaut

Berger, Sven
see: Otten, Kees

Munrow, David
see: Laird, Michael, 1)

van der Beek, Andrew
see: Laird, Michael, 1)

Cow horn

Berger, Sven
see: Otten, Kees

Jakobsson, Pelle
see: Potpourri, 3)

Lumsden, Alan
see: Laird, Michael, 1)

Crumhorn (Cromorne / Krummhorn)
[includes all ranges]

Bixler, Martha
see: Montesi, Robert, 4), 6)

Brookes, Oliver
see: Laird, Michael, 1), 2), 3), 13)
see: Smithers, Don, 3)

Davenport, LaNoue
see: Davenport, LaNoue
see: Montesi, Robert, 4), 5), 6)

Eckert, Franz
see: Eichhorn, Holger
see: Idinger, Matthias

Fendt, Leopold
see: Neunhoeffer, Frieder
see: Renz, Albrecht, 6), 7)

Fest, Fritjof
see: Tarr, Edward, 10), 18), 28)

Fiedler, Eric
see: Cook, Richard

Fries, Vimala
see: Otto, Joachim

Göldner, Nicolo-Heinrich
see: Renz, Albrecht, 1)
see: Tarr, Edward, 10), 18)

Gruskin, Shelley
see: Davenport, LaNoue
see: Montesi, Robert, 3), 4), 5), 6)

Gulland, Brian
see: Potpourri, 67)

Hartl, Wolfgang
see: Idinger, Matthias

Harvey, Richard
see: Potpourri, 67)

Höller, Günther
see: Caudle, Theresa

Jurkovič, Pavel
see: Pok, František, 6)

Kastner, Gerhard
see: Tarr, Edward, 10), 18), 28)

Klebel, Bernhard
see: Idinger, Matthias

Matoušek, Lukás
see: Pok, František, 6)

Maurer, Paul
see: Idinger, Matthias

Meilink, Leo
see: Otten, Kees

Miedema, Barbara
see: Otten, Kees

Miller, Tess
see: Smithers, Don, 2)

Morrow, Michael
see: Smithers, Don, 2)

Munrow, David
see: Laird, Michael, 1), 2), 3), 13)
see: Smithers, Don, 2), 3)

Nitz, Martin
see: Hagge, Detlef

Nováková, Jana
see: Pok, František, 6)

Otten, Kees
see: Otten, Kees

Oxenham, Michael
see: Smithers, Don, 2)

Picket, Philip
see: Smithers, Don, 3)

Pugsley, David
see: Laird, Michael, 2)

Reich, Kurt
see: Smithers, Don, 12)

Sallay, Imre
see: Stradner, Gerhard

Sanvoisin, Michel
see: Thibaud, Pierre, 14)

Simon, Christine
see: Hagge, Detlef

Smithers, Don
see: Smithers, Don, 2)

Sonneck, Gerald
see: Stradner, Gerhard

Steinkopf, Otto
see: Tarr, Edward, 10), 18), 28)

Teichert, Almut
see: Hagge, Detlef

Tenta, Franz
see: Eichhorn, Holger

Tenta, Hilde
see: Eichhorn, Holger

Thomas, Bernard
see: Potpourri, 67)
see: Smithers, Don, 2)

Turner, John
see: Laird, Michael, 2), 13)

Tyler, James
see: Laird, Michael, 1), 2), 3), 13)
see: Smithers, Don, 3)

van Altena, Marius
see: Otten, Kees

van der Beek, Andrew
see: Laird, Michael, 1), 2), 13)

Veilhan, J.-C.
see: Thibaud, Pierre, 14)

von Huene, Friedrich
see: Cook, Richard

Wollitz, Kenneth
see: Montesi, Robert, 6)

Curtal (Dulcian)
[includes various ranges]

Brombey, Elke
see: Hagge, Detlef

Fleischmann, Otto
see: Potpourri, 49), 50), 64)
see: Spindler, Josef, 7)
see: Stradner, Gerhard
see: Tarr, Edward, 45)

Göldner, Nicolo-Heinrich
see: Tarr, Edward, 10)

Hartl, Wolfgang
see: Idinger, Matthias
see: Stradner, Gerhard

Hildebrand, Renate
see: Hagge, Detlef

Junghänel, Bernhard
see: Eichhorn, Holger

Khosro, Soltan
see: Stradner, Gerhard

Kroissenbrunner, Hans
see: Stradner, Gerhard

Munrow, David
see: Laird, Michael, 1), 3), 13)
see: Smithers, Don, 2), 3)

Roth, Kenneth
see: Cook, Richard

Steinkopf, Otto
see: Tarr, Edward, 10), 20)

Stiftner, Walter
see: Caudle, Theresa
see: Eichhorn, Holger

van der Beek, Andrew
see: Laird, Michael, 1), 2), 13)

von Busch, Hans
see: Hagge, Detlef

Wagner, Käthe
see: Hagge, Detlef

Wollitz, Kenneth
see: Montesi, Robert, 6)

Didjeridu

Staley, James
see: Sasaki, Ray

Double pipes
(Bolivian folk instrument)

Munrow, David
see: Laird, Michael, 1)

Double-reed slide music stand

Lickman, Stephen
see: Platt, Seymour

Electronium

Bojé, Harald
see: Miller, John
see: Stockhausen, Markus, 4)

English horn
[cross-referenced under oboe]

Barnett, James John
see: Ellinghaus, Wolfram

Beiman, Melvin
see: Schwarz, Gerard, 13)

Casier, Pierre
see: André, Maurice, 6)

Casier, Robert
see: André, Maurice, 6)

Chambon, Jacques
see: Gleissle, Walter, 3)
see: Lagorce, Marcel

Checker, Maurice
see: Webb, Gordon, 2)

Christ, Peter
see: Stevens, Thomas, 11)

de Nattes, Michel
see: André, Maurice, 120)

Dittrich, Erich
see: Spindler, Josef, 2)

Elliot, Gladys
see: Miller, Rodney
see: Perry, Brian

Fink, Marc
see: Potpourri, 38)

Goltzer, Albert
see: Glantz, Harry, 1)

Goy, Jean-Paul
see: Touvron, Guy, 10)

Gruber, Karl
see: Rudolf, Richard

Haas, George
see: Anderson, Ronald, 3)
see: Dean, Allan, 6)
see: Nagel, Robert, 20)

Häberling, Markus
see: Touvron, Guy, 10)

Hadady, Laszlo
see: Vasse, Claude

Hausmann, Kurt
see: Lachenmeir, Paul

Hertel, Alfred
see: Libiseller, Hansjörg

Jaeger, Don Th.
see: Rapier, Leon, 1)

Kirkpatrick, Vernon
see: Geisler, Lloyd

Korman, Fred
see: Murtha, Roger

Krall, Ernst
see: Libiseller, Hansjörg
see: Spindler, Josef, 2), 3)

Krylov, Leonid
see: Margolin, Veniamin

Miller, Robin
see: Miller, John

Nicklin, Celia
see: Laird, Michael, 4)

Pateau, Didier
see: Cure, Antoine

Pierlot, Pierre
see: Gleissle, Walter, 3)
see: Lagorce, Marcel
see: Thibaud, Pierre, 9)

Post, Gary
see: Sullivan, William

Richards, Ronald
see: Kuehn, David

Rosso, Pierre
see: Adelbrecht, Henri, 3)

Rullman, Charles
see: Potpourri, 5)

Schmalfuss, Gernot
see: Potpourri, 2)

Schwinn, Andreas
see: Lachenmeir, Paul
see: Potpourri, 11)

Stacy, Thomas
see: Smith, Philip, 1)

Swingley, Richard
see: Mear, Sidney, 1), 3)

Taylor, Stephen
see: Anderson, Ronald, 6)

Thorstenberg, Laurence
see: Ghitalla, Armando, 7)

Timm, Joel
see: Carroll, Edward, 4)

Tustin, Whitney
see: Burke, James, 5), 6)

Weber, Hanspeter
see: André, Maurice, 138)

Wenzel, Wilhelm
see: Potpourri, 19)

West, Philip
see: Nagel, Robert, 19)

Winfield, Michael
see: Lang, William

Fiddle
[includes various types and sizes]

Brix-Meinert, Ilse
see: Renz, Albrecht, 2), 3)

Collette, Joannes
see: Otten, Kees

Dittrich, Michael
see: Pok, František, 2), 4)

Harnoncourt, Nikolaus
see: Tarr, Edward, 45)

Höbarth, Hermann
see: Tarr, Edward, 45)

Macrow, Mary
see: Otten, Kees

Maier, Franz-Josef
see: Renz, Albrecht, 2), 3)

Obermayer, Ernst
see: Neunhoeffer, Frieder
see: Renz, Albrecht, 6), 7)

Olsson, Hjort Anders
see: Potpourri, 3)

Pols, Anneke
see: Otten, Kees

Rantos, Spiros
see: Pok, František, 4)

Ruhland, Elisabeth
see: Neunhoeffer, Frieder
see: Renz, Albrecht, 6)

Schnitzler, Heide
see: Stradner, Gerhard

Sloan, Eleanor
see: Laird, Michael, 1)

Stradner, Gerhard
see: Stradner, Gerhard

Thurmair, Veronika
see: Neunhoeffer, Frieder
see: Renz, Albrecht, 6)

Zosso, René
see: Pok, František, 4)

Fife

Berger, Sven
see: Otten, Kees

Hart, David
see: Dudgeon, Ralph

Flügelhorn
[cross-referenced under trumpet]

Anderson, Ronald
see: Anderson, Ronald, 6)

André, Maurice
see: André, Maurice, 4), 8),
   61), 88), 120), 212)

Birch, Robert
see: Birch, Robert

Braz, Dirceu
see: Braz, Dirceu, 1), 2)

Bush, Irving
see: Bush, Irving

Cantie, Jean
see: André, Maurice, 120)

Delmas, Serge
see: André, Maurice, 120)

Driscoll, Phil
see: Driscoll, Phil

Halldén, Leif
see: Potpourri, 3)

Hausamann, Ernst
see: McCann, Phillip

Lecluse, Michel
see: André, Maurice, 120)

Lieberman, Harold J.
see: Lieberman, Harold J.

Nystrom, Kaj
see: Nystrom, Kaj

Romm, Ronald
see: Canadian Brass, 3)

Schultz, Erik
see: Schultz, Erik, 8)

Schwarz, Gerard
see: Schwarz, Gerard, 10)

Steele-Perkins, Crispian
see: Steele-Perkins, Crispian,
15)

Stevens, Thomas
see: Stevens, Thomas, 2), 3), 5)

Stone, Fred
see: Stone, Fred

Thomas, Peggy Paton
see: Thomas, Peggy Paton

Tolley, Richard
see: Tolley, Richard

Flute
[includes various sizes & ranges]

Aarons, Martha
see: Plog, Anthony, 7)

Achilles, Michael
see: Schmidt, Ingus

Adeney, Richard
see: Clift, Dennis
see: Jackson, Harold
see: Jones, Philip, 2), 8), 11)
see: Mason, David, 4), 5)
see: Potpourri, 9)
see: Webb, Gordon, 7)
see: Wilbraham, John, 27)

Adorjan, Andras
see: André, Maurice, 130)

Aitken, Robert
see: Berinbaum, Martin
see: Chenette, Stephen
see: Umbrico, Joseph

Akroyd, Arthur
see: Scherbaum, Adolf, 3)

Anderson, Lynn
see: Birch, Robert

Asin, Nadine
see: Potpourri, 38)

Auge, Gérard
see: André, Maurice, 120)

Baker, Frederick
see: Logan, Jack

Baker, Julius
see: Friestadt, Harry
see: Glantz, Harry, 4)
see: Nagel, Robert, 1), 5), 14)
see: Vacchiano, William, 2)
see: Wobisch, Helmut, 14)

Ballot, Jacques
see: André, Maurice, 160)

Baron, Samuel
see: Broiles, Melvin
see: Ghitalla, Armando, 10)
see: Weis, Theodore, 1)

Barwahser, Hubert
see: Groot, Willem (Wim)

Barwell, Nina
see: Hoffman, Edward

Beauregard, Lawrence
see: Vasse, Claude

Beda, Dmitri
see: Margolin, Veniamin

Behrmann, K.
see: Zickler, Heinz, 5)

Bell, Sebastian
see: Miller, John
see: Snell, Howard
see: Watson, James

Bennett, Harold
see: Butterfield, Billy
see: Voisin, Roger, 6), 8)

Bennett, William
see: Jones, Philip, 3)
see: Laird, Michael, 21), 22)
see: Potpourri, 4)
see: Soustrot, Bernard, 5)
see: Steele-Perkins, Crispian,
14)
see: Wilbraham, John, 1), 11),
18)

Bentzon, Johann
see: Hovaldt, Knud

Beznosiuk, Lisa
see: Laird, Michael, 8)
see: Steele-Perkins, Crispian,
16)

Biamonte, Louis
see: Butterfield, Billy

Birkelund, Poul
see: Hovaldt, Knud

Blau, Andreas
see: Groth, Konradin

Bobzien, Karl
see: Bauer, Willibald, 4)

Böckheler, Wiltrud
see: Schmid, Bernhard, 10), 11)

Bopp, Joseph
see: Haneuse, Arthur
see: Tarr, Edward, 11)
see: Zeyer, Adam

Bourdin, Roger
see: André, Maurice, 180), 199)
see: Delmotte, Roger, 16), 29),
32)

Boyer, Paul
see: Greenho, David

Braun, Gerhard
see: André, Maurice, 138)
see: Tarr, Edward, 17)

Breiden
see: Spörri, Paul

Briggs, Anne
see: Holmgren, Fred

Brook, Paige
see: Ghitalla, Armando, 10)

Brown, Elizabeth
see: Carroll, Edward, 3), 5)
see: Gould, Mark

Bruderhans, Zdenek
see: André, Maurice, 196)

Brüggen, Frans
see: Bryant, Ralph, 5)
see: Potpourri, 51), 59), 60),
61)
see: Rippas, Claude
see: Smithers, Don, 13)
see: Spindler, Josef, 11), 15)

Büchel, Willi
see: Tarr, Edward, 27)

Bye, Torkil
see: Christiansen, Jan

Calle, Régis
see: André, Maurice, 120)

Carucci, James
see: Schwarz, Gerard, 13)

Castagner, Jacques
see: André, Maurice, 172)
see: Delmotte, Roger, 2)
see: Jones, Philip, 11)

Čech, František
see: André, Maurice, 220)
see: Horák, Jiří, 3), 4), 5)

Chambers, Colin
see: Webb, Gordon, 1), 2)

Cherrier, Sophie
see: Cure, Antoine

Chugg, Richard
see: Roberts, Standish

Cleghorn, Arthur
see: Eskdale, George, 4)

Clemenčić, René
see: Pok, František, 4)

Clement, Marianne
  see: Touvron, Guy, 10)

Cohen, Raymond
  see: Wilbraham, John, 28)

Conwesser, Laura
  see: Dean, Allan, 3)

Cortet, R.
  see: Mule, Marcel

Cotton, Rémy
  see: Thibaud, Pierre, 9)

Crocker, Conrad
  see: Hopkins, Kenneth

Dailey, Jan
  see: Henderson, Douglas

Dalley, Nancy
  see: Nagel, Robert, 2)

Davies, Paul Edmund
  see: Steele-Perkins, Crispian, 14)

Debost, Michel
  see: André, Maurice, 49), 180)
  see: Calvayrac, Albert
  see: Delmotte, Roger, 30)
  see: Ménardi, Louis
  see: Wilbraham, John, 21)

Diederich, Claus
  see: Zickler, Heinz, 2)

Dilloo, Kraft Thorwald
  see: André, Maurice, 171)
  see: Gleissle, Walter, 1)

Di Tullio, Louise
  see: Plog, Anthony, 1), 3)

Dohn, Robert
  see: André, Maurice, 16)
  see: Goethel, Siegfried

Duckles, Larry
  see: Metzger, Charles

Dufrêne, Fernand
  see: Delmotte, Roger, 4)

Dunigan, Philip
  see: Broiles, Melvin
  see: Weis, Theodore, 1)

Dunkel, Paul
  see: Dean, Allan, 1), 2), 4), 5), 6), 7), 8)
  see: Haneuse, Arthur
  see: Potpourri, 5)
  see: Ranger, Louis
  see: Wise, Wilmer

Dwyer, Doriot Anthony
  see: Ghitalla, Armando, 7)
  see: Voisin, Roger, 11)

Dzionora, Michael
  see: André, Maurice, 171)

Eichar, Ralph
  see: Vacchiano, William, 2)

Endsley, Pamela
  see: Hickman, David, 2)

Estrin, Harvey
  see: Crisara, Raymond, 2)

Eustache, Jean-Pierre
  see: André, Maurice, 122), 188)
  see: Schneidewind, Helmut, 10)

Fiore, Nicholas
  see: Chevanelle, Serge
  see: LeComte, Jacques

Fischer, C.
  see: Flugel, J.

Fonville, John
  see: Sasaki, Ray

Francis, John
  see: Mason, David, 3)

Fried, Paul
  see: Metzger, Charles

Fuge, Francis
  see: Rapier, Leon, 4)

Fulton, Jack
  see: Butterfield, Billy

Fulton, John
  see: Burke, James, 8)

Futschik, Johann
  see: Spindler, Josef, 3)

Gaertner, W.
  see: Haas, Rudolf

Galway, James
  see: Krug, Willi, 1)
  see: Stevens, Thomas, 3)

Garside, Patricia
  see: Plog, Anthony, 11)

Gazzelloni, Severino
  see: Adelbrecht, Henri, 4), 7)
  see: André, Maurice, 194), 201)
  see: Touvron, Guy, 14)

Gérard, Jean-Claude
  see: Thibaud, Pierre, 9)

Gilbert, David
  see: Anderson, Ronald, 3)
  see: Potpourri, 5)

Gilbert, Geoffrey
  see: Gay, Bram

Giles, Anne Diener
  see: Parker, Craig B.
  see: Romm, Ronald
  see: Stevens, Thomas, 2), 5),
    12)

Glas, Willy
  see: Scherbaum, Adolf, 5)

Gleghorn, Arthur
  see: Heinrich, Robert
  see: Nagel, Robert, 4)

Goldbeck, Gudrun
  see: Brass-zination

Goldberg, B.
  see: Mule, Marcel

Golishiev, Alexandre
  see: Dokshitser, Timofei, 12)

Goody, P.
  see: Gay, Bram

Goudey, Jacqueline
  see: Schwarz, Gerard, 13)

Graef, Richard
  see: Vosburgh, George

Graf, Anna-Katharina
  see: Sommerhalder, Max

Graf, Erich Louis
  see: Anderson, Ronald, 1)

Graf, Peter-Lukas
  see: Sauter, Hermann, 7), 8),
    9), 10), 13), 14), 15), 16)
  see: Schmid, Bernhard, 4), 5),
    6), 9)
  see: Unidentified, Trumpet(s),
    5)
  see: Wolf, Hans, 9)

Graitzer, Murray
  see: Crisara, Raymond, 9)

Green, Harlan
  see: Lowrey, Alvin

Greenberg, Susan
  see: Schwarz, Gerard, 1)

Greiss, Renate
  see: Läubin, Hannes, 3)

Gross, Michel
  see: André, Maurice, 120)

Gruskin, Shelley
  see: Berinbaum, Martin
  see: Davenport, LaNoue
  see: Montesi, Robert, 3), 4), 5),
    6)

Guiot, Raymond
  see: André, Maurice, 13), 178)
  see: Potpourri, 36), 37)

Gulbransen, Ornulf
  see: Nagel, Robert, 2)
  see: Nowak, Henry

Haag, Wolfgang
  see: Potpourri, 11)

Haldemann, Hugo
  see: Haneuse, Arthur

Hambelton, Patrice
  see: Burkhart, David

Hampe, Konrad
see: Wolf, Hans, 1)
see: Zickler, Heinz, 1), 2), 3)

Harnoncourt, Elisabeth
see: Bryant, Ralph, 4)

Harras, Manfred
see: Wolf, Hans, 11)

Hart, David
see: Dudgeon, Ralph

Harvey, Richard
see: Potpourri, 67)

Harzer, A.
see: Spörri, Paul

Hechtl, Gottfried
see: Potpourri, 51), 53), 60)
see: Rudolf, Richard
see: Spindler, Josef, 10), 13)

Heck, Josef
see: Holy, Walter, 2)

Hecl, Jan
see: Junek, Václav, 3), 5)
see: Kejmar, Miroslav, 13)

Heim, F. William
see: Vacchiano, William, 4)

Heiss, John
see: Dean, Allan, 2)
see: Potpourri, 5)

Hellmann, Christiane
see: Kierski, Eckhard

Hériché, Robert
see: Delmotte, Roger, 3)
see: Vaillant, Ludovic, 7)

Herlinger, Jan
see: Miller, Rodney

Hester, Byron
see: Austin, James

Hill, Rodney
see: Eggers, Carter

Hlavsa, Lutobor
see: Horák, Jiří, 3), 5)

Hoffman (Gofman), Albert
see: Fomin, Evgeny
see: Maximenko, Anatoly, 2)

Holler, Günter
see: Tarr, Edward, 21)

Höller, Günther
see: Basch, Wolfgang, 1)
see: Potpourri, 22)
see: Schneidewind, Helmut, 2)
see: Tarr, Edward, 11), 18), 28)

Honner, Derek
see: Webb, Gordon, 2)

Howard, Alexander
see: Burke, James, 5)

Howell, Thomas
see: Ferrantino, Kenneth

Hünteler, Konrad
see: Immer, Friedemann, 12)

Ikeda, Utako
see: Steele-Perkins, Crispian, 16)

Indermühle, Heidi
see: Sauter, Hermann, 8)

Islas, Rubén
see: León, Felipe

Jaunet, André
see: Scherbaum, Adolf, 1)

Jenne, Peter
see: André, Maurice, 25)

Jorns, Rotraud
see: Schmid, Bernhard, 12)

Josífko, Jaroslav
see: Mičaník, Jaroslav

Jurriaanse, Govert
see: Floore, John

Kägi, V.
see: Zeyer, Adam

Kane, Trudy
see: Crisara, Raymond, 1)

Kanji, Ricardo
see: Immer, Friedemann, 14)

Kaplan, Phillip
see: Voisin, Roger, 1)

Kelber, Sebastian
see: Otto, Joachim
see: Tarr, Edward, 12), 17)

Keller-Sanwald, Sibylle
see: Friedrich, Reinhold
see: McGregor, Rob Roy, 6)
see: Sauter, Hermann, 14)
see: Schmid, Bernhard, 10), 11)
see: Wolf, Hans, 5)

Kincaid, William
see: Johnson, Gilbert, 1)
see: Krauss, Sam

King, April
see: Metzger, Charles

Kirschner, Fritz
see: Bauer, Willibald, 3)

Knight, Norman
see: Mason, David, 4)

Koch, Johannes
see: Renz, Albrecht, 2)

Koch-Hoffer, Marianne
see: Schmid, Bernhard, 12)

Korneyev, Alexander
see: Popov, Sergei, 3), 5)

Kout, Trix
see: Hoffman, Edward
see: Potpourri, 5)

Kovács, Lóránt
see: Csiba, József

Kozlov, Alexandre
see: Popov, Sergei, 2)

Kraber, Karl
see: Anderson, Ronald, 4)
see: Dean, Allan, 1)

Krell, John
see: Blee, Eugene

Kripl, Jack
see: Soloff, Lew
see: Wise, Wilmer

Krueger, Christopher
see: Holmgren, Fred

Kuijken, Barthold
see: Bodenröder, Robert
see: Potpourri, 22), 57)

Kulikov, Fedor
see: Gorokhov, Vitaly

Kuzmin, Oleg
see: Yudashkin, Georgy

Lagerquist, John
see: Ghitalla, Armando, 1)

Lane, Timothy
see: Dolce, Christine

Lardé, Christian
see: André, Maurice, 89)
see: Couëffé, Yves
see: Pollin, Pierre
see: Scherbaum, Adolf, 4)

Larrieu, Maxence
see: André, Maurice, 13), 57),
102), 124), 151), 201), 226),
227)
see: Gleissle, Walter, 4), 5), 6)
see: Unidentified, Trumpet(s),
13)
see: Vaillant, Ludovic, 1)

Laurent, Georges
see: Mager, Georges
see: Voisin, Roger, 9)

Lavaillotte, Lucien
see: Delmotte, Roger, 3)

Laws, Hubert
see: Carroll, Edward, 2)

Le Roy, Rene
see: Ghitalla, Armando, 10)

Levy, Gerardo
see: Anderson, Ronald, 4)

Lewis, Robert
see: Platt, Seymour

Linde, Hans-Martin
see: André, Maurice, 21), 25), 30)
see: Immer, Friedemann, 3)
see: Renz, Albrecht, 3)
see: Scherbaum, Adolf, 14), 24)
see: Tarr, Edward, 11), 12), 37)

Löckle, Michael
see: Scholz, Walter

Lolya, Andrew
see: Burke, James, 5), 6)
see: Dean, Allan, 5)
see: Schwarz, Gerard, 13)

Lumsden, Alan
see: Laird, Michael, 1)

Lynden, Patricia
see: Laird, Michael, 15)

Magnin, Alexandre
see: Millière, Gérard

Mahler, Carla
see: Spindler, Josef, 15)

Mann, Wallace
see: Geisler, Lloyd

Mansfield, Gwyndolyne
see: Mase, Raymond

Marek, V.
see: Mičaník, Jaroslav

Mariano, Joseph
see: Mear, Sidney, 1), 2), 4)

Marion, Alain
see: André, Maurice, 110), 152)
see: Couëffé, Yves
see: Delmotte, Roger, 30)
see: Touvron, Guy, 13)

McGegan, Nicholas
see: Laird, Michael, 5)

McKibben, Maureen
see: Hoffman, Edward

Meisen, Paul
see: André, Maurice, 17), 93)
see: Basch, Wolfgang, 8), 10)
see: Scherbaum, Adolf, 35)

Mess, Karl Friedrich
see: Scherbaum, Adolf, 5), 30)

Meylan, Raymond
see: Adelbrecht, Henri, 2)

Middleton, Peter
see: Logan, Jack

Milzkott, Erwin
see: Potpourri, 19)

Mochida, Hiroshi
see: Sauter, Hermann, 26)

Möhring, Hans Jürgen
see: Schneidewind, Helmut, 1), 2), 7), 12)

Monteux, Claude
see: Crisara, Raymond, 3)
see: Glantz, Harry, 4)
see: Tuckwell, Barry
see: Wilbraham, John, 19)

Morgan, Carole
see: Potpourri, 38)

Moritz, Roland
see: Stevens, Thomas, 12)

Morris, Gareth
see: Jackson, Harold
see: Mason, David, 2)
see: Scherbaum, Adolf, 3)

Morris, Robert
see: Crisara, Raymond, 9)
see: Vacchiano, William, 4)

Moulton, Marie
see: Miller, Rodney
see: Perry, Brian

Moÿse, Louis
see: Eskdale, George, 2)

Moÿse, Marcel
see: Eskdale, George, 2)

Munclinger, Milan
see: André, Maurice, 220)

Munrow, David
see: Laird, Michael, 1), 3)

Nanzetta, Virginia
see: Levy, Robert

Nicolet, Aurèle
see: André, Maurice, 179)
see: Eichler, Horst
see: Frei, Marcel
see: Scherbaum, Adolf, 6)
see: Thibaud, Pierre, 8)
see: Touvron, Guy, 4), 6)

Noack, Valery
see: Schneidewind, Helmut, 4)
see: Tarr, Edward, 18), 19),
21), 28)

Nyfenger, Thomas
see: Nagel, Robert, 18), 19),
20)
see: Schwarz, Gerard, 6)

Øien, Per
see: Christiansen, Jan
see: Kvebaek, Harry

Oostdam, Leo
see: Groot, Willem (Wim)

Otto, Gerhard
see: Scherbaum, Adolf, 33)

Paar, Hans
see: Tarr, Edward, 27)

Palma, Susan
see: Burns, Stephen
see: Dean, Allan, 3)
see: Ranger, Louis

Panitz, Murray
see: Burke, James, 5), 6)

Pappoutsakis, James
see: Voisin, Roger, 11)

Parloff, Michael
see: Carroll, Edward, 1)

Parshley, Thomas
see: Karpilovsky, Murray

Paschek, Joseph
see: Scholz, Walter

Passin, Karl-Heinz
see: Güttler, Ludwig, 8), 11),
12), 13), 14), 21)

Pasveer, Kathinka
see: Stockhausen, Markus, 1)

Pearce, Judith
see: Evans, Laurie

Peck, Donald
see: Herseth, Adolph, 3), 6)

Pecover, Joan
see: Lowrey, Alvin

Pellerite, James
see: Davidson, Louis
see: Nagel, Robert, 4)

Pépin, André
see: Longinotti, Paolo

Perepelkin, Lev
see: Margolin, Veniamin

Perz, Gerhard
see: Spindler, Josef, 2)

Peschke, Werner
see: Schmid, Bernhard, 13)

Pierlot, Philippe
see: André, Maurice, 167)
see: Pollin, Pierre

Plockyn, Michel
see: Delmotte, Roger, 42), 43)
see: Jeannoutot, Bernard

Pohl, Günther
see: McGregor, Rob Roy, 6)

Pohlers, Klaus
see: Zickler, Heinz, 8)

Preston, Stephen
 see: Immer, Friedemann, 1), 4)
 see: Laird, Michael, 5)

Pugsley, David
 see: Laird, Michael, 2)

Purswell, Patrick
 see: Bastin, Ernie

Rampal, Jean-Pierre
 see: André, Maurice, 82), 95),
  108), 110), 116), 124), 140),
  152), 167), 173), 184), 191),
  211)
 see: Bernard, André, 12)
 see: Delmotte, Roger, 1), 20)
 see: Potpourri, 45), 47)
 see: Scherbaum, Adolf, 31)
 see: Schneidewind, Helmut, 5)
 see: Spindler, Josef, 6)
 see: Thibaud, Pierre, 1)
 see: Vaillant, Ludovic, 2), 4),
  7)

Redel, Kurt
 see: André, Maurice, 93), 183),
  204)
 see: Bauer, Willibald, 3)
 see: Jeannoutot, Bernard
 see: Scherbaum, Adolf, 27), 28)
 see: Zeyer, Adam

Renzi, Paul
 see: Potpourri, 31)

Reskin, David
 see: Hoffman, Edward

Reznicek, Hans
 see: Wobisch, Helmut, 1), 2),
  12)

Richter, Werner
 see: Bernard, André, 2)
 see: Preis, Ivo

Riessberger, Helmut
 see: Spindler, Josef, 2), 3), 4)

Ring, Christine
 see: Potpourri, 67)

Rosenfeld, Jayn
 see: Burns, Stephen

Roth, Nancy Joyce
 see: Hoffman, Edward

Roy, Alphonse
 see: Longinotti, Paolo

Rumpel, Günter
 see: Adelbrecht, Henri, 1), 3)

Rütters, Matthias
 see: Scherbaum, Adolf, 12)

Sanvoisin, Michel
 see: Calvayrac, Albert
 see: Thibaud, Pierre, 14)

Sanwald, Sibylle
 see: André, Maurice, 123)

Sarge, Ann
 see: Hoffman, Edward

Sauveur, Cornelie
 see: Tarr, Edward, 44)

Schaefer, Lois
 see: Voisin, Roger, 1)

Schaeffer, Burghard
 see: Scherbaum, Adolf, 7), 35)

Scheck, Gustav
 see: Zeyer, Adam

Schecter, Margaret
 see: Nagel, Robert, 18)

Schlenker, Barbara
 see: Schmid, Bernhard, 10)

Schlenker, Peter
 see: Schmid, Bernhard, 11)

Schmidtmann, Friedrich
 see: Tarr, Edward, 19)

Schochow, K.
 see: Scherbaum, Adolf, 35)

Schoene, Arndt
 see: Haas, Rudolf

Schwegler, Wilhelm
 see: Holy, Walter, 2)
 see: Scherbaum, Adolf, 27)

Tassinari, Gastone
see: Adelbrecht, Henri, 4)

Taub, Paul
see: Pressley, Richard

Thalheimer, Peter
see: Sauter, Hermann, 9), 27)
see: Schmitt, Siegfried

Theurer, Walter
see: Scherbaum, Adolf, 9)

Thomas, Friedrich
see: Spörri, Paul

Townsend, Richard
see: Geisler, Lloyd

Tromp, Joost
see: André, Maurice, 221)
see: Groot, Willem (Wim)

Troob, Jolie
see: Hoffman, Edward

Turetzky, Nancy
see: Murtha, Roger

Turner, John
see: Laird, Michael, 1), 2)

Tyler, James
see: Laird, Michael, 1), 2), 3)

Urbain, Luc
see: Touvron, Guy, 11)

Válek, Jiří
see: Kejmar, Miroslav, 5), 8)

van Hauwe, Walter
see: Potpourri, 60)

Veilhan, J.-C.
see: Thibaud, Pierre, 14)

Veretchnikova, Anatoly
see: Dokshitser, Timofei, 16)

Vester, Frans
see: André, Maurice, 221), 225)
see: Groot, Willem (Wim)

Vogel, H.
see: Flugel, J.

Voisin, Jean-Claude
see: André, Maurice, 120)

von Huene, Friedrich
see: Cook, Richard

Walklate, Audrey
see: Roberts, Standish

Walter, Bernhard
see: Bauer, Willibald, 3), 4)

Wanausek, Camillo
see: Holler, Adolf
see: Rudolf, Richard
see: Scherbaum, Adolf, 36)

Watson, Thaddeus
see: Hunger, Helmut, 4)

Wavre, Pierre
see: Touvron, Guy, 10)

Weinreb, Alice
see: Ghitalla, Armando, 1)

Weissberg, Herbert
see: Rudolf, Richard

Weitz, Gertrude
see: Zeh, Karl Heinz

Wendel, Martin
see: Sauter, Hermann, 14), 16)

Whaley, Anne
see: Potpourri, 38)

White, Nathaniel
see: Hood, Donald

Whittaker, Douglas
see: Webb, Gordon, 4)

Wichmann, Ernst
see: Holy, Walter, 10)

Wilkins, Frederick
see: Glantz, Harry, 6)

Williams, Guy
see: Steele-Perkins, Crispian, 16)

Willoughby, Robert
see: Young, Gene

Wilson, Ransom
see: Stubbs, James

Wincenz, Carol
see: Potpourri, 6)

Winkelmann, Wilfried
see: Gass, Josef

Wolf, Robert
see: Potpourri, 62)

Woll, Gernot
see: Potpourri, 11)

Wummer, John
see: Baker, Bernard
see: Broiles, Melvin
see: Mule, Marcel
see: Vacchiano, William, 4)

Yokoyama, Sadako
see: Hoffman, Edward

Zentner, Miles
see: Stevens, Thomas, 14)

Zöller, Karlheinz
see: Groth, Konradin
see: Potpourri, 16)
see: Scherbaum, Adolf, 12)
see: Tarr, Edward, 18)

Zuckerman, Sharon
see: Hoffman, Edward

Zverev, Valentin
see: Maximenko, Anatoly, 3)

Flute (Bolivian folk instrument)

Munrow, David
see: Laird, Michael, 1)

Flûte de berger

Clemenčić, René
see: Pok, František, 4)

Flûte de corne

Clemenčić, René
see: Pok, František, 4)

Gemshorn

Munrow, David
see: Laird, Michael, 1), 3)

Otten, Kees
see: Otten, Kees

Guitar
[includes various types: historic &
modern, acoustic & electric]

Almeida, Laurindo
see: Méndez, Rafael, 14)

Andreotti, Clemer
see: Braz, Dirceu, 2)

Atkins, Chet
see: Hirt, Al

Behrend, Siegfried
see: Scherbaum, Adolf, 24)

Berliner, Jay
see: Dean, Allan, 5)

Bertoncini, Eugene
see: Crisara, Raymond, 2)

Böttner, Karlheinz
see: Tarr, Edward, 14)

Boyd, Liona
see: Canadian Brass, 3)

Bruck, Wilhelm
see: Schoof, Manfred

Bushler, Herb
see: Crisara, Raymond, 2)

Clarke, Bruce
see: Victorian Trumpet Trio

Collins, Howie
see: Lieberman, Harold J.

Damian, John
see: Metzger, Charles

Diaz, Alirio
see: Wobisch, Helmut, 14)

Finckel, Chris
see: Miller, Rodney

Förster, Anton
see: Luithle, Rainer

Fox, Stuart
see: Stevens, Thomas, 16)

Ghirardi, Thérèse
see: Cure, Antoine

Grzeschik, Peter
see: Schmid, Bernhard, 13)

Gwiazda, Henry
see: Metzger, Charles

Hall, Jim
see: Murtha, Roger

Henderson, Forbes
see: Steele-Perkins, Crispian, 6)

Hollestelle, Hans
see: Grin, Freddy, 7)

Hollestelle, Jan
see: Grin, Freddy, 7)

Mann, Bob
see: Schultz, Erik, 8)

Mason, Patrick
see: Potpourri, 6)

Morell, John
see: Bush, Irving

North, Nigel
see: Laird, Michael, 2)

Piltch, Rob
see: Canadian Brass, 3)

Pirie, James
see: Schultz, Erik, 8)

Rave, Wallace
see: Bastin, Ernie

Remnant, Mary
see: Laird, Michael, 1)

Ritz, Lyle
see: Bush, Irving

Rogério, José
see: Braz, Dirceu, 2), 5)

Rooley, Anthony
see: Potpourri, 67)

Russell, Brian
see: Canadian Brass, 3)

Sanders, Jack
see: Plog, Anthony, 4)

Scheit, Karl
see: Eichhorn, Holger
see: Wobisch, Helmut, 5)

Schöllmann, Jürgen
see: Stockhausen, Markus, 2)

Silverman, Stanley
see: Anderson, Ronald, 5)
see: Nagel, Robert, 19)

Spencer, Robert
see: Laird, Michael, 1)

Starobin, David
see: Potpourri, 6)
see: Ranger, Louis

Szczesniak, Tom
see: Schultz, Erik, 8)

Tackett, Fred
see: Stevens, Thomas, 2)

Thomas, Bobby
see: Dallas Brass

Tyler, James
see: Laird, Michael, 1)

Vogt, Johannes
see: Braz, Dirceu, 2)

Williams, John
see: Potpourri, 4)
see: Wilbraham, John, 30)

Yepes, Narcisso
see: André, Maurice, 30)

Zaczek, Brigitte
see: Spindler, Josef, 5)

Hardart

Schickele, Peter
see: Platt, Seymour

Harmonica

Cipriani, Guy-Joel
see: André, Maurice, 49)

Harp
[includes various types: historic & modern]

Adams, Anne
see: Haug, Edward

Agostini, Gloria
see: Butterfield, Billy

Bernard, Joëlle
see: André, Maurice, 64), 84), 227)

Blankenship, Shirley
see: Potpourri, 66)

Cassedanne(-Hasse), Charlotte
see: Schmid, Bernhard, 13)
see: Schneidewind, Helmut, 2)

Cifani, Elizabeth
see: Miller, Rodney
see: Perry, Brian

Dobrinský, Bedřich
see: Mičaník, Jaroslav

Dulova, Vera
see: Dokshitser, Timofei, 12)

Ellis, Osian
see: Jones, Philip, 2), 11)

Fletcher, Elizabeth
see: Miller, John
see: Webb, Gordon, 2)

Goodman, Erica
see: Canadian Brass, 3)
see: Chenette, Stephen
see: Schultz, Erik, 8)

Goossens, Sidonie
see: Wilbraham, John, 30)

Hobson, Ann
see: Metzger, Charles

Hogwood, Christopher
see: Laird, Michael, 1), 3), 12), 13)

Holliger, Ursula
see: Potpourri, 47)
see: Tarr, Edward, 32)

Jamet, Marie-Claire
see: Cure, Antoine
see: Zickler, Heinz, 8)

Jelinek, Hubert
see: Eichhorn, Holger

Jolles, Susan
see: Dean, Allan, 3), 4), 6)
see: Nagel, Robert, 19)
see: Ranger, Louis

Kanga, Skaila
see: McCann, Phillip

Kauffungen, Eva
see: Adelbrecht, Henri, 1)
see: Sommerhalder, Max

Laban, U.
see: Tarr, Edward, 20)

Laskine, Lily
see: André, Maurice, 82), 112), 124)
see: Potpourri, 47)
see: Thibaud, Pierre, 14)

Lawrence, Lucille
see: Glantz, Harry, 6)

Loman, Judy
see: Umbrico, Joseph

Meyer, Sylvia
see: Geisler, Lloyd

Moskvitina, Emily
see: Paniotov, Kharlampi

Neill, Lou Anne
see: Guarneri, Mario

Okuniewski, Laura
see: Dolce, Christine

Owen, Thelma
see: Steele-Perkins, Crispian,
17)

Patras, Karel
see: Junek, Václav, 5)
see: Mičaník, Jaroslav

Pierre, Francis
see: Jones, Philip, 11)
see: Thibaud, Pierre, 1)

Reid, Gillian
see: Laird, Michael, 1)

Remsen, Dorothy
see: Heinrich, Robert
see: Nagel, Robert, 4)
see: Stevens, Thomas, 2), 5)

Ross, Margaret
see: Karpilovsky, Murray

Shameyeva, Nataly
see: Dokshitser, Timofei, 12)

Stavrache, Christine
see: Vacchiano, William, 4)

Sylvestre, Brigitte
see: Bauer, Adam

Tieu, Teresia
see: Floore, John

Vachalová, Libuše
see: Pok, František, 6)

Wilson, Brian
see: Potpourri, 67)

Wurtzler, Aristid
see: Vacchiano, William, 4)

Zabaleta, Nicanor
see: Scherbaum, Adolf, 26)

Zoff, Jutta
see: Krug, Willi, 2)

Harpsichord

Alain, Marie-Claire
see: Gleissle, Walter, 4)

Alain, Olivier
see: Potpourri, 15)
see: Scherbaum, Adolf, 18)

Anderson, R. Kinloch
see: Clift, Dennis

Andrae, Hans
see: Eichhorn, Holger

Angerer, Paul
see: Holler, Adolf

Attinger, Günter
see: Schneidewind, Helmut, 3)

Aveling, Valda
see: Webb, Gordon, 4)
see: Wilbraham, John, 23)

Bach, Gottfried
see: André, Maurice, 192), 194),
196)
see: Friedrich, Reinhold
see: Potpourri, 42), 44)
see: Schneidewind, Helmut, 2)

Bagger, Louis
see: Mase, Raymond

Beckensteiner, Anne-Marie
see: André, Maurice, 12), 15),
89), 90), 102), 111), 151),
152), 169), 177), 211), 215)
see: Greffin, Jean Jacques
see: Tarr, Edward, 31)

Beckett, John
see: Potpourri, 67)
see: Unidentified, Trumpet(s),
1)

Behringer, Michael
see: Läubin, Hannes, 4), 5)
see: Send, Peter

Bernstein, Heinz
see: Scherbaum, Adolf, 33)

491

Bernstein, Leonard
see: Vacchiano, William, 4)

Bernstein, Walter Heinz
see: Güttler, Ludwig, 3), 4), 8),
14), 21), 26), 27)

Berstel, Béatrice
see: Parramon, Henry

Bilgram, Hedwig
see: André, Maurice, 18), 19),
20), 23), 24), 26), 27), 28),
29), 31), 33)
see: Bauer, Willibald, 1), 4)
see: Potpourri, 15)
see: Scherbaum, Adolf, 8)
see: Thibaud, Pierre, 8)
see: Webb, Gordon, 3)

Birch, John
see: Bernard, André, 12)

Bohne, A.
see: Tarr, Edward, 20)

Boudlot, F.
see: Scherbaum, Adolf, 4)

Boulay, Laurence
see: André, Maurice, 13), 14),
178), 194), 195), 197), 200),
203)
see: Delmotte, Roger, 32)
see: Potpourri, 36), 37), 42),
44), 45)

Boyes, Shibley
see: Stevens, Thomas, 14)

Brejcha, Antonín
see: Buriánek, Jindřich

Brewer, Edward
see: Carroll, Edward, 4), 6)
see: Gould, Mark
see: Schwarz, Gerard, 8)

Carno, Zita
see: Crisara, Raymond, 2)
see: Stevens, Thomas, 12)

Charbonnier, Marcelle
see: Delmotte, Roger, 24)

Chirat, Denise
see: Delmotte, Roger, 15)

Christie, William
see: Laird, Michael, 7)

Churchill, John
see: Potpourri, 9)
see: Wilbraham, John, 12)

Conant, Robert
see: Smith, James

Constable, John
see: Goetting, Chandler
see: Hardenberger, Håkan

Cooper, Kenneth
see: Schwarz, Gerard, 4), 20)

Coquillat, R.
see: Thibaud, Pierre, 14)

Dähler, Jörg Ewald
see: Zapf, Gerd

Dart, Thurston
see: Clift, Dennis
see: Tuckwell, Barry

Davis, Andrew
see: André, Maurice, 195)
see: Potpourri, 29)
see: Wilbraham, John, 4), 6),
7), 15)

Davis, Sharon
see: Plog, Anthony, 6), 7)

Dawkes, Hubert
see: Jones, Philip, 10)

de Carli, Maria-Isabella
see: Tarr, Edward, 1)

Doll-Bittlmayer, Suzanne
see: André, Maurice, 58)
see: Reinhart, Carole Dawn, 2)

Drewanz, Hans
see: Zeyer, Adam

Earle, Eugenia
see: Broiles, Melvin
see: Nagel, Robert, 14)

Kraus, Greta
see: Anderson, George

Kreuger, Patricia
see: Weeks, Larry

Krieger, Günter
see: Hunger, Helmut, 4)

Kruttge, E.
see: Spörri, Paul

Lancelot, James
see: Laird, Michael, 14)

Langfort, Hilde
see: Libiseller, Hansjörg
see: Spindler, Josef, 3), 5)

Laredo, Ruth
see: Nowak, Henry

Leach, Andrew
see: Laird, Michael, 14)

Lechner, Irmgard
see: Scherbaum, Adolf, 5)

Ledger, Philip
see: Mason, David, 4)
see: Steele-Perkins, Crispian, 14)
see: Tuckwell, Barry

Lehrndorfer, Franz
see: Bodenröder, Robert

Leonhardt, Gustav
see: André, Maurice, 221), 222), 223), 224), 225)
see: Groot, Willem (Wim)
see: Mertens, Theo, 7)
see: Rippas, Claude
see: Tarr, Edward, 35), 36), 37), 45)

Leppard, Raymond
see: André, Maurice, 195)
see: Mason, David, 2)
see: Tuckwell, Barry
see: Webb, Gordon, 4)
see: Wilbraham, John, 27)

Lester, Harold
see: Berinbaum, Martin
see: Potpourri, 67)
see: Rudolf, Richard
see: Wilbraham, John, 31)

Levine, James
see: Herseth, Adolph, 3)

Lindorff, Joyce
see: Smedvig, Rolf

Lücker, Martin
see: Junge, Harald

Mabee, Patricia
see: Hood, Boyde

Maddox, Arthur
see: Miller, Rodney

Malcolm, George
see: Bernard, André, 1), 12)
see: Clift, Dennis
see: Gay, Bram
see: Scherbaum, Adolf, 3), 36)
see: Tuckwell, Barry
see: Unidentified, Trumpet(s), 18)
see: Wilbraham, John, 11), 16), 19)

Marlow, Sylvia
see: Vacchiano, William, 2)

Mauriello, Marina
see: André, Maurice, 115)

Maynard, Paul
see: Davenport, LaNoue
see: Montesi, Robert, 3), 4)

Meyer, Wolfgang
see: André, Maurice, 180), 199)
see: Tarr, Edward, 18)

Miedema, Barbara
see: Otten, Kees

Miremont, Josiane
see: Parramon, Henry

Moll, Philip
see: Groth, Konradin

Müller, Eduard
see: Haneuse, Arthur
see: Tarr, Edward, 11)
see: Zeyer, Adam

Münch, Roland
see: Krug, Willi, 1)
see: Potpourri, 20)

Murray, Edward
see: Dean, Allan, 6)

Murray, Gordon
see: Ferry, Dennis

Murray the Klavierkitzler
see: Nagel, Robert, 6)

Nebois, Josef
see: Holler, Adolf
see: Wobisch, Helmut, 1)

Nerokas, Johannes
see: Preis, Ivo

Neumann, Fritz
see: Flugel, J.

Neumeyer, Fritz
see: Tarr, Edward, 35), 38)
see: Vaillant, Ludovic, 2)
see: Wobisch, Helmut, 7)

Newman, Anthony
see: Berinbaum, Martin

Nicholson, Paul
see: Impett, Jonathan
see: Steele-Perkins, Crispian, 10)

Nicotri, Nunzia
see: Dassé, Jean-Luc

Noé, Hilde
see: André, Maurice, 20), 23), 31), 33), 34)

Norell, Judith
see: Carroll, Edward, 1)
see: Schwarz, Gerard, 2)

Nygaard, Jens
see: Weis, Theodore, 1)

Oberle, Grover
see: Nashan, Rudolph

Oxentyan, N.
see: Potpourri, 30)

Parrott, Lelan
see: Nagel, Robert, 18)

Party, Lionel
see: Immer, Friedemann, 13)

Pearson, Leslie
see: André, Maurice, 41), 46)
see: Lang, William
see: Webb, Gordon, 1)
see: Wilbraham, John, 26), 28)

Pertis, Zsuzsa
see: André, Maurice, 41), 43), 44), 53), 57), 67), 226), 227)
see: Csiba, József
see: Petz, Pál

Petit, Françoise
see: Jeannoutot, Bernard

Petrenz, Siegfried
see: Sauter, Hermann, 27)

Pflüger, Hans Georg
see: Sauter, Hermann, 25)
see: Schmitt, Siegfried

Picht-Axenfeld, Edith
see: Scherbaum, Adolf, 12)
see: Tarr, Edward, 18)

Pinkham, Daniel
see: Nashan, Rudolph

Pinnock, Trevor
see: Laird, Michael, 8), 10)

Pontet, Joël
see: André, Maurice, 119)
see: Soustrot, Bernard, 3)

Preston, Simon
see: Potpourri, 42), 45), 46)
see: Smithers, Don, 1), 4)

Priegnitz, Hans
see: Scherbaum, Adolf, 27)

Sirotskaya, Nataly
see: Yudashkin, Georgy

Skernick, Linda
see: Schwarz, Gerard, 7)

Šlechta, Milan
see: Horák, Jiří, 1), 2)

Smith, Edward
see: Montesi, Robert, 6)

Smith, William
see: Johnson, Gilbert, 8)

Soly, Geneviève
see: Thompson, James

Sonnleitner, Johann
see: Basch, Wolfgang, 8), 10)

Stadelmann, Li
see: Potpourri, 14), 15)
see: Scherbaum, Adolf, 13), 19), 25), 26)

Stubbs, Stephen
see: Eichhorn, Holger

Švihlíková, Viktorie
see: André, Maurice, 220)

Tachezi, Herbert
see: Immer, Friedemann, 16)
see: Potpourri, 49), 50), 64)
see: Spindler, Josef, 8), 9)
see: Wobisch, Helmut, 5), 6), 11)

Thalheim, Armin
see: Güttler, Ludwig, 3)

Thoene, Walter
see: Potpourri, 16)
see: Steinkopf, Otto
see: Tarr, Edward, 18), 21)

Thuri, František Xaver
see: Kejmar, Miroslav, 5), 8)
see: Rejlek, Vladimir

Tilney, Colin
see: Stringer, Alan, 1)
see: Tuckwell, Barry
see: Wilbraham, John, 4), 5), 15)

Toll, John
see: Bernard, André, 12)

Trimborn, Roswitha
see: Immer, Friedemann, 11)
see: Schneidewind, Helmut, 12)

Uittenbosch, Anneke
see: André, Maurice, 225)
see: Mertens, Theo, 7)

Valenti, Fernando
see: Vacchiano, William, 2)

van Asperen, Bob
see: Rippas, Claude

van der Ven, Elza
see: Tarr, Edward, 12)

van der Ven-Ulsamer, Elza
see: Otto, Joachim

Vaucher-Clerc, Germaine
see: Longinotti, Paolo
see: Scherbaum, Adolf, 31)

Vaughan, Denis
see: Eskdale, George, 5)

Veyron-Lacroix, Robert
see: André, Maurice, 93), 116), 124), 149), 169)
see: Delmotte, Roger, 7), 26)
see: Jones, Philip, 8)
see: Schneidewind, Helmut, 5)

Volle, Sverre
see: Volle, Bjarne

Wadsworth, Charles
see: Schwarz, Gerard, 3)

Wallfisch, Lory
see: Preis, Ivo

Watson, Ian
see: Steele-Perkins, Crispian, 5)

Weaver, James
see: Ghitalla, Armando, 3)
see: Immer, Friedemann, 13)

Werdermann, Hermann
see: André, Maurice, 171)
see: Gleissle, Walter, 1)

Wering, Janny Van
see: Groot, Willem (Wim)

White, John
see: Murtha, Roger

Widensky, Peter
see: Pok, František, 2)

Wolinsky, Robert
see: Burns, Stephen

Wuorinen, Charles
see: Ferrantino, Kenneth

Zanaboni, Giuseppe
see: Battagliola, Anania

Zartner, Rudolf
see: Fink, Werner
see: Quinque, Rolf, 7)
see: Ziegler, Albert

Horn
[includes natural horn & corno da caccia]

Achen, Eric
see: Schwarz, Gerard, 1)

Afanasyev, Boris
see: Dokshitser, Timofei, 1)
see: Popov, Sergei, 3)

Alfing, Heinrich
see: Basch, Wolfgang, 8)
see: Bodenröder, Robert
see: Schneidewind, Helmut, 7)
see: Tarr, Edward, 12)

Alfing, Konrad
see: Basch, Wolfgang, 1), 8)
see: Schneidewind, Helmut, 7)
see: Tarr, Edward, 12), 28)

Alonge, Ray
see: Burke, James, 6)
see: Ghitalla, Armando, 10)

Anderer, Joseph
see: Dean, Allan, 8)
see: Wise, Wilmer

André, Maurice
see: André, Maurice, 152)

Arnold, Karl
see: André, Maurice, 171)
see: Gleissle, Walter, 1), 9), 10), 11)
see: Scholz, Walter

Baccelli, Umberto
see: Haneuse, Arthur
see: Wobisch, Helmut, 8)
see: Zeyer, Adam

Bachmaier, F.
see: Scherbaum, Adolf, 36)

Baker, Julian
see: Bernard, André, 12)

Ball, Jerry
see: Rapier, Leon, 4)

Barboteu, Georges
see: André, Maurice, 12), 14), 92), 96), 98), 104), 110)
see: Calvayrac, Albert
see: Delmotte, Roger, 5)
see: Scherbaum, Adolf, 11)
see: Thibaud, Pierre, 9)

Barrows, John
see: Burke, James, 5), 6)

Bartoli, Augusto
see: André, Maurice, 130)

Baumann, Hermann
see: André, Maurice, 26), 100),
107), 222), 225)
see: Bryant, Ralph, 1), 2), 3)
see: Groot, Willem (Wim)
see: Immer, Friedemann, 16)
see: Lachenmeir, Paul
see: Smithers, Don, 13)
see: Spindler, Josef, 14)
see: Tarr, Edward, 17), 25)
see: Thibaud, Pierre, 8)
see: Touvron, Guy, 14)

Beck, Willi
see: André, Maurice, 17), 93)

Benjamin, Barry
see: Anderson, Ronald, 1)
see: Dean, Allan, 1)
see: Potpourri, 5)

Beránek, Rudolf
see: André, Maurice, 220)
see: Horák, Jiří, 4), 5)
see: Kejmar, Miroslav, 7)

Berg, Richard
see: Crisara, Raymond, 2)

Berger, Othmar
see: Bryant, Ralph, 1)
see: Potpourri, 57)

Bergés, Michel
see: André, Maurice, 172)

Bernard, Paul
see: André, Maurice, 92)

Berv, Arthur
see: Butterfield, Billy
see: Glantz, Harry, 7)

Berv, Harry
see: Butterfield, Billy

Bij de Leij, Simon
see: Grin, Freddy, 7)

Birdwell, Edward
see: Schwarz, Gerard, 13)

Black, Edwin
see: Schwarz, Gerard, 13)

Blank, Kurt
see: André, Maurice, 180)

Bloom, Myron
see: Nagel, Robert, 2)

Boldrev, B.
see: Paniotov, Kharlampi

Bos, Jan
see: Groot, Willem (Wim)

Both, André
see: André, Maurice, 160)
see: Touvron, Guy, 7)

Bradford, Fred
see: Kuehn, David

Bradley, Francis
see: Eskdale, George, 2)

Brain, Aubrey
see: Eskdale, George, 2)

Brandt, Christoph
see: Potpourri, 11)

Brazda, Joseph
see: Soustrot, Bernard, 1)

Brejza, Jozef
see: Immer, Friedemann, 3)

Brevot, Emmanuel
see: André, Maurice, 120)

Briegleb, Arthur
see: Stevens, Thomas, 4), 8)

Brown, Timothy
see: Bernard, André, 12)
see: Immer, Friedemann, 2)
see: Jones, Philip, 3)
see: Laird, Michael, 21)

Bryant, Jeffrey
see: Webb, Gordon, 1), 4)

Bryant, Ralph
see: Potpourri, 61)

Buffington, James
see: Burke, James, 5), 6)

Burden, John
  see: Jones, Philip, 11)

Burke, Tony
  see: Watson, James

Burroughs, Mary
  see: Potpourri, 66)

Butterworth, John
  see: Miller, John

Büttner, Werner
  see: Gleissle, Walter, 1)

Buurman, Jos
  see: Grin, Freddy, 9)

Buyanovsky, Vitaly
  see: Dokshitser, Timofei, 22)
  see: Margolin, Veniamin
  see: Potpourri, 30)

Carlisle, Robert
  see: Gould, Mark
  see: Soloff, Lew
  see: Wise, Wilmer

Carr, Gordon
  see: Steele-Perkins, Crispian, 19)
  see: Watson, James

Ceck, Jan
  see: Ghitalla, Armando, 15)

Cerminaro, John
  see: Stevens, Thomas, 6)

Černý, Vladimír
  see: Horák, Jiří, 5)

Chapin, Earl
  see: Burke, James, 5)
  see: Schwarz, Gerard, 6)

Chausow, Gene
  see: Perry, Brian

Chidell, Anthony
  see: Steele-Perkins, Crispian, 14)

Civil, Alan
  see: Scherbaum, Adolf, 3), 12)
  see: Wallace, John, 1)
  see: Wilbraham, John, 21)

Civil, Peter
  see: Watson, James

Clark, John T.
  see: Ranger, Louis

Clevenger, Dale
  see: Herseth, Adolph, 1), 6)

Cobaut, Ronny
  see: Mertens, Theo, 1), 3)

Čoček, Alois
  see: Kejmar, Miroslav, 13)

Corrado, Donald
  see: Broiles, Melvin
  see: Butterfield, Billy

Coursier, Gilbert
  see: André, Maurice, 12), 14), 92), 96), 110)
  see: Calvayrac, Albert
  see: Mule, Marcel

Crain, Robert
  see: McGuffey, Patrick

Crüts, Hubert
  see: Bodenröder, Robert

Damm, Peter
  see: Haas, Rudolf
  see: Krug, Willi, 3)

Dannhausen, K. (Clemens?)
  see: Zickler, Heinz, 5)

Davis, Robin
  see: Jones, Philip, 3)

del Vescovo, Pierre
  see: André, Maurice, 89)
  see: Vaillant, Ludovic, 7)

Delvigne, Georges
  see: André, Maurice, 151)

Delwande, Xavier
  see: André, Maurice, 92)
  see: Delmotte, Roger, 47)

Guy, Marc
see: Ghitalla, Armando, 1)

Halloin, Elizabeth
see: Potpourri, 7)

Halstead, Anthony
see: Jones, Philip, 6)
see: Laird, Michael, 8)
see: Wilbraham, John, 27)

Hanke, Kurt
see: Adelbrecht, Henri, 3)

Harper, Ian
see: Wilbraham, John, 26)

Harris, Ronald
see: Webb, Gordon, 1)

Haucke, Gerd
see: André, Maurice, 201)

Hauptmann, Norbert
see: Groth, Konradin

Hefti, Jakob
see: Adelbrecht, Henri, 1)

Henderson, Robert
see: Stevens, Thomas, 11)

Hill, Douglas
see: Dean, Allan, 8)
see: Potpourri, 38)

Hill, Nicholas
see: Laird, Michael, 21)

Hoekmeyer, Peter
see: Ros, Ad

Hoekstra, Theo
see: Grin, Freddy, 7)

Hofmann, Franz
see: Spindler, Josef, 6)

Högner, Günther
see: André, Maurice, 32)

Holden, Thomas
see: Ferrantino, Kenneth

Holzer, Kurt
see: Adelbrecht, Henri, 3)

Hopkins, Shirley
see: Scherbaum, Adolf, 12)

Horton, Colin
see: Webb, Gordon, 4)

Hoyt, David
see: Lowrey, Alvin

Hrdina, Emanuel
see: Mičaník, Jaroslav

Hustis, Gregory
see: Giangiulio, Richard

Huth, Fritz
see: Scherbaum, Adolf, 35)

Hyde, George
see: Stevens, Thomas, 8)

Immer, Friedemann
see: Immer, Friedemann, 14),
15)
see: Potpourri, 61)

Ingraham, Paul
see: Burns, Stephen
see: Dean, Allan, 2), 4), 5), 6)
see: Mills, Fred

Irmscher, Helmuth
see: Scherbaum, Adolf, 5)
see: Schneidewind, Helmut, 13)

James, Ifor
see: Howarth, Elgar
see: Mason, David, 4)
see: Watson, James

Johnson, A. Robert
see: Berinbaum, Martin
see: Nagel, Robert, 2)

Johnson, David
see: Sommerhalder, Max

Jolley, David
see: Anderson, Ronald, 6)
see: Berinbaum, Martin
see: Stubbs, James

Maries, Keith
see: Laird, Michael, 7)

McGavin, Andrew
see: Wilbraham, John, 26)

McGregor, Rob Roy
see: McGregor, Rob Roy, 3), 4)
see: Potpourri, 17)

McKee, William
see: Henderson, Douglas

Mealy, George
see: Burkhart, David

Meek, Harold
see: Voisin, Roger, 13)

Meissonier, Guy
see: André, Maurice, 120)

Mensenkamp, Rut
see: Grin, Freddy, 7)

Meyendorf, Werner
see: André, Maurice, 26)
see: Lachenmeir, Paul
see: Thibaud, Pierre, 8)

Michalec, V.
see: Mičaník, Jaroslav

Michelsen, I.
see: Hovaldt, Knud

Miller, Todd
see: Stevens, Thomas, 4), 8)

Molnar, Jozsef
see: Touvron, Guy, 10)

Morel, Yves
see: André, Maurice, 120)

Mühlbacher, Ernst
see: Rudolf, Richard
see: Spindler, Josef, 10)

Navasse, R.
see: André, Maurice, 89)
see: Scherbaum, Adolf, 4)

Neunecker, Marie-Louise
see: Schmid, Bernhard, 10)

Nicolaas, Herman
see: Mertens, Theo, 1), 3)

Nitsch, Herwig
see: Rudolf, Richard

Odmark, Robert
see: Ghitalla, Armando, 1)

Oheim, Martin
see: Schneidewind, Helmut, 5)

Olsen, K.E.
see: Hovaldt, Knud

Ondracek, Paul
see: Miller, Rodney

Page, Graeme
see: Canadian Brass, 1), 2), 3),
    4), 5), 6), 7)
see: Malone, Michael
see: Potpourri, 32), 33)

Penzel, Erich
see: André, Maurice, 179), 201)
see: Holy, Walter, 6)
see: Lösch, Reinhold
see: Potpourri, 2), 16)
see: Sauter, Hermann, 26)
see: Schneidewind, Helmut, 4),
    13)
see: Tarr, Edward, 28), 37)

Petr, Miloš
see: Junek, Václav, 1)
see: Kejmar, Miroslav, 3), 9)

Pichal, André
see: Mertens, Theo, 3)

Pigneguy, John
see: Steele-Perkins, Crispian,
    19)
see: Watson, James
see: Wilbraham, John, 26)

Pontiggia, Claudio
see: Touvron, Guy, 10)

Prince, William
see: Laird, Michael, 7)

Tuckwell, Barry
  see: Clift, Dennis
  see: Jones, Philip, 6)
  see: Stringer, Alan, 1), 4)
  see: Tuckwell, Barry

Tyler, Basil
  see: Bastin, Ernie

Tylšar, Bedřich
  see: Kejmar, Miroslav, 5), 7)
  see: Quinque, Rolf, 7)

Tylšar, Zdeněk
  see: Kejmar, Miroslav, 5), 7)
  see: Quinque, Rolf, 7)

Tynyakin, N.
  see: Paniotov, Kharlampi

Ulleberg, Odd
  see: Christiansen, Jan

van Aeken, Alex
  see: Mertens, Theo, 5)

van der Wal, Bernard
  see: Grin, Freddy, 7)

van Driessche, André
  see: Mertens, Theo, 1), 3)

van Woudenberg, Adriaan
  see: André, Maurice, 222), 225)
  see: Groot, Willem (Wim)
  see: Potpourri, 58)
  see: Sevenstern, Harry
  see: Spindler, Josef, 11), 14)

Vaughn, James D.
  see: Brass-zination

Vermeulen, Jeroen
  see: Grin, Freddy, 7)

Vošický, B.
  see: Mičaník, Jaroslav

Waas, Roy
  see: Kuehn, David

Wakefield, David
  see: Potpourri, 38)

Wallendorf, Klaus
  see: Preis, Ivo

Warhol, Cindy
  see: Potpourri, 66)

Warné, Hans
  see: Zickler, Heinz, 5)

Warne, Ralf
  see: Basch, Wolfgang, 14)

Watt, Robert
  see: Guarneri, Mario

Weiver, Jane
  see: Potpourri, 66)

Whitmore, Keith
  see: Webb, Gordon, 2)

Wilber, Weldon
  see: Vacchiano, William, 2)

Williams, Gail
  see: Perry, Brian

Woodburn, Andrew
  see: Scherbaum, Adolf, 3)

Wunder, Oscar
  see: Schneidewind, Helmut, 5)

Zarzo, Vicente
  see: León, Felipe

Hurdy-gurdy

Hogwood, Christopher
  see: Laird, Michael, 1)

Renz, Frederick
  see: Potpourri, 67)

Jew's harp
[includes guimbarde]

Kecskés, András
  see: Pok, František, 4)

Tyler, James
  see: Laird, Michael, 1)

Keyed bugle

Dudgeon, Ralph
see: Dudgeon, Ralph

Impett, Jonathan
see: Impett, Jonathan

Sheldon, Robert
see: Sheldon, Robert

Keyed fiddle

Sahlström, Eric
see: Potpourri, 3)

Kindertrompete (toy trumpet)

Tarr, Edward
see: Tarr, Edward, 29)

Left-handed sewer flute

Lewis, Robert
see: Platt, Seymour

Lira da braccio

Melkus, Eduard
see: Eichhorn, Holger

Sothcott, John
see: Potpourri, 67)

Lute
[includes various types: bandora,
chitarrone, orpharion, pandora,
theorbo, ect.]

Buetens, Stanley
see: Platt, Seymour

Cohen, Joel
see: Cook, Richard

Crawford, Timothy
see: Steele-Perkins, Crispian,
10)

Dupré, Desmond
see: Potpourri, 42)
see: Smithers, Don, 1), 3), 4)
see: Wilbraham, John, 20)

Funk, Eike
see: Potpourri, 47)
see: Tarr, Edward, 32)

Gerrits, Paul
see: Otto, Joachim

Gerwig, Kristian
see: Tarr, Edward, 31)

Gerwig, Walter
see: Scherbaum, Adolf, 7)
see: Wobisch, Helmut, 7)

Goldschmidt, Gusta
see: Otten, Kees
see: Tarr, Edward, 45)

Gruenmayer, Christa
see: Spindler, Josef, 3)

Hübscher, Jürgen
see: Touvron, Guy, 7)

Imamura, Yasunori
see: Immer, Friedemann, 11)

Junghänel, Konrad
see: Caudle, Theresa

Just, Franz
see: Haas, Rudolf

Kecskés, András
see: Pok, František, 2), 4)

Kirsch, Dieter
see: Otto, Joachim

Müller-Dombois, Eugen
see: André, Maurice, 221), 224)
see: Holy, Walter, 5)
see: Potpourri, 47)
see: Steinkopf, Otto
see: Tarr, Edward, 10), 18),
21), 27), 32)

North, Nigel
see: Laird, Michael, 1), 2)

O'Brien, Patrick
see: Carroll, Edward, 8), 9)

O'dette, Paul
see: Keavy, Stephen

Pok, František
see: Pok, František, 4)

Ragossnig, Konrad
see: Otto, Joachim

Robert, Guy
see: Thibaud, Pierre, 14)

Rooley, Anthony
see: Laird, Michael, 3)
see: Potpourri, 67)

Rubin, Jonathan
see: Ferry, Dennis

Schäffer, Michael
see: Potpourri, 47)
see: Tarr, Edward, 10), 12),
   18), 19), 20), 27), 31), 32)

Scheit, Karl
see: Eichhorn, Holger
see: Scherbaum, Adolf, 24)
see: Spindler, Josef, 3)

Segerman, Ephraim
see: Potpourri, 67)

Spencer, Robert
see: Laird, Michael, 1), 13), 14)
see: Smithers, Don, 3)

Stradner, Friderike
see: Stradner, Gerhard

Stubbs, Stephen
see: Eichhorn, Holger

Tucholski, Gerhard
see: Tarr, Edward, 18)

Tyler, James
see: Davenport, LaNoue
see: Laird, Michael, 1), 3), 11),
   12), 13)
see: Potpourri, 67)
see: Smithers, Don, 2), 3)

Zimmer, Roland
see: Haas, Rudolf

Lyre
[includes cithara]

Brookes, Oliver
see: Laird, Michael, 1)

Rollin
see: Caens, Thierry

Sloan, Eleanor
see: Laird, Michael, 1)

Mandolin
[includes various types: mandole,
mandora, etc.]

Bianchi, Bonifacio
see: Leroy, Jean-Paul

Bolotine, Leonid
see: Carroll, Edward, 1)

de Filippis, Carlo
see: Vacchiano, William, 4)

del Vescovo, Gino
see: Adelbrecht, Henri, 4)
see: André, Maurice, 195)

Fietz, Elisabeth
see: Haas, Rudolf

Fietz, Erhard
see: Haas, Rudolf

Grund, Paul
see: Zickler, Heinz, 8)

Mason, Patrick
see: Potpourri, 6)

Melkus, Thomas
see: Eichhorn, Holger

Ochi, Silvia
see: Biessecker, Friedhelm

Ochi, Takashi
see: André, Maurice, 30)
see: Biessecker, Friedhelm
see: Erb, Helmut, 1)
see: Goethel, Siegfried

Pok, František
see: Pok, František, 4)

Ruta, Tommaso
see: Adelbrecht, Henri, 4)
see: André, Maurice, 195)

Saint-Clivier, André
see: Calvayrac, Albert
see: Cure, Antoine
see: Potpourri, 4)

Schneider, Christian
see: Calvayrac, Albert
see: Potpourri, 4)
see: Touvron, Guy, 13)

Tyler, James
see: Laird, Michael, 1), 2), 21)

Vicari, Giovanni
see: Vacchiano, William, 4)

Wootton, Douglas
see: Laird, Michael, 21)

Mediaeval cornett (tuohitorvi)

Laird, Michael
see: Laird, Michael, 1)

Melodeon
[suction operated reed-organ]

Kalish, Gilbert
see: Sheldon, Robert

Mezzo-soprano
[cross-referenced under soprano]

Allen, Betty
see: Mills, Fred

Baker, Janet
see: Wilbraham, John, 22)

Berberian, Cathy
see: Heinrich, Robert

Biswenger, Annette
see: Schmitt, Siegfried

Bonazzi, Elaine
see: Anderson, Ronald, 5)
see: Burns, Stephen

Davis, Eleanor
see: Nashan, Rudolph

DeGaetani, Jan
see: Dean, Allan, 4), 6), 7)
see: Miller, Rodney
see: Nagel, Robert, 19)
see: Romm, Ronald
see: Sheldon, Robert

de Montmollin, Marie-Lise
see: Longinotti, Paolo

Edmonds, Katherine
see: Cook, Richard

Farris, Mary Lee
see: Rapier, Leon, 6)

Hamm-Albrecht, Helga
see: Stockhausen, Markus, 4)

Jones, Isola
see: Herseth, Adolph, 4)
see: Perry, Brian

Kotova, Raisa
see: Gorokhov, Vitaly

Martin, Pauline
see: Longinotti, Paolo

Morgan, Beverly
see: Metzger, Charles

Murray, Ann
see: Vasse, Claude

Noorman, Jantina
see: Potpourri, 67)

Palade, Dorothea
see: Hyatt, Jack

Pilgrim, Neva
see: Anderson, Ronald, 5)

Plantamura, Carol
see: Burkhart, David

Quivar, Florence
see: Weeks, Larry

Robbin, Catherine
see: Steele-Perkins, Crispian, 18)

Salvetti, A.
see: Thibaud, Pierre, 14)

Schaer, Hanna
see: Caens, Thierry

Schwartz, Magali
see: Tarr, Edward, 32)

Terhoeven, Ursula
see: Tarr, Edward, 27)

Troyanos, Tatiana
see: Eichhorn, Holger

Verrett, Shirley
see: Heinrich, Robert

von Otter, Anne Sofie
see: Steele-Perkins, Crispian, 4)

von Stade, Frederica
see: Schwarz, Gerard, 3)

Muschelhorn

Tarr, Edward
see: Tarr, Edward, 29)

Nafir (Arabian trumpet)

Tarr, Edward
see: Tarr, Edward, 29)

Narrator

Albrecht, Gerd
see: Adelbrecht, Henri, 1)

Alvan, Ameen
see: Plog, Anthony, 6)

Ashcroft, Peggy
see: Evans, Laurie

Auclair, Michel
see: Delmotte, Roger, 35)

Audel, Stephane
see: Longinotti, Paolo

Aumont, Jean Pierre
see: Weis, Theodore, 4)

Basescu, Elinor
see: Romm, Ronald

Berberian, Cathy
see: Mason, David, 5)

Berthet, François
see: Cuvit, Michel

Bookspan, Janet
see: Broiles, Melvin

Bookspan, Martin
see: Potpourri, 67)

Böse, Joachim
see: Schmid, Bernhard, 13)

Boult, Sir Adrian
see: Webb, Gordon, 2)

Burke, Harold
see: Umbrico, Joseph

Carrat, Gérard
see: Cuvit, Michel

Cattand, Gabriel
see: Ghitalla, Armando, 8)

Clay, Philippe
see: Ghitalla, Armando, 8)

Cocteau, Jean
see: André, Maurice, 181)

Costinescu, Gheorghe
see: Hyatt, Jack

Courtenay, Tom
see: Ghitalla, Armando, 9)

Desailly, Jean
see: Thibaud, Pierre, 9)

Smith, Hal
see: Plog, Anthony, 4), 6)

Striebeck, Peter
see: Ghitalla, Armando, 6)

Tear, Robert
see: Mason, David, 5)

Thomas, John P.
see: Schwarz, Gerard, 18)

Ustinov, Peter
see: André, Maurice, 181)

Warriner, Frederic
see: Unidentified, Trumpet(s), 22)

Weaver, Fritz
see: Unidentified, Trumpet(s), 22)

Zorina, Vera
see: Johnson, Gilbert, 1)

Natural trumpet (Baroque trumpet)
[may be incomplete listing, and is cross-referenced under trumpet]

Bäckvall, Arne
see: Eklund's Baroque Ensemble

Basch, Wolfgang
see: Basch, Wolfgang, 1), 14)

Bengtsson, Helene
see: Eklund's Baroque Ensemble

Bodenröder, Robert
see: Bodenröder, Robert
see: Potpourri, 47)
see: Tarr, Edward, 18), 20), 21), 32)

Brandes, Lothar
see: Tarr, Edward, 30), 43)

Bryant, Ralph
see: Immer, Friedemann, 18)
see: Potpourri, 61), 62)
see: Tarr, Edward, 3)

Carlsson, Lars-Göran
see: Eklund's Baroque Ensemble

Chappuis, Paul
see: Tarr, Edward, 3)

Dolk, Pieter
see: Bodenröder, Robert
see: Tarr, Edward, 18), 20), 21)

Edefors, Ake
see: Eklund's Baroque Ensemble

Eklund, Bengt
see: Eklund's Baroque Ensemble

Eriksson, Lars
see: Eklund's Baroque Ensemble

Faller, Robert
see: Tarr, Edward, 30), 43)

Federowitz, Kurt
see: Potpourri, 47)
see: Tarr, Edward, 3), 32)

Ferry, Dennis
see: Ferry, Dennis

Finke, Helmut
see: Holy, Walter, 3)

Gekker, Chris
see: Holmgren, Fred

Goetting, Chandler
see: Tarr, Edward, 3)

Gössling, Christhard
see: Immer, Friedemann, 18)

Gottfried, Karl Heinz
see: Immer, Friedemann, 18)

Gustavsson, Jan
see: Eklund's Baroque Ensemble

Held, Friedrich
see: Immer, Friedemann, 18)

Hermann, Emil
see: Potpourri, 47)
see: Tarr, Edward, 32)

Hoffmann, Ernst
see: Spindler, Josef, 7)

Roos, Ingemar
  see: Eklund's Baroque Ensemble

Rudolf, Richard
  see: Immer, Friedemann, 14),
    15), 17)
  see: Potpourri, 49), 51), 52),
    53), 54), 56), 60), 62), 64)
  see: Spindler, Josef, 7), 8), 9),
    10), 12), 13), 14), 15), 16)

Schmidt, Ingus
  see: Holy, Walter, 2)
  see: Spindler, Josef, 9)

Schmidt, Kurt
  see: Holy, Walter, 5)

Schmitt, Helmut
  see: Potpourri, 47)
  see: Tarr, Edward, 32)

Schneidewind, Helmut
  see: Holy, Walter, 2), 3)

Schöber, Hermann
  see: Immer, Friedemann, 14),
    15)
  see: Potpourri, 49), 50), 51),
    52), 53), 54), 55), 56), 60)
  see: Spindler, Josef, 7), 8), 9),
    10), 12), 13), 14), 15), 16)

Schwammeis, Richard
  see: Potpourri, 56), 60)

Skar, Bard
  see: Eklund's Baroque Ensemble

Sköld, Lars-Gunnar
  see: Eklund's Baroque Ensemble

Smith, Malcolm
  see: Laird, Michael, 1), 7)

Smithers, Don
  see: Immer, Friedemann, 14)
  see: Potpourri, 57), 59), 61),
    63), 67)
  see: Smithers, Don, 6), 7), 10),
    13), 14), 15)
  see: Spindler, Josef, 14)

Spindler, Günter
  see: Idinger, Matthias
  see: Pok, František, 2)
  see: Potpourri, 49), 50), 56)
  see: Spindler, Josef, 7), 9), 13)

Spindler, Josef
  see: Idinger, Matthias
  see: Potpourri, 49), 50), 51),
    52), 53), 54), 55), 56), 58),
    64)
  see: Spindler, Josef, 7), 8), 9),
    10), 11), 12), 13), 14), 15),
    16)

Spjut, Paul
  see: Eklund's Baroque Ensemble

Staff, David
  see: Steele-Perkins, Crispian,
    7), 16)

Steele-Perkins, Crispian
  see: Immer, Friedemann, 18)
  see: Steele-Perkins, Crispian,
    5), 7), 9), 10), 15), 16)

Steiner, Michael
  see: Tarr, Edward, 20)

Stenvik, Rigmor
  see: Eklund's Baroque Ensemble

Sundberg, Annemarie
  see: Eklund's Baroque Ensemble

Sykes, Mark
  see: Eklund's Baroque Ensemble

Tarr, Edward
  see: Potpourri, 47)
  see: Tarr, Edward, 3), 7), 17),
    18), 20), 21), 30), 32), 33),
    35), 36), 37), 40), 41), 43)

Ullrich, Marc
  see: Tarr, Edward, 17), 41)

Wenth, Andreas
  see: Spindler, Josef, 7)

Westerlund, Börie
  see: Eklund's Baroque Ensemble

Willig, Claes
see: Eklund's Baroque Ensemble

Wilson, Ian
see: Immer, Friedemann, 1)
see: Laird, Michael, 5), 6), 11),
19)
see: Smithers, Don, 6), 14)

Oboe
[includes oboe d'amore, oboe da
caccia & English horn, (and may
include Baroque oboe)]

Adamczyk, Peter
see: Potpourri, 2)

Adamus, Jan
see: Rejlek, Vladimir

Albrecht, Erich
see: Sauter, Hermann, 1)

Alcalá, Robert
see: Potpourri, 55), 56)

Alvarosi, Alberto
see: Battagliola, Anania

Alves, Karl-Heinz
see: Scherbaum, Adolf, 13),
19), 25)

Amedyan, Sergei
see: Dokshitser, Timofei, 12)

André, Béatrice
see: André, Maurice, 39)

Arner, Leonard
see: Broiles, Melvin

Arrignon, Daniel
see: André, Maurice, 47), 48),
119)

Arrowsmith, William
see: Burke, James, 5), 6)

Bachert, Willi
see: Preis, Ivo
see: Sauter, Hermann, 26)

Barnett, James John
see: Ellinghaus, Wolfram

Barrington, Sara
see: Wilbraham, John, 18), 26)

Barry, Tom
see: Hickman, David, 2)

Bartonikova, Hana
see: Potpourri, 40)

Bartonikova, Josef
see: Potpourri, 40)

Baskin, Theodore
see: Thompson, James

Bauman, Perry
see: Chevanelle, Serge
see: LeComte, Jacques
see: Lowrey, Alvin

Beiman, Melvin
see: Schwarz, Gerard, 13)

Berman, Melvin
see: Schultz, Erik, 8)

Black, Neil
see: Clift, Dennis
see: Jones, Philip, 3)
see: Potpourri, 4)
see: Steele-Perkins, Crispian,
13), 14), 17)
see: Tuckwell, Barry
see: Wilbraham, John, 26), 27)

Blech, Rhonda
see: Birch, Robert

Bloom, Robert
see: Baker, Bernard
see: Vacchiano, William, 2)

Bode, Albrecht
see: Junge, Harald

Bolz, Erich
see: André, Maurice, 10)

Bolz, Jörg
see: Fink, Werner

Borggrefe, Siegfried
see: Bodenröder, Robert

Botti, Robert
see: Gould, Mark

Bourgue, Maurice
see: André, Maurice, 63), 68),
   201)
see: Scherbaum, Adolf, 11), 23)
see: Touvron, Guy, 4), 6)
see: Wilbraham, John, 21)

Brenner, Englebert
see: Vacchiano, William, 4)

Brewer, Virginia
see: Berinbaum, Martin
see: Carroll, Edward, 11)
see: Holmgren, Fred
see: Schwarz, Gerard, 8)

Broggia, Daniel
see: Ullrich, Marc

Brown, James
see: Clift, Dennis
see: Steele-Perkins, Crispian,
   13), 14)
see: Wilbraham, John, 26), 27)

Bruch, O.
see: Flugel, J.

Brückner, Hans
see: Bauer, Willibald, 3)

Caldwell, James
see: Immer, Friedemann, 13)

Camden, Anthony
see: Laird, Michael, 11)
see: Snell, Howard

Canter, Robin
see: Steele-Perkins, Crispian,
   18)

Caroldi, Alberto
see: Battagliola, Anania
see: Unidentified, Trumpet(s),
   24)

Casier, Pierre
see: André, Maurice, 6)

Casier, Robert
see: André, Maurice, 6), 172)
see: Calvayrac, Albert
see: Delmotte, Roger, 3), 41)
see: Ménardi, Louis

Cattermole, Robert
see: Webb, Gordon, 4)

Chambon, Jacques
see: André, Maurice, 6), 75),
   81), 83), 87), 89), 94),
   107), 109), 111), 113), 116),
   125), 128), 136), 149), 151),
   152), 168), 169), 217)
see: Bernard, André, 7)
see: Delmotte, Roger, 30)
see: Gabel, Bernard, 3)
see: Gleissle, Walter, 3), 6), 7)
see: Lagorce, Marcel
see: Sauter, Hermann, 24)
see: Touvron, Guy, 11)

Chavana, Jean-Philippe
see: André, Maurice, 119)

Checker, Maurice
see: Clift, Dennis
see: Webb, Gordon, 2), 4)

Christ, Peter
see: Nagel, Robert, 2)
see: Plog, Anthony, 9)
see: Stevens, Thomas, 11)

Clement, Manfred
see: André, Maurice, 17), 26)
see: Bauer, Willibald, 3)
see: Potpourri, 11)
see: Schmid, Bernhard, 6)
see: Thibaud, Pierre, 7), 8)
see: Wolf, Hans, 7)

Cowart, Robert
see: Stevens, Thomas, 12)

Cramer, Wilhelm
see: Preis, Ivo

Craxton, Janet
see: Clift, Dennis
see: Miller, John
see: Wilbraham, John, 22)

Czaja, Alfons
  see: Köpp, Rudolf

Daraux, René
  see: Delmotte, Roger, 15)

Darke, Valerie
  see: Laird, Michael, 8)
  see: Potpourri, 62)
  see: Steele-Perkins, Crispian, 16), 18)

Davis, Barry
  see: Bernard, André, 12)
  see: Laird, Michael, 21), 22)

Debray, Lucien
  see: André, Maurice, 95), 172)

Dekant, Helmut
  see: Fink, Werner

de Lancie, John
  see: Johnson, Gilbert, 8)

de Nattes, Michel
  see: André, Maurice, 120)

Dent, Simon
  see: Miller, Rodney
  see: Schmid, Bernhard, 5)
  see: Wolf, Hans, 10)

Dhont, Pieter
  see: Bryant, Ralph, 4)
  see: Immer, Friedemann, 14)
  see: Rippas, Claude
  see: Smithers, Don, 14), 15)

Dicker, Judith
  see: Potpourri, 6)

di Domenica, Robert
  see: Nagel, Robert, 3)

Dienes, Gábor
  see: Petz, Pál

Dittrich, Erich
  see: Spindler, Josef, 2)

Dobson, Michael
  see: Clift, Dennis

Dombrecht, Paul
  see: Rippas, Claude
  see: Smithers, Don, 13)

Dondeyne, Marc
  see: André, Maurice, 120)

Dorsey, Richard
  see: Berinbaum, Martin

Driehuys, Leo
  see: Adelbrecht, Henri, 4), 6)

Duste, Raymond
  see: Haug, Edward

Dutka, Alfred
  see: Spindler, Josef, 3)

Earle, Richard
  see: Steele-Perkins, Crispian, 16), 18)

Ebach, Klaus
  see: Tarr, Edward, 18), 21), 38)
  see: Wolf, Hans, 1)

Ebbinge, Ku
  see: Bryant, Ralph, 2), 4)
  see: Immer, Friedemann, 4), 14)
  see: Potpourri, 52), 57), 58), 59), 60), 61), 63)
  see: Rippas, Claude
  see: Smithers, Don, 13), 14), 15)
  see: Spindler, Josef, 13), 14), 15)
  see: Steele-Perkins, Crispian, 9)

Eggers, H.
  see: Scherbaum, Adolf, 33)

Elhorst, Hans
  see: Soustrot, Bernard, 5)

Eliscu, Robert
  see: Potpourri, 11)
  see: Thibaud, Pierre, 7)

Elliot, Gladys
  see: Miller, Rodney
  see: Perry, Brian

Fedorov, E.
see: Gorokhov, Vitaly

Ferber, Nils
see: Immer, Friedemann, 3)

Ferrero, Alessandro
see: Unidentified, Trumpet(s), 24)

Fest, Frithjof
see: André, Maurice, 180), 199)

Figatner, Nancy
see: Immer, Friedemann, 14)
see: Potpourri, 62)

Fink, Marc
see: Potpourri, 38)

Fischer, Fritz
see: Krug, Willi, 5)
see: Scherbaum, Adolf, 5), 31)

Francz, Katalin
see: André, Maurice, 44), 53), 227)

Franklin, Ian
see: Schultz, Erik, 7)

Germann, G.
see: Zickler, Heinz, 5)

Germann, Kurt
see: Potpourri, 34), 35)
see: Preis, Ivo
see: Zickler, Heinz, 7)

Giacobassi, Julie
see: Ghitalla, Armando, 1)

Gillet, Fernand
see: Voisin, Roger, 9)

Giuliani, Giuliano
see: André, Maurice, 105)

Glaetzner, Burkhard
see: Güttler, Ludwig, 12), 18), 19), 21)

Gleitsman, Stefan
see: Preis, Ivo

Gombai, József
see: Petz, Pál

Gomberg, Harold
see: Vacchiano, William, 4)

Gomberg, Ralph
see: Ghitalla, Armando, 7), 10)
see: Voisin, Roger, 11)

Goodwin, Paul
see: Steele-Perkins, Crispian, 16)

Goossens, Leon
see: Gay, Bram
see: Wilbraham, John, 30)

Goritzki, Ingo
see: Basch, Wolfgang, 8), 10)
see: Güttler, Ludwig, 12)
see: Potpourri, 25)
see: Sauter, Hermann, 7), 21)
see: Schmid, Bernhard, 4), 9)
see: Tarr, Edward, 37)
see: Wolf, Hans, 11), 12)

Goy, Jean-Paul
see: Touvron, Guy, 10)

Graeme, Peter
see: Clift, Dennis
see: Eskdale, George, 5)
see: Jones, Philip, 2)
see: Mason, David, 4)
see: Potpourri, 9)
see: Wilbraham, John, 28)

Grigorivich, V.
see: Krylov, Gleb

Grimm, Wilhelm
see: André, Maurice, 93)

Gruber, Karl
see: Bryant, Ralph, 1), 3)
see: Holy, Walter, 9)
see: Potpourri, 49), 50), 51), 53), 54), 64)
see: Rudolf, Richard
see: Spindler, Josef, 7), 8), 10), 11), 12), 13)

Gürke, Dieter
see: Immer, Friedemann, 5)

Gütz, Klaus-Peter
  see: Güttler, Ludwig, 4), 8),
    12), 14)

Haas, George
  see: Dean, Allan, 2), 4), 5), 6),
    8)
  see: Nagel, Robert, 18), 19),
    20)
  see: Ranger, Louis

Häberling, Markus
  see: Touvron, Guy, 10)

Hadady, Laszlo
  see: Vasse, Claude

Hailperin, Paul
  see: Bryant, Ralph, 1), 2), 3),
    4), 5)
  see: Potpourri, 51), 53), 54),
    55), 56), 57), 59), 60), 61)
  see: Spindler, Josef, 11), 12),
    13), 14), 15), 16)

Hammer, Stephen
  see: Holmgren, Fred
  see: Immer, Friedemann, 13)

Hanták, František
  see: Junek, Václav, 3), 5)

Harrison, Earnest
  see: Geisler, Lloyd

Hart, Terry
  see: Lowrey, Alvin

Hauck, Hans-Ludwig
  see: Tarr, Edward, 24), 26), 27)

Hausmann, Kurt
  see: André, Maurice, 17)
  see: Bauer, Willibald, 1)
  see: Lachenmeir, Paul
  see: Quinque, Rolf, 7)
  see: Scherbaum, Adolf, 9)

Haynes, Bruce
  see: Bryant, Ralph, 4), 5)
  see: Immer, Friedemann, 14)
  see: Potpourri, 57), 58), 59),
    60), 61), 63)
  see: Smithers, Don, 13), 14),
    15)
  see: Spindler, Josef, 13), 14),
    15)

Heidrich, Günter
  see: Güttler, Ludwig, 26)

Henderson, Guy
  see: Webb, Gordon, 5)

Hertel, Alfred
  see: Libiseller, Hansjörg
  see: Spindler, Josef, 2), 4), 13)

Hewett, Stevens
  see: Johnson, Gilbert, 8)

Hickel, Heinrich
  see: Potpourri, 34), 35)
  see: Zickler, Heinz, 5), 7)

Hildebrand, Renate
  see: Immer, Friedemann, 3)

Hill, Mark
  see: Carroll, Edward, 11)

Hinrichs, Hans Heinrich
  see: Zeh, Karl Heinz

Hofmann, Klaus
  see: Sauter, Hermann, 2)

Holliger, Heinz
  see: Adelbrecht, Henri, 6)
  see: André, Maurice, 194), 201)
  see: Bernard, André, 1), 12)
  see: Potpourri, 45)
  see: Touvron, Guy, 14)

Hopf, Siegfried
  see: Gleissle, Walter, 11)

Horowitz, Irving
  see: Butterfield, Billy

Hoth, Wolfgang
  see: Köpp, Rudolf

Klement, Karel
see: Schneidewind, Helmut, 8)

Kneissl, Willi
see: Bauer, Willibald, 4)

Knight, Janice
see: Steele-Perkins, Crispian, 14)

Knip, Wim
see: Groot, Willem (Wim)

Koch, Gerhard
see: Erb, Helmut, 6)

Koch, Helmut
see: André, Maurice, 171)
see: Immer, Friedemann, 6)
see: Sauter, Hermann, 7)
see: Scholz, Walter

Koch, Lothar
see: Scherbaum, Adolf, 12)
see: Tarr, Edward, 18)

Koch, Rolf Julius
see: André, Maurice, 180), 199)
see: Sauter, Hermann, 21)
see: Schmid, Bernhard, 12)

Kochnev, Stanislav
see: Fomin, Evgeny

Korbus, Bernd
see: Schneidewind, Helmut, 11)

Korman, Fred
see: Murtha, Roger

Korner, Fritz
see: Sauter, Hermann, 26)

Krall, Ernst
see: Libiseller, Hansjörg
see: Spindler, Josef, 2), 3)

Krauss, Manfred
see: Haas, Rudolf

Krebs, Friedrich C.
see: Potpourri, 22)

Krilov, Arthur
see: Haneuse, Arthur

Kühn, Michel
see: Zickler, Heinz, 5)

Kull, Hans
see: André, Maurice, 201)

Kurlin, Vladimir
see: Margolin, Veniamin

Kuskin, Charles
see: Dean, Allan, 1)

Lange, Christian
see: Tarr, Edward, 17)

Lännerholm, Torleif
see: Schrello, Mark

Lardrot, André
see: Adelbrecht, Henri, 2)
see: Scherbaum, Adolf, 1)
see: Wobisch, Helmut, 5), 14)

Laubin, Alfred
see: Broiles, Melvin

Leadbetter, Susan
see: Laird, Michael, 22)

Lesser, Diane
see: Burns, Stephen

Linder, Martin
see: Gleissle, Walter, 1)

Liubimov, Anatoly
see: Maximenko, Anatoly, 2), 3)

Logemann, Sally
see: Berinbaum, Martin

Lord, Roger
see: Wilbraham, John, 11), 18), 19)

Lorenz, Andreas
see: Güttler, Ludwig, 20)

Lugue, Michel
see: André, Maurice, 120)

Lützen, Ludolf
see: Tarr, Edward, 28)

Macdonagh, Terence
see: Jones, Philip, 8)

Mack, John
see: Mule, Marcel
see: Nagel, Robert, 2)
see: Nowak, Henry

Mahn, Kurt
see: Haas, Rudolf

Maisonneuve, Claude
see: André, Maurice, 95), 152)
see: Couëffé, Yves
see: Delmotte, Roger, 2), 45)
see: Jeannoutot, Bernard

Malgoire, Jean-Claude
see: André, Maurice, 6)
see: Delmotte, Roger, 42), 43)

Marx, Josef
see: Anderson, Ronald, 1)
see: Mueller, Herbert

Mater, Adolf (Ad)
see: André, Maurice, 221), 223), 224)
see: Groot, Willem (Wim)
see: Tarr, Edward, 28), 38)

Mattern, Norbert
see: Ridder, Jean de

Maugras, Gaston
see: Ménardi, Louis
see: Scherbaum, Adolf, 20)

Mayousse, Emile
see: Scherbaum, Adolf, 11), 23)

Mayrhofer, Karl
see: Wobisch, Helmut, 2), 12)

McAninch, Daniel
see: Rapier, Leon, 4)

McKenna, Sophia
see: Laird, Michael, 7), 8), 17)
see: Steele-Perkins, Crispian, 7), 16), 18)

Meidhof, Adolf
see: Sauter, Hermann, 8), 26)
see: Zickler, Heinz, 5)

Menzel, Fabian
see: Läubin, Hannes, 8)

Merrienne, Jean-Paul
see: Ullrich, Marc

Meshkov, N.
see: Volodin, Lev

Meyer, Gustav
see: André, Maurice, 17)
see: Bauer, Willibald, 4)

Mihule, Jiří
see: André, Maurice, 220)
see: Horák, Jiří, 5)
see: Kejmar, Miroslav, 5), 8)

Milde, Friedrich
see: André, Maurice, 123), 138)
see: Gleissle, Walter, 10), 11)
see: Scherbaum, Adolf, 30)
see: Schneidewind, Helmut, 3)

Miller, Mitchell
see: Friestadt, Harry

Miller, Robin
see: Miller, John
see: Steele-Perkins, Crispian, 1)

Miller, Tess
see: André, Maurice, 36)
see: Hardenberger, Håkan
see: Jones, Philip, 5)
see: Laird, Michael, 7), 11), 15)
see: Wilbraham, John, 11), 19)

Mirschel, Andreas
see: Tarr, Edward, 17)

Miyamoto, Fumiaki
see: Immer, Friedemann, 5), 6)
see: Potpourri, 25)
see: Wolf, Hans, 6)

Mogi, Daisuke
see: Läubin, Hannes, 5), 7)

Mörchen, Hans-Ludwig
see: Güttler, Ludwig, 8), 26)

Morgan, Richard
see: Clift, Dennis
see: Webb, Gordon, 1), 2)

Morris, Charles M.
see: Johnson, Gilbert, 8)

Muggeridge, Donald
  see: Stevens, Thomas, 12)

Muhlbach, Bernhard
  see: Haas, Rudolf

Navrátil, V.
  see: Mičaník, Jaroslav

Neuranter, Roland
  see: André, Maurice, 120)

Newbury, Peter
  see: Scherbaum, Adolf, 3)

Nicklin, Celia
  see: André, Maurice, 36)
  see: Bernard, André, 12)
  see: Hardenberger, Håkan
  see: Jones, Philip, 3)
  see: Laird, Michael, 4), 15),
    21), 22)
  see: Wilbraham, John, 27)

Nikonchuk, Kirill
  see: Margolin, Veniamin

Nordbruch, Heinz
  see: Scherbaum, Adolf, 7), 35)
  see: Schmidt, Ingus

Northcutt, Barbara
  see: Plog, Anthony, 11)

Northrup, Jean
  see: Nashan, Rudolph

O'Meara, John
  see: Nashan, Rudolph

Parolari, Egon
  see: Hausdoerfer, Fred

Passin, Günther
  see: André, Maurice, 180), 199)
  see: Friedrich, Reinhold
  see: Läubin, Hannes, 3), 4), 5),
    6), 7), 8)
  see: McGregor, Rob Roy, 1),
    2), 3), 4), 5), 6)
  see: Potpourri, 48)
  see: Sauter, Hermann, 12), 13),
    14), 15), 16), 17), 19), 20),
    21), 35)
  see: Schmid, Bernhard, 5), 6),
    7), 8), 9), 10), 11)
  see: Schneidewind, Helmut, 6),
    11), 12)
  see: Send, Peter
  see: Unidentified, Trumpet(s),
    5)
  see: Wolf, Hans, 3), 5), 6), 7),
    8), 12)

Pateau, Didier
  see: Cure, Antoine
  see: Vasse, Claude

Pellerin, Louise
  see: LeComte, Jacques

Pence, Judith
  see: Greenho, David

Pierlot, Pierre
  see: André, Maurice, 12), 13),
    14), 75), 81), 83), 87), 89),
    92), 93), 94), 95), 99),
    100), 102), 106), 107), 110),
    113), 116), 122), 124), 125),
    126), 128), 143), 149), 152),
    168), 169), 172), 177), 188),
    211), 216), 217)
  see: Bernard, André, 7)
  see: Delmotte, Roger, 1), 29)
  see: Gleissle, Walter, 2), 3), 4),
    6), 7)
  see: Greffin, Jean Jacques
  see: Lagorce, Marcel
  see: Scherbaum, Adolf, 27)
  see: Schneidewind, Helmut, 5)
  see: Thibaud, Pierre, 1), 9)
  see: Unidentified, Trumpet(s),
    15)
  see: Vaillant, Ludovic, 2), 4)

Piguet, Michel
see: Immer, Friedemann, 4),
13)
see: Tarr, Edward, 2), 11), 28),
33)

Plath
see: Braeunig, Herbert

Plesnicar, Donald
see: Schwarz, Gerard, 13)

Pongrácz, Péter
see: André, Maurice, 44), 53),
227)
see: Csiba, József

Pope, Gordon
see: Stevens, Thomas, 13)

Priebe, Cheryl
see: Hoffman, Edward

Quendler, Hans
see: Spindler, Josef, 2)

Raoult, André
see: Adelbrecht, Henri, 1)
see: Scherbaum, Adolf, 1)

Rast, H.G.
see: Holy, Walter, 8)

Rau, Joachim
see: Läubin, Hannes, 3)

Ravelli, Carlo
see: Adelbrecht, Henri, 6)

Reichenberg, David
see: Bryant, Ralph, 4), 5)
see: Immer, Friedemann, 16),
17)
see: Laird, Michael, 8)
see: Potpourri, 54), 55), 57),
58), 59), 60), 61), 62)
see: Spindler, Josef, 15), 16)
see: Steele-Perkins, Crispian, 7)

Renner, Hans-Georg
see: Bodenröder, Robert
see: Potpourri, 22)
see: Tarr, Edward, 17)

Renzi, Paolo
see: Potpourri, 31)

Řepka, J.
see: Mičaník, Jaroslav

Reuter, Gerard
see: Burns, Stephen

Richards, Ronald
see: Nagel, Robert, 2)

Robson, Anthony
see: Steele-Perkins, Crispian, 5)

Rohde, Burkhard
see: Groth, Konradin

Roseman, Ronald
see: Berinbaum, Martin
see: Broiles, Melvin
see: Romm, Ronald
see: Schwarz, Gerard, 2), 6),
8), 13), 23)

Rosso, Pierre
see: Adelbrecht, Henri, 3)

Roth, Kenneth
see: Holmgren, Fred

Rothweiler, Hedda
see: Friedrich, Reinhold
see: Immer, Friedemann, 5), 6)
see: Läubin, Hannes, 3), 4), 5),
6), 7), 8)
see: McGregor, Rob Roy, 1),
2), 3), 4), 6)
see: Miller, Rodney
see: Sauter, Hermann, 1), 12),
13), 14), 15), 16), 17), 20),
21), 23), 24), 27), 35)
see: Schmid, Bernhard, 2), 3),
4), 5), 6), 7), 8), 9), 10),
11)
see: Send, Peter
see: Wolf, Hans, 2), 3), 5), 6),
7), 8), 9), 10), 11), 12)

Rothwell, Evelyn
see: Eskdale, George, 2), 4)

Row, Terry
see: Schwarz, Gerard, 1)

Rullman, Charles
  see: Potpourri, 5)

Schachman, Marc
  see: Holmgren, Fred

Schaeftlein, Jürg
  see: Bryant, Ralph, 1), 2), 3),
    4), 5)
  see: Holy, Walter, 9)
  see: Immer, Friedemann, 14),
    15), 16), 17)
  see: Potpourri, 49), 50), 51),
    52), 53), 54), 55), 56), 57),
    58), 59), 60), 61), 62), 63),
    64)
  see: Scherbaum, Adolf, 36)
  see: Spindler, Josef, 8), 10),
    11), 12), 13), 14), 15), 16)

Schaumann, Heinz
  see: André, Maurice, 171)

Schellenberger, Hansjörg
  see: Groth, Konradin
  see: Sauter, Hermann, 23)
  see: Schmid, Bernhard, 2)

Schenkel, Bernard
  see: André, Maurice, 57), 226),
    227)

Schie, Martin
  see: Junge, Harald

Schiele, Ulrike
  see: Erb, Helmut, 6)

Schmalfuss, Gernot
  see: André, Maurice, 25), 192),
    194), 196)
  see: Goethel, Siegfried
  see: Potpourri, 2), 42)
  see: Schneidewind, Helmut, 2)

Schneider, Christian
  see: Bodenröder, Robert
  see: Tarr, Edward, 28)

Schneider, Horst
  see: André, Maurice, 171)
  see: Gleissle, Walter, 1), 8)

Schnell, Willy
  see: Holy, Walter, 8)
  see: Quinque, Rolf, 7)
  see: Schneidewind, Helmut, 13)
  see: Tarr, Edward, 4)
  see: Zickler, Heinz, 2), 3)

Schöpbach, Marie-Lise
  see: Wolf, Hans, 12)

Schulz, Werner
  see: Tarr, Edward, 24), 25), 26)

Schulze, Theodora
  see: Potpourri, 34), 35)
  see: Statter, Arthur

Schuman, Henry
  see: Weis, Theodore, 1)

Schwarz, Georg
  see: Erb, Helmut, 6)

Schwarz, Thomas
  see: Sauter, Hermann, 6), 9),
    10), 11), 12), 14), 15), 35)
  see: Unidentified, Trumpet(s),
    5)

Schweinfurter, Fred
  see: Scherbaum, Adolf, 5)

Schwesinger, Heinz
  see: Scherbaum, Adolf, 7)

Schwinn, Andreas
  see: Lachenmeir, Paul
  see: Potpourri, 11)

Scott, Peter
  see: Schwarz, Gerard, 1)

Seifert, Leonhard
  see: André, Maurice, 93)
  see: Bauer, Willibald, 4)

Seigel, Joshua
  see: Berinbaum, Martin

Seitz, Richard
  see: Ziegler, Albert

Selwyn, Edward
  see: Eskdale, George, 5)
  see: Jones, Philip, 5)
  see: Wilbraham, John, 28)

Shanks, Clare
see: Immer, Friedemann, 1), 4)
see: Laird, Michael, 7), 19)

Shann, Edgar
see: André, Maurice, 17)
see: Haneuse, Arthur
see: Scherbaum, Adolf, 9)

Shapiro, Bernard
see: Pressley, Richard

Shulman, Harry
see: Crisara, Raymond, 9)
see: Karpilovsky, Murray
see: Nagel, Robert, 14)

Sirucek, Jerry
see: Davidson, Louis

Siviero, Gino
see: André, Maurice, 105)

Smith, Stanley
see: Scherbaum, Adolf, 3)

Smyles, Harry
see: Broiles, Melvin

Sous, Alfred
see: André, Maurice, 225)
see: Potpourri, 21), 34), 35)
see: Tarr, Edward, 4), 12), 37),
    38)
see: Tasa, David
see: Wolf, Hans, 1)
see: Zickler, Heinz, 1), 2), 3),
    9)

Sprenkle, Robert
see: Mear, Sidney, 1), 2), 4)

Stancliffe, Martin
see: Laird, Michael, 19)

Stannard, Warren
see: Hopkins, Kenneth

Steinert, Gustav
see: Holy, Walter, 8)
see: Scherbaum, Adolf, 31)
see: Schneidewind, Helmut, 13)

Steins, Karl
see: Scherbaum, Adolf, 12)

Stempnik, Gerhard
see: Groth, Konradin

Still, Ray
see: Herseth, Adolph, 1), 3), 6)

Storch, Laila
see: Mule, Marcel

Stotijn, Haakon
see: Groot, Willem (Wim)
see: Sevenstern, Harry

Strowitzky, Fritz
see: Gleissle, Walter, 1)

Sutcliffe, Herbert
see: Jackson, Harold

Sutcliffe, Sidney
see: Jackson, Harold
see: Scherbaum, Adolf, 3)
see: Webb, Gordon, 1)

Suzuki, Takashi
see: Junge, Harald

Swillens, Victor
see: Doets, Jas

Szabo, Herbert
see: Wobisch, Helmut, 3)

Tabuteau, Marcel
see: Krauss, Sam
see: Mule, Marcel

Taillefer, Paul
see: Scherbaum, Adolf, 20)

Taran, Anatoly
see: Gorokhov, Vitaly

Taylor, Robert
see: McGuffey, Patrick

Taylor, Stephen
see: Anderson, Ronald, 6)
see: Burns, Stephen
see: Carroll, Edward, 1), 3), 4),
    5)
see: Gould, Mark

Tennick, Angela
see: Bernard, André, 12)

Thieme, Peter
see: Güttler, Ludwig, 20)

Thorstenberg, Laurence
see: Ghitalla, Armando, 7)

Timm, Joel
see: Gould, Mark

Töttcher, Hermann
see: Scherbaum, Adolf, 7)

Trenz, Ludwig
see: André, Maurice, 10)

Turner, Joseph
see: Nowak, Henry

Tustin, Whitney
see: Burke, James, 5), 6)

Vagoun, Jaroslav
see: Kejmar, Miroslav, 8)

Valentin, Paul
see: Longinotti, Paolo

Van Den Berg, Sally
see: León, Felipe

van den Brinck, Michiel
see: Touvron, Guy, 14)

van Tright, Evert
see: Adelbrecht, Henri, 4)

Verner, Pavel
see: Kejmar, Miroslav, 8)

Vetter, Gerhard
see: Basch, Wolfgang, 6)

Vogel, Allan
see: Hood, Boyde
see: McGregor, Rob Roy, 1),
2), 5)
see: Plog, Anthony, 1), 3)
see: Schmid, Bernhard, 3)
see: Schwarz, Gerard, 1)
see: Wolf, Hans, 2), 3), 5), 8)

Wächter, Friedrich
see: Holler, Adolf
see: Rudolf, Richard

Wätzig, Hans-Werner
see: Güttler, Ludwig, 3)
see: Potpourri, 19)

Weber, Hanspeter
see: André, Maurice, 16), 123)
see: Sauter, Hermann, 5), 7),
8), 9), 13), 14), 15), 35)
see: Scherbaum, Adolf, 5), 31)
see: Schneidewind, Helmut, 3)

Wehrle, Rene
see: Unidentified, Trumpet(s),
14)

Weiner, Susan
see: Schwarz, Gerard, 8)

Weiss, David
see: Stevens, Thomas, 12)

Wells, Rosemary
see: Clift, Dennis

West, Philip
see: Broiles, Melvin
see: Miller, Rodney
see: Weis, Theodore, 1)

Westermann, Hans-Peter
see: Basch, Wolfgang, 1)
see: Immer, Friedemann, 3),
12)
see: Potpourri, 48)

Wiedenhoff, Martin
see: Hunger, Helmut, 4)

Wilson, Sophia
see: Laird, Michael, 19)

Winfield, Michael
see: Mason, David, 2)
see: Webb, Gordon, 1)
see: Wilbraham, John, 22)

Winfield, Roger
see: Webb, Gordon, 4)

Winschermann, Helmut
see: André, Maurice, 10), 16), 25), 179)
see: Basch, Wolfgang, 8)
see: Ellinghaus, Wolfram
see: Holy, Walter, 1), 2), 3)
see: Potpourri, 2), 14), 42)
see: Scherbaum, Adolf, 6)
see: Schneidewind, Helmut, 1), 2), 7)
see: Wobisch, Helmut, 8)
see: Zeyer, Adam

Winter, Otto
see: André, Maurice, 142)
see: Potpourri, 21), 34), 35)
see: Sauter, Hermann, 4), 5), 6), 7), 8), 9), 10), 11), 12), 13), 35)
see: Unidentified, Trumpet(s), 5)
see: Wolf, Hans, 1)
see: Zickler, Heinz, 1), 9)

Winters, Barbara
see: Stevens, Thomas, 12)

Wolf, Marie
see: Immer, Friedemann, 14), 15), 16)
see: Potpourri, 62), 63)

Wolfgang, Randall
see: Potpourri, 38)

Wolsing, Waldemar
see: Hovaldt, Knud

Zanfini, Renato
see: Hunger, Helmut, 2)

Zeh, Manfred
see: Scherbaum, Adolf, 13), 19), 25)

Zonn, Wilma
see: Sasaki, Ray

Zorn, Günther
see: André, Maurice, 194), 196)
see: Basch, Wolfgang, 8), 10)
see: Potpourri, 42)

Oboe d'amore
[cross-referenced under oboe]

Adamczyk, Peter
see: Potpourri, 2)

Bachert, Willi
see: Sauter, Hermann, 26)

Barnett, James John
see: Ellinghaus, Wolfram

Casier, Robert
see: André, Maurice, 6)
see: Calvayrac, Albert

Chambon, Jacques
see: André, Maurice, 94), 111)
see: Gleissle, Walter, 6)

Clement, Manfred
see: André, Maurice, 17)
see: Bauer, Willibald, 3)
see: Schmid, Bernhard, 6)
see: Thibaud, Pierre, 7)
see: Wolf, Hans, 7)

Craxton, Janet
see: Wilbraham, John, 22)

Czaja, Alfons
see: Köpp, Rudolf

Darke, Valerie
see: Potpourri, 62)
see: Steele-Perkins, Crispian, 16)

Ebach, Klaus
see: Wolf, Hans, 1)

Ebbinge, Ku
see: Immer, Friedemann, 14)
see: Potpourri, 57), 59), 60), 61)
see: Smithers, Don, 15)

Eliscu, Robert
see: Thibaud, Pierre, 7)

Glaetzner, Burkhard
see: Güttler, Ludwig, 18)

Passin, Günther
see: Friedrich, Reinhold
see: Läubin, Hannes, 3), 4), 6), 8)
see: McGregor, Rob Roy, 1), 2), 5), 6)
see: Potpourri, 48)
see: Sauter, Hermann, 12), 14), 16), 20)
see: Schmid, Bernhard, 5), 6), 7), 8), 10), 11)
see: Unidentified, Trumpet(s), 5)
see: Wolf, Hans, 3), 5)

Pierlot, Pierre
see: André, Maurice, 94), 99), 110)
see: Gleissle, Walter, 2), 4), 6)

Reichenberg, David
see: Bryant, Ralph, 4)
see: Potpourri, 59), 60), 62)

Renner, Hans-Georg
see: Potpourri, 22)

Roseman, Ronald
see: Broiles, Melvin

Roth, Kenneth
see: Holmgren, Fred

Rothweiler, Hedda
see: Friedrich, Reinhold
see: Immer, Friedemann, 5)
see: Läubin, Hannes, 6), 8)
see: McGregor, Rob Roy, 2), 6)
see: Miller, Rodney
see: Sauter, Hermann, 12), 20)
see: Schmid, Bernhard, 6), 7), 8), 10), 11)
see: Wolf, Hans, 5), 7), 11)

Schachman, Marc
see: Holmgren, Fred

Schaeftlein, Jürg
see: Bryant, Ralph, 1), 3), 4), 5)
see: Immer, Friedemann, 15)
see: Potpourri, 51), 53), 54), 55), 56), 58), 59), 60), 61), 62), 63)
see: Spindler, Josef, 10), 11), 12), 16)

Schneider, Horst
see: Gleissle, Walter, 8)

Schnell, Willy
see: Zickler, Heinz, 2)

Schwarz, Thomas
see: Unidentified, Trumpet(s), 5)

Seifert, Leonhard
see: Bauer, Willibald, 4)

Shanks, Clare
see: Immer, Friedemann, 1)

Shann, Edgar
see: André, Maurice, 17)
see: Scherbaum, Adolf, 9)

Sous, Alfred
see: Tarr, Edward, 12)
see: Wolf, Hans, 1)
see: Zickler, Heinz, 1), 2)

Taylor, Stephen
see: Carroll, Edward, 3), 4), 5)

Vogel, Allan
see: McGregor, Rob Roy, 2), 5)
see: Wolf, Hans, 5)

Weber, Hanspeter
see: André, Maurice, 16)
see: Sauter, Hermann, 8)

West, Philip
see: Broiles, Melvin

Westermann, Hans-Peter
see: Basch, Wolfgang, 1)

Winschermann, Helmut
see: André, Maurice, 16)
see: Ellinghaus, Wolfram
see: Holy, Walter, 2)
see: Schneidewind, Helmut, 1),
7)

Winter, Otto
see: Sauter, Hermann, 4), 5),
8), 12)
see: Wolf, Hans, 1)

Wolf, Marie
see: Immer, Friedemann, 15)

Oboe da caccia
[cross-referenced under oboe]

Brewer, Virginia
see: Holmgren, Fred

Chambon, Jacques
see: André, Maurice, 94)

Craxton, Janet
see: Wilbraham, John, 22)

Dhont, Pieter
see: Bryant, Ralph, 4)
see: Immer, Friedemann, 14)
see: Smithers, Don, 15)

Earle, Richard
see: Steele-Perkins, Crispian,
16)

Ebbinge, Ku
see: Bryant, Ralph, 2)

Gruber, Karl
see: Bryant, Ralph, 1)
see: Spindler, Josef, 11), 12)

Gürke, Dieter
see: Immer, Friedemann, 5)

Hailperin, Paul
see: Bryant, Ralph, 1), 5)
see: Potpourri, 53), 55), 57),
59), 60)
see: Spindler, Josef, 11)

Hauck, Hans-Ludwig
see: Tarr, Edward, 24)

Hertel, Alfred
see: Spindler, Josef, 13)

Hucke, Helmut
see: Basch, Wolfgang, 1)

Juschka, Frank
see: Holy, Walter, 1)

Keller, Dietmar
see: Immer, Friedemann, 5), 6)
see: Läubin, Hannes, 5), 8)
see: McGregor, Rob Roy, 3), 4)
see: Potpourri, 25)
see: Sauter, Hermann, 20), 21),
23)
see: Schmid, Bernhard, 2), 3)
see: Wolf, Hans, 9), 10)

Kneissl, Willi
see: Bauer, Willibald, 4)

Koch, Helmut
see: Immer, Friedemann, 6)

Lange, Christian
see: Tarr, Edward, 17)

Meyer, Gustav
see: André, Maurice, 17)
see: Bauer, Willibald, 4)

Mogi, Daisuke
see: Läubin, Hannes, 7)

Pierlot, Pierre
see: André, Maurice, 94)

Renner, Hans-Georg
see: Potpourri, 22)
see: Tarr, Edward, 17)

Rothweiler, Hedda
see: McGregor, Rob Roy, 3)
see: Sauter, Hermann, 20), 23)
see: Schmid, Bernhard, 2), 3)
see: Wolf, Hans, 10)

Schaeftlein, Jürg
see: Bryant, Ralph, 1), 2), 3),
5)
see: Potpourri, 57)
see: Spindler, Josef, 11), 16)

Schöpbach, Marie-Lise
  see: Wolf, Hans, 12)

Shann, Edgar
  see: André, Maurice, 17)

Weber, Hanspeter
  see: Sauter, Hermann, 8), 9),
      14), 15)

Westermann, Hans-Peter
  see: Basch, Wolfgang, 1)

Winfield, Michael
  see: Wilbraham, John, 22)

Winschermann, Helmut
  see: Holy, Walter, 1)

Wolf, Marie
  see: Potpourri, 62)

Ocarina

Schickele, Peter
  see: Platt, Seymour

Ondes Martenot

Loriod, Jeanne
  see: André, Maurice, 82)

Rzewski, Fredric
  see: Dean, Allan, 4)

Sibon-Simonovitch, Arlette
  see: Dean, Allan, 4)

One-handed flute

Berger, Sven
  see: Otten, Kees

One-keyed flute

Sheldon, Robert
  see: Sheldon, Robert

Organ
[includes various types: historic &
modern, pipe & electronic, regal,
etc.]

Alain, Marie-Claire
  see: André, Maurice, 35), 71),
      76), 78), 96), 97), 102),
      104), 105), 118), 124), 134),
      139), 215), 218)
  see: Gleissle, Walter, 2), 3), 4)
  see: Jeannoutot, Bernard
  see: Potpourri, 47)
  see: Vaillant, Ludovic, 6)

Alain, Olivier
  see: Greffin, Jean Jacques
  see: Scherbaum, Adolf, 20)
  see: Tarr, Edward, 31)

Albright, William
  see: Ranger, Louis

Arnold, Robert
  see: Smith, James

Bach, Gottfried
  see: André, Maurice, 192)

Bailbé, B.
  see: Lopez, Vincente

Bair, Johannes
  see: Potpourri, 48)

Bales, Gerald
  see: Chenette, Stephen

Barber, Clarence H.
  see: Coursier, Gérard

Barrett, John
  see: Victorian Trumpet Trio

Baudry-Godard, Jeanne
  see: Jorand, Jean-Claude

Beckensteiner, Anne-Marie
  see: André, Maurice, 9), 177)
  see: Tarr, Edward, 31)

Beckett, John
  see: Potpourri, 67)

Belsky, Vratislav
see: Potpourri, 40)

Bernard, Paul
see: Laird, Michael, 1)

Bernstein, Walter Heinz
see: Güttler, Ludwig, 8)

Berruti, Achille
see: André, Maurice, 114), 115)

Bickenbach, Christfried
see: Tarr, Edward, 10), 18), 21)

Biggs, E. Power
see: Ghitalla, Armando, 5)
see: Voisin, Roger, 1), 2)

Bilgram, Hedwig
see: André, Maurice, 17), 22),
27), 28), 29), 33), 35), 40),
45), 55), 59), 65), 77),
131), 141), 144), 145), 150),
156), 215), 227)
see: Goetting, Chandler
see: Lachenmeir, Paul
see: Potpourri, 11)
see: Scherbaum, Adolf, 9)
see: Thibaud, Pierre, 7)

Bjorklund, Ingegerd
see: Nystrom, Kaj

Blöchliger, Imelda
see: Schmid, Bernhard, 1)

Blümle, Heide
see: Schetsche, Walter

Bodson, Dominique
see: Capouillez, Luc
see: Waltzing, Gast

Boldrey, Richard
see: Geyer, Charles

Bovet, Guy
see: Urfer, Eric

Bowers-Broadbent,
Christopher
see: Steele-Perkins, Crispian,
17)

Boyer
see: Caens, Thierry

Brausinger, Günther
see: André, Maurice, 205)

Brewer, Edward
see: Carroll, Edward, 3), 5), 6),
7), 8), 9), 10), 11)
see: Holmgren, Fred
see: Potpourri, 32), 33)

Brough, George
see: Umbrico, Joseph

Busato, Paul
see: Schultz, Erik, 9)

Butler, Douglas
see: Sautter, Fred

Campbell, John
see: Blair, Stacy

Carl, Martin
see: Send, Peter

Celeghin, Luigi
see: Riggione, Angelo

Chapelet, Francis
see: Hardy, Francis

Childs, David
see: Potpourri, 6)

Christie, James David
see: Holmgren, Fred

Cintins, Olgerts
see: Dokshitser, Timofei, 18)

Clemenčić, René
see: Pok, František, 4)

Cleobury, Stephen
see: Steele-Perkins, Crispian,
15)

Cochereau, Pierre
see: André, Maurice, 185), 186),
187), 189), 198), 202)
see: Delmotte, Roger, 38), 39),
44)
see: Potpourri, 33), 35), 41),
43), 44)

535

Karau, Günther
see: André, Maurice, 110), 122)

Karius, Wolfgang
see: André, Maurice, 69)
see: Potpourri, 48)
see: Touvron, Guy, 12), 16),
18), 19), 20), 21)

Kauffmann, Werner
see: Zeh, Karl Heinz

Kaufmann, Diethelm
see: Erb, Helmut, 5)

Kaufmann, Eduard
see: Scherbaum, Adolf, 26)

Kaufmann, Gerd
see: Tarr, Edward, 13), 17)

Keller, Jörg-Neithardt
see: Ellinghaus, Wolfram
see: Holy, Walter, 4)

Kent, George
see: Eklund's Baroque Ensemble
see: Tarr, Edward, 39), 40), 41)

Kiel, Piet
see: Grin, Freddy, 1)

Kircheis, Christoph
see: Güttler, Ludwig, 2), 6),
22)

Kircheis, Friedrich
see: Güttler, Ludwig, 4), 6),
15), 21), 23), 24)

Klinda, Ferdinand
see: Kejmar, Miroslav, 1)

Klomp, Dick
see: Grin, Freddy, 3)

Knüsel, Guido
see: Conrad, Jörg

Kobayashi, Michio
see: Tamiya, Kenji

Koch, Johannes
see: Renz, Albrecht, 1), 2), 3)

Koch, P. Ambros
see: Rippas, Claude

Kolafa, Jiří
see: Pok, František, 5)

Kontarsky, Aloys
see: Jurča, Vladimir

Koopman, Ton
see: Spindler, Josef, 13)

Kraemer, Nicholas
see: Laird, Michael, 2)

Krämer, Leo
see: Grin, Freddy, 4)

Krapp, Edgar
see: Bernard, André, 4), 9), 11)
see: Webb, Gordon, 3)

Krček, Jaroslav
see: Pok, František, 6)

Kröll, Georg
see: Schoof, Manfred

Krüger, Irmtraud
see: Tarr, Edward, 7), 8), 44)

Krumbach, Wilhelm
see: Scherbaum, Adolf, 17)

Kümmerlin, Ludwig
see: Braz, Dirceu, 3)

Laberge, André
see: Chatel, Jean-Louis

Lancaster, Sam
see: Endsley, Gerald

Lancelot, James
see: Laird, Michael, 14)

Landale, Susan
see: Groth, Konradin

Langlais, Jean
see: André, Maurice, 78)

Larson, Janåke
see: Hardenberger, Håkan

Lauterbach, Peter
see: Wolf, Hans, 13)

Leach, Andrew
  see: Laird, Michael, 14)

Leclerc, Michelle
  see: Cure, Antoine

Lécot, Jean-Paul
  see: Loustalot, Alain

Lehmann, Christoph
  see: Immer, Friedemann, 11),
  18)

Lehrndorfer, Franz
  see: Bauer, Willibald, 4)
  see: Potpourri, 22)
  see: Unidentified, Trumpet(s),
  21)

Leonhardt, Gustav
  see: André, Maurice, 222), 223),
  224), 225)
  see: Bryant, Ralph, 2), 4), 5)
  see: Groot, Willem (Wim)
  see: Immer, Friedemann, 14)
  see: Potpourri, 51), 52), 57),
  58), 59), 60), 61), 63)
  see: Smithers, Don, 13), 14),
  15)
  see: Spindler, Josef, 11), 13),
  14), 15)

Lester, Harold
  see: Rudolf, Richard

Liedecke, Herbert
  see: Maier, Hans Walter

Lohman, Ludger
  see: Tamiya, Kenji

Louchart, Jean-Michel
  see: Parramon, Henry

Luy, André
  see: André, Maurice, 163), 164)

Malcolm, George
  see: Wilbraham, John, 11), 16)

Mann, Sy
  see: Lieberman, Harold J.

Manz, André
  see: Scherbaum, Adolf, 32)

Maranca, Elisabeth
  see: Wolf, Hans, 5)

Marichal, Jacques
  see: Gaudon, Jean-Jacques

Marion, Sander van
  see: Grin, Freddy, 8)

Martin, Carol Feather
  see: Birch, Robert

May, Ernest
  see: Chesnut, Walter

Maynard, Paul
  see: Davenport, LaNoue
  see: Montesi, Robert, 3), 4), 5)

Maysenhölder, Günther
  see: Rehm, Klaus

Mencke, Herfried
  see: Rausch, Heiner

Metten, Elfried
  see: Renz, Albrecht, 7)

Meyer, Hannes
  see: Schmidhäusler, Francis &
  René

Meyer, Wolfgang
  see: Tarr, Edward, 19), 20)

Miedema, Barbara
  see: Otten, Kees

Mitterhofer, Alfred
  see: André, Maurice, 40), 42),
  50), 159), 227)

Morançon, Guy
  see: Gabel, Bernard, 2)

Morisset-Bailier,
  Marie-Andrée
  see: Morisset, Michel

Morris, Richard
  see: Berinbaum, Martin

Muhr, Roland
  see: Zapf, Gerd

Müller, Eduard
see: André, Maurice, 26), 30)
see: Wobisch, Helmut, 8)

Murray, Edward
see: Dean, Allan, 4)

Murray, Gordon
see: Ferry, Dennis

Neary, Martin
see: Wilbraham, John, 23)

Nebois, Josef
see: Wobisch, Helmut, 1)

Neil, William
see: Hickman, David, 6)
see: Smithers, Don, 6), 7), 9)

Neuhaus, Wilhelm
see: Tarr, Edward, 19)

Neumann, Peter
see: Basch, Wolfgang, 1)

Newman, Anthony
see: Carroll, Edward, 12)

Nicholson, Paul
see: Steele-Perkins, Crispian, 10)

Niel, Gabriel
see: Bouche

Nitzschke, Rüdiger
see: Potpourri, 2)

Obermayer, Ernst
see: Renz, Albrecht, 6)

Ochse, Orpha
see: Plog, Anthony, 10)

Oehms, Wolfgang
see: Unidentified, Trumpet(s), 21)

Okano, Ryoko
see: Braz, Dirceu, 1)

Orlinski, Heinz-Bernhard
see: Grin, Freddy, 5)

Overduin, Jan
see: Schultz, Erik, 2), 3), 4), 10)

Oxentyan, N.
see: Potpourri, 30)

Pagenel, André
see: Dutot, Pierre

Pangritz, Thomas
see: Yamamoto, Eisuke

Parker-Smith, Jane
see: André, Maurice, 38), 40), 42), 44), 52), 67), 227)

Paterson, Donald R. M.
see: Stith, Marice, 6)

Pearson, Leslie
see: Potpourri, 1)
see: Wilbraham, John, 3), 24), 26)

Pearson, Tom
see: Crisara, Raymond, 2)

Pertis, Zsuzsa
see: André, Maurice, 43), 57), 227)

Petrenz, Siegfried
see: André, Maurice, 16)

Pflüger, Hans Georg
see: Schmitt, Siegfried

Pierront, Noëellie
see: André, Maurice, 71)

Pinkham, Daniel
see: Voisin, Roger, 3)

Pontremoli, Anita
see: Dolce, Christine

Preston, Simon
see: Laird, Michael, 7)
see: Läubin, Hannes, 2)
see: Potpourri, 42), 46)
see: Smithers, Don, 1), 4)
see: Stringer, Alan, 4)
see: Wilbraham, John, 19)

Pulfer, Jean-Marc
see: André, Maurice, 70)
see: Thibaud, Pierre, 9)

Rabol, Georges
see: Molénat, Claude

Rainer, Ingomar
see: Stradner, Gerhard

Raver, Leonard
see: Dean, Allan, 9)

Rawsthorne, Noel
see: Stringer, Alan, 3)

Ricken, Johannes
see: Basch, Wolfgang, 5)

Riddle, Pauline
see: Thomas, Peggy Paton

Riedo, Paul
see: Giangiulio, Richard

Rifkin, Joshua
see: Holmgren, Fred

Riley, Doug
see: Schultz, Erik, 8)

Robertson, Eric
see: Schultz, Erik, 8)

Rodgers, James
see: McGuffey, Patrick

Rogg, Lionel
see: Potpourri, 47)
see: Tarr, Edward, 32)

Romanov, Boris
see: Unidentified, Trumpet(s),
16)

Ropek, Jiří
see: Junek, Václav, 5)

Ross, Alastair
see: Steele-Perkins, Crispian,
16)
see: Wilbraham, John, 18)

Roth, Daniel
see: Perinelli, René

Rothe, David
see: Winslow, Richard

Rübsam, Wolfgang
see: Basch, Wolfgang, 11)

Ruhland, Elisabeth
see: Neunhoeffer, Frieder

Scheidegger, Rudolf
see: Tarr, Edward, 3), 34)

Schloter, Elmar
see: André, Maurice, 19)
see: Thibaud, Pierre, 7)

Schmid, Bärbel
see: Miller, Rodney

Schmid, Bernhard
see: Sauter, Hermann, 2)

Schneider, Gisbert
see: Holy, Walter, 1)

Schneider, Michael
see: André, Maurice, 2)
see: Zeyer, Adam

Schneider, Norbert J.
see: Läubin, Hannes, 9)

Schnorr, Klemens
see: Michel, Jean-François

Scholz, Rudolf
see: Eichhorn, Holger

Schönstedt, Arno
see: Holy, Walter, 3)
see: Schneidewind, Helmut, 2)

Schönstedt, Rolf
see: Rhoten, Bruce

Schuba, Konrad Philipp
see: Quinque, Rolf, 3)

Schuster, Martha
see: Läubin, Hannes, 5), 8)
see: McGregor, Rob Roy, 6)
see: Sauter, Hermann, 4), 5),
    6), 7), 8), 9), 10), 11), 12),
    13), 14), 15), 16), 17), 18),
    21), 22), 35)
see: Schmid, Bernhard, 4)
see: Unidentified, Trumpet(s),
    5)

Sherman, Roger
see: Sautter, Fred

Sibertin-Blanc, Antoine
see: Gabel, Bernard, 4)

Siedel, Mathias
see: Holy, Walter, 6)

Silvester, F.C.
see: Anderson, George

Sirotskaya, Nataly
see: Yudashkin, Georgy

Šlechta, Milan
see: Horák, Jiří, 1), 2)
see: Kejmar, Miroslav, 13)
see: Kozderka, Vladislav
see: Pok, František, 5)

Slimáček, Jan
see: Buriánek, Jindřich

Sluys, Jozef
see: Capouillez, Luc

Smalley, Roger
see: Stockhausen, Markus, 4)

Smith, Edward
see: Montesi, Robert, 6)

Sojcic, Zeljko
see: Tschotschev,
    Nicolai-Dimitrov

Soly, Geneviève
see: Thompson, James

Somerville, Murray
see: Wiggans, Brian

Sonnleitner, Johann
see: Bryant, Ralph, 1)
see: Potpourri, 53), 55), 58),
    60)
see: Spindler, Josef, 11)

Suter, Jeremy
see: Laird, Michael, 16)

Swearingen, Madolyn
see: Plog, Anthony, 2)

Tachezi, Herbert
see: Bryant, Ralph, 1), 3), 4),
    5)
see: Immer, Friedemann, 14),
    15), 17)
see: Potpourri, 49), 50), 51),
    52), 53), 54), 55), 56), 57),
    58), 59), 60), 61), 62), 63),
    64)
see: Spindler, Josef, 7), 9), 10),
    11), 12), 13), 14), 15), 16)
see: Tarr, Edward, 45)
see: Wobisch, Helmut, 6), 11)

Tagliavini, Luigi-Ferdinando
see: André, Maurice, 105), 114),
    115)

Tambyeff, Raphaël
see: Gabel, Bernard, 5)

Teeuwsen, Christiaan
see: Laughton, Stuart

Thalben-Ball, George
see: Jackson, Harold

Thalheim, Armin
see: Güttler, Ludwig, 3)

Thomas, Ladd
see: Plog, Anthony, 5)

Tilney, Colin
see: Tuckwell, Barry

Torrent, Montserrat
see: Sauter, Hermann, 23), 24)
see: Schmid, Bernhard, 2)

Vad, Knud
see: Gabel, Bernard, 1)

Valach, Jan
see: Unidentified, Trumpet(s), 19)

van Asperen, Bob
see: Bryant, Ralph, 2), 4), 5)
see: Immer, Friedemann, 14)
see: Potpourri, 52), 57), 58), 59), 60), 61), 63)
see: Smithers, Don, 13), 14), 15)
see: Spindler, Josef, 14), 15)

van Hoof, Harry
see: Grin, Freddy, 6), 7)

van Twillert, Willem
see: Hopman, Herman

Vaughan, Denis
see: Eskdale, George, 5)

Vidrich, Arthur
see: Pearson, Byron

Volkov, A.
see: Orvid, Georgy

Volle, Sverre
see: Volle, Bjarne

von Karajan, Hedy
see: Eichhorn, Holger

von Karajan, Wolfgang
see: Eichhorn, Holger

Voppel, Konrad
see: Krystek, Ulrich

Walcha, Helmut
see: André, Maurice, 26)
see: Scherbaum, Adolf, 14)

Walter, Fritz
see: Wolf, Hans, 8)

Weinberger, Gerhard
see: Erb, Helmut, 2)
see: Quinque, Rolf, 4)

Weinmann, Hildegard
see: Send, Peter

Westenholz, Elisabeth
see: Tarr, Edward, 5)

Westermann, Klaus
see: Potpourri, 44)

Weyer, Martin
see: Hartog, Thomas

Widensky, Peter
see: Idinger, Matthias
see: Pok, František, 2)

Wilkesmann, Dorothea
see: Krystek, Ulrich

Wills, Arthur
see: Read, David

Wilson, Glenn
see: Smithers, Don, 15)

Wisskirchen, Paul
see: Haas, Wolfgang

Withrow, Scott
see: McGuffey, Patrick

Wolfe, Gerlad
see: Stith, Marice, 9)

Wyrick, Julie
see: Tolley, Richard

Zanaboni, Giuseppe
see: Battagliola, Anania

Zartner, Rudolf
see: Fink, Werner
see: Holy, Walter, 5)
see: Tarr, Edward, 23)

Oriental shawm

Munrow, David
see: Laird, Michael, 1)

Panpipes (Panflute)

Fonville, John
see: Sasaki, Ray

Kelber, Sebastian
see: Tarr, Edward, 12)

Turner, John
see: Laird, Michael, 1)

Percussion
[includes timpani]

Applebaum, Terry
see: Miller, Rodney
see: Perry, Brian

Armengol, R.
see: Foriscot, J.

Arnold, David
see: Watson, James

Bähr, Frank
see: Schneidewind, Helmut, 11)

Bähr, Heinz
see: Tarr, Edward, 28)

Bailey, Eldon
see: Mueller, Herbert
see: Potpourri, 31)

Baker, Don
see: Potpourri, 66)
see: Sasaki, Ray

Baker, James
see: Burns, Stephen

Bardach, Nicholas
see: Touvron, Guy, 18), 19)

Bauer, Vincent
see: Cure, Antoine

Baumgartner, Virgil
see: Bastin, Ernie

Beckett, John
see: Potpourri, 67)

Begun, Fred
see: Geisler, Lloyd
see: Ghitalla, Armando, 10)

Bender, Karlheinz
see: Scholz, Walter

Berlioz, Pierre
see: André, Maurice, 92)

Bernas, Richard
see: Stockhausen, Markus, 4)

Bernhardt, Lynn
see: Carroll, Edward, 12)

Bittrich, Lilofee
see: Braz, Dirceu, 2)

Blackshere, Lawrence
see: Metzger, Charles

Blades, James
see: Clift, Dennis
see: Jones, Philip, 2)
see: Mason, David, 3), 5)

Blankfort, William
see: Potpourri, 31)

Blegen, Niles
see: Potpourri, 66)

Bookspan, Michael
see: Ghitalla, Armando, 10)

Borodkin, Sam
see: Glantz, Harry, 6)

Bramvall, Anders
see: Eklund's Baroque Ensemble

Bratman, Carroll
see: Crisara, Raymond, 9)

Braugham, Charles
see: Bastin, Ernie
see: Potpourri, 66)

Britton, Peter
see: Miller, John

Brown, Ashley
see: Wallace, John, 6)

Cambreling, Benoît
see: Touvron, Guy, 21)

Camozi, Jean
see: André, Maurice, 92)

Carlyss, Gerald
see: Johnson, Gilbert, 8)

Casadesus, Jean-Claude
see: André, Maurice, 82)

Caskel, Christoph
see: Bauer, Adam
see: Holy, Walter, 6)
see: Tarr, Edward, 14)

Castagne, Robert
see: André, Maurice, 120)

Castka, Joseph
see: Glantz, Harry, 6)

Catin, Charles
see: Ghitalla, Armando, 10)

Cauberghs, Louis
see: Mertens, Theo, 1), 3)

Cavaillé, André
see: Ménardi, Louis

Cavallaro, Armand
see: Molénat, Claude

Cerutti, Michel
see: Cure, Antoine

Charbonneau, Louis
see: LeComte, Jacques

Ciampolini, Daniel
see: Cure, Antoine

Claiborne, Tom
see: Henderson, Douglas

Clemenčič, René
see: Pok, František, 2), 4)

Cohen, Joel
see: Cook, Richard

Cole, Nicholas
see: Watson, James

Combs, J.C.
see: Potpourri, 6)

Corkhill, David
see: Laird, Michael, 1), 2), 11), 19)
see: Miller, John
see: Smithers, Don, 3), 6)

Culley, James
see: Dolce, Christine

Cypriani, Guy
see: Thibaud, Pierre, 9)

Dahlgren, Marvin
see: Chenette, Stephen

D'Amico, Achilles
see: Schwarz, Gerard, 13)

D'Amico, Louis
see: Schwarz, Gerard, 13)

D'Angelo, Robert
see: Miller, Rodney

Davis, Alan
see: Bastin, Ernie

Debij, Louis
see: Grin, Freddy, 7)

Dejean, Pierre
see: Delmotte, Roger, 7), 26)

DeLancey, Charles
see: Bush, Irving

Delécluse, Jacques
see: André, Maurice, 92)
see: Ménardi, Louis

Delmas, Yvan
see: André, Maurice, 120)

Denov, Sam
see: Herseth, Adolph, 4)

Depannemaker, Serge
see: Thibaud, Pierre, 9)

DesRoches, Raymond
see: Anderson, Ronald, 1), 3), 4), 6)
see: Dean, Allan, 1), 3), 4), 5), 6), 7), 8)
see: Ferrantino, Kenneth
see: Nagel, Robert, 18), 20)
see: Romm, Ronald

Donaldson, Charles
see: Clift, Dennis

Donaldson, John
see: Laird, Michael, 13)
see: Smithers, Don, 3)

Dorn, William
see: Glantz, Harry, 6)
see: Potpourri, 31)

Dotson, James
see: Hohstadt, Thomas

Drouet, Jean-Pierre
see: André, Maurice, 82)

Druckman, Daniel
see: Burns, Stephen

Engelman, John R.
see: Rapier, Leon, 3)

Engelman, Robin
see: Chenette, Stephen

Epstein, Frank
see: Metzger, Charles

Erickson, Robert
see: Logan, Jack

Ernst, Marcus
see: Adelbrecht, Henri, 3)
see: Potpourri, 47)
see: Tarr, Edward, 32)

Fabrizio, Art
see: Henderson, Douglas

Fairchild, Fred
see: Bastin, Ernie

Farberman, Harold
see: Ghitalla, Armando, 10)
see: Weis, Theodore, 2)

Fein, Paul
see: Montesi, Robert, 3)

Fennell, Frederick
see: Hohstadt, Thomas

Fiebig, Eckhard
see: Adelbrecht, Henri, 1)

Fine, Elliot
see: Chenette, Stephen

Firth, Everett
see: Ghitalla, Armando, 5), 6),
7), 8), 9)

Fischer, Wolfgang
see: Held, Friedrich

Fitz, Richard
see: Anderson, Ronald, 1), 3)
see: Crisara, Raymond, 1)
see: Dean, Allan, 3), 4), 5), 6),
7), 8)
see: Nagel, Robert, 18)
see: Romm, Ronald

Fletcher, Charles
see: Jones, Philip, 11)

Flower, Reginald
see: Jones, Philip, 11)

Forestier, Jean-Claude
see: Adelbrecht, Henri, 3)

François, Jean-Charles
see: André, Maurice, 82)

Frazeur, Theodore
see: Hohstadt, Thomas

Freeman, Harold
see: Glantz, Harry, 6)

Friedman, David
see: Crisara, Raymond, 2)

Fry, Allan
see: Jones, Philip, 11)
see: Webb, Gordon, 2)

Fry, Tristan
see: Izan, Bernard
see: Webb, Gordon, 2)
see: Wilbraham, John, 1)

Fullbrook, Charles
see: Laird, Michael, 7)
see: Steele-Perkins, Crispian, 7)

Gaber, George
see: Potpourri, 31)

Garrido, Gabriel
see: André, Maurice, 64), 227)

Gartner, Hans
see: Wobisch, Helmut, 3)

Gasquet, Pierre
see: Jarmasson, Jacques

Gauger, Thomas
see: Metzger, Charles

Georgin, Guy
see: André, Maurice, 120)

Glamsch, Harald
see: Adelbrecht, Henri, 3)

Goldberg, Arnold
see: Ghitalla, Armando, 10)

Goldberg, Morris
see: Glantz, Harry, 6)

Goodwin, Bill
see: Mase, Raymond

Goodwin, Walter
see: Bush, Irving
see: Stevens, Thomas, 4)

Gordon, James
see: Miller, Rodney

Gordy (III), Marvin B.
see: Guarneri, Mario

Gottlieb, Gordon
see: Anderson, Ronald, 4)
see: Carroll, Edward, 10)
see: Dean, Allan, 4), 6)
see: Potpourri, 6)
see: Schwarz, Gerard, 6), 7)
see: Stubbs, James

Grant, P.
see: Burke, James, 6)

Green, Michael
see: Herseth, Adolph, 4)

Gregory, Scott
see: Henderson, Douglas

Grimes, John
see: Logan, Jack

Gualda, Sylvio
see: André, Maurice, 145)

Gubin, Sol
see: Butterfield, Billy

Guillon, Patrice
see: Aquitaine Brass Ensemble

Guntern, Michael
see: Sommerhalder, Max

Haas, Jonathan
see: Potpourri, 38)

Hammer, Kurt
see: Immer, Friedemann, 14), 15)
see: Potpourri, 51), 52), 53), 54), 55), 56), 60), 62)
see: Spindler, Josef, 7), 8), 9), 10), 12), 13), 14), 15), 16)

Hanicot, René
see: André, Maurice, 92)
see: Delmotte, Roger, 35)

Hanson, Eileen
see: Bastin, Ernie

Harbold, Lynn
see: Kuehn, David

Harms, Ben
see: Holmgren, Fred

Harris, Herbert
see: Broiles, Melvin
see: Crisara, Raymond, 2), 5)

Hartenberger, Russell
see: Malone, Michael
see: Mills, Fred

Hassbecker, Siegfried
see: Güttler, Ludwig, 21), 23)

Heim, Alyn
see: Schwarz, Gerard, 13)

Heldrich, Claire L.
see: Anderson, Ronald, 1), 4), 6)
see: Dean, Allan, 4), 6), 8)
see: Potpourri, 5)

Herdi, Urs
see: Adelbrecht, Henri, 3)

Herzog, Roland
see: Luithle, Rainer

Hinger, Fred
see: Schwarz, Gerard, 13)

Hochrainer, R.
see: Eichhorn, Holger

Hoffnung, Benedict
see: Watson, James

Hogwood, Christopher
see: Laird, Michael, 1), 3)

Holland, James
see: Jones, Philip, 11)
see: Miller, John
see: Snell, Howard

Hollard
see: Pollin, Pierre

Holm, Mathias
see: Potpourri, 11)

Horowitz, Richard
see: Potpourri, 31)

Howard, Alfred
see: Ghitalla, Armando, 10)
see: Nagel, Robert, 1), 7)

Howard, Douglas
see: Giangiulio, Richard

Howarth, Jackson
see: Ghitalla, Armando, 10)

Howes, Robert
see: Steele-Perkins, Crispian, 10)

Humair, Daniel
see: André, Maurice, 8)

Israel, Brian
see: Stith, Marice, 4)

Jabara, Martin
see: Plog, Anthony, 11)

Jacquillat, Jean-Pierre
see: André, Maurice, 92)

Jeffery, John
see: Watson, James

Jonak, Anton
see: Spindler, Josef, 1)

Jones, Brian
see: Lowrey, Alvin

Joosten, Arndt
see: Pohle, Wolfgang

Junge, Wieland
see: Sauter, Hermann, 24)

Junghänel, Konrad
see: Caudle, Theresa

Kaenzig, Fritz
see: Potpourri, 66)

Kasas, Speros
see: Potpourri, 31)

Kassica, John
see: Crisara, Raymond, 2)

Kauffmann, Jean-Pierre
see: André, Maurice, 120)

Kecskés, András
see: Pok, František, 4)

Kilgore, Brian
see: Parker, Craig B.

King, Frederick
see: Montesi, Robert, 4), 6)

Kizer, Kevin
see: Potpourri, 66)

Kocmieroski, Mathew
see: Pressley, Richard

Köhler, Walter
see: Adelbrecht, Henri, 1)

Kohloff, Roland
see: Schwarz, Gerard, 20)

Kopf, Richard
see: Ghitalla, Armando, 10)

Koss, Donald
see: Herseth, Adolph, 4), 6)
see: Vosburgh, George

Kraft, William
  see: Brady, Charles
  see: Bush, Irving

Kraus, Phil
  see: Butterfield, Billy

Krček, Jaroslav
  see: Buriánek, Jindřich

Kregal, Jesse
  see: Geisler, Lloyd

Krell, Stanley
  see: Potpourri, 31)

Kühn, Werner
  see: Schmitt, Siegfried

Küttner, Michael
  see: Stockhausen, Markus, 2)

Kvistad, Richard
  see: Metzger, Charles

Lake, Donald
  see: Bastin, Ernie

Lamb, Christopher
  see: Carroll, Edward, 12)

Lane, James
  see: Herseth, Adolph, 4)

Lang, Morris
  see: Ghitalla, Armando, 10)
  see: Jandorf, D.

Laverack, William
  see: Schwarz, Gerard, 13)

Leavitt, Joseph
  see: Geisler, Lloyd

Lemaire, Gérard
  see: André, Maurice, 147)

Leonard, Brian
  see: Canadian Brass, 3)
  see: Schultz, Erik, 8)

Lesbines, Tele
  see: Murtha, Roger

Leue, Eckhard
  see: Immer, Friedemann, 18)

Lighton, Ernest
  see: Roberts, Standish

Lindenfeld, Harris
  see: Stith, Marice, 4)

Magadini, Peter
  see: Mills, Fred

Manigley, Roland
  see: Adelbrecht, Henri, 3)

Marcus, Abraham
  see: Ghitalla, Armando, 10)
  see: Potpourri, 31)

Marotti, Artie
  see: Smith, Bramwell "Bram"

Marsh, George
  see: Bastin, Ernie

Masson, Diego
  see: André, Maurice, 82)

Mawson, John
  see: Victorian Trumpet Trio

McCarty, Frank
  see: Logan, Jack

McCormick, John
  see: Lowrey, Alvin

McKenzie, Kevan
  see: Schultz, Erik, 8)

Metral, Pierre
  see: Cuvit, Michel

Meyn, Rob
  see: Grin, Freddy, 7)

Millar, Keith
  see: Evans, Laurie

Miller, Gary
  see: Schwarz, Gerard, 13)

Mitchell, Danlee
  see: Logan, Jack

Montagu, Jeremy
  see: Potpourri, 67)

Morehouse, Chauncey
see: Burke, James, 5), 6)
see: Crisara, Raymond, 10)

Morel, M.
see: Foveau, Eugène

Müller, Horst
see: Gass, Josef

Neff, Jerome
see: Metzger, Charles

Nemish, Barry
see: Lowrey, Alvin

Neuhaus, Max
see: Mills, Fred

Newton, Rodney
see: Watson, James

Nikulin, R.
see: Volodin, Lev

Ogorodnikov, A.
see: Dokshitser, Timofei, 29)

Otte, Allen
see: Dolce, Christine

Ouderits, Leo
see: Mertens, Theo, 1), 3)

Parsons, William
see: Bastin, Ernie
see: Potpourri, 5)

Passaro, Joseph
see: Dean, Allan, 6)
see: Ranger, Louis

Payson, Albert
see: Herseth, Adolph, 4)

Pazzaro, Louis
see: Ghitalla, Armando, 10)

Peck, Norman
see: Burkhart, David

Peinecke, Karl-Heinz
see: Sauter, Hermann, 7), 8),
17), 18)

Peinkofer, Karl
see: Basch, Wolfgang, 14)
see: Tarr, Edward, 38)

Peinkofer, Ralph
see: Potpourri, 22)

Pennington, Roy
see: Stubbs, James

Pérotin, Gérard
see: André, Maurice, 49)
see: Gabel, Bernard, 2)
see: Thibaud, Pierre, 9)

Peschier, Charles
see: André, Maurice, 181)
see: Longinotti, Paolo

Peters, Gordon
see: Herseth, Adolph, 4)
see: Hohstadt, Thomas

Peters, Mitchell
see: Bush, Irving
see: Guarneri, Mario
see: Hohstadt, Thomas
see: Stevens, Thomas, 1), 2),
4), 5), 10), 16)

Petsch, Gerhard
see: Gass, Josef

Pluth, Linda Schell
see: Logan, Jack

Pok, František
see: Pok, František, 4)

Ponemba, Edward
see: Miller, Rodney

Poremba, Edward
see: Perry, Brian

Pratt, Daryl
see: Harkins, Edwin

Press, Arthur
see: Ghitalla, Armando, 5), 10)

Price, Paul
see: Nagel, Robert, 5)

551

Seaman, Christopher
see: Webb, Gordon, 2)

See, Cees
see: Schoof, Manfred

Shimizu, Yukio
see: Kierski, Eckhard

Shoemake, Charlie
see: Stevens, Thomas, 9)

Simon, Jimmy
see: Ghitalla, Armando, 10)

Sinatra, Frank
see: Geisler, Lloyd

Singer, Erich
see: Tarr, Edward, 3), 17), 34)

Sirotta, Michael
see: Miller, Rodney

Sitar, Helmut
see: Hardenberger, Håkan

Siwe, Thomas
see: Ferrantino, Kenneth
see: Miller, Rodney

Skinner, Michael
see: Watson, James

Slivka, Meyer
see: Haug, Edward

Smith, Charles
see: Voisin, Roger, 10)

Smith, David
see: Miller, Rodney

Smith
see: Hyatt, Jack

Snegirev, Valentin
see: Maximenko, Anatoly, 3)
see: Volodin, Lev

Snyder, Jane
see: Henderson, Douglas

Snyder, Terry
see: Butterfield, Billy

Spangler, Ward
see: Burkhart, David

Spinney, Bradley
see: Burke, James, 5), 6)

Šprunk, Petr
see: Horák, Jiří, 3), 5)
see: Junek, Václav, 4)

Steedman, Heather
see: Watson, James

Steinberger, Karl
see: Bauer, Willibald, 3)

Stepanov, Boris
see: Maximenko, Anatoly, 1)

Stout, Gordon
see: Levy, Robert

Studer, Fredy
see: Stockhausen, Markus, 6)

Stuttsman, James
see: Bastin, Ernie

Surnachev, Vladimir
see: Gorokhov, Vitaly

Szulc, Roman
see: Voisin, Roger, 2)

Szymanski, Norbert
see: Miller, Rodney

Tavernier, J.C.
see: Pollin, Pierre

Taylor, Norman
see: Watson, James

Thärichen, Werner
see: Touvron, Guy, 19)

Thrailkill
see: Patti, Douglas

Tilkin, Morris
see: Potpourri, 31)

Tolansky, Jonathan
see: Watson, James

Traxler, Gene
see: Lieberman, Harold J.

Truyens, Herman
see: Mertens, Theo, 1), 3)

Tyler, James
see: Laird, Michael, 1)

Udow, Michael
see: Sasaki, Ray

Ulsamer, Josef
see: Otto, Joachim

Vandersteene, Zeger
see: Pok, František, 4)

van der Ven-Ulsamer, Elza
see: Otto, Joachim

Van Hyning, Howard
see: Anderson, Ronald, 1), 4)
see: Dean, Allan, 4), 6), 8)

Verbeeck, Alois
see: Mertens, Theo, 1)

Vérité
see: Caens, Thierry

Waddell, Douglas
see: Potpourri, 38)

Waggott, Colin
see: Garside, Derek M.

Wallez, Gus
see: André, Maurice, 69), 70)

Wallin, Peter
see: Hardenberger, Håkan

Ward, Robert
see: Dallas Brass

Wasson, John
see: Dallas Brass

Wendrich, Kenneth
see: Hohstadt, Thomas

Wherry, Donald
see: Umbrico, Joseph

Whittaker, Stephen
see: Jones, Philip, 2)

Wilhelm, Willy
see: Sauter, Hermann, 2)

Wilson, Larry
see: Schwarz, Gerard, 20)

Wimmer, Rudolf
see: Spindler, Josef, 2)

Wirweitzki, Peter
see: Schmid, Bernhard, 11)

Woodhull, David
see: Miller, Rodney

Woud, Nick
see: Bryant, Ralph, 5)
see: Immer, Friedemann, 14)
see: Potpourri, 58)
see: Smithers, Don, 14)

Wuliger, David
see: Weast, Robert

Wyre, John
see: Nowak, Henry

Youhass, William
see: Dolce, Christine
see: Levy, Robert

Zambrano, Rafael
see: Adelbrecht, Henri, 3)

Piano
[includes "prepared piano" & electric keyboards]

Adamec, Petr
see: Kejmar, Miroslav, 7)

Alexeev, Dmitri
see: Jones, Philip, 4)

Aller, Victor
see: Klein, Manny

Andersen, Jørgen
see: Christensen, Ketil

Anderson, Leroy
see: Burke, James, 1)

Andrievskaya, Tatiana
see: Dokshitser, Timofei, 21)

Angeleri, Franco
see: Leroy, Jean-Paul

Angeleri, Micaela Mingardo
see: Leroy, Jean-Paul

Argerich, Martha
see: Adelbrecht, Henri, 3)

Arutunian, Alexander
see: Balyan, Yuri

Asmaryan, T.
see: Balyan, Yuri

Auer, Edward
see: Adelbrecht, Henri, 3)

Baloghová, Dagmar
see: Kejmar, Miroslav, 4)

Balsam, Artur
see: Mills, Fred

Barbizet, Pierre
see: Delmotte, Roger, 4)

Barth, Helmuth
see: Schmidt, Ingus

Baudo, Serge
see: Delmotte, Roger, 18)

Bergmann, Maria
see: Potpourri, 39)
see: Scholz, Walter

Bernardi, Mario
see: LeComte, Jacques

Bernstein, Leonard
see: Vacchiano, William, 1)

Bernstein, Seymour
see: Ware, John

Béroff, Michel
see: André, Maurice, 49)

Bilson, Malcolm
see: Stith, Marice, 3)

Blackwood, Easley
see: Vosburgh, George

Bles, Theo
see: Ros, Ad

Bodin, Esther
see: Schrello, Mark

Bogin, Abba
see: Burke, James, 7)

Bolcom, William
see: Schwarz, Gerard, 19)

Bolling, Claude
see: André, Maurice, 8)

Bovet, Guy
see: Urfer, Eric

Bradshaw, Susan
see: Jones, Philip, 11)

Bratlie, Jens Harald
see: Kvebaek, Harry

Brejcha, Antonín
see: Buriánek, Jindřich

Brown, Harold
see: Hopkins, Kenneth

Brüninghaus, Rainer
see: Stockhausen, Markus, 6)

Bunger, Richard
see: Stevens, Thomas, 16)

Burnham, Lucille
see: Karpilovsky, Murray

Bussotti, Carlo
see: Nagel, Robert, 12)

Carno, Zita
see: Crisara, Raymond, 2)
see: McNab, Malcolm
see: Stevens, Thomas, 4), 6),
7), 9), 16)

Catelinet, Philip B.
see: Reynolds, George

Chang, Yi-An
see: Anderson, Ronald, 1)

Charpentier, Maryse
see: Ménardi, Louis

Chen, You-hsiu
see: Yeh, Shu-han

Ciccolini, Aldo
see: Lagorce, Antoine

Cobb, John
see: Miller, Rodney

Collard, Jean-Philippe
see: André, Maurice, 49)

Collier, Jay
see: Burkart, Richard

Constable, John
see: Miller, John

Cooper, H. Rex
see: Haneuse, Arthur

Cooper, Kenneth
see: Schwarz, Gerard, 21)

Cope, David
see: Levy, Robert

Corea, Chick
see: Carroll, Edward, 2)

Covert, Mary Ann
see: Ode, James

Craft, Robert
see: Heinrich, Robert

Crane, Fredrick
see: Dudgeon, Ralph

Crisara, Margaret
see: Crisara, Raymond, 6), 7), 8)

Crowson, Lamar
see: Jones, Philip, 2)

Czapski, Jutta
see: Gass, Josef

Dalberto, Michel
see: Thibaud, Pierre, 11)

Dalheim, Eric
see: Hickman, David, 4)

d'Arco, Annie
see: André, Maurice, 82), 103), 129), 145)
see: Ménardi, Louis

Darré, Jeanne-Marie
see: Delmotte, Roger, 36)

Davis, Sharon
see: Plog, Anthony, 4), 5), 6), 7), 9), 10), 11)

Dawes, Marylou
see: House, Lawrence

Dean, Roger
see: Wallace, John, 6)

Degerman, Johannes
see: Potpourri, 3)

Dello Joio, Norman
see: Mueller, Herbert

Derungs, Martin
see: Soustrot, Bernard, 1)

Descaves, Lucette
see: Delmotte, Roger, 18)

Dobler, Charles
see: Scholz, Walter

Dodd, Neil
see: Naess, Lars

Donohoe, Peter
see: Warren, Wesley

Dosse, Marylène
see: Holy, Walter, 10)

Duchable, François-René
see: André, Maurice, 167)

Duval, Henri
see: Sevenstern, Harry

Dyakov, A.B.
see: Yeryomin, Sergei Nikolaivich

Ellington, Duke
see: Hirt, Al

Eshpai, Andrei
see: Maximenko, Anatoly, 1)

Fcinbcrg, Alan
see: Burns, Stephen

Février, Jacques
see: André, Maurice, 172)
see: Wilbraham, John, 21)

Fiedler, Tamara
see: Margolin, Veniamin

Fiorillo, Alexander
see: Nagel, Robert, 8)

Fischer, Edwin
see: Jackson, Harold

Fizdale, Robert
see: Vacchiano, William, 5)

Foss, Lukas
see: Voisin, Roger, 11)

Fowke, Philip
see: Warren, Wesley

Frantz, Roslyn
see: Haug, Edward

Freeman, Joann
see: Miller, Rodney

Freire, Nelson
see: Adelbrecht, Henri, 3)

Fuks, Ekaterina Filippovna
see: Polonsky, Naum E.

Gabor, Joszcf
see: Potpourri, 39)

Garvey, John
see: Logan, Jack

Genuit, Werner
see: Goethel, Siegfried

Gibbons, Bruce
see: Chunn, Michael

Gigliotti, Charles
see: Murtha, Roger

Gillis, Don
see: Canadian Brass, 3)

Gilson, L.
see: Roelant, Alain

Glass, Philip
see: Wise, Wilmer

Glazer, Frank
see: Crisara, Raymond, 9)
see: Haneuse, Arthur

Gold, Arthur
see: Vacchiano, William, 5)

Goldblatt, Rose
see: LeComte, Jacques

Gonnermann, Wilhelm
see: Potpourri, 19)

Gottlieb, J.
see: Caens, Thierry

Gould, Glenn
see: Johnson, Gilbert, 6)

Govorova, Nataly
see: Kafelnikov, Vladimir

Grabko, Larisa
see: Kafelnikov, Vladimir

Grierson, Ralph
see: Stevens, Thomas, 1), 2),
4), 8)

Grinberg, Maria
see: Popov, Sergei, 1)

Gurt, Joseph
see: Eggers, Carter

Hala, Josef
see: Potpourri, 39)

Hambro, Leonid
see: Vacchiano, William, 3)

Hartsuiker, Ton
see: Floore, John

Hawkins, John
see: Chenette, Stephen

Haynie, Marilyn Hindsley
see: Haynie, John, 1), 2)

Helmer, Paul
  see: Stone, Fred

Herting, Michael
  see: Stockhausen, Markus, 2)

Hindart, Kerstin
  see: Schrello, Mark

Hirsch, Albert
  see: Weast, Robert

Holeček, Alfréd
  see: Junek, Václav, 4)

Holeňa, Jiří
  see: Kozderka, Vladislav

Hollmann, Otakar
  see: Lisý, Rudolf

Horszowski, Mieczyslaw
  see: Unidentified, Trumpet(s),
    20)

Hubbell, Harriss
  see: Burke, James, 2)

Hubeau, Jean
  see: André, Maurice, 148)

Hunt, Robert
  see: Blair, Stacy

Husson, Suzanne
  see: Adelbrecht, Henri, 3)

Hyatt, Ruby
  see: Hyatt, Jack

Isakova, Aida
  see: Klushkin, Yuri

Israel, Brian
  see: Stith, Marice, 2), 4)

Istomin, Eugene
  see: Mule, Marcel

Jacobs, Paul
  see: Anderson, Ronald, 4)
  see: Nagel, Robert, 3)

James, Thomas
  see: Anderson, Ronald, 5)

Jílek, Zdeněk
  see: Junek, Václav, 1), 6)

Johannesen, Grant
  see: Unidentified, Trumpet(s),
    6), 7)

Johansson, Jan
  see: Potpourri, 3)

Johnson, Roy Hamlin
  see: Head, Emerson

Joly, Catherine
  see: Unidentified, Trumpet(s),
    11)

Jones, Lawson
  see: Autrey, Byron L.

Jones, Maureen
  see: Jones, Philip, 6)

Kalish, Gilbert
  see: Dean, Allan, 1), 2), 4), 5),
    6), 7), 8)
  see: Ghitalla, Armando, 7)
  see: Nagel, Robert, 3), 10), 11),
    18), 19), 20), 21)
  see: Potpourri, 38)
  see: Ranger, Louis
  see: Sheldon, Robert

Kaplan, Arnold
  see: Dokshitser, Timofei, 5), 7),
    9), 27), 35), 39)

Karis, Aleck
  see: Anderson, Ronald, 6)

Kashkin, Alla Scott
  see: Cesare, James

Kaye, Milton
  see: Wilder, Joseph B.

Kazaryan, Y.
  see: Balyan, Yuri

Keller, Christoph
  see: Sommerhalder, Max

Keyes, Christopher
  see: Metzger, Charles

Kieser, Karen
see: Malone, Michael

Kocsis, Zoltán
see: Geiger, György

Kogan, Yuliya
see: Usov, Yuri

Kokhanova, Elena
see: Dokshitser, Timofei, 12)

Kontarsky, Aloys
see: Bauer, Adam

Krainyev, Vladimir
see: Kafelnikov, Vladimir
see: Korolev, Alexandre

Krieger, Günter
see: Hunger, Helmut, 4)

Krilova, Olga
see: Malkov, Valentin

Kröll, Georg
see: Schoof, Manfred

Kuehefuhs, Gertrude
see: Amstutz, Keith

Kuzanov, G.
see: Balyan, Yuri

Laforge, Jean
see: Lagorce, Antoine

Lam, Bun Ching
see: Pressley, Richard

Lancaster, Sam
see: Endsley, Gerald

Larson, Janåke
see: Hardenberger, Håkan

Laugs, Richard
see: Lösch, Reinhold

Layton, Bentley
see: Unidentified, Trumpet(s),
2)

Leigh, Mitchell
see: Terracini, Paul

Leighton, Bernard
see: Smith, Leonard B.

Lenom, Marthe
see: Potpourri, 28)

Lettvin, Theodore
see: Wilson, Alex

Levy, Amy Lou
see: Levy, Robert

Lewis, Harmon
see: McNab, Malcolm

Lifchitz, Max
see: Romm, Ronald
see: Stubbs, James

Lindgren, Ingrid
see: Potpourri, 3)

List, Eugene
see: Korolev, Alexandre
see: Wesenigk, Fritz

Loriod, Yvonne
see: Delmotte, Roger, 2)

Lüthy, Susy
see: Rippas, Claude

Lytle, Cecil
see: Harkins, Edwin

Maddox, Arthur
see: Miller, Rodney
see: Sasaki, Ray

Madge, Geoffrey
see: Ros, Ad

Mancinelli, Judith
see: Henderson, Douglas

Mann, Sy
see: Lieberman, Harold J.

Mason, Lucas
see: Levy, Robert

Masselos, William
see: Crisara, Raymond, 5)
see: Glantz, Harry, 2), 5)
see: Mueller, Herbert
see: Weis, Theodore, 3)

Massey, Michael
  see: Lowrey, Alvin

Matsushita, Koyoko
  see: Kierski, Eckhard

Mauldin, Michael
  see: Birch, Robert

Maxin, Jack
  see: Nagel, Robert, 7)

Mehta, Dady
  see: Eggers, Carter

Meshchaninov, Petr (Pyotr)
  see: Ikov, Andrei
  see: Krivosheyev, Yuri
  see: Maximenko, Anatoly, 1)

Miansarova, T.
  see: Volkov, Vitaly

Miller, Donald C.
  see: Masters, Edward L.

Miller, Robert
  see: Anderson, Ronald, 3), 4)
  see: Dean, Allan, 1)
  see: Nagel, Robert, 3)
  see: Young, Gene

Mitchell, Johnlyn
  see: Ritter, David

Mizukami, Keiko
  see: Kierski, Eckhard

Moore, William B.
  see: Lewis, E. Leonard

Morishima, Eiko
  see: Tobe, Yutaka

Motard, Alain
  see: Delmotte, Roger, 33)

Muntyan, Mikhail
  see: Dokshitser, Timofei, 29)

Muraco, Thomas
  see: Schwarz, Gerard, 22)

Nasedkin, Alexei
  see: Dokshitser, Timofei, 17)

Nelson, Roger
  see: Pressley, Richard

Nero, Peter
  see: Hirt, Al

Neveux, Alain
  see: Cure, Antoine

Nicholson, Paul
  see: Impett, Jonathan

Nodaïra, Ichiro
  see: Thibaud, Pierre, 2)

Nuridzhanian, Nora
  see: Margolin, Veniamin

Oertel, Helmut
  see: Potpourri, 19)

Ogdon, John
  see: Wilbraham, John, 8)

Olson, Judith
  see: Ghitalla, Armando, 11), 12), 13)

Oppens, Ursula
  see: Anderson, Ronald, 5)
  see: Schwarz, Gerard, 18)
  see: Unidentified, Trumpet(s), 7)

Ortiz, Cristina
  see: Senior, Rodney

Ots, Meely
  see: Ots, Aavo

Owen, Benjamin
  see: Rapier, Leon, 2)

Paik, Kun Woo
  see: Schwarz, Gerard, 12)

Páleníček, Josef
  see: Horák, Jiří, 4)
  see: Popov, Sergei, 3)

Palmer, Robert
  see: Stith, Marice, 7)

Panenka, Jan
  see: Junek, Václav, 6)
  see: Mičaník, Jaroslav

Panzer, Siegbert
see: Erb, Helmut, 1), 4)

Paterson, Donald R. M.
see: Stith, Marice, 5)

Pawlyk, John
see: Wilbraham, John, 30)

Peyton, Malcolm
see: Dolce, Christine

Pflüger, Hans Georg
see: Schmitt, Siegfried

Phillips, Robert
see: Potpourri, 6)

Pichaureau, Claude
see: Thibaud, Pierre, 12)

Pinter, Margot
see: Bauer, Willibald, 5)

Pires, Maria Joao
see: Potpourri, 47)

Podolskaya, V.
see: Orvid, Georgy

Podshivailyenko, L.
see: Dokshitser, Timofei, 28)

Pokorná, M.
see: Sejpal, Stanislav

Pokorný, Jiří
see: Kejmar, Miroslav, 7)

Pommer, Max
see: Potpourri, 19)

Ponce, Walter
see: Anderson, Ronald, 2)
see: Dean, Allan, 1)

Ponti, Michael
see: Giangiulio, Richard

Pöntinen, Roland
see: Hardenberger, Håkan

Pontremoli, Anita
see: Dolce, Christine

Post, Trudi
see: Tolley, Richard

Poulenc, Francis
see: André, Maurice, 172)
see: Delmotte, Roger, 1), 51)

Pressler, Menahem
see: Glantz, Harry, 3), 4)

Previn, André
see: Vacchiano, William, 1), 5)

Pryor, Gwynneth
see: Webb, Gordon, 7)

Pustinová, D.
see: Rejlek, Vladimir

Raleigh, Stuart W.
see: Stith, Marice, 7), 8)

Rauch, František
see: Junek, Václav, 6)

Reid, Richard
see: Gardner, Ned

Reinelt, Manfred
see: Potpourri, 19)

Renzulli, Franco
see: Potpourri, 6)

Rice, Virginia
see: Amstutz, Keith

Richter, Sviatoslav
see: Zikov, Vladimir

Riesman, Michael
see: Soloff, Lew
see: Wise, Wilmer

Riley, Doug
see: Schultz, Erik, 8)

Robertson, Eric
see: Schultz, Erik, 8)

Rodina, I.
see: Sveshnikov, Mikhail

Rosen, Charles
see: Heinrich, Robert
see: Nagel, Robert, 4)

Rosenberg, Ron
see: Victorian Trumpet Trio

Rosenberger, Carol
see: Burns, Stephen

Rosenohl-Grinhauz, Berta
see: LeComte, Jacques

Roussel, L.
see: Perinelli, René

Rouvier, Jacques
see: Thibaud, Pierre, 9)

Rowland, Bill
see: Smith, Bramwell "Bram"

Rzewski, Frederic
see: Dean, Allan, 1)

Sampen, Marilyn
see: Potpourri, 6)

Sanders, Samuel
see: Benedetti, Donald

Sargon, Simon
see: Giangiulio, Richard

Sauer, Mary
see: Herseth, Adolph, 4)

Schenly, Paul
see: Herseth, Adolph, 4)

Schickele, Peter
see: Mase, Raymond

Schrama, Cees
see: Grin, Freddy, 7)

Schub, André-Michel
see: Herseth, Adolph, 4)

Schwartz, Elliott
see: Dean, Allan, 9)
see: Patti, Douglas

Schwartz, Joseph
see: Young, Gene

Serbo, Emma
see: Klushkin, Yuri

Serkin, Rudolf
see: Eskdale, George, 2)
see: Nagel, Robert, 2)

Sheppard, Craig
see: Marsalis, Wynton, 3)

Shetler, Norman
see: Rudolf, Richard

Shkolnik, Sheldon
see: Geyer, Charles

Shostakovich, Dmitri
see: Popov, Sergei, 1)
see: Vaillant, Ludovic, 5)
see: Volovnik, Iosif

Shostakovich, Maxim
see: Volovnik, Iosif

Shostakovich (Jr.), Dmitri
see: Thompson, James

Shuhan, Alex
see: Dallas Brass

Sidoti, Genevieve
see: Darling, James

Sipley, Shirley J.
see: Smith, Philip, 3)

Smendzianka, Regina
see: Piórkowski, Zygmunt

Smirnova, Tatiana
see: Usov, Yuri

Smith, Brooks
see: Glantz, Harry, 7)

Smolko, James
see: Dean, Allan, 2)

Soderholm, Pauline
see: Hickman, David, 3)

Solodovnik, Sergei
see: Dokshitser, Timofei, 19)

Solter, Fany
see: Schnackenberg, Friedemann

Somer, Hilde
see: Crisara, Raymond, 3)

Stein, Joan
see: Mase, Raymond

Stern, Robert
see: Young, Gene

Stevens, Delores
see: Stevens, Thomas, 13)

Stöckigt, Siegfried
see: Potpourri, 19)

Stokman, Abraham
see: Perry, Brian

Swan, Andrea
see: Perry, Brian

Swiatkowski, Chet
see: Stevens, Thomas, 5)

Takahashi, Aki
see: Soken, Hosei

Talroze, G.
see: Krylov, Gleb

Tartak, Marvin
see: Metzger, Charles

Thome, Diane
see: Henderson, Douglas

Thomson, Virgil
see: Mills, Fred

Tower, Joan
see: Potpourri, 5)

Trythall, Richard
see: Anderson, Ronald, 4)

Tudor, David
see: Floore, John
see: Nagel, Robert, 7)

Turrin, Joseph
see: Smith, Philip, 2)

Uhlhorn, Herman
see: Ros, Ad

Vanden Eynden, Jean-Claude
see: Reinhart, Carole Dawn, 9)

Vendice, William
see: Herseth, Adolph, 4)

Venzago, Mario
see: Sommerhalder, Max

Veyron-Lacroix, Robert
see: Delmotte, Roger, 24)

Volle, Sverre
see: Volle, Bjarne

Vosgerchian, Luise
see: Unidentified, Trumpet(s), 2)

Wadsworth, Charles
see: Schwarz, Gerard, 3)

Wallfisch, Lory
see: Patti, Douglas

Weast, Janice
see: Weast, Robert

Weaver, James
see: Ghitalla, Armando, 2)

Weinberg, Moisse
see: Volovnik, Iosif

Wentworth, Jean
see: Nagel, Robert, 21)

Wentworth, Kenneth
see: Nagel, Robert, 21)

Westenholz, Elisabeth
see: Tarr, Edward, 6)

Wheatley, David
see: Stevens, Thomas, 9)

Wild, Earl
see: Glantz, Harry, 2)

Wingreen, Harriet
see: Nagel, Robert, 15), 16), 17)
see: Schwarz, Gerard, 14), 15), 16)
see: Wilder, Joseph B.

Wong, Shirley
see: Logan, Jack

Wood, Kathie
see: Thomas, Peggy Paton

Wuorinen, Charles
see: Anderson, Ronald, 1)

Wyner, Yehudi
see: Nagel, Robert, 5)

Yavryan, Igor
see: Balyan, Yuri

Zatin, Anatoly
see: Dokshitser, Timofei, 22)

Zelka, Charlotte
see: Parker, Craig B.

Zhak, Abram
see: Dokshitser, Timofei, 2), 3),
5), 7), 9), 27), 31), 34),
35), 36), 38), 39)

Zichová (-Lochmanová),
Zorka
see: Junek, Václav, 5)

Zuckerman, Evelyn
see: Potpourri, 5)

Piccolo
[cross-referenced under flute]

Adeney, Richard
see: Jones, Philip, 2), 11)
see: Mason, David, 5)

Asin, Nadine
see: Potpourri, 38)

Baker, Julius
see: Wobisch, Helmut, 14)

Baron, Samuel
see: Ghitalla, Armando, 10)

Bell, Sebastian
see: Snell, Howard

Bennett, William
see: Jones, Philip, 3)
see: Wilbraham, John, 1)

Bourdin, Roger
see: Delmotte, Roger, 16)

Brook, Paige
see: Ghitalla, Armando, 10)

Brüggen, Frans
see: Potpourri, 59)

Cotton, Rémy
see: Thibaud, Pierre, 9)

Dailey, Jan
see: Henderson, Douglas

Debost, Michel
see: André, Maurice, 49)

Di Fazio, Louis
see: Dean, Allan, 4)

Dunkel, Paul
see: Dean, Allan, 4), 5), 6), 7),
8)

Fonville, John
see: Sasaki, Ray

Francis, John
see: Mason, David, 3)

Fulton, John
see: Burke, James, 8)

Gazzelloni, Severino
see: Adelbrecht, Henri, 7)

Gérard, Jean-Claude
see: Thibaud, Pierre, 9)

Gilbert, David
see: Potpourri, 5)

Goudey, Jacqueline
see: Schwarz, Gerard, 13)

Green, Harlan
see: Lowrey, Alvin

Gross, Michel
see: André, Maurice, 120)

Harnoncourt, Elisabeth
see: Bryant, Ralph, 4)

Harras, Manfred
see: Wolf, Hans, 11)

Heim, F. William
see: Vacchiano, William, 4)

Herlinger, Jan
see: Miller, Rodney

Honner, Derek
see: Webb, Gordon, 2)

Kane, Trudy
see: Crisara, Raymond, 1)

Kincaid, William
see: Johnson, Gilbert, 1)

King, April
see: Metzger, Charles

Korneyev, Alexander
see: Popov, Sergei, 3)

Kout, Trix
see: Hoffman, Edward

Kozlov, Alexandre
see: Popov, Sergei, 2)

Kuijken, Barthold
see: Bodenröder, Robert

Lagerquist, John
see: Ghitalla, Armando, 1)

Larrieu, Maxence
see: André, Maurice, 102)

Linde, Hans-Martin
see: Scherbaum, Adolf, 14), 24)

Lolya, Andrew
see: Burke, James, 5), 6)

McKibben, Maureen
see: Hoffman, Edward

Monteux, Claude
see: Crisara, Raymond, 3)

Morgan, Carole
see: Potpourri, 38)

Moulton, Marie
see: Miller, Rodney
see: Perry, Brian

Nyfenger, Thomas
see: Dean, Allan, 4)
see: Nagel, Robert, 19)

Pearce, Judith
see: Evans, Laurie

Pecover, Joan
see: Lowrey, Alvin

Rampal, Jean-Pierre
see: André, Maurice, 108)
see: Vaillant, Ludovic, 4)

Rumpel, Günter
see: Adelbrecht, Henri, 3)

Sanvoisin, Michel
see: Calvayrac, Albert

Sauveur, Cornelie
see: Tarr, Edward, 44)

Shanley, Gretel
see: Stevens, Thomas, 11)

Solum, John
see: Weis, Theodore, 2)

Spencer, Patricia
see: Anderson, Ronald, 6)

Strebel, Hartmut
see: Wolf, Hans, 11)

Swinfield, Ray
see: Izan, Bernard

Tanzer, Stephen
see: Hoffman, Edward

Townsend, Richard
see: Geisler, Lloyd

Turetzky, Nancy
see: Murtha, Roger

Veretchnikova, Anatoly
see: Dokshitser, Timofei, 16)

Walklate, Audrey
see: Roberts, Standish

Weissberg, Herbert
see: Rudolf, Richard

Prepared piano
[cross-referenced under piano]

    Bunger, Richard
      see: Stevens, Thomas, 16)

Psaltery (small harp)
[includes psaltérion]

    Kecskés, András
      see: Pok, František, 4)

    Leach, John
      see: Potpourri, 67)

    Reid, Gillian
      see: Laird, Michael, 1)

Qobuz
(2-stringed fiddle)

    Kecskés, András
      see: Pok, František, 2), 4)

Rabâb

    Rantos, Spiros
      see: Pok, František, 4)

Racket (Rankett / Rackett)
[includes various sizes]

    Lumsden, Alan
      see: Laird, Michael, 1)

    Munrow, David
      see: Laird, Michael, 1)
      see: Smithers, Don, 2), 3)

    Otten, Kees
      see: Otten, Kees

    Roth, Kenneth
      see: Cook, Richard

    Tenta, Franz
      see: Eichhorn, Holger

    Thomas, Bernard
      see: Potpourri, 67)

    Turner, John
      see: Laird, Michael, 1)

    van der Beek, Andrew
      see: Laird, Michael, 1), 2)

    Wollitz, Kenneth
      see: Montesi, Robert, 6)

Rebec (3-strings)
[includes rubebe]

    Brookes, Oliver
      see: Laird, Michael, 1), 13)

    Dupré, Desmond
      see: Potpourri, 67)

    Jones, Trevor
      see: Laird, Michael, 13)
      see: Potpourri, 67)

    Kecskés, András
      see: Pok, František, 4)

    Mackintosh, Catherine
      see: Potpourri, 67)

    North, Nigel
      see: Laird, Michael, 13)

    Rantos, Spiros
      see: Pok, František, 4)

    Skeaping, Adam
      see: Potpourri, 67)

    Sloan, Eleanor
      see: Laird, Michael, 1), 13)
      see: Potpourri, 67)

    Waterfield, Polly
      see: Laird, Michael, 13)

Recorder
[includes various sizes]

    Angerer, Paul
      see: Holler, Adolf
      see: Scherbaum, Adolf, 36)
      see: Wobisch, Helmut, 2)

    Beckett, Rachel
      see: Laird, Michael, 8)

Bixler, Martha
see: Broiles, Melvin
see: Montesi, Robert, 3), 4), 6)

Boeke, Kees
see: Bryant, Ralph, 2), 3)
see: Potpourri, 63)
see: Rippas, Claude
see: Spindler, Josef, 14), 15)

Böhm, Bernhard
see: Neunhoeffer, Frieder

Braun, Gerhard
see: André, Maurice, 138)
see: Schneidewind, Helmut, 13)
see: Tarr, Edward, 4)

Brookes, Oliver
see: Laird, Michael, 1), 3)

Brüggen, Frans
see: André, Maurice, 201), 221),
   222), 225)
see: Bryant, Ralph, 2)
see: Potpourri, 59)
see: Rippas, Claude
see: Spindler, Josef, 15)

Carp, David
see: Gould, Mark

Clemenčić, René
see: André, Maurice, 114)
see: Idinger, Matthias
see: Pok, František, 1), 2), 4)

Conrad, Ferdinand
see: Holy, Walter, 1)
see: Scherbaum, Adolf, 33)

Cook, Richard
see: Cook, Richard

Copley, Michael
see: Touvron, Guy, 14)

Czidra, Lászlo
see: Csiba, József

Daehn-Wilke, Rosemarie
see: Tarr, Edward, 10), 19)

Davenport, LaNoue
see: Broiles, Melvin
see: Davenport, LaNoue
see: Montesi, Robert, 3), 4), 5),
   6)

Derschmidt, Walther
see: André, Maurice, 114)

Dolmetsch, Carl
see: Jones, Philip, 8)

Duschenes, Mario
see: André, Maurice, 111), 116)

Erig, Richard
see: Hagge, Detlef

Fiedler, Eric
see: Cook, Richard

Finkel, Klaus
see: Soustrot, Bernard, 8)

Gabriel, Wolfgang
see: Eichhorn, Holger

Geiger, Johannes
see: Neunhoeffer, Frieder

Grubb, Francis
see: Smithers, Don, 2)

Gruskin, Shelley
see: Berinbaum, Martin
see: Davenport, LaNoue
see: Montesi, Robert, 3), 4), 5),
   6)

Gulland, Brian
see: Potpourri, 67)

Gund, Klaus
see: Eichhorn, Holger

Hammer, Stephen
see: Gould, Mark

Hampe, Konrad
see: Zickler, Heinz, 3)

Hanisch, Sieglinde
see: Zeh, Karl Heinz

Harnoncourt, Elisabeth
see: Bryant, Ralph, 3)
see: Immer, Friedemann, 16)
see: Potpourri, 57), 62)
see: Spindler, Josef, 16)

Harras, Manfred
see: Läubin, Hannes, 3)

Harvey, Richard
see: Potpourri, 67)

Hildebrand, Renate
see: Hagge, Detlef

Hofmann, Klaus
see: Sauter, Hermann, 2)

Hofstötter, Rudolf
see: Eichhorn, Holger

Höller, Günther
see: Caudle, Theresa
see: Preis, Ivo
see: Sauter, Hermann, 28)
see: Schneidewind, Helmut, 1),
5)
see: Schoof, Manfred
see: Tarr, Edward, 37), 38)
see: Thibaud, Pierre, 8)
see: Touvron, Guy, 6)
see: Zickler, Heinz, 5)

Hunt, Edgar
see: Jones, Philip, 8)

Iwami, Atsuko
see: Stockhausen, Markus, 4)

Jenne, Peter
see: Immer, Friedemann, 3)
see: Potpourri, 11)

Junghänel, Bernhard
see: Eichhorn, Holger

Jurkovič, Pavel
see: Pok, František, 6)

Kastner, Gerhard
see: Tarr, Edward, 10)

Kelber, Sebastian
see: Otto, Joachim
see: Tarr, Edward, 12)

Keldorfer, Felicitas
see: Idinger, Matthias

Klebel, Bernhard
see: Tarr, Edward, 45)

Klement, Karel
see: Pok, František, 5)

Klement, Miloslav
see: Pok, František, 5)

Koch, Hans Oskar
see: Preis, Ivo
see: Soustrot, Bernard, 6), 8)

Koch, Johannes
see: Renz, Albrecht, 1)

Krainis, Bernard
see: Immer, Friedemann, 13)

Leber, Eric
see: Montesi, Robert, 4)

Lee, Richard
see: Wilbraham, John, 20)

Lehmann-Isenbart, Gundula
see: Zeh, Karl Heinz

Linde, Hans-Martin
see: André, Maurice, 21), 25)
see: Immer, Friedemann, 3)
see: Potpourri, 14)
see: Renz, Albrecht, 1), 2), 3)
see: Scherbaum, Adolf, 6), 26),
33)
see: Schneidewind, Helmut, 5)
see: Tarr, Edward, 11), 36),
37), 38)
see: Thibaud, Pierre, 8)

Lucke, Annegret
see: Bernard, André, 2)

Lumsden, Alan
see: Laird, Michael, 1), 2), 9),
13)

Lüthi, Marianne
see: Läubin, Hannes, 3)

Martin, Judith
see: Montesi, Robert, 6)

Thieme, Ulrich
see: Touvron, Guy, 6)

Thomas, Bernard
see: Potpourri, 67)
see: Smithers, Don, 2)

Toncourt, Elisabeth
see: André, Maurice, 114)

Trötzmüller, Karl
see: Holler, Adolf
see: Scherbaum, Adolf, 36)
see: Wobisch, Helmut, 2)

Turner, John
see: Immer, Friedemann, 1)
see: Laird, Michael, 1), 2), 11), 13), 17)
see: Smithers, Don, 3)
see: Tuckwell, Barry
see: Webb, Gordon, 1), 4)
see: Wilbraham, John, 20), 27), 31)

Tutschek, Helga
see: Potpourri, 49), 64)
see: Tarr, Edward, 45)

Tyler, James
see: Laird, Michael, 1), 3)

Ulsamer, Josef
see: Otto, Joachim

Unger, Robert
see: Idinger, Matthias

Urbanek, Hannaliese
see: Eichhorn, Holger

van der Beek, Andrew
see: Laird, Michael, 1), 2), 13)

van der Ven-Ulsamer, Elza
see: Otto, Joachim

van Hauwe, Walter
see: Basch, Wolfgang, 8), 10)
see: Bryant, Ralph, 3)
see: Potpourri, 59), 63)
see: Spindler, Josef, 14)

van Wingerden, Jeanette
see: André, Maurice, 201)

Veilhan, J.-C.
see: Thibaud, Pierre, 14)

Vetter, Michael
see: Stockhausen, Markus, 4)

von Huene, Friedrich
see: Cook, Richard

von Sparr, Thea
see: Scherbaum, Adolf, 6), 26)

Wagner, Käthe
see: Hagge, Detlef

Walch, Hans
see: Renz, Albrecht, 6), 7)

Waldbauer, T.
see: Krug, Willi, 5)

Weber, Helga
see: Hagge, Detlef

Weill, Sabine
see: Immer, Friedemann, 4)

Widensky, Peter
see: Idinger, Matthias

Wolf, Marie
see: Immer, Friedemann, 16)
see: Potpourri, 62)

Wollitz, Kenneth
see: Montesi, Robert, 6)

Zlatníková, Kateřina
see: Pok, František, 6)

Reed pipe

Munrow, David
see: Laird, Michael, 1)

Saxhorn
[includes various sizes]

Camenzind, James
see: André, Maurice, 120)

Candelle, Marc
see: André, Maurice, 120)

Desmeulles, Léopold
see: André, Maurice, 120)

Desruennes, Jacques
see: André, Maurice, 120)

Dubois, Bernard
see: André, Maurice, 120)

Firmin, Daniel
see: André, Maurice, 120)

Langlois, Paul
see: André, Maurice, 120)

Saxophone
[includes various sizes]

Abato, Vincent J.
see: Burke, James, 5), 6)
see: Potpourri, 31)
see: Weis, Theodore, 2), 3)

Allard, Joseph
see: Burke, James, 6)

Ballion, Jean
see: André, Maurice, 120)

Beckenstein, Raymond
see: Mills, Fred

Bensmann, Detlef
see: Kierski, Eckhard
see: Send, Peter

Brymer, Jack
see: Mason, David, 5)

Burns, Robert
see: Jones, Philip, 11)

Campbell, Kirby
see: Glantz, Harry, 6)

Catenne, Daniel
see: André, Maurice, 120)

Caumont, Francis
see: André, Maurice, 120)

Cohn, Al
see: Nagel, Robert, 7)

Crowley, Charles
see: Roberts, Standish

Dankworth, John
see: Izan, Bernard

Davoine, Patrice
see: André, Maurice, 120)

Deffayet, Daniel
see: Delmotte, Roger, 33)
see: Thibaud, Pierre, 1)

Douse, Kenneth
see: Geisler, Lloyd

Ehrhardt, Rainer
see: Kierski, Eckhard

Estrin, Harvey
see: Broiles, Melvin
see: Crisara, Raymond, 2)
see: Dean, Allan, 6)

Gallodoro, Alfred
see: Burke, James, 5), 6)

Gibson, Jon
see: Wise, Wilmer

Green, Lloyd A.
see: Anderson, Ronald, 2)

Greenberg, Roger
see: Stevens, Thomas, 11)

Hacker, Alan
see: Evans, Laurie

Heller, Volker
see: Kierski, Eckhard

Howard, Alexander
see: Burke, James, 5), 6)

Jousset, Alain
see: André, Maurice, 120)

Kaufman, Bernie
see: Butterfield, Billy

Klink, Albert
see: Burke, James, 5), 6)

Krautgartner, Karel
see: Junek, Václav, 2)

573

Krem, Michael
see: Mason, David, 3)

Kripl, Jack
see: Soloff, Lew

Legrand, Gaston
see: André, Maurice, 120)

Livingston, Larry
see: Logan, Jack

Morosco, Victor
see: Nagel, Robert, 20)

Mule, Marcel
see: Ménardi, Louis
see: Mule, Marcel

Niehaus, Manfred
see: Schoof, Manfred

Peck, Richard
see: Wise, Wilmer

Pengue, Romeo
see: Butterfield, Billy

Perry, P.J.
see: Lowrey, Alvin

Peters, Gregoire
see: Kierski, Eckhard

Plank, Max
see: Eggers, Carter

Puech, Edmond
see: André, Maurice, 120)

Regni, Albert
see: Anderson, Ronald, 2), 5)
see: Crisara, Raymond, 1)
see: Dean, Allan, 5), 7)

Ricci, Paul
see: Burke, James, 5), 6)

Richman, Boomie
see: Butterfield, Billy

Ross, Hank
see: Butterfield, Billy

Rousseau, Eugene
see: Davidson, Louis

Sampen, John
see: Potpourri, 6)

Saucy, Michel
see: André, Maurice, 120)

Schmied-Forthmann,
  Eberhard
see: Kierski, Eckhard

Shaposhnikova, Margarita
see: Dokshitser, Timofei, 16)

Soufflet, René
see: André, Maurice, 120)

Taggert, Mark
see: Reese, Rebecca

Terrill, Harry
see: Butterfield, Billy

Thompson, Robin
see: Miller, John

Tofani, David
see: Dean, Allan, 7)

Trier, Stephen
see: Wilbraham, John, 1)

Vignaud, Jean-Luc
see: André, Maurice, 120)

Schryari
[Schreyepfeifen = shouting pipes (a
type of shawm)]

Gruskin, Shelley
see: Davenport, LaNoue
see: Montesi, Robert, 4), 5)

Serpent

Gumz, Hubert
see: Hagge, Detlef

Lumsden, Alan
see: Laird, Michael, 1)

Orosz, Josef
see: Voisin, Roger, 13)

Shawm
[includes various types & sizes:
bombard, musette, pommer,
rauschpfeife & schalmei]

Boisits, Gottfried
see: Eichhorn, Holger

Brombey, Elke
see: Hagge, Detlef

Brookes, Oliver
see: Laird, Michael, 1)

Erig, Richard
see: Hagge, Detlef
see: Pok, František, 4)

Fendt, Leopold
see: Renz, Albrecht, 6), 7)

Fest, Fritjof
see: Tarr, Edward, 10), 28)

Göldner, Nicolo-Heinrich
see: Renz, Albrecht, 1), 2), 3)
see: Tarr, Edward, 10), 28)

Gruber, Karl
see: Tarr, Edward, 45)

Gruskin, Shelley
see: Montesi, Robert, 6)

Hartl, Wolfgang
see: Stradner, Gerhard

Hertel, Alfred
see: Pok, František, 4)

Hildebrand, Renate
see: Hagge, Detlef
see: Pok, František, 4)

Hucke, Helmut
see: Caudle, Theresa
see: Renz, Albrecht, 1), 2), 3)
see: Tarr, Edward, 19)

Kaplan, Melvin
see: Montesi, Robert, 1)

Kelber, Sebastian
see: Otto, Joachim

Klebel, Bernhard
see: Idinger, Matthias

Klement, Karel
see: Pok, František, 6)

Kroissenbrunner, Hans
see: Stradner, Gerhard

Logemann, Sally
see: Potpourri, 67)

Martin, Judith
see: Montesi, Robert, 6)

Maurer, Paul
see: Idinger, Matthias

Mauruschat, Werner
see: Tarr, Edward, 19)

Meilink, Leo
see: Otten, Kees

Munrow, David
see: Laird, Michael, 1), 2), 3),
9), 12), 13)
see: Smithers, Don, 2)

Newman, Morris
see: Montesi, Robert, 1), 2), 3),
4)

Otten, Kees
see: Otten, Kees

Plesnicar, Donald
see: Montesi, Robert, 6)

Quendler, Margit
see: Stradner, Gerhard

Roseman, Ronald
see: Montesi, Robert, 2), 3), 4),
5), 6)

Schaeftlein, Jürg
see: Tarr, Edward, 45)

Soltani, Khosro
see: Pok, František, 2)

Steinkopf, Otto
see: Tarr, Edward, 10), 28)

Teichert, Almut
see: Hagge, Detlef

Thomas, Bernard
see: Potpourri, 67)

Turner, John
see: Laird, Michael, 2), 13)

Tyler, James
see: Laird, Michael, 1)

Ulsamer, Josef
see: Otto, Joachim

van der Beek, Andrew
see: Laird, Michael, 1), 2), 13)

von Busch, Hans
see: Hagge, Detlef

Wagner, Käthe
see: Hagge, Detlef

Weber, Helga
see: Hagge, Detlef

West, Philip
see: Montesi, Robert, 3), 4)

Sitar

Sherry, Fred
see: Dean, Allan, 7)

Six-holed pipe (Peruvian folk instrument)

Munrow, David
see: Laird, Michael, 1)

Soprano (voice)
[includes coloratura & mezzo-soprano]

Addison, Adele
see: Broiles, Melvin
see: Nagel, Robert, 3)
see: Vacchiano, William, 7)

Alarie, Pierrette
see: Wobisch, Helmut, 15)

Albert, Adrienne
see: Heinrich, Robert

Allen, Betty
see: Mills, Fred

Ameling, Elly
see: André, Maurice, 16), 192)
see: Bauer, Willibald, 4)
see: Laird, Michael, 14), 15)
see: Tarr, Edward, 24), 25), 26)
see: Wilbraham, John, 2), 22)

Amini, Nancy
see: Sauter, Hermann, 19)

Anderfuhren, Isabelle
see: Caudle, Theresa

Anderson, George
see: Montesi, Robert, 2)

Angelici, Martha
see: André, Maurice, 97)

Archimbaud, Jean
see: Coursier, Gérard

Argenta, Nancy
see: Steele-Perkins, Crispian, 4), 16)

Armstrong, Sheila
see: Groot, Willem (Wim)

Augér, Arleen
see: Eichhorn, Holger
see: Immer, Friedemann, 5), 6)
see: Läubin, Hannes, 3), 4), 5), 6), 7)
see: McGregor, Rob Roy, 1), 2), 3), 4), 6)
see: Miller, Rodney
see: Potpourri, 23), 24), 25)
see: Sauter, Hermann, 19), 20), 21), 22), 23), 24)
see: Schmid, Bernhard, 2), 3), 4), 5), 6), 7), 8), 9)
see: Send, Peter
see: Wolf, Hans, 2), 3), 4), 5), 6), 8), 9), 10), 11), 12)

Backus, Carolyn
see: Montesi, Robert, 5)

Baird, Julianne
see: Holmgren, Fred

Barr, Glenna
see: Geyer, Charles

Barraud, Dany
see: Perinelli, René

Battle, Kathleen
see: Herseth, Adolph, 3)
see: Weeks, Larry

Baumann, Hubertus
see: Tarr, Edward, 17)

Beardslee, Bethany
see: Anderson, Ronald, 5)
see: Dolce, Christine

Beatty, Sarah
see: Geyer, Charles

Beery, Leigh
see: Carroll, Edward, 1)

Bell, Matthew
see: Laird, Michael, 7)

Berberian, Cathy
see: Heinrich, Robert

Bergius, Alan
see: Immer, Friedemann, 14),
   15)
see: Potpourri, 63)

Bernát-Klein, Gundula
see: Ellinghaus, Wolfram
see: Köpp, Rudolf

Beverley, Mary
see: Laird, Michael, 11)

Bichler, Maria
see: Renz, Albrecht, 4), 5), 6),
   7)

Bing, Barbara
see: Plog, Anthony, 2)

Bise, Juliette
see: Tarr, Edward, 32)

Biswenger, Annette
see: Schmitt, Siegfried

Bjorklund, Ingegerd
see: Nystrom, Kaj

Blegen, Judith
see: Schwarz, Gerard, 3), 4)

Bogard, Carole
see: Dean, Allan, 10)
see: Ghitalla, Armando, 3)

Boháčová, Marta
see: Pok, František, 5)

Bonazzi, Elaine
see: Anderson, Ronald, 5)
see: Burns, Stephen

Bondi, Anna-Maria
see: Soustrot, Bernard, 8)

Bratschke, Detlef
see: Bryant, Ralph, 5)
see: Potpourri, 58)

Bruce, Phyllis
see: Levy, Robert

Brumaire, Jacqueline
see: Delmotte, Roger, 51)

Bryden, Jane
see: Holmgren, Fred

Bryn-Julson, Phyllis
see: Dean, Allan, 3), 6)
see: Nagel, Robert, 18)

Buckel, Ursula
see: Potpourri, 2)
see: Unidentified, Trumpet(s),
   8)

Burns, Nancy
see: Potpourri, 24)
see: Sauter, Hermann, 5), 6),
   35)

Burrowes, Norma
see: Laird, Michael, 11), 14)

Byram-Wigfield, Timothy
see: Laird, Michael, 15)

Caccavallo, Catherine
see: Geyer, Charles

Cantelo, April
see: Eskdale, George, 5)
see: Unidentified, Trumpet(s),
18)

Carroll, Dara
see: Wiggans, Brian

Čechová, Jitka
see: Pok, František, 6)

Chamonin, Jocelyne
see: André, Maurice, 71), 78),
97)
see: Greffin, Jean Jacques
see: Jeannoutot, Bernard
see: Thibaud, Pierre, 14)

Charleston, Elsa
see: Miller, Rodney

Clarke, Christina
see: Jones, Philip, 7), 9)

Coe, Cathy
see: Potpourri, 66)

Collart, Claudine
see: Coursier, Gérard

Cowart, Judy
see: Potpourri, 66)

Cranmer, Richard
see: Laird, Michael, 7)

Csapò, Eva
see: Sauter, Hermann, 18)

Cuccaro, Costanza
see: Friedrich, Reinhold
see: Läubin, Hannes, 8)
see: Schmid, Bernhard, 10)

Curry, Corinne
see: Unidentified, Trumpet(s),
2)

Curtin, Phyllis
see: Nashan, Rudolph

Danco, Suzanne
see: Longinotti, Paolo

Davis, Eleanor
see: Nashan, Rudolph

Davrath, Netania
see: Rudolf, Richard

Dawson, Lynn
see: Steele-Perkins, Crispian,
12)

Debnam, Poyas
see: Montesi, Robert, 2)

DeGaetani, Jan
see: Dean, Allan, 4), 6), 7)
see: Miller, Rodney
see: Montesi, Robert, 5)
see: Nagel, Robert, 19)
see: Romm, Ronald
see: Sheldon, Robert

de Montmollin, Marie-Lise
see: Longinotti, Paolo

Donath, Helen
see: André, Maurice, 48)
see: Güttler, Ludwig, 28)
see: Potpourri, 24)
see: Sauter, Hermann, 9), 11),
12), 13), 14), 16), 35)
see: Tarr, Edward, 19)
see: Unidentified, Trumpet(s),
5)
see: Webb, Gordon, 3)

Dunkley, Sally
see: Laird, Michael, 11)

Eckert, Thomasa
see: Pressley, Richard

Eda-Pierre, Christiane
see: Thibaud, Pierre, 9)

Edmonds, Katherine
see: Cook, Richard

Endich, Saramae
see: Broiles, Melvin

Erler, Jörg
see: Smithers, Don, 14)

Evans, Simon
see: Laird, Michael, 7)

Hall, Carol
  see: Steele-Perkins, Crispian, 16)

Hamari, Julia
  see: McGregor, Rob Roy, 6)

Hamm, Helen
  see: Bastin, Ernie

Hamm-Albrecht, Helga
  see: Stockhausen, Markus, 4)

Hansmann, Rotraud
  see: Groot, Willem (Wim)
  see: Spindler, Josef, 10)
  see: Tarr, Edward, 45)

Hardy, Rosemary
  see: Laird, Michael, 11)

Harper, Heather
  see: Lang, William

Harris, Adrian
  see: Laird, Michael, 7)

Harsanyi, Janice
  see: Mills, Fred

Harwood, Elizabeth
  see: Jones, Philip, 1)

Heichele, Hildegard
  see: Immer, Friedemann, 17)
  see: Quinque, Rolf, 4)

Hennig, Sebastian
  see: Immer, Friedemann, 14)
  see: Potpourri, 61), 63)

Himmler, Hesther
  see: Potpourri, 18)

Hinterreiter, Peter
  see: Bryant, Ralph, 2)
  see: Potpourri, 22)

Hlobilová, Eva
  see: Pok, František, 5)

Hofweber, Marianne
  see: Quinque, Rolf, 4)

Hornbacker, Mary Beth
  see: Potpourri, 66)

Houghton, Lucinda
  see: Steele-Perkins, Crispian, 16)

Huber, Markus
  see: Potpourri, 61), 62)

Humes, Elizabeth
  see: Davenport, LaNoue
  see: Montesi, Robert, 5)

Humphreys, Wendy
  see: Laughton, Stuart

Hurt, Phyllis
  see: Potpourri, 66)

Ihle, Andrea
  see: Güttler, Ludwig, 20), 28)

Iiyama, Emiko
  see: Spindler, Josef, 10)

Inoue, Setsko
  see: Maier, Hans Walter

Inoue-Heller, Shihomi
  see: Schmid, Bernhard, 11)

Isayeva, L.
  see: Novikov, Vadim

Ivanoff, Alexandria
  see: Potpourri, 6)

Jacobeit, Irmgard
  see: Tarr, Edward, 45)

Jaffe, Jann
  see: Herseth, Adolph, 4)

Jakschitsch, Rosmarie
  see: Schetsche, Walter

James, Jason
  see: Laird, Michael, 15)

Janowitz, Gundula
  see: André, Maurice, 17), 19)

Jelosits, Peter
see: Potpourri, 54), 55), 56),
57)
see: Spindler, Josef, 15)

Jenkin, Nicola
see: Steele-Perkins, Crispian,
16)

Jespers, Liane
see: André, Maurice, 132)

Jirglová, Milada
see: Pok, František, 6)

Jones, Isola
see: Herseth, Adolph, 4)
see: Perry, Brian

Keglmaier, Christa
see: Renz, Albrecht, 4), 5), 6),
7)

Khouri, David
see: Montesi, Robert, 2)

King, Matthew
see: Laird, Michael, 7)

Kirkby, Emma
see: Laird, Michael, 7), 18), 19)
see: Steele-Perkins, Crispian,
16)

Kirschstein, Leonore
see: Zickler, Heinz, 2)

Kitchen, Jeremy
see: Laird, Michael, 7)

Klein, Marcus
see: Potpourri, 59), 60)
see: Smithers, Don, 14), 15)

Knibbs, Jean
see: Steele-Perkins, Crispian,
16)

Kobow, Jan
see: Tamiya, Kenji

Kolganová, Jaroslava
see: Pok, František, 6)

Kotova, Raisa
see: Gorokhov, Vitaly

Kronwitter, Seppi
see: Potpourri, 55), 56)
see: Smithers, Don, 13)

Kweksilber, Marjanne
see: Smithers, Don, 13)
see: Steele-Perkins, Crispian, 8)

Kwella, Patrizia
see: Steele-Perkins, Crispian,
16)

Lacquet, JoAnne
see: Potpourri, 66)

Laki, Krisztina
see: Schmid, Bernhard, 10)
see: Soustrot, Bernard, 2)

Lamoree, Valarie
see: Ferrantino, Kenneth

Lane, Elizabeth
see: Laird, Michael, 17)

Larsen, Susan
see: Cook, Richard

Lehmann, Charlotte
see: Sauter, Hermann, 26)

Lengert, Claus
see: Bryant, Ralph, 4)

Leonard, Sarah
see: Steele-Perkins, Crispian,
16)

Le Sage, Sally
see: Jones, Philip, 5)

Lieb, Linda
see: Cook, Richard

Lloyd, Prudence
see: Laird, Michael, 17)

Lutter, Judith
see: Geyer, Charles

Maksimova, Valentina
see: Popov, Sergei, 5)

Maliponte, Adriana
see: Potpourri, 18)

Mancini, J.
see: Battagliola, Anania

Mandac, Evelyn
see: Ware, John

Marino, E.
see: Battagliola, Anania

Marshall, Lois
see: Anderson, George

Marshall, Margaret
see: Steele-Perkins, Crispian,
18)

Martin, Barbara
see: Ranger, Louis

Martin, Pauline
see: Longinotti, Paolo

Mathis, Edith
see: Holy, Walter, 5)
see: Lachenmeir, Paul
see: Potpourri, 11)
see: Tarr, Edward, 15), 18)
see: Thibaud, Pierre, 6), 7)
see: Unidentified, Trumpet(s),
9)
see: Zickler, Heinz, 1), 3)

Matsushita, Koyoko
see: Kierski, Eckhard

Mayorga, Lorie
see: Levy, Robert

Meier, Johanna
see: Anderson, Ronald, 2)

Mellor, Rupert
see: Laird, Michael, 7)

Meriweather, Annette
see: Stockhausen, Markus, 3),
4)

Mesplé, Mady
see: André, Maurice, 71)
see: Greffin, Jean Jacques

Metten, Irmengard
see: Renz, Albrecht, 4), 5), 6),
7)

Milner, Laurie
see: Laird, Michael, 7)

Minton, Yvonne
see: André, Maurice, 16)

Morgan, Beverly
see: Metzger, Charles

Morison, Elsie
see: Jackson, Harold

Morrison, Mary
see: Chenette, Stephen
see: Umbrico, Joseph

Moser, Edda
see: Eichhorn, Holger

Munger, Forrest
see: Montesi, Robert, 2)

Murray, Ann
see: Vasse, Claude

Murray-Brown, James
see: Laird, Michael, 7)

Nelson, Judith
see: Ferry, Dennis
see: Holmgren, Fred
see: Laird, Michael, 7), 17),
18), 19)

Nielsen, Inga
see: Läubin, Hannes, 6)
see: Schmid, Bernhard, 6), 7)
see: Wolf, Hans, 10)

Nixon, Marni
see: Stevens, Thomas, 10), 13)

Noorman, Jantina
see: Potpourri, 67)
see: Unidentified, Trumpet(s),
1)

Olleson, Andrew
see: Laird, Michael, 7)

Ornest, Dorothy
see: Young, Gene

Palade, Dorothea
see: Hyatt, Jack

Palmer, Felicity
see: Immer, Friedemann, 17)

Parcells, Elisabeth
see: Ridder, Jean de

Patterson, Rebecca
see: Geyer, Charles

Pearson, Barbara
see: Geyer, Charles

Perrin, Yvonne
see: Tarr, Edward, 32), 43)

Petel, Bernard
see: Thibaud, Pierre, 9)

Peters, Roberta
see: Schwarz, Gerard, 11)

Peterson, Patricia
see: Geyer, Charles

Pierre, Christiane Eda
see: Greffin, Jean Jacques

Pilgrim, Neva
see: Anderson, Ronald, 5)
see: Miller, Rodney

Plantamura, Carol
see: Burkhart, David

Poli, Liliana
see: Scholz, Walter

Pond, Nicholas
see: Laird, Michael, 7)

Popp, Lucia
see: Reinhart, Carole Dawn, 2)

Pound, Christine
see: Laird, Michael, 11)

Price, Janet
see: Snell, Howard

Price, Margaret
see: Goetting, Chandler

Pütz, Ruth-Margret
see: Schneidewind, Helmut, 3)

Quirke, Saul
see: Steele-Perkins, Crispian, 18)

Quivar, Florence
see: Weeks, Larry

Radecker, Helga
see: Renz, Albrecht, 4), 5), 6), 7)

Raskin, Judith
see: Adelstein, Bernard
see: Heinrich, Robert
see: Smith, James

Reichelt, Ingeborg
see: Gleissle, Walter, 2), 3), 8)
see: Holy, Walter, 2)
see: Sauter, Hermann, 4)

Reischl, Ute Herbert
see: Tasa, David

Renzi, Dorothy
see: Crisara, Raymond, 5)

Retchitzka, Basia
see: Adelbrecht, Henri, 3)
see: Potpourri, 18)

Rinaldi, Margherita
see: Hunger, Helmut, 2)

Robbin, Catherine
see: Steele-Perkins, Crispian, 18)

Roberts, Deborah
see: Impett, Jonathan

Rondelli, Barbara
see: Sauter, Hermann, 8)

Ross, Gill
see: Steele-Perkins, Crispian, 16)

Rosso, Margaret
see: Potpourri, 66)

Ruhland, Elisabeth
see: Renz, Albrecht, 4), 5), 6), 7)

Sahesch-Pur, Frank
see: Tarr, Edward, 17)

Sailer, Friederike
see: Gleissle, Walter, 5), 6), 7),
11)
see: Steinkopf, Otto

Salvetti, A.
see: Thibaud, Pierre, 14)

Saneva, Claudie
see: Delmotte, Roger, 29), 32)

Saque, Elsa
see: Gabel, Bernard, 4)

Sarti, Laura
see: Tarr, Edward, 32)

Sautereau, Nadine
see: André, Maurice, 71)

Schaer, Hanna
see: Caens, Thierry

Scherrer, Denise Jeanne
see: Scherbaum, Adolf, 32)

Schlick, Barbara
see: Immer, Friedemann, 10)
see: Sauter, Hermann, 2)
see: Scherbaum, Adolf, 21)
see: Touvron, Guy, 10)

Schlick-Eras, Barbara
see: Basch, Wolfgang, 1)

Schonbrun, Sheila
see: Davenport, LaNoue
see: Montesi, Robert, 5)

Schulz, Gertrud
see: Stradner, Gerhard

Schwartz, Magali
see: Tarr, Edward, 32)

Schwarzkopf, Elisabeth
see: Jackson, Harold
see: Mason, David, 1)

Schwarzweller, Lisa
see: Zeh, Karl Heinz

Scovotti, Jeanette
see: Kutik, Ronald

Seers, Mary
see: Steele-Perkins, Crispian,
16)

Selig, Edith
see: André, Maurice, 106), 110)
see: Jeannoutot, Bernard
see: Scherbaum, Adolf, 11)
see: Unidentified, Trumpet(s),
14)

Shelton, Lucy
see: Carroll, Edward, 8), 9)
see: Mase, Raymond

Sheppard, Honor
see: Jones, Philip, 7)
see: Rudolf, Richard

Silva, Joana
see: Gabel, Bernard, 4)

Simmons, Mary
see: Chevanelle, Serge

Slater, Mark
see: Laird, Michael, 7)

Smith, Jennifer
see: Steele-Perkins, Crispian, 7)

Smith, Sally
see: Cook, Richard

Solet, David
see: Montesi, Robert, 2)

Sonntag, Ulrike
see: Läubin, Hannes, 7)

Speiser, Elisabeth
see: Tarr, Edward, 4)

Spoorenberg, Erna
see: Wolf, Hans, 1)

Spring, Andrew
see: Laird, Michael, 7)

Stader, Maria
  see: Bauer, Willibald, 1), 2)
  see: Scherbaum, Adolf, 9)
  see: Unidentified, Trumpet(s), 8)

Stämpfli, Wally
  see: Tarr, Edward, 32), 43)

Steffen, Stuart
  see: Endsley, Gerald
  see: Hickman, David, 2)

Sterling, Thomas
  see: Montesi, Robert, 2)

Stich-Randall, Teresa
  see: André, Maurice, 1), 11)
  see: Mackintosh, Jack
  see: Wobisch, Helmut, 1), 7), 8)

Stoneham, Sandra
  see: Potpourri, 66)

Strádalová, Cecilie
  see: Pok, František, 5)

Sutherland, Joan
  see: Stringer, Alan, 5)

Sydnor, Fabian
  see: Dean, Allan, 3)

Tattermuschová, Helena
  see: Junek, Václav, 4)

Te Kanawa, Kiri
  see: Herseth, Adolph, 2)
  see: Steele-Perkins, Crispian, 17)

Terhoeven, Ursula
  see: Tarr, Edward, 27)

Thomas, Mary
  see: Jones, Philip, 2)
  see: Rudolf, Richard
  see: Snell, Howard

Thurmair, Veronika
  see: Renz, Albrecht, 4), 5), 6), 7)

Ticinelli-Fattori, Luciana
  see: Tarr, Edward, 30), 43)

Todd, Ailene
  see: Henderson, Douglas

Töpler-Marizy, Annemarie
  see: Ellinghaus, Wolfram

Troth, Marilyn
  see: Steele-Perkins, Crispian, 16)

Troyanos, Tatiana
  see: Eichhorn, Holger
  see: Thibaud, Pierre, 5)

van Bork, Hanneke
  see: Potpourri, 18)

Vandersteene, Zeger
  see: Hagge, Detlef

van Duyn, Ina
  see: Grin, Freddy, 5)

Vaughan, Elizabeth
  see: Jones, Philip, 3)

Venuti, Maria
  see: Reinhart, Carole Dawn, 8)

Verrett, Shirley
  see: Heinrich, Robert

Viredaz, Fabienne
  see: Touvron, Guy, 10)

von Otter, Anne Sofie
  see: Steele-Perkins, Crispian, 4)

von Stade, Frederica
  see: Schwarz, Gerard, 3)

Vyvyan, Jennifer
  see: Bravington, Eric
  see: Egan, Dennis
  see: Jackson, Harold

Wearing, Edmund
  see: Laird, Michael, 7)

Webber, Lynn
  see: Hyatt, Jack

Weber, Gunthild
see: Zeyer, Adam

Wehrung, Harrad
see: Ellinghaus, Wolfram
see: Holy, Walter, 3)

White, Marilyn
see: Potpourri, 66)

Wickham, Henry
see: Laird, Michael, 7)

Wiedl, Wilhelm
see: Bryant, Ralph, 4), 5)
see: Potpourri, 58), 59), 60)
see: Spindler, Josef, 16)

Wieninger, Elisabeth
see: Stradner, Gerhard

Wiens, Edith
see: Sauter, Hermann, 17)

Wilfinger, Grete
see: Stradner, Gerhard

Williamson, Simon
see: Laird, Michael, 7)

Wirtz, Dorothea
see: Basch, Wolfgang, 2)

Wolf, Simon
see: Wilbraham, John, 20)

Woodland, Rae
see: Wilbraham, John, 23)

Yakar, Rachel
see: Touvron, Guy, 15), 16)

Young, Nancy
see: Dean, Allan, 3)

Yureneva, Nadezhda
see: Margolin, Veniamin

Zahariades, Bruce
see: Montesi, Robert, 2)

Zedelius, Maria
see: Immer, Friedemann, 8)

Zylis-Gara, Teresa
see: Eichhorn, Holger
see: Tarr, Edward, 23), 27)

Sordone

Smithers, Don
see: Smithers, Don, 2)

Synthesizer

Britton, Peter
see: Miller, John
see: Stockhausen, Markus, 4)

Brüninghaus, Rainer
see: Stockhausen, Markus, 6)

Dubrovay, Laszlo
see: Geiger, György

Gabe, Ralf
see: Braz, Dirceu, 2)

Pomanti, Lou
see: Schultz, Erik, 8)

Riesman, Michael
see: Soloff, Lew

Subotnick, Morton
see: Guarneri, Mario

Thompson, Robin
see: Miller, John

Watts, John
see: Levy, Robert

Tenor (voice)

Aler, John
see: Weeks, Larry

Altay, Eric
see: Potpourri, 66)

Altmeyer, Theo
see: Ellinghaus, Wolfram
see: Potpourri, 2), 22), 24)
see: Sauter, Hermann, 5), 6),
  35)
see: Schneidewind, Helmut, 3)
see: Steinkopf, Otto
see: Tarr, Edward, 10), 24),
  25), 26), 32)
see: Zickler, Heinz, 3)

Baldin, Aldo
see: Immer, Friedemann, 5)
see: Läubin, Hannes, 5), 6), 7)
see: Sauter, Hermann, 2), 14),
  16), 21), 30)
see: Schmid, Bernhard, 7), 8),
  10)
see: Send, Peter
see: Unidentified, Trumpet(s),
  5)
see: Wolf, Hans, 4), 6), 8), 9)

Bamber, Peter
see: Laird, Michael, 17)

Barrows, Stuart
see: Webb, Gordon, 3)

Bartle, Donald
see: Umbrico, Joseph

Berger, Helmut
see: Renz, Albrecht, 6)

Bichler, Hans
see: Neunhoeffer, Frieder
see: Renz, Albrecht, 4), 5), 6),
  7)

Blazer, Pierre-André
see: Adelbrecht, Henri, 3)

Blochwitz, Hans Peter
see: Steele-Perkins, Crispian, 4)

Bottazzo, Pietro
see: André, Maurice, 11)

Brandon, Ernest
see: Potpourri, 66)

Bressler, Charles
see: Dean, Allan, 10)
see: Montesi, Robert, 1), 2)

Brienes, Harold
see: Nagel, Robert, 6)

Brink, Phil
see: Potpourri, 66)

Brooks, William
see: Potpourri, 66)

Brown, Wilfred
see: Eskdale, George, 5)
see: Renz, Albrecht, 1)
see: Unidentified, Trumpet(s),
  18)

Brownless, Edmund
see: Holmgren, Fred

Brunder, Wolfgang
see: Stradner, Gerhard

Büchner, Eberhard
see: Güttler, Ludwig, 10), 17),
  28)

Bufkens, Roland
see: André, Maurice, 132)

Burrows, Stuart
see: Goetting, Chandler

Byers, Alan
see: Laird, Michael, 17)

Caldwell, Don
see: Potpourri, 66)

Cassolas, Constantine
see: Burns, Stephen

Cave, Philip
see: Laird, Michael, 7)

Christophers, Harry
see: Laird, Michael, 10)

Clemens, Helmut
see: Stockhausen, Markus, 4)

Corazza, Rémy
see: André, Maurice, 97)

Cordes, Manfred
see: Tamiya, Kenji

Covey-Crump, Rogers
see: Laird, Michael, 11), 12)

Creech, Philip
see: Herseth, Adolph, 4)

Crook, Howard
see: Potpourri, 66)

Crowley, John
see: Laird, Michael, 7)

Cuenod, Hugues
see: Stracker, Wilhelm
see: Tarr, Edward, 30), 43)

Cunningham, Davis
see: Johnson, Gilbert, 5)

Davies, Maldwyn
see: Steele-Perkins, Crispian,
12)

Dekker, David
see: Montesi, Robert, 2)

DeVoll, Ray
see: Davenport, LaNoue
see: Montesi, Robert, 5)

Dodds, David
see: Montesi, Robert, 2), 5)

Driscoll, Loren
see: Crisara, Raymond, 5)
see: Heinrich, Robert

Dudley, John
see: Potpourri, 67)

Dufour, Olivier
see: Tarr, Edward, 32), 43)

Duxberry, John
see: Potpourri, 18)

Duykers, John
see: Pressley, Richard

Eckert, Rinde
see: Pressley, Richard

Ellenbeck, Hans-Dieter
see: Ellinghaus, Wolfram

Elliott, Paul
see: Laird, Michael, 2), 7), 11),
12), 13), 17)
see: Steele-Perkins, Crispian,
7), 8)

Elwes, John
see: Hagge, Detlef
see: Immer, Friedemann, 10)
see: Laird, Michael, 9)

English, Gerald
see: Renz, Albrecht, 1)
see: Wiggans, Brian

Equiluz, Kurt
see: Bryant, Ralph, 1), 2), 3),
4), 5)
see: Eichhorn, Holger
see: Groot, Willem (Wim)
see: Immer, Friedemann, 14),
15), 17)
see: McGregor, Rob Roy, 2), 4)
see: Potpourri, 51), 52), 53),
54), 55), 56), 57), 58), 59),
60), 61), 62), 63)
see: Sauter, Hermann, 10), 16),
20), 22), 23), 31)
see: Schmid, Bernhard, 2)
see: Smithers, Don, 13), 14),
15)
see: Spindler, Josef, 7), 10),
11), 12), 13), 14), 15), 16)
see: Touvron, Guy, 10)
see: Wolf, Hans, 3)
see: Zickler, Heinz, 2)

Esswood, Paul
see: Potpourri, 60)

Etchebarne
see: Caens, Thierry

Farber, Jesse
see: Montesi, Robert, 1)

Fassett, Charles
see: Montesi, Robert, 1)

Fendt, Leopold
see: Neunhoeffer, Frieder
see: Renz, Albrecht, 4), 5), 6),
7)

Fink, Manfred
  see: Soustrot, Bernard, 2)

Fleet, Edgar
  see: Potpourri, 67)

Fromme, Wolfgang
  see: Stockhausen, Markus, 4)

Gázarra, G.
  see: Battagliola, Anania

Gedda, Nicolai
  see: Mason, David, 1)

Geraerts, Harry
  see: Tamiya, Kenji

Gianotti, Pierre
  see: Coursier, Gérard

Gilvan, Raimund
  see: Sauter, Hermann, 26)

Ginzel, Reinhart
  see: Güttler, Ludwig, 20)

Greer, Albert
  see: Umbrico, Joseph

Griffett, James
  see: Hagge, Detlef
  see: Laird, Michael, 9)

Haefliger, Ernst
  see: André, Maurice, 19)
  see: Lachenmeir, Paul
  see: Scherbaum, Adolf, 9)
  see: Unidentified, Trumpet(s),
    8)

Hallmark, Rufus
  see: Cook, Richard

Hamel, Michel
  see: Longinotti, Paolo

Hansen, Kurt R.
  see: Geyer, Charles

Harder, Lutz-Michael
  see: Basch, Wolfgang, 1)
  see: Immer, Friedemann, 6)
  see: Miller, Rodney
  see: Schmid, Bernhard, 5), 7)
  see: Wolf, Hans, 10)

Herbert, William
  see: Egan, Dennis

Hess, William
  see: Mueller, Herbert

Hill, Martyn
  see: Laird, Michael, 2), 3), 11),
    12), 13), 14), 17), 18), 19)
  see: Wilbraham, John, 29)

Hochhalter, Clayton
  see: Geyer, Charles

Hoefflin, Johannes
  see: Ellinghaus, Wolfram
  see: Holy, Walter, 3)

Hoffmeister, Frank
  see: Cook, Richard
  see: Holmgren, Fred
  see: Mase, Raymond

Hopfner, Heiner
  see: Tarr, Edward, 17)

Huber, Kurt
  see: André, Maurice, 123), 138)
  see: Tarr, Edward, 4)

Jeffes, Rory
  see: Laird, Michael, 7)

Jelden, Georg
  see: André, Maurice, 106), 110)
  see: Holy, Walter, 1), 2), 5)
  see: Köpp, Rudolf
  see: Lagorce, Marcel
  see: Unidentified, Trumpet(s),
    14)

Jenkins, Neil
  see: Jones, Philip, 7)

Jochims, Wilfred
  see: Zickler, Heinz, 1)

Johnson, David
  see: Wilbraham, John, 23)

Johnstone, Don
  see: Cook, Richard

Jonen, Alfons
  see: Tarr, Edward, 19)

Jurkovič, Pavel
  see: Pok, František, 6)

Kirby, Gordon
  see: Smith, Philip, 3)

Kondo, Nobumasa
  see: Schmitt, Siegfried

Kraus, Adalbert
  see: Friedrich, Reinhold
  see: Immer, Friedemann, 6)
  see: McGregor, Rob Roy, 1),
    2), 3), 5), 6)
  see: Miller, Rodney
  see: Potpourri, 23), 24), 58)
  see: Sauter, Hermann, 4), 5),
    6), 7), 8), 9), 10), 11), 12),
    13), 14), 15), 17), 18), 19),
    21), 22), 24), 35)
  see: Schmid, Bernhard, 3), 4),
    6), 8), 9), 10)
  see: Smithers, Don, 14)
  see: Unidentified, Trumpet(s),
    5)
  see: Wolf, Hans, 2), 5), 7), 8),
    9), 10), 12)

Krebs, Helmut
  see: André, Maurice, 94), 99),
    100), 107)
  see: Gleissle, Walter, 2), 3), 4),
    5), 6), 7), 8)
  see: Unidentified, Trumpet(s),
    13), 15)

Krejčík, Vladimír
  see: Pok, František, 5)

Krenn, Werner
  see: André, Maurice, 16)
  see: Wolf, Hans, 1)

Kühner, Hartwig
  see: Hagge, Detlef

Lange, Klaus
  see: Pfann, Karl

Langridge, Philip
  see: Immer, Friedemann, 17)
  see: Laird, Michael, 3)
  see: Wilbraham, John, 2)

Laubenthal, Horst
  see: Bauer, Willibald, 4)

Lauterbach, William
  see: Pier, Fordyce

Lesueur, Jean-Jacques
  see: Jeannoutot, Bernard

Lewington, James
  see: Hagge, Detlef
  see: Laird, Michael, 9)

Lewis, Keith
  see: Herseth, Adolph, 2)

Lewis, Richard
  see: Smith, James

Litten, Jack D.
  see: Ferrantino, Kenneth

Lloyd, David
  see: Vacchiano, William, 7)

MacBone, Thomas
  see: Miller, Rodney

Mackenzie, Neil
  see: Laird, Michael, 7)

Maier, Theophil
  see: Unidentified, Trumpet(s),
    23)

Maran, George
  see: Bravington, Eric

Martell, Frederick
  see: Levy, Robert

Marten, Heinz
  see: Zeyer, Adam

McKellar, Kenneth
  see: Stringer, Alan, 5)

Melzer, Friedrich
  see: Ellinghaus, Wolfram

Metten, Elfried
  see: Neunhoeffer, Frieder
  see: Renz, Albrecht, 4), 5), 6),
    7)

Meurant, André
see: André, Maurice, 186)
see: Thibaud, Pierre, 14)

Milner, Howard
see: Steele-Perkins, Crispian, 16)

Moser, Thomas
see: Immer, Friedemann, 17)

Murgatroyd, Andrew
see: Laird, Michael, 7)
see: Steele-Perkins, Crispian, 16)

Nagel, Theodor
see: Soustrot, Bernard, 8)

Neunhoeffer, Frieder
see: Neunhoeffer, Frieder

Newell, Robert
see: Potpourri, 66)

Nobile, Alfredo
see: Battagliola, Anania

Orfenov, A.
see: Novikov, Vadim

Partridge, Ian
see: Wilbraham, John, 22)

Pavarotti, Luciano
see: Mantovani, Alberto

Pears, Peter
see: Jackson, Harold

Pfaff, Oly
see: Schmid, Bernhard, 11)

Pool, William
see: Steele-Perkins, Crispian, 16)

Porrello, Joseph
see: Montesi, Robert, 2)

Pugh, Guy
see: Levy, Robert

Regul, Norbert
see: Neunhoeffer, Frieder
see: Renz, Albrecht, 4), 5), 6), 7)

Reich, Kurt
see: Smithers, Don, 12)

Render, Charles
see: Potpourri, 66)

Resch, Rudolf
see: Eichhorn, Holger

Roberts, John
see: Hyatt, Jack

Roberts, Stephen
see: Laird, Michael, 9)

Robertson, Nicolas
see: Steele-Perkins, Crispian, 16)

Robinson, Douglas
see: Sauter, Hermann, 19)

Rogers, Nigel
see: Caudle, Theresa
see: Jones, Philip, 5)
see: Smithers, Don, 12)
see: Tarr, Edward, 45)
see: Unidentified, Trumpet(s), 1)

Rolf-Johnson, Anthony
see: Laird, Michael, 14)
see: Steele-Perkins, Crispian, 4), 16), 18)
see: Vasse, Claude

Romani, Arturo
see: Tasa, David

Rotzsch, Hans Joachim
see: Potpourri, 19)
see: Tarr, Edward, 4)
see: Zeh, Karl Heinz

Rowader, Darrell
see: Geyer, Charles

Ruhland, Konrad
see: Neunhoeffer, Frieder
see: Renz, Albrecht, 4), 5), 7)

Wohlers, Rüdiger
see: Touvron, Guy, 15), 16)

Wunderlich, Fritz
see: André, Maurice, 17), 205)
see: Gleissle, Walter, 11)
see: Steinkopf, Otto
see: Tarr, Edward, 18)

Young, Alexander
see: Mackintosh, Jack
see: Wilbraham, John, 20)

Zelnis, Edward
see: Geyer, Charles

Života, Josef
see: Pok, František, 6)

Tenor viola
(Tenor Bratsche)

Harnoncourt, Nikolaus
see: Potpourri, 49), 50), 64)
see: Spindler, Josef, 9)

Smithers, Janet
see: Smithers, Don, 6)

Stradner, Gerhard
see: Stradner, Gerhard

Theiner, Kurt
see: Potpourri, 49), 50), 64)
see: Spindler, Josef, 7), 9)
see: Tarr, Edward, 45)

Theorbo (bass lute)
[cross-referenced under lute]

Crawford, Timothy
see: Steele-Perkins, Crispian,
10)

Gerrits, Paul
see: Otto, Joachim

Imamura, Yasunori
see: Immer, Friedemann, 11)

Just, Franz
see: Haas, Rudolf

Kirsch, Dieter
see: Otto, Joachim

Müller-Dombois, Eugen
see: André, Maurice, 221), 224)
see: Holy, Walter, 5)

O'Brien, Patrick
see: Carroll, Edward, 8), 9)

O'dette, Paul
see: Keavy, Stephen

Rubin, Jonathan
see: Ferry, Dennis

Schäffer, Michael
see: Tarr, Edward, 12)

Scheit, Karl
see: Eichhorn, Holger

Tyler, James
see: Laird, Michael, 1), 11)

Zimmer, Roland
see: Haas, Rudolf

Theremin

Siwe, Thomas
see: Bastin, Ernie

Timpani
[cross-referenced under percussion]

Bähr, Frank
see: Schneidewind, Helmut, 11)

Bähr, Heinz
see: Tarr, Edward, 28)

Bardach, Nicholas
see: Touvron, Guy, 18), 19)

Begun, Fred
see: Geisler, Lloyd

Bernhardt, Lynn
see: Carroll, Edward, 12)

Blades, James
see: Clift, Dennis
see: Jones, Philip, 9)

Howes, Robert
  see: Steele-Perkins, Crispian,
    10)

Joosten, Arndt
  see: Pohle, Wolfgang

Junge, Wieland
  see: Sauter, Hermann, 24)

Kohloff, Roland
  see: Schwarz, Gerard, 20)

Koss, Donald
  see: Herseth, Adolph, 4), 6)

Kühn, Werner
  see: Schmitt, Siegfried

Leue, Eckhard
  see: Immer, Friedemann, 18)

Montagu, Jeremy
  see: Potpourri, 67)

Nemish, Barry
  see: Lowrey, Alvin

Newton, Rodney
  see: Watson, James

Peinecke, Karl-Heinz
  see: Sauter, Hermann, 7), 8),
    17), 18)

Peinkofer, Karl
  see: Basch, Wolfgang, 14)
  see: Tarr, Edward, 38)

Peinkofer, Ralph
  see: Potpourri, 22)

Pérotin, Gérard
  see: Gabel, Bernard, 2)
  see: Thibaud, Pierre, 9)

Pricha, Wenzel
  see: Potpourri, 16)
  see: Tarr, Edward, 18), 20),
    21), 23), 24), 26), 28)

Radbauer, Hans
  see: Idinger, Matthias

Rémy, Jacques
  see: André, Maurice, 6), 92),
    98)
  see: Delmotte, Roger, 7), 26)
  see: Scherbaum, Adolf, 11), 23)

Rockstroh, Siegfried
  see: Schneidewind, Helmut, 2)

Schacht, Hans-Joachim
  see: Schmid, Bernhard, 4), 9)
  see: Wolf, Hans, 12)

Schad, Karl
  see: Sauter, Hermann, 8), 9),
    12), 13), 14), 19), 20), 21),
    35)
  see: Scherbaum, Adolf, 31)
  see: Schmid, Bernhard, 3)
  see: Wolf, Hans, 3)

Schaude, Rolf
  see: Immer, Friedemann, 7)

Scherz, Friedel
  see: Potpourri, 2)

Schmitt, Norbert
  see: Immer, Friedemann, 6)
  see: Läubin, Hannes, 2), 3), 4),
    5), 7), 8)
  see: Schmid, Bernhard, 10)
  see: Send, Peter

Schmukalla, Hans Joachim
  see: Sauter, Hermann, 15)

Schuller, Aloys
  see: Sauter, Hermann, 26)

Schwander, Hermann
  see: Fink, Werner

Seaman, Christopher
  see: Webb, Gordon, 2)

Singer, Erich
  see: Tarr, Edward, 3), 17), 34)

Siwe, Thomas
  see: Hickman, David, 6)
  see: Miller, Rodney

Šprunk, Petr
  see: Horák, Jiří, 3), 5)
  see: Junek, Václav, 4)

Steinberger, Karl
  see: Bauer, Willibald, 3)

Szulc, Roman
  see: Voisin, Roger, 2)

Tavernier, J.C.
  see: Pollin, Pierre

Taylor, Alan
  see: Eskdale, George, 5)

Taylor, Norman
  see: Watson, James

Thärichen, Werner
  see: Touvron, Guy, 19)

Wilhelm, Willy
  see: Sauter, Hermann, 1), 2)

Wilson, Larry
  see: Schwarz, Gerard, 20)

Wimmer, Rudolf
  see: Spindler, Josef, 2)

Wirweitzki, Peter
  see: Schmid, Bernhard, 11)

Woud, Nick
  see: Bryant, Ralph, 5)
  see: Immer, Friedemann, 14)
  see: Potpourri, 58)
  see: Smithers, Don, 14)

Wyre, John
  see: Nowak, Henry

Tromba marina

Brookes, Oliver
  see: Laird, Michael, 1)

Pok, František
  see: Pok, František, 4)

Schindler, A.
  see: Haas, Rudolf

Zindler, J.
  see: Haas, Rudolf

Trombone
[includes all sizes, historic & modern]

Addison, Susan
  see: Impett, Jonathan
  see: Keavy, Stephen

Aigro, Ervin
  see: Ots, Aavo

Allain, René
  see: André, Maurice, 114)
  see: Delmotte, Roger, 2)
  see: Thibaud, Pierre, 9), 10)

Anderson, Early
  see: Mase, Raymond

Armstrong, Jay
  see: McGuffey, Patrick

Arqué, Henri
  see: André, Maurice, 176)

Ascher, Bob
  see: Smith, Bramwell "Bram"

Ascherl, Helmut
  see: Idinger, Matthias
  see: Stradner, Gerhard

Aubapan, Pierre
  see: Longinotti, Paolo

Badia, Miquel
  see: Espigoli, Jaume
  see: Foriscot, J.

Banens, Jacques
  see: Groot, Willem (Wim)

Barnhill, Allen
  see: Geyer, Charles

Barron, Ronald
  see: Schwarz, Gerard, 21)

Bartee, Neal
  see: Potpourri, 66)

Barteld, Harry
see: Steinkopf, Otto
see: Tarr, Edward, 10), 19),
20), 28)

Bastaens, Frans
see: Mertens, Theo, 1), 3)

Batashev, Viktor
see: Popov, Sergei, 3)

Becquet, Michel
see: André, Maurice, 157)
see: Delmotte, Roger, 44)
see: Touvron, Guy, 9), 17)

Beer, Paul
see: Laird, Michael, 2)

Berger, Helmut
see: Neunhoeffer, Frieder
see: Renz, Albrecht, 4), 5), 6),
7)

Beyer, Herbert
see: Grin, Freddy, 4)

Bichler, Hans
see: Renz, Albrecht, 4), 5), 6),
7)

Biddlecome, James A.
see: Anderson, Ronald, 1)

Biddlecome, Robert E.
see: Anderson, Ronald, 1)
see: Dean, Allan, 4)
see: Schwarz, Gerard, 13)

Blokker, Cees
see: Groot, Willem (Wim)

Bobowski, Wolfgang
see: Eichhorn, Holger

Bolter, Norman
see: Schwarz, Gerard, 21)

Bortl, Luděk
see: Kejmar, Miroslav, 7)

Bradley, Will
see: Smith, Bramwell "Bram"

Brenner, Roger
see: Jones, Philip, 9)
see: Laird, Michael, 1), 2), 3),
9), 12), 13)
see: Potpourri, 67)
see: Smithers, Don, 3)
see: Wilbraham, John, 14), 17)

Brevig, Per
see: Schwarz, Gerard, 11)

Brezna, Josef
see: Stradner, Gerhard

Brodersen, Fritz
see: Hagge, Detlef

Brown, Keith
see: Nagel, Robert, 4), 5), 8)

Brown, Raymond
see: Wilbraham, John, 6), 14),
17)

Buchanan, James
see: Schwarz, Gerard, 13)

Bulen, Jay Charles
see: Guarneri, Mario

Burne, Bobby
see: Smith, Bramwell "Bram"

Busby, Colin
see: Jones, Philip, 9)

Carlsson, Lars-Göran
see: Eklund's Baroque Ensemble

Chappuis, Paul
see: Tarr, Edward, 3)

Christen, Jo-Ann
see: Schwarz, Gerard, 13)

Cichos, Gerhard
see: Miller, Rodney
see: Potpourri, 24), 25)
see: Schmid, Bernhard, 5), 8),
13)
see: Wolf, Hans, 2), 4), 6)

Clark, John
see: Burke, James, 5), 6)

Coffey, John
see: Mager, Georges

Cohen, Gilbert
see: Montesi, Robert, 1), 2), 3),
4), 5)

Cravens, Terry
see: Plog, Anthony, 9), 11)

Cutler, Ray
see: Cook, Richard

d'Agostino, John
see: Butterfield, Billy
see: Smith, Bramwell "Bram"

Danilov, G.
see: Potpourri, 30)

Dauwe, Willy
see: Mertens, Theo, 1), 3)

Davenport, LaNoue
see: Montesi, Robert, 5)

Dellos
see: Foveau, Eugène

Dempster, Stuart
see: Pressley, Richard

Derens, Frans
see: Potpourri, 52)

Destanque, Guy
see: André, Maurice, 157)

d'Haene, Guido
see: Mertens, Theo, 1), 3)

DiBiase, Neal
see: Crisara, Raymond, 9)
see: Weis, Theodore, 3)

Dietermann, Harry
see: Potpourri, 52)
see: Ros, Ad

Dion, Jean-Jacques
see: Aquitaine Brass Ensemble

Donatelle, Marc
see: Plog, Anthony, 9)

Dorfner, Josef
see: Eichhorn, Holger

Dormeier, Walter
see: Stradner, Gerhard

Dowden, John
see: Malone, Michael

Durand, Claude
see: André, Maurice, 157)

Edelfors, Ake
see: Eklund's Baroque Ensemble

Edelman, Douglas
see: Schwarz, Gerard, 21)

English, Jon
see: Potpourri, 5)

Eriksson, Lars
see: Eklund's Baroque Ensemble

Erwin, Edward
see: Mills, Fred

Fauconnier, Eric
see: André, Maurice, 120)

Favre, Yves
see: Touvron, Guy, 9)

Feck, Josef
see: Schneidewind, Helmut, 2)
see: Tarr, Edward, 20)

Federovich, D.
see: Popov, Sergei, 3)

Federowitz, Kurt
see: Holy, Walter, 4)
see: Potpourri, 2), 47)
see: Steinkopf, Otto
see: Tarr, Edward, 3), 10), 18),
19), 20), 28), 32)

Fevrier, François
see: André, Maurice, 120)

Fiedler, Eberhard
see: Hagge, Detlef

Filippov, N.
see: Paniotov, Kharlampi

Forsyth, Malcolm
see: Lowrey, Alvin
see: Pier, Fordyce

Foucher, Max
see: Thibaud, Pierre, 10)

Fourquet, Jacques (Jacky)
see: André, Maurice, 157)
see: Delmotte, Roger, 44)
see: Touvron, Guy, 9)

Fourquet, Jean-Michel
see: Aquitaine Brass Ensemble

Fraser, Noel
see: Watson, James

Friedman, Jay
see: Geyer, Charles
see: Herseth, Adolph, 4), 6)
see: Vosburgh, George

Fromme, Arnold
see: Montesi, Robert, 1), 2), 3),
4), 5), 6)

Galiègue, Marcel
see: André, Maurice, 172)
see: Delmotte, Roger, 35)

Gallot, Bernard
see: André, Maurice, 176)

Gamble, Steven
see: Potpourri, 7)

Gardner, Richard
see: Potpourri, 6)

Geyer, Wilfried
see: Eichhorn, Holger

Gibson, William
see: Ghitalla, Armando, 5), 6),
7), 8), 9)

Girard, Pierre
see: André, Maurice, 120), 157)

Globokar, Vinko
see: Tarr, Edward, 14)

Goodwin, Peter
see: Laird, Michael, 2), 13)
see: Smithers, Don, 3)

Gosset, André
see: André, Maurice, 185), 198)
see: Potpourri, 41), 43)

Gössling, Christhard
see: Immer, Friedemann, 18)

Gottfried, Karl Heinz
see: Immer, Friedemann, 18)

Grätzig, Günter
see: Ellinghaus, Wolfram
see: Potpourri, 2)
see: Tarr, Edward, 10), 19),
20), 28)

Green, Urbie
see: Butterfield, Billy

Grin, Hans
see: Potpourri, 52)

Grivillers, A.
see: Kemblinsky, A.

Guenther, Roy
see: Ghitalla, Armando, 1)

Guizien, Christian
see: Thibaud, Pierre, 13)

Gumz, Hubert
see: Hagge, Detlef

Haines, Clifford
see: Anderson, Ronald, 6)

Hainzl, Erik
see: Spindler, Günter

Hallberg, Gordon
see: Ghitalla, Armando, 7)

Halt, Fred
see: Kuehn, David

Hanks, Thompson
see: Dean, Allan, 4)

Hauck, Robert
see: Crisara, Raymond, 3)

Haug, Jürgen
see: Ellinghaus, Wolfram
see: Holy, Walter, 4)

Havel, Jaromír
see: Horák, Jiří, 4)

Heather, Cliff
see: Smith, Bramwell "Bram"

Hecker, John
see: Potpourri, 66)

Heincke, Helmuth
see: Tarr, Edward, 4)

Hejda, Miroslav
see: Horák, Jiří, 4)

Held, Friedrich
see: Immer, Friedemann, 18)

Henry, Martin
see: Brass-zination

Herbert, Trevor
see: Potpourri, 67)

Hermann, Theo
see: Grin, Freddy, 4)

Hixon, Richard
see: Nagel, Robert, 1), 4)

Hoekstra, Wouter
see: Grin, Freddy, 2), 7)

Hoffmann, Ernst
see: Bryant, Ralph, 1), 3), 5)
see: Potpourri, 49), 52), 53),
56), 57), 62), 64)
see: Spindler, Josef, 7)
see: Tarr, Edward, 45)

Holmes, Toby L.
see: Guarneri, Mario

Huber, Heinrich
see: Potpourri, 47)
see: Tarr, Edward, 3), 32)

Hudeček, František
see: Jurča, Vladimir

Hutt, Alan
see: Jones, Philip, 9)

Iveson, John
see: Howarth, Elgar
see: Jones, Philip, 6), 9)
see: Wilbraham, John, 6), 14),
17), 21)

James, Derek
see: Jones, Philip, 9)
see: Webb, Gordon, 2)

Jampen, René
see: Brass-zination

Janda, Franz
see: Scherbaum, Adolf, 16),
22), 23)

Jeitler, Karl
see: Bryant, Ralph, 3)

Jensen, Arild
see: Christiansen, Jan

Kahila, Kauko
see: Ghitalla, Armando, 5)

Kahlenbach, Hermann Josef
see: Wolf, Hans, 4), 6), 7)

Katarzynski, Raymond
see: André, Maurice, 185), 198)
see: Potpourri, 41), 43)
see: Thibaud, Pierre, 13)

Kautzky, Karl
see: Pok, František, 2)

Kellner, Erwin
see: Idinger, Matthias

Kenreich, Glenn
see: Anderson, Ronald, 6)

Ketchen, James
see: Watson, James

Kettner, Antonín
see: Horák, Jiří, 4)
see: Lisý, Rudolf

Khersonsky, Grigory
see: Volodin, Lev

Kitzman, John
see: Giangiulio, Richard

Klemann, Jaap
  see: Groot, Willem (Wim)

Klyuchinsky, I.
  see: Popov, Sergei, 3)

Knaub, Donald
  see: Potpourri, 32), 33)

Kohlert, Walfried
  see: Hagge, Detlef

König, Wolfgang
  see: Stockhausen, Markus, 4)

Korshunov, N.
  see: Potpourri, 30)

Kozlov, Akim
  see: Margolin, Veniamin
  see: Potpourri, 30)

Krol, Sebastian
  see: Tamiya, Kenji

Küblöck, Dietmar
  see: Potpourri, 62)

Küblöck, Horst
  see: Bryant, Ralph, 5)
  see: Potpourri, 53), 56), 57),
    62)
  see: Stradner, Gerhard

Kuhner, Hans
  see: Potpourri, 24), 25)
  see: Schmid, Bernhard, 5), 8)

Ladilov, K.
  see: Volodin, Lev

Laird, Michael
  see: Laird, Michael, 1)

Lake, Leslie
  see: Watson, James

Langlitz, David
  see: Carroll, Edward, 7)

Langston, Sidney
  see: Walton, Richard

Laukamp, Bernd
  see: Stockhausen, Markus, 2)

Lawrence, Mark
  see: Metzger, Charles

Leisenring, John
  see: Ferrantino, Kenneth
  see: Potpourri, 66)

Leroy, Jean-Claude
  see: André, Maurice, 120)

Levin, Michael
  see: Dallas Brass

Linsner, Art
  see: Geyer, Charles

List, Garrett
  see: Dean, Allan, 4)
  see: Stubbs, James

Lister, Richard A.
  see: Immer, Friedemann, 18)
  see: Tarr, Edward, 3)

Lisý, Jaroslav
  see: Kejmar, Miroslav, 13)

Livesay, Dan
  see: Burkhart, David
  see: Metzger, Charles

Lumsden, Alan
  see: Laird, Michael, 1), 2), 9),
    12), 13)
  see: Smithers, Don, 1), 2)

Lund, Erik
  see: Potpourri, 66)

Maasen, Hans
  see: Groot, Willem (Wim)

Manfrin, Alain
  see: André, Maurice, 157)
  see: Delmotte, Roger, 44)

Marsteller, Robert
  see: Brady, Charles

Masson, Gabriel
  see: André, Maurice, 172), 185),
    198)
  see: Delmotte, Roger, 30)
  see: Ménardi, Louis
  see: Potpourri, 41), 43)

601

Mattern, James
  see: Miller, Rodney
  see: Perry, Brian

McElhone, Gerard
  see: Jones, Philip, 9)

Menken, Julien
  see: Ghitalla, Armando, 10)

Miller, Donald
  see: Kuehn, David

Millière, Gilles
  see: Delmotte, Roger, 44)

Mitchell, Tom
  see: Crisara, Raymond, 2)
  see: Smith, Bramwell "Bram"

Moore, Arthur
  see: Floore, John

Moore, Tony
  see: Smithers, Don, 2)

Mosheimer, Herbert
  see: Idinger, Matthias

Mueller, Thomas
  see: Carroll, Edward, 7)

Myers, Richard
  see: Kuehn, David

Naulais, Jérôme
  see: Cure, Antoine
  see: Vasse, Claude

Nicholls, Martin
  see: Laird, Michael, 1), 2), 3),
    9), 12), 13)
  see: Smithers, Don, 3)

Norden, Robert
  see: Schwarz, Gerard, 13)

Orosz, Josef
  see: Voisin, Roger, 2), 13)

Pavolka, David
  see: Greenho, David

Pearlstein, Abraham
  see: Crisara, Raymond, 3)

Peebles, Byron
  see: Stevens, Thomas, 4)

Pelikán, J.
  see: Mičaník, Jaroslav

Perkins, Geoffrey
  see: Watson, James

Peters, Gerard
  see: Grin, Freddy, 9)

Petrov, E.
  see: Popov, Sergei, 3)

Pillu, Vaino
  see: Ots, Aavo

Poindexter, Porter
  see: Anderson, Ronald, 4)
  see: Carroll, Edward, 7)
  see: Ranger, Louis

Posten, Robert
  see: Ghitalla, Armando, 1)

Pöttler, Hans
  see: Bryant, Ralph, 1), 3), 4),
    5)
  see: Potpourri, 49), 50), 52),
    57), 64)
  see: Rudolf, Richard
  see: Spindler, Josef, 7)
  see: Tarr, Edward, 45)

Poulet, Bernard
  see: Aquitaine Brass Ensemble

Powell, Michael
  see: Potpourri, 38)

Powell, Morgen
  see: Sasaki, Ray

Premru, Raymond
  see: Wilbraham, John, 6), 14),
    17)

Price, Erwin
  see: Ghitalla, Armando, 10)
  see: Nagel, Robert, 1)

Pritchard, John G.
  see: Smithers, Don, 2)
  see: Webb, Gordon, 2)

Pryor, Arthur
  see: Potpourri, 8)

Pugh, James
  see: Soloff, Lew
  see: Wise, Wilmer

Pulec, Zdeněk
  see: Kejmar, Miroslav, 3), 7),
    10)

Pulis, Gordon
  see: Glantz, Harry, 7)

Purser, David
  see: Miller, John
  see: Watson, James

Raichman, Jacob
  see: Mager, Georges
  see: Voisin, Roger, 2), 10)

Ramin, Jürgen
  see: Scholz, Walter

Ramsey, George
  see: Dean, Allan, 4)

Rankin, Herbert
  see: Plog, Anthony, 8)

Raph, Alan
  see: Soloff, Lew
  see: Wise, Wilmer

Reynolds, Jeffrey
  see: Stevens, Thomas, 4)

Richards, Ian
  see: Garside, Derek M.

Ricketts, Ronald
  see: Chenette, Stephen

Roos, Ingemar
  see: Eklund's Baroque Ensemble

Rosin, Armin
  see: Bauer, Adam
  see: Sauter, Hermann, 13)
  see: Wilbraham, John, 10)
  see: Wolf, Hans, 13)

Rouyer, Roger
  see: André, Maurice, 172)

Rückert, Hans
  see: Potpourri, 24), 25)
  see: Schmid, Bernhard, 5), 8)
  see: Wolf, Hans, 2)

Rudin, Emil
  see: Potpourri, 47)
  see: Tarr, Edward, 12), 32)

Rudolf, Richard
  see: Potpourri, 52)

Samborski, Robert
  see: Potpourri, 66)

Sanabria, Clemente
  see: León, Felipe

Sarro, Armand
  see: Geisler, Lloyd

Satterfield, Jack
  see: Butterfield, Billy

Sauer, Ralph
  see: Chenette, Stephen
  see: Stevens, Thomas, 4), 6), 7)

Saunders, Steven
  see: Watson, James

Schlagmüller, Paul
  see: Adelbrecht, Henri, 1)

Schmidt, Paul-Gerhard
  see: Güttler, Ludwig, 21), 26)

Schmitt, Helmut
  see: Ellinghaus, Wolfram
  see: Holy, Walter, 4), 5)
  see: Potpourri, 2), 47)
  see: Renz, Albrecht, 1), 2), 3)
  see: Steinkopf, Otto
  see: Tarr, Edward, 10), 18),
    19), 20), 28), 31), 32), 38)

Schnorkh, Roland
  see: André, Maurice, 181)
  see: Cuvit, Michel
  see: Potpourri, 47)
  see: Tarr, Edward, 32)

Schreckenberger, Paul
  see: Lösch, Reinhold

Schwab, Gerrit
see: Wolf, Hans, 2)

Schyns, José
see: Mertens, Theo, 3), 5)

Seisenbacher, Gerhard
see: Eichhorn, Holger

Sexton, John
see: Potpourri, 66)

Sheen, Colin
see: Smithers, Don, 3)

Singer, Wolfgang
see: Potpourri, 53)

Skarba, Hans
see: Wolf, Hans, 13)

Slokar, Branimir
see: Adelbrecht, Henri, 3)

Sluchin, Benny
see: Vasse, Claude

Smith, Henry Charles
see: Johnson, Gilbert, 1), 2), 6)

Smith, Robert D.
see: Patti, Douglas

Smith, Roger
see: Wilson, Alex

Sommer, Peter
see: Stockhausen, Markus, 4)

Soosirv, Tinu
see: Ots, Aavo

Spain, Harold
see: Jones, Philip, 9)

Staley, James
see: Potpourri, 66)
see: Sasaki, Ray

Štindl, Miroslav
see: Horák, Jiří, 4)
see: Lisý, Rudolf

Strutz, Harald
see: Hagge, Detlef

Suzan, Gérard
see: André, Maurice, 114)

Suzan, Maurice
see: André, Maurice, 98), 114), 176)
see: Delmotte, Roger, 6)

Svanberg, Carsten
see: Hovaldt, Knud

Swails, Jan
see: Wolf, Hans, 4), 6)

Swallow, John
see: Burke, James, 5), 6)
see: Dean, Allan, 2), 4), 5), 6), 7), 8)
see: Nagel, Robert, 18), 19), 20)
see: Schwarz, Gerard, 5)
see: Weis, Theodore, 4)

Sweeney, Gordon
see: Mills, Fred

Szabo, Robert
see: Montesi, Robert, 6)

Taylor, Christopher
see: Pier, Fordyce

Taylor, David
see: Carroll, Edward, 7)

Thompson, J.
see: Jandorf, D.

Thompson, James
see: Mills, Fred

Toet, Charles
see: Dickey, Bruce

Toulon, Jacques
see: Caens, Thierry

Tschedemnig, Johannes (Hans)
see: Idinger, Matthias
see: Potpourri, 56)
see: Stradner, Gerhard

Tuinstra, Luuk
see: Grin, Freddy, 7)

Tuinstra, Stef
  see: Grin, Freddy, 7)

Uber, David
  see: Burke, James, 5), 6)

Ueno, Yoshihisa
  see: Wolf, Hans, 13)

Urban, Josef
  see: Lisý, Rudolf

Vaisse, André
  see: Perinelli, René

van Balen, Hans
  see: Grin, Freddy, 2)

van Bergen, Henk
  see: Grin, Freddy, 2)

van Hecke, Pierre
  see: Mertens, Theo, 1)

Veeh, Alvin
  see: Plog, Anthony, 9)

Vengbo, Lyder
  see: Christiansen, Jan

Venglovsky, Victor
  see: Margolin, Veniamin
  see: Potpourri, 30)
  see: Yudashkin, Georgy

Verdier, Camille
  see: André, Maurice, 114), 176)
  see: Thibaud, Pierre, 13)

Viel, Guy
  see: André, Maurice, 120)

Votava, Josef
  see: Kejmar, Miroslav, 13)
  see: Mičaník, Jaroslav

Walter, Willy
  see: Schneidewind, Helmut, 2)

Waters, David
  see: Schwarz, Gerard, 13)

Watkin, Evan
  see: Jones, Philip, 9)

Watts, Eugene
  see: Canadian Brass, 1), 2), 3),
     4), 5), 6), 7)
  see: Malone, Michael
  see: Potpourri, 32), 33)

Weber, Karl-Heinz
  see: Caudle, Theresa
  see: Ellinghaus, Wolfram

Weinman, Lawrence
  see: Chenette, Stephen

Weiss, Robert
  see: Potpourri, 66)

Wells, Wayne
  see: Ghitalla, Armando, 1)

Welsch, Chauncey
  see: Crisara, Raymond, 2)

Wendlandt, Wilhelm
  see: Holy, Walter, 4), 5)
  see: Tarr, Edward, 10), 18),
     19), 20), 28)

Wendt, Heinz
  see: Stradner, Gerhard

Wenth, Andreas
  see: Bryant, Ralph, 1)
  see: Potpourri, 49), 52), 64)
  see: Spindler, Josef, 7)
  see: Tarr, Edward, 45)

Wetz, Erhard
  see: Grin, Freddy, 4)

Wick, Denis
  see: Clift, Dennis

Wilson, Arthur
  see: Jones, Philip, 2)

Winkler, Harald
  see: Krug, Willi, 2)

Winthorpe, Tom
  see: Watson, James

Witzer, Steve
  see: Geyer, Charles

Wright, Robert
see: Crisara, Raymond, 3)
see: Nagel, Robert, 18)

Würzler, Fritz
see: Idinger, Matthias
see: Spindler, Josef, 1)

Yamamoto, Masaaki
see: Wolf, Hans, 13)

Zellmer, Steven
see: Chenette, Stephen

Zettler, Richard
see: Tarr, Edward, 4)

Zinke, Lothar
see: Schneidewind, Helmut, 2)

Zuskin, Joseph
see: Chevanelle, Serge

Trumpet
[includes various types & ranges,
historic & modern: cornet, flügelhorn,
piccolo trumpet, natural trumpet
(Baroque trumpet, Jägertrompete,
Tromba da tirarsi); cornetto is
excluded but is indexed separately]

Ackermann, Wilhelm
see: André, Maurice, 123)
see: Potpourri, 21), 34), 35)
see: Zickler, Heinz, 7)

Adelbrecht, Henri
see: Adelbrecht, Henri

Adelstein, Bernard
see: Adelstein, Bernard

Adriano, Albert
see: Delmotte, Roger, 9), 14),
15), 23), 27), 40), 45), 46),
47)

Akoka, Lucien
see: André, Maurice, 92)

Albach, Carl
see: Giangiulio, Richard

Ametrano, Stephen
see: Carroll, Edward, 10)
see: Potpourri, 32)

Amstutz, Keith
see: Amstutz, Keith

Andersen, Ole
see: Andersen, Ole

Andersen, Tim
see: Dallas Brass

Anderson, George
see: Anderson, George

Anderson, Ronald
see: Anderson, Ronald
see: Dean, Allan, 4)
see: Potpourri, 5), 38)

André, Lionel
see: André, Maurice, 3), 43),
57), 74), 85), 86), 119),
153), 211), 215)

André, Maurice
see: André, Maurice
see: Delmotte, Roger, 37)
see: Potpourri, 13), 14), 15),
18), 32), 33), 35), 36), 37),
41), 42), 43), 44), 45), 47),
68)

André, Nicolas
see: André, Maurice, 39)

André, Raymond
see: André, Maurice, 77), 131),
140), 150), 208), 215)
see: Molénat, Claude
see: Soustrot, Bernard, 7)

Archibald, Paul
see: Watson, James

Austin, James
see: Austin, James
see: Hohstadt, Thomas

Autrey, Byron L.
see: Autrey, Byron L.

Avonds, Eddy
see: Mertens, Theo, 1)

Bäckvall, Arne
see: Eklund's Baroque Ensemble

Baker, Bernard (Benny)
see: Baker, Bernard

Baker, Sidney
see: Baker, Sidney

Baldwin, David
see: Baldwin, David

Balm, Neil
see: Carroll, Edward, 7), 9), 10)
see: Potpourri, 32), 33)
see: Schwarz, Gerard, 7)

Balyan, Yuri
see: Balyan, Yuri

Banz, Erwin
see: Ullrich, Marc

Barker, Horace
see: Clift, Dennis

Basch, Jürgen
see: Schneidewind, Helmut, 11)

Basch, Wolfgang
see: Basch, Wolfgang

Bastin, Ernie
see: Bastin, Ernie
see: Potpourri, 5)

Battagliola, Anania
see: Battagliola, Anania

Battagliola, Walter
see: Battagliola, Anania

Bauer, Adam
see: Bauer, Adam

Bauer, Willibald
see: Bauer, Willibald

Beacraft, Ross
see: Perry, Brian

Bell, Glen
see: Giangiulio, Richard

Benedetti, Donald
see: Benedetti, Donald

Bengtsson, Helene
see: Eklund's Baroque Ensemble

Benzinger, Karl
see: Bauer, Willibald, 3), 4)
see: Benzinger, Karl

Berg, Willi
see: Schneidewind, Helmut, 11)

Berginc, Charles
see: Giangiulio, Richard

Berinbaum, Martin
see: Berinbaum, Martin

Bernard, André
see: Bernard, André
see: Potpourri, 36), 37)

Bernes, André
see: Calvayrac, Albert

Biessecker, Friedhelm
see: Biessecker, Friedhelm

Biessecker, Sigrid
see: Biessecker, Friedhelm

Bilger, David
see: Bilger, David
see: Carroll, Edward, 12)

Birch, Robert
see: Birch, Robert

Birk, Neeme
see: Ots, Aavo

Blackburn, Roger
see: Blackburn, Roger

Blair, Stacy
see: Blair, Stacy

Blank, Isodor
see: Broiles, Melvin

Blasaditsch, Otto
see: Basch, Wolfgang, 7)

Blee, Eugene
see: Blee, Eugene

607

Bush, Irving
  see: Bush, Irving
  see: Plog, Anthony, 5)
  see: Stevens, Thomas, 8)

Butler, Barbara
  see: Butler, Barbara
  see: Geyer, Charles

Butterfield, Billy
  see: Butterfield, Billy

Caens, Thierry
  see: André, Maurice, 47)
  see: Caens, Thierry
  see: Touvron, Guy, 2)

Calvayrac, Albert
  see: Calvayrac, Albert

Camp, William
  see: Potpourri, 7)

Cantie, Jean
  see: André, Maurice, 120)

Capouillez, Luc
  see: Capouillez, Luc

Carl, Michael
  see: Parker, Craig B.

Carlsson, Lars-Göran
  see: Eklund's Baroque Ensemble

Carrière, Guy
  see: Delmotte, Roger, 23), 26),
    28), 29)

Carroll, Edward
  see: Carroll, Edward
  see: Potpourri, 4), 32), 33)
  see: Schwarz, Gerard, 7)
  see: Soloff, Lew

Caston, Saul
  see: Cohen, Sol

Cesare, James
  see: Cesare, James

Chaine, Paul
  see: Delmotte, Roger, 15), 23)

Chandler, Cameron
  see: Giangiulio, Richard

Chappuis, Paul
  see: Tarr, Edward, 3)

Charlet, William
  see: André, Maurice, 6)

Chatel, Jean-Louis
  see: Chatel, Jean-Louis

Chenette, Stephen
  see: Chenette, Stephen

Chesnut, Walter
  see: Chesnut, Walter

Chevanelle, Serge
  see: Chevanelle, Serge

Chmel, Miloslav
  see: Buriánek, Jindřich

Christensen, Ketil
  see: Christensen, Ketil

Christiansen, Jan
  see: Christiansen, Jan

Chunn, Michael
  see: Chunn, Michael
  see: Hickman, David, 6)

Clarke, Herbert L.
  see: Clarke, Herbert L.

Clift, Dennis
  see: Clift, Dennis
  see: Eskdale, George, 5)
  see: Potpourri, 9)

Cohen, Sol
  see: Cohen, Sol

Collins, Philip
  see: Potpourri, 32), 33)

Collura, Frank
  see: Kuehn, David

Come, Andre
  see: Ghitalla, Armando, 5), 7)
  see: Hirt, Al

Conrad, Jörg
  see: Conrad, Jörg

Conrath, Gerald
see: Wobisch, Helmut, 3)

Cooper, Grant
see: Cooper, Grant

Couëffé, Yves
see: André, Maurice, 157)
see: Couëffé, Yves
see: Pollin, Pierre
see: Touvron, Guy, 21)

Coursier, Gérard
see: Coursier, Gérard
see: Pollin, Pierre

Cowell, Johnny
see: Cowell, Johnny

Coyne, Stephen
see: Parker, Craig B.

Cran, David
see: Ghitalla, Armando, 1)

Crisara, Raymond
see: Burke, James, 3), 5), 6)
see: Crisara, Raymond
see: Glantz, Harry, 2), 5), 6)

Cronshaw, Brian
see: Garside, Derek M.

Csiba, József
see: Csiba, József

Csizmadia, Gabor
see: Potpourri, 39)

Cure, Antoine
see: Cure, Antoine

Curnow, Jeffrey
see: Carroll, Edward, 12)

Cuvit, Michel
see: Cuvit, Michel
see: Potpourri, 29), 37)

Darling, James
see: Darling, James

Dassé, Jean-Luc
see: Dassé, Jean-Luc

Daval, Charles
see: Geyer, Charles

Davidson, Louis
see: Davidson, Louis

Dean, Allan
see: Carroll, Edward, 10)
see: Dean, Allan
see: Nagel, Robert, 11)
see: Potpourri, 32), 33)
see: Schwarz, Gerard, 5), 20), 21)
see: Weis, Theodore, 1)

de Antoni, Charles
see: André, Maurice, 11), 79), 114)

Debonneville, Michel
see: Cuvit, Michel
see: Potpourri, 37)

de Hauwere, Florent
see: Mertens, Theo, 1), 3)

Delmas, Serge
see: André, Maurice, 120)

Delmotte, Roger
see: André, Maurice, 172)
see: Delmotte, Roger
see: Potpourri, 37), 41), 43), 44), 68)

de Ridder, Jean
see: Ridder, Jean de

Derras, Dominique
see: Delmotte, Roger, 44)

Deside
see: Deside

Despretz, Gilbert
see: Coursier, Gérard
see: Delmotte, Roger, 7), 15), 23), 26)

Didrickson, Luther
see: Miller, Rodney

Dillon, G. Burnette
see: Plog, Anthony, 4)

Dion, Jean-François
see: Aquitaine Brass Ensemble

Dityatkin, Alexandre
see: Volodin, Lev

DiVall, Robert
see: DiVall, Robert
see: Plog, Anthony, 5)
see: Stevens, Thomas, 8)

Dobson, George
see: Victorian Trumpet Trio

Doets, Jas
see: Doets, Jas

Dokshitser, Timofei
see: Dokshitser, Timofei

Dolce, Christine
see: Dolce, Christine

Dolk, Pieter
see: Bodenröder, Robert
see: Potpourri, 16), 22)
see: Tarr, Edward, 18), 20),
    21), 28)

Dougherty, Patrick
see: Cesare, James

Douglas, Priscilla
see: Schwarz, Gerard, 13)

Driscoll, Phil
see: Driscoll, Phil

Dudgeon, Ralph
see: Dudgeon, Ralph

Dupisson, Ferdinand
see: Vaillant, Ludovic, 6)

Duquénoy, Louis
see: Tarr, Edward, 23)

Dutot, Pierre
see: Delmotte, Roger, 44)
see: Dutot, Pierre
see: Loustalot, Alain

Dweir, Fred
see: Sauter, Hermann, 3)

Early, Robert
see: Thompson, James

Ebner, Ludwig
see: Potpourri, 23), 27)
see: Schmid, Bernhard, 4)

Edefors, Ake
see: Eklund's Baroque Ensemble

Egan, Dennis
see: Egan, Dennis
see: Potpourri, 9)

Egger, Alfons
see: Spindler, Josef, 2)

Eggers, Carter
see: Eggers, Carter

Eichler, Horst
see: Eichler, Horst

Eklund, Bengt
see: Eklund's Baroque Ensemble
see: Tarr, Edward, 39), 40)

Ellinghaus, Wolfram
see: Ellinghaus, Wolfram

Ellison, Sidney
see: Clift, Dennis

Endsley, Gerald
see: Endsley, Gerald

Epp, Peter
see: Held, Friedrich

Erb, Helmut
see: Erb, Helmut

Eriksson, Lars
see: Eklund's Baroque Ensemble

Eskdale, George
see: Eskdale, George

Espigoli, Jaume
see: Espigoli, Jaume

Evans, Laurie
see: Evans, Laurie

Faber, Albert
see: Grin, Freddy, 7)

Falcone, Frank
see: Glantz, Harry, 2), 5), 6)

Falentin, Paul
see: Falentin, Paul

Faller, Robert
see: Tarr, Edward, 30), 43)

Fauconnier, Hubert
see: André, Maurice, 120)

Feck, Josef
see: Tarr, Edward, 28)

Federowitz, Kurt
see: Potpourri, 47)
see: Tarr, Edward, 3), 32)

Ferguson, Simon
see: Watson, James

Ferrantino, Kenneth
see: Ferrantino, Kenneth
see: Lowrey, Alvin
see: Potpourri, 66)

Ferry, Dennis
see: Ferry, Dennis

Fink, Werner
see: Fink, Werner

Finke, Helmut
see: Holy, Walter, 3)
see: Tarr, Edward, 38)

Flecheux, José
see: André, Maurice, 120)

Flik, Geert
see: Grin, Freddy, 7)

Floch, Duane B.
see: Brass-zination

Floore, John
see: Floore, John

Flugel, J.
see: Flugel, J.

Fomin, Evgeny
see: Fomin, Evgeny

Fontanella, Claude
see: Schwarz, Gerard, 13)

Foriscot, J.
see: Foriscot, J.

Foveau, Eugène
see: Foveau, Eugène

Frautschi, Fritz
see: McCann, Phillip

Frei, Marcel
see: Frei, Marcel

Friedli, Bernhard
see: McCann, Phillip

Friedman, Stanley
see: Giangiulio, Richard

Friedrich, Reinhold
see: Friedrich, Reinhold

Friestadt, Harry
see: Friestadt, Harry

Gabel, Bernard
see: André, Maurice, 143), 168), 169), 216)
see: Gabel, Bernard
see: Thibaud, Pierre, 10)

Gabel, Gérard
see: Thibaud, Pierre, 9)

Gardner, Ned
see: Gardner, Ned

Garreau, André
see: Delmotte, Roger, 42), 43)
see: Garreau, André

Garside, Derek M.
see: Garside, Derek M.

Gass, Josef
see: Gass, Josef

Gaudon, Jean-Jacques
see: Gaudon, Jean-Jacques
see: Vasse, Claude

Gay, Bram
see: Gay, Bram

Geiger, György
see: Geiger, György

Geisler, Lloyd
see: Geisler, Lloyd

Gekker, Chris
see: Holmgren, Fred
see: Potpourri, 38)

Gerloff, Wolfgang
see: Güttler, Ludwig, 21), 23)

Gevorkyan, Sergei
see: Popov, Sergei, 3)

Geyer, Charles
see: Butler, Barbara
see: Geyer, Charles

Ghitalla, Armando
see: Ghitalla, Armando
see: Voisin, Roger, 2), 3)

Giangiulio, Richard
see: Giangiulio, Richard
see: Potpourri, 33)

Giehl, Paul
see: Holy, Walter, 7), 8)

Ginetsinsky, Daniel
see: Potpourri, 30)

Glantz, Harry
see: Burke, James, 5), 6)
see: Glantz, Harry
see: Potpourri, 31)
see: Voisin, Roger, 5), 8)

Gleaves, Charles
see: Kuehn, David

Gleissle, Walter
see: André, Maurice, 123)
see: Gleissle, Walter
see: Potpourri, 34), 35)

Goethel, Siegfried
see: Goethel, Siegfried

Goetting, Chandler
see: Goetting, Chandler
see: Tarr, Edward, 3), 34)

Goguen, Gerard
see: Ghitalla, Armando, 5)

Gonczarowski, Jerzy
see: Piórkowski, Zygmunt

Gordyczukowski, Borys
see: Piórkowski, Zygmunt

Gorokhov, Vitaly
see: Gorokhov, Vitaly

Gössling, Christhard
see: Immer, Friedemann, 18)

Gottfried, Karl Heinz
see: Immer, Friedemann, 18)

Gould, Mark
see: Carroll, Edward, 1), 6), 7),
    9), 10), 11)
see: Gould, Mark
see: Potpourri, 32), 33)
see: Schwarz, Gerard, 5), 7),
    20), 21)

Gräber, Wolfgang
see: Gräber, Wolfgang

Grčar, Anton
see: Grčar, Anton

Green, Donald
see: Plog, Anthony, 10)

Greenho, David
see: Greenho, David

Greffin, Jean Jacques
see: Greffin, Jean Jacques

Greffin, M.
see: Greffin, M.

Grin, Freddy
see: Grin, Freddy
see: Groot, Willem (Wim)

Groot, Willem (Wim)
see: Groot, Willem (Wim)

Groth, Konradin
see: Groth, Konradin

Grzesiak, Jan
see: Piórkowski, Zygmunt

Guarneri, Mario
  see: Guarneri, Mario
  see: Plog, Anthony, 5)
  see: Stevens, Thomas, 4), 8)

Guggenberger, Wolfgang
  see: Quinque, Rolf, 4)

Gursch, Heinz
  see: Krug, Willi, 2)

Gustavsson, Jan
  see: Eklund's Baroque Ensemble

Güttler, Ludwig
  see: Güttler, Ludwig

Guyot, Jean
  see: Jarmasson, Jacques

Haas, Rudolf
  see: Haas, Rudolf

Haas, Wolfgang
  see: Haas, Wolfgang

Hagemeyer, Jan
  see: Doets, Jas

Halder, Karl-Heinz
  see: Wolf, Hans, 12)

Hall, Malcolm
  see: Watson, James

Halldén, Leif
  see: Potpourri, 3)

Haneuse, Arthur
  see: Delmotte, Roger, 15), 23),
    49), 50)
  see: Haneuse, Arthur
  see: Potpourri, 68)

Hanžl, Z.
  see: Mičaník, Jaroslav

Hardenberger, Håkan
  see: Hardenberger, Håkan

Hardy, Francis
  see: Hardy, Francis
  see: Potpourri, 44)

Harkins, Edwin
  see: Harkins, Edwin

Hartog, Thomas
  see: Hartog, Thomas

Hasselmann, Ronald
  see: Chenette, Stephen

Haubold, Rudolf
  see: Potpourri, 14), 15)
  see: Scherbaum, Adolf, 19),
    22), 23), 24), 25), 26)

Haug, Edward
  see: Haug, Edward

Hausamann, Ernst
  see: McCann, Phillip

Hausberger, Josef
  see: Potpourri, 17), 23), 27)
  see: Schmid, Bernhard, 3), 4),
    9), 11)
  see: Send, Peter

Hausdoerfer, Fred
  see: Hausdoerfer, Fred

Häusler, Siegfried
  see: André, Maurice, 199)

Hawkins, Richard
  see: Rehm, Klaus

Haynie, John
  see: Haynie, John, 1), 2), 3),
    4), 5)

Head, Emerson
  see: Head, Emerson

Heinisch, Heinz
  see: Güttler, Ludwig, 21), 23)

Heinrich, Robert
  see: Heinrich, Robert

Held, Friedrich
  see: Held, Friedrich
  see: Immer, Friedemann, 18)

Hell, Josef
  see: Wobisch, Helmut, 3)

Helmacy, Robert
see: Schwarz, Gerard, 13)

Henderson, Douglas
see: Henderson, Douglas

Hendrickx, Ivo
see: Mertens, Theo, 3)

Hendrie, Andrew
see: Watson, James

Hengst, Berndt
see: Güttler, Ludwig, 21), 23)
see: Haas, Rudolf

Herdlitschka, Heinrich
see: Spindler, Josef, 2)

Hermann, Emil
see: Potpourri, 22), 47)
see: Tarr, Edward, 23), 24),
26), 32)

Herrick, Carol
see: Giangiulio, Richard

Herseth, Adolph
see: Herseth, Adolph

Hertel, Karl
see: Bauer, Willibald, 4)

Hickman, David
see: Hickman, David

Hidalgo, José Luis
see: Hidalgo, José Luis

Higgins, Henry
see: Potpourri, 8)

Himmelreich, Leo
see: Grin, Freddy, 2)

Hindmarsh, Martin
see: Hopkins, Peter

Hirt, Al
see: Hirt, Al

Hobart, Edward
see: Laird, Michael, 22)

Hobart, Edwin
see: Steele-Perkins, Crispian,
19)

Hoffman, Edward
see: Hoffman, Edward

Hoffman, Melanie
see: Parker, Craig B.

Hoffmann, Ernst
see: Spindler, Josef, 7)

Hohstadt, Thomas
see: Hohstadt, Thomas

Holland, Jack
see: Holland, Jack

Holler, Adolf
see: Holler, Adolf
see: Wobisch, Helmut, 3), 4),
6), 11), 14)

Holmes, Allan
see: Garside, Derek M.

Holmgren, Fred
see: Holmgren, Fred

Holy, Walter
see: Holy, Walter
see: Potpourri, 16), 42), 44)
see: Spindler, Josef, 9)
see: Tarr, Edward, 18), 20),
21), 27), 28)

Hood, Boyde
see: Hood, Boyde
see: Stevens, Thomas, 9)

Hood, Donald
see: Hood, Donald

Hopkins, Kenneth
see: Hopkins, Kenneth

Hopkins, Peter
see: Hopkins, Peter

Hopman, Herman
see: Grin, Freddy, 7)
see: Hopman, Herman

Jorand, Jean-Claude
  see: Jorand, Jean-Claude

Juarez, Rosalio
  see: Juarez, Rosalio

Junek, Václav
  see: Horák, Jiří, 3), 5)
  see: Junek, Václav

Junge, Harald
  see: Junge, Harald

Jurča, Vladimir
  see: Jurča, Vladimir

Kafelnikov, Vladimir
  see: Kafelnikov, Vladimir

Kan, Vasily
  see: Yudashkin, Georgy

Karon, Robert
  see: Plog, Anthony, 4)

Karpilovsky, Murray
  see: Karpilovsky, Murray
  see: Voisin, Roger, 5), 8)

Katscher, Horst
  see: Zeh, Karl Heinz

Kauffman, Jean
  see: Delmotte, Roger, 23), 26),
    28), 29)

Keavy, Stephen
  see: Keavy, Stephen
  see: Steele-Perkins, Crispian,
    10), 16)

Kejmar, Miroslav
  see: Horák, Jiří, 3), 5)
  see: Kejmar, Miroslav
  see: Zapf, Gerd

Kelber, Fritz
  see: Potpourri, 2)
  see: Zickler, Heinz, 1), 2)

Kemblinsky, A.
  see: Kemblinsky, A.

Kempton, Jeff
  see: Potpourri, 66)

Keneke, Emil
  see: Potpourri, 8)

Kent, George
  see: Eklund's Baroque Ensemble
  see: Tarr, Edward, 28)

Ketch, James
  see: Hickman, David, 6)

Khanin, Mikhail
  see: Prokopov, Vyacheslav

Kidd, Russell
  see: Plog, Anthony, 5), 10)

Kierski, Eckhard
  see: Kierski, Eckhard

Kipfer, Paul
  see: McCann, Phillip

Klein, Manny
  see: Klein, Manny

Kleren, Guy
  see: Waltzing, Gast

Klette, Manfred
  see: Potpourri, 11)

Klishans, Yanis
  see: Klishans, Yanis

Klochkov, Pavel
  see: Klochkov, Pavel

Klushkin, Yuri
  see: Klushkin, Yuri

Knudsvig, Peter
  see: Brass-zination

Köpp, Rudolf
  see: Junge, Harald
  see: Köpp, Rudolf

Korolev, Alexandre
  see: Korolev, Alexandre

Kozderka, Vladislav
  see: Kejmar, Miroslav, 13)
  see: Kozderka, Vladislav
  see: Potpourri, 40)

Lecointre, Jacques
  see: André, Maurice, 185), 198)
  see: Pollin, Pierre
  see: Potpourri, 41), 43)

LeComte, Jacques
  see: LeComte, Jacques

Lemos, Alexandre Vasilievich
  see: Lemos, Alexandre
    Vasilievich

León, Felipe
  see: León, Felipe

Leroy, Jean-Paul
  see: André, Maurice, 47), 157)
  see: Leroy, Jean-Paul
  see: Soustrot, Bernard, 4)
  see: Touvron, Guy, 2)

Leutscher, Lubertus
  see: Grin, Freddy, 4)

Levine, Jesse
  see: Holmgren, Fred

Levy, Robert
  see: Levy, Robert

Lewark, Egbert
  see: Lewark, Egbert

Lewis, E. Leonard
  see: Lewis, E. Leonard

Libiseller, Hansjörg
  see: Idinger, Matthias
  see: Libiseller, Hansjörg

Lieberman, Harold J.
  see: Lieberman, Harold J.

Lindeborg, Jimm
  see: Eklund's Baroque Ensemble

Lindeke, Per-Olov
  see: Eklund's Baroque Ensemble

Lindtvedt, Gunnar
  see: Eklund's Baroque Ensemble

Lippert, Lloyd
  see: Plog, Anthony, 10)

Lisenbee, Thomas
  see: Dean, Allan, 4), 5)
  see: Schwarz, Gerard, 20)

Lister, Richard A.
  see: Immer, Friedemann, 18)
  see: Tarr, Edward, 3)

Lisý, Rudolf
  see: Lisý, Rudolf

Logan, Jack
  see: Logan, Jack

Longinotti, Paolo
  see: Longinotti, Paolo
  see: Potpourri, 29)

Lopez, Vincente
  see: Lopez, Vincente

Lösch, Reinhold
  see: Lösch, Reinhold
  see: Schneidewind, Helmut, 2)

Loustalot, Alain
  see: Loustalot, Alain

Lowrey, Alvin
  see: Lowrey, Alvin
  see: Pier, Fordyce

Luithle, Rainer
  see: Luithle, Rainer

Lumsden, Alan
  see: Laird, Michael, 1)

Maalouf, Nassim
  see: Maalouf, Nassim

Macintosh, Ian
  see: Wilbraham, John, 26)

Mackintosh, Jack
  see: Mackintosh, Jack

Mager, Georges
  see: Mager, Georges

Maier, Hans Walter
  see: Maier, Hans Walter

Malkov, Valentin
  see: Malkov, Valentin
  see: Potpourri, 30)

Malone, Michael
see: Malone, Michael

Männel, Armin
see: Güttler, Ludwig, 7)

Mantovani, Alberto
see: Mantovani, Alberto

Margolin, Veniamin
see: Margolin, Veniamin

Marinus, Jan
see: Marinus, Jan

Marrs, Dale
see: Tarr, Edward, 3), 34)

Marsalis, Wynton
see: Marsalis, Wynton

Mas, Jacques
see: André, Maurice, 10), 92), 95)

Mase, Raymond
see: Holmgren, Fred
see: Mase, Raymond
see: Schwarz, Gerard, 7), 20)

Mason, David
see: Mason, David

Masters, Edward L.
see: Masters, Edward L.

Mathez, Jean-Pierre
see: Adelbrecht, Henri, 4), 5), 6), 7)
see: Tarr, Edward, 28), 42)

Maximenko, Anatoly
see: Maximenko, Anatoly

Maxwell, Jimmy
see: Butterfield, Billy

Mayer, Eugen
see: Potpourri, 23), 24), 26), 27)
see: Sauter, Hermann, 1), 7), 8), 9), 12), 13), 14), 15), 17), 18), 19), 20), 21), 24), 26), 30), 32), 33), 34), 35), 36)

Mazeau, Serge
see: André, Maurice, 120)

Mazurowicz, Andrzej
see: Piórkowski, Zygmunt

McCann, Phillip
see: McCann, Phillip

McComas, Donald E.
see: Johnson, Gilbert, 8)

McGaw, Laurie
see: Schwarz, Gerard, 13)

McGregor, Rob Roy
see: McGregor, Rob Roy
see: Potpourri, 17), 26)
see: Stevens, Thomas, 9)

McGuffey, Patrick
see: McGuffey, Patrick

McKiever, Gerald
see: Potpourri, 66)

McNab, Malcolm
see: McNab, Malcolm
see: Stevens, Thomas, 8)

Mear, Sidney
see: Mear, Sidney

Meek, Henk
see: Grin, Freddy, 7)

Meer, Moritz
see: Rehm, Klaus

Meinen, Ernst
see: McCann, Phillip

Ménardi, Louis
see: André, Maurice, 6), 11)
see: Ménardi, Louis
see: Potpourri, 28), 33)

Méndez, Rafael
see: Méndez, Rafael

Méndez, Ralph
see: Méndez, Rafael, 19), 24)

Méndez, Robert
see: Méndez, Rafael, 19), 24)

Mertens, Theo
see: Mertens, Theo

Messler, Guy
see: Touvron, Guy, 10)
see: Ullrich, Marc

Metzger, Charles
see: Metzger, Charles

Mičaník, Jaroslav
see: Horák, Jiří, 1), 2)
see: Kejmar, Miroslav, 14)
see: Mičaník, Jaroslav

Michel, Jean-François
see: Michel, Jean-François

Miller, James
see: Schwarz, Gerard, 7)

Miller, John
see: Miller, John
see: Watson, James

Miller, Rodney
see: Miller, Rodney
see: Potpourri, 26)

Millière, Gérard
see: Millière, Gérard

Mills, Fred
see: Canadian Brass, 1), 2), 3),
4), 5), 6), 7)
see: Malone, Michael
see: Mills, Fred
see: Potpourri, 32), 33)

Modell, Ronald
see: Logan, Jack

Mogilnicki, Robert
see: Hirt, Al

Möhlheinrich, Ernst
see: Scherbaum, Adolf, 31)

Molénat, Claude
see: Molénat, Claude

Molostov, Alexandre
see: Volodin, Lev

Monogenis, Statios
see: Zickler, Heinz, 3)

Moore, Albert
see: Potpourri, 6)

Morisset, Michel
see: Morisset, Michel

Morrison, David
see: Potpourri, 66)

Mueller, Herbert
see: Mueller, Herbert

Mugdan, Albrecht
see: Immer, Friedemann, 7),
18)

Murphy, Maurice
see: Murphy, Maurice

Murtha, Roger
see: Murtha, Roger

Myers, Walter
see: Potpourri, 6)

Naess, Lars
see: Eklund's Baroque Ensemble
see: Naess, Lars

Nagel, Robert
see: Burke, James, 5), 6)
see: Dean, Allan, 2)
see: Heinrich, Robert
see: Nagel, Robert
see: Voisin, Roger, 5), 6), 8)

Nashan, Rudolph
see: Nashan, Rudolph

Nayuki, Takanori
see: Tobe, Yutaka

Neal, Ronald
see: Umbrico, Joseph

Nelson, John
see: Giangiulio, Richard

Nicolson, Graham
see: Immer, Friedemann, 9)

Nilsson, Bo
see: Eklund's Baroque Ensemble
see: Tarr, Edward, 44)

Novikov, Vadim
see: Novikov, Vadim

Nowak, Henry
see: Nowak, Henry

Nowicki, August
see: Nowicki, August

Nystrom, Kaj
see: Nystrom, Kaj

Oberli, Ernst
see: McCann, Phillip

Ode, James
see: Ode, James

Oesterle, Albert
see: Basch, Wolfgang, 7), 14)

Okuyama, Taizo
see: Tobe, Yutaka

Opalesky, Louis
see: Nowak, Henry

Orvid, Georgy
see: Orvid, Georgy

Osterloh, Klaus
see: Immer, Friedemann, 7),
18)

Ots, Aavo
see: Ots, Aavo

Paniotov, Kharlampi
see: Paniotov, Kharlampi

Parker, Craig B.
see: Parker, Craig B.

Parker, R. Ted
see: Parker, R. Ted

Parramon, Henry
see: Parramon, Henry

Pasch, Wolfgang
see: Potpourri, 21), 34), 35),
65)
see: Zickler, Heinz, 7)

Patrylak, Daniel
see: Potpourri, 32), 33)

Patti, Douglas
see: Patti, Douglas

Pauli, Otto
see: McCann, Phillip

Pearson, Byron
see: Pearson, Byron

Peers, Harry
see: Potpourri, 34), 35)
see: Statter, Arthur

Peress, Maurice
see: Potpourri, 34), 35)
see: Statter, Arthur

Perinelli, René
see: Aquitaine Brass Ensemble
see: Perinelli, René

Perry, Brian
see: Perry, Brian

Perucca, Alain
see: André, Maurice, 120)

Petit, Gilbert
see: Petit, Gilbert
see: Ullrich, Marc

Petz, Pál
see: Petz, Pál

Pfann, Karl
see: Pfann, Karl

Phillippe, André
see: Phillippe, André

Picavais, Lucien
see: André, Maurice, 92)
see: Delmotte, Roger, 15), 23)

Pichel, Willi
see: Holy, Walter, 7), 8)

Pichl, Anton
see: Spindler, Josef, 7)

Pier, Fordyce
see: Pier, Fordyce

Piórkowski, Zygmunt
see: Piórkowski, Zygmunt

Pirot, Jean
see: André, Maurice, 74), 153),
  157), 176), 185), 198)
see: Potpourri, 41), 43)

Platt, Seymour
see: Platt, Seymour

Pliquett, Joachim
see: Pliquett, Joachim

Plog, Anthony
see: Plog, Anthony
see: Stevens, Thomas, 8)

Plunkett, Paul
see: Plunkett, Paul
see: Tarr, Edward, 17), 34)

Pohle, Wolfgang
see: Pohle, Wolfgang

Pok, František
see: Pok, František, 2)

Pollin, Pierre
see: André, Maurice, 92), 157)
see: Pollin, Pierre

Polonsky, Naum E.
see: Polonsky, Naum E.

Poper, Roy
see: Stevens, Thomas, 4)

Popov, Sergei
see: Popov, Sergei

Porté, Patrice
see: Ullrich, Marc

Pöschl, Josef
see: Idinger, Matthias

Pöttler, Hans
see: Spindler, Josef, 7)

Prager, Nathan
see: Glantz, Harry, 2), 5), 6)
see: Vacchiano, William, 4)

Preis, Ivo
see: Preis, Ivo
see: Schmid, Bernhard, 3)

Preisendanz, Dieter
see: Maier, Hans Walter

Pressley, Richard
see: Pressley, Richard

Prokopov, Vyacheslav
see: Prokopov, Vyacheslav
see: Volodin, Lev

Quinque, Rolf
see: Quinque, Rolf

Raber, Paul
see: Schmid, Bernhard, 10)
see: Send, Peter

Ranger, Louis
see: Dean, Allan, 4)
see: Ranger, Louis
see: Schwarz, Gerard, 10), 13),
  20)

Rapier, Leon
see: Rapier, Leon

Rausch, Heiner
see: Rausch, Heiner

Read, David
see: Read, David

Reber, Peter
see: McCann, Phillip

Reese, Rebecca
see: Reese, Rebecca

Rehm, Klaus
see: Rehm, Klaus
see: Tarr, Edward, 34)

Rehnberg, Torben
see: Potpourri, 3)

Reichen, Roland
see: McCann, Phillip

Reinecke, Konrad
see: Scherbaum, Adolf, 31)

Reinhart, Carole Dawn
see: Reinhart, Carole Dawn

Rejlek, Vladimir
see: Rejlek, Vladimir

Relave, Jean-Claude
see: André, Maurice, 120)

Rettig, Georg
see: Potpourri, 17), 23), 27)
see: Schmid, Bernhard, 3), 4)

Reyes, Arturo
see: Reyes, Arturo

Reynolds, George
see: Reynolds, George

Rhea, John
see: Voisin, Roger, 4), 5), 6),
8)

Rhoten, Bruce
see: Rhoten, Bruce

Richter, Hans
see: Potpourri, 16)
see: Tarr, Edward, 21)

Riebesel, Otto
see: Ellinghaus, Wolfram

Riggione, Angelo
see: Riggione, Angelo

Rilling, Emil
see: Sauter, Hermann, 7)

Rilling, Eugen
see: Sauter, Hermann, 2)

Rippas, Claude
see: Rippas, Claude
see: Schmid, Bernhard, 10)

Ritter, David
see: Ritter, David

Riva, Bruno
see: Aquitaine Brass Ensemble

Roberts, Standish
see: Roberts, Standish
see: Victorian Trumpet Trio

Roberts, Wilfred
see: Burke, James, 5), 6)

Robertson, John
see: Robertson, John

Roelant, Alain
see: Roelant, Alain

Romm, Ronald
see: Canadian Brass, 1), 2), 3),
4), 5), 6), 7)
see: Malone, Michael
see: Potpourri, 32), 33)
see: Romm, Ronald

Roos, Ingemar
see: Eklund's Baroque Ensemble

Ros, Ad
see: Ros, Ad

Rosenfeld, Seymour
see: Johnson, Gilbert, 8)

Rosenthal, Heribert
see: André, Maurice, 16)
see: Schetsche, Walter

Rosenzweig, Stanley
see: Schwarz, Gerard, 10)

Rotzoll, Manfred
see: André, Maurice, 199)

Rotzoll, Winfried
see: André, Maurice, 199)

Rudd, Wiff
see: Dallas Brass

Rudolf, Richard
see: Immer, Friedemann, 14),
15), 17)
see: Potpourri, 49), 51), 52),
53), 54), 56), 60), 62), 64)
see: Rudolf, Richard
see: Spindler, Josef, 7), 8), 9),
10), 11), 12), 13), 14), 15),
16)

Rudolph, Roland
see: Güttler, Ludwig, 21), 23)

Ruecktenwald, Philip
see: Wise, Wilmer

Rührlinger, Helmut
see: Fink, Werner

Sabarich, Raymond
see: Potpourri, 28)

Sanchez, Adel
see: Crisara, Raymond, 3)

Sandau, Kurt
see: Güttler, Ludwig, 3), 10),
12), 13), 14), 15), 18), 19),
20), 21), 23), 27)

San Filippo, Richard
see: Crisara, Raymond, 2)
see: Weis, Theodore, 1)

Sasaki, Ray
see: Hickman, David, 6)
see: Potpourri, 66)
see: Sasaki, Ray

Sauter, Hermann
see: Potpourri, 23), 24), 26),
27), 35)
see: Sauter, Hermann
see: Schmid, Bernhard, 2)

Sautter, Fred
see: Sautter, Fred

Schatz, Heiner
see: Potpourri, 24), 26), 27)
see: Sauter, Hermann, 1), 2),
7), 8), 9), 12), 13), 14),
15), 17), 18), 19), 20), 21),
26), 30), 32), 33), 34), 35),
36)

Scherbaum, Adolf
see: Potpourri, 12), 13), 14),
15)
see: Scherbaum, Adolf

Schermerhorn, Kenneth
see: Nashan, Rudolph

Schetsche, Walter
see: André, Maurice, 16)
see: Potpourri, 17), 21), 34),
35)
see: Schetsche, Walter
see: Wolf, Hans, 3), 13)
see: Zickler, Heinz, 7)

Schmahl, Larry
see: Parker, Craig B.

Schmid, Bernhard
see: Immer, Friedemann, 6)
see: Potpourri, 17), 23), 25),
27)
see: Sauter, Hermann, 23)
see: Schmid, Bernhard

Schmidhäusler, Francis
see: Schmidhäusler, Francis &
René

Schmidhäusler, René
see: Schmidhäusler, Francis &
René

Schmidt, Ingus
see: Holy, Walter, 2), 6)
see: Schmidt, Ingus
see: Spindler, Josef, 9)

Schmidt, Kurt
see: Holy, Walter, 5)

Schmitt, Helmut
see: Potpourri, 47)
see: Tarr, Edward, 28), 32)

Schmitt, Rainer
see: Tarr, Edward, 28)

Schmitt, Siegfried
see: Schmitt, Siegfried

Schmutzler, Mathias
see: Güttler, Ludwig, 21), 23)

Schnackenberg, Friedemann
see: Schnackenberg, Friedemann

Schneidewind, Helmut
see: Holy, Walter, 2), 3)
see: Potpourri, 16), 21), 34),
35), 65)
see: Schneidewind, Helmut
see: Zickler, Heinz, 7)

Schöber, Hermann
see: Immer, Friedemann, 14),
15)
see: Potpourri, 49), 50), 51),
52), 53), 54), 55), 56), 60)
see: Spindler, Josef, 2), 7), 8),
9), 10), 12), 13), 14), 15),
16)

Stith, Marice
  see: Stith, Marice

Stockhausen, Markus
  see: Stockhausen, Markus

Stone, Fred
  see: Stone, Fred

Stracker, Wilhelm
  see: Stracker, Wilhelm

Streitwieser, Franz Xaver
  see: Streitwieser, Franz Xaver
  see: Tarr, Edward, 28)

Stringer, Alan
  see: Potpourri, 1)
  see: Stringer, Alan

Stubbs, James
  see: Stubbs, James

Stuchlý, Josef
  see: Horák, Jiří, 3), 4), 5)

Stucki, Jacqueline
  see: McCann, Phillip

Suggs, Robert
  see: Ghitalla, Armando, 1)

Sugiki, Mineo
  see: André, Maurice, 143), 168),
    169), 216)

Sullivan, William
  see: Sullivan, William

Sundberg, Annemarie
  see: Eklund's Baroque Ensemble

Svejkovský, Josef
  see: Junek, Václav, 1)
  see: Kejmar, Miroslav, 8), 13)
  see: Svejkovský, Josef

Sveshnikov, Mikhail
  see: Sveshnikov, Mikhail

Sykes, Mark
  see: Eklund's Baroque Ensemble

Tamiya, Kenji
  see: Tamiya, Kenji

Tarr, Edward
  see: Haas, Wolfgang
  see: Holy, Walter, 4)
  see: Potpourri, 16), 18), 20),
    21), 22), 34), 35), 47), 65)
  see: Rehm, Klaus
  see: Tarr, Edward

Tasa, David
  see: Tarr, Edward, 34)
  see: Tasa, David

Terracini, Paul
  see: Terracini, Paul

Tessin, Jerry
  see: Potpourri, 66)

Testenière, Michel
  see: Jarmasson, Jacques

Thal, Herbert
  see: Holy, Walter, 7), 8)
  see: Potpourri, 2), 21), 34),
    35), 65)
  see: Zickler, Heinz, 1), 2), 3),
    8), 9)

Thibaud, Pierre
  see: Potpourri, 11), 12), 15)
  see: Thibaud, Pierre

Thomas, Peggy Paton
  see: Thomas, Peggy Paton

Thompson, James
  see: Hoffman, Edward
  see: Thompson, James

Thornburg, Scott
  see: Carroll, Edward, 12)

Thunderburke, Mike
  see: Thunderburke, Mike

Ticheli, Frank
  see: Giangiulio, Richard

Tison, Donald
  see: Pearson, Byron

Tobe, Yutaka
  see: Tobe, Yutaka

Tolley, Richard
see: Tolley, Richard

Touvron, Guy
see: André, Maurice, 47), 58),
119), 143), 168), 169), 216)
see: Potpourri, 10), 48)
see: Touvron, Guy

Truax, Bert
see: Giangiulio, Richard
see: Potpourri, 33)

Tschotschev,
Nicolai-Dimitrov
see: Tschotschev,
Nicolai-Dimitrov

Ullrich, Marc
see: Petit, Gilbert
see: Tarr, Edward, 17), 34), 41)
see: Ullrich, Marc

Ulrich, Rudolf
see: Held, Friedrich

Umbrico, Joseph
see: Umbrico, Joseph

Urfer, Eric
see: Urfer, Eric

Usov, Yuri
see: Usov, Yuri

Vacchiano, William
see: Vacchiano, William

Vaillant, Ludovic
see: Delmotte, Roger, 20)
see: Vaillant, Ludovic, 1), 2),
3), 4), 5), 6), 7)

van der Merk, Auke
see: Grin, Freddy, 7)

van der Poel, Frank
see: Mertens, Theo, 3)

van Haren, Jos
see: Grin, Freddy, 7)

van Kerckhoven, François
see: Mertens, Theo, 1), 5)

van Langenhove, Willy
see: Mertens, Theo, 1), 3)

van Loo, Peter
see: Grin, Freddy, 2), 9)

Vasse, Claude
see: Gabel, Bernard, 2)
see: Thibaud, Pierre, 13)
see: Vasse, Claude

Vizzutti, Allen
see: Vizzutti, Allen

Voisin, Roger
see: Ghitalla, Armando, 14)
see: Voisin, Roger

Volkov, Vitaly
see: Volkov, Vitaly

Volle, Bjarne
see: Volle, Bjarne

Volodin, Lev
see: Volodin, Lev

Volovnik, Iosif
see: Volovnik, Iosif

Volpe, Clement
see: Chenette, Stephen

von Kaenel, Andreas
see: McCann, Phillip

Vosburgh, George
see: Vosburgh, George

Vrijens, Gé
see: Grin, Freddy, 2)

Wallace, John
see: Wallace, John

Walton, Richard
see: Walton, Richard

Waltzing, Gast
see: Waltzing, Gast

Ware, John
see: Burke, James, 3)
see: Schwarz, Gerard, 20)
see: Ware, John

Warren, Wesley
  see: Warren, Wesley

Watson, James
  see: Potpourri, 1)
  see: Watson, James

Weast, Robert
  see: Weast, Robert

Webb, Gordon
  see: Webb, Gordon

Weeks, Larry
  see: Cowell, Johnny
  see: Weeks, Larry

Weinstock, Manny
  see: Burke, James, 5), 6)

Weis, Theodore
  see: Burke, James, 5), 6)
  see: Ghitalla, Armando, 10)
  see: Nagel, Robert, 1), 4), 6)
  see: Voisin, Roger, 5), 6), 8)
  see: Weis, Theodore

Wendlandt, Wilhelm
  see: Tarr, Edward, 28)

Wenth, Andreas
  see: Spindler, Josef, 7)

Werner, Horst
  see: Wolf, Hans, 1)

Wesenigk, Fritz
  see: Wesenigk, Fritz

Westerlund, Börie
  see: Eklund's Baroque Ensemble

Wiendl, Josef
  see: Bauer, Willibald, 3)

Wiggans, Brian
  see: Wiggans, Brian

Wilbraham, John
  see: Jones, Philip, 3), 9), 10)
  see: Potpourri, 1), 11), 29),
    44), 46)
  see: Wilbraham, John

Wilder, Joseph B.
  see: Crisara, Raymond, 2)
  see: Wilder, Joseph B.

Willig, Claes
  see: Eklund's Baroque Ensemble

Willwerth, Paul
  see: Willwerth, Paul

Wilson, Alex
  see: Wilson, Alex

Wilson, Ian
  see: Immer, Friedemann, 1)
  see: Laird, Michael, 1), 5), 6),
    11), 19)
  see: Smithers, Don, 6), 14)
  see: Wilbraham, John, 26)

Winslow, Richard
  see: Winslow, Richard

Wise, Wilmer
  see: Nowak, Henry
  see: Wise, Wilmer

Witecki, Franz
  see: Potpourri, 19)

Wobisch, Helmut
  see: Wobisch, Helmut

Wolf, Hans
  see: McGregor, Rob Roy, 1),
    6), 7)
  see: Potpourri, 17), 24), 25),
    26)
  see: Wolf, Hans

Woolard, Wes
  see: Mertens, Theo, 1)

Woomert, Bart
  see: Cowell, Johnny

Würsch, Markus
  see: Conrad, Jörg

Yamamoto, Eisuke
  see: Yamamoto, Eisuke

Yeh Shu-han
  see: Yeh, Shu-han

Yenne, Forest W.
  see: Giangiulio, Richard

Yeryomin, Sergei Nikolaivich
  see: Yeryomin, Sergei
    Nikolaivich

Young, Gene
  see: Young, Gene

Yudashkin, Georgy
  see: Yudashkin, Georgy

Yudin, Valentin
  see: Orvid, Georgy

Zaiser, Uwe
  see: McGregor, Rob Roy, 6)
  see: Wolf, Hans, 12)

Zapf, Gerd
  see: Zapf, Gerd

Zeh, Karl Heinz
  see: Zeh, Karl Heinz

Zeyer, Adam
  see: Zeyer, Adam

Zickler, Heinz
  see: Holy, Walter, 7), 8)
  see: Potpourri, 2), 21), 34),
    35), 65)
  see: Schneidewind, Helmut, 3)
  see: Zickler, Heinz

Ziegler, Albert
  see: Ziegler, Albert

Zikov, Vladimir
  see: Zikov, Vladimir

Trumpet mouthpiece

Platt, Seymour
  see: Platt, Seymour

Tarr, Edward
  see: Tarr, Edward, 29)

Tuba

Augustin, Rüdiger
  see: Lösch, Reinhold

Baram, V.
  see: Paniotov, Kharlampi

Barber, William
  see: Ghitalla, Armando, 10)

Bauchens, Robert
  see: Perry, Brian

Beauregard, Cherry
  see: Potpourri, 32), 33)

Bell, William
  see: Butterfield, Billy

Blakeslee, Donald
  see: Grin, Freddy, 2)

Bobo, Roger
  see: Stevens, Thomas, 2), 4),
    8), 16)

Budin, Paul
  see: André, Maurice, 120)

Butterfield, Donald
  see: Anderson, Ronald, 3)

Carper, Gary
  see: Dallas Brass

Cunningham, John
  see: Potpourri, 66)

Daellenbach, Charles
  see: Canadian Brass, 1), 2), 3),
    4), 5), 6), 7)
  see: Malone, Michael
  see: Potpourri, 32), 33)

Desmeulles, Léopold
  see: André, Maurice, 157)

Eger, Franz
  see: Adelbrecht, Henri, 1)

Fiol, Francisco
  see: Grin, Freddy, 9)

Fletcher, John
  see: Howarth, Elgar
  see: Watson, James

Frazier, Richard
  see: Potpourri, 7)

631

Hanks, Thompson
see: Dean, Allan, 2), 5)

Hoza, Václav
see: Kejmar, Miroslav, 7)

Hylas, F.
see: Mičaník, Jaroslav

Johns, Steve
see: Ranger, Louis

Kaenzig, Fritz
see: Potpourri, 66)

Kotsaftis, Ted
see: Butterfield, Billy

Lewin, William
see: Geisler, Lloyd

Lind, Michael
see: Hovaldt, Knud

Mullins, Mary Anne
see: McGuffey, Patrick

Orosz, Josef
see: Voisin, Roger, 13)

Pauwels, Jozef
see: Mertens, Theo, 1)

Peeters, Gerard
see: Mertens, Theo, 3), 5)

Perantoni, Daniel
see: Hickman, David, 5)
see: Potpourri, 66)
see: Sasaki, Ray

Phillips, Harvey
see: Burke, James, 5), 6)
see: Rapier, Leon, 1)

Price, Herbert
see: Schwarz, Gerard, 13)

Raynaud, Elie
see: André, Maurice, 185), 198)
see: Potpourri, 41), 43)

Saywell, Victor
see: Webb, Gordon, 2)

Sládek, Josef
see: Lisý, Rudolf

Smith, John F.
see: Watson, James

Smith, John Robert
see: Eggers, Carter

Spodar, Franck
see: Aquitaine Brass Ensemble

Swallow, John
see: Crisara, Raymond, 3)

Tomey, Guus
see: Grin, Freddy, 7)

Torchinsky, Abe
see: Johnson, Gilbert, 6)

Tucci, Robert
see: Bauer, Adam
see: Kuehn, David

van der Berg, Rijk
see: Grin, Freddy, 7)

Vihuela (Spanish guitar)
[cross-referenced under guitar]

Tyler, James
see: Laird, Michael, 1)

Viola

Alessandri, Giuliano
see: Dassé, Jean-Luc

Altenburger, Sylvie
see: Cure, Antoine

Andrix, George
see: Lowrey, Alvin

Angerer, Paul
see: Holler, Adolf
see: Wobisch, Helmut, 2)

Aronowitz, Cecil
see: Clift, Dennis
see: Jones, Philip, 2), 11)
see: Smithers, Don, 1)

Assayaf, Richard
see: Guarneri, Mario

Bachmann, Klaus-Dieter
see: Schmidt, Ingus

Bacon, Brian
see: Thompson, James

Ballardie, Quintin
see: Clift, Dennis
see: Steele-Perkins, Crispian, 14)
see: Webb, Gordon, 2)
see: Wilbraham, John, 27)

Balout, Jacques
see: Ménardi, Louis

Barber, Julian
see: Crisara, Raymond, 3)

Barchet, Reinhold
see: Gleissle, Walter, 1)

Bargen, Karl
see: Gould, Mark

Barritt, Jonathan
see: Steele-Perkins, Crispian, 14)

Barrus, Clynn
see: Spindler, Josef, 10)

Bauer, Fritz
see: Stradner, Gerhard

Beaudry, Anne
see: Thompson, James

Bell, E.
see: Haug, Edward

Best, Roger
see: Bernard, André, 12)

Beyer, Franz
see: Longinotti, Paolo
see: Potpourri, 22)
see: Tarr, Edward, 35), 36), 37), 38)

Biro, Nicholas
see: Vacchiano, William, 2)

Blume, Norbert
see: Steele-Perkins, Crispian, 14)

Bohlscheid, Erich
see: Tarr, Edward, 10)

Bolle, Linda
see: Perry, Brian

Borgatti, Franco
see: Dassé, Jean-Luc

Breitschmid, Gabi
see: Sauter, Hermann, 27)

Breslaw, Irene
see: Berinbaum, Martin

Brickley, Joan
see: Laird, Michael, 7)
see: Steele-Perkins, Crispian, 18)

Cappone, Giusto
see: Groth, Konradin

Careau, Suzanne
see: Thompson, James

Catchpole, Christopher
see: Berinbaum, Martin

Caudle, Theresa
see: Keavy, Stephen
see: Steele-Perkins, Crispian, 10)

Cauhape, Jean
see: Ghitalla, Armando, 2)

Caussé, Gérard
see: Cure, Antoine

Chailley, Marie-Thérèse
see: André, Maurice, 104)
see: Haneuse, Arthur

Christ, Wolfram
see: Groth, Konradin
see: Schneidewind, Helmut, 11)

Clarke, Brian
see: Clift, Dennis

Cleminson, Nicola
  see: Steele-Perkins, Crispian,
    16)

Cochrane, Lisa
  see: Keavy, Stephen

Cole, P.
  see: Warren, Wesley

Collot, Serge
  see: André, Maurice, 49)
  see: Delmotte, Roger, 2)
  see: Thibaud, Pierre, 1)

Cooley, Carlton
  see: Johnson, Gilbert, 2)

Corti, Ottavio
  see: Jones, Philip, 6)

Crafoord, Henrik
  see: Adelbrecht, Henri, 3)

Crouse, Wayne
  see: Austin, James

Daugareil, Noëlle
  see: Cure, Antoine

Davis, John
  see: Jones, Philip, 10)

de Sordi, Josef
  see: Bryant, Ralph, 4), 5)
  see: Holy, Walter, 9)
  see: Immer, Friedemann, 14),
    15), 16), 17)
  see: Potpourri, 58), 59), 60),
    61), 62), 63)
  see: Spindler, Josef, 7), 9), 12),
    16)

de Veritch, Alan
  see: Stevens, Thomas, 12)

Dexter, John
  see: Gould, Mark

Doktor, Paul
  see: Wise, Wilmer

Druce, Duncan
  see: Laird, Michael, 17), 19)

Dunham, James
  see: Guarneri, Mario

Dupin, Marc-Olivier
  see: Cure, Antoine

Dutt, Hank
  see: Wise, Wilmer

Eddy, Timothy
  see: Dean, Allan, 2)

Edwards, Gwynne
  see: Jones, Philip, 5)

Ellis, Nancy
  see: Metzger, Charles

Empt, Wilhelm
  see: Tarr, Edward, 38)

Engel, Wilfried
  see: Immer, Friedemann, 3),
    11)
  see: Schneidewind, Helmut, 11)

Epstein, Jerry
  see: Guarneri, Mario

Essex, Kenneth
  see: Webb, Gordon, 1)

Etter, Philippe
  see: Chenette, Stephen

Falkove, Al
  see: Stevens, Thomas, 10)

Fennell, Dorothy
  see: McGuffey, Patrick

Fima, Louis
  see: Cure, Antoine

Fine, Burton
  see: Ghitalla, Armando, 7)

Finkelman, Jody
  see: Cesare, James

Fischer, Martin
  see: Scherbaum, Adolf, 6)

Fischle, Ruth
  see: Sauter, Hermann, 27)

Fisher, Marlow
see: Plog, Anthony, 11)

Fogg, Cynthia
see: Parker, Craig B.

Frasca-Colombier, Monique
see: André, Maurice, 30)

Fuchs, Lillian
see: Mills, Fred

Funcke, Sibylle
see: Potpourri, 2)

Gabriel, Lilo
see: Eichhorn, Holger

Gahlbeck, Siegfried
see: André, Maurice, 180)

Gallien, Michele
see: Anderson, Ronald, 3)

Garvey, John
see: Bastin, Ernie

Gilly, Andreas
see: Immer, Friedemann, 3)

Girard, J.
see: Thibaud, Pierre, 14)

Giuranna, Bruno
see: Haas, Rudolf

Glick, Jacob
see: Anderson, Ronald, 4)
see: Burns, Stephen
see: Dean, Allan, 4), 6), 8)
see: Nagel, Robert, 18), 19), 20)

Goldberg, Szymon
see: Groot, Willem (Wim)

Graf, Heinz-Otto
see: Bodenröder, Robert

Graham, John
see: Anderson, Ronald, 2)
see: Burns, Stephen
see: Dean, Allan, 2)

Grainger, Eileen
see: Clift, Dennis
see: Jones, Philip, 8), 10)

Green, Rosemary
see: Clift, Dennis

Greitzer, Sol
see: Wise, Wilmer

Gunes, Rüsen
see: Wilbraham, John, 27)

Händschke, Fritz
see: Rudolf, Richard
see: Spindler, Josef, 5)

Harnoncourt, Alice
see: Holy, Walter, 9)
see: Immer, Friedemann, 16)
see: Spindler, Josef, 12)

Harnoncourt, Nikolaus
see: Bryant, Ralph, 1)
see: Spindler, Josef, 11), 12)

Harriott, Harold
see: Jones, Philip, 5)

Harris, Mary
see: Thompson, James

Hart, Katherine
see: Eichhorn, Holger
see: Laird, Michael, 7), 11), 19)
see: Steele-Perkins, Crispian, 16), 18)

Hedrich, Christian
see: Wolf, Hans, 9)

Held, Günter
see: Sauter, Hermann, 27)

Heman, Christine
see: Tarr, Edward, 11)

Hesseling, Ruth
see: Immer, Friedemann, 14)
see: Potpourri, 57), 58), 59), 60), 61), 63)
see: Smithers, Don, 13), 14)
see: Spindler, Josef, 15)

Hill, Janet Lyman
  see: Anderson, Ronald, 6)
  see: Smithers, Don, 2)

Hirschfeld, Franz
  see: Adelbrecht, Henri, 1)

Höbarth, Erich
  see: Immer, Friedemann, 14),
    16)
  see: Potpourri, 63)

Holzman, Carrie
  see: Plog, Anthony, 11)

Hood, Maurice
  see: Potpourri, 6)

Hübner, Wilhelm
  see: Wobisch, Helmut, 2)

Huggett, Monica
  see: Immer, Friedemann, 1)

Hurwitz, Emanuel
  see: Jones, Philip, 8)

Iglitzin, Alan
  see: Mills, Fred

Ireland, Patrick
  see: Clift, Dennis

Irvine, Jeffrey
  see: Potpourri, 38)

Isserlis, Annette
  see: Laird, Michael, 7), 8)
  see: Steele-Perkins, Crispian,
    7), 16), 18)

Jaffe, Jill
  see: Wise, Wilmer

James, Mary
  see: Haug, Edward

Jamieson, Nannie
  see: Clift, Dennis

Jappe, Dorothea
  see: Immer, Friedemann, 3),
    11)

Jeppesen, Laura
  see: Immer, Friedemann, 13)

Jones, Trevor
  see: Immer, Friedemann, 4)
  see: Laird, Michael, 7), 8), 11),
    17), 19)
  see: Steele-Perkins, Crispian,
    7), 10)

Jopen, Heinz
  see: Steinkopf, Otto
  see: Tarr, Edward, 10), 20)

Kägi, Lotte
  see: Tarr, Edward, 11)

Kägi, Walter
  see: Haneuse, Arthur
  see: Zeyer, Adam

Kahlson, Erik
  see: Blee, Eugene

Kato, Roland
  see: Schwarz, Gerard, 1)

Katz, Harold
  see: Miller, Rodney

Kavafian, Ida
  see: Schwarz, Gerard, 3)

Kelly, Martin
  see: Steele-Perkins, Crispian, 5)

Kirchner, Heinz
  see: Longinotti, Paolo
  see: Tarr, Edward, 18)

Kitching, Colin
  see: Laird, Michael, 7)

Klár, Vladimír
  see: Junek, Václav, 4)

Klatz, Harold
  see: Miller, Rodney

Klegel, Elisabeth
  see: Friedrich, Reinhold

Knieps, Wolfgang
  see: André, Maurice, 171)

Knudsen, Ronald
  see: Metzger, Charles

Koch, Barbara
see: Pok, František, 2)

Koch, Ulrich
see: André, Maurice, 171)
see: Scherbaum, Adolf, 6)
see: Schneidewind, Helmut, 13)
see: Wolf, Hans, 1)

Kochanowski, John
see: Anderson, Ronald, 4)
see: Dean, Allan, 2)

Krakow, Bernd
see: Preis, Ivo

Kriss, Ernst
see: Wobisch, Helmut, 2)

Kroft
see: Horák, Jiří, 4)

Kuijken, Sigiswald
see: Rippas, Claude

Kussmaul, Jürgen
see: André, Maurice, 192)
see: Goethel, Siegfried

Lakatos, Janet
see: Hood, Boyde
see: Schwarz, Gerard, 1)

Lamy, M.
see: Thibaud, Pierre, 14)

Lapointe, Vincent
see: Thompson, James

Lemmen, Günter
see: André, Maurice, 15)
see: Bodenröder, Robert
see: Schneidewind, Helmut, 1),
7)
see: Tarr, Edward, 35), 37), 38)

Lemoine, Micheline
see: André, Maurice, 82)

Lequien, C.
see: Thibaud, Pierre, 14)

Lessing, Alfred
see: Tarr, Edward, 10)

Letofsky, Kurt
see: Holy, Walter, 9)

Levine, Lynne
see: Ghitalla, Armando, 1)

Levy, Jane
see: Plog, Anthony, 11)

Lincer, William
see: Vacchiano, William, 2)

Lormand, Charles
see: André, Maurice, 152)

Lormand, Christian
see: André, Maurice, 151)
see: Cure, Antoine

Lucas, Theodore
see: Bastin, Ernie

Lurata, Norboru
see: Friedrich, Reinhold

Majer, Marianne
see: Haneuse, Arthur
see: Tarr, Edward, 11)
see: Zeyer, Adam

Major, Margaret
see: Groot, Willem (Wim)
see: Tuckwell, Barry

Marsh, Mary
see: Potpourri, 5)

Martin, Michel
see: André, Maurice, 152)

Menuhin, Ychudi
see: Clift, Dennis

Miller, David
see: Holmgren, Fred
see: Immer, Friedemann, 13)

Mishnayevsky, M.
see: Volodin, Lev

Mitterer, Anita
see: Immer, Friedemann, 16)

Müller-Ney, Ingeborg
see: Preis, Ivo

Naegele, Philipp
  see: Bernard, André, 2)
  see: Preis, Ivo

Nalden, Rosemary
  see: Steele-Perkins, Crispian, 5)

Naumann, Herbert
  see: André, Maurice, 180)
  see: Tarr, Edward, 10)

Niehaus, Manfred
  see: Schoof, Manfred

Nishi, Elinor
  see: Metzger, Charles

Norman, Jane
  see: Keavy, Stephen

Ochsenhofer, Hans-Peter
  see: Spindler, Josef, 13)

Oldeman, Gerrit
  see: Floore, John

Olshausen, Detlev
  see: Haug, Edward

Orlamünde, Arnim
  see: Gass, Josef

Pachla, Fredrik
  see: Basch, Wolfgang, 1)

Paris, Massimo
  see: Touvron, Guy, 14)

Parnas, Richard
  see: Geisler, Lloyd

Pasquier, Bruno
  see: Cure, Antoine
  see: Lagorce, Antoine

Paulon, Sergio
  see: André, Maurice, 130)

Peabody, Paul
  see: Gould, Mark

Pecha, Peter
  see: Adelbrecht, Henri, 2)

Peeters, Wiel
  see: Bryant, Ralph, 2), 4), 5)
  see: Potpourri, 51), 52), 57),
    58), 59), 60)
  see: Rippas, Claude
  see: Smithers, Don, 13), 14),
    15)
  see: Spindler, Josef, 11), 13),
    14), 15)

Perich, Guillermo
  see: Sasaki, Ray

Phillips, Karen
  see: Berinbaum, Martin
  see: Romm, Ronald

Polifrone, Sharon
  see: Potpourri, 38)

Proulx, Jacques
  see: Thompson, James

Queille, Annette
  see: André, Maurice, 13), 14)

Rab, Eduard
  see: Wobisch, Helmut, 2)

Řehák, Karel
  see: Horák, Jiří, 5)

Reher, Sven
  see: Stevens, Thomas, 10), 13)

Resa, Neithard
  see: Groth, Konradin

Rhodes, Samuel
  see: Nagel, Robert, 3)

Riddle, Frederick
  see: Jones, Philip, 8)

Robbins, B.
  see: Broiles, Melvin

Roehr, Gideon
  see: Schrello, Mark

Roth, Max
  see: Scholz, Walter

Rowland-Jones, Simon
  see: Laird, Michael, 7), 17)

Rubin, Nathan
see: Burkhart, David

Ruf, Fritz
see: Schneidewind, Helmut, 13)

Ruymen, Gérard
see: Bauer, Adam

Sangiorgi, Ferruccio
see: André, Maurice, 130)

Schäfer, Hansjörg
see: Gleissle, Walter, 1)

Schessl, Franz
see: André, Maurice, 93)

Schlapp, Jan
see: Immer, Friedemann, 4)
see: Laird, Michael, 8)
see: Steele-Perkins, Crispian,
7), 16), 18)

Schmid, Georg
see: André, Maurice, 93)
see: Scherbaum, Adolf, 28)

Schonbach, Sanford
see: Heinrich, Robert
see: Nagel, Robert, 4)

Schulman, Louis
see: Ranger, Louis

Seidl, Mathes
see: Scherbaum, Adolf, 21)

Seiler, Emil
see: Scherbaum, Adolf, 24)
see: Steinkopf, Otto
see: Tarr, Edward, 10), 20)
see: Wobisch, Helmut, 7)

Sheidin, Alexandre
see: Dokshitser, Timofei, 12)

Shingles, Stephen
see: Bernard, André, 12)
see: Tuckwell, Barry
see: Wilbraham, John, 11), 19)

Silpigni, Constance
see: Greenho, David

Sinnhoffer, Ingo
see: Thibaud, Pierre, 8)

Sklar, Arnold
see: Miller, Rodney

Slaughter, Robert
see: Miller, Rodney

Smithers, Janet
see: Smithers, Don, 7)

Soloman, Stanley
see: Schultz, Erik, 8)

Soloyov, Vissarion
see: Margolin, Veniamin

Sonneveld, Martin
see: Spindler, Josef, 13), 14)

Soultanian, Joel
see: Schwarz, Gerard, 1)

Souster, Tim
see: Stockhausen, Markus, 4)

Sparey, Caroline
see: Laird, Michael, 11)

Špelina, Karel
see: Buriánek, Jindřich
see: Horák, Jiří, 5)

Spiga, Umberto
see: Touvron, Guy, 14)

Steeb, Karlheinz
see: Bodenröder, Robert
see: Potpourri, 22)

Stepner, Daniel
see: Immer, Friedemann, 13)

Stier, Kurt-Christian
see: Thibaud, Pierre, 8)

Stierhof, Karl
see: Adelbrecht, Henri, 2)

Stockhammer, David
see: Stevens, Thomas, 10)

Streatfield, Simon
see: Potpourri, 9)
see: Wilbraham, John, 13)

Weiner, Stanley
see: Tarr, Edward, 44)

Weller, Ira
see: Burns, Stephen

Wellington, Christopher
see: Webb, Gordon, 1)

Westman, T. Burns
see: Hood, Donald

Wilgowicz, Gérard
see: Cure, Antoine

Williams, Andrew
see: Wilbraham, John, 27)

Wilson, Nancy
see: Immer, Friedemann, 13)

Wolff-Malm, Doris
see: Tarr, Edward, 35), 37)

Wright, Barbara
see: Hunger, Helmut, 4)

Yokell, B.
see: Broiles, Melvin

Zaratzian, Harry
see: Nagel, Robert, 5)

Zaslaw, Bernard
see: Broiles, Melvin

Zlatoff-Mirsky, Everett
see: Miller, Rodney

Zukerman, Pinchas
see: Stevens, Thomas, 12)

Viola d'amore

Frasca-Colombier, Monique
see: André, Maurice, 30)

Giuranna, Bruno
see: Haas, Rudolf

Huggett, Monica
see: Immer, Friedemann, 1)

Lemmen, Günter
see: André, Maurice, 15)
see: Schneidewind, Helmut, 1),
7)
see: Tarr, Edward, 35)

Seiler, Emil
see: Scherbaum, Adolf, 24)
see: Wobisch, Helmut, 7)

Viola da braccio

Bauer, Fritz
see: Stradner, Gerhard

Engel, Wilfried
see: Immer, Friedemann, 3)

Harnoncourt, Alice
see: Immer, Friedemann, 16)

Höbarth, Erich
see: Immer, Friedemann, 16)

Jappe, Dorothea
see: Immer, Friedemann, 3)

Kägi, Walter
see: Zeyer, Adam

Koch, Barbara
see: Pok, František, 2)

Koch, Ulrich
see: Schneidewind, Helmut, 13)

Majer, Marianne
see: Zeyer, Adam

Miller, David
see: Immer, Friedemann, 13)

Ruf, Fritz
see: Schneidewind, Helmut, 13)

Schnitzler, Heide
see: Stradner, Gerhard

Wilson, Nancy
see: Immer, Friedemann, 13)

Viola da gamba
[includes various sizes & designations]

Alexander, Rolf
see: André, Maurice, 93)

Arico, Fortunato
see: Gould, Mark

Bauer, Alwin
see: Schneidewind, Helmut, 7)

Baxa, Jiří
see: Pok, František, 6)

Bogatin, Barbara
see: Gould, Mark
see: Immer, Friedemann, 13)

Bols, Hans
see: Groot, Willem (Wim)

Bonnal, Laurence
see: Touvron, Guy, 14)

Brookes, Oliver
see: Laird, Michael, 1), 2), 3),
    11), 12), 14), 17)
see: Smithers, Don, 3)
see: Webb, Gordon, 1)

Cervera, Marçal
see: Potpourri, 47)
see: Tarr, Edward, 32)

Charlsdotter-Lahrs,
  Rosemarie
see: Ellinghaus, Wolfram

Coin, Christophe
see: Canihac, Jean-Pierre
see: Immer, Friedemann, 16)

Cook, Adrienne
see: Cook, Richard

Cordier, R.
see: Thibaud, Pierre, 14)

Davenport, Patricia
see: Montesi, Robert, 4)

Davidoff, Judith
see: Berinbaum, Martin
see: Davenport, LaNoue
see: Montesi, Robert, 4), 5), 6)

de Ligt, Ben
see: Otten, Kees

Dupré, Desmond
see: Clift, Dennis
see: Smithers, Don, 1)

Eggers, Wolfgang
see: Caudle, Theresa
see: Tarr, Edward, 19), 20)

Fink, Johannes
see: Smithers, Don, 12)
see: Thibaud, Pierre, 8)

Fisher, Cynthia
see: Montesi, Robert, 4)

Fowle, Alison
see: Cook, Richard

Friedrich, Roswitha
see: Ellinghaus, Wolfram

Fries, Vimala
see: Ellinghaus, Wolfram
see: Otto, Joachim

Gabriel, Lilo
see: Eichhorn, Holger

Gammie, Ian
see: Laird, Michael, 11)

Gauntlet, Ambrose
see: Clift, Dennis

Glatt, Adelheid
see: Potpourri, 59)
see: Rippas, Claude

Guttmann, Veronika
see: Stradner, Gerhard

Häferland, Heinrich
see: Ellinghaus, Wolfram
see: Holy, Walter, 5)
see: Schneidewind, Helmut, 1),
    13)
see: Tarr, Edward, 10), 19), 20)

Hampe, Veronika
    see: André, Maurice, 221), 224)

Harnoncourt, Nikolaus
    see: Holy, Walter, 9)
    see: Immer, Friedemann, 16)
    see: Potpourri, 49), 50), 58),
        64)
    see: Spindler, Josef, 7)
    see: Wobisch, Helmut, 2)

Haupt, Werner
    see: André, Maurice, 180)

Hedler, Horst
    see: Holy, Walter, 5)
    see: Steinkopf, Otto
    see: Tarr, Edward, 10), 19), 20)

Horák, Jaroslav
    see: Pok, František, 6)

Hsu, John
    see: Immer, Friedemann, 13)

Hunt, William
    see: Laird, Michael, 8)

Hussong, Christina
    see: Otto, Joachim

Jaksch, Werner
    see: Preis, Ivo

Jappe, Michael
    see: Immer, Friedemann, 3)

Jones, Trevor
    see: Laird, Michael, 1), 2)

Kaiser, Michael
    see: Spindler, Josef, 5)

Klotz, Udo
    see: Smithers, Don, 12)

Knava, Ernst
    see: Holy, Walter, 9)

Koch, Hans
    see: Hagge, Detlef

Koch, Johannes
    see: Ellinghaus, Wolfram
    see: Scherbaum, Adolf, 7)
    see: Schneidewind, Helmut, 13)
    see: Tarr, Edward, 35), 37), 38)
    see: Wobisch, Helmut, 7)

Krásná, Zora
    see: Pok, František, 6)

Kubizek, Elli
    see: Potpourri, 49), 50), 64)
    see: Spindler, Josef, 7)
    see: Tarr, Edward, 45)

Kuijken, Wieland
    see: Rippas, Claude

Lamy, J.
    see: Thibaud, Pierre, 14)

Lentz, Piet
    see: Groot, Willem (Wim)

Lessing, Alfred
    see: Holy, Walter, 5)
    see: Tarr, Edward, 10), 18),
        19), 20)

Loosli, Annelies
    see: Potpourri, 47)
    see: Tarr, Edward, 32)

Ludvík, Brětislav
    see: Pok, František, 6)

Mackintosh, Catherine
    see: Laird, Michael, 1)

Medlam, Charles
    see: Laird, Michael, 8)

Melziarek, Egon
    see: André, Maurice, 180)

Mueser, Barbara
    see: Montesi, Robert, 3), 4)

Münch-Holland, Gunhild
    see: Ellinghaus, Wolfram

Naumann, Gerhard
    see: Tarr, Edward, 18)

Naumann, Herbert
    see: Tarr, Edward, 10), 20)

Uhlenhoff, Jens-Peter
see: Ellinghaus, Wolfram

Ulsamer, Josef
see: Ellinghaus, Wolfram
see: Otto, Joachim
see: Tarr, Edward, 12)
see: Wobisch, Helmut, 8)

van der Ven-Ulsamer, Elza
see: Otto, Joachim

Vel, Peter
see: Laird, Michael, 17)
see: Wilbraham, John, 27)

Waterfield, Polly
see: Laird, Michael, 1), 2)

Wellisch, Caecilia
see: Stradner, Gerhard

Wenzinger, August
see: Gleissle, Walter, 2)

Winzap, Françoise
see: Potpourri, 47)
see: Tarr, Edward, 32)

Viola pomposa

Funcke, Sibylle
see: Potpourri, 2)

Hampe, Charlotte
see: Zeh, Karl Heinz

Violin
[includes violino piccolo]

Abramenkov, Andrei
see: Popov, Sergei, 3)

Adamo, Giovanni
see: André, Maurice, 114)
see: Dassé, Jean-Luc

Adams, Richard
see: Blee, Eugene

Aiken, Jeanne
see: Guarneri, Mario

Aiken, Patricia
see: Schwarz, Gerard, 1)

Aki, Syoko
see: Schwarz, Gerard, 6), 7)

Albert, Thomas
see: Eichhorn, Holger

Alès, Georges
sec: Delmotte, Roger, 6), 35), 37)

Allen, Sanford
see: Wise, Wilmer

Alshuth, Ulrich
see: Schmidt, Ingus

Altenburger, Christian
see: Basch, Wolfgang, 8), 10)

Altheimer, Christel
see: Sauter, Hermann, 27)

Angelis, Brigitte
see: Gabel, Bernard, 3)

Apostoli, Arnaldo
see: Touvron, Guy, 14)

Appel, Toby
see: Burns, Stephen

Armand, Georges
see: Calvayrac, Albert

Armin, Adèle
see: Chenette, Stephen

Armin, Otto
see: Läubin, Hannes, 3)

Armuzzi-Romei, Gabriella
see: André, Maurice, 105), 114), 115)

Artur, Danièle
see: André, Maurice, 200)

Ashikawa, Lori
see: Plog, Anthony, 11)

Auriacombe, Aimée
see: Calvayrac, Albert

Ayo, Felix
see: Adelbrecht, Henri, 4), 6)
see: André, Maurice, 194), 201)

Baines, June
see: Laird, Michael, 11), 19)

Baker, Israel
see: Brady, Charles
see: Heinrich, Robert
see: McNab, Malcolm
see: Nagel, Robert, 4)

Balian, Haig
see: Guarneri, Mario
see: Stevens, Thomas, 10)

Ballard, J.
see: Warren, Wesley

Banchini, Chiara
see: Ferry, Dennis

Baranov, Mark
see: Popov, Sergei, 2)

Barber, Michael
see: Ghitalla, Armando, 1)

Barbieri, Vittorio
see: Dassé, Jean-Luc

Barchet, Reinhold
see: André, Maurice, 93)
see: Gleissle, Walter, 1), 2), 3), 5), 7)
see: Longinotti, Paolo
see: Scherbaum, Adolf, 27)
see: Unidentified, Trumpet(s), 14)

Barton, James
see: Clift, Dennis

Baumgartner, Doris
see: Tarr, Edward, 11)

Baumgartner, Rudolf
see: Potpourri, 14)
see: Scherbaum, Adolf, 6), 24), 26)

Bean, Hugh
see: Scherbaum, Adolf, 3)
see: Webb, Gordon, 1)

Beetz, Ulrich
see: Bodenröder, Robert
see: Potpourri, 22)

Beguin, Liliane
see: André, Maurice, 90)

Bělčík, Bruno
see: Junek, Václav, 6)

Belensky, L.
see: Volodin, Lev

Benac, Andrew
see: Schultz, Erik, 8)

Benjamin, Jeanne
see: Anderson, Ronald, 1), 3), 4)
see: Dean, Allan, 1), 4), 5), 6), 7)
see: Ferrantino, Kenneth
see: Nagel, Robert, 19), 20)

Berg, Bruce
see: Steele-Perkins, Crispian, 16)

Berman, Joel
see: Ghitalla, Armando, 1)

Bertshinger, Edith
see: Wobisch, Helmut, 9)

Beths, Vera
see: Berinbaum, Martin

Beznosiuk, Pavlo
see: Keavy, Stephen

Bignami, William
see: André, Maurice, 114)
see: Dassé, Jean-Luc

Bischof, Andrea
see: Immer, Friedemann, 14), 15), 16), 17)
see: Potpourri, 62), 63)

Bodamer, Cornelie
see: Sauter, Hermann, 27)

Boesen, Albert
see: McGregor, Rob Roy, 3),
    4), 6)
see: Sauter, Hermann, 19), 20)

Bondarenko, Helena
see: Streitwieser, Franz Xaver

Bor, Edward
see: Clift, Dennis

Borries, Siegfried
see: Spörri, Paul

Boskovsky, Willi
see: Scherbaum, Adolf, 36)
see: Wobisch, Helmut, 14)

Brandis, Thomas
see: Groth, Konradin
see: Scherbaum, Adolf, 7)
see: Wobisch, Helmut, 8)

Braun, Matitiahu
see: Schwarz, Gerard, 2)

Brickley, Joan
see: Laird, Michael, 19)

Brière, Christian
see: Gabel, Bernard, 3)

Brink, Robert
see: Nashan, Rudolph

Brix-Meinert, Ilse
see: Renz, Albrecht, 1)

Brouwer, Henk
see: Doets, Jas

Brown, Iona
see: André, Maurice, 36), 48)
see: Goethel, Siegfried
see: Jones, Philip, 3)
see: Laird, Michael, 15), 21)
see: Smithers, Don, 1)
see: Tuckwell, Barry
see: Wilbraham, John, 2), 12),
    22)

Brünig, Johannes
see: Schmidt, Ingus
see: Zickler, Heinz, 4)

Brusilow, Anshel
see: Johnson, Gilbert, 2)

Buccarella, Claudio
see: Touvron, Guy, 14)

Buchberger, Hubert
see: Läubin, Hannes, 4)
see: Schmid, Bernhard, 8)

Buchmann, Rudolf
see: Eichhorn, Holger

Büchner, Otto
see: André, Maurice, 17)
see: Bauer, Willibald, 1)
see: Lachenmeir, Paul
see: Quinque, Rolf, 1)
see: Scherbaum, Adolf, 9)

Bünte, Hans
see: André, Maurice, 113)

Burgin, Richard
see: Voisin, Roger, 9), 10), 11)

Bury, Alison
see: Laird, Michael, 17)
see: Steele-Perkins, Crispian,
    7), 9), 16), 18)

Busch, Adolf
see: Eskdale, George, 2)

Bushee, Kevin
see: Dudgeon, Ralph

Carles, Ginette
see: André, Maurice, 89), 102)
see: Tarr, Edward, 31)

Carmirelli, Pina
see: Touvron, Guy, 14)

Carol, Norman
see: Johnson, Gilbert, 8)

Carpenter-Jacobs, Susan
see: Laird, Michael, 7)
see: Steele-Perkins, Crispian,
    16)

Carracilly, Yvon
see: André, Maurice, 13)

Carter, T.
see: Jones, Philip, 8)

Caudle, Theresa
see: Keavy, Stephen

Ceasar, James
see: Potpourri, 6)

Chirila, Vasile
see: Adelbrecht, Henri, 3)

Chumachenko, Nicolas
see: Cuvit, Michel

Cirillo, Nancy
see: Dean, Allan, 2)

Clarkson, N.
see: Wilbraham, John, 30)

Claudio, Silvio
see: Haug, Edward

Cleaver, Sylvia
see: Jones, Philip, 7)

Cleminson, Nicola
see: Laird, Michael, 11), 17), 19)
see: Steele-Perkins, Crispian, 7)

Cohen, Isodore
see: Blee, Eugene
see: Heinrich, Robert
see: Romm, Ronald

Colandrea, Italo
see: Touvron, Guy, 14)

Collette, Joannes
see: Otten, Kees

Colò, Giovanni
see: Dassé, Jean-Luc

Comberti, Michaela
see: Laird, Michael, 7), 8), 11)
see: Steele-Perkins, Crispian, 7)

Connoh, Trevor
see: Wilbraham, John, 12)

Corigliano, John
see: Vacchiano, William, 4)

Cotogni, Anna Maria
see: Adelbrecht, Henri, 6)
see: Touvron, Guy, 14)

Cowan, Carole
see: Potpourri, 38)

Cracknell, Graham
see: Steele-Perkins, Crispian, 7), 16), 18)

Crayford, Marcia
see: Miller, John

Cruthirds, JoAnn
see: McGuffey, Patrick

D'Antonio, Franklin
see: Stevens, Thomas, 10)

D'Antonio, Joy
see: Stevens, Thomas, 10)

Darrieux, Marcel
see: Foveau, Eugène

Déat, Huguette
see: André, Maurice, 151), 211), 215)

Deeks, Stuart
see: Laird, Michael, 19)

de Ligt, Mary
see: Potpourri, 52)

del Maria, Joe
see: Schwarz, Gerard, 3)

Dentan, Maurice
see: Immer, Friedemann, 3)

de Pasquale, William
see: Johnson, Gilbert, 8)

de Sordi, Josef
see: Bryant, Ralph, 1), 3)
see: Holy, Walter, 9)
see: Potpourri, 49), 50), 51), 52), 53), 54), 55), 56), 57), 64)
see: Spindler, Josef, 8), 10), 11), 12), 13), 14), 15)
see: Tarr, Edward, 45)

Fetz, Anton
see: Adelbrecht, Henri, 1)

Figueroa, Guillermo
see: Carroll, Edward, 8), 9)

Finkel, Christopher
see: Dean, Allan, 2)

Finotti, Leonardo
see: Dassé, Jean-Luc

Flügel, Gertrude
see: Tarr, Edward, 11)

Folty, Laszlo
see: Eichhorn, Holger

Forchert, Walter
see: André, Maurice, 142)
see: Immer, Friedemann, 5), 6)
see: Läubin, Hannes, 3), 6)
see: McGregor, Rob Roy, 1), 5)
see: Potpourri, 25)
see: Sauter, Hermann, 17), 20), 24)
see: Schmid, Bernhard, 5), 6), 9)
see: Wolf, Hans, 7), 10), 12)

Frasca-Colombier, Monique
see: Scherbaum, Adolf, 4), 20)
see: Soustrot, Bernard, 3)

Friedman, Leonard
see: Eskdale, George, 5)

Friend, Rodney
see: Webb, Gordon, 2), 4), 7)

Fröhlich, Josef
see: Steele-Perkins, Crispian, 14)

Frydén, Lars
see: Tarr, Edward, 11)

Fuchs, Joseph
see: Mills, Fred

Fuglesang, Kare
see: Christiansen, Jan

Führlinger, Siegfried
see: Holy, Walter, 9)
see: Rudolf, Richard

Fülöp, Maria
see: Quinque, Rolf, 7)

Furini, Guido
see: André, Maurice, 130)

Furney, Jo Anne
see: Patti, Douglas

Futer, A.
see: Volodin, Lev

Gabsch, Brigitte
see: Güttler, Ludwig, 20)

Gali, Lionel
see: Lagorce, Antoine

Galimir, Felix
see: Broiles, Melvin
see: Nagel, Robert, 3)

Gallozzi, Walter
see: Adelbrecht, Henri, 5)
see: Touvron, Guy, 14)

Garcia, José Luis
see: Steele-Perkins, Crispian, 14)
see: Wilbraham, John, 20), 27)

Garcia-Reichel, Rodrigo
see: Hunger, Helmut, 4)

Garvey, John
see: Ferrantino, Kenneth
see: Potpourri, 66)

Gatti, Enrico
see: Ferry, Dennis

Gauthier, Jeffrey
see: Plog, Anthony, 11)

Gawriloff, Saschko
see: André, Maurice, 196)
see: Bauer, Adam

Gazeau, Sylvie
see: Vasse, Claude

Geiger, Hans
see: Webb, Gordon, 1)

Geller, Irving
see: Stevens, Thomas, 10)

Gerle, Robert
see: Rudolf, Richard

Geyer, Albert
see: Sauter, Hermann, 27)

Ghestem, Jacques
see: Delmotte, Roger, 2)
see: Thibaud, Pierre, 1)

Giersch, Klaus
see: Basch, Wolfgang, 1)
see: Tarr, Edward, 38)

Gilliard, Roy
see: Jones, Philip, 3)

Gilmore, Peggy
see: Laird, Michael, 17)

Giordano, Oreste
see: Calvayrac, Albert

Goberman, Max
see: Nagel, Robert, 14)

Goldberg, Szymon
see: Groot, Willem (Wim)
see: Spörri, Paul

Golding, Miles
see: Laird, Michael, 7), 8)
see: Steele-Perkins, Crispian,
    7), 16), 18)

Golub, Elliott
see: Miller, Rodney
see: Perry, Brian

Goodman, Roy
see: Keavy, Stephen
see: Laird, Michael, 7), 8)
see: Steele-Perkins, Crispian,
    7), 10), 16), 18)

Goren, Eli
see: Clift, Dennis
see: Eskdale, George, 5)

Gorski, Paul
see: Potpourri, 5)

Grach, Eduard
see: Dokshitser, Timofei, 29)

Granat, Endre
see: Plog, Anthony, 9)

Gravoin, Jean-René
see: Delmotte, Roger, 42), 43)

Gray, Ella Marie
see: Pressley, Richard

Grehling, Ulrich
see: Vaillant, Ludovic, 2)
see: Wobisch, Helmut, 7)

Griensteidl, Lotte
see: Eichhorn, Holger

Grinhauz, Luis
see: LeComte, Jacques

Grinke, Frederick
see: Eskdale, George, 4)

Grobholz, Werner
see: Goethel, Siegfried

Grüb, Evelyne
see: Sauter, Hermann, 27)

Guilet, Daniel
see: Glantz, Harry, 4)
see: Potpourri, 31)

Gurevich, Paul
see: Berinbaum, Martin

Guyot, Michel
see: Touvron, Guy, 13)

Haase, Ralf-Rainer
see: Gass, Josef

Hall, Lucia
see: Thompson, James

Hamann, Bernhard
see: Scherbaum, Adolf, 33)

Hammer, Mosha
see: Schultz, Erik, 8)

Hansen, Leo
see: Hovaldt, Knud
see: Mason, David, 2)

651

Hori, Masafumi
see: Bernard, André, 2)
see: Preis, Ivo

Höver, Herbert
see: Immer, Friedemann, 3)
see: Scherbaum, Adolf, 24)

How, Liang-Ping
see: Carroll, Edward, 8), 9)

Howard, Anthony
see: Clift, Dennis
see: Potpourri, 9)
see: Wilbraham, John, 12)

Howard, Penelope
see: Smithers, Don, 2)

Hübner, Wilhelm
see: Wobisch, Helmut, 1)

Hudeček, Vaclav
see: Soustrot, Bernard, 1)

Hudson, Benjamin
see: Anderson, Ronald, 6)
see: Burns, Stephen
see: Dean, Allan, 3)

Huggett, Monica
see: Laird, Michael, 5), 7), 11), 17), 18), 19)

Humphreys, Sydney
see: Clift, Dennis

Hurwitz, Emanuel
see: Gay, Bram
see: Jones, Philip, 2), 5), 11)
see: Mason, David, 4)

Igleman, Otis
see: Heinrich, Robert
see: Nagel, Robert, 4)

Igolnikov, Albert
see: Vosburgh, George

Isaacs, Kelly
see: Clift, Dennis

Isselmann, Wilhelm
see: Zeyer, Adam

Isserlis, Rachael
see: Laird, Michael, 7)

Ivanov, Vassil
see: Ridder, Jean de

Jacquerod, Jean
see: Potpourri, 47)
see: Tarr, Edward, 32)
see: Touvron, Guy, 10)

Jacquillat, Cécile
see: André, Maurice, 13)

Jahn, Jörg-Wolfgang
see: Preis, Ivo
see: Zickler, Heinz, 5)

Jarry, Gérard
see: André, Maurice, 49), 136), 151), 152), 209), 211), 215)
see: Gabel, Bernard, 3)
see: Thibaud, Pierre, 1)
see: Touvron, Guy, 9), 11)

Jarvis, Gerald
see: Potpourri, 9)
see: Webb, Gordon, 4)
see: Wilbraham, John, 13)

Jennings, Andrew
see: Anderson, Ronald, 4)
see: Dean, Allan, 2)

Jilka, Alfred
see: Wobisch, Helmut, 2)

Jones, Granville
see: Clift, Dennis
see: Jackson, Harold
see: Jones, Philip, 10)

Jones, Stuart
see: Stockhausen, Markus, 4)

Joubert, Ursula
see: Immer, Friedemann, 3)

Justh, Gottfried
see: Potpourri, 59), 60), 61)

Kagan, Oleg
see: Zikov, Vladimir

Kägi, Walter
  see: Zeyer, Adam

Kaine, Carmel
  see: Jones, Philip, 3)
  see: Potpourri, 46)
  see: Wilbraham, John, 11), 19)

Kakuska, Thomas
  see: Rudolf, Richard

Kalafusz, Hans
  see: Quinque, Rolf, 7)

Kalup, Rudolf
  see: Libiseller, Hansjörg
  see: Spindler, Josef, 3)

Kantarjian, Gerrard
  see: Schultz, Erik, 8)

Kaplan, Lewis
  see: Anderson, Ronald, 2)
  see: Dean, Allan, 1)

Karrer, Emily
  see: Sommerhalder, Max

Katai, Gyola
  see: Friedrich, Reinhold

Katt, Peter
  see: Potpourri, 61), 62), 63)

Kavafian, Ani
  see: Berinbaum, Martin
  see: Schwarz, Gerard, 3)

Kavafien, Ida
  see: Berinbaum, Martin

Kawahara, Karl
  see: Holmgren, Fred

Keen, Erika
  see: Haug, Edward

Keene, James
  see: Lowrey, Alvin

Kegl, Gaspar
  see: Eichhorn, Holger

Keller, Andrea
  see: Immer, Friedemann, 11)

Kellerman, Wolfgang
  see: Clift, Dennis

Keltsch, Werner
  see: Sauter, Hermann, 6), 9),
    10), 11), 12), 27), 35)
  see: Tarr, Edward, 4)

Kernerman, Morry
  see: Schultz, Erik, 8)

Kessler, Jack
  see: Hopkins, Kenneth

Kimstedt, Rainer
  see: Wolf, Hans, 11)

Kirch, Willy
  see: Scherbaum, Adolf, 7)

Kling, Paul
  see: Rapier, Leon, 2)

Kluppelberg, Helmut
  see: Tarr, Edward, 18), 21)

Knetsch, Reinier
  see: Potpourri, 6)

Knowles, Leslie
  see: Schultz, Erik, 8)

Koeckert, Rudolf
  see: Bauer, Willibald, 4)

Kok, F.
  see: Warren, Wesley

Kolberg, Hugo
  see: Vacchiano, William, 2)

Kolouch
  see: Horák, Jiří, 4)

Korda, Robert
  see: Guarneri, Mario

Kornacker, Thomas
  see: Dean, Allan, 4), 5)
  see: Potpourri, 5)

Korngold, Kathrin
  see: Plog, Anthony, 11)

Kortner, Ottavia
  see: Bernard, André, 2)

Koutzen, Nadia
see: Broiles, Melvin

Krachmalnick, Jacob
see: Krauss, Sam

Kransberg, Marjorie
see: Schwarz, Gerard, 1)

Krasznai, István
see: Tarr, Edward, 17)

Krauth, Martin
see: Wolf, Hans, 7)

Krips, Alfred
see: Ghitalla, Armando, 14), 16)
see: Voisin, Roger, 1)

Krotzinger, Werner
see: Scherbaum, Adolf, 5), 21)

Kuijken, Sigiswald
see: Potpourri, 51)
see: Rippas, Claude
see: Smithers, Don, 13)
see: Spindler, Josef, 13), 15)

Kupka, Connie
see: Plog, Anthony, 11)

Kussmaul, Rainer
see: André, Maurice, 196)
see: Immer, Friedemann, 11)
see: Sauter, Hermann, 25)
see: Zickler, Heinz, 5)

Kwalwasser, Helen
see: Broiles, Melvin
see: Nagel, Robert, 14)

Labella, Peter
see: Potpourri, 38)

Lakatos, Janet
see: Stevens, Thomas, 10)

Langbein, Brenton
see: Jones, Philip, 6)

Laroque, Nicole
see: André, Maurice, 13), 14)

Larsens, Gunars
see: Touvron, Guy, 5)

Latchem, Malcolm
see: Laird, Michael, 15)
see: Wilbraham, John, 12)

Lautenbacher, Susanne
see: Gleissle, Walter, 11)
see: Holy, Walter, 10)
see: Scherbaum, Adolf, 30)
see: Schneidewind, Helmut, 13)
see: Tarr, Edward, 4)
see: Zickler, Heinz, 8), 10), 11)

Lavers, Marjorie
see: Clift, Dennis

Lee, Mi-Kyung
see: Biessecker, Friedhelm

Lehmann, Ulrich
see: Adelbrecht, Henri, 3)
see: Scherbaum, Adolf, 1)

Leonhardt, Marie
see: André, Maurice, 221)
see: Bryant, Ralph, 2), 4), 5)
see: Immer, Friedemann, 14)
see: Potpourri, 51), 52), 57),
  58), 59), 60), 61), 63)
see: Smithers, Don, 13), 14),
  15)
see: Spindler, Josef, 11), 13),
  14), 15)

Lepinte, Nicole
see: André, Maurice, 13)

Lester, Joel
see: Burns, Stephen
see: Dean, Allan, 3)

Levin, Michael
see: Hoffman, Edward

Levine, Adrian
see: Wilbraham, John, 27)

Lewis, Roy
see: Gould, Mark

Lieberman, V.
see: Potpourri, 30)

Lin, Cho-Liang
see: Marsalis, Wynton, 5)

Lin, Marjorie
see: Bastin, Ernie

Lindenau, Wolfgang
see: Tarr, Edward, 27)

Loković, Edith
see: Immer, Friedemann, 3)

Loveday, Alan
see: Jones, Philip, 3)
see: Tuckwell, Barry
see: Wilbraham, John, 6), 12),
19)

Löwe, Wolfgang
see: Gass, Josef

Lutski, Grigori
see: Margolin, Veniamin

Lyne, Allison
see: Thompson, James

Lysell, Bernt
see: Schrello, Mark

Lywen, Werner
see: Geisler, Lloyd

Mackintosh, Catherine
see: Immer, Friedemann, 4)
see: Laird, Michael, 5), 7), 11),
17), 18), 19)

Macrow, Mary
see: Otten, Kees

Madison, David
see: Johnson, Gilbert, 8)

Maetzl, Klaus
see: Spindler, Josef, 10)

Magad, Samuel
see: Herseth, Adolph, 3), 4)

Magaziner, Elliot
see: Crisara, Raymond, 9)

Magnes, Frances
see: Nagel, Robert, 7)

Maguire, Hugh
see: Clift, Dennis
see: Webb, Gordon, 1)

Maiben, Dana
see: Dickey, Bruce

Maier, Franz-Josef
see: André, Maurice, 225)
see: Bodenröder, Robert
see: Potpourri, 22)
see: Renz, Albrecht, 1)
see: Tarr, Edward, 35), 36),
37), 38)

Malan, Roy
see: Metzger, Charles

Mansfield, Newton
see: Schwarz, Gerard, 20)

Marquardt, Ulrich
see: Sauter, Hermann, 27)

Marriner, Neville
see: Wilbraham, John, 6), 12),
13)

Martin, Anthony
see: Holmgren, Fred
see: Immer, Friedemann, 13)

Martin, Victor
see: Foriscot, J.

Masters, Robert
see: Clift, Dennis

Matsuda, Yoko
see: Ferrantino, Kenneth
see: Guarneri, Mario

Maurer, James
see: Hickman, David, 2)

Mayer-Schierning, Ernst
see: Basch, Wolfgang, 10)
see: Tarr, Edward, 11)

McCartney, Corol
see: Schultz, Erik, 8)

McDonald, Marilyn
see: Immer, Friedemann, 13)

McMahon, Ivor
see: Jones, Philip, 5)

Meacham, Charles
see: Haug, Edward

Medina, Marisol
see: Thompson, James

Melcher, Wilhelm
see: McGregor, Rob Roy, 2)
see: Sauter, Hermann, 23)
see: Schmid, Bernhard, 2), 6)
see: Wolf, Hans, 6)

Melkus, Eduard
see: André, Maurice, 25)
see: Bauer, Willibald, 3)
see: Eichhorn, Holger
see: Pok, František, 5)
see: Tarr, Edward, 11)

Menollu, Petru
see: Haneuse, Arthur

Menuhin, Yehudi
see: Clift, Dennis
see: Wilbraham, John, 21)

Merckel, Henri
see: Mule, Marcel

Mergl, Wilhelm
see: Bryant, Ralph, 1), 3), 4),
5)
see: Immer, Friedemann, 16)
see: Potpourri, 49), 50), 51),
52), 53), 54), 55), 56), 57),
58), 59), 60), 61), 62), 63),
64)
see: Spindler, Josef, 10), 11),
12), 13), 14), 15), 16)

Meyer, Paul
see: Schultz, Erik, 8)

Meyer-Schierning, Ernst
see: Potpourri, 2)
see: Schneidewind, Helmut, 9),
12)

Michaelian, Ernest
see: Haug, Edward

Michelucci, Roberto
see: Adelbrecht, Henri, 4)

Miller, Julie
see: Laird, Michael, 7), 19)
see: Steele-Perkins, Crispian,
7), 16), 18)

Mirring, Peter
see: Haas, Rudolf

Mischakoff, Mischa
see: Baker, Bernard

Mitter, Helmut
see: Immer, Friedemann, 14),
15), 17)
see: Potpourri, 62), 63)

Mitterer, Anita
see: Bryant, Ralph, 4), 5)
see: Immer, Friedemann, 14),
15), 16), 17)
see: Potpourri, 55), 56), 57),
58), 59), 60), 61), 62), 63)
see: Spindler, Josef, 16)

Moglia, Alain
see: André, Maurice, 49)

Monosoff, Sonya
see: Sheldon, Robert

Moonen, Nicolette
see: Potpourri, 61)

Moosmann, Alois
see: Ziegler, Albert

Morin, Françoise
see: Thompson, James

Motz, Richard
see: Potpourri, 63)

Moulton, Roger
see: Miller, Rodney

Mountain, Peter
see: Webb, Gordon, 1)

Mowatt, Roy
see: Steele-Perkins, Crispian,
10)

Mühlberger, Klaus
see: Calvayrac, Albert

Mullen, William
see: Bastin, Ernie

Müller, Miloš
see: Pok, František, 5)

Muroya, Takahiro
see: Quinque, Rolf, 7)

Musaelyan, Alexandre
see: Volodin, Lev

Naegele, Philipp
see: Bernard, André, 2)
see: Hunger, Helmut, 4)
see: Immer, Friedemann, 7)
see: Preis, Ivo

Nakaten, Matthias
see: Holy, Walter, 5)
see: Tarr, Edward, 19), 38)

Neininger, Wolfgang
see: Bodenröder, Robert
see: Potpourri, 22)

Nelson, Norman
see: Chenette, Stephen
see: Potpourri, 9)
see: Wilbraham, John, 12), 13)

Neuhaus, Werner
see: Bodenröder, Robert
see: Holy, Walter, 5)
see: Potpourri, 22)
see: Steinkopf, Otto
see: Tarr, Edward, 10), 18),
19), 21), 23), 24), 25), 27),
35), 37)

Neuhaus, Wolfgang
see: Tarr, Edward, 38)

Neumann, Franz
see: Immer, Friedemann, 11)

Nielen, Ruth
see: Basch, Wolfgang, 1)
see: Bodenröder, Robert
see: Potpourri, 22)

Niessen, Joseph
see: Immer, Friedemann, 12)

Nilsson, Stig
see: Christiansen, Jan

Noel, Michael
see: Lagorce, Antoine

Novák, Antonín
see: Horák, Jiří, 5)

Novosad
see: Horák, Jiří, 4)

Obermayer, Ernst
see: Renz, Albrecht, 6)

Ohnheiser, Gerhard
see: Bernard, André, 2)
see: Preis, Ivo

Oistrakh, David
see: Scherbaum, Adolf, 26)

Oistrakh, Igor
see: Fomin, Evgeny

Okada, Yoshiko Nakura
see: Wolf, Hans, 11)

Oomens, Radboud
see: Läubin, Hannes, 6), 8)
see: Schmid, Bernhard, 11)
see: Send, Peter

O'Reilly, Brendan
see: Webb, Gordon, 1)

Orsler, Helen
see: Steele-Perkins, Crispian,
16), 18)

Ortner, Annemarie
see: Immer, Friedemann, 17)

Ovčarek, Vladimir
see: Krylov, Gleb
see: Margolin, Veniamin

Ovens, Raymond
see: Chenette, Stephen

Paik, Hyung Sun
see: Schwarz, Gerard, 1)

Palm, Eberhard
see: Güttler, Ludwig, 8), 14),
18)

Parikian, Manoug
  see: André, Maurice, 181)
  see: Jackson, Harold

Parker, Nicholas
  see: Steele-Perkins, Crispian,
    16)

Paulu, Norman
  see: Hood, Donald

Peabody, Paul
  see: Gould, Mark

Pellegrino, Pasquale
  see: Touvron, Guy, 14)

Perez, José Antonio
  see: André, Maurice, 138)

Perez-Ruiz, Antonio
  see: Touvron, Guy, 14)

Perron, Jasmine
  see: Thompson, James

Peters, Gerhard
  see: Bodenröder, Robert

Petrell, Sigrid
  see: Immer, Friedemann, 11)

Pfeiffer, Walter
  see: Bryant, Ralph, 1), 3), 4),
    5)
  see: Immer, Friedemann, 14),
    15), 16)
  see: Potpourri, 49), 50), 51),
    52), 53), 54), 55), 56), 57),
    58), 59), 60), 61), 62), 63),
    64)
  see: Spindler, Josef, 7), 8), 9),
    10), 11), 12), 13), 14), 15),
    16)
  see: Tarr, Edward, 45)

Phillips, Daniel
  see: Burns, Stephen
  see: Schwarz, Gerard, 3)

Phillips, Leo
  see: Biessecker, Friedhelm

Pichler, Günter
  see: André, Maurice, 135), 169),
    210), 216)

Pignotti, Alfio
  see: Eggers, Carter

Pini, Carl
  see: Bernard, André, 12)
  see: Clift, Dennis
  see: Wilbraham, John, 31)

Pitchon, Joel
  see: Gould, Mark

Plott, Stefan
  see: Holy, Walter, 9)
  see: Potpourri, 49), 50), 64)
  see: Spindler, Josef, 7), 8), 10)

Poggi, Gino
  see: André, Maurice, 130)

Poleyes, L.
  see: Popov, Sergei, 3)

Pollikoff, Max
  see: Murtha, Roger

Pols, Anneke
  see: Otten, Kees

Pool, Carol
  see: Wise, Wilmer

Pougnet, Jean
  see: Jones, Philip, 8)

Prévost, Christian
  see: Thompson, James

Proto, Secondo
  see: Crisara, Raymond, 3)

Prystawski, Walter
  see: André, Maurice, 30)
  see: Scherbaum, Adolf, 24)

Purger, Bohuslav
  see: Pok, František, 5)

Purich, Peter
  see: Thompson, James

Pynchon, William
  see: Haug, Edward

659

Rösch, Wolfgang
see: Sauter, Hermann, 24)
see: Schmitt, Siegfried
see: Wolf, Hans, 10)

Rosenberger, Celia
see: Metzger, Charles

Rosenboom, David
see: Bastin, Ernie

Rosenfeld, Julie
see: Schwarz, Gerard, 1)

Rosoff, Elliot
see: Wise, Wilmer

Rossi, Christiano
see: André, Maurice, 114), 115)

Roth, Fred
see: Güttler, Ludwig, 18)

Rothstein, Jack
see: Clift, Dennis

Rubin, Nathan
see: Haug, Edward

Ruder, Philip
see: Giangiulio, Richard

Ruhland, Elisabeth
see: Renz, Albrecht, 6)

Ryber, Peter
see: Jandorf, D.

Sambuco, Gino
see: Nagel, Robert, 3)

Saulesco, Mircea
see: Schrello, Mark

Sax, Sidney
see: Wilbraham, John, 29)

Schaeffer, Ralph
see: Stevens, Thomas, 10)

Schäfer, Adelheid
see: Tarr, Edward, 38)

Schaller, Herlinde
see: Immer, Friedemann, 17)

Schärnack, Otto
see: Tarr, Edward, 11)

Schellenberger, Ilsebill
see: Basch, Wolfgang, 1)

Schich, Günther
see: Eichhorn, Holger

Schmahl, Gustav
see: Krug, Willi, 2)

Schmidt, Christopher
see: Immer, Friedemann, 3)
see: Tarr, Edward, 11)

Schmidt, Veronika
see: Bryant, Ralph, 4), 5)
see: Potpourri, 57), 58), 59)
see: Spindler, Josef, 16)

Schneeberger, Hansheinz
see: André, Maurice, 26)
see: Thibaud, Pierre, 8)

Schneider, Alexander
see: Mule, Marcel
see: Nagel, Robert, 1), 2)

Schneider, Claudia
see: Immer, Friedemann, 11)

Schneider, David
see: Haug, Edward

Schneiderhan, Hans
see: Scherbaum, Adolf, 26)

Schneiderhan, Wolfgang
see: Holler, Adolf
see: Scherbaum, Adolf, 6), 24)

Schnitzler, Heide
see: Stradner, Gerhard

Schoberwalter, Peter
  see: Bryant, Ralph, 1), 3), 4),
    5)
  see: Immer, Friedemann, 14),
    15), 16), 17)
  see: Potpourri, 49), 50), 51),
    52), 53), 54), 55), 56), 57),
    58), 59), 60), 61), 62), 63),
    64)
  see: Spindler, Josef, 7), 8), 9),
    10), 11), 12), 13), 14), 15),
    16)
  see: Tarr, Edward, 45)

Scholefield, Walter
  see: Tasa, David

Schor, Joseph
  see: Crisara, Raymond, 3)

Schröder, Jaap
  see: André, Maurice, 221), 222),
    223), 224), 225)
  see: Groot, Willem (Wim)
  see: Immer, Friedemann, 13)
  see: Mertens, Theo, 7)
  see: Smithers, Don, 11)

Schroeder, Jan
  see: Immer, Friedemann, 4)

Schulte, Rolf
  see: Unidentified, Trumpet(s),
    7)

Schulz, Rudolf
  see: Scherbaum, Adolf, 7)

Schumacher, Helmut
  see: Schmid, Bernhard, 13)

Schumann, Robert
  see: Hunger, Helmut, 4)

Schunk, Heinz
  see: Güttler, Ludwig, 21), 26)

Schwalbé, Michel
  see: Longinotti, Paolo
  see: Scherbaum, Adolf, 12)

Sedláček, Jan
  see: Buriánek, Jindřich

Seeger, Brigitte
  see: Tarr, Edward, 35), 37)

Seifert, Ingrid
  see: Bryant, Ralph, 4), 5)
  see: Potpourri, 55), 56), 57),
    58), 59)
  see: Spindler, Josef, 16)

Seitz, Gerhard
  see: Bauer, Willibald, 4)

Semenovich, Denise
  see: Gould, Mark

Seplow, Kathy
  see: Immer, Friedemann, 13)

Sestak, Tomislav
  see: Spindler, Josef, 5)

Shapiro, Eudice
  see: Stevens, Thomas, 10)

Sherba, John
  see: Wise, Wilmer

Shermont, Roger
  see: Ghitalla, Armando, 2)

Shindaryov, Daniel
  see: Schwarz, Gerard, 1)

Shumsky, Oscar
  see: Broiles, Melvin

Shure, Paul
  see: Hood, Boyde
  see: Plog, Anthony, 8)
  see: Schwarz, Gerard, 1)
  see: Stevens, Thomas, 10)

Sillito, Kenneth
  see: Berinbaum, Martin
  see: Bernard, André, 12)
  see: Smithers, Don, 1)
  see: Webb, Gordon, 1)

Silpigni, Constance
  see: Greenho, David

Silverstein, Joseph
  see: Ghitalla, Armando, 6), 7),
    8), 9)

Silzer, Giorgio
see: Scherbaum, Adolf, 7)

Simon, Pierre
see: Ménardi, Louis

Simons, Matthias
see: Zapf, Gerd

Šinder, L.
see: Krylov, Gleb

Sinnhoffer, Ingo
see: Potpourri, 11)

Siskovics, Curt
see: Hunger, Helmut, 4)

Skeaping, Roderick
see: Laird, Michael, 19)
see: Smithers, Don, 2)

Skerjanc, Edvard
see: Thompson, James

Skvor, Petr
see: Kejmar, Miroslav, 5)

Sloan, Eleanor
see: Laird, Michael, 2), 11),
17), 19)
see: Smithers, Don, 3)

Smirnoff, Joel
see: Miller, Rodney

Smith, Hazel
see: Wallace, John, 6)

Smithers, Janet
see: Smithers, Don, 6)

Snítil, Vaclav
see: André, Maurice, 220)

Socher, Barry
see: Plog, Anthony, 11)

Sokol, Mark
see: Anderson, Ronald, 4)
see: Dean, Allan, 2)

Sonnleitner, Fritz
see: Zapf, Gerd

Sorkin, Herbert
see: Jandorf, D.
see: Karpilovsky, Murray

Sortomme, Richard
see: Schwarz, Gerard, 3)
see: Wise, Wilmer

Spierer, Leon
see: Groth, Konradin

Standage, Simon
see: Laird, Michael, 2), 8), 11),
14), 19)
see: Smithers, Don, 3)
see: Wilbraham, John, 27)

Stanic, Jelka
see: Adelbrecht, Henri, 2)

Staryk, Steven
see: Berinbaum, Martin
see: Mills, Fred

Stenske, David
see: Parker, Craig B.
see: Plog, Anthony, 11)

Stevens, Cyrus
see: Burns, Stephen

Stier, Kurt Christian
see: Lachenmeir, Paul
see: Potpourri, 22)

Stowell, Robin
see: Laird, Michael, 7), 17)

Straumer, Roland
see: Güttler, Ludwig, 20)

Streng, Rudolf
see: Wobisch, Helmut, 1), 2)

Stuurop, Alda
see: Bryant, Ralph, 2)
see: Immer, Friedemann, 14)
see: Potpourri, 51), 52), 57),
58), 59), 60), 61), 63)
see: Rippas, Claude
see: Smithers, Don, 13), 14),
15)
see: Spindler, Josef, 11), 13),
14), 15)

Suk, Josef
see: Touvron, Guy, 6)

Suske, Karl
see: Güttler, Ludwig, 18)
see: Krug, Willi, 5)

Suske, Kurt
see: Güttler, Ludwig, 12), 21)

Svatek, Ferdinand
see: Spindler, Josef, 10)

Svendsen, Troels
see: Smithers, Don, 13)
see: Spindler, Josef, 15)

Sweet, Marti
see: Wise, Wilmer

Szeryng, Henryk
see: Bernard, André, 12)

Szigeti, Joseph
see: Mule, Marcel

Takada, Miohisa
see: Burns, Stephen

Talassi, Glauco
see: André, Maurice, 130)

Talvi, Ilkka
see: Hood, Boyde
see: Schwarz, Gerard, 1)

Tamponi, Franco
see: Adelbrecht, Henri, 5), 6)

Tanabe, Roy
see: Guarneri, Mario
see: Stevens, Thomas, 10)

Tarack, Gerald
see: Heinrich, Robert
see: Mase, Raymond

Tarling, Judith
see: Keavy, Stephen

Tarnowsky, Vera
see: Schultz, Erik, 8)

TeBrake, Nelva
see: Holmgren, Fred

Teco, Romuald
see: Romm, Ronald
see: Stubbs, James

Terebesi, György
see: André, Maurice, 94), 99), 171)
see: Quinque, Rolf, 7)

Terranova, Samual
see: McGuffey, Patrick

Tessier, Georges
see: Delmotte, Roger, 3)
see: Ménardi, Louis

Theiner, Kurt
see: Potpourri, 49), 50), 64)

Thoene, Helga
see: Steinkopf, Otto
see: Tarr, Edward, 10)

Thurmair, Veronika
see: Renz, Albrecht, 6)

Titmus, Florence
see: Plog, Anthony, 11)

Tomasow, Jan
see: Spindler, Josef, 1)
see: Wobisch, Helmut, 2), 12), 14)

Topolski, Zlatko
see: Spindler, Josef, 5)

Toso, Piero
see: André, Maurice, 130), 209)

Townley, Alison
see: Steele-Perkins, Crispian, 16), 18)

Toyoda, Koji
see: André, Maurice, 180)

Trauner, Wolfgang
see: Immer, Friedemann, 15), 17)

Travers, Patricia
see: Mueller, Herbert

Trent, Janet
see: Laird, Michael, 19)

Walker, Urs
see: Sommerhalder, Max

Wallez, Jean-Pierre
see: André, Maurice, 13), 14),
188)
see: Bernard, André, 3), 7), 8),
11)

Walta, Jaring
see: Floore, John

Wang, Tze-Koong
see: Guarneri, Mario

Warren-Green, Christopher
see: André, Maurice, 38), 41),
46)
see: Wallace, John, 3)

Watanabe, Keiko
see: Bryant, Ralph, 4), 5)
see: Potpourri, 58)
see: Smithers, Don, 14), 15)

Waterfield, Polly
see: Laird, Michael, 1), 2), 7),
17)

Waterhouse, William
see: Nashan, Rudolph

Waterman, Frits Joël
see: Reinhart, Carole Dawn, 2)

Waterman, Robert
see: Reinhart, Carole Dawn, 2)

Waterman, Ruth
see: Carroll, Edward, 3), 5)
see: Gould, Mark

Watkinson, Andrew
see: Steele-Perkins, Crispian, 6)

Wayne, Henrietta
see: Steele-Perkins, Crispian,
16)

Webb, Carol
see: Schwarz, Gerard, 3)

Weigmann, Günther
see: Gleissle, Walter, 8)

Weiner, Stanley
see: Tarr, Edward, 44)

Weingart, Edmund
see: Haug, Edward

Weintrob, Neil
see: Henderson, Douglas

Welch, Robin
see: Plog, Anthony, 11)

Westphal, Hans-Joachim
see: Groth, Konradin
see: Scherbaum, Adolf, 7)

Wieck, Michael
see: André, Maurice, 16)

Wilcock, Elizabeth
see: Laird, Michael, 7), 8), 19)
see: Steele-Perkins, Crispian,
7), 18)

Williams, Hildburg
see: Steele-Perkins, Crispian,
7), 16), 18)

Williams, Trevor
see: Clift, Dennis
see: Wilbraham, John, 23)

Wilson, Nancy
see: Holmgren, Fred
see: Immer, Friedemann, 13)

Wirz, Ruth
see: Tarr, Edward, 11)

Wittrig, Janis
see: Plog, Anthony, 11)

Wolfe, Marlin
see: Lowrey, Alvin

Wolff-Malm, Doris
see: Bodenröder, Robert
see: Potpourri, 22)

Wood, Deborah
see: Miller, Rodney

Woodcock, David
see: Steele-Perkins, Crispian, 5)

Wührer, Friedrich
see: Scherbaum, Adolf, 35)

Yankelev, Yosef
see: Berinbaum, Martin

Zaks, Leon
see: Dokshitser, Timofei, 12)

Zampieri, Fernando
see: Dassé, Jean-Luc

Zannella, Bruno
see: Dassé, Jean-Luc

Zeavin, Carol
see: Anderson, Ronald, 6)
see: Dean, Allan, 3)

Zeidler, Max
see: Scherbaum, Adolf, 21)

Zienkowsky, Edward
see: Tasa, David

Zimansky, Robert
see: Berinbaum, Martin
see: Scherbaum, Adolf, 32)
see: Sommerhalder, Max

Zlatoff-Mirsky, Everett
see: Miller, Rodney
see: Perry, Brian

Zolotarev, Alexandre
see: Yudashkin, Georgy

Zukerman, Pinchas
see: Stevens, Thomas, 12)

Zukofsky, Paul
see: Dean, Allan, 8)
see: Nagel, Robert, 18), 19),
 20)
see: Soloff, Lew

Violino piccolo
[cross-referenced under violin]

Ayo, Felix
see: André, Maurice, 201)

Felicani, Rodolfo
see: Wobisch, Helmut, 8)
see: Zeyer, Adam

Garcia, José Luis
see: Wilbraham, John, 27)

Hamann, Bernhard
see: Scherbaum, Adolf, 33)

Harnoncourt, Alice
see: Bryant, Ralph, 5)
see: Holy, Walter, 9)
see: Immer, Friedemann, 16)

Höver, Herbert
see: Immer, Friedemann, 3)

Kuijken, Sigiswald
see: Rippas, Claude

Lautenbacher, Susanne
see: Schneidewind, Helmut, 13)

Maier, Franz-Josef
see: Tarr, Edward, 37)

Melkus, Eduard
see: Eichhorn, Holger

Menuhin, Yehudi
see: Clift, Dennis

Pini, Carl
see: Bernard, André, 12)
see: Clift, Dennis
see: Wilbraham, John, 31)

Ritchie, Stanley
see: Holmgren, Fred

Sillito, Kenneth
see: Webb, Gordon, 1)

Standage, Simon
see: Laird, Michael, 8)

Suske, Kurt
see: Güttler, Ludwig, 12)

Tomasow, Jan
see: Wobisch, Helmut, 2)

Waterman, Ruth
see: Gould, Mark

Violone
[cross-referenced under Bass (string)]

Baines, Francis
see: Laird, Michael, 11), 14),
    17)

Berg, Christian
see: Immer, Friedemann, 3)

Brookes, Oliver
see: Laird, Michael, 1), 2)
see: Smithers, Don, 3)

Franklin, Brian
see: Immer, Friedemann, 11)

Hruza, Eduard
see: Bryant, Ralph, 1), 3), 4),
    5)
see: Holy, Walter, 9)
see: Immer, Friedemann, 14),
    15), 16), 17)
see: Potpourri, 49), 50), 51),
    52), 53), 54), 55), 56), 57),
    58), 59), 60), 61), 62), 63),
    64)
see: Spindler, Josef, 7), 8), 9),
    10), 11), 12), 13), 14), 15),
    16)
see: Tarr, Edward, 45)

MacNamara, Amanda
see: Laird, Michael, 8)
see: Steele-Perkins, Crispian,
    10)

Marjoram, Keith
see: Laird, Michael, 8)

Oboda, Jaroslav
see: Pok, František, 2)

Pap, Nicholas
see: Immer, Friedemann, 14)
see: Potpourri, 61), 63)

Planyavsky, Alfred
see: Eichhorn, Holger

Pošta, František
see: Pok, František, 5)

Ros, Pere
see: Immer, Friedemann, 3)

Skeaping, Adam
see: Smithers, Don, 1), 2)

Spicker, Heiner
see: Holy, Walter, 5)
see: Tarr, Edward, 10), 19), 20)

Strehl, Laurenzius
see: Tarr, Edward, 12)

Swinkels, Piet
see: Potpourri, 51)
see: Spindler, Josef, 11), 13)

Uhl, Siegfried
see: Schneidewind, Helmut, 13)

Ulsamer, Josef
see: Tarr, Edward, 17)

Viale, Angelo
see: Tarr, Edward, 3)

Willens, Michael
see: Holmgren, Fred
see: Immer, Friedemann, 13)

Woodrow, Anthony
see: Bryant, Ralph, 2), 4), 5)
see: Immer, Friedemann, 14)
see: Potpourri, 51), 52), 57),
    58), 59), 60), 63)
see: Rippas, Claude
see: Smithers, Don, 13), 14),
    15)
see: Spindler, Josef, 11), 13),
    14), 15)

Virginal

Hogwood, Christopher
see: Laird, Michael, 1)

Holman, Peter
see: Steele-Perkins, Crispian,
    10)

Leonhardt, Gustav
see: Tarr, Edward, 45)

Lester, Harold
see: Potpourri, 67)

Nicholson, Paul
see: Impett, Jonathan

Vocals
(background singing)

Bello, Dal
see: Schultz, Erik, 8)

Fowler, Bernard
see: Wise, Wilmer

Massey, Curt
see: Méndez, Rafael, 4)

Pendarvis, Janice
see: Wise, Wilmer

Perry, Douglas
see: Wise, Wilmer

Pirie, Diane
see: Schultz, Erik, 8)

Roche, Maggie
see: Wise, Wilmer

Roche, Suzzy
see: Wise, Wilmer

Roche, Terre
see: Wise, Wilmer

Ronstadt, Linda
see: Wise, Wilmer

Williams, Sharon Lee
see: Schultz, Erik, 8)

Voice
(unidentified singing voice type)

Baucomont, Janette
see: Thibaud, Pierre, 13)

Bortoluzzi, Paolo
see: Stockhausen, Markus, 2)

Chédeville
see: Caens, Thierry

Clary, Robert
see: Stevens, Thomas, 15)

Donat, Peter
see: Stevens, Thomas, 15)

Feussner, Alfred
see: Tarr, Edward, 16)

Gertken, Klaus
see: Kierski, Eckhard

Gilbert, Ramon
see: Dean, Allan, 7)

Giroux
see: Caens, Thierry

Johansson, Karin Edvards
see: Potpourri, 3)

Jonsson, Dansar Edvard
see: Potpourri, 3)

Jonsson, Finn Jonas
see: Potpourri, 3)

Larsson, Björs Olof
see: Potpourri, 3)

Legrand, Christiane
see: Thibaud, Pierre, 13)

Meunier, Claudine
see: Thibaud, Pierre, 13)

Pearson, William
see: Tarr, Edward, 16)

Rhodes, Julia
see: Kierski, Eckhard

Robin, N.
see: Caens, Thierry

Sanguineti, Edoardo
see: Thibaud, Pierre, 13)

Schickele, Peter
see: Mase, Raymond

Voices
(spoken voice parts, but not necessarily narration)

Hellermann, Jacqueline
see: Schwarz, Gerard, 18)

Immanuel, Marsha
see: Schwarz, Gerard, 18)

O'Brien, Michael
see: Schwarz, Gerard, 18)

Thomas, John P.
see: Schwarz, Gerard, 18)

Wine bottle

Schickele, Peter
see: Platt, Seymour

Zither
[includes various types & sizes: bûche, citole, cittern, Scheitholtz, kanoun, etc.]

Achcar, Elie
see: Maalouf, Nassim

Corkhill, David
see: Laird, Michael, 1)

Gerrits, Paul
see: Otto, Joachim

Harwood, Ian
see: Smithers, Don, 3)

Kirsch, Dieter
see: Otto, Joachim

Leach, John
see: Potpourri, 67)

Osnowycz, Anne
see: Pok, František, 4)

Tyler, James
see: Laird, Michael, 1), 2)
see: Potpourri, 67)

Waldburg, Klaus
see: Schoof, Manfred

Zanetti, Sandro
see: Potpourri, 47)
see: Tarr, Edward, 32)

BIBLIOGRAPHY

Record Catalogues

Bielefelder Katalog, Schallplatten, Compact Discs, Klassik.
Vereinigte Motor-Verlag, Leuschnerstrasse 1, 7000 Stuttgart, West Germany.

Catalogo Generale Italia (Tutti i dischi, musicassette, stereo8: musica classica).
Catalogo Generale Italia, piazza S. Angelo 2, 20121 Milano, Italy.

Diapason, Catalogue général classique.
Diapason-Microsillon, 6, rue Jules Simon, 92100 Boulogne, France.

Gramophone Classical Catalogue.
117-179 Kenton Road, Harrow, Middlesex, HA3 OHA, England.

Perrault International.
C.P. 250, St-Hyacinthe, Québec   J2S 7B6, Canada.
(73 East Allen Street, Winooski, Vermont   05404)

Schwann.
Schwann Catalogs, 535 Boylston St., Boston, Massachusetts   02116.

Plus catalogues from various recording companies:
CBC, CBS, Coronet, CRI, Crystal, Decca (England), Deutsche Grammophon, Erato, Golden Crest, Mark Records, Musical Heritage Society, Nonesuch, Panton, Philips, Supraphon...

[It should be noted that each issue of the *Bielefelder, Diapason, Gramophone &
Schwann* catalogues includes current addresses of record companies and distributors.]

Periodicals

Brass Bulletin, 1971-1987.
(Jean-Pierre Mathez, Editor) CH-1630 Bulle, Switzerland

The Brass World, 1965-1974.
(Robert Weast, Editor) College of Fine Arts, Drake University, Des Moines, Iowa   50311

International Trumpet Guild Newsletter, 1975-1982.
(Anne [Farr-] Hardin, Editor) P.O. Drawer 2025, Columbia, South Carolina   29202

International Trumpet Guild Journal, 1976-1987.
(Anne [Farr-] Hardin, Editor) P.O. Drawer 2025, Columbia, South Carolina   29202

BIBLIOGRAPHY

Discographies and Record Guides

Bennett, John R. *Melodiya: A Soviet Russian L.P. Discography*. Westport,
Connecticut & London, England: Greenwood Press, 1981.
ISBN: 0-313-22596-6   LCCN: 81-4247
(Discographies, ISSN: 0192-334X; no. 6)

Clough, Francis F. & G.J. Cuming. *The World's Encyclopædia of Recorded Music
(1950).* ₍Includes *First Supplement (April 1950 to May-June 1951),*
p. 725-860₎ London: The London Gramophone Corporation & Sidgwick and
Jackson Limited, 1952.
LCCN: A 52-8431

Clough/Cuming/E.A. Hughes. *Second Supplement to The World's Encyclopædia of
Recorded Music (May 1951 - December 1952).* London: Sidgwick and Jackson
Limited (in association with The Decca Record Company Limited & London
Records Inc.), 1953.
LCCN: A 52-8431

Clough/Cuming/Hughes/Angela Noble. *Third Supplement to The World's
Encyclopædia of Recorded Music (January 1953 - December 1955).* London:
Sidgwick and Jackson Limited (in association with The Decca Record Company
Limited & London Records Inc.), 1957. ₍Reprint, 1969₎
LCCN: A 52-8431

Clough/Cuming/Hughes/Noble. *The World's Encyclopædia of Recorded Music*
₍1950-1955₎. (Reprint of 3 volumes: 1950-1951; 1951-1952; 1953-1955). Westport,
Connecticut: Greenwood Press, 1970.
LCCN: 71-100214

Cooper, David Edwin. *International Bibliography of Discographies: Classical Music
and Jazz & Blues, 1962-1972.* Littleton, Colorado: Libraries Unlimited, Inc.,
1975.
ISBN: 0-87287-108-8   LCCN: 75-4516

Creighton, James. *Discopaedia of the Violin, 1889-1971.* Toronto: University of
Toronto Press, 1974.
ISBN: 0-8020-1810-6   LCCN: 79-185708

Fellers, Frederick P. & Betty Meyers. *Discographies of Commercial Recordings of
the Cleveland Orchestra (1924-1977) and the Cincinnati Symphony Orchestra
(1917-1977).* Westport, Connecticut: Greenwood Press, 1978.
ISBN: 0-313-20375-X   LCCN: 78-3122

Gramophone Shop Encyclopedia of Recorded Music. New York: Simon and
Schuster, 1942.

Gramophone Shop Encyclopedia of Recorded Music. New York: Crown Publishers,
1948.

Lowrey, Alvin L. *Trumpet Discography.* (Includes Volume I: Maurice André;
Volume II: Individual Trumpet Performers; Volume III: Brass Ensembles)
Denver: National Trumpet Symposium, University of Denver School of Music,
1970.

Lowrey, Alvin & Michel Laplace. *Roger Delmotte Discography.* Nashville:
Supplement to ITG *Journal*, May, 1985.

BIBLIOGRAPHY

Maleady, Antoinette O. *Index to Record and Tape Reviews: A Classical Music Buying Guide*. Metuchen, New Jersey: Scarecrow Press, Inc., 1973-76. San Anselmo, California: Chulainn Press, 1976-82.

Myers, Kurtz. *Index to Record Reviews*. (based on material originally published in *Notes*, the quarterly journal of the Music Library Association between 1949 and 1977) Boston: G.K. Hall, 1978-1980.
    ISBN: 0-8161-0087-X   LCCN: 79-101459

Myers, Kurtz. *Index to Record Reviews*. (based on material originally published in *Notes*, the quarterly journal of the Music Library Association between 1978 and 1983) Boston: G.K. Hall, 1985.
    ISBN: 0-8161-0435-2

Poulton, Alan. *A Discography: Sir William Walton*. Kidderminster: Bravura Publications, 1980.
    ISBN: 0-906959-00-4

Rust, Brian. *American Dance Band Discography, 1917-1942*. (2 volumes). New Rochelle, New York: Arlington House, 1975.
    ISBN: 0-8700-0248-1   LCCN: 75-033689

Rust, Brian. *Jazz Records, 1897-1942*. (5th revision, 2 volumes). Chigwell, England: Storyville Publications, 1982?.
    ISBN: 0-9023-9104-6 (set)   LCCN: 78-001693

Thematic Catalogues

Bell, A. Craig. *Handel: Chronological Thematic Catalogue*. Darley: Grian-aig Press, 1972.

Brook, Barry, S. *Thematic Catalogues in Music. An Annotated Bibliography*. Hillsdale, New York: Pendragon Press, 1972.
                                        LCCN: 72-7517

Dufourcq, Norbert. *Notes et Références pour servir a une histoire de Michel-Richard Delalande*. Paris: Éditions A. & J. Picard & Co., 1957.

Giegling, Franz. *Giuseppe Torelli: Ein Beitrag zur entwicklungsgeschichte des Italienischen Konzerts*. Kassel: Bärenreiter-Verlag, 1948.

Hoffmann, Adolf. *Die Orchestersuiten Georg Philipp Telemanns, TWV 55. (mit thematisch-bibliographischen Werkverzeichnis)*. Zürich: Möseler Verlag Wolfenbuttel, 1969.

Kross, Siegfried. *Das Instrumentalkonzert bei G. Ph. Telemann*. Tutzing: Hans Schneider, 1969.

Oesch, Hans & Hans Joachim Marx. *Arcangelo Corelli: Historisch-kritische Gesamtausgabe der musikalischen Werke. (Supplementband: Die Überlieferung der Werke Arcangelo Corellis, Catalogue raisonné, - H.J. Marx)*. Köln: Arno Volk Verlag - Hans Gerig KG, 1980.
    ISBN: 3-87252-121-7

Payne, May DeForest. [McAll, May DeForest]. *Melodic Index to the Works of Johann Sebastian Bach*. New York: C.F. Peters, 1962 ₜorig. copyright 1938₎

Priestman, Brian. "Catalogue thématique des œuvres de Jean-Baptist, John et Jacques Lœillet", *Révue belge de musicologie*, vi (1952), 219-74. (Brussels)

Ruhnke, Martin. *Georg Philipp Telemann: Thematisch-Systematisches Verzeichnis seiner Werke*. Kassel: Bärenreiter-Verlag, 1984.

Ryom, Peter. *Répertoire des Œuvres d'Antonio Vivaldi*. Copenhagen: Engstrøm & Sødring A.S. Musikforlag, 1986.
ISBN: 87-87091-19-4

Schmieder, Wolfgang. *Thematisch-systematisches Verzeichnis der Werke Johann Sebastian Bachs*. Leipzig: Breitkopf & Härtel, 1961 [orig. copyright 1950]

Schneider, Herbert. *Chronologisch-Thematisches Verzeichnis Sämtlicher Werke von Jean-Baptiste Lully (LWV)*. Tutzing: Hans Schneider, 1981.
ISBN: 3-7952-0323-6

Talbot, Michael. *Albinoni — Leben und Werk*. Adliswil, Switzerland: Edition Kunzelmann, 1980.
ISBN: 3-85662-006-0

Viollier, Renée. *Jean-Joseph Mouret: le musicien des grâces, 1682-1738*. Paris: Librarie Floury, 1950. Genève: Minkoff Reprint, 1976.
ISBN: 2-8266-0632-8

Wienandt, Elwyn A. *Johann Pezel (1639-1694): A Thematic Catalogue of his Instrumental Works*. New York: Pendragon Press, 1983.
ISBN: 0-918728-23-1   LCCN: 82-12288

Wotquenne, Alfred. *Thematisches Verzeichnis der Werke von Carl Philipp Emanuel Bach*. Leipzig: 1905. Wiesbaden: Breitkopf & Härtel, 1964.

Zimmerman, Franklin B. *Henry Purcell: An analytical catalogue of his music*. London: Macmillan & Co. Ltd., 1963.

Zimmerman, Franklin B. *Henry Purcell: Melodic and Intervallic Indexes to his complete works*. Philadelphia: Smith-Edwards-Dunlap, 1975.
ISBN: 8443-0068-3   LCCN: 72-80707

Repertoire

Carnovale, Norbert. *Twentieth-Century Music for Trumpet and Orchestra: An Annotated Bibliography*. Nashville: The Brass Press, 1975.
ISBN: 0-914282-08-5   LCCN: 75-29090

Cunning, Carol. *Composium Directory of New Music. An Index of Contemporary Compositions*. [annual editions] Sedro Woolley, Washington: Crystal Musicworks, 1972-1983.

Dale, Delbert A. *Trumpet Technique*. London: Oxford University Press, 1965. [Second Edition, 1985]
ISBN: 0-19-322128-4   LCCN: 86-162172

de Lerma, Dominique-René. *Charles Ives, 1874-1954: A Bibliography of His Music*. Kent, Ohio: Kent State University Press, 1970.
ISBN: 0-87338-057-6   LCCN: 72-99083

BIBLIOGRAPHY

Eslinger, Gary S. & F. Mark Daugherty. *Sacred Choral Music in Print*. Second
Edition. (2 volumes). Philadelphia: Musicdata, Inc., 1985.
ISBN: 0-88478-017-1 (set) LCCN: 85-15368

Fantini, Girolamo. *Modo per Imparare a sonare di Tromba tanto di guerra Quanto
Musicalmente in Organo, con Tromba Sordina, col Cimbalo, e ogn'altro
istrumento*. (1638). Facsimile edition. Nashville: The Brass Press, 1972. Facsimile
study score edition. Nashville: The Brass Press, 1978.
ISBN: 0-914282-22-0

Gregory, Robin. *The Horn. A Comprehensive Guide to the Modern Horn & its
Music*. London: Faber and Faber, 1969.
ISBN: 571 04667 3

Havlice, Patricia Pate. *Popular Song Index*. Metuchen, New Jersey: Scarecrow Press,
Inc., 1975.
ISBN: 0-8108-0820-X LCCN: 75-9896

Havlice, Patricia Pate. *Popular Song Index*. First Supplement. Metuchen,
New Jersey: Scarecrow Press, Inc., 1978.
ISBN: 0-8108-1099-9 LCCN: 77-25219

Havlice, Patricia Pate. *Popular Song Index*. Second Supplement. Metuchen,
New Jersey: Scarecrow Press, Inc., 1984.
ISBN: 0-8108-1642-3 LCCN: 83-7692

Kinkle, Roger D. *The Complete Encyclopedia of Popular Music and Jazz
1900-1950*. (4 volumes). New Rochelle, New York: Arlington House, 1974.
ISBN: 0-87000-229-5

Rilling, Helmuth. *Texte zu den Kirchenkantaten von Johann Sebastian Bach*.
(Z. Philip Ambrose, English translation: *The Texts to Johann Sebastian Bach's
Church Cantatas*). Neuhausen-Stuttgart: Hänssler-Verlag, 1984.
ISBN: 3-7751-0970-6

Shapiro, Nat. *Popular Music, An Annotated Index of American Popular Songs*.
New York: Adrian Press, 1964-73.

Vol. 1. 1950-1959 (pub. 1964)
Vol. 2. 1940-1949 (pub. 1965)
Vol. 3. 1960-1964 (pub. 1967)
Vol. 4. 1930-1939 (pub. 1968)
Vol. 5. 1920-1929 (pub. 1969)
Vol. 6. 1965-1969 (pub. 1973)

LCCN: 64-23761

Smithers, Don Leroy. *The Music & History of the Baroque Trumpet before 1721*.
London: J.M. Dent & Sons Ltd., 1973.
ISBN: 0-460-03991-1

BIBLIOGRAPHY

Biographical References

Anderson, Ruth E. *Contemporary American Composers. A biographical dictionary.*
Second Edition. Boston: G.K. Hall & Co., 1982.
ISBN: 0-8161-8223-X   LCCN: 81-7047

ASCAP Biographical Dictionary. Fourth Edition. [edited by the Jaques Cattell
Press] New York & London: R.R. Bowker Company, 1980.
ISBN: 0-8352-1283-1   LCCN: 80-65351

Bull, Storm. *Index to Biographies of Contemporary Composers*, Vol. 1. New York:
Scarecrow Press, Inc., 1964.
                               LCCN: 64-11781

Bull, Storm. *Index to Biographies of Contemporary Composers*, Vol. 2. New York:
Scarecrow Press, Inc., 1974.
ISBN: 0-8108-0734-3   LCCN: 64-11781

Bull, Storm. *Index to Biographies of Contemporary Composers*, Vol. 3. Metuchen,
New Jersey: Scarecrow Press, Inc., 1987.
ISBN: 0-8108-1930-9   LCCN: 64-11781

Cohen, Aaron I. *International Encyclopedia of Women Composers.* Second Edition.
New York & London: Books & Music (USA) Inc, 1987.
ISBN: 0-9617485-2-4   LCCN: 86-72857

Greene, Frank. *Composers on Record.* (An Index to Biographical Information on
14,000 Composers...) Metuchen, New Jersey, & London: Scarecrow Press, 1985.
ISBN: 0-8108-1816-7   LCCN: 85-8238

Hitchcock, H. Wiley & Stanley Sadie. *The New Grove Dictionary of American
Music.* (4 volumes). London: Macmillan Publishers Limited; New York: Grove's
Dictionaries of Music, Inc., 1986.
ISBN: 0-943818-36-2 (set)

Kallman, Helmut, Gilles Potvin & Kenneth Winters. *Encyclopedia of Music in
Canada.* Toronto: University of Toronto Press, 1981.
ISBN: 0-8020-5509-5

Kenton, Egon. *Life and Works of Giovanni Gabrieli.* Roma: American Institute of
Musicology, 1967.

McDonald, Donna. *The Odyssey of The Philip Jones Brass Ensemble.* Bulle,
Switzerland: Éditions BIM, 1986.
ISBN: 2-88039-006-0

McNeil, Barbara & Miranda C. Herbert. *Performing Arts Biography Master Index.*
(A consolidated index to over 270,000 biographical sketches...) Detroit: Gale
Research Company, 1981.
ISBN: 0-8103-1097-X   LCCN: 81-20145

Sadie, Stanley, ed. *The New Grove Dictionary of Music and Musicians.*
(20 volumes). London: Macmillan Publishers Limited; New York: Grove's
Dictionaries of Music, Inc., 1980.
ISBN: 0-333-23111-2   LCCN: 79-26207

BIBLIOGRAPHY

Slonimsky, Nicolas, ed. *Baker's Biographical Dictionary of Musicians*. Seventh Edition. New York: G. Schirmer, 1984.
ISBN: 0-02-870270-0   LCCN: 84-5595

Thompson, Kenneth. *A Dictionary of Twentieth-Century Composers (1911-1971)*. London: Faber & Faber, 1973.
ISBN: 0-571-09002-8

Toomey, Kathleen M. & Stephen C. Willis. *Musicians in Canada: a bio-bibliographical finding list (Musiciens au Canada: Index bio-bibliographique)*. Ottawa: Canadian Association of Music Libraries, 1981.
ISBN: 0-9690583-1-4   LCCN: C81-090058-OE

Vodarsky-Shiraeff, Alexandria. *Russian Composers and Musicians. A Biographical Dictionary*. New York: Da Capo Press, 1969.
LCCN: 71-76422

Who's Who in American Music: Classical. First Edition. ₍edited by the Jaques Cattell Press₎ New York & London: R.R. Bowker Company, 1983.
ISBN: 0-8352-1725-6
ISSN: 0737-9137

Who's Who in American Music: Classical. Second Edition. ₍edited by the Jaques Cattell Press₎ New York: R.R. Bowker Company, c1985.
ISBN: 0-8352-2074-5

Unpublished references

Carnovale, Norbert. *A Comprehensive Performance Project in Trumpet Literature with an Essay on Published Music Composed Since ca. 1900 for Solo Trumpet Accompanied by Orchestra*. ₍dissertation - University of Iowa, 1973₎

Carlson, Stephen. *The Life, Career and Influence of Herbert L. Clarke*. (Appendix E includes list of 150 discs and cylinders) ₍dissertation - Catholic University of America, 1980₎

Häfner, Klaus. *Johann Melchior Molter*. (In preparation: to include thematic catalogue of 450 compositions)

Haynie, John. *A Classified Listing of Music for Trumpet in the Holdings of Willis Library*. North Texas State University, 1982.

Hedwig, Douglas Frederick. *The Trumpet and Organ as Recital Ensemble - A Comprehensive Research and Performance Project: Including Discography, Bibliography of Authentic Baroque Music, and Iconography of Trumpet and Organ*. ₍dissertation - Juilliard School of Music, 1986₎

Parker, Craig B.   Handout for *Herbert L. Clarke: His Life and Works, with Personal Remembrances* by Dr. Leonard B. Smith. ITG Conference, Western Michigan University, 1987.

Pier, Fordyce Chilcen. *Italian Baroque Instrumental Music with Solo Trumpet from the Emilian School: Cazzati to Torelli*. ₍dissertation - Boston University, 1964₎

Pier, Fordyce Chilcen. *Unaccompanied Trumpet Solos*. (An annotated list of 83 compositions.) University of Alberta, 1982.